murach's
Java
servlets and
JSP

2ND EDITION

murach's
Java
servlets and
JSP
2ND EDITION

Joel Murach
Andrea Steelman

MIKE MURACH & ASSOCIATES, INC.

1-800-221-5528 • (559) 440-9071 • Fax: (559) 440-0963
murachbooks@murach.com • www.murach.com

Authors:	Joel Murach
	Andrea Steelman
Editor:	Mike Murach
Cover Design:	Zylka Design
Production:	Tom Murach
	Cynthia Vasquez
	Judy Taylor

Two books for Java developers

Murach's Java SE 6
Murach's Oracle SQL and PL/SQL

Seven books for .NET developers

Murach's C# 2010
Murach's ADO.NET 4 Database Programming with C# 2010
Murach's ASP.NET 4 Web Programming with C# 2010

Murach's Visual Basic 2010
Murach's ADO.NET 4 Database Programming with VB 2010
Murach's ASP.NET 4 Web Programming with VB 2010

Murach's SQL Server 2008 for Developers

Three books for Web developers

Murach's HTML, XHTML, and CSS
Murach's JavaScript and DOM Scripting
Murach's PHP and MySQL

For more on Murach books, please visit us at www.murach.com

Contents

Expanded contents

Section 2   Essential servlet and JSP skills

Chapter 4   A crash course in HTML

Chapter 5   How to develop JavaServer Pages

Chapter 6 How to develop servlets

Chapter 7 How to structure a web application with the MVC pattern

Chapter 8   How to work with sessions and cookies

Chapter 9   How to use standard JSP tags with JavaBeans

Chapter 10   How to use the JSP Expression Language (EL)

Chapter 11   How to use the JSP Standard Tag Library (JSTL)

Chapter 12   How to use custom JSP tags

Section 3   Essential database skills

Chapter 13   How to use MySQL as the database management system

Chapter 14   How to use JDBC to work with a database

Section 4 Advanced servlet and JSP skills

Section 5   The Music Store web site

Introduction

Ever since the late 1990s when Java servlets and JavaServer Pages (JSPs) came into widespread use, web site developers have been switching from CGI scripting languages to servlets and JSPs. As a result, there has been tremendous growth in the use of servlets and JSPs. Today, there's little doubt that servlet and JSP technology is here to stay.

From the start, though, servlets and JSPs have been a training problem because web programming with them requires so many different skills and so much conceptual background. That's why it's been so hard to organize and teach these skills and concepts in a single book or course. But now, by reading just this book, you can master all the skills that you need for developing e-commerce applications. And to prove that, you can download our illustrative e-commerce web site that uses just the skills that are presented in this book.

Why you'll learn faster and better with this book

When we started writing the first edition of this book, we knew we had to take a new approach if we wanted to teach you everything you need to know in a way that's faster and better than the other books. In this edition, we've fine-tuned that approach to make it work even more effectively for today's Java web developer. Here, then, are a few of the ways in which our book differs from the others:

- Chapter 2 shows you how to install and use the free Tomcat web server so you can run web applications on your own computer. In contrast, most competing books let you figure this out on your own.

- Chapter 3 shows you how to install and use the free NetBeans IDE for developing web applications. This is the IDE that we recommend for doing the exercises and running the applications for this book. By using an IDE, you'll learn faster and better than you will without one. And here again, most competing books don't give you any help with this.

- Chapter 4 of this book provides a crash course in HTML. Since this is essential background for the use of JSPs, this means you won't have to use a second book to figure out how HTML works.

- Chapters 5 through 7 show you how JSPs work, how servlets work, and how to use the MVC pattern (or Model 2 architecture) to get the most from JSPs and servlets. From that point on, you'll use servlets when they're appropriate for the task at hand and JSPs when they're appropriate. As a result, you won't waste your time learning how to use servlets for tasks that should be handled by JSPs, or vice versa.

- Like all of our books, this one includes hundreds of examples that range from the simple to the complex. That way, you can quickly see how a feature works by looking at the simple examples. But you can also see how the feature is used in more complex, real-world examples, including the complete e-commerce application that's presented in section 5.

- Like most of our books, this one has exercises at the end of each chapter that help you practice what you've learned. They also encourage you to experiment and challenge you to apply what you've learned in new ways. To help you get the most practice in the least time, you'll start these exercises from existing applications.

- If you page through this book, you'll see that all of the information is presented in "paired pages," with the essential syntax, guidelines, and examples on the right page and the perspective and extra explanation on the left page. This helps you learn faster by reading less...and this is the ideal reference format when you need to refresh your memory about how to do something.

What you'll learn in this book

- In section 1, you'll learn the concepts and terms that you need for web programming. You'll learn how to install and use Tomcat, the server software that lets you use servlets and JSPs for web applications. And you'll learn how to use the NetBeans IDE for developing web applications. When you're done with this section, you'll have set up the development environment you need to code and run servlets and JSPs on your own computer.

- In section 2, you'll get a crash course in HTML, which is essential to the use of JSPs. Then, you'll learn the skills for creating servlets and JSPs that you'll need for almost every application. These chapters move from the simple to the complex as they show you how to work with JSPs, servlets, the MVC pattern, sessions, cookies, JavaBeans, Expression Language (EL), the JSP Standard Tag Library (JSTL), and custom JSP tags.

- In section 3, you'll learn how to use servlets and JSPs to work with a database. Since MySQL is a popular open-source database that works well with Java and is commonly used for web applications, this section presents the details for working with MySQL. However, these principles can be applied to the use of any database management system, including Oracle and SQL Server.

- In section 4, you'll learn the advanced servlet and JSP skills that you will need for certain types of web applications. This includes the use of JavaMail, SSL, authentication, advanced HTTP skills, listeners, and filters. Since the chapters in this section have been designed to work independently of each other, you can read them in any order you want. This makes it easy for you to learn new skills whenever you need them.

- To complete your Java web programming skills, section 5 presents an e-commerce web site that puts the skills presented in the first four sections into context. This downloadable application illustrates best practices and provides code that you can use in your own applications. Once you understand how this web site works, you will have all the skills you need for creating your own web applications.

Who this book is for

This book assumes that you have basic Java skills, the kind you should get from any core Java course. But you don't need any web programming experience at all.

As you read this book, though, you may discover that your Java skills aren't as strong as they ought to be. In that case, we recommend that you get a copy of our latest Java book (currently, *Murach's Java SE 6*). That book will get you up to speed with the language, and show you how to use all of the other basic skills that you need for developing servlets and JSPs. In fact, we see our core Java book as the perfect companion to our servlets and JSP book.

How to get the software you need for this book

You can download all of the software that you need for this book for free from the Internet. To make that easier for you, appendix A shows you how to download and install Java and MySQL. Chapter 2 shows you how to download and install the Tomcat web server. And chapter 3 shows you how to download and install NetBeans.

How our downloadable files make learning easier

To make learning easier, you can download the source code for all the web applications presented in this book from our web site (www.murach.com). This includes the Music Store e-commerce application. Then, you can view the complete code for these applications as you read each chapter; you can compile and run these applications to see how they work; and you can copy portions of code for use in your own web applications.

You can also download the source code that you need for doing the exercises in this book. That way, you don't have to start every exercise from scratch. This takes the busywork out of doing these exercises. For complete download instructions, please refer to appendix A.

Support materials for trainers and instructors

If you're a corporate trainer or a college instructor who would like to use this book for a course, we offer an Instructor's CD that includes: (1) a complete set of PowerPoint slides that you can use to review and reinforce the content of the book; (2) instructional objectives that describe the skills a student should have upon completion of each chapter; (3) the solutions to the exercises in this book; (4) projects that the students start from scratch; (5) solutions to those projects; and (6) test banks that measure mastery of the instructional objectives.

To learn more about this Instructor's CD and to find out how to get it, please go to our web site at www.murach.com and click on the Trainers link or the Instructors link. Or, if you prefer, you can call Kelly at 1-800-221-5528 or send an email to kelly@murach.com.

Please let us know how this book works for you

When we started the first edition of this book, our goal was to teach you how to develop real-world web applications with Java servlets and JSPs as quickly and easily as possible. Now, with this second edition, we hope we've taken that to a new level. So if you have any comments, please send an email to us at murachbooks@murach.com.

Thanks for buying this book. Thanks for reading it. And good luck with your web programming.

Joel Murach

Andrea Steelman

Section 1

Introduction to servlet and JSP programming

The three chapters in this section provide the background information that you need for developing web applications with servlets and JavaServer Pages (JSPs). In chapter 1, you'll learn what web programming is and how servlets and JSPs work. In chapter 2, you'll learn how to install and use the Tomcat server that you can use to run servlets and JSPs on your own computer.

Then, in chapter 3, you'll learn how to use the NetBeans IDE (Integrated Development Environment) for developing Java web applications with servlets and JSPs. This is the IDE that we recommend for doing the exercises and developing new applications as you use this book.

1

An introduction to web programming with Java

This chapter introduces you to the concepts and terms that you need for working with servlets and JavaServer Pages (JSPs) as you create web applications. In particular, this chapter introduces you to the software that you need to be able to write, deploy, and run servlets and JSPs.

An introduction to web applications

A *web application* is a set of web pages that are generated in response to user requests. The Internet has many different types of web applications, such as search engines, online stores, auctions, news sites, discussion groups, and games.

A typical web application

Figure 1-1 shows the first two pages of the shopping cart application that's available from www.murach.com. Here, the first page presents some information about our beginning Java book. This page contains two buttons: a View Cart button and an Add To Cart button. When you click the Add To Cart button, the web application adds the book to your cart and displays the second page in this figure, which shows all of the items in your cart.

The second page lets you change the quantity for an item or remove an item from the cart. It also lets you continue shopping or begin the checkout process. In this book, you'll learn all the skills you need to create a shopping cart application like this one.

If you take a closer look at these web pages, you can learn a little bit about how this application works. For the first page, the Address box of the browser shows an address that has an htm extension. This means that the HTML code for this page is probably stored in file with an htm extension.

In contrast, the Address box for the second page shows the address of a servlet that was mapped to the cart/displayCart URL. This means that the HTML code for this page was generated by the servlet. After the servlet address, you can see a question mark and one parameter named productCode that has a value of "jse6". This is the parameter that was passed from the first page.

The first page of a shopping cart application

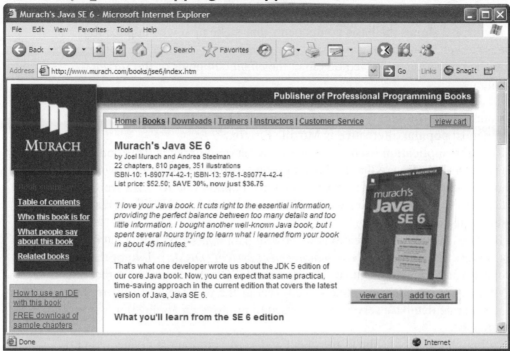

The second page of a shopping cart application

Figure 1-1   A typical web application

The components of a web application

Figure 1-2 shows the basic components that make up a web application. Because a web application is a type of *client/server application*, the components of a web application are stored on either the *client* computer or the *server* computer.

To access a web application, you use a *web browser* that runs on a client computer. The most widely used web browser is Microsoft's Internet Explorer, and the most popular alternative is Mozilla Firefox.

The web application itself is stored on the server computer. This computer runs *web server* software that enables it to send web pages to web browsers. Although there are many web servers, the most popular one for Java web applications is the Apache Software Foundation's *Apache HTTP Server*, which is usually just called *Apache*.

Because most web applications work with data that's stored in a database, most servers also run a *database management system* (*DBMS*). Two of the most popular for Java development are *Oracle* and *MySQL*. Note, however, that the DBMS doesn't have to run on the same server as the web server software. In fact, a separate database server is often used to improve an application's overall performance.

Although this figure shows the client and server computers connected via the Internet, this isn't the only way a client can connect to a server in a web application. If the client and the server are on the same *Local Area Network* (*LAN*), they function as an *intranet*. Since an intranet uses the same protocols as the Internet, a web application works the same on an intranet as it does on the Internet.

Components of a web application

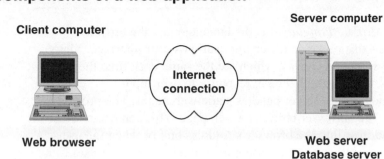

Description

- Web applications are a type of *client/server application*. In a client/server application, a user at a *client* computer accesses an application at a *server* computer. For a web application, the client and server computers are connected via the Internet or an intranet.

- In a web application, the user works with a *web browser* at the client computer. The web browser provides the user interface for the application. The most widely used web browser is Microsoft's Internet Explorer, but other web browsers such as Mozilla Firefox arc also widely used.

- A web application runs on the server computer under the control of *web server* software. For Java web applications, the *Apache* server is the most widely used web server.

- For most web applications, the server computer also runs a *database management system* (*DBMS*). For servlet and JSP applications, *Oracle* and *MySQL* are two of the most popular database management systems.

Figure 1-2   The components of a web application

How static web pages work

HTML (*Hypertext Markup Language*) is the language that the browser renders to the web pages that make up a web application's user interface. Many of these web pages are *static web pages*, which are the same each time they are viewed. In other words, they don't change in response to user input.

Figure 1-3 shows how a web server handles static web pages. The process begins when a user at a web browser requests a web page. This can occur when the user enters a web address into the browser's Address box or when the user clicks a link that leads to another page. In either case, the web browser uses a standard Internet protocol known as *Hypertext Transfer Protocol* (*HTTP*) to send a request known as an *HTTP request* to the web site's server.

When the web server receives an HTTP request from a browser, the server gets the requested HTML file from disk and sends the file back to the browser in the form of an *HTTP response*. The HTTP response includes the HTML document that the user requested along with any other resources specified by the HTML code such as graphics files.

When the browser receives the HTTP response, it renders the HTML document into a web page that the user can view. Then, when the user requests another page, either by clicking a link or typing another web address in the browser's Address box, the process begins again.

How a web server processes static web pages

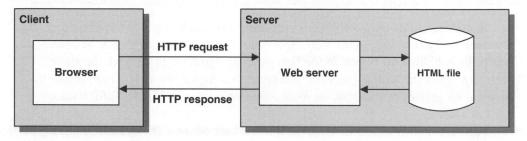

Description

- *Hypertext Markup Language* (*HTML*) is the language that the web browser converts into the web pages of a web application.

- A *static web page* is an HTML document that's stored in a file and does not change in response to user input. Static web pages have a filename with an extension of .htm or .html.

- *Hypertext Transfer Protocol* (*HTTP*) is the protocol that web browsers and web servers use to communicate.

- A web browser requests a page from a web server by sending the server a message known as an *HTTP request*. For a static web page, the HTTP request includes the name of the HTML file that's requested.

- A web server replies to an HTTP request by sending a message known as an *HTTP response* back to the browser. For a static web page, the HTTP response includes the HTML document that's stored in the HTML file.

Figure 1-3   How static web pages work

How dynamic web pages work

In contrast to a static web page, a *dynamic web page* changes based on the parameters that are sent to the web application from another page. For instance, when the Add To Cart button in the first page in figure 1-1 is clicked, the static web page calls the web application and sends one parameter to it. Then, the web application generates the dynamic web page and sends the HTML for it back to the browser.

Figure 1-4 shows how this works. When a user enters data into a web page and clicks the appropriate button, the browser sends an HTTP request to the server. This request contains the address of the next web page along with any data entered by the user. Then, when the web server receives this request and determines that it is a request for a dynamic web page, it passes the request back to the web application.

When the web application receives the request, it processes the data that the user entered and generates an HTML document. Next, it sends that document to the web server, which sends the document back to the browser in the form of an HTTP response. Then, the browser displays the HTML document that's included in the response so the process can start over again.

How a web server processes dynamic web pages

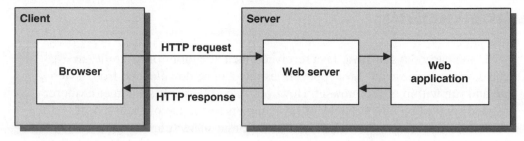

Description

- A *dynamic web page* is an HTML document that's generated by a web application. Often, the web page changes according to parameters that are sent to the web application by the web browser.

- When a web server receives a request for a dynamic web page, the server passes the request to the web application. Then, the application generates a response, which is usually an HTML document, and returns it to the web server. The web server, in turn, wraps the generated HTML document in an HTTP response and sends it back to the browser.

- The browser doesn't know or care whether the HTML was retrieved from a static HTML file or was dynamically generated by the web application. Either way, the browser displays the HTML document that is returned.

Figure 1-4   How dynamic web pages work

An introduction to Java web programming

In the early days of Java, Java received much attention for its ability to create *applets*. These are Java applications that can be downloaded from a web site and run within a web browser. However, once Microsoft's Internet Explorer stopped supporting new versions of Java, applets lost much of their appeal. As a result, many developers switched their attention to *servlets* and *JavaServer Pages* (*JSPs*). These technologies allow developers to write Java web applications that run on the server.

The components of a Java web application

Figure 1-5 shows the primary software components for a Java web application. By now, you should understand why the server must run web server software. To run a Java application, though, the server must also run a software product known as a *servlet/JSP engine*, or *servlet/JSP container*. This software allows a web server to run servlets and JSPs.

Sun's *Java Enterprise Edition* (*Java EE*) specification describes how a servlet/JSP engine should interact with a web server. Since all servlet/JSP engines must implement this specification, all servlet/JSP engines should work similarly. In theory, this makes servlet/JSP code portable between servlet/JSP engines and web servers. In practice, though, there are minor differences between each servlet/JSP engine and web server. As a result, you may need to make some modifications to your code when switching servlet/JSP engines or web servers.

Tomcat is a free, open-source servlet/JSP engine that was developed by the Jakarta project at the Apache Software Foundation. This engine is the official reference implementation of the servlet/JSP specification set forth by Sun, and it's one of the most popular servlet/JSP engines. In the next chapter, you'll learn how to install and use Tomcat on your own computer.

For a servlet/JSP engine to work properly, the engine must be able to access the *Java Development Kit (JDK)* that comes as part of the *Java Standard Edition* (*Java SE*). The JDK contains the Java compiler and the core classes for working with Java. It also contains the *Java Runtime Environment* (*JRE*) that's necessary for running compiled Java classes. Since this book assumes that you already have some Java experience, you should already be familiar with the JDK and the JRE.

Many large websites also use a Java technology known as *Enterprise JavaBeans* (*EJBs*). To use EJBs, the server must run an additional piece of software known as an *EJB server*, or *EJB container*. Although there are some benefits to using EJBs, they're more difficult to use when you're first learning how to code Java web applications, and they can make web applications unnecessarily complex. That's why this book shows how to develop web applications without using EJBs.

The components of a Java web application

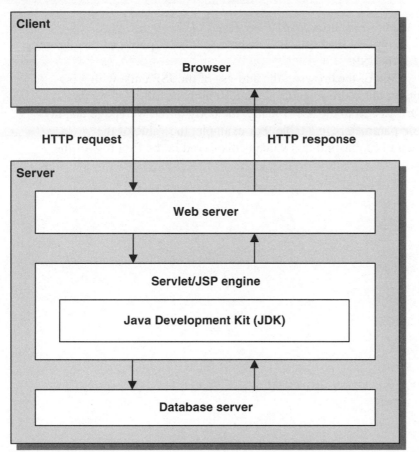

Description

- Java web applications consist of JavaServer Pages and servlets. You'll learn more about them in the next two figures.

- A *servlet/JSP engine*, or *servlet/JSP container*, is the software that allows the web server to work with servlets and JSPs.

- The *Java Enterprise Edition* (*Java EE*) specification describes how web servers can interact with servlet/JSP engines. *Tomcat* is one of the most popular servlet/JSP engines. It was developed by the Jakarta project at the Apache Software Foundation.

- For a servlet/JSP engine to work, it must have access to Java's *Java Development Kit* (*JDK*), which comes as part of the *Java Standard Edition* (*Java SE*). Among other things, the JDK contains the core Java class libraries, the Java compiler, and the *Java Runtime Environment* (*JRE*).

- Java web applications that use *Enterprise JavaBeans* (*EJBs*) require an additional server component known as an *EJB server*, or *EJB container*. As a result, they won't run on the Tomcat server.

Figure 1-5   The components of a Java web application

An introduction to JavaServer Pages

To give you a better idea how *JavaServer Pages* (*JSPs*) work, part 1 of figure 1-6 shows a simple JSP displayed in a browser. Then, part 2 of this figure shows the code for the JSP.

In the Address box of the browser, the address of the JSP ends with a jsp extension. After that, the address includes a question mark followed by the parameters that are passed to the JSP. Finally, the body of the web page displays the values of these parameters in a table. For example, the value of the firstName parameter is John, and this value is displayed in the first row of the table.

A JSP that displays three parameters entered by the user

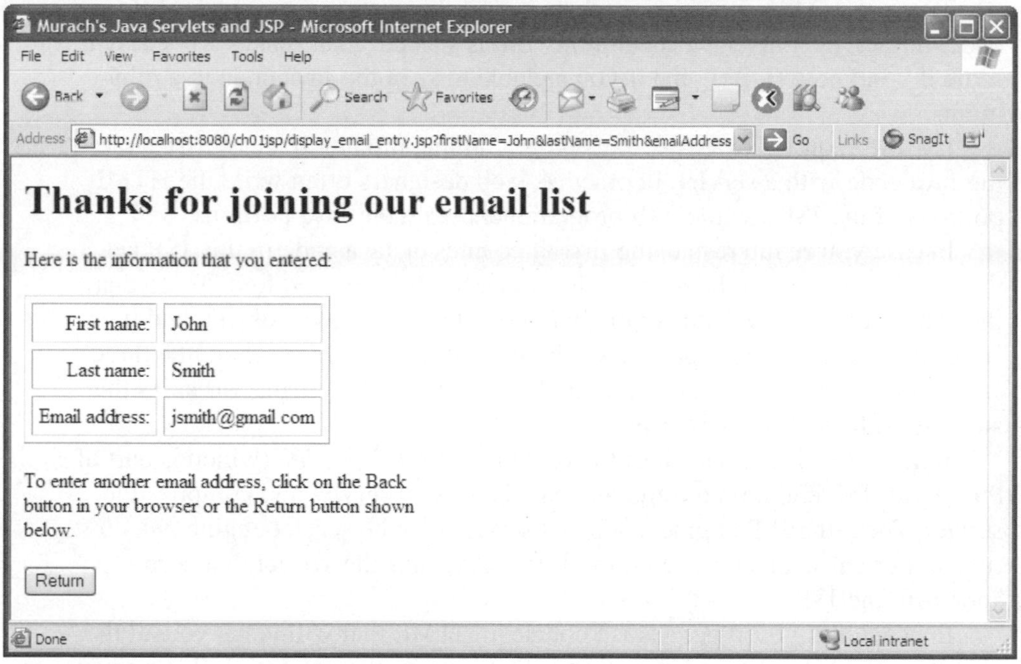

Description

- A *JavaServer Page*, or *JSP*, consists of Java code that is embedded within HTML code. This makes it easy to write the HTML portion of a JSP, but harder to write the Java code.

- When a JSP is first requested, the JSP engine translates it into a servlet and compiles it. Then, the servlet is run by the servlet engine.

Figure 1-6   An introduction to JavaServer Pages (part 1 of 2)

In part 2 of this figure, you can see the code for this JSP. If you're already familiar with HTML, you can see that most of this code consists of HTML code. In fact, the only Java code in this JSP is shaded. That makes JSPs easy to write if you know HTML and if you are able to keep the Java code to a minimum.

If a JSP requires extensive Java programming, though, it's easier to write the Java code with a servlet. In practice, web designers often write the HTML portions of the JSPs, while web programmers write the Java portions.

In case you're interested, the first three lines of Java code in this JSP get three parameters from the request object that has been passed to it. To do that, the code uses the getParameter method of the built-in request object, and it stores the values of these parameters in three String variables. Then, the three Java expressions that are used later in the JSP refer to the String variables that store the values of the parameters.

When a JSP is requested for the first time, the *JSP engine* (which is part of the servlet/JSP engine) converts the JSP code into a servlet and compiles the servlet. Then, the JSP engine loads that servlet into the servlet engine, which runs it. For subsequent requests, the JSP engine runs the servlet that corresponds to the JSP.

In chapter 4, you'll get a crash course in HTML that will teach you all the HTML you need to know for writing JSPs. Then, in chapter 5, you'll learn how to combine HTML code with Java code as you write JSPs. When you're done with those chapters, you'll know how to write significant JSPs of your own.

The code for the JSP

```
<!DOCTYPE HTML PUBLIC "-//W3C//DTD HTML 4.01 Transitional//EN"
    "http://www.w3.org/TR/html4/loose.dtd">

<html>
<head>
    <title>Murach's Java Servlets and JSP</title>
</head>
<body>
    <%
        // get parameters from the request
        String firstName = request.getParameter("firstName");
        String lastName = request.getParameter("lastName");
        String emailAddress = request.getParameter("emailAddress");
    %>

    <h1>Thanks for joining our email list</h1>

    <p>Here is the information that you entered:</p>

    <table cellspacing="5" cellpadding="5" border="1">
        <tr>
            <td align="right">First name:</td>
            <td><%= firstName %></td>
        </tr>
        <tr>
            <td align="right">Last name:</td>
            <td><%= lastName %></td>
        </tr>
        <tr>
            <td align="right">Email address:</td>
            <td><%= emailAddress %></td>
        </tr>
    </table>

    <p>To enter another email address, click on the Back <br>
    button in your browser or the Return button shown <br>
    below.</p>

    <form action="join_email_list.html" method="get">
        <input type="submit" value="Return">
    </form>

</body>
</html>
```

Figure 1-6   An introduction to JavaServer Pages (part 2 of 2)

An introduction to servlets

To give you a better idea of how *servlets* work, figure 1-7 shows a servlet that generates the same web page as the JSP in figure 1-6. In short, a servlet is a Java class that runs on a server and does the processing for the dynamic web pages of a web application. That's why servlets for a web application are written by web programmers, not web designers. After the processing is done, a servlet can return HTML code to the browser by using the println method of an out object. Note, however, that this makes it more difficult to code the HTML.

If you study the code in this figure, you can see that each servlet is a Java class that extends (or inherits) the HttpServlet class. Then, each servlet can override the doGet method of the inherited class, which receives both a request and a response object from the web server, and the servlet can get the parameters that have been passed to it by using the getParameter method of the request object. After that, the servlet can do whatever processing is required by using normal Java code.

In chapter 6, you'll learn the details for coding servlets. When you complete that chapter, you'll be able to write significant servlets of our own.

How to combine servlets and JSPs in a web application

When you're developing Java web applications, you will usually want to use a combination of servlets and JSPs so you get the benefits of both. As you have seen, servlets are actually Java classes. As a result, it makes sense to use them for the processing requirements of a web application. Similarly, JSPs are primarily HTML code so it makes sense to use them for the design of the web pages in an application. But how can you do that in an efficient way?

The solution is for the servlets to do the processing for the application and then forward the request and response objects to a JSP. That way, the servlet does the processing, and the JSP provides the HTML for the user interface. With this approach, the JSP requires a minimum of embedded Java code. And that means that the web designer can write the JSPs with minimal interaction with the Java programmer, and the Java programmer can write the servlets without worrying about the HTML.

In chapter 7, you'll learn how to use this approach for developing web applications. You'll also learn how to use the Model-Controller-View (MVC) pattern to structure your applications so they're easy to manage and maintain. When you finish that chapter, you'll know how to develop Java web applications in a thoroughly professional manner.

The code for a servlet that works the same as the JSP in figure 1-6

```java
package email;

import java.io.*;
import javax.servlet.*;
import javax.servlet.http.*;

public class DisplayEmailListServlet extends HttpServlet
{
    protected void doGet(
        HttpServletRequest request,
        HttpServletResponse response)
        throws ServletException, IOException
    {
        // get parameters from the request
        String firstName = request.getParameter("firstName");
        String lastName = request.getParameter("lastName");
        String emailAddress = request.getParameter("emailAddress");

        // return response to browser
        response.setContentType("text/html;charset=UTF-8");
        PrintWriter out = response.getWriter();
        out.println(
          "<!doctype html public \"-//W3C//DTD HTML 4.0 Transitional//EN\">\n"
        + "<html>\n"
        + "<head>\n"
        + "  <title>Murach's Java Servlets and JSP</title>\n"
        + "</head>\n"
        + "<body>\n"
        + "<h1>Thanks for joining our email list</h1>\n"
        + "<p>Here is the information that you entered:</p>\n"
        + "  <table cellspacing=\"5\" cellpadding=\"5\" border=\"1\">\n"
        + "  <tr><td align=\"right\">First name:</td>\n"
        + "      <td>" + firstName + "</td>\n"
        + "  </tr>\n"
        + "  <tr><td align=\"right\">Last name:</td>\n"
        + "      <td>" + lastName + "</td>\n"
        + "  </tr>\n"
        + "  <tr><td align=\"right\">Email address:</td>\n"
        + "      <td>" + emailAddress + "</td>\n"
        + "  </tr>\n"
        + "  </table>\n"
        + "<p>To enter another email address, click on the Back <br>\n"
        + "button in your browser or the Return button shown <br>\n"
        + "below.</p>\n"
        + "<form action=\"join_email_list.html\" >\n"
        + "  <input type=\"submit\" value=\"Return\">\n"
        + "</form>\n"
        + "</body>\n"
        + "</html>\n");
        out.close();
    }
}
```

Figure 1-7   An introduction to servlets

An introduction to Java web development

This topic introduces you to servlet/JSP development. In particular, it presents some of the hardware and software options that you have as you develop Java web applications.

Three environments for servlet and JSP development

Figure 1-8 shows the three possible environments that you can use to develop servlets and JSPs. First, you can use a single computer. Second, you can use a Local Area Network (or LAN). Third, you can use the Internet.

When you use a single computer, you need to install all of the required software on that computer. That includes the JDK, the web server software, the servlet/JSP engine, and the database management system. To make this easy, you can use Tomcat as both the web server and the servlet/JSP engine. Then, you can use MySQL as the database server. In the next chapter, you'll learn how to install Tomcat, and you can learn how to install the other components in appendix A.

When you work over a LAN, it functions as an intranet. In this development environment, you can use the same software components as you do on your own computer, but you divide them between client and server. To compile and run servlets on the server, the server requires the JDK, a web server and servlet/JSP engine like Tomcat, and a DBMS like MySQL. Then, the client just needs the JDK and the JAR files for any classes that aren't available from the JDK. For example, to compile servlets on a client, the client requires the servlet.jar file, which contains all of the classes required for servlet development. These JAR files come with Tomcat, and you'll learn more about them in the next chapter.

When you work over the Internet, you use the same general components as you do when you work over an intranet. To improve performance, though, you can use a dedicated web server like Apache together with a dedicated servlet/JSP engine like Tomcat. If necessary, you can also improve the performance of an intranet application by using Apache as the web server.

Since the JDK, Apache, Tomcat, and MySQL can be run by most operating systems, Java web developers aren't tied to a specific operating system. In fact, the Windows operating system is commonly used for the client computers during development. But when the applications are ready for use, they are often deployed to a Unix or Solaris server.

Three environments for servlet and JSP development

Stand-alone development

JDK
Tomcat
MySQL

Local Area Network development

JDK
Java EE JAR files

————LAN connection————

Client

JDK
Tomcat
MySQL

Server

Internet development

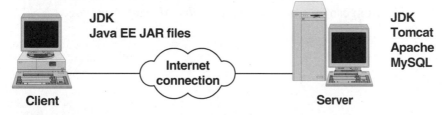

JDK
Java EE JAR files

Internet
connection

Client

JDK
Tomcat
Apache
MySQL

Server

Description

- When you develop web applications, you can set up your development environment in several different ways.

- If you want to develop web applications on your own computer, you need to install the JDK, a web server, a servlet/JSP engine, and a DBMS. In this case, it's common to use Tomcat as both the web server and the servlet/JSP engine, and MySQL as the DBMS.

- If you're working in a group over an intranet, the server can run Tomcat as the web server and the servlet/JSP engine, and it can run MySQL as the DBMS. Then, the client just needs the JDK and the JAR files for any classes that aren't available from the JDK. At the least, the client will need the servlet-api.jar, jsp-api.jar, and el-api.jar files that contain standard Java EE classes for working with servlets and JSPs.

- If you're working in a group over the Internet, you may want to use a web server such as Apache and a dedicated servlet/JSP engine like Tomcat. Otherwise, this works the same as when you're working over a LAN.

Figure 1-8   Three environments for servlet and JSP development

The architecture for a Java web application

Figure 1-9 shows the architecture for a typical web application that uses servlets and JSPs. This architecture uses three layers: (1) the *presentation layer*, or *user interface layer*, (2) the *business rules layer*, and (3) the *data access layer*. In theory, the programmer tries to keep these layers as separate and independent as possible. In practice, though, these layers are often interrelated, and that's especially true for the business and data access layers.

The presentation layer consists of HTML pages and JSPs. Typically, a web designer will work on the HTML stored in these pages to create the look and feel of the user interface. Later, a Java programmer may need to edit these pages so they work properly with the servlets of the application.

The business rules layer uses servlets to control the flow of the application. These servlets may call other Java classes to store or retrieve data from a database, and they may forward the results to a JSP or to another servlet. Within the business layer, Java programmers often use a special type of Java class known as a *JavaBean* to temporarily store and process data. A JavaBean is typically used to define a business object such as a User or Invoice object.

The data layer works with data that's stored on the server's disk. For a serious web application, this data is usually stored in a relational database. However, this data can also be stored in text files and binary files. In addition, the data for an application can be stored in an *Extensible Markup Language* (*XML*) file.

The architecture for a typical Java web application

Presentation layer

> HTML files

> JSP files

Business rules layer

> Servlets

> JavaBeans

> Other Java classes

Data access layer

> Data access classes

Database   Text files   Binary files   XML files

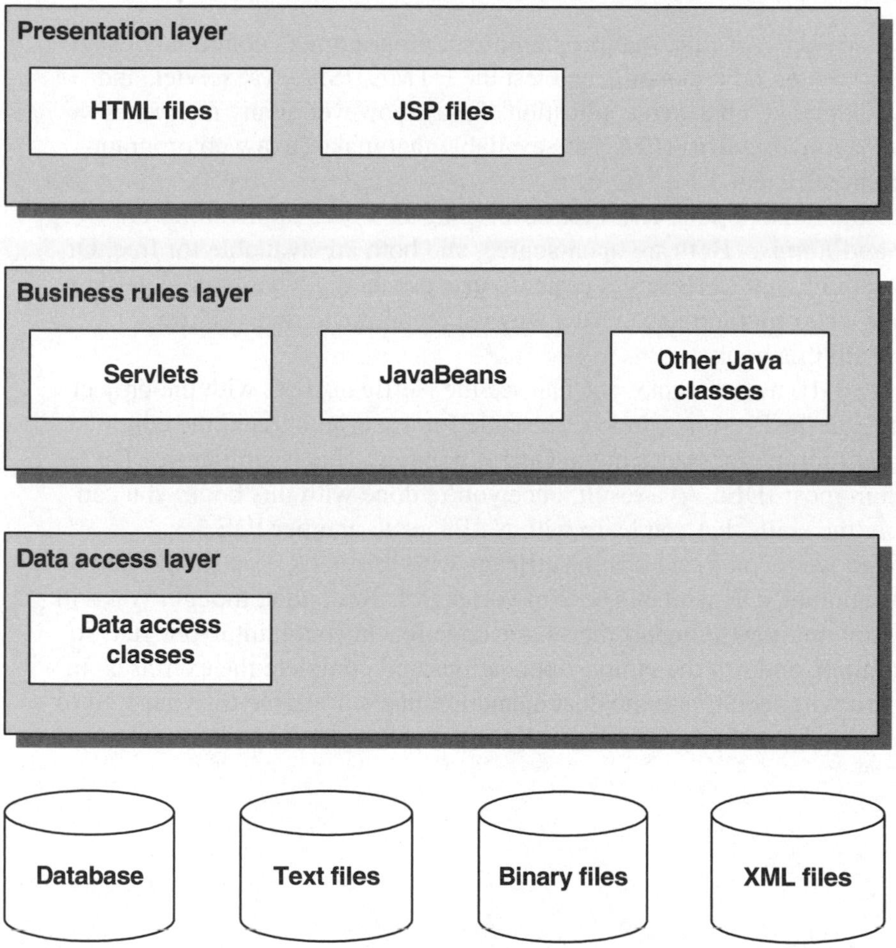

Description

- The *presentation layer* for a typical Java web application consists of HTML pages and JSPs.

- The *business rules layer* for a typical Java web application consists of servlets. These servlets may call other Java classes including a special type of Java class known as a *JavaBean*. In chapters 9 and 10, you'll learn how to use several special types of tags within a JSP to work with JavaBeans.

- The *data access layer* for a typical Java web application consists of classes that read and write data that's stored on the server's disk drive.

- For a serious web application, the data is usually stored in a relational database. However, it may also be stored in binary files, in text files, or in *Extensible Markup Language* (or *XML*) files.

Figure 1-9   The architecture for a Java web application

IDEs for developing Java web applications

In the early days of Java web programming, programmers commonly used text editors to enter, edit, compile, and test the HTML, JSP, Java, servlet, and XML files that make up a web application. Today, however, many *Integrated Development Environments* (*IDEs*) are available that make Java web programming far more efficient.

Two of the most popular IDEs for developing Java web applications are *NetBeans* and *Eclipse*. Both are open-source, and both are available for free. Of the two, we think that NetBeans is easier to use, especially when you're getting started with web programming. That's why we recommend that you use NetBeans with this book.

In figure 1-10, for example, you can see the NetBeans IDE with the project for chapter 7 in the Projects window, the code for a servlet class in the editor window, and runtime messages in the Output window. This is similar to what you'll find in most IDEs. As a result, once you're done with this book, you can easily apply the skills that you learn with NetBeans to another IDE.

Although we recommend using NetBeans with this book, you should be able to use another IDE with this book if you prefer. To do that, though, you will need to figure out how to import the source code for this book into your IDE so you can compile and run the sample applications and complete the exercises. In addition, you will need to use the documentation that's available for your IDE to learn how to perform the tasks presented in chapter 3.

The NetBeans IDE

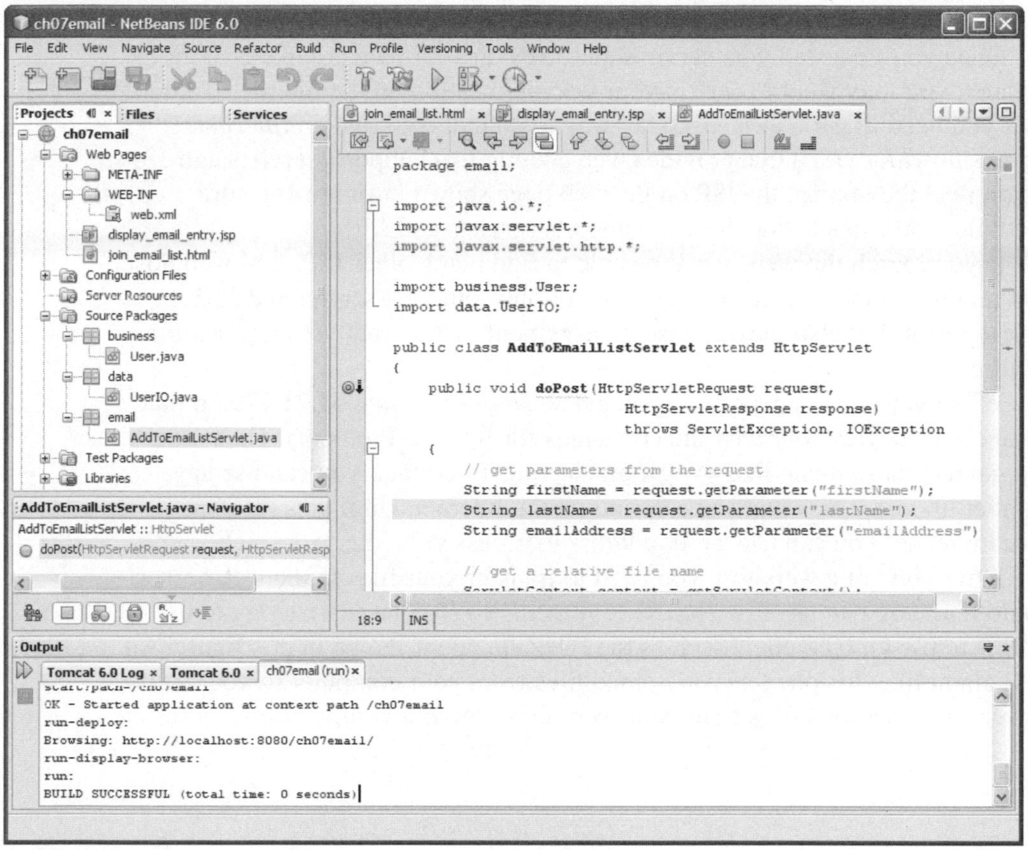

Popular IDEs for Java web development

NetBeans

Eclipse

JBuilder

IntelliJ IDEA

Description

- An *Integrated Development Environment* (*IDE*) is a tool that provides all of the functionality that you need for developing web applications.

- *NetBeans* and *Eclipse* are popular IDEs for Java web development that are open-source and free.

- In chapter 3, you will learn how to use NetBeans for developing Java web applications. This is the IDE that we recommend for use with this book.

Figure 1-10   IDEs for developing Java web applications

Tools for deploying Java web applications

Once you've tested your servlets and JSPs on your own computer or an intranet, you may want to deploy your web application on the Internet. To do that, you need to get a *web host*. One way to do that is to find an *Internet service provider* (*ISP*) that provides web hosting that supports servlets and JSPs. If you read the text for the ISP on the web page shown in figure 1-11, for example, you can see that this ISP supports servlets and JSPs.

If you search the web, you'll be able to find many other ISPs and web hosts. Just make sure that the one you choose not only supports servlet and JSP development, but also the database management system that your application requires.

When you select a web host, you get an *IP address* like 64.71.179.86 that uniquely identifies your web site (IP stands for Internet Protocol). Then, you can get a *domain name* like www.murach.com. To do that, you can use any number of companies that you can find on the Internet. Until you get your domain name, you can use the IP address to access your site.

After you get a web host, you need to transfer your files to the web server. To do that, you can use *File Transfer Protocol* (*FTP*). The easiest way to use FTP is to use an FTP client such as the FileZilla client shown in this figure. An FTP client like this one lets you upload files from your computer to your web server and download files from your web server to your computer.

An ISP that provides web hosting that supports servlets and JSPs

The FileZilla program

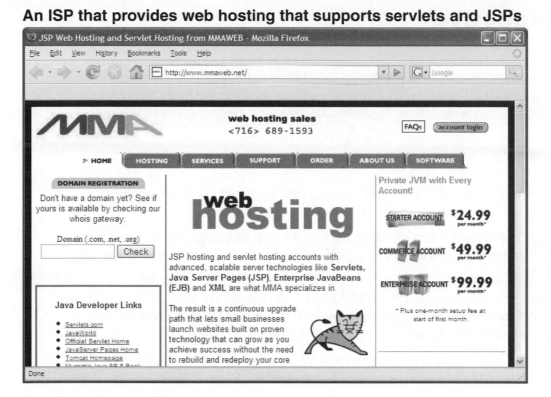

Figure 1-11   Tools for deploying Java web applications

Perspective

The goal of this chapter has been to provide the background that you need for developing servlets and JSPs. Now, if this chapter has succeeded, you should be ready to install Tomcat on your own computer as shown in the next chapter. Then, you'll be ready to install the NetBeans IDE on your computer as shown in chapter 3.

Summary

- A *web application* is a set of web pages that are generated in response to user requests.

- To run a web application, the client requires a web browser and the server requires *web server* software. The server may also require a *database management system* (*DBMS*).

- *Hypertext Markup Language* (*HTML*) is the language that the browser converts into the user interface, while *Hypertext Transfer Protocol* (*HTTP*) is the protocol that web browsers and web servers use to communicate.

- A web browser requests a page from a web server by sending an *HTTP request*. A web server replies by sending an *HTTP response* back to the browser.

- A *static web page* is generated from an HTML document that doesn't change, while a *dynamic web page* is generated by a web application based on the parameters that are included in the HTTP request.

- To run Java web applications, the server requires the *Java Development Kit* (*JDK*) and a *servlet/JSP engine* like Tomcat.

- A *JavaServer Page* (*JSP*) consists of HTML with embedded Java code. When it is requested, the JSP engine generates a servlet from the JSP and compiles that servlet. Then, the servlet engine runs that servlet.

- A *servlet* is a Java class that runs on a server. For web applications, a servlet extends the HttpServlet class. To pass HTML back to the browser, a servlet can use the println method of the out object.

- When you develop a Java web application, you can use servlets to do the processing that's required and JSPs to present the user interface.

- You can develop servlets and JSPs on your own computer, on a *Local Area Network* (*LAN*) that functions as an *intranet*, and on the Internet. When you use the Internet, it's common to use a web server that's separate from the servlet/JSP engine.

- As you develop a Java web application, you try to divide its classes into three layers: *presentation*, *business rules*, and *data access*. This makes it easier to manage and maintain the application.

2

How to install and use Tomcat

As you learned in the last chapter, Tomcat can be used as both the web server and the servlet and JSP engine for web applications. In this chapter, you'll learn how to install and use Tomcat on your own computer. Along the way, you should take the time to install Tomcat. When you're through with this chapter, you'll be able to run some of the downloadable applications for this book.

How to get started with Tomcat

This topic shows how to get started with Tomcat. Although the examples shown in this topic use Windows as the operating system, similar concepts apply to all operating systems. As a result, if you're using another operating system, you may be able to get the installation done by modifying the procedures shown in this topic so they're appropriate for your operating system. Otherwise, you can go to the Tomcat web site to get information about installing Tomcat on your system.

How to install Tomcat

Figure 2-1 shows how to install Tomcat 6. This version of Tomcat supports the 2.5 servlet and 2.1 JSP specifications.

Since the Apache Software Foundation is continually updating its web site, the procedure in this figure may be out of date by the time you read this. As a result, you may have to do some searching to find the current version of Tomcat. Once you do, you shouldn't have any trouble following the procedure shown in this figure to install Tomcat.

After you've installed Tomcat, its top-level directory is apache-tomcat-6.0.X. This can be referred to as the *Tomcat home directory*. To make it easier to refer to this directory later on, we recommend that you change its name to tomcat as specified by step 7 in this figure.

The last step in this procedure is to copy (not move) the JAR files shown in this figure from Tomcat's lib directory to the JDK's jre\lib\ext directory. In case you need to refresh your memory, a *Java Archive* (*JAR*) *file* contains a group of Java classes in a compressed format. The JAR files shown in this figure allow the Java Runtime Environment (JRE) to work with servlets, JSPs, the Expression Language (EL), and database connection pooling (DBCP). Although you can get the same result by adding Tomcat's lib directory to the classpath, it's usually easier to copy the JAR files.

The Tomcat web site

`http://tomcat.apache.org/`

How to install Tomcat

1. Go to the Tomcat web site.

2. Navigate to the Download page for Tomcat 6.X.

3. Navigate to the Binary Distributions heading for the latest stable release. To do that, avoid any headings labeled as alpha or beta releases. Beneath the Core subheading, click on the link for the zip file.

4. Save the zip file to your hard disk. By default, this file should be named something like apache-tomcat-6.0.10.zip.

5. Use a zip program to extract the files from the zip file.

6. If necessary, move the apache-tomcat directory to your C drive.

7. Rename the apache-tomcat directory to tomcat.

8. Copy the JAR files shown below from Tomcat's lib directory to the JDK's jre\lib\ext directory.

The JAR files that need to be available to the JRE

```
servlet-api.jar
jsp-api.jar
el-api.jar
tomcat-dbcp.jar
```

Description

- The directory that holds the files for Tomcat is known as the *Tomcat home directory*. By default, this directory is apache-tomcat-6.0.X. However, to save yourself typing, we recommend that you rename this directory to tomcat.

- The Java Archive (JAR) files shown above contain the Java classes that need to be available to the JDK and JRE when you develop servlets and JSPs. By copying these JAR files from Tomcat's lib subdirectory to the JDK's jre\lib\ext subdirectory, you make the classes available to the JDK and JRE.

- Although it's possible to download the source distribution for Tomcat and build Tomcat from the source code, web developers only need to download and install the binary distribution.

Figure 2-1   How to install Tomcat

A summary of Tomcat's directories and files

Figure 2-2 shows the directories and files for the Tomcat home directory, which has been changed to c:\tomcat. Of the directories, the most important are the bin, conf, lib, logs, webapps, and work directories.

The bin directory holds the binary files that let you start and stop Tomcat. You'll learn how to do that later in this chapter.

The webapps directory contains a few web applications that come with Tomcat. You can run these applications to make sure Tomcat has been installed properly. Later, when you develop your own web applications, you will store them under this directory.

The lib directory contains the JAR files that contain the Java class libraries that are available to all web applications running on the server. In the previous figure, you learned how to make some of these JAR files available to the JDK and the JRE.

The conf directory contains some XML files that you may need to edit as you configure Tomcat, and the logs directory contains text files that Tomcat uses to log its operations. You can open these XML and log files in a text editor to learn more about how Tomcat works.

The work directory is used by Tomcat to store the source code and class files for the servlets that the JSP engine generates. In chapter 5, you'll learn how to view these files.

In the Tomcat home directory, you can also find two text files. The RELEASE-NOTES file contains some general information about the current release of Tomcat. The running.txt file contains more information about installing, starting, and stopping Tomcat. Although most of this information is presented in this chapter, you can check the running.txt file if you encounter any problems installing and running Tomcat. In particular, this file includes directions for Unix users, and it includes directions for how to install Tomcat on a server so it can be shared by multiple users across a network.

The file structure of Tomcat

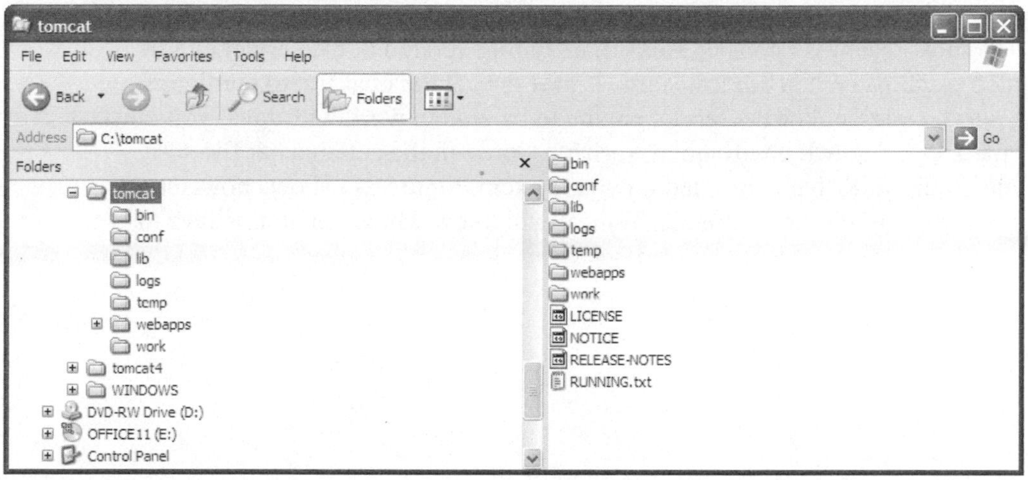

The subdirectories

Directory	Description
bin	Files for working with Tomcat such as the startup and shutdown batch files.
conf	Files for configuring Tomcat such as server.xml, context.xml, and web.xml.
lib	JAR files that contain classes that are available to all web applications. As a result, you can put any JAR files you want to make available to all web applications in this directory.
logs	Log files.
temp	Temporary files used by the JVM.
webapps	The directories and files for the web applications.
work	The source code and class files for the servlets that Tomcat generates for the JSPs.

The files

File	Description
RELEASE-NOTES	General information about the current release of Tomcat.
running.txt	Instructions for installing, starting, and stopping Tomcat.

Figure 2-2   A summary of Tomcat's directories and files

How to set the JAVA_HOME environment variable

In most recent versions of Tomcat, including version 6, the servlet engine is named Catalina. When Tomcat starts, it runs the catalina.bat file to configure this servlet engine. For the servlet engine to be able to work with Java, you must set the JAVA_HOME environment variable stored in the catalina.bat file so it points to the JDK that's installed on your system. Figure 2-3 shows how. Once you set this environment variable, Tomcat will know which version of Java to use.

The catalina batch file opened for editing

```
TextPad - [C:\tomcat\bin\catalina.bat]
File  Edit  Search  View  Tools  Macros  Configure  Window  Help

catalina.bat

36  rem
37  rem    JPDA_ADDRESS    (Optional) Java runtime options used when the "jpd
38  rem                    command is executed. The default is "jdbconn".
39  rem
40  rem    JPDA_SUSPEND    (Optional) Java runtime options used when the "jpd
41  rem                    command is executed. Specifies whether JVM should
42  rem                    execution immediately after startup. Default is "r
43  rem
44  rem    JPDA_OPTS       (Optional) Java runtime options used when the "jpd
45  rem                    command is executed. If used, JPDA_TRANSPORT, JPDA
46  rem                    and JPDA_SUSPEND are ignored. Thus, all required j
47  rem                    options MUST be specified. The default is:
48  rem
49  rem                    -Xdebug -Xrunjdwp:transport=%JPDA_TRANSPORT%,
50  rem                        address=%JPDA_ADDRESS%,server=y,suspend=%JPDA_
51  rem
52  rem $Id: catalina.bat 500710 2007-01-28 00:24:33Z markt $
53  rem --------------------------------------------------------------------
54
55  set JAVA_HOME=C:\Program Files\Java\jdk1.6.0
56
57  rem Guess CATALINA_HOME if not defined
58  set CURRENT_DIR=%cd%
59  if not "%CATALINA_HOME%" == "" goto gotHome
60  set CATALINA_HOME=%CURRENT_DIR%
61  if exist "%CATALINA_HOME%\bin\catalina.bat" goto okHome
62  cd ..
63  set CATALINA_HOME=%cd%
64  cd %CURRENT_DIR%
65  :gotHome
66  if exist "%CATALINA_HOME%\bin\catalina.bat" goto okHome
67  echo The CATALINA_HOME environment variable is not defined correctly
68  echo This environment variable is needed to run this program
69  goto end

ANSI Characters

33  !
34  "
35  #
36  $
37  %
38  &
39  '
40  (
41  )
42  *
43  +
44  ,
45  -
46  .

55    1    Read Ovr Block Sync Rec Caps
```

How to set the JAVA_HOME environment variable

1. Use a text editor like NotePad to open the catalina.bat file located in the c:\tomcat\bin directory. One way to do that is to right-click on the name of the file in the Windows Explorer and choose Edit.

2. Scroll down past the remarks at the beginning of the file. These lines begin with "rem".

3. After the remarks at the beginning of the file, enter a set statement that sets the JAVA_HOME variable to the directory that contains the JDK that's installed on your system. When you enter this statement, put an equals sign (=) between the variable and the directory path.

4. Save your changes to the catalina.bat file.

5. If necessary, stop and restart Tomcat.

Figure 2-3   How to set the JAVA_HOME environment variable

How to start and stop Tomcat

Figure 2-4 shows how to start and stop Tomcat. To do that, you open up a DOS prompt window and run the startup and shutdown batch files that are stored in Tomcat's bin directory. Before you do that, though, you need to use the cd command to change the current directory to Tomcat's bin directory so DOS will know where to find the batch files.

When you start Tomcat, several message lines are displayed in the DOS prompt window including two that show the Tomcat and Java home directories. Then, Tomcat displays a console in a second window. This console shows that Tomcat is running and is ready to receive requests for HTML pages, servlets, and JSPs.

If you're using Unix, you can use a procedure that's similar to the one in this figure to start and stop Tomcat. After you start a Unix command prompt, you use the cd command to change the current working directory to Tomcat's bin directory. When using Unix, though, you use front slashes in the directory path instead of the backslashes that are required by DOS. Then, to start and stop Tomcat, you use the startup.sh and shutdown.sh commands.

When you start Tomcat for the first time, Tomcat will display one or more messages if you haven't done the installation and configuration properly. Most of the time, you can use these messages to solve any configuration problems. For some older versions of Windows, you may get an "out of environment space" message. In that case, you can follow the troubleshooting directions that are at the end of the running.txt file that's in Tomcat's home directory.

DOS commands for starting Tomcat

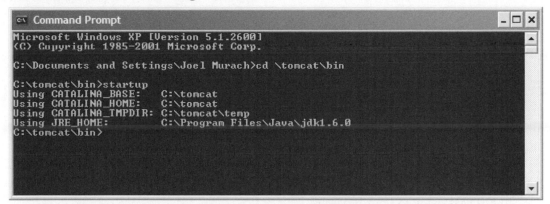

The console that Tomcat displays when it's running

How to use the DOS Prompt window to start and stop Tomcat

1. Open a DOS Prompt window and use the cd command to change the current directory to Tomcat's bin directory.

2. To start Tomcat, type "startup" and press the Enter key. To stop Tomcat, type "shutdown" and press the Enter key.

How to solve the "out of environment space" problem

- You may get an "out of environment space" error if you're using Windows 95, 98, or ME. To solve this problem, follow the troubleshooting directions that are at the end of the running.txt file that's in Tomcat's root directory.

Figure 2-4 How to start and stop Tomcat

How to test Tomcat

On most systems, you can view an HTML document without using a web server. To do that, you can use the Windows Explorer to navigate to the HTML file for the page and double-click on it. This starts your web browser and displays the HTML document. Another way to view an HTML document is to start your web browser and enter the path and filename for the HTML file.

To view a web page that's generated by a JSP or servlet, though, you need to use HTTP to request the web page through Tomcat as shown in figure 2-5. After you start Tomcat and your browser, you enter a *Uniform Resource Locator*, or *URL*, in the browser. Then, Tomcat finds the servlet for the page that you've requested, runs the servlet to generate the HTML for the page, and sends the HTML back to your browser.

The Address box of the Internet Explorer browser that's shown in this figure contains a URL that you can use to test Tomcat to make sure it's running properly. This URL requests an HTML page from one of the web applications that's included with Tomcat. Here, the URL begins with the *protocol*, which is Hypertext Transfer Protocol (HTTP). This protocol is followed by a colon and two slashes.

After the protocol, the URL must specify the *host*, which is the server that's hosting the web application. To specify the local system, you can use the localhost keyword. To specify another computer, though, you usually use an address that includes the domain name like *www.murach.com*. The other alternative is to use a specific IP address like 64.71.179.86, but you rarely have to do that.

After the host, the URL must specify the *port*. By default, the port for Tomcat is 8080. If another application uses the same port, though, you may need to change that port number as shown in figure 2-7.

After the port, you specify the *path* and the *filename* of the resource. In this figure, for example, the complete URL requests the index.html file that's stored in Tomcat's examples/servlets directory. Please note that front slashes are used to separate the components of a path in a URL.

If you display the index page for the examples/servlets directory, you'll see that it lets you run several of the servlet examples that come with Tomcat. To make sure that the Tomcat servlet engine is installed properly on your system, you can run some of them. If, for example, you scroll down to the Hello World application and click on the Execute link, the application should use a servlet to display "Hello World!" in your browser. This shows that your servlet engine is working properly.

Similarly, if you display the index page for the examples/jsp directory, you can use it to run several of the JSP examples that come with Tomcat. To make sure that the JSP engine is configured properly, you can run some of these examples.

The default Tomcat home page

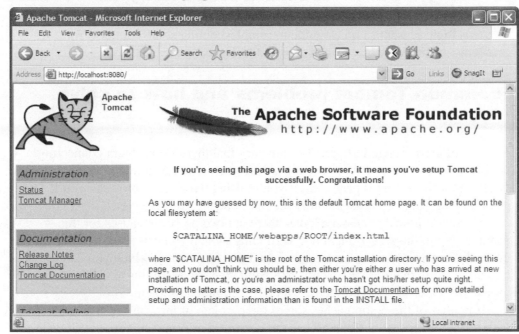

The components of an HTTP URL

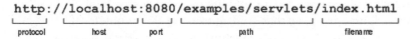

`http://localhost:8080/examples/servlets/index.html`

protocol   host   port   path   filename

HTTP URLs that you can use to test Tomcat

```
http://localhost:8080/
http://localhost:8080/examples/servlets/
http://localhost:8080/examples/jsp/
```

How to view a web page via an HTTP URL

1. Start Tomcat.
2. Start your web browser.
3. Type an HTTP URL into your web browser and press Enter.

Description

- You can use the syntax shown above to specify a *Uniform Resource Locator* (*URL*).
- When Tomcat is running on your local machine, you can use the "localhost" keyword to specify the host machine.
- The default port for Tomcat is 8080. If another application is already using this port, you can change the default port as shown in figure 2-7.

Figure 2-5   How to test Tomcat to make sure it's running

A quick guide to troubleshooting

This topic presents a quick guide to troubleshooting some common Tomcat problems. For more help, you can consult the Tomcat web site.

Two common Tomcat problems and how to solve them

The first error page in figure 2-6 indicates that there's a problem connecting the browser to Tomcat. If you're using a different version of Internet Explorer, you'll see a similar error page. And if you're using the Firefox browser, you'll get a message that says that the browser can't connect to the server.

No matter how the message looks, there are two probable causes for this problem. First, the server might not be running, which you can fix by starting Tomcat. Second, you may have entered the URL incorrectly, which you can fix by making sure that the URL points to a valid web server. In this example, the user didn't enter the port correctly, which is a common problem.

If neither of these approaches solves the problem, it may be because another web server or process is trying to use the same port as Tomcat. If so, you'll need to change the port used by Tomcat as shown in the next figure.

The second error page in this figure shows that the browser has successfully connected to the server, but the server can't find the page requested by the browser. This is the default error page that Tomcat uses for this problem. If you're running Tomcat on a local Windows machine, you can use the Windows Explorer to make sure the directory in the URL really exists.

Since it's a common practice to substitute a custom error page for the default error page, the error page that you get when you encounter a 404 error might look different than the one in this figure. Later in this book, you'll learn how to create your own custom error page and how to configure Tomcat to display that page when it encounters various types of errors.

The Internet Explorer's error page

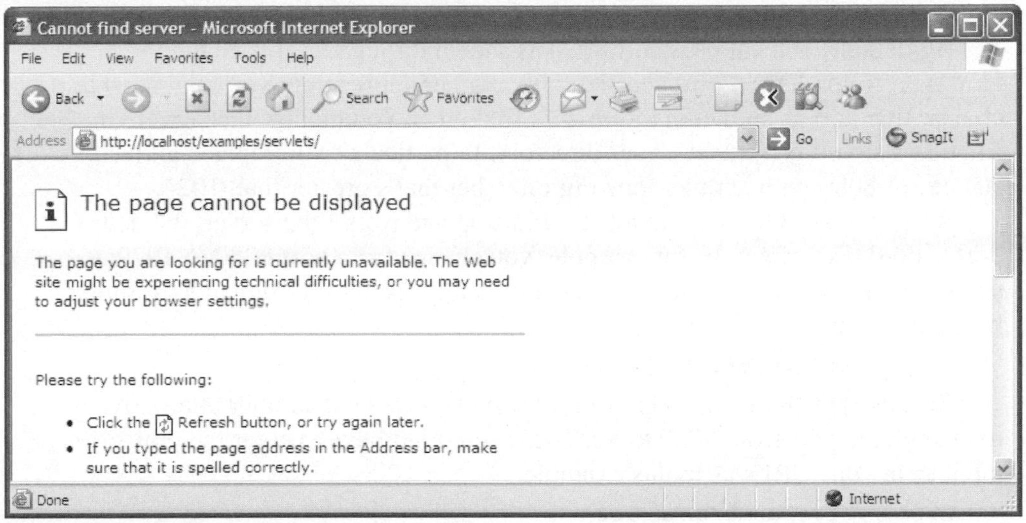

Tomcat's default 404 error page

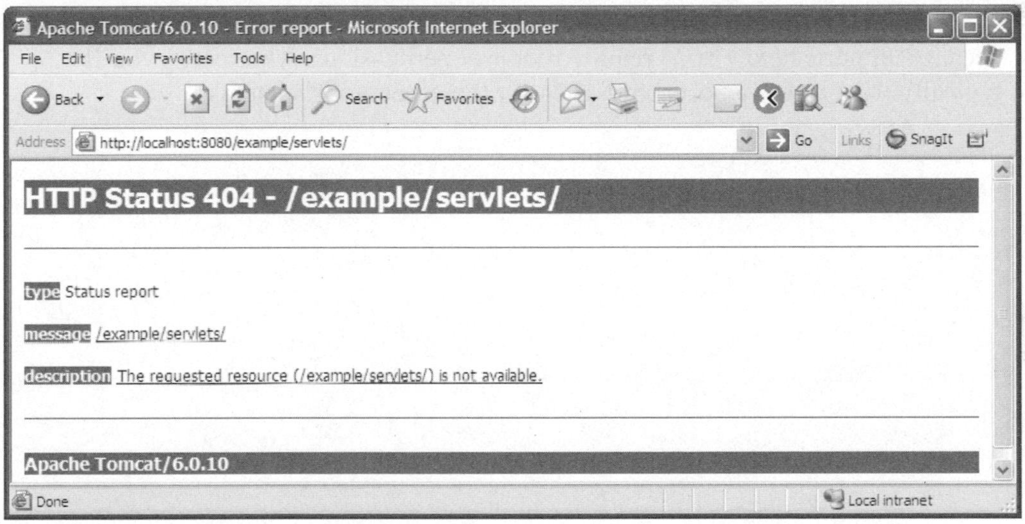

Description

- If the browser displays an error page like the first one above, the HTTP request isn't connecting with a web server. To solve this problem, make sure that the Tomcat engine is running, and make sure that you've entered a valid host name and port number.

- If the browser displays an error page like the second one above, Tomcat is receiving the HTTP request, but it can't find the requested resource. To solve this problem, make sure that you've entered the path and filename of the URL correctly.

Figure 2-6   How to solve common Tomcat problems

How to change the port that's used by Tomcat

By default, Tomcat uses port 8080 as shown throughout this chapter. However, if you have a port conflict with another application, you may need to change that port as shown in figure 2-7. To do that, you modify the server.xml file that's stored in Tomcat's conf directory. In particular, you replace all instances of 8080 with another four-digit number that's greater than 1024.

After you save the server.xml file and stop and restart the server, the new port should take effect. If, for example, you change from port 8080 to 1979 as shown in this figure, you can access the directory listing for Tomcat's examples by entering this URL:

```
http://localhost:1979/examples
```

Because port 80 is the default port for most browsers, another alternative is to change the port from 8080 to 80. Then, you don't have to enter the port number in your URLs as in this example:

```
http://localhost/examples
```

Since this can save some typing, you may want to try this. However, if this causes a port conflict, you will have to change to another port.

In addition, port 80 is more difficult to configure for a Unix or Linux system because all ports below 1024 require root user permissions. As a result, you'll typically want to use a port above 1024 for those operating systems.

The server.xml file

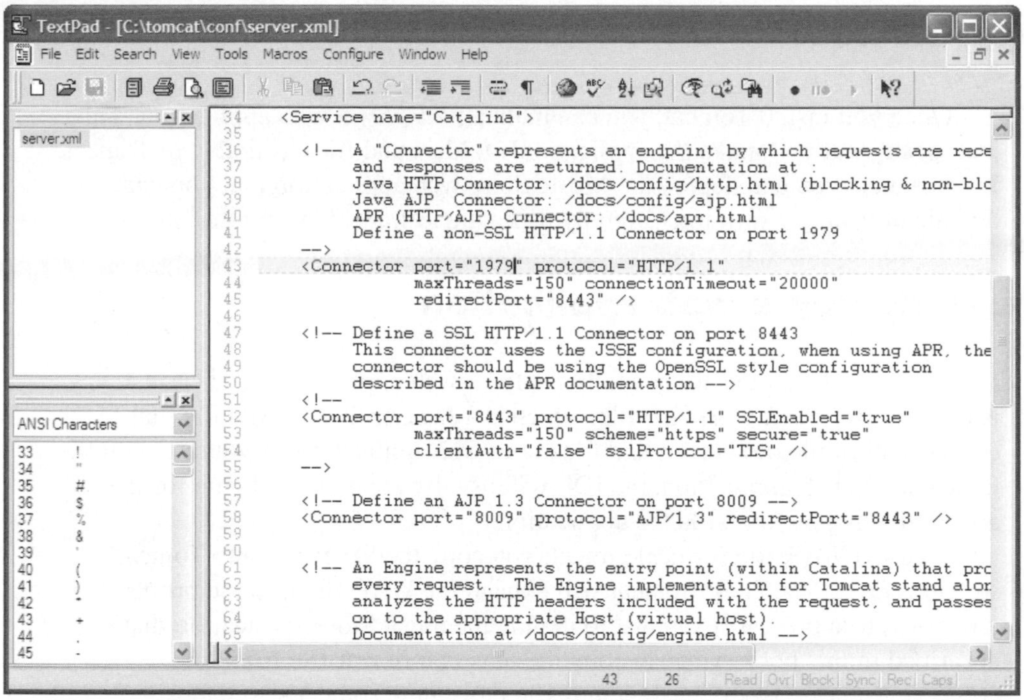

How to change the port that's used by Tomcat

1. Use the Windows Explorer to navigate to Tomcat's conf directory and open the server.xml file in a text editor.
2. Replace all instances of the current port, which is 8080 by default, to a four-digit number that's greater than 1024 or to 80. To do this, you may want to use the Find and Replace feature of your text editor.
3. Save the changes to the server.xml file.
4. Stop and restart Tomcat.

Description

- If you have a port conflict with another application, you can change the default port from 8080 to a four-digit number that's greater than 1024.
- If you don't enter a port when you specify a URL, your browser will use port 80. As a result, if you change Tomcat's default port from 8080 to 80, you don't need to enter a port when entering a URL in the browser. Then, assuming that there isn't a port conflict, you can view a web page by entering a URL like this:

```
http://localhost/examples/servlets
```

Figure 2-7   How to change the port that's used by Tomcat

How to manually deploy and run a web application

Once you install Tomcat, you can manually *deploy* a web application. This just means that you make the application's folders and files available to Tomcat. For instance, you can deploy the Music Store web application that you can download from www.murach.com by using the techniques in figure 2-8.

How to deploy a web application

These are two ways to manually deploy a web application. The easiest way is to use a *Web Archive (WAR)* file, which is a Java Archive (JAR) file that contains all of the directories and files for a web application. If you use an IDE to develop a web application, the IDE will usually create a WAR file for the application when you build the application.

To use a WAR file for deployment, you copy the WAR file into Tomcat's webapps directory. Then, Tomcat will expand the WAR file into the proper directory structure. For example, to deploy the musicStore application that's described in this book, you can copy the musicStore.war file from the c:/murach/servlet_jsp/manual_deploy directory into Tomcat's webapps directory.

If you don't have a WAR file available, you can manually deploy a web application by copying the directories and files for the application into Tomcat's webapps directory. If you're running Tomcat on your computer or on a net-worked computer, you can use a tool like the Windows Explorer to copy the files to the appropriate directories. However, if you need to deploy a web application to a server that's running on the Internet, you need to use an FTP program to upload your files to the appropriate directories on the web server.

How to run a web application

Once you've copied the files for a web application to the appropriate directory, you can manually run the pages for the web application by entering a URL that points to a web page. Or, you can click on a link that points to a web page. In this figure, the URL points to the index page for the musicStore directory that's stored in Tomcat's webapps directory. If you know that you will frequently run a page like this, you can use your web browser to bookmark the page. Then, you can use the bookmark to run the page without having to type the URL for the page.

The home page for the musicStore application

Two ways to manually deploy a web application

- With Tomcat running, copy the WAR file for the application into Tomcat's webapps directory. Then, Tomcat expands the WAR file into the proper directory structure.
- Copy the files for the application into Tomcat's webapps directory.

How to run a web application

- Start Tomcat and enter the URL for the application into your browser.

Description

- A *Web Archive* (*WAR*) file is a Java Archive (JAR) file that contains all of the directories and files for a web application. When you use an IDE to build a web application, the IDE usually creates a WAR file for the application automatically.
- In chapter 3, you'll learn how you can use an IDE to automatically deploy and run a web application.

Figure 2-8   How to manually deploy and run a web application

The standard directories and files for a web application

Figure 2-9 shows a simplified version of the directory structure for the Music Store application that's presented in this book. Some of these directories are part of the servlet and JSP specifications. As a result, they are standard for all web applications. For example, all web applications that use servlets must have the WEB-INF and WEB-INF\classes directories. In addition, you can optionally include other standard directories such as the WEB-INF\lib directory or the META-INF directory.

Of course, to organize and structure an application, a programmer can create other directories within these directories. In this figure, for example, the admin, cart, and download directories are used to organize the Administration, Cart, and Download sections of the Music Store application.

To start, each web application must have a root directory. This directory can be referred to as the *document root directory*, or just *document root*. In this figure, the document root directory is named musicStore, and it is subordinate to Tomcat's webapps directory. Then, all of the other directories and files for the application must be subordinate to this document root directory.

The WEB-INF directory that's subordinate to the document root directory must contain the web.xml file for the application. You'll learn more about this file in the next figure. In addition, you can use this directory or any of its subdirectories to store other files that you don't want to be directly accessible from the web. For example, some applications in this book use the WEB-INF directory to store data files. This prevents users from directly accessing these files.

The WEB-INF directory also has a few standard directories that are subordinate to it. In particular, the WEB-INF\classes directory is the root directory for all Java classes for the application that aren't stored in JAR files, including servlets. Typically, these are the classes that you write. In contrast, the WEB-INF\lib directory contains the JAR files that contain any Java class libraries for the application. Typically, you get these JAR files from a third party. Remember, though, that Tomcat's lib directory stores the JAR files for the class libraries that are available to all web applications running on the web server. As a result, you only use the WEB-INF\lib directory if you want to make the JAR file available to just that one application.

To organize the classes that you create for the application, you can store them in *packages*. In that case, you need to create one subdirectory for each package. For example, this figure shows five packages. Three of these packages (music.admin, music.cart, and music.download) contain servlets that work with the Administration, Cart, and Download sections of the application while the other two contain the Java classes that provide the business objects (music.business) and data access objects (music.data) for the application.

As you progress through this book, you'll learn how to use some other standard directories and files to deploy web applications. For example, if you want to use the database connection pool that's available from Tomcat, you can

The directory structure for a web application named musicStore

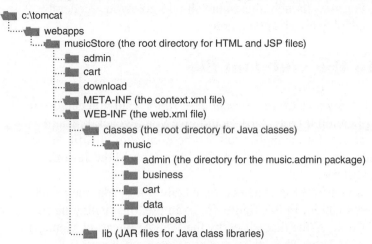

A summary of the directories and files for a web application

Directory	Description
(root)	This directory and its subdirectories typically contain the HTML and JSP files for the application.
\WEB-INF	This directory must contain a file named web.xml. This file can be used to configure the servlets and other components that make up the application. In addition, this directory is not directly accessible from the web.
\WEB-INF\classes	This directory and its subdirectories contain the servlets and other Java classes for your application. Each subdirectory must correspond with the package for the Java class.
\WEB-INF\lib	This directory contains any JAR files that contain Java class libraries that are used by the web application.
\META-INF	This directory contains the context.xml file. This file can be used to configure the web application context.

Description

- The top-level directory for a web application is known as its *root directory*.

- A Java web application is a hierarchy of directories and files in a standard layout defined by the Java EE specification. All Java web applications must use the first three directories that are summarized above.

- To make classes within a JAR file available to more than one web application, you can put the JAR file in Tomcat's lib directory.

Figure 2-9   The standard directories and files for a web application

modify the context.xml file that's stored in the META-INF directory as described in chapter 14. For now, though, this figure should give you a general idea of what it takes to deploy a web application.

An introduction to the web.xml file

The web.xml file is known as the *deployment descriptor*, and you can use it to configure a web application. Figure 2-10 should give you a general idea of what the web.xml file can do for an application. At the minimum, this file must contain the shaded code. This code defines the XML version and the Java EE standards for the web.xml file.

Typically, though, a web.xml file contains some additional code that's used to configure the web application. In this figure, for example, the display-name element specifies the display name that's used by the Web Application Manager that's shown later in this chapter. Then, the description element specifies a description for the application that may be useful to other programmers.

After the name and description elements, the servlet element specifies a name for the servlet class that's stored in the music.email package. This name is used by the servlet-mapping element to map the servlet class to a user-friendly URL. As a result, you can use the specified URL to call the servlet class. For now, all you need to know is that the web.xml file typically maps the servlets for the application to URLs. In chapter 6, you'll learn more about mapping servlets to URLs.

In addition, a web.xml file typically defines one or more welcome pages. Then, if a browser specifies a URL that only includes a directory, Tomcat will attempt to display one of the welcome pages for the application. In this figure, for example, Tomcat will start by attempting to display the index.jsp page. If this page doesn't exist in the directory, it will attempt to display the index.html page. And so on.

As you progress through this book, you'll learn some specifics for working with a web.xml file. In chapter 6, for example, you'll learn how to work with servlet mapping. In chapter 7, you'll learn how to define initialization parameters and how to enable custom error pages. And in chapter 17, you'll learn how to restrict access to the pages within a web application.

A web.xml file

```xml
<?xml version="1.0" encoding="ISO-8859-1"?>

<web-app xmlns="http://java.sun.com/xml/ns/javaee"
    xmlns:xsi="http://www.w3.org/2001/XMLSchema-instance"
    xsi:schemaLocation="http://java.sun.com/xml/ns/javaee
        http://java.sun.com/xml/ns/javaee/web-app_2_5.xsd"
    version="2.5">
```

```xml
    <display-name>Murach's Servlets and JSP: Music Store site</display-name>

    <description>The Music Store web site that's described in Murach's Java
        Servlets and JSP (second edition)</description>

    <!-- Enable servlet mapping -->
    <servlet>
        <servlet-name>AddToEmailListServlet</servlet-name>
        <servlet-class>music.email.AddToEmailListServlet</servlet-class>
    </servlet>

    <!-- Map servlets to URL patterns -->
    <servlet-mapping>
        <servlet-name>AddToEmailListServlet</servlet-name>
        <url-pattern>/email/addToEmailList</url-pattern>
    </servlet-mapping>

    <!-- Specify index pages -->
    <welcome-file-list>
        <welcome-file>index.jsp</welcome-file>
        <welcome-file>index.html</welcome-file>
        <welcome-file>index.htm</welcome-file>
    </welcome-file-list>
```

```xml
</web-app>
```

What the web.xml file can do

- Enable servlet mapping so you can call a servlet using any URL or URL pattern.
- Define initialization parameters for a servlet or the entire application.
- Define error pages for an entire application.
- Provide security constraints to restrict access to certain web pages and servlets.

Description

- Every web application requires a web.xml file in the WEB-INF directory. This file is known as the *deployment descriptor* for the web application. At the minimum, this file must contain the information that's highlighted above.

Figure 2-10   An introduction to the web.xml file for an application

How to work with Tomcat's Web Application Manager

When multiple web applications are running on a Tomcat server, you may want to stop and restart one of the web applications without having to stop and restart the rest of the applications. This is particularly true if you're working in a production environment. Fortunately, Tomcat comes with a web-based tool known as the Web Application Manager that allows you to stop, start, and undeploy individual applications that are running on the Tomcat server.

How to start the Web Application Manager

Before you can start the Tomcat Web Application Manager, you must edit the tomcat-users.xml file that's in Tomcat's conf directory so it includes a username and password for the manager role as shown in figure 2-11.

Once you do that, you can start the manager just as you would start any web application. In particular, you can start a web browser and enter the URL for the manager application. When you do, Tomcat will prompt you for a username and password. If you supply a valid username and password for the manager role, you will be able to view the manager as shown in the next figure.

The tomcat-users.xml file

```
<?xml version='1.0' encoding='utf-8'?>
<tomcat-users>
  <role rolename="manager"/>
  <user username="admin" password="sesame" roles="manager"/>
</tomcat-users>
```

The default URL for accessing the Web Application Manager

```
http://localhost:8080/manager/html
```

The Authentication Required dialog box

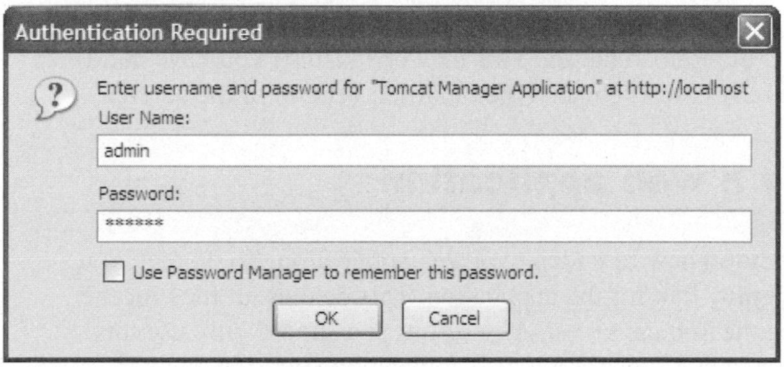

Authentication Required

Enter username and password for "Tomcat Manager Application" at http://localhost
User Name:

admin

Password:

******

☐ Use Password Manager to remember this password.

OK   Cancel

Description

- To add a username and password for the manager role, you can open the tomcat-users.xml file that's in Tomcat's conf directory in a text editor. Then, you can add a role element that defines the manager role, and you can add a user element that provides a username and password for the manager role.

- If Tomcat is running when you add users to the tomcat-users.xml file, you need to restart Tomcat after you close the file so Tomcat will recognize the changes.

- To start the Web Application Manager, start a web browser and enter the URL shown above. When you do, Tomcat will prompt you for a username and password. If you supply a valid username and password for the manager role, you will be able to view the Web Application Manager as shown in the next figure.

Figure 2-11   How to start Tomcat's Web Application Manager

How to start and stop web applications

Once you start the Web Application Manager, it will display all of the web applications that are running on the specified Tomcat server. In figure 2-12, for example, the Web Application Manager shows several of the applications that are included with Tomcat as well as the musicStore application that you learned how to deploy earlier in this chapter.

To stop any of these applications, you can click on the Stop button for the application. Then, once the application has stopped, you can start it by clicking on its Start button. This causes all of the servlets for the application to be reloaded. However, if you just want to reload all of the servlets for the application, you can click on the Reload button. This may be useful if you have modified a servlet and Tomcat hasn't reloaded the modified version of the servlet.

How to undeploy a web application

This figure also shows how to undeploy a web application. To do that, you can click on the Undeploy link for the application. This deletes all files for the web application from the Tomcat server. As a result, you should only use this option if you have the source files for the web application stored in another location. For example, you can safely undeploy the musicStore application from the Tomcat server because you know that a copy of this application is stored with the other downloadable files for this book.

The index page for Tomcat's Web Application Manager

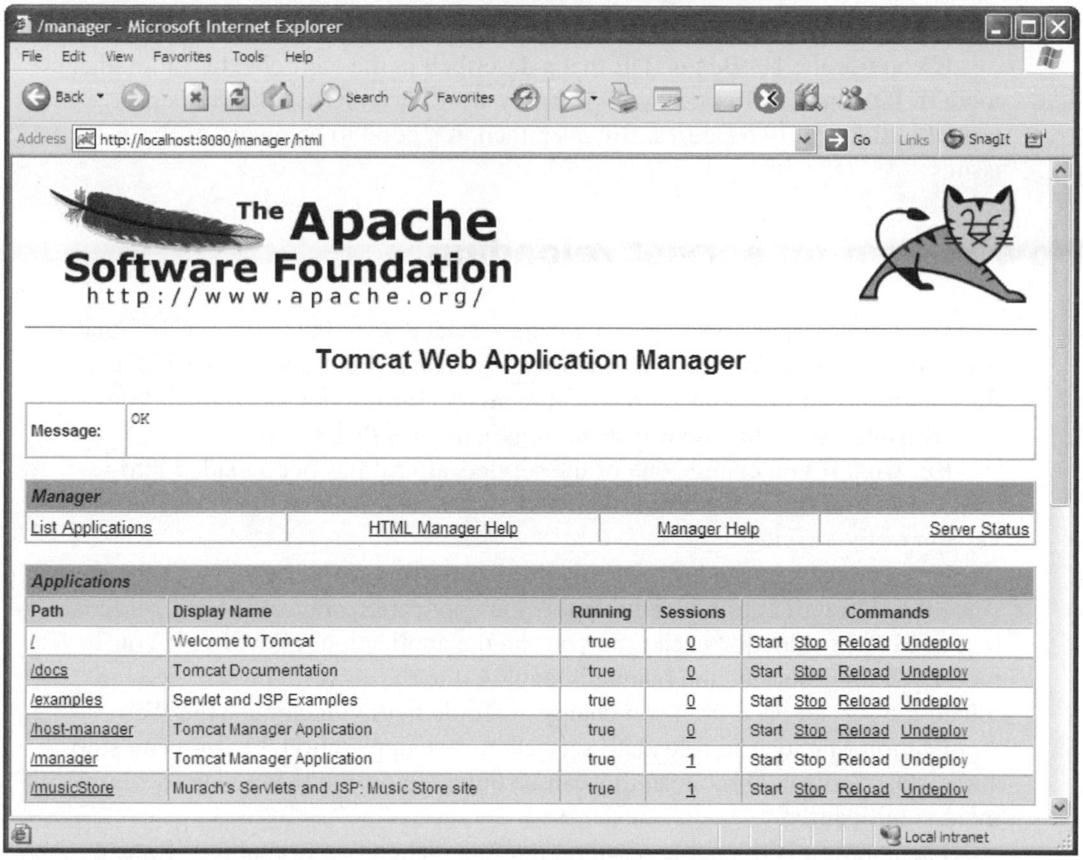

Description

- To reload all of the classes for an application, click on the Reload link for the application.

- To stop an application, click on the Stop link for the application.

- To start an application, click on the Start link for the application.

- To undeploy an application, click on the Undeploy link for the application. This deletes all files for the web application from Tomcat's server.

Figure 2-12   How to use Tomcat's Web Application Manager

Two more configuration issues

If you use the NetBeans IDE that's described in the next chapter or another modern IDE such as Eclipse, you probably won't need to use the skills presented in the next two figures. But even then, it's good to be aware of these issues.

How to turn on servlet reloading

When you request a servlet, Tomcat's servlet engine loads the servlets that users request from disk into internal memory. Then, if there's another request for one of the servlets that's already in memory, Tomcat doesn't reload the servlet from disk to memory. Instead, it uses the one that's in memory.

But what if you change one of the servlets after it has been loaded into memory? How does the servlet engine know that it should use the changed version of the servlet?

If you're using a modern IDE like NetBeans, this won't be an issue for you since the IDE will automatically deploy the application and reload any servlets that need to be reloaded each time you run the application. However, if you modify a single servlet and manually deploy it to the server, you will need to reload the servlet each time you change it. To do that, you can use the Web Application Manager to reload all servlets for the application. Or, you can stop and restart Tomcat. Of course, this can be quite tedious and slow your development significantly.

The solution is to enable *servlet reloading*. When this is enabled, Tomcat checks to make sure the requested servlet in memory is the same as the one on disk. Then, if the one on disk has been modified, Tomcat reloads the servlet before it runs it.

To enable servlet reloading, you add some code to the context.xml file that's stored in Tomcat's conf directory. The procedure for making this change is shown in figure 2-13.

When you're developing a web application, you may want to enable servlet reloading. However, checking to make sure each servlet in memory hasn't been changed requires some overhead. As a result, you usually don't want servlet reloading enabled on a production server.

The context.xml file

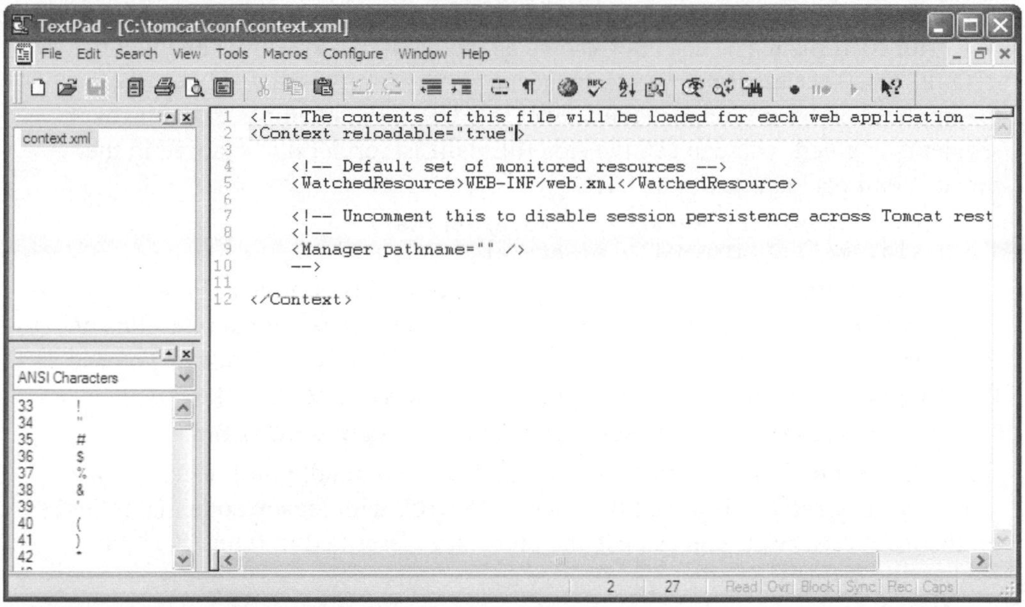

```
TextPad - [C:\tomcat\conf\context.xml]
File  Edit  Search  View  Tools  Macros  Configure  Window  Help

context.xml
 1   <!-- The contents of this file will be loaded for each web application -->
 2   <Context reloadable="true">
 3
 4       <!-- Default set of monitored resources -->
 5       <WatchedResource>WEB-INF/web.xml</WatchedResource>
 6
 7       <!-- Uncomment this to disable session persistence across Tomcat rest
 8       <!--
 9       <Manager pathname="" />
10       -->
11
12   </Context>

ANSI Characters
33  !
34  "
35  #
36  $
37  %
38  &
39  '
40  (
41  )
42  *

                                                    2    27   Read Ovr Block Sync Rec Caps
```

How to turn on servlet reloading

1. Use a text editor to open the context.xml file in Tomcat's conf directory.
2. Add the reloadable attribute to the Context element and set this attribute to true like this:

    `<Context reloadable="true">`
3. Save the changes to the context.xml file
4. If necessary, stop and restart Tomcat.

Description

-   If *servlet reloading* isn't on, which is the default setting, you have to stop and restart Tomcat each time that you change one of the classes that's in memory.

-   If you turn servlet reloading on, Tomcat checks the modification dates of the classes in memory and automatically reloads the ones that have changed. Although this is useful in development, it can cause performance problems in a production environment.

-   The context.xml file is an XML file that controls how the Tomcat engine is configured. Tomcat reads this file every time it starts to configure itself. You can use a text editor to edit this file. Then, you can stop and restart Tomcat to put the changes into effect.

-   This is a global setting that affects all web applications running on this instance of Tomcat. In the next chapter, you'll learn how to set this for a single web application.

Figure 2-13   How to turn on servlet reloading

How to map the invoker servlet

Prior to Tomcat 4.1, a servlet known as the *invoker servlet* was enabled by default. This servlet allows you to request a servlet even if the web.xml file for the application hasn't mapped the servlet to a URL. For example, if the invoker servlet is enabled, you can call the AddToEmailListServlet that's stored in the music.email package with this URL:

```
http://localhost:8080/musicStore/servlet/
music.email.AddToEmailListServlet
```

However, there are a couple of disadvantages to this approach. First, it creates some security issues since it shows the locations of your servlet files on the server. Second, it requires a long and unwieldy URL. In contrast, if you use the mapping shown in figure 2-10, you can call the same servlet like this:

```
http://localhost:8080/musicStore/email/addToEmailList
```

Since this results in a URL that's shorter and easier to read, you'll usually want to map your servlets. However, if you need to work with legacy code that relies on the invoker servlet, you can use the procedure described in figure 2-14 to enable this servlet.

Note that this procedure modifies the web.xml file that's stored in Tomcat's conf directory. This is the default web.xml file for all web applications running on this instance of the server. As a result, this will enable the invoker servlet for all web applications on the current server.

However, if you only want to enable the invoker servlet for one application, you can copy the servlet and servlet-mapping elements shown here into the web.xml file in the application's WEB-INF directory. That way, these elements will remain commented out in the web.xml file in Tomcat's conf directory, but they will be enabled for the web.xml file in the application's WEB-INF directory.

The web.xml file

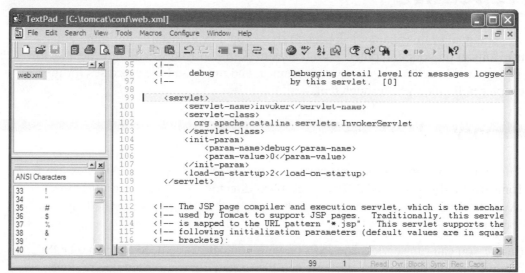

The element that defines the invoker servlet

```
<servlet>
    <servlet-name>invoker</servlet-name>
    <servlet-class>
        org.apache.catalina.servlets.InvokerServlet
    </servlet-class>
    <init-param>
        <param-name>debug</param-name>
        <param-value>0</param-value>
    </init-param>
    <load-on-startup>2</load-on-startup>
</servlet>
```

The element that maps the invoker servlet

```
<!-- The mapping for the invoker servlet -->
<servlet-mapping>
    <servlet-name>invoker</servlet-name>
    <url-pattern>/servlet/*</url-pattern>
</servlet-mapping>
```

How to map the invoker servlet

1. Use a text editor to open the context.xml file in Tomcat's conf directory.
2. Add the privileged attribute to the Context element and set this attribute to true like this:
    ```
    <Context reloadable="true" privileged="true">
    ```
3. Save the changes to the context.xml file
4. Use a text editor to open the web.xml file in Tomcat's conf directory.
5. Remove the comments from the element that defines the invoker servlet.
6. Scroll down and remove the comments from the element that maps the invoker servlet.

Figure 2-14   How to map the invoker servlet

Perspective

The goal of this chapter has been to show you how to install, configure, and use Tomcat on your computer. With that as background, you should now be able to deploy the Music Store application to Tomcat and run it, and the exercises for this chapter will guide you through that.

Summary

- After you install Tomcat on your computer, you need to copy some JAR files from Tomcat's lib directory to the JDK's jre\lib\ext directory. You also need to set the JAVA_HOME environment variable so it points to the JDK that's installed on your computer.

- Before you can run servlets and JSPs on your computer, you need to open a DOS prompt window and use the startup batch file to start Tomcat. When you're done with Tomcat, you use the shutdown batch file to turn Tomcat off.

- When Tomcat is running, you can use your web browser to enter a *Uniform Resource Locator* (*URL*) that accesses an HTML document, a JSP, or a servlet.

- Two common problems that occur when you enter a URL into your browser are (1) that Tomcat isn't running so the browser can't connect with the web server, and (2) that the URL is incorrect so Tomcat can't find the page you want. In either case, an error message is displayed.

- If Tomcat's default *port* is used by another application on your system, you may need to change the default port by modifying the server.xml file.

- A Java web application consists of a hierarchy of directories and files in a standard layout that's defined by the Java EE specification. This layout includes a *document root directory*, a WEB-INF directory, a WEB-INF\classes directory, and a WEB-INF\lib directory.

- The web.xml file for an application is also known as the *deployment descriptor*. This file can be used to configure the servlets and other components that make up the application, and it must be stored in the WEB-INF directory.

- You can use Tomcat's Web Application Manager to start, stop, and undeploy web applications.

- If you want Tomcat to recognize changes that are made to the servlet classes after they have been loaded into memory, you need to turn on *servlet reloading* by modifying the context.xml file in Tomcat's conf directory.

- If you want Tomcat to let you call servlets without mapping them to a URL, you need to enable the *invoker servlet* by modifying the web.xml file in Tomcat's conf directory.

Before you do the exercises for this chapter

If you haven't already done so, you need to install Java SE 6 and the source code for this book as described in figures A-2 and A-3 of appendix A. If you're comfortable with the use of databases, you can also install MySQL and its related components as described in figures A-4 through A-7. The exercises that follow will help you make sure that you've done these installations correctly.

Exercise 2-1   Install and test Tomcat

This exercise will insure that you've installed and configured Tomcat correctly so it's ready to run the applications that you develop.

1. Install and configure Tomcat as shown in figures 2-1 through 2-3.

2. Start Tomcat as shown in figure 2-4. If Tomcat displays any error messages, fix them. Then, stop and restart Tomcat.

3. Run some of the Tomcat examples as shown in figure 2-5.

Exercise 2-2   Run one of the chapter applications

This exercise has you run one of the chapter applications to make sure that our downloadable applications have been installed correctly. Then, in chapter 3, you'll learn how to run these applications by using the NetBeans IDE.

1. With Tomcat running, deploy the ch02cart application for by copying the ch02cart.war file from the c:\murach\servlet_jsp\manual_deploy directory to Tomcat's webapps directory.

2. Use the Windows Explorer to review the directories and files for the ch02cart application. Note that Tomcat has automatically extracted all of the directories and files from the war file.

3. Start the ch02cart application by entering the URL for its root directory. Then, test the application by entering the required data and clicking on the Submit button. This is a partial application that lets you add items to a cart, but hasn't yet implemented the checkout pages.

Exercise 2-3   Run the Music Store application

This exercise has you run the Music Store application that's described in the last section of this book. This will test whether you've installed MySQL and the databases for this book correctly.

1. With Tomcat running, deploy the Music Store application by copying the musicStore.war file from the c:\murach\servlet_jsp\manual_deploy directory to Tomcat's webapps directory.

2. Use the Windows Explorer to review the directories and files for the Music Store application.

3. Start the Music Store application by entering the URL for its root directory. This should display the application's home page. Then, bookmark this page so you can easily run the application again.

4. Click on the "Browse through our catalog" link on the home page, and click on one of the album links on the page that follows. If this works, you have installed MySQL correctly and the application is getting data from the Music Store database.

5. If you can't run the pages that require database access, you can review the procedures in figures A-4 through A-7 in appendix A to make sure you've done them all and done them all correctly. If this doesn't fix the problem, you can fix it after you read chapters 13 and 14, but it's worth taking the time to get this working right now.

Exercise 2-4   Use the Web Application Manager

1. Edit the tomcat-users.xml file so it provides a username and password for the manager role as described in figure 2-11.

2. Start Tomcat's Web Application Manager and enter the username and password as described in figure 2-11.

3. Note the web applications that are running on the Tomcat server. If you did exercise 2-2 and 2-3, the ch02cart and musicStore applications should still be running on this server.

4. Use the Web Application Manager to stop and restart the musicStore application. Then, use the Manager to reload the classes of the musicStore application. Note the difference between these approaches.

5. Use the Web Application Manager to undeploy the ch02cart and musicStore applications. Use the Windows Explorer to review the directories and files for these applications. Note how undeploying the application causes Tomcat to delete all directories and files for the application from the server.

6. Close the browser window for the Web Application Manager.

7. Stop Tomcat.

3

How to use the NetBeans IDE

This chapter shows how to use the NetBeans IDE for developing Java web applications with servlets and JavaServer Pages. We recommend that you use this IDE with this book because it makes it easier for you to enter, edit, deploy, and run the various files that make up a web application.

If you prefer to use another IDE or you don't want to use an IDE at all, you can do that. But our recommendation is that you use NetBeans with this book because it will help you learn more efficiently. Then, when you're done with this book, you can switch to whatever IDE or development method you prefer.

How to install and configure NetBeans

NetBeans is a software framework for developing *Integrated Development Environments (IDEs)*. The NetBeans IDE for Java is built on this framework. NetBeans is open-source, available for free from the NetBeans web site, and runs on all modern operating systems.

This topic shows how to install NetBeans and how to configure it with a Tomcat server. This topic also shows how to register the MySQL database connections for our downloadable applications with NetBeans. However, these skills also apply to other web servers and database management systems.

How to install NetBeans

Once you have installed a JDK and Tomcat as described in appendix A and chapter 2, you're ready to install the NetBeans IDE. Since most Java development is done under Windows, figure 3-1 shows how to install NetBeans on a Windows system.

In summary, once you download the exe file for the NetBeans installation program, you run this installation program and respond to the resulting dialog boxes. Then, the installation program will install NetBeans and create a shortcut to the NetBeans.exe file in your Start menu. Since this works like most Windows installation programs, you shouldn't have any trouble with this procedure.

If you encounter any problems, you can view the documentation that's available from the NetBeans web site and consult the troubleshooting tips. If you want to install NetBeans on another operating system such as Linux, Solaris, or Mac OS X, you can follow the instructions that are available from the NetBeans web site.

The NetBeans web site

`www.netbeans.org`

How to install NetBeans

1. Go to the NetBeans web site.

2. Download the Web and Java EE pack for NetBeans 6.0. On a Windows system, the exe file should be named something like netbeans-6.0-javaee-windows.exe. This download will include a bundled version of Tomcat.

3. Run the install file and respond to the resulting dialog boxes. If you've already installed Tomcat as described in chapter 2, you can uncheck the Tomcat box when that option is offered so it isn't installed again.

The default installation folder

`C:\Program Files\NetBeans 6.0`

Description

- Although this procedure is for downloading and installing NetBeans for Windows, you can use a similar procedure for non-Windows systems.

- For information about installing NetBeans on other operating systems or about trouble-shooting installation problems, you can refer to the documentation that's available from the NetBeans web site.

Figure 3-1   How to install NetBeans

How to start NetBeans

Once you've installed the NetBeans IDE, you can start it by selecting it from the Start menu. When you start NetBeans for the first time, it should display a Start Page tab like the one in figure 3-2. If it doesn't, you can display this page by selecting the Start Page command from the Help menu. Since you don't need this Start Page tab to work with NetBeans, you can close it if you like. To do that, click the X that's displayed on the right side of the tab.

If you're curious to see what version of Java the NetBeans IDE uses by default, you can select the Java Platforms command from the Tools menu to display the Java Platform Manager dialog box. By default, NetBeans uses the latest version of Java that's installed on your system, which is usually what you want. However, if you want to use another version of Java, you can install that version of Java on your system and use the Java Platform Manager to specify that version of Java.

The Welcome page

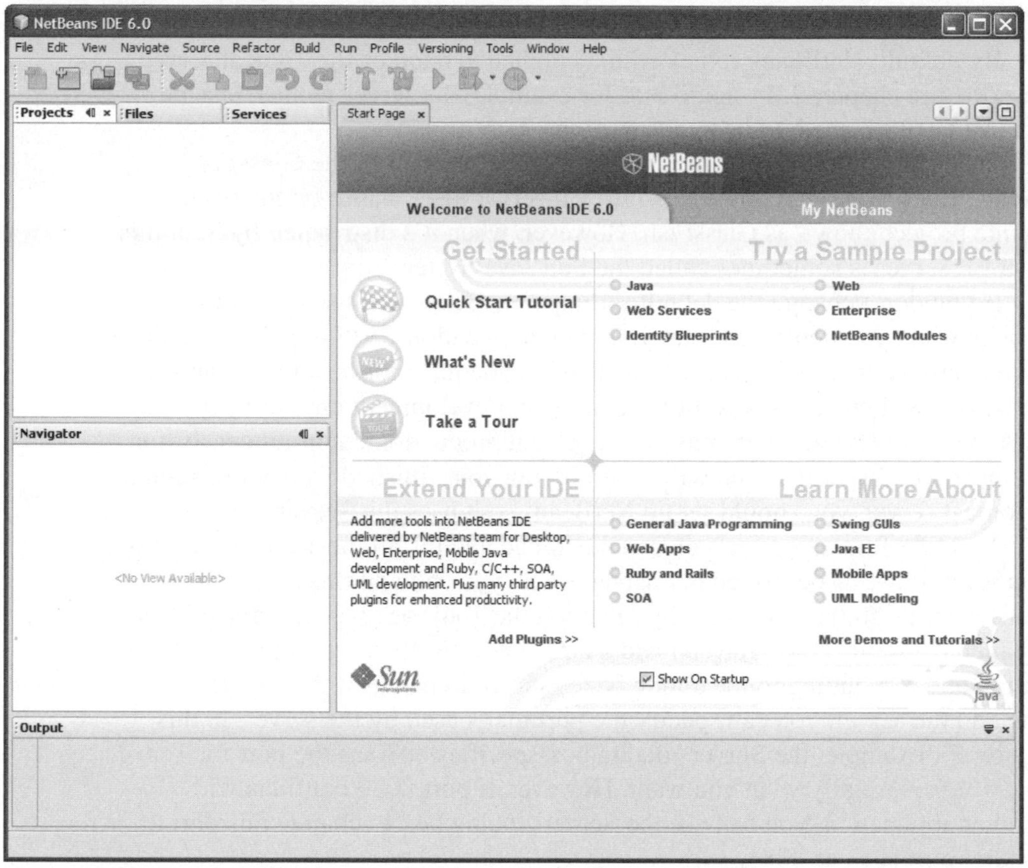

Description

- You can start NetBeans by selecting it from the Start menu just as you would for any other program. When you start NetBeans for the first time, it usually displays a Start Page tab like the one shown above.

- If the Start Page tab isn't displayed on startup, you can display it by selecting the Start Page command from the Help menu.

- You can use the Tools→Java Platforms command to find out what version of Java the NetBeans IDE is using.

Figure 3-2   How to start NetBeans

How to configure a Tomcat server

By default, NetBeans comes with a bundled version of the Tomcat server described in chapter 2. In figure 3-3, for example, the server named Apache Tomcat 6.0.14 is the bundled version of the Tomcat server.

In addition, NetBeans comes with a bundled version of the GlassFish application server, which is a free Java EE server that's based on the open-source project known as GlassFish. However, when it's distributed by Sun, this Java EE server is sometimes called the Sun Java System Application Server.

If you don't change the default settings, NetBeans will use one of these servers when you deploy and run your web applications. Although both of these servers are commercial-grade servers that are adequate for developing applications, you will most likely want to set up your development environment so it uses the same Java EE server as your eventual production environment. If, for example, you know that you will be deploying your finished web application to a Tomcat server, you should set up NetBeans so it uses this server.

To add a Tomcat server, you can download and install the Tomcat server that you want to use as described in chapter 2, and you can add this server to NetBeans. To do that, you start by selecting the Tools→Servers command from the menu system. Then, you can add a new server by clicking on the Add Server button and responding to the dialog boxes shown in part 2 of this figure. After you add the server, you can specify the port that's used by the server. In this figure, for example, the Servers dialog box specifies 8080 as the port for Tomcat, which is usually what you want. However, if port 8080 conflicts with another application, you can use the Servers dialog box to change this port to another port such as 8081.

Although installing a new Tomcat server requires more work than using the built-in Tomcat server, it allows you to set up your development environment exactly the way you want it. For this book, we recommend that you install the Tomcat 6.0 server as described in chapter 2 and configure it as shown in this figure. That way, you can be sure that the downloadable applications for this book will work as described in the text.

The Servers dialog box

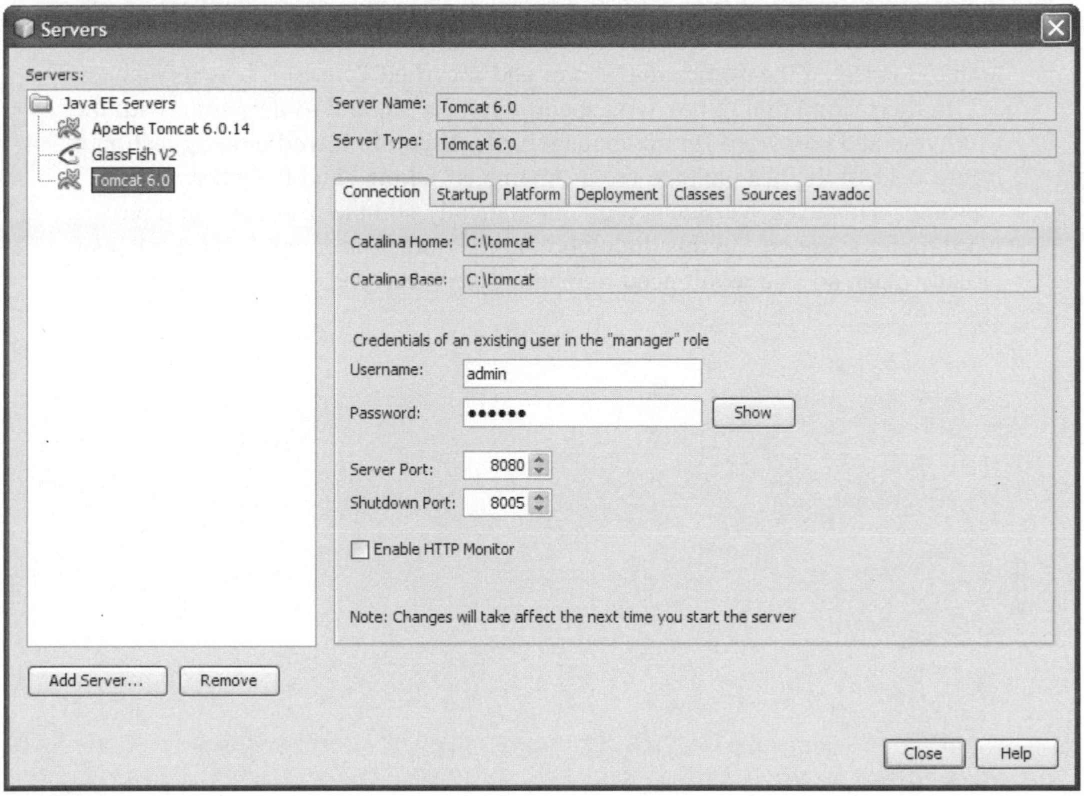

Description

- To view the available servers, select the Tools→Servers command from the menu system.
- By default, NetBeans comes with a bundled version of Tomcat named Apache Tomcat that runs on port 8084.
- By default, NetBeans comes with a bundled version of the Glassfish application server, which is also known as the Sun Java System Application Server.
- To change the settings for a server, select the server in the Servers pane and use the other tabs to modify the settings for that server.
- To add another server, click on the Add Server button and respond to the dialog boxes shown in part 2 of this figure.
- After you add a server, you can specify the port that's used by the server. For example, you can use the Servers dialog box to change the port for Tomcat to 8080, which is the default port for Tomcat.
- To remove a server, select the server in the Servers pane and click the Remove button.

Figure 3-3   How to configure a Tomcat server (part 1 of 2)

When you click on the Add Server button in the Servers dialog box, the first dialog box in part 2 of figure 3-3 is displayed. Then, you select the version of Tomcat that you want to add and specify a name for it. In this figure, for example, I selected the Tomcat 6.0 server and specified Tomcat 6.0 as its name.

In the second dialog box, you specify Tomcat's home folder along with the username and password for the manager role. If you followed our suggestion in figure 2-11 of the last chapter, the username is "admin" and the password is "sesame." However, NetBeans will automatically add the username and password that you specify in this dialog box to the tomcat-users.xml file if it doesn't already exist, so you won't need to manually edit this file.

The first Add Server Instance dialog box

```
Add Server Instance                                          [X]

Steps                    Choose Server
1.  Choose Server
2.  ...                  Server: BEA WebLogic Server
                                 GlassFish V1
                                 GlassFish V2
                                 JBoss Application Server
                                 Sun Java System Application Server
                                 Tomcat 5.0
                                 Tomcat 5.5
                                 Tomcat 6.0

                         Name:   Tomcat 6.0

              < Back   Next >   Finish   Cancel   Help
```

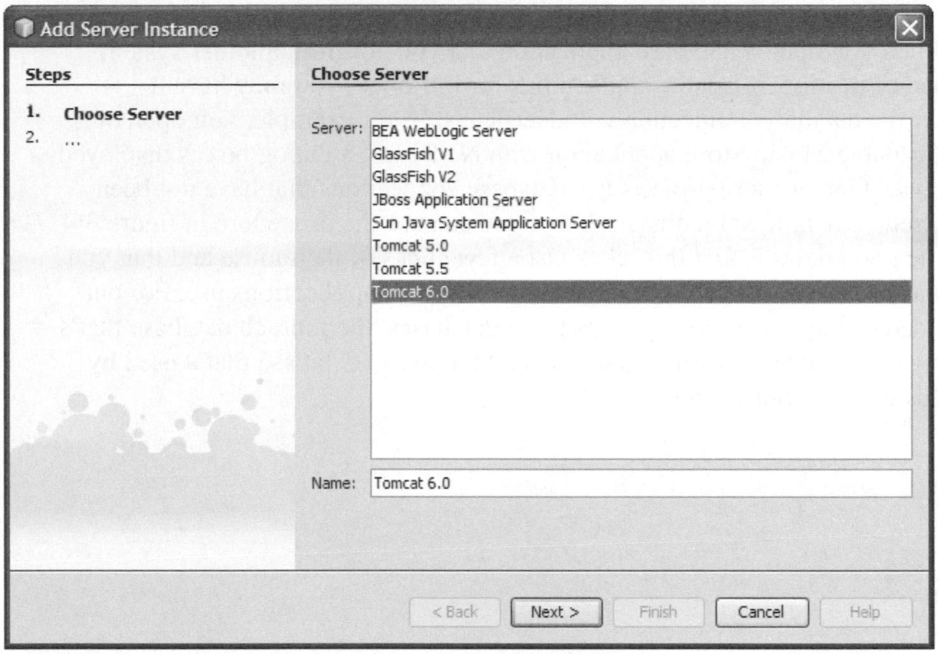

The second Add Server Instance dialog box

```
Add Server Instance                                          [X]

Steps                    Installation and Login Details
1.  Choose Server        Specify the installation folder (Catalina Home) and login details
2.  Installation and Login
    Details              Catalina Home:  C:\tomcat            Browse ...

                         [ ] Use Private Configuration Folder (Catalina Base)

                         Catalina Base:                       Browse ...

                         Enter the credentials of an existing user in the "manager" role
                         Username:  admin
                         Password:  ••••••
                                    [✓] Create user if it does not exist

              < Back   Next >   Finish   Cancel   Help
```

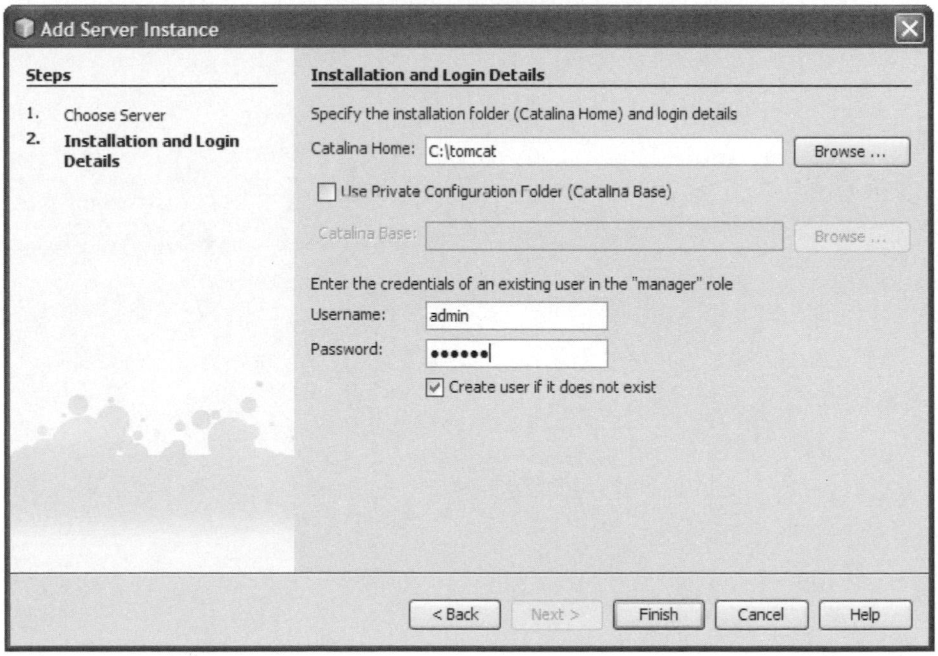

Figure 3-3   How to configure a Tomcat server (part 2 of 2)

How to register a database connection

When you open a database application that you got from another system, like one of the downloadable applications for this book, you may have to register the database connection with NetBeans. If, for example, you open our downloadable Music Store application with NetBeans, a dialog box is displayed that says, "One or more projects use database connections that have not been registered." Then, to solve this problem, you can use the procedure in figure 3-4.

The good news is that this takes just a few clicks of the mouse and that you only have to do this once for each database that your applications use. For our downloadable applications, that's just two databases: the murach database that's used by the applications for chapter 14, and the music database that's used by the Music Store application.

The dialog box for resolving a database connection

Resolve Data Sources

To resolve, select a Data Source name below then click Add Connection.

Database Connections for the Data Sources referenced in this project could not be located.

musicDB

Add Connection...

Close

The dialog box for registering the database connection

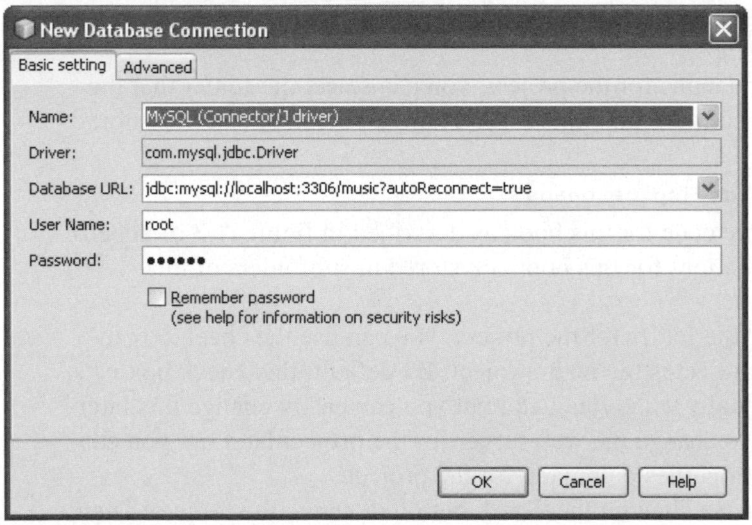

New Database Connection

Basic setting | Advanced

Name: MySQL (Connector/J driver)
Driver: com.mysql.jdbc.Driver
Database URL: jdbc:mysql://localhost:3306/music?autoReconnect=true
User Name: root
Password: ●●●●●●

☐ Remember password
  (see help for information on security risks)

OK   Cancel   Help

How to register a database connection for a project

1. Right-click on the project in the Project window and select the Resolve Data Source Problem command to display the Resolve Data Sources dialog box.
2. Select the data source that you want to resolve, and click the Add Connection button to display the New Database Connection dialog box.
3. If necessary, change any of the entries for the connection. Then, click on the OK button to register the database connection.

Figure 3-4   How to register a database connection

How to get started with NetBeans

Once you've got NetBeans installed and configured, you can use it to create new applications, to open old applications, and to build, deploy, and run applications. The topics that follow will get you started with these skills.

How to create a new web application

Figure 3-5 shows how to create a new NetBeans project for a web application. Essentially, a *project* is a folder that contains all of the files that make up an application. To create a new project, select the New Project command from the File menu. Then, NetBeans will display a New Project dialog box like the first one in this figure.

In the New Project box, you select the Web category and the Web Application option. Then, when you click on the Next button, NetBeans will display a New Web Application dialog box like the second one in this figure. In this dialog box, you can enter a name for the project. In this figure, for example, the project name is "testApp".

After you enter the name for the project, you can select the folder that the project should be stored in. In this figure, for example, the application is stored in this folder:

```
C:\murach\servlet_jsp\netbeans
```

If you install the source code for this book as described in figure A-3 of appendix A, all of the applications for this book are stored in subfolders of this NetBeans folder.

After you specify the folder for the project, you can use the check box to specify whether this project is the main project. By default, this check box is selected, and that's usually what you want, but you can easily change this later on. Also, if you want to change the web server for the project later on, you can do that by using the Properties command for the project.

At this point, you can click on the Finish button to create the project. Then, NetBeans creates a folder that corresponds to the project name. This folder contains the folders and files for a web application that contains a single JSP. It also contains some other files that are used to configure the project.

These configuration files include a *build script* that's automatically generated by NetBeans. This build script is used to specify how NetBeans builds and deploys the application when you run the application. Since this build script usually works the way you want it to, you'll rarely need to modify it. However, you should know that this script is required and that NetBeans uses it when you build, run, and debug your project.

Please note that if you click on the Next button instead of the Finish button in the second dialog box in this figure, a third dialog box for selecting Frameworks is displayed. However, you won't need to select any of these frameworks as you use this book. As a result, you can click on the Finish button in the third dialog box to create the new project.

The first dialog box for creating a new web application

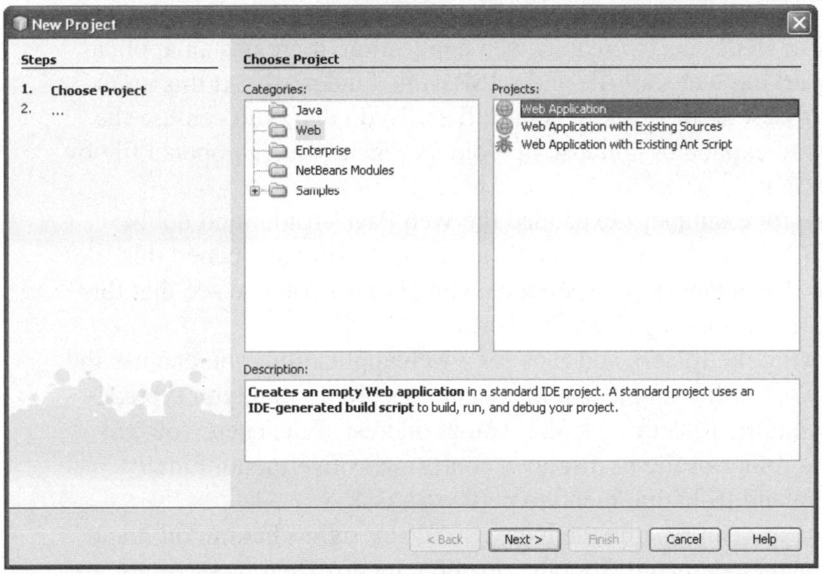

The second dialog box for creating a new web application

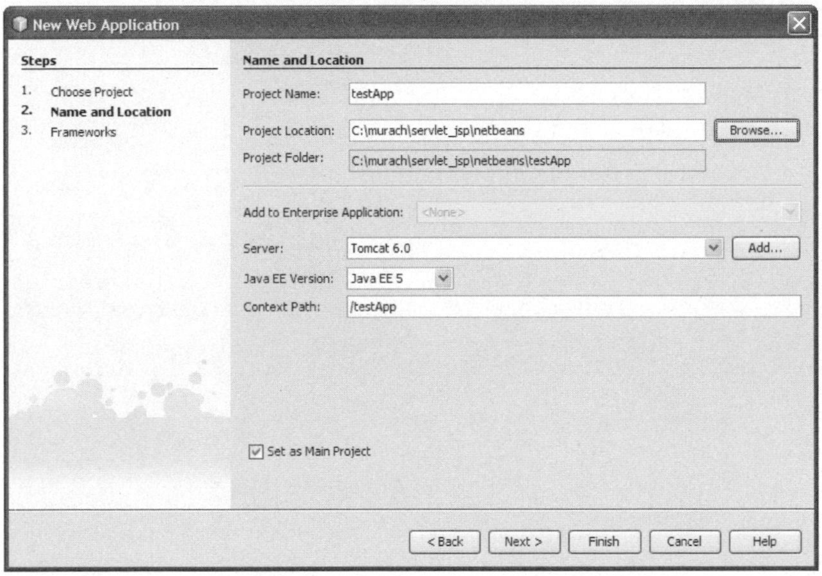

Description

- To create a new project, select the File→New Project command. When you complete the second dialog box, you can click on the Finish button. Or, you can click on the Next button to display a third dialog box, make no entries, and then click the Finish button.

- If you want to change the server later, you can select the File→Properties command for the project, select the Run group, and select another server.

Figure 3-5   How to create a new web application

How to use the Projects window

When you use NetBeans to create a web application, it creates an application that has a working web.xml file and a JSP named index.jsp. At this point, you may want to view some of these default files. To do that, you can use the Projects window to expand or collapse the folders. Then, you can open a file by double-clicking on it.

In figure 3-6, for example, I expanded the Web Pages folder and double-clicked on the JSP file named index.jsp. When I did, NetBeans opened this file in its text editor. If you have any experience with HTML, you can see that this file displays some text that says, "Hello World!".

Besides viewing the folders and files for a web application, you can use the Projects window to work with these folders and files. To do that, you typically begin by displaying the folder or file that you're interested in. Then, you can right-click on the folder or file to display a context-sensitive menu. Finally, you can select a command from that menu to perform a task.

For example, you can rename the index.jsp file by right-clicking on it and selecting the Rename command from the resulting menu. Then, you can use the resulting dialog box to rename the file. Or, you can delete the index.jsp file by right-clicking on it and selecting the Delete command from the resulting menu.

The default web application

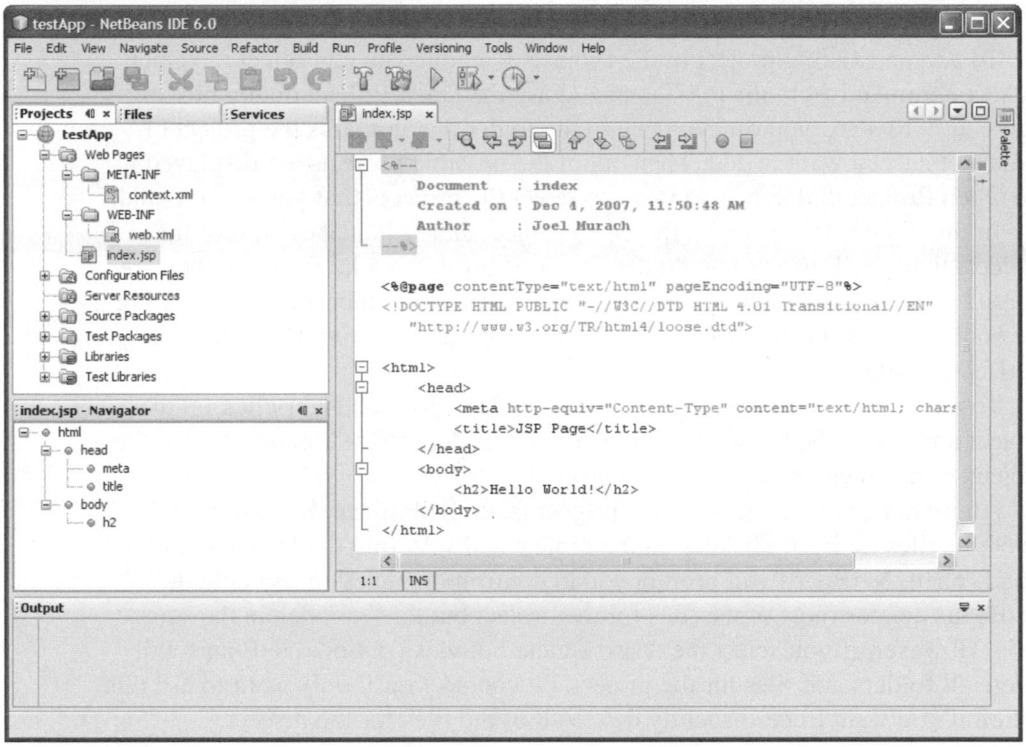

Description

- When you use NetBeans to create a web application, it creates a web application that includes a working web.xml file and a JSP that displays some text.
- To view the files that are available for a web application, you can expand or collapse the folders that are available in the Projects window.
- To open a file in the appropriate editor, you can double-click on the file.
- To rename a file, you can right-click on it, select the Rename command, and respond to the resulting dialog box.
- To delete a file, you can right-click on it, select the Delete command, and respond to the resulting dialog box.
- To display the Projects window if it isn't visible, use the Window→Projects command.

Figure 3-6   How to use the Projects window

How to open and close projects

To add an existing project to the Projects window, you can select the Open Project command from the File menu and use the Open Project dialog box in figure 3-7. To start, you can navigate to the folder that contains the project or projects that you want to add. Then, all of the possible projects are displayed in the Open Project dialog box so you can select the projects that you want to add.

In this figure, for example, the Open Project dialog box shows all of the projects that you'll use as you do the exercises for this book. Note that they are stored in the ex_starts subfolder that's in the NetBeans folder. In contrast, all of the book applications are stored in the book_apps subfolder that's in the NetBeans folder.

To remove a project from the Projects window, you can right-click on the project and select the Close command. Since this doesn't delete the files for the project, you can easily re-open the project.

Alternately, you can remove the project from the Projects window and delete its files by right-clicking on the project and selecting the Delete command. Then, NetBeans will prompt you to confirm the deletion. By default, NetBeans deletes most of the files for the project but does not delete the source code. However, if you select the "Also Delete Sources" option, NetBeans will delete all folders and files for the project. Of course, you'll only want to use this option if you want to permanently delete all of the files for the project.

How to set the main project

When you have several projects open in the Project window, the *main project* is displayed in bold. In this figure, for example, the testApp project is the main project. As a result, if you execute the Run Main Project command as shown in the next figure, NetBeans will run this project. To change the main project, though, you just right-click on the project in the Project window and select the Set Main Project command.

Note also that the Open Project dialog box has an Open as Main Project check box. If this box is checked when you open a project, that project becomes the main project. In this figure, for example, the ch03email project will become the main project.

The Open Project dialog box

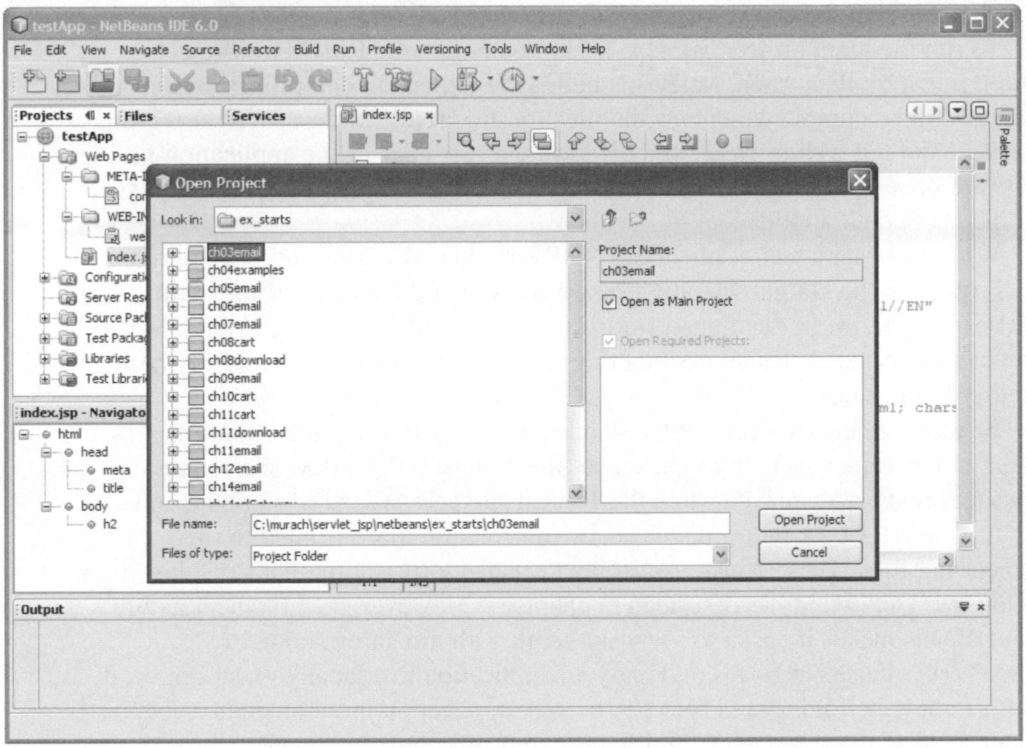

Description

- To open a project, select the File→Open Project command. Then, use the Open Project dialog box to locate the folder for the project and click on the Open Project button.

- When two or more projects are open at the same time, the *main project* is displayed in bold in the Projects window.

- To change the main project, right-click on a different project and select the Set Main Project command.

- To remove a project from the Projects window, right-click on the project in the Projects window and select the Close command.

Figure 3-7   How to work with existing projects

How to build, deploy, and run a web application

To run the main project, you can press F6 or click the Run Main Project button in the toolbar. Then, NetBeans builds the project by compiling all files that need to be compiled, deploys the files for the project to the specified server, starts the default web browser, and displays the first page of the application in that web browser. In figure 3-8, for example, the browser displays the first page for the ch03email application.

When you run a web application, NetBeans displays information about the run process in the Output window that's displayed at the bottom of the main NetBeans window. In this figure, for example, the "ch03email (run)" tab displays information that shows that this application has been successfully built, deployed, and run.

In addition, the two Tomcat 6.0 windows display information about the status of the Tomcat server. In particular, the Tomcat 6.0 window shows the messages that are displayed when the Tomcat server is started or stopped, and the Tomcat 6.0 Log window displays any information that's printed to the Tomcat log files. These windows display the same information that's displayed by the two DOS windows described in chapter 2. However, the graphical nature of NetBeans makes it easier to view and work with this information.

When you use NetBeans to deploy an application to a local Tomcat server, it doesn't copy the folders and files for the web application into Tomcat's webapps folder. Instead, it copies an XML file into Tomcat's conf\Catalina\localhost folder. Here, for example, is the Context element from the XML file for the ch03email application:

```
<Context docBase="C:\murach\servlet_jsp\netbeans\ex_starts
\ch03email\build\web" path="/ch03email"/>
```

This maps the folders and files for the application to the root folder on the web server, which has the same effect as copying all of the folders and files for the web application into Tomcat's webapps folder.

When you test a web application, you may want to display another page besides the first page of the web application. Or, you may want to test a servlet without running a JSP first. To do that, you can run a specific file by right-clicking on the file and selecting the Run File command. This deploys the web application and displays the file in the default web browser.

In addition, you may want to make sure that your web application runs correctly with all types of web browsers. To do that, you can test the web application with multiple web browsers. In this figure, the Internet Explorer is the default browser. But you can change the default browser by selecting the Tools→Options command, selecting the General category, and selecting any browser that's installed on your computer.

The web browser that's displayed when you run a project

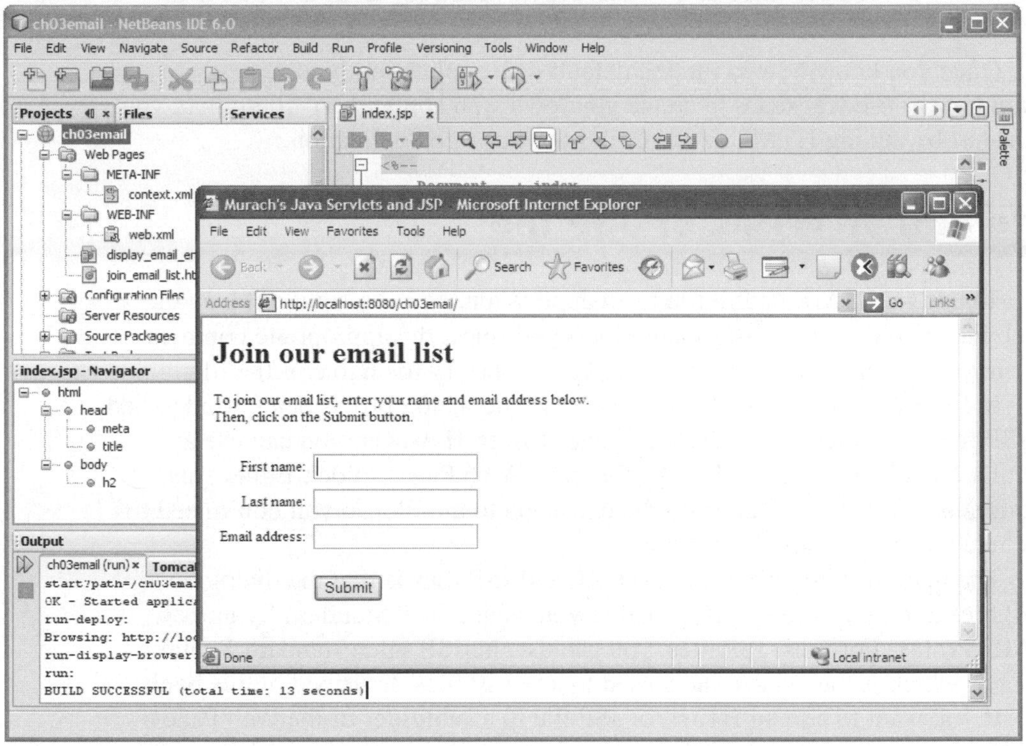

Description

- To run the main project, press F6 or select the Run Main Project command from the toolbar or the Run menu.

- When you run a web application, NetBeans automatically compiles all files that need to be compiled, deploys the files for the project to the specified server, starts the default web browser, and displays the first page of the application in that browser.

- To run a specific file, right-click on the file and select the Run File command. This deploys the web application and displays the file in the default web browser.

- To change the default browser, select the Tools→Options command, select the General category, and select the browser that you want to use.

- To view information about a test run, use the tabs in the Output window. To open this window, use the Window→Output command. To clear the data from one of the tabs, right-click in the window and select the Clear command.

- When NetBeans deploys an application to a local Tomcat server, it copies an XML file for the web application into Tomcat's conf\Catalina\localhost folder. This XML file maps these folders and files to its root folder on the web server.

Figure 3-8   How to build, deploy, and run a web application

How to work with HTML and JSP files

Once you know how to run the default web application, you're ready to learn how to use NetBeans to create your own web application. To do that, you can start by adding HTML and JSP files to your web application.

How to add an HTML or JSP file

To add an HTML or JSP file to an application, you can right-click on the Web Pages folder or one of its subfolders and select the appropriate command. Then, you can use the resulting dialog box to specify the name of the file.

In figure 3-9, for example, the New JSP File dialog box is being used to add a JSP file named test.jsp to the Web Pages folder. However, you can use a similar technique to add an HTML file to the Web Pages folder. Either way, NetBeans will automatically add the extension to the file, so you don't need to include the extension in the filename.

The main difference between HTML and JSP files is that the dialog box for JSP files allows you to specify whether you want to use Standard Syntax or XML Syntax. For most JSP files, you can use the JSP File (Standard Syntax) option, which is the syntax that's used by the JSP files described in this book.

If you want to add an HTML or JSP file to a subfolder of the Web Pages folder, you can right-click on that folder in the Projects window and select the appropriate command. If, for example, you have a folder named cust_serv, you can right-click on that folder to add a file to it. Or, if you have already displayed a dialog box like the one in this figure, you can use the Folder text box to specify a location or to create a new subfolder. Either way, the Created File text box shows the complete path and filename for the file that will be created.

The New File dialog box

Steps

1. Choose File Type
2. **Name and Location**

Name and Location

JSP File Name: test

Project: testApp

Location: Web Pages

Folder: Browse...

Created File: C:\murach\servlet_jsp\netbeans\testApp\web\test.jsp

Options: ⦿ JSP File (Standard Syntax)   ◯ JSP Document (XML Syntax)

☐ Create as a JSP Segment

Description:

A JSP file using JSP standard syntax.

[< Back] [Next >] [Finish] [Cancel] [Help]

Description

- To add an HTML file, right-click on the Web Pages folder or one of its subfolders and select the New→HTML command. Then, use the resulting dialog box to specify the name and location of the file.

- To add a JSP file, right-click on the Web Pages folder or one of its subfolders and select the New→JSP command. Then, use the resulting dialog box to specify the name and location of the file.

- To enter a name for the HTML or JSP file, enter the name in the File Name text box. Note that you don't need to enter the extension for the file.

- To specify a location, you can use the Folder text box. To create a new subfolder, enter the name in the Folder text box. To select an existing folder, click the Browse button to the right of the Folder text box and use the resulting dialog box to select the folder where you want to store the file.

- The Created File text box shows the complete path and filename for the file that will be created.

- For most JSP files, you can use the JSP File (Standard Syntax) option. The XML Syntax is rarely used and isn't covered in this book.

Figure 3-9   How to add an HTML or JSP file

How to edit an HTML or JSP file

When you add an HTML or JSP file to a web site, NetBeans will include some starting code. Before you can use these files in your application, you need to delete or modify this code so it's appropriate for your application. To do that, you can use the Projects window to open the file in a text editor that's designed for working with HTML and JSP files, as shown in figure 3-10.

In general, you can use the same types of techniques with this editor that you use with other text editors. However, since this editor is specifically designed to work with HTML and JSP files, it provides several features that can help you work more efficiently with HTML and JSP tags.

First, this editor displays different parts of the HTML and JSP syntax in different colors, which makes it easier to work with the code. In particular, this editor clearly identifies JSP tags so you can tell them apart from HTML tags. In this figure, for example, the JSP tags are shaded while the HTML tags aren't shaded.

Second, when you enter an HTML or JSP tag, the *code completion* feature often helps you complete the code for the tags. If it doesn't, you can activate this feature by pressing Ctrl+Spacebar as you make your entries. In this figure, for example, you can see the list of entries that are automatically displayed after you enter the starting bracket for a tag.

Third, if you don't want to enter a tag manually, you can use the Palette window to add HTML or JSP tags to the file. To do that, you can drag the tag you want to add from the Palette window and drop it into the appropriate location in the editor window. Then, NetBeans may prompt you with a dialog box that gets some information about the tag before it inserts the code for the tag into the window.

Fourth, NetBeans displays yellow or red markers if you enter a tag incorrectly. Then, you can position the mouse pointer over a marker or click on a marker to get more information about an error. This will help you avoid some entry errors that can take a long time to fix without this kind of help.

When you do the exercises for this chapter, you'll get a chance to experiment with these features. At this point, though, you don't need to understand the code. You just need to understand how to use this editor to edit the code. Then, in the next two chapters, you'll learn how to write code like this.

The HTML and JSP editor

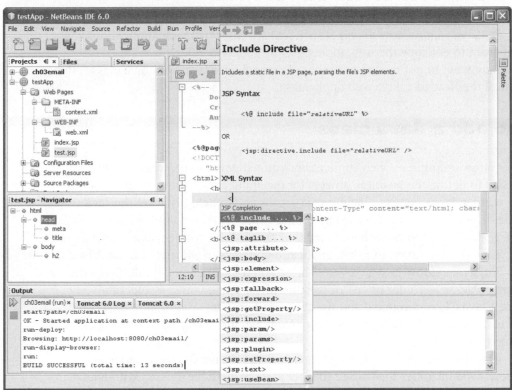

Description

- When you add a new HTML or JSP file to a web application, NetBeans includes some starting code. You can delete this code or modify it for use in your application.

- To edit source code, you can use the same techniques that you use with other text editors.

- After you enter the starting bracket for an HTML or JSP tag, the *code completion* feature provides a list of possible entries. Then, you can select an item and press the Tab or Enter key to insert the starting code for the tag.

- To insert the ending code for a tag right after the starting tag, press Ctrl+Spacebar. You can also press Ctrl+Spacebar to activate the code completion feature at other points in your entries.

- To open the Palette window, use the Window→Palette command. Then, to add HTML or JSP tags, drag the tag you want to add from the Palette window into the code editor. Or, move the insertion point to where you want to insert the code and double-click on the tag in the Palette window. For most of these tags, NetBeans will prompt you with a dialog box that gets some information before it inserts the code into the code editor.

- To identify lines of code with entry errors, NetBeans displays yellow or red markers in the bar at the left of the editor window. Then, you can position the mouse pointer over a marker or click on a marker to get more information about an error.

Figure 3-10   How to edit an HTML or JSP file

How to work with Java files

Once you know how to add HTML and JSP files to a web application, you may want to enhance the web application by adding regular Java classes. Or, you may want to define one or more *servlets*, which are special Java classes that control the flow of a Java web application.

How to add a Java class

For any significant web application, you will want to use regular Java classes to define the business objects for the application. You may also want to use regular Java classes to handle data access and to help organize the Java code. If you have some Java programming experience or if you've read *Murach's Java SE 6*, you should already know how to code regular Java classes.

To add a Java class to a web application, you can right-click on the folder in the Projects window in which you want to add the class. By default, that's the Source Packages folder or one of its subfolders. Then, you can select the New→Java Class command and use the New Java Class dialog box to specify the name of the file. In figure 3-11, for example, the dialog box creates a class named User.

If necessary, you can also specify a package for the file. A *package* is a special type of folder that's used to store and organize the classes within an application or library. In this figure, for example, the dialog box creates the User class in the business package, which is stored in the Source Packages folder.

If you don't enter a package when you add a new class, the New Java Class dialog box will display a message that encourages you to enter a package for the class. Although you don't have to specify a package for every class, it's a good programming practice, and all of the classes presented in this book are stored in packages.

The New Java Class dialog box

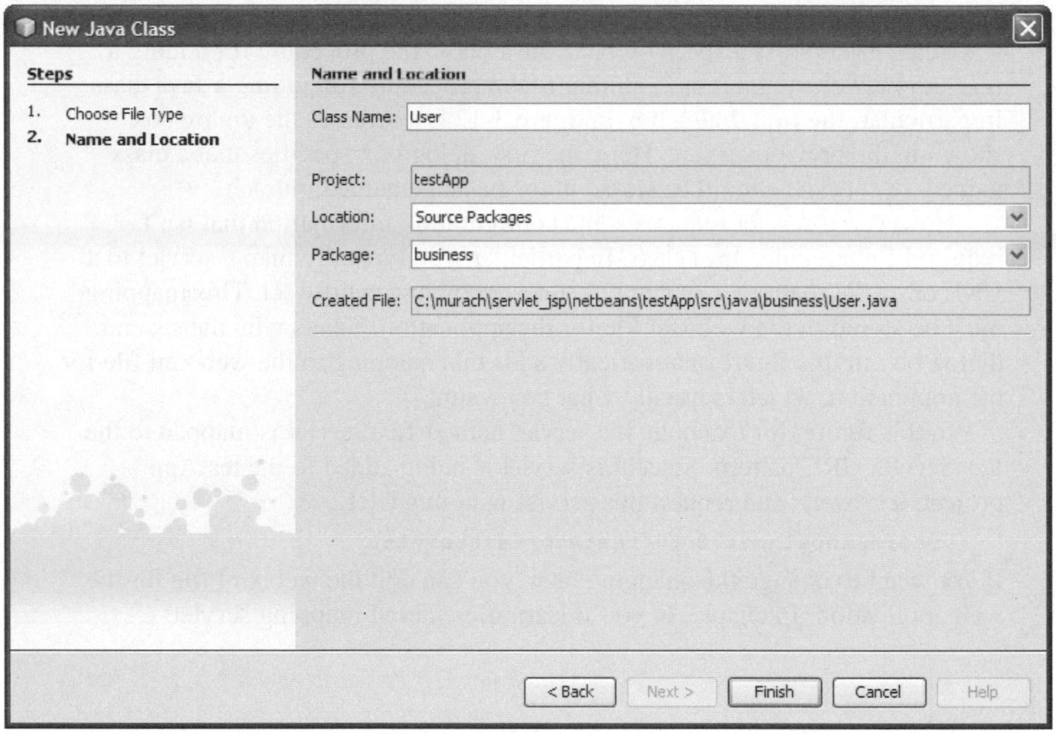

Description

- To add a Java class, right-click on one of the project folders and select the New→Java Class command. Then, use the resulting dialog box to specify the name and location of the file.
- To specify a package for the class, use the Package combo box to select an existing package or to enter the name for a new package.

Figure 3-11   How to add a Java class

How to add a servlet

Since a servlet is a special type of Java class, the procedure for adding a servlet to a web application is similar to the procedure for adding a Java class. In particular, the first dialog box in figure 3-12 is similar to the dialog box shown in the previous figure. Here, the first dialog box specifies that a class named TestServlet should be stored in the package named murach.

However, a servlet requires some configuration information that isn't required for a regular Java class. In particular, you typically map a servlet to a URL or a URL pattern so it can be requested by a web browser. This mapping must be stored in the web.xml file for the application. That's why the second dialog box in this figure automatically adds this mapping to the web.xml file for the application, which is usually what you want.

In this figure, for example, the servlet named TestServlet is mapped to the /testServlet URL pattern. Since this servlet is being added to the testApp project, a browser can request this servlet with this URL:

`http://localhost:8080/testApp/testServlet`

If you want to change this mapping later, you can edit the web.xml file for the web application. In chapter 6, you'll learn more about mapping servlets.

The first New Servlet dialog box

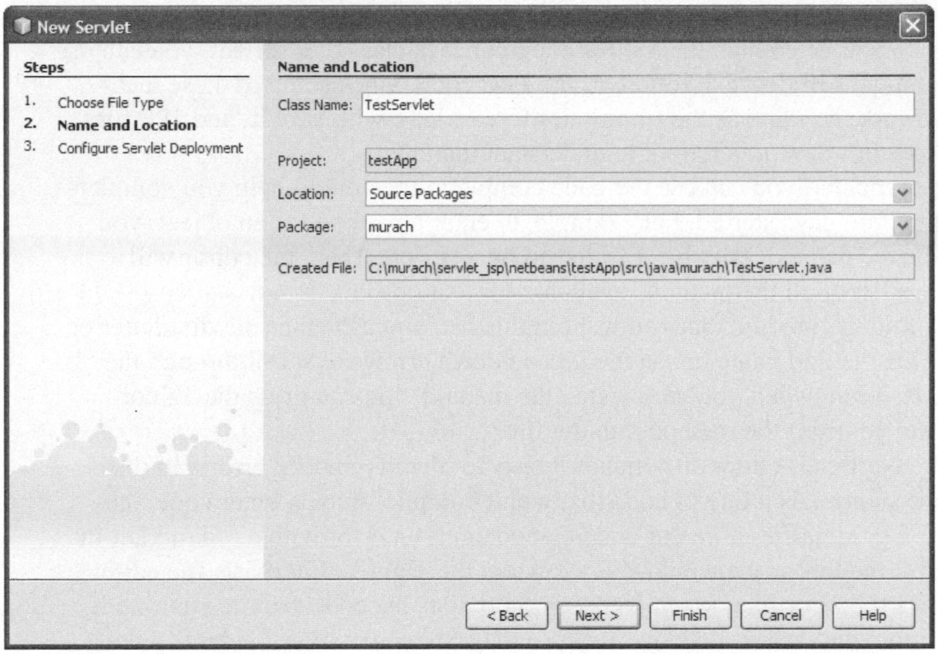

The second dialog box

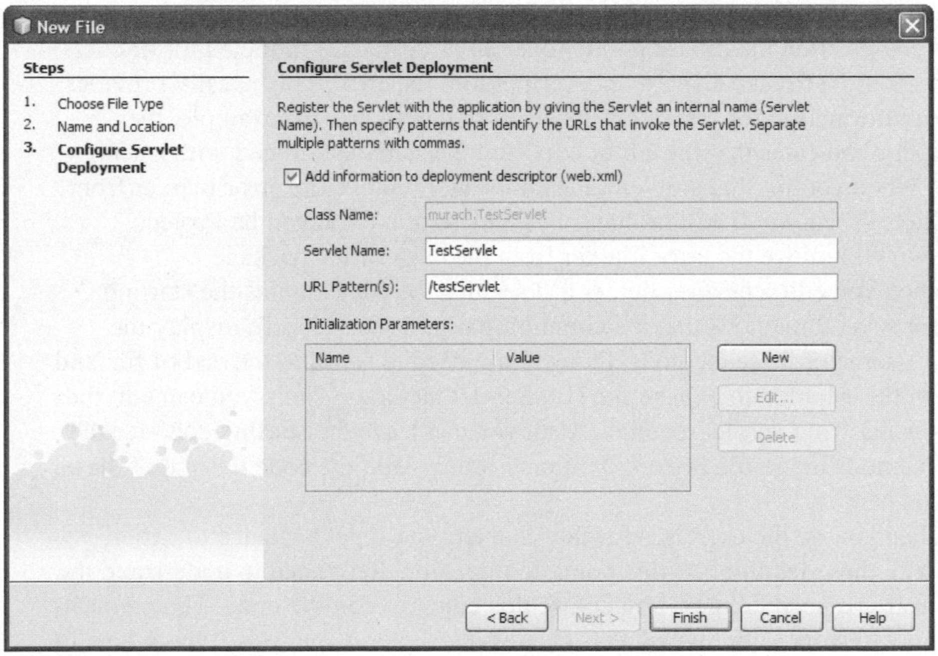

Description

- To add a servlet, right-click on the package, select the New→Servlet command, and use the resulting dialog boxes to specify a name and URL for the servlet.

Figure 3-12   How to add a servlet

How to edit a Java file

Once you've created the file for a regular Java class or a servlet, you can use the techniques in figure 3-13 to edit the Java code. Since some of these techniques work the same as the techniques for working with HTML and JSP files, you shouldn't have much trouble understanding them.

In particular, you can use the code completion feature to help you complete code that you have started. For example, to enter a method for an object, you can type the name of the object followed by a period. Then, the editor will display a list of all the methods available for that object.

To find the method that you want in this list, you can enter the first letter or two of the method name or use the up and down arrows to scroll through the methods. Then, when you've selected the method, you can press the Tab or Enter key to insert the method into the file.

The NetBeans editor also makes it easy to identify and fix errors. In this context, an *error* is a line of code that won't compile. As you enter code, the editor often identifies a line of code that contains an error with a red marker in the bar at the left of the window as shown in this figure. Otherwise, the editor identifies the error lines when NetBeans compiles the code prior to running it. In addition, the Project window may use the same red marker to identify the parts of the project that contain errors. In this figure, for example, the Project window uses four red markers to show that there's an error with the servlet class in the email package.

If you position the mouse pointer over an error marker in the editor or click on a marker, NetBeans displays a description of the error. This usually provides enough information for you to fix the error. In this figure, for example, the description indicates that the editor expected the statement to end with a semi-colon. When you fix this problem, the editor will remove the error marker from the editor. When you fix all problems for a class or a package, the Project window will remove the error marker from the class or the package.

When you edit a new servlet, you'll see that the file contains the starting code for several methods that are commonly used in servlets. To display the code for some of these methods, though, you need to scroll to the end of file and click on the + button to expand the HttpServlet methods. Then, you can edit the methods that your servlet requires. Also, you can leave the starting code for the other methods in the file because you may want to add the code for one of these methods later on.

When you do the exercises for this chapter, you'll get a chance to experiment with these features. At this point, though, you don't need to understand the code. You just need to know how to use this editor to edit the code. Then, you'll learn how to work with regular Java classes in chapter 5, and you'll learn how to work with servlets in chapter 6.

The Java editor with an error displayed

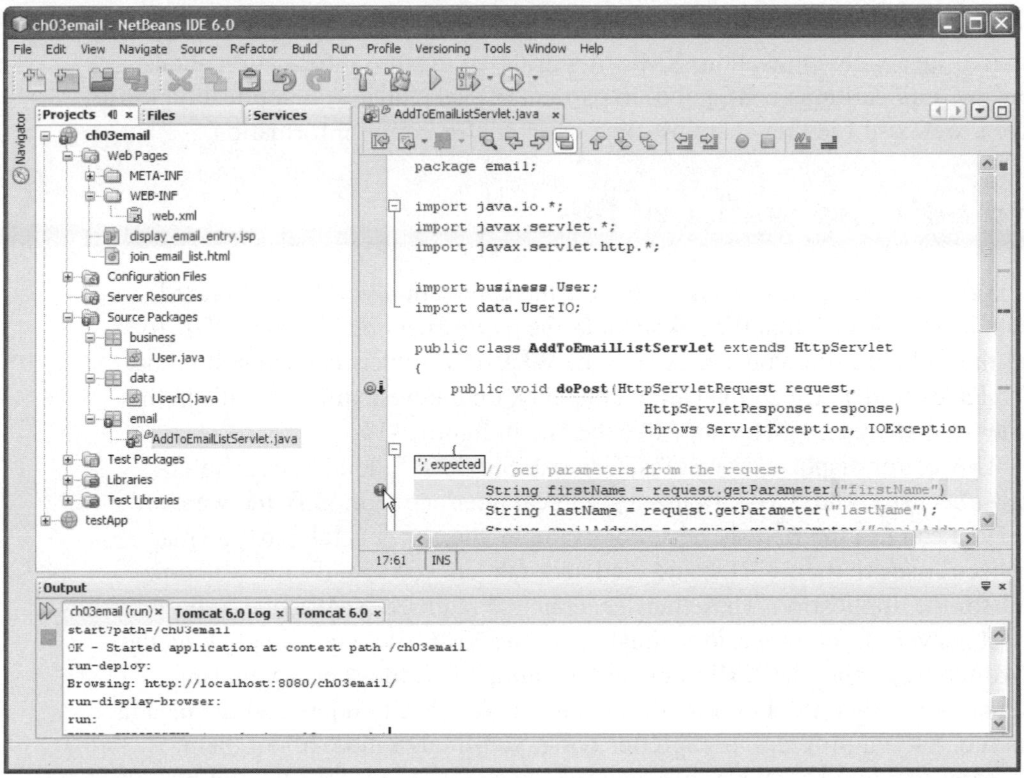

Description

- When you add a Java class or servlet to a web application, NetBeans includes some starting code. You can delete this code or modify it for use in your application.
- To enter and edit source code, you can use the same types of techniques that you use with most code editors.
- After you enter a class or object name and a period, the code completion feature provides a list of possible entries. Then, you can select an item and press the Tab or Enter key to insert the code into the file.
- To activate the code completion feature at other points in your entries, you can press Ctrl+Spacebar.
- To identify lines of code that contain errors, NetBeans displays red markers in the bar at the left of the code editor window. Then, you can position the mouse pointer over a marker or click on a marker to get more information about an error.

Figure 3-13   How to edit a Java file

How to work with XML files

In a Java web application, XML files are used to store information about how the application is configured. In particular, every Java web application must have a web.xml file that contains some basic configuration information.

How to edit the web.xml file

Since the web.xml file describes how the application will be configured when it is deployed, this file is known as the *deployment descriptor (DD)*. To edit the web.xml file, you can expand the WEB-INF folder that's stored in the Web Pages folder. Then, you can double-click on the web.xml file that's in this folder to display an XML editor like the one in figure 3-14.

This editor displays seven tabs: General, Servlets, Filters, Pages, References, Security, and XML. To use a graphical interface to modify the web.xml file, you can use the first six tabs. For example, the Servlets tab lets you map servlet classes to their URLs, and the Pages tab lets you specify the welcome files for the application. These tabs generate the required XML code.

However, if you prefer to manually edit the XML file, you can click on the XML tab to display the XML tags for the entire XML file. Then, you can manually edit this file. For now, don't worry if you don't understand the tags in this file. As you progress through this book, you'll learn more about them.

After you edit a web.xml file, you can check to see if it is still valid by checking it against its *XML schema*, which is an XML file that specifies what elements are valid. To do that, you can right-click on the file and select the Validate XML command from the resulting menu. Then, the results of the validation will be displayed within the Output window, including any errors.

When you modify a web.xml file and use NetBeans to run the application, NetBeans automatically saves the file and forces Tomcat to read it again. However, if you notice that the changes to the web.xml file aren't taking effect, you may need to save the web.xml file and restart Tomcat. That's because Tomcat reads the web.xml file for an application when it starts. Later in this chapter, you'll learn one easy way to use NetBeans to restart Tomcat.

How to edit other XML files

To edit any XML file, you can double-click on it in the Projects window. Then, NetBeans will open the file in an XML editor that looks similar to the second screen in this figure. For example, when you use NetBeans to create a new web application, it automatically adds an XML file named context.xml to the META-INF folder. To view or edit this file, you can begin by double-clicking on it in the Projects window.

The XML editor with the Pages tab displayed

The XML editor with the XML tab displayed

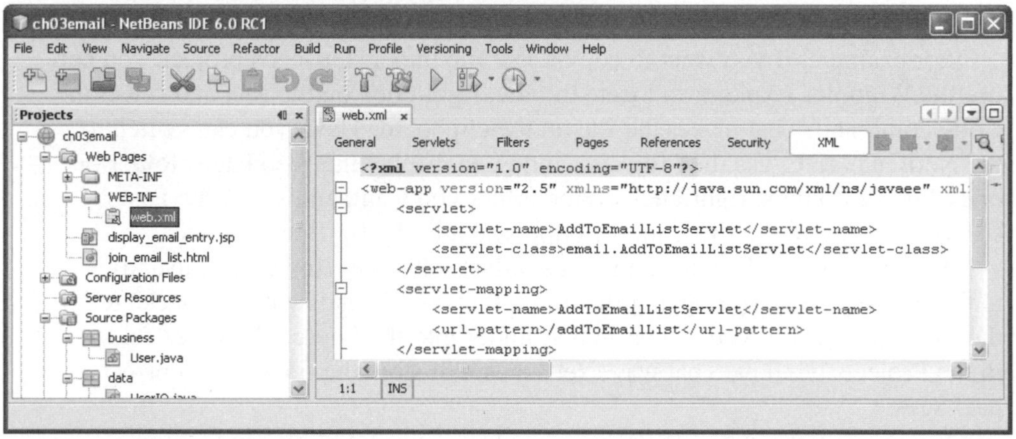

Description

- The web.xml file is known as the *deployment descriptor* (*DD*).

- To edit an XML file, double-click on it to open it. Then, you can use the seven tabs across the top of the page to modify the web.xml file. Of these tabs, you can use the XML tab to manually edit the file in the XML editor.

- To validate an XML file against its schema, you can right-click on the file and select the Validate XML command from the resulting menu. Then, the results of the validation will be displayed in an XML Check window within the Output window.

- When you run an application after you modify its web.xml file, NetBeans saves the file and forces Tomcat to read it again so the changes will take effect. Then, if the elements in the web.xml file aren't in the correct order or if there is another problem with the file, the errors will be noted in the Tomcat and Tomcat Log windows within NetBeans.

Figure 3-14   How to work with XML files

Other skills for working with web applications

This chapter concludes by presenting some other skills that you will need as you develop web applications with NetBeans.

How to add existing files to a project

If you're converting from another IDE to NetBeans, you may have existing HTML, JSP, or Java files available to you that aren't stored in a NetBeans project. In that case, you may want to add those files to a NetBeans project. To do that, you can use the Windows Explorer to copy the files into an appropriate folder in the Projects window.

For example, if you want to copy a JSP file into a NetBeans project, you can use the Windows Explorer to locate the file, right-click on the file, and select the Copy command. That places the file on the clipboard. Then, you can switch to the NetBeans IDE, use the Projects window to display the Web Pages folder or one of its subfolders, right-click on the folder you want, and select the Paste command to paste the file from the clipboard into the NetBeans project.

To copy a Java file, you can use a similar technique. However, it usually makes sense to start by copying the folder that corresponds with the package for the Java class. Then, you can paste that folder into the Source Packages folder in the Projects window. That way, NetBeans will store the files in the correct packages.

When you work with the Projects window, you should realize that the folders in this window aren't the actual folders that are stored on your hard drive. Instead, NetBeans maps these folders to the actual folders that are stored on your hard drive. If you want to view the actual folders that are stored on your hard drive, you can use the Files window as shown in figure 3-15. Here, the Web Pages folder in the Projects window maps to the web folder in the Files window, and the Source Packages folder in the Projects window maps to the src folder in the Files window.

In addition, the build\web folder in the Files window contains the files for the web application after it has been built, and the dist folder contains the WAR file for the application. As you learned in chapter 2, a WAR file is a compressed file that contains all of the files in the build\web directory.

How to deploy a web application to a remote server

When you're done developing and testing a web application, you can deploy it to a remote server by copying its WAR file from the dist folder to the appropriate folder on the remote server. To do that, you may need to use an FTP

The Files window for the ch03email project

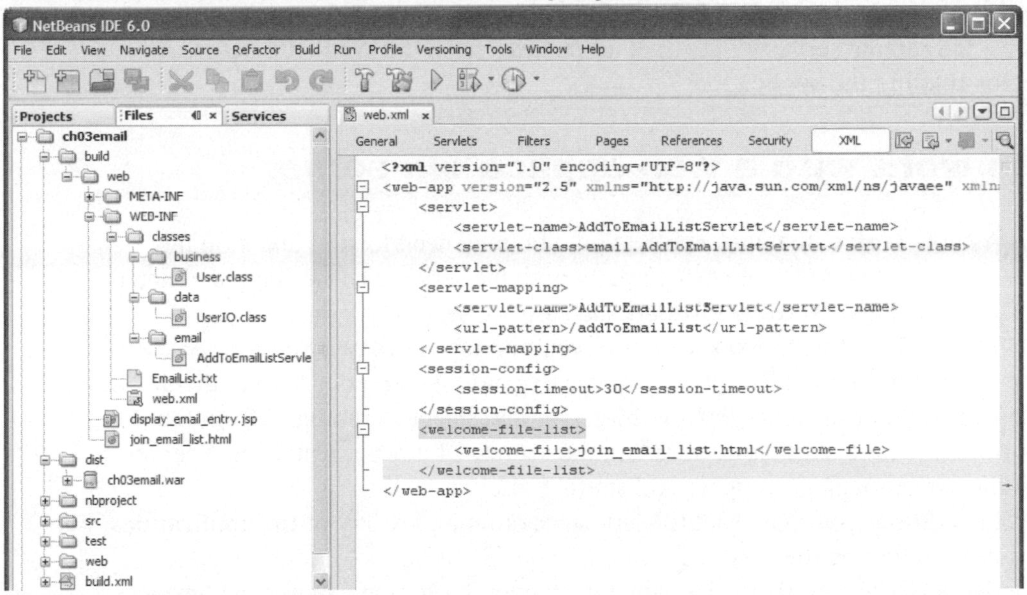

The folders that NetBeans uses

Folder	Description
build\web	Contains all necessary folders and files for the web application after it has been built.
dist	Contains the WAR file for the application.
nbproject	Contains the configuration files and build scripts for the NetBeans project.
src	Contains the source code for the Java files and servlets.
test	Contains the source code for any automated testing for the project.
web	Contains the HTML, JSP, and XML files for the application.

How to add existing files to a project

- Copy the files from the Windows Explorer and paste them into an appropriate folder in the Projects window or the Files window.

How to deploy an application to a remote server

- Copy the WAR file for the application from the dist folder to the appropriate folder for web applications on the remote server.

Description

- The Files window shows the actual folder structure that's used for storing the files of an application. The Projects window shows the logical structure of these folders and files.

Figure 3-15   How to use the Files window

application like the one described in chapter 1. Once the WAR file has been copied to the remote server, the server can run the web application. In most cases, the remote server will extract all the files from the WAR file before it begins running the application.

How to work with a web application server

As you work with a web application, you may need to start and stop the server. To do that, you can work directly with the server as described in chapter 2. Or, you can use NetBeans to start and stop the server.

To use NetBeans to work with a server, you first display a Services window like the one in figure 3-16. Then, you can expand the Servers group to display a server, and you can right-click on the server and select a command from the resulting menu to start, stop, or restart the server. Of course, restarting a server has the same effect as stopping and starting a server.

In addition, you may want to start, stop, or undeploy any of the applications that are running on the server. To do that, you can use a tool like the Web Application Manager that's described in chapter 2. Or, you can use the Services window shown in this figure. For example, you can undeploy an application by right-clicking on the application and selecting the Undeploy command from the resulting menu.

The Services window with the Servers group displayed

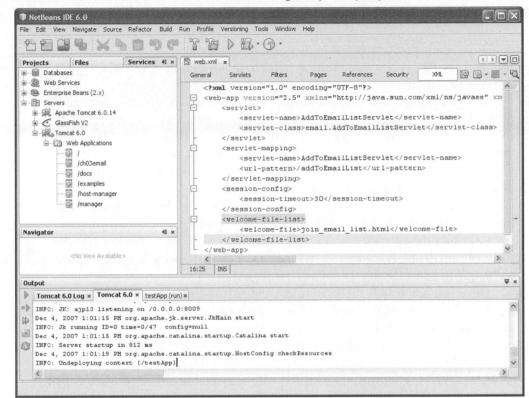

Description

- To open the Services window, use the Window→Services command. The Services window shows the services and other runtime resources that are available to NetBeans.

- To view a server, expand the Servers group. Then, you can start, stop, restart, or refresh the server by right-clicking on the server and selecting the appropriate command.

- To view the web applications that are running on the Tomcat server, expand the Web Applications folder for the server. Then, you can start, stop, or undeploy a web application by right-clicking on the application and selecting the appropriate command.

Note

- You can also start, stop, restart, or refresh the Tomcat server, by clicking on one of the symbols to the left of the Tomcat tab in the Output window or by right-clicking in the Tomcat tab in the Output window and selecting a command from the resulting menu.

Figure 3-16   How to use the Services window

How to add a class library or a JAR file to a project

Most of the projects in this book only use classes that are in the *class libraries* for JDK 1.6 and for Tomcat 6.0. These libraries are available to all projects by default.

To use classes that are stored in other libraries, though, you can right-click on the Libraries folder, select the Add Library command, and use the resulting dialog box to select the library that you want to use. In figure 3-17, for example, the Add Library dialog box is about to add the JSTL 1.1 library that's needed to work with JSTL tags as described in chapter 11. This class library actually consists of two JAR files: jstl.jar and standard.jar.

If the classes you want to use are stored in a JAR file that isn't a standard library, you can still make them available to your project. To do that, you can right-click on the Libraries folder, select the Add JAR/Folder command, and use the resulting dialog box to select the JAR file. For example, you can use this technique to add a database driver to the project.

Once you add a JAR file to a project, the JAR file will appear under the Libraries folder in the Projects window and your application will be able to use any classes within the JAR file when it is deployed. Sometimes, however, your project won't be able to find a JAR file even though you've added it to the Libraries folder. In that case, you can copy the JAR file into the JDK's jre\lib\ext folder. That way, the JAR file will be available to your project as part of the JDK's default library. This has the added benefit of making the JAR file available to all of your projects.

The Add Library dialog box for the JSTL 1.1 library

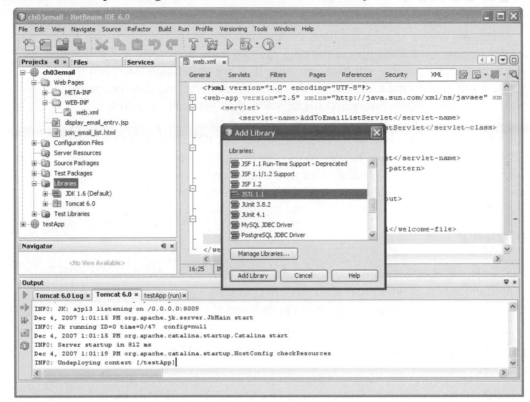

Description

- If you add a library or a JAR file to a project, the JRE will be able to find and run any of the classes within the JAR files that are added to the project. When the application is deployed, these JAR files will be stored in the application's WEB-INF\lib folder.

- To add a library file to the libraries for a project, right-click on the Libraries folder, select the Add Library command, and use the resulting dialog box to select the library. This may add one or more JAR files to the project.

- To add a JAR file to a project, right-click on the Libraries folder, select the Add JAR/ Folder command and use the resulting dialog box to select the JAR file. If that doesn't work, copy the JAR file into the JDK's jre\lib\ext folder.

- To remove a JAR file from the libraries for a project, right-click on the JAR file and select the Remove command.

Figure 3-17   How to add a class library or a JAR file to a project

Perspective

The goal of this chapter has been to show you how to use the NetBeans IDE for developing Java web applications. Because we think that NetBeans will help you learn faster than you will with any other IDE, we recommend that you use NetBeans as you do the exercises for this book. That's why our downloadable source files have the directory and file structure that NetBeans requires.

If you prefer to use some other IDE, you will have to convert the NetBeans directory and file structure so it's appropriate for that IDE. If you're comfortable with doing that, you should be able to use this book with your IDE. If not, we recommend that you use NetBeans for doing the exercises for this book. Then, when you're done with this book, you can switch to the other IDE.

Summary

- The NetBeans IDE is open-source, available for free from the NetBeans web site (www.netbeans.org), and runs on all modern operating systems. You can configure the NetBeans IDE so it uses Tomcat as the web server.

- A *project* is a folder that contains all of the folders and files that make up an application. You can use the Projects window to work with the folders and files of a project.

- You can run the *main project* by pressing F6 or by clicking the Run Main Project button in the toolbar. You can set a project as the main project by right-clicking on it and selecting the Set Main Project command.

- You can use NetBeans to add and edit HTML, JSP, Java, servlet, and XML files. When you edit a file, you can use the *code completion* feature to help you enter code.

- Since the web.xml file describes how the application will be configured when it is deployed, this file is known as the *deployment descriptor* (*DD*). Every web application must have a web.xml file in its WEB-INF folder.

- You can use the Files window to view the physical locations of the folders and files for a project.

- You can add existing folders and files to a project by copying them to the appropriate folders.

- You can deploy a web application to a remote server by copying its WAR file from the dist folder for a project to the appropriate folder on the remote server.

- You can use the Services window to start, stop, or undeploy a web application on a Tomcat server.

Before you do the exercises for this chapter

If you haven't already done so, you should install Java and the source files for this book as described in appendix A. You should also read chapter 2, install Tomcat, and do the exercises for chapter 2.

When you install the source files for this book, they are stored in these directories:

```
C:\murach\servlet_jsp\netbeans\book_apps
C:\murach\servlet_jsp\netbeans\ex_starts
```

Then, you'll find the book applications in the book_apps directory and the starting applications for the exercises in the ex_starts directory. When you do the exercises in this book, you'll be using the applications in the ex_starts directory.

Exercise 3-1   Install and use the NetBeans IDE

This exercise will insure that you've installed and configured NetBeans so it will work with the Tomcat 6.0 server that you installed on your computer.

Install and test the NetBeans IDE

1. Install NetBeans and configure it to work with your Tomcat server as described in figures 3-1 through 3-3.

2. Create a new project for a web application named testApp as described in figure 3-5, but save it in the \netbeans\ex_starts directory. Also, make sure that this project uses the Tomcat server.

3. Use the Projects window to review the folders and files for the testApp project as shown in figure 3-6. Then, run the testApp web application as described in figure 3-8, and review the information that's in the NetBeans Output window.

Add a JSP file to the project and modify the web.xml file

4. With the testApp project for exercise 3-1 still open, add a JSP file named test.jsp as described in figure 3-9.

5. Use the techniques in figure 3-10 to edit the code for the test.jsp file so it includes this tag within its Body tags:

```
<h2>Test JSP</h2>
```

   To do that, type an opening bracket (<), select the h2 tag from the resulting list, and press the Enter key. Next, press Ctrl+Spacebar to complete the tag, and type "Test JSP" within the tag. Then, right-click on the file in the Projects window, and select the Run File command to see what this JSP looks like.

6. Use the Window→Palette command to open the Palette window, and click on the plus signs for HTML, HTML Forms, and JSP to expand these items. Then, drag the Text Input item to the test.jsp file right after the h2 tag that you just entered. In the dialog box that opens, type TestName for the Name and click on the OK button. Now, note the code that has been entered into the file, right-click on the file, and select the Run File command to see the changes.

7. Press the F6 button to run the application. Note that the index.jsp file runs instead of the test.jsp file. To change that, modify the web.xml file for the application as in figure 3-14 so the welcome-file tag specifies the test.jsp file. Then, press F6 to run the application again and make sure this works.

Add a servlet file to the project

8. Add a Java servlet named TestServlet to a package named murach as in figure 3-12, and map it to the /testServlet URL.

9. In the editor window, scroll to the bottom of the TestServlet file and click on the + sign before the HttpServlet methods. That will expand the starting code for these methods. Then, note that the doGet and doPost methods call the processRequest method that's earlier in the servlet. You'll learn how to code the doGet and doPost methods of a servlet in chapter 6.

10. In the Projects window, right-click on the TestServlet file and select the Run File command. At this point, NetBeans will display a blank browser window. But note that NetBeans uses the URL that you specified in step 8 to call the servlet.

Exercise 3-2   Experiment with an existing application

This exercise gives you a chance to run and review one of the applications that has been downloaded from our web site.

1. Open the ch03email project in the ex_starts directory as shown in figure 3-7. Then, use the Project window to view the code that's stored in the HTML, JSP, Java, servlet, and XML files for this application.

2. Run this application to make sure that it runs correctly on your system. Then, enter a first name, last name, and email address into the application and click on the Submit button. This should display the second page for the application.

3. Use the Files window to view the files for this application as in figure 3-15. Double-click on the EmailList.txt file that's in the WEB-INF folder to open it. Note that this file stores the email address that you entered in step 2.

4. Use the Services window to view the applications running on the Tomcat server as in figure 3-16. Then, use the Windows Explorer to view the files that are stored in Tomcat's conf\Catalina\localhost folder. Note that there is an XML file for each web application that NetBeans has deployed to this server.

5. Double-click on one of the XML files in Tomcat's localhost folder. That will display the file in your web browser. Note how this file maps the files for the build\web folder for the application to Tomcat.

6. Use the Services window to undeploy the ch03email application. Then, use the Windows Explorer to view the files that are stored in Tomcat's localhost folder. Note that the XML file for the ch03email application has been deleted.

7. Close the ch03email and testApp projects.

Exercise 3-3   Run our database applications

If you completed exercise 2-3 in chapter 2, you used a WAR file to deploy our Music Store application to a Tomcat server. Since that application uses a MySQL database, that proved that you had Tomcat and MySQL installed right.

Now, this exercise will give you a chance to run this application from NetBeans, which will force you to register the connection for the music database. This exercise will also give you a chance to run one of the applications for chapter 14, which will force you to register the connection for the murach database.

Use the murach database

1. Open the ch14email project that's in the book_apps directory. That should cause a dialog box to be displayed that says the database connection needs to be registered with NetBeans. Click on the Close button for this dialog box.

2. Use the procedure in figure 3-4 to resolve the data source problem and register the database connection for the murach database.

3. Run the application to see how it works. After you enter your name and email address and click on the Submit button, your entries are saved to a MySQL database.

4. Close the project.

Use the music database

5. Open the musicStore application that's in the book_apps directory.

6. Use the procedure in figure 3-4 to resolve the data source problem and register the database connection for the music database.

7. Run the application to see how it works. When you browse through the catalog, the application is getting data from a MySQL database.

8. Close the project.

Were you able to do both parts of this exercise successfully?

If so, all of the software that you'll need for this book has been successfully installed and configured. Congratulations!

Section 2

Essential servlet and JSP skills

The best way to learn how to develop web applications in Java is to start developing them. That's why the chapters in this section take a hands-on approach to application development. When you complete this section, you'll have the essential skills that you need for designing, coding, and testing web applications that use JSPs and servlets.

To get you started right, chapter 4 shows you how to code HTML pages, which is a prerequisite for coding servlets or JavaServer Pages (JSPs). Then, chapter 5 shows you how to code JSPs, which is one way to develop web applications. Chapter 6 shows you how to code servlets, which is another way to develop web applications. And chapter 7 shows you how to structure your web applications so you combine the best features of JSPs and servlets.

With that as background, you'll be ready to learn the other web programming essentials. Then, chapter 8 shows you how to work with sessions and cookies so your application can keep track of its users. Chapter 9 shows you how to build better applications by using JavaBeans. Chapter 10 shows you how to use JSP Expression Language (EL) to reduce the amount of Java code that's in your JSPs. And chapters 11 and 12 show you how to further reduce the amount of Java code that's in your JSPs by using the JSP Standard Tag Library (JSTL) and custom JSP tags.

4

A crash course in HTML

In a typical web application, HyperText Markup Language (HTML) is used to provide the user interface. Then, the user can navigate through the HTML pages to view data, and the user can enter data into HTML forms that pass that data to JavaServer Pages (JSPs) and servlets. That's why you need to have a basic set of HTML skills before you can code JSPs or servlets. And that's why this chapter presents a crash course in HTML.

If you already know how to code HTML, of course, you can skip this chapter. And if you want to learn more about HTML after you read this chapter, you can get a book that's dedicated entirely to HTML. However, this chapter presents all of the HTML skills that you will need as you use this book.

How to code HTML documents

This topic presents all the skills you need to code HTML documents. To start, you'll learn how to code a simple HTML document that uses the basic HTML tags. Then, you'll learn how to use the HTML tags that are used in most commercial web pages. These, of course, are the tags that Java web developers need to know and understand.

Tools for working with HTML

When you're working with HTML pages, you can use a general text editor like Notepad. Or, you can use a tool that's specifically designed for working with HTML such as Macromedia's Dreamweaver. However, if you're going to be doing any serious Java web development, you'll want to use an *Integrated Development Environment* (*IDE*) that's designed for working with HTML, JSP, XML, and Java files.

As you learned in chapter 3, we recommend that you use NetBeans with this book. This IDE includes an excellent HTML editor that uses color to identify various parts of the HTML syntax. This editor also provides other features that can help you enter and edit HTML code.

An HTML document

Figure 4-1 shows a simple *HTML page* in a browser along with the *HTML document* that contains the HTML code for the page. Within the HTML code, *HTML tags* define the elements of the HTML page. Each of these tags is coded within an opening bracket (<) and a closing bracket (>).

Since HTML tags aren't case sensitive, you can use upper or lowercase letters when you code your tags. Since lowercase is easier to read and type, most programmers use lowercase when coding HTML tags, and that's how the tags are coded in this book.

When coding an HTML document, you can use spaces, indentation, and blank lines to make your code easier to read. In this HTML document, for example, blank lines separate the Head and Body sections, and all tags within the Head and Body sections are indented. As a result, it's easy to tell where these sections begin and end. Similarly, the text after the heading in the body section is broken into two lines to make the code easier to read. However, the web browser displays this text as a single line.

An HTML page viewed in a browser

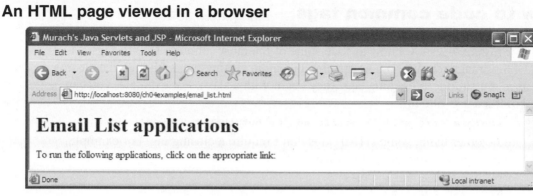

The HTML document for the page

```
<!DOCTYPE HTML PUBLIC "-//W3C//DTD HTML 4.01 Transitional//EN">

<html>

<head>
    <title>Murach's Java Servlets and JSP</title>
</head>

<body>
    <h1>Email List applications</h1>
    <p>To run the following applications,
        click on the appropriate link:</p>
</body>

</html>
```

Description

- *HyperText Markup Language* (*HTML*) is used to provide the user interface for web applications.

- To write and edit HTML code and JSPs, you can use a general text editor like NotePad, a text editor that's specifically designed for working with HTML, or an *Integrated Development Environment*, or *IDE*, that's designed for developing web applications.

- An *HTML document* is used to define each *HTML page* that's displayed by a web browser.

- Within an HTML document, *HTML tags* define how the page will look when it is displayed. Each of these HTML tags is coded within a set of brackets (< >).

- Since HTML tags aren't case sensitive, you can use upper or lowercase letters for your tags.

- To make your code easier to read, you can use spaces, indentation, and blank lines.

Figure 4-1   An HTML document

How to code common tags

Figure 4-2 shows how to code some of the most common HTML tags. Most of these tags require both an opening tag and a closing tag. Although the closing tags are similar to opening tags, they begin with a slash. For example, you can boldface text like this:

```
<b>This text will be boldfaced</b> but this text won't be.
```

On the other hand, some HTML tags don't require a closing tag. For example, you can insert a line break like this:

```
The text for line 1<br>
The text for line 2
```

To start the HTML document, the code in this figure uses a DocType tag that identifies the type of document that's being sent to the browser:

```
<!DOCTYPE HTML PUBLIC "-//W3C//DTD HTML 4.01 Transitional//EN">
```

This tag lets the browser know that this HTML document is an HTML 4.0 document that transitionally conforms to the W3C standard and is in the English language. As a Java programmer, you don't need to completely understand this tag, but you usually begin your web pages with this DocType tag or one that's similar to it. Some HTML editors will automatically insert this tag for you when you create a new HTML page.

After the DocType tag, the opening HTML tag identifies the start of the HTML document, and the closing HTML tag identifies the end of the HTML document. Then, within the HTML tags, the Head and Body tags identify the Head and Body sections of the HTML document. Within the Head tags, the Title tag identifies the title that's displayed in the title bar of the browser. Within the Body tags, the H1 tag identifies a level-1 heading, the H2 tag identifies a level-2 heading, and the P tag identifies a paragraph. Since these tags are coded within the Body tags, they're displayed within the main browser window.

To document your HTML code, you can use *comments* in the same way that you use them in other languages. In this figure, for example, comments are used to identify the beginning of the Head and Body sections, but that's just for the purpose of illustration. You can also use comments to "comment out" portions of HTML code that you don't want displayed by the browser. In this figure, for example, the second P tag is commented out and won't be displayed by the browser. Then, if you want to display this tag, you can just remove the opening and closing comment tags that are coded around it.

The code for an HTML document that contains comments

```
<!DOCTYPE HTML PUBLIC "-//W3C//DTD HTML 4.01 Transitional//EN">

<html>

<!-- begin the Head section of the HTML document -->
<head>
    <title>Murach's Java Servlets and JSP</title>
</head>

<!-- begin the Body section of the HTML document -->
<body>
    <h1>Email List applications</h1>
    <p>To run the following applications,
       click on the appropriate link:</p>
    <!--
    <p>Links to come.</p>
    -->
</body>

</html>
```

Basic HTML tags

Tag	Description
`<!doctype ... >`	Identifies the type of HTML document. This tag is often inserted automatically by the HTML editor.
`<html> </html>`	Marks the beginning and end of an HTML document.
`<head> </head>`	Marks the beginning and end of the Head section of the HTML document.
`<title> </title>`	Marks the title that is displayed in the title bar of the browser.
`<body> </body>`	Marks the beginning and end of the Body section of the HTML document.
`<h1> </h1>`	Tells the browser to use the default format for a heading-1 paragraph.
`<h2> </h2>`	Tells the browser to use the default format for a heading-2 paragraph.
`<p> </p>`	Tells the browser to use the default format for a standard paragraph.
` `	Inserts a line break.
`<b> </b>`	Marks text as bold.
`<i> </i>`	Marks text as italic.
`<u> </u>`	Marks text as underlined.
`<!-- -->`	Defines a comment that is ignored by the browser.

Description

- *Comments* can be used anywhere within an HTML document to document portions of code or to tell the browser not to process portions of code.

Figure 4-2   How to code common tags

How to code links

Any web site or web application is a series of web pages that are connected by *links*. To code a link to another web page, you can use an A (anchor) tag as shown in figure 4-3. Within the opening tag, you code an *attribute* named href that contains a *value* that identifies the linked page. Between the opening and closing tags, you code the text that describes the link. When viewed in a browser, this text is usually underlined. Then, the user can click on the link to jump to the page that's specified by the link.

To code an attribute, you code the name of the attribute, the equals sign, and the value, with no intervening spaces. However, if you code two or more attributes within a single tag, you separate the attributes with spaces. Although it's generally considered a good coding practice to include quotation marks around the attribute's value, that's not required. As a result, you may come across HTML code that doesn't include the quotation marks.

The first group of examples in this figure shows how to use a *relative link*. Here, the first link specifies a web page named join.html that's in the same directory as the current web page. Then, the second link specifies the join.html page that's stored in the email subdirectory of the current directory. If necessary, you can code a link that navigates down several directories like this:

```
books/java/ch01/toc.html
```

The second group of examples shows how to navigate up the directory hierarchy. To do that, you can start your link with a slash or two periods (..). Here, the first example navigates up one directory, and the second example navigates up two directory levels.

Since these examples and the ones that follow don't include the name of a web page, they select the index page for that directory. By default, Tomcat looks for index pages with these names: index.html, index.htm, and index.jsp. However, you can change this behavior for each application by modifying the web.xml file for the application. To learn how to do that, see chapter 7.

The third group of examples shows how to use a slash to navigate to the directory that's defined as the web applications directory by your web server. For Tomcat, this directory is the webapps directory, and the first example goes to this directory. In contrast, the second example specifies the musicStore directory that's in the web applications directory of the web server.

The fourth group of examples shows how to use an *absolute link* to specify a web page. Here, the first link shows how to specify a web page that's stored in the email subdirectory of the root HTML directory for the www.murach.com web site. The second link specifies the same web page, but it uses an IP address instead of a URL. Although you rarely need to use IP addresses, you may need to use them for sites that are under development and haven't yet been assigned their domain names.

Two Anchor tags viewed in a browser

The Email List application 1
The Email List application 2

Examples of Anchor tags

Anchor tags with URLs that are relative to the current directory

```
<a href="join.html">The Email List application 1</a><br>
<a href="email/join.html">The Email List application 2</a><br>
```

Anchor tags with relative URLs that navigate up the directory structure

```
<a href="../">Go back one directory level</a><br>
<a href="../../">Go back two directory levels</a><br>
```

Anchor tags with URLs that are relative to the webapps directory

```
<a href="/">Go to the default root directory for the web server</a><br>
<a href="/musicStore">Go to the root directory of the musicStore app</a>
```

Anchor tags with absolute URLs

```
<a href="http://www.murach.com/email">An Internet address</a>
<a href="http://64.71.179.86/email">An IP address</a>
```

The Anchor tag

Tag	Description
`<a> </a>`	Defines a link to another URL. When the user clicks on the text that's displayed by the tag, the browser requests the page that is identified by the Href attribute of the tag.

One attribute of the Anchor tag

Attribute	Description
`href`	Specifies the URL for the link.

How to code attributes for tags

* Within the starting tag, code a space and the attribute name. Then, if the attribute requires a value, code the equals sign followed by the value between quotation marks with no intervening spaces.
* If more than one attribute is required, separate the attributes with spaces.

Description

* A tag can have one or more *attributes*, and most attributes require values. Although it's considered a good coding practice to code values within quotation marks, the quotation marks aren't required.
* When you code a *relative URL* in the Href attribute, the URL can be relative to the current directory, which is the one for the current HTML page, or the URL can be relative to the web server's directory for web applications.
* When you code an *absolute URL*, you code the complete URL. To do that, you can code the name of the host or the IP address for the host.

Figure 4-3   How to code links to other HTML pages

How to code tables

As you work with HTML, you will need to use one or more *tables* to present data in *rows* and *columns* as shown in figure 4-4. To start, you use the Table tag to identify the start and end of the table. Within the Table tag, you use the TR (table row) tag to specify a new row, and you use the TD (table data) tag, to specify a new column. In this figure, for example, the table contains three rows and two columns.

The intersection of a row and column is known as a *cell*. Typically, each cell of a table stores text as shown in this figure. However, cells can store any type of data including links, images, controls, and even other tables. In fact, it's common for a web page to contain one or more tables nested within other tables.

The HTML code for a table

```
<p>Here is the information that you entered:</p>

<table cellspacing="5" cellpadding="5" border="1">
    <tr>
        <td align="right">First name:</td>
        <td>John</td>
    </tr>
    <tr>
        <td align="right">Last name:</td>
        <td>Smith</td>
    </tr>
    <tr>
        <td align="right">Email address:</td>
        <td>jsmith@hotmail.com</td>
    </tr>
</table>
```

The table displayed in a browser

Here is the information that you entered:

First name:	John
Last name:	Smith
Email address:	jsmith@hotmail.com

The tags for working with tables

Tag	Description
`<table> </table>`	Marks the start and end of the table.
`<tr> </tr>`	Marks the start and end of each row.
`<td> </td>`	Marks the start and end of each data cell within a row.

Description

- A *table* consists of *rows* and *columns*. The intersection of a row and column creates a *cell* that can hold data.

- Although this figure shows a single table that stores text within each cell, it's common to store other types of data within a cell such as images, links, or even another table.

- The attributes shown in part 2 of this figure can be used with the Table, TR, and TD tags to control the formatting of the table.

Figure 4-4   How to code tables (part 1 of 2)

When coding the HTML for a table, you usually need to use some of the attributes that are summarized in part 2 of figure 4-4. In part 1, for example, you can see the use of the Border, CellSpacing, and CellPadding attributes of the Table tag. They make the table border visible and add some spacing and padding between the cells of the table. That example also uses the Align attribute of the TD tag to align the text in the first column with the right edge of that column.

When you're creating and modifying tables, you can set the Border attribute to 1 so you can see the cells within the table. This makes it easier to organize the rows and columns of the table and to set the attributes of the table. Then, when you've got the table the way you want it, you can set the Border attribute to 0 to hide the borders of the table.

Although this figure doesn't present all of the attributes for working with tables, it does present the most useful ones. If you experiment with them, you should be able to figure out how they work. In addition, a good HTML editor will provide pop-up lists of other attributes that you can use when you're working with tables.

When working with a table, you can use *pixels* to specify most height and width measurements. Pixels are the tiny dots on your computer's monitor that display the text and images that you see. Today, many computers display a screen that's 1280 pixels wide by 1024 pixels tall. Other common screen resolutions are 1024 by 728 pixels and 800 by 600 pixels.

When coding a table, then, it's a good practice to make the total width of your table less than the total number of pixels for your target resolution. That usually means coding tables where all cell spacing and width measurements add up to be less than 780 (800 pixels wide minus 20 pixels for the vertical scroll bar).

Attributes of the Table tag

Attribute	Description
border	Specifies the visual border of the table. To turn the border off, specify a value of 0. To specify the width of the border in pixels, specify a value of 1 or greater.
cellspacing	Specifies the number of pixels between cells.
cellpadding	Specifies the number of pixels between the contents of a cell and the edge of the cell.
width	Specifies the width of the table. To specify the width in pixels, use a number such as 300. To specify a percent of the browser's display space, use a number followed by the percent sign such as 60%.
height	Specifies the height of the table in pixels or as a percentage of the browser's display space. This works like the Width attribute.

Attributes of the TR tag

Attribute	Description
valign	Specifies the vertical alignment of the contents of the row. Acceptable values include Top, Bottom, and Middle.

Attributes of the TD tag

Attribute	Description
align	Specifies the horizontal alignment of the contents of the cell. Acceptable values include Left, Right, and Center.
colspan	Specifies the number of columns that the cell will span.
rowspan	Specifies the number of rows that the cell will span.
height	Specifies the height of the cell in pixels.
width	Specifies the width of the cell in pixels.
valign	Specifies the vertical alignment of the contents of the row. Acceptable values include Top, Bottom, and Middle and will override any settings in the TR tag.

Description

- Although there are other attributes for working with tables, these are the ones that are commonly used.

Figure 4-4   How to code tables (part 2 of 2)

How to include images

Although text and links are an important part of any web site, most web pages include one or more images. Figure 4-5 shows how to use the Img (image) tag to display an image. Unlike most of the tags presented so far, the Img tag doesn't have a closing tag. As a result, you just need to code the tag and its attributes.

The example in this figure shows how to code an Img tag and its three required attributes. Here, you must code the Src (source) attribute to specify the image that you want to include. In this case, the Src attribute specifies the filename of an image that's stored in the images directory. If you have any trouble specifying the file for the image, please refer to figure 4-3 because many of the skills that apply to the Href attribute of the A tag also apply to the Src attribute of the Img tag.

After the Src attribute, you can code the Width and Height attributes. The values for these attributes must specify the height and width of the image in pixels. If you use one of your HTML editor's tools to insert an image, all three of these attributes may be automatically specified for you. Otherwise, you may need to open the image in an image editor to determine the number of pixels for the width and height.

The last five attributes described in this figure aren't required, but they're commonly used. For example, the Alt attribute is commonly used to specify text that's displayed if an image can't be loaded. This text is usually displayed when a web browser takes a long time to load all of the images on a page, but it can also be displayed for text-only browsers. If you experiment with the attributes described in this list, you shouldn't have any trouble using them.

When you include images in a web page, you can use a *Graphic Interchange Format (GIF)* file, or you can use a *Joint Photographic Experts Group (JPEG)* file. Typically, a web designer will use imaging software such as Adobe Photoshop to create and maintain these files for a web site and will save these files in a directory named images or graphics. In this book, for example, all images used by the applications are stored in an images subdirectory of the applications root directory. GIF files are stored with a GIF extension, and JPEG files can be stored with either a JPEG or JPG extension.

HTML code that includes an image

```
<p>Here is the image for the Murach logo:</p>
<img src="images/murachlogo.jpg" width="100" height="100">
```

The HTML code displayed in a browser

The Image tag

Tag	Description
`<img>`	Specifies how to place a GIF or JPEG image within an HTML page.

Common attributes of the Image tag

Attribute	Description
`src`	Specifies the relative or absolute URL for the GIF or JPEG file.
`height`	Specifies the height of the image in pixels.
`width`	Specifies the width of the image in pixels.
`alt`	Specifies the text that's displayed when the image can't be displayed.
`border`	Specifies the width of the border in pixels with 0 specifying no border at all.
`hspace`	Specifies the horizontal space in pixels. This space is added to the left and right of the image.
`vspace`	Specifies the vertical space in pixels. This space is added to the top and bottom of the image.
`align`	Specifies the alignment of the image on the page. Acceptable values include Left, Right, Top, Bottom, and Middle.

Other examples

```
<img src="java.gif" width="175" height="243">

<img src="../../images/murachlogo.jpg" width="100" height="100">

<img src="http://www.murach.com/images/murachlogo.jpg" width="100"
height="100">
```

Description

- The two types of image formats that are supported by most web browsers are the *Graphic Interchange Format* (*GIF*) and the *Joint Photographic Experts Group* (*JPEG*). JPEG files, which have a JPEG or JPG extension, are typically used for photographs and scans, while GIF files are typically used for other types of images.

Figure 4-5   How to include images in an HTML page

How to use a style sheet

Although you can code formatting attributes such as fonts, colors, margins, and alignment within a web page, most commercial web sites store this information in a file known as a *style sheet*. That way, all of the web pages within a site will have a uniform look that can be quickly and easily modified if necessary. Figure 4-6 shows how you can code a style sheet and link it to your web pages.

To start, this figure shows the code for a style sheet that's stored in a file named murach.css in the styles subdirectory of the current directory. Since this style sheet is stored in its own file and must be linked to web pages, it's known as an *external style sheet* or a *linked style sheet*. The first style in this sheet sets a font and font size for the Body tag, which sets the base font and font size for the rest of the tags. Then, the rest of the styles in the sheet set the font, color, indentation, and alignment for the A, H1, H2, and H3 tags. A style sheet like this is normally developed by the web designer.

Next, this figure shows how to link a web page to an external style sheet. To do that, you can code the Link tag and its attributes in the Head section of the HTML document. Here, you should always set the Rel attribute to "stylesheet". Then, the Href attribute works like it does for the Anchor tag in figure 4-3. In this figure, for example, the Href attribute specifies a style sheet named murach.css that's stored in the styles subdirectory of the current directory.

Web programmers often use external style sheets so the styles developed by a web designer are used in the pages that are being developed or modified by the programmer. An external style sheet represents the highest level of a series of *cascading style sheets*. To override the styles in an external style sheet, you can code a style sheet within an opening and closing Style tag in the Head section of an HTML document. Similarly, you can override a Style tag coded in the Head section by coding a Style attribute within a tag that's in the Body section. Most programmers, though, don't need to override or modify styles. Instead, they use the external style sheet developed by the web designer.

Incidentally, the a:hover notation in the third style in this figure refers to the Anchor tag when the mouse pointer is hovering over the link that it presents. This lets you set two styles for the link: one for its normal display and one for when the mouse is hovering over it. In this example, the color of the link changes when the mouse hovers over it.

The code for a style sheet

```
body { font-family: Arial, sans-serif; font-size: 12px }

a { text-decoration : underline }
a:hover { text-decoration : underline; color : #CC0000 }

h1 { font-size: 16px; color: #003366;
     vertical-align: top; margin-top: 10px; margin-bottom: 0px }
h2 { font-size: 16px; color: #003366 }
h3 { font-size: 14px; color: #003366 }
```

The code in the HTML document that links to a style sheet

```
<head>
    <title>Murach's Java Servlets and JSP</title>
    <link rel="stylesheet" href="styles/murach.css">
</head>
```

An HTML page after the style sheet above has been applied to it

Email List applications

To run the following applications, click on the appropriate link:

The Email List application 1
The Email List application 2

The Link tag

Tag	Description
`<link>`	Specifies the external style sheet.

Attributes of the Link tag

Attribute	Description
`href`	Specifies the location of the style sheet.
`rel`	Specifies the type of link. To specify a style sheet, supply a value of "stylesheet".

Description

- A *style sheet* can be used to define the font *styles* that are applied to the text of an HTML page. To identify the location of the style sheet that should be used for a page, you use the Link tag within the Head tags of the page.

- This type of style sheet can be referred to as an *external style sheet*, or *linked style* sheet, and it is actually the top style sheet in a series of *cascading style sheets*. An external style sheet is typically stored in its own directory, and css is used as the extension for its file name.

Figure 4-6   How to use a style sheet

How to code HTML forms

This topic shows how to code an HTML *form* that contains one or more *controls* such as text boxes and buttons. In this topic, you'll learn how to code 11 types of controls to gather data. In the next chapter, you'll learn how to process the data that's gathered by these controls.

How to code a form

Figure 4-7 shows how to code a form that contains three controls: two text boxes and a button. To code a form, you begin by coding the opening and closing Form tags. Within the opening Form tag, you must code an Action attribute that specifies the servlet or JSP that will be called when the user clicks on the Submit button. In addition, you can code a Method attribute that specifies the HTTP method that will be used. Between the two Form tags, you code the controls for the form.

This example shows a form that contains two text boxes and a Submit button. When the user clicks on the Submit button, the data that's in the text boxes will be passed to the JSP named entry.jsp that's specified by the Action attribute of the form. Although a form can have many controls, it should always contain at least one control that executes the Action attribute of the form. Typically, this control is a Submit button like the one shown in this figure.

When you code the Action attribute, you can specify a JSP page as shown in this figure. Or, you can specify a servlet like this:

```
action="writeEntry"
```

However, this code assumes that a servlet is mapped to the URL specified by the Action attribute. For now, don't worry if this is a little confusing. In chapter 6, you'll learn how to code servlets and how to map them to URLs.

You can use the Input tag to code several types of controls. This figure shows how to use the Input tag to code a text box and a button, but you'll learn more about coding these controls in the following figures.

When coding controls, you can use the Name attribute to specify a name that you can use in your Java code to access the parameter that's passed from the HTML form to a servlet or JSP. To access the data in the two text boxes in this figure, for example, you can use firstName to access the data that's been entered in the first text box, and you can use lastName to access the data in the second text box.

In contrast, you can use the Value attribute to specify a value for a control. This works differently depending on the control. If, for example, you're working with a button, the Value attribute specifies the text that's displayed on a button. But if you're working with a text box, the Value attribute specifies the default text that's displayed in the box.

The HTML code for a form

```
<p>Here's a form that contains two text boxes and a button:</p>
<form action="entry.jsp" method="get">
    <p>
    First name: <input type="text" name="firstName"><br>
    Last name: <input type="text" name="lastName">
    <input type="submit" value="Submit">
    </p>
</form>
```

The form displayed in a browser before the user enters data

Here's a form that contains two text boxes and a button:

First name: [   ]
Last name: [   ] [Submit]

Tags for working with a simple form

Tag	Description
`<form> </form>`	Defines the start and end of the form.
`<input>`	Defines the input type. You'll learn more about this tag in the following figures.

Attributes of the Form tag

Attribute	Description
`action`	The Action attribute specifies the URL of the servlet or JSP that will be called when the user clicks on the Submit button. You'll learn more about specifying this attribute in the following figures and chapters.
`method`	The Method attribute specifies the HTTP method that the browser will use for the HTTP request. The default method is the Get method, but the Post method is also commonly used. You'll learn more about these methods in the next chapter.

Common control attributes

Attribute	Description
`name`	The name of the control. When writing Java code, you can use this attribute to refer to the control.
`value`	The default value of the control. This varies depending on the type of control. For a text box, this attribute sets the default text that's displayed in the box. For a button, this attribute sets the text that's displayed on the button.

Description

- A *form* contains one or more *controls* such as text boxes, buttons, check boxes, and list boxes.

Figure 4-7   How to code a form

How to code text boxes, password boxes, and hidden fields

Figure 4-8 shows how to use the Input tag to code three types of *text boxes*. You can use a *standard text box* to accept text input from a user. You can use a *password box* to let a user enter a password that is displayed as one asterisk for each character that's entered. And you can use a *hidden field* to store text that you don't want to display on the HTML page.

To create a text box, you set the Type attribute to Text, Password, or Hidden. Then, you code the Name attribute so you'll be able to access the text that's stored in the text box from your Java code.

If you want the text box to contain a default value, you can code the Value attribute. Although all three of the text boxes shown in this figure have Value attributes, you often don't need to code them for standard text boxes and password boxes. Then, the user can enter values for these text boxes. In contrast, since a user can't enter text into a hidden field, you commonly code a Value attribute for a hidden field.

When coding text boxes, you can use the Size attribute to control the width of the text box. To set this attribute, you should specify the approximate number of characters that you want to display. However, since the Size attribute is based upon the average width of the character for the font that's used, it isn't exact. As a result, to be sure that a text box is wide enough to hold all of the characters, you can add a few extra characters. If, for example, you want a text box to be able to display 40 characters, you can set the size attribute to 45.

You can also use the MaxLength attribute to specify the maximum number of characters that can be entered into a text box. This can be helpful if you create a database that can only store a fixed number of characters for certain fields. If, for example, the FirstName field in the database accepts a maximum of 20 characters, you can set the MaxLength attribute of its textbox to 20. That way, the user won't be able to enter more than 20 characters for this field.

The code for three types of text controls

```
<p>Here's a form that contains a text box and a hidden text box:</p>
<form action="checkPassword" method="get">
    Username: <input type="text" name="username" value="jsmith"><br>
    Password: <input type="password" name="password" value="opensesame"><br>
            <input type="hidden" name="productCode" value="jr01"><br>
</form>
```

The text controls displayed in a browser

Here's a form that contains a text box and a hidden text box:

Username: jsmith

Password: ••••••••••

Attributes of these text controls

Attribute	Description
type	Specifies the type of input control. Acceptable types for text boxes are Text, Password, and Hidden.
name	Specifies the name of the control. This is the name that is used to refer to the data in the control from a servlet or JSP.
value	Specifies the value of data in the control.
size	The width of the text control field in characters based on the average character width of the font.
maxlength	The maximum number of characters that can be entered into the text box.

Description

- The Type attribute identifies the type of *text box* to be used. A value of Text creates a *standard text box*. A value of Password creates a *password box* that displays asterisks instead of text. And a value of Hidden creates a *hidden field* that can store text but isn't shown by the browser.

- For a standard text box or password box, you can use the Value attribute to provide a default value. For a hidden field, you always use the Value attribute to supply a value that can be used by a servlet or JSP.

- Since the Size attribute specifies an approximate number of characters, you may want to make a text box slightly larger than necessary to make sure that all characters will fit within the box.

Figure 4-8   How to code text boxes, password boxes, and hidden fields

How to code buttons

Figure 4-9 shows how to use the Input tag to code three types of *buttons*. A *submit button* executes the Action attribute that's specified in the Form tag. A *reset button* resets all controls on the current form to the default values that are set by their Value attributes. And a *JavaScript button* executes the JavaScript method that's specified by its OnClick attribute.

To create a button, you set the Type attribute of the Input tag to Submit, Reset, or Button. Then, you can code a Value attribute that contains the text that's displayed on the button. For submit and reset buttons, that's all you need to do.

For a JavaScript button, though, you also need to code an OnClick attribute that specifies the JavaScript method that should be called. In chapter 7, you'll learn how to code some simple JavaScript methods for data validation so don't be bothered if you don't know JavaScript right now. In this example, the JavaScript button calls a JavaScript method named validate that accepts the current form as an argument. To specify the current form, this code uses the *this* keyword and the *form* keyword.

When coding a web page, you often need to have two or more buttons per page that link to different servlets or JSPs. However, each form can only contain one submit button. As a result, you often need to code more than one form per page. In some cases, that means that you code a form that only contains one button. For instance, the second example in this figure actually shows two forms where the first form contains only the Continue Shopping button and the second form contains only the Checkout button.

The code for three types of buttons

```
<input type="submit" value="Submit">
<input type="reset" value="Reset">
<input type="button" value="Validate" onclick="validate(this.form)">
```

The buttons displayed in a browser

Submit Reset Validate

The code for two submit buttons on the same page

```
<form action="displayQuickOrder" method="post">
    <input type="submit" name="continue" value="Continue Shopping">
</form>
<form action="checkUser" method="post">
    <input type="submit" name="checkout" value="Checkout">
</form>
```

The buttons displayed in a browser

Continue Shopping

Checkout

Attributes of these buttons

Attribute	Description
type	Specifies the type of input control. Acceptable types are Submit, Reset, and Button.
onclick	Specifies the JavaScript method that the button will execute when the user clicks the button.

Description

- The Type attribute identifies the type of *button* to be used.
- A Type attribute of Submit creates a *submit button* that activates the Action attribute of the form when it's clicked.
- A Type attribute of Reset creates a *reset button* that resets all controls on the form to their default values when it's clicked.
- A Type attribute of Button creates a *JavaScript button*. When this type of button is clicked, the JavaScript method that's specified by the OnClick attribute of the button is executed.
- To pass the current form to a JavaScript method in the OnClick attribute, you can use the *this* keyword and the *form* keyword. You'll learn more about JavaScript in chapter 7.

Figure 4-9   How to code buttons

How to code check boxes and radio buttons

Figure 4-10 shows how to use the Input tag to code *check boxes* and *radio buttons*. Although check boxes work independently of other check boxes, radio buttons can be set up so the user can select only one radio button from a group of radio buttons. In this figure, for example, you can select only one of the three radio buttons. However, you can select or deselect any combination of check boxes.

To create a check box, you set the Type attribute of the Input tag to Checkbox. Then, you can set the Name attribute for the check box so you can access the value from your Java code. If you want the check box to be checked by default, you can also code the Checked attribute. Unlike the Type and Name attributes, you don't need to supply a value for the Checked attribute.

To create a radio button, you can set the Type attribute of the Input tag to Radio. Then, you can set the Name attribute just as you do for other controls. However, you can specify the same name for all of the radio buttons in a group. In this figure, for example, all three radio buttons are named contactVia. That way, the user will only be able to select one of these radio buttons at a time. When coding radio buttons, you typically supply a value for each radio button. Later, when you write your Java code, you can access the value that's coded for the selected radio button.

The code for four checkboxes and three radio buttons

```
<form action="addToMailingList" method="get">
    <input type="checkbox" name="addEmail" checked>
    Yes, add me to your mailing list.<br>
    <br>
    Contact me by:<br>
    <input type="radio" name="contactVia" value="Email">Email
    <input type="radio" name="contactVia" value="Postal Mail">Postal mail
    <input type="radio" name="contactVia" value="Both" checked>Both<br>
    <br>
    I'm interested in these types of music:<br>
    <input type="checkbox" name="rock">Rock<br>
    <input type="checkbox" name="country">Country<br>
    <input type="checkbox" name="bluegrass">Bluegrass<br>
</form>
```

The check boxes and radio buttons when displayed in a browser

Attributes of these buttons

Attribute	Description
type	Specifies the type of control. A value of Checkbox creates a check box while a value of Radio creates a radio button.
checked	Selects the control. When several radio buttons share the same name, only one radio button can be selected at a time.

Description

- You can use *check boxes* to allow the user to supply a true/false value.
- You can use *radio buttons* to allow a user to select one option from a group of options. To create a group of radio buttons, use the same name for all of the radio buttons.
- If you don't group radio buttons, more than one can be on at the same time.

Figure 4-10   How to code check boxes and radio buttons

How to code combo boxes and list boxes

Figure 4-11 shows how to code *combo boxes* and *list boxes*. You can use a combo box to allow the user to select one option from a drop-down list, and you can use a list box to allow the user to select one or more options. In this figure, for example, the combo box lets you select one country, and the list box lets you select more than one country.

To code a combo or list box, you must use the Select tag and two or more Option tags. To start, you code an opening and closing Select tag. Within the opening Select tag, you must code the Name attribute. Within the two Select tags, you can code two or more Option tags. These tags supply the options that are available for the box. Within each Option tag, you must code a Value attribute. After the Option tag, you must supply the text that will be displayed in the list. This text is often similar to the text of the Value attribute.

The Multiple attribute of the Select tag allows you to create a list box. If you don't code this attribute, the Select tag will produce a combo box that lets the user select one option. If you do code this attribute, the Select tag will produce a list box that lets the user select multiple options. In fact, the only difference between the combo box and list box in this figure is that the Multiple attribute is supplied for the list box.

If you want to select a default option for a combo or list box, you can code the Selected attribute within the Option tag. Since a combo box only allows one option to be selected, you should only code one Selected attribute per combo box. However, for a list box, you can code the Selected attribute for one or more options.

The code for a combo box

```
<form action="writeCountry" method="get">
    Select a country:<br>
    <select name="country">
        <option value="USA" selected>United States
        <option value="Canada">Canada
        <option value="Mexico">Mexico
    </select><br>
</form>
```

The combo box displayed in a browser

How to convert a combo box to a list box

```
<select name="country" multiple>
```

The combo box displayed as a list box

Attributes of the Select tag

Attribute	Description
multiple	Converts a combo box to a list box.

Attributes of the Option tag

Attribute	Description
selected	Selects the option.

Description

- A *combo box* provides a drop-down list that lets the user select a single option. A *list box* provides a list of options and lets the user select one or more of these options.

- To select adjacent options from a list box, the user can click the top option, hold down the Shift key, and click the bottom option.

- To select non-adjacent options from a list box, the user can click one option, hold down the Ctrl key, and click other options.

Figure 4-11   How to code combo boxes and list boxes

How to code text areas

Figure 4-12 shows how to code a *text area*. Although a text area is similar to a text box, a text area can display multiple lines of text. By default, a text area wraps each line of text to the next line and provides a vertical scroll bar that you can use to scroll up and down through the text.

To code a text area, you can begin by coding the opening and closing TextArea tags. Within the opening TextArea tag, you can code a Name attribute so you can access the control through Java. You can also code the Rows attribute to specify the number of visible rows, and you can code the Cols attribute to specify the width of the text area. Here, the Cols attribute works like the Width attribute of a text box.

Within the opening and closing TextArea tags, you can code any default text that you want to appear in the text area. By default, a text area automatically wraps text to the next line.

The code for a text area

```
Comments:<br>
<textarea name="comment" rows="5" cols="60"></textarea>
```

The text area displayed in a browser

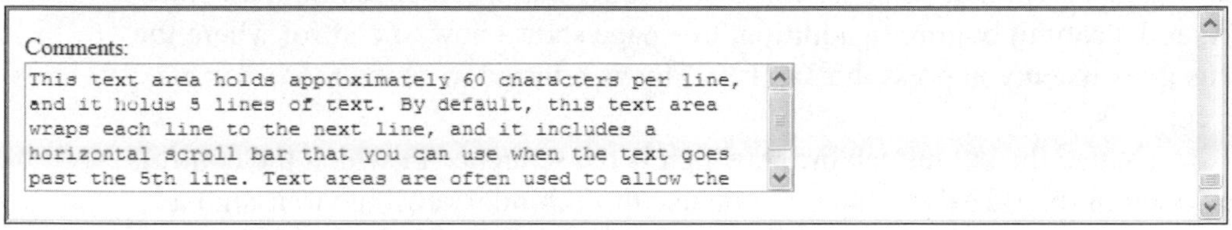

Attributes of the TextArea tag

Attribute	Description
rows	Specifies the number of visible lines in the text area. If the number of lines in the text box exceeds this setting, the text area will display a vertical scroll bar.
cols	Specifies the width of the text area based on the average character width of the font that's being used.

Description

- A *text area* is similar to a text box, but it can display multiple lines of text.
- To specify a default value for a text area, you can code the text within the opening and closing TextArea tags.

Figure 4-12   How to code text areas

How to set the tab order of controls

Figure 4-13 shows an HTML page that takes many of the skills described in this chapter and puts them all together. This page uses an external style sheet, tables, and a form that contains text boxes, radio buttons, a check box, a combo box, and a submit button. In addition, this page shows how to control where the focus goes when you press the Tab key. This is referred to as the *tab order* of the controls.

To change the default tab order, which is the sequence in which the controls are coded in the HTML document, you use the TabIndex attribute to assign a number to each control. In this figure, for example, the TabIndex attribute has been set so the focus moves from the text boxes to the first radio button and then to the submit button. In other words, it skips the check box and the combo box. In this case, modifying the default tab order isn't that useful, but it can be when the default tab order doesn't work the way you want it to.

An HTML page for a survey

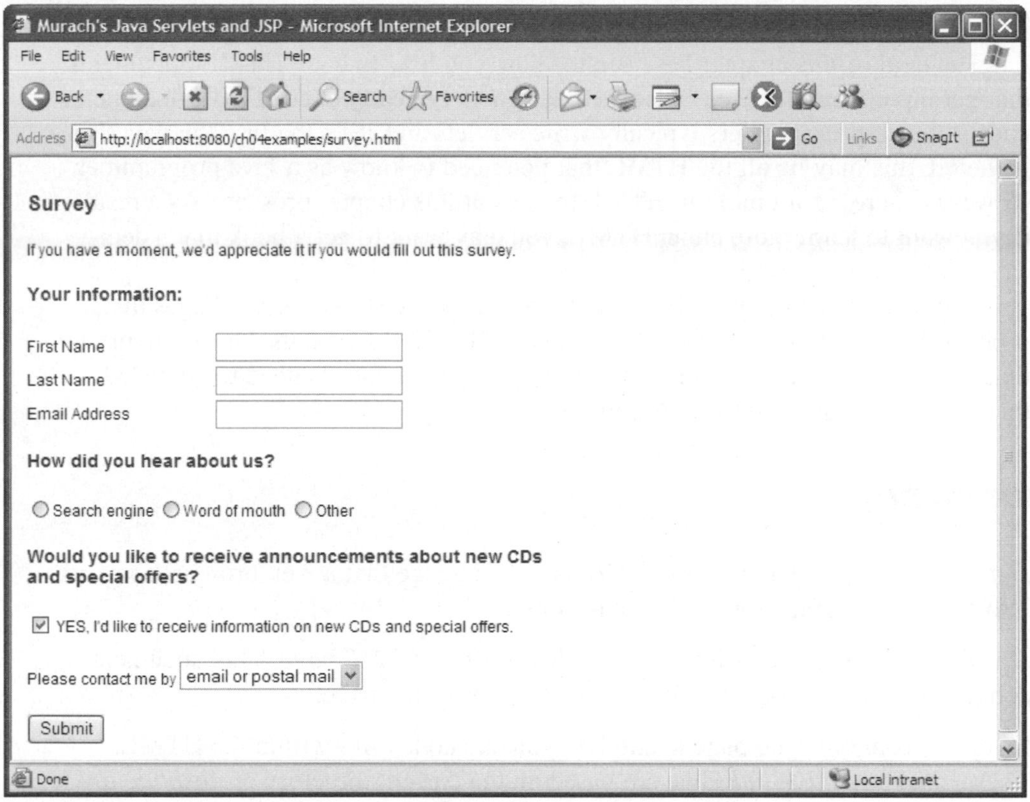

Code that controls the tab order of the survey page

```
<input type="text" name="firstName" size="20" tabindex="1">
<input type="text" name="lastName" size="20" tabindex="2">
<input type="text" name="emailAddress" size="20" tabindex="3">
<input type=radio name="heardFrom" value="Search Engine" tabindex="4">
<input type=submit value="Submit" tabindex="5">
```

Description

- The *tab order* determines the sequence in which the controls on a form will receive the focus when the Tab key is pressed. By default, the tab order is the same as the sequence in which the controls are coded in the HTML document.

- To modify the default tab order, you can use the TabIndex attribute of any visible control. Then, if you omit the TabIndex attribute for some controls, they will be added to the tab order after the controls that have TabIndex attributes.

- The TabIndex attribute only works for the first radio button in a group.

- To view the complete code for this page, open the survey.html file that's included with the downloadable files for the book.

Figure 4-13   How to set the tab order of controls

Perspective

The goal of this chapter has been to show you how to code HTML documents that get input from the user. Since web designers typically code HTML documents and Java web programmers typically write servlets and JSPs that use the data that's gathered, this may be all the HTML that you need to know as a Java programmer. However, there's a lot more to HTML than what this chapter presents. As a result, if you want to learn more about HTML, you may want to get a book that's dedicated entirely to the subject.

In the next chapter, you'll learn how to code and test JavaServer Pages that process the data that's sent from the forms on HTML documents. Once you master that, you will have a better understanding of how the controls need to be coded so their values can be used by JSPs and servlets.

Summary

- *HyperText Markup Language* (*HTML*) is the language that a web browser converts into the user interface for a web application.

- An *HTML document* consists of the HTML for one *HTML page*. This document contains the *HTML tags* that define the elements of the page.

- To move from one web page to another, you can code *links* within the HTML. These can be *relative links* that are based on the current directory or *absolute links*.

- *Tables* that consist of *rows* and *columns* are used for the design of many web pages. The *cells* within the table can be used to store links, images, controls, and even other tables.

- An HTML page can include images in Graphic Interchange Format (GIF) or Joint Photographic Experts Group (JPEG) format.

- To insure consistent formatting, the formatting for the web pages of an application can be stored in an *external style sheet*, or just *style sheet*. Then, each web page can refer to that style sheet.

- An *HTML form* contains one or more controls like text boxes, check boxes, radio buttons, combo boxes, and list boxes. It should also contain a submit button that calls a JSP or servlet when the user clicks it. If necessary, one HTML document can contain two or more forms.

- The *tab order* of the controls on a form determines where the focus goes when the user presses the Tab key.

Exercise 4-1   Modify the survey page

In this exercise, you'll view and modify the survey.html page that's shown in figure 4-13. As you modify the file, take advantage of the features that your IDE offers like the NetBeans Palette. After you modify this file, you may need to save the file before you view it or click on the Refresh button in your browser to view the latest version of the page, although you won't have to do that with NetBeans.

Open the file, review the HTML, and view the survey page

1. Open the ch04examples project in the ex_starts directory.
2. Open the survey.html page in your editor, and review the HTML code that it contains. Note that the entire body of the page is within a table.
3. Run the survey.html page. Then, note that the URL that's used to request the page uses the Tomcat server.
4. Open the Windows Explorer and double-click on the survey.html file that's in the ch04examples/web folder to display the page in your web browser. Note that the URL that's used to request the page doesn't use the Tomcat server.

Modify the survey page

After each step that follows, run the page to make sure the changes are correct.

5. Edit the survey.html page so it displays the image for the Murach logo at the top of the page. This image is in the images directory of your web application.
6. After the row in the table that lets the user enter an email address, add another row that lets the user enter a date of birth.
7. Turn the Search engine button on as the default button for the group of radio buttons.
8. Add an Advertising radio button before the Other radio button.
9. Add a Direct Mail radio button after the Advertising radio button.
10. After the check box, add another check box with a name of emailOK and text that says, "YES, it's okay to send me email announcements." Then, make sure that this box is checked.
11. Add a text area for comments before the Submit button.
12. When you've got everything working right, close the project.

5

How to develop JavaServer Pages

In this chapter, you'll learn how to develop a web application that consists of HTML pages and JavaServer Pages (JSPs). As you will see, JSPs work fine as long as the amount of processing that's required for each page is limited. When you complete this chapter, you should be able to use JSPs to develop simple web applications of your own.

The Email List application

This topic introduces you to a simple web application that consists of one HTML page and one *JavaServer Page* (*JSP*). Once you get the general idea of how this application works, you'll be ready to learn the specific skills that you need for developing JSPs.

The user interface for the application

Figure 5-1 shows the two pages that make up the user interface for the Email List application. The first page is an HTML page that asks the user to enter a first name, last name, and email address. Then, when the user clicks on the Submit button, the HTML page calls the JSP and passes the three user entries to that page.

When the JSP receives the three entries, it can process them by checking them for validity, writing them to a file or database, and so on. In this simple application, though, the JSP just passes the three entries back to the browser so it can display the second page of this application. From this page, the user can return to the first page by clicking the Back button in the web browser or by clicking the Return button that's displayed on this page.

As simple as this application is, you're going to learn a lot from it. In this chapter, you'll learn how to enhance this application so it uses regular Java classes to save the user entries in a text file. Then, in later chapters, you'll learn how to modify this application to illustrate other essential skills that apply to servlet and JSP programming.

The HTML page

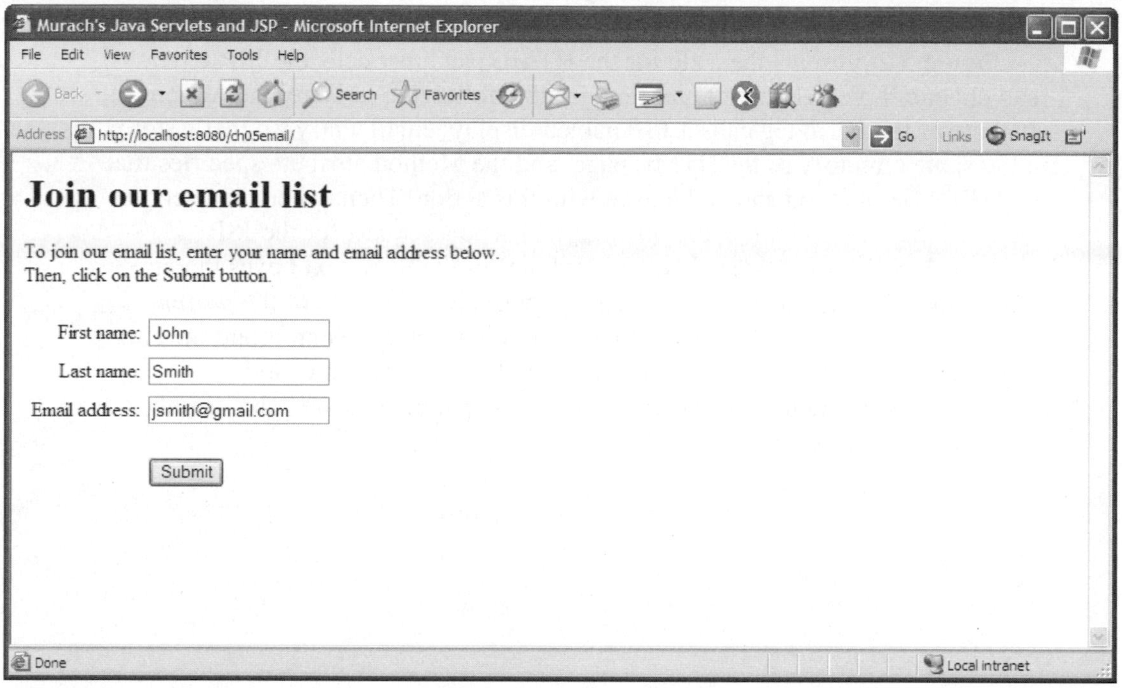

The JSP

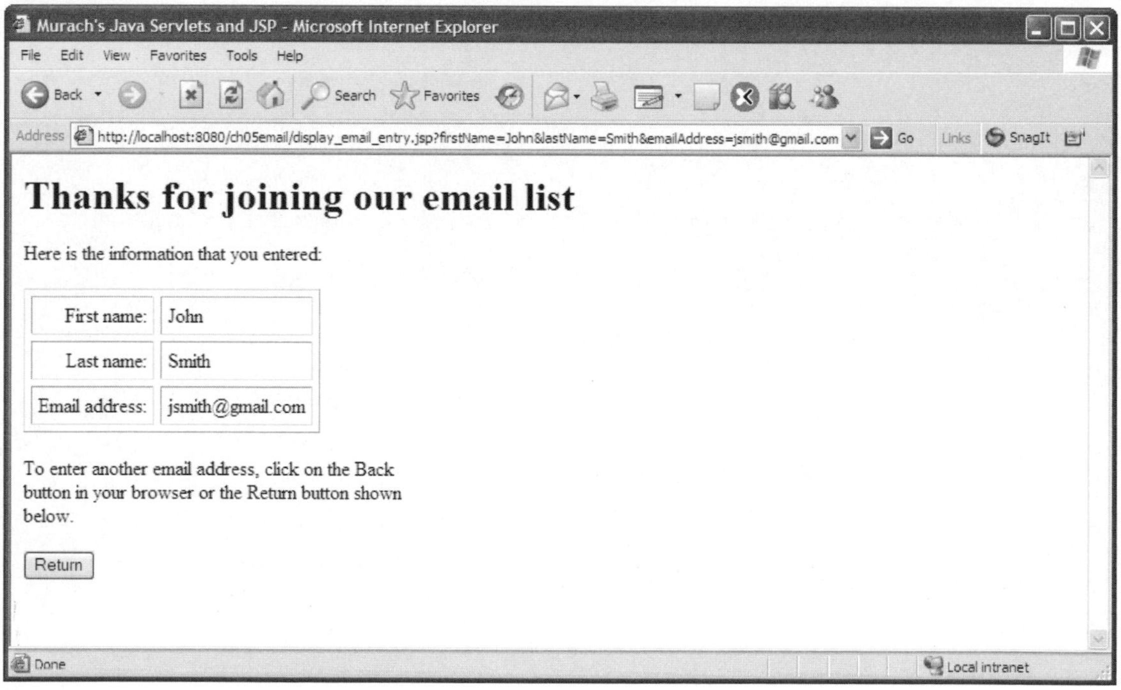

Figure 5-1   The user interface for the application

The code for the HTML page that calls the JSP

Figure 5-2 presents the code for the HTML page that calls the JSP. If you've read chapter 4, you shouldn't have any trouble following it. Here, the Action attribute of the Form tag calls a JSP named display_email_entry.jsp that's stored in the same directory as the HTML page, and the Method attribute specifies that the HTTP Get method should be used with this action. Then, when the user clicks on the Submit button, the browser will send a request for the JSP.

You should also notice the Name attributes of the three text boxes that are used in the table within this HTML page. These are the names of the *parameters* that are passed to the JSP when the user clicks on the Submit button. This figure shows that the parameter names are firstName, lastName, and emailAddress. In figure 5-1, the values for those parameters are John, Smith, and jsmith@gmail.com.

The code for the HTML page

```
<!DOCTYPE HTML PUBLIC "-//W3C//DTD HTML 4.01 Transitional//EN">

<html>

<head>
    <title>Murach's Java Servlets and JSP</title>
</head>

<body>
    <h1>Join our email list</h1>
    <p>To join our email list, enter your name and
     email address below. <br>
     Then, click on the Submit button.</p>

    <form action="display_email_entry.jsp" method="get">
    <table cellspacing="5" border="0">
        <tr>
            <td align="right">First name:</td>
            <td><input type="text" name="firstName"></td>
        </tr>
        <tr>
            <td align="right">Last name:</td>
            <td><input type="text" name="lastName"></td>
        </tr>
        <tr>
            <td align="right">Email address:</td>
            <td><input type="text" name="emailAddress"></td>
        </tr>
        <tr>
            <td></td>
            <td><br><input type="submit" value="Submit"></td>
        </tr>
    </table>
    </form>
</body>

</html>
```

Description

- The Action and Method attributes for the Form tag set up a request for a JSP that will be executed when the user clicks on the Submit button.

- The three text boxes represent *parameters* that will be passed to the JSP when the user clicks the Submit button.

- The parameter names are firstName, lastName, and emailAddress, and the parameter values are the strings that the user enters into the text boxes.

Figure 5-2   The code for the HTML page that calls the JSP

The code for the JSP

Figure 5-3 presents the code for the JSP. As you can see, most of this code is HTML. In addition, some Java code is embedded within the HTML code in the form of JSP *scriptlets* and *expressions*. Typically, a scriptlet is used to execute one or more Java statements while a JSP expression is used to display text. To identify scriptlets and expressions, you use special tags. To distinguish these tags from HTML tags, you can refer to them as *JSP tags*.

When you code a JSP, you can use the methods of the *request object* in your scriptlets or expressions. Since you don't have to explicitly create this object when you code JSPs, this object is sometimes referred to as the *implicit request object*. The scriptlet in this figure contains three statements that use the getParameter method of the request object. Each of these statements returns the value of the parameter that is passed to the JSP from the HTML page. Here, the argument for each getParameter method is the name of the textbox on the HTML page.

Once the scriptlet is executed, the values for the three parameters are available as variables to the rest of the page. Then, the three expressions can display these variables. Since these expressions are coded within the HTML tags for a table, the browser will display these expressions within a table.

After the table, the JSP contains some HTML that defines a form. This form contains only one control, a submit button named Return. When it is clicked, it takes the user back to the first page of the application. If you have any trouble visualizing how this button or the rest of the page will look when displayed by a browser, please refer back to figure 5-1.

As you read this book, remember that it assumes that you already know the basics of Java programming. If you have any trouble understanding the Java code in this chapter, you may need a refresher course on Java coding. To quickly review the basics of Java coding, we recommend that you use *Murach's Java SE 6* because it contains all the Java skills that you'll need for working with this book.

The code for the JSP

```html
<!DOCTYPE HTML PUBLIC "-//W3C//DTD HTML 4.01 Transitional//EN"
    "http://www.w3.org/TR/html4/loose.dtd">

<html>
<head>
    <title>Murach's Java Servlets and JSP</title>
</head>
<body>
    <%
        // get parameters from the request
        String firstName = request.getParameter("firstName");         JSP scriptlet
        String lastName = request.getParameter("lastName");
        String emailAddress = request.getParameter("emailAddress");
    %>

    <h1>Thanks for joining our email list</h1>

    <p>Here is the information that you entered:</p>

    <table cellspacing="5" cellpadding="5" border="1">
        <tr>
            <td align="right">First name:</td>
            <td><%= firstName %></td>
        </tr>
        <tr>
            <td align="right">Last name:</td>                         JSP expressions
            <td><%= lastName %></td>
        </tr>
        <tr>
            <td align="right">Email address:</td>
            <td><%= emailAddress %></td>
        </tr>
    </table>

    <p>To enter another email address, click on the Back <br>
    button in your browser or the Return button shown <br>
    below.</p>

    <form action="join_email_list.html" method="post">
        <input type="submit" value="Return">
    </form>

</body>
</html>
```

Description

- A JSP contains HTML tags and embedded Java code.

- To code a *scriptlet* that contains one or more Java statements, you use the <% and %> tags.

- To code an *expression* that can be converted to a string, you use the <%= and %> tags.

- To get the values of the parameters that are passed to the JSP, you can use the getParameter method of the *implicit request object* named request.

Figure 5-3   The code for the JSP

How to code a JSP

Now that you have a general idea of how JSPs are coded, you're ready to learn some specific skills for coding a JSP. To start, you need to know more about coding scriptlets and expressions.

How to code scriptlets and expressions

Figure 5-4 summarizes the information you need for coding scriptlets and expressions within a JSP. To code a scriptlet, for example, you code Java statements that end with semicolons within the JSP scriptlet tags. To code an expression, you code any Java expression that evaluates to a primitive data type such as an int value or an object such as a String object.

If an expression evaluates to a primitive type like an int value or a double value, the JSP will automatically convert the primitive type to a string that represents the value. If, on the other hand, the expression evaluates to an object, the JSP will call the object's toString method to get a string that represents the object. As a result, if you code an expression that evaluates to an object, you need to make sure that the object has a toString method that returns a string that represents the object. Otherwise, the object will use the toString method of the Object class, which includes the class name and hash code for the object.

When you're coding a scriptlet or an expression, you can use any of the methods of the implicit request object. In this figure, only the getParameter method is used, but you'll learn about two more methods of the request object in the next figure.

In this figure, the first two examples show different ways that you can display the value of a parameter. The first example uses a scriptlet to return the value of the firstName parameter and store it in a String object. Then, this example uses an expression to display the value. In contrast, the second example uses an expression to display the value of the firstName parameter without creating the firstName object.

The last example in this figure shows how two scriptlets and an expression can be used to display an HTML line five times while a Java variable within the HTML line counts from 1 to 5. Here, the first JSP scriptlet contains the code that begins a while loop. Then, a line of HTML code uses a JSP expression to display the current value of the counter for the loop. And finally, the second scriptlet contains the code that ends the loop.

The syntax for a JSP scriptlet

```
<% Java statements %>
```

The syntax for a JSP expression

```
<%= any Java expression that can be converted to a string %>
```

The syntax for getting a parameter from the implicit request object

```
request.getParameter(parameterName);
```

Examples that use scriptlets and expressions

A scriptlet and expression that display the value of the firstName parameter

```
<%
    String firstName = request.getParameter("firstName");
%>
The first name is <%= firstName %>.
```

An expression that displays the value of the firstName parameter

```
The first name is <%= request.getParameter("firstName") %>.
```

Two scriptlets and an expression that display an HTML line 5 times

```
<%
    int numOfTimes = 1;
    while (numOfTimes <= 5)
    {
%>
    <h1>This line is shown <%= numOfTimes %> of 5 times in a JSP.</h1>
<%
        numOfTimes++;
    }
%>
```

Description

- Within a scriptlet, you can code one or more Java statements. You must end each Java statement with a semicolon.

- Within a JSP expression, you can code any Java expression that evaluates to a Java object or to a primitive type. Since an expression isn't a statement, you don't end it with a semicolon.

Figure 5-4   How to code scriptlets and expressions

How to use the methods of the request object

In the last figure, you learned how to use the getParameter method to return the value that the user entered into a textbox. Now, figure 5-5 summarizes that method and illustrates it in a new context. This figure also summarizes and illustrates two more methods of the implicit request object.

In most cases, the getParameter method returns the value of the parameter. For a textbox, that's usually the value entered by the user. But for a group of radio buttons or a combo box, that's the value of the button or item selected by the user.

For checkboxes or independent radio buttons that have a Value attribute, the getParameter method returns that value if the checkbox or button is selected and a null value if it isn't. For checkboxes or independent radio buttons that don't have a Value attribute, though, the getParameter method returns an "on" value if the checkbox or button is selected and a null value if it isn't. This is illustrated by the first example in this figure.

To retrieve multiple values for one parameter name, you can use the getParameterValues method as illustrated by the second example. This method is useful for controls like list boxes that allow multiple selections. After you use the getParameterValues method to return an array of String objects, you can use a loop to get the values from the array.

To get the names of all the parameters sent with a request, you can use the getParameterNames method to return an Enumeration object that contains the names. Then, you can search through the Enumeration object to get the parameter names, and you can use the getParameter method to return the value for each parameter name. This is illustrated by the third example.

If you're not familiar with the Enumeration class, you can learn more about it by looking it up in the documentation for the Java SE 6 API specification. For most purposes, though, you only need to know that an Enumeration object is a collection that can be searched element by element. To determine if more elements exist in the collection, you can use the hasMoreElements method, which returns a Boolean value. And to get the next element in the collection, you can use the nextElement method.

Three methods available from the request object

Method	Description
getParameter(String param)	Returns the value of the specified parameter as a string if it exists or null if it doesn't. Often, this is the value defined in the Value attribute of the control in the HTML page or JSP.
getParameterValues(String param)	Returns an array of String objects containing all of the values that the given request parameter has or null if the parameter doesn't have any values.
getParameterNames()	Returns an Enumeration object that contains the names of all the parameters contained in the request. If the request has no parameters, the method returns an empty Enumeration object.

A scriptlet that determines if a checkbox is checked

```
<%
    // returns the value or "on" if checked, null otherwise.
    String rockCheckBox = request.getParameter("Rock");
    if (rockCheckBox != null)
    {
%>
        You checked Rock music!
<%
    }
%>
```

A scriptlet that reads and displays multiple values from a list box

```
<%
    // returns the values of the items selected in a list box.
    String[] selectedCountries = request.getParameterValues("country");
    for (int i = 0; i < selectedCountries.length; i++)
    {
%>
        <%= selectedCountries[i] %> <br>
<%
    }
%>
```

A scriptlet that reads and displays all request parameters and values

```
<%
    Enumeration parameterNames = request.getParameterNames();
    while (parameterNames.hasMoreElements())
    {
        String parameterName = (String) parameterNames.nextElement();
        String parameterValue = request.getParameter(parameterName);
%>
        <%= parameterName %> has value <%= parameterValue %>. <br>
<%
    }
%>
```

Figure 5-5   How to use the methods of the request object

How to get the real path for a file

When you work with JSPs and servlets, you typically use relative paths to refer to files that are available within the web application. Sometimes, though, you need to get the real path for one of these files.

To do that, you can use the technique shown in figure 5-6. First, you call the getServletContext method from the JSP or servlet to get a ServletContext object. Then, you call the getRealPath method of the ServletContext object to return the real path for the specified file. When you use the getRealPath method, a front slash navigates to the root directory for the current application, so

```
getRealPath("/EmailList.txt")
```

specifies the EmailList.txt file in the current application's root directory.

In this figure, the first example gets the real path for a file named EmailList.txt that's stored in the WEB-INF subdirectory of the application. Here, the getRealPath method returns a string for an absolute path to this file. If, for example, this method is used in the ch05email application that's in the NetBeans directory that's used for our downloadable applications, the getRealPath method will return the path shown in this figure.

If you store a file in a directory that's web accessible, such as the root directory for a web application, the file can be accessed by any user who enters the correct URL. Keep in mind, though, that the WEB-INF directory isn't web-accessible. As a result, if you want to keep a file private, you can store it in the WEB-INF directory or one of its subdirectories. Or, you can restrict access to the file or directory as described in chapter 17.

A method of the GenericServlet class

Method	Description
getServletContext()	Returns a ServletContext object that contains information about the application's context.

A method of the ServletContext class for working with paths

Method	Description
getRealPath(String path)	Returns a String object for the real path of the specified relative path.

Code that gets the real path for a file

```
ServletContext sc = this.getServletContext();
String path = sc.getRealPath("/WEB-INF/EmailList.txt");
```

The value for the real path variable if the application is ch05email in the netbeans directory

```
C:\murach\servlet_jsp\netbeans\book_apps\ch05email\build\web\
WEB-INF\EmailList.txt
```

Description

- All servlets and JSPs inherit the GenericServlet class. As a result, the getServletContext method is available to all servlets and JSPs.

- In addition to working with relative paths as described here, you can use the ServletContext object to read global initialization parameters, to work with global variables, and to write data to log files. You'll learn more about these skills as you progress through this book.

Figure 5-6   How to get the real path for a file

How to request a JSP

After you code a JSP, you need to be able to request it. That way, you can view it in a browser and test it to make sure it's working properly.

How to request a JSP with the HTTP Get method

Figure 5-7 shows several ways to request a JSP. The first example shows how to use a Form tag to request a JSP. When you use this technique, you code the Action attribute of the form to provide a path and filename that point to the JSP. In this figure, for example, the first Form tag requests a JSP that's stored in the same directory as the calling form. However, if the JSP is stored in a different directory, you can specify a relative or absolute path for the Action attribute.

When you use a Form tag to request a JSP, you can use the Method attribute to specify the HTTP method that's used for the request. By default, the Get method is used for a Form tag, but you can also explicitly specify the Get method. In the first set of examples in this figure, both of the Form tags use the Get method. In the next figure, you'll learn when and how to use the Method attribute to specify the Post method.

When you use the Get method to request a JSP from another page, any parameters that are passed to the JSP will be displayed in the browser's URL address. In the bitmap in this figure, for example, you can see the two parameters that have been appended to the URL. In the next figure, you'll learn that the Post method doesn't display the parameters in the URL.

When you test a JSP, you will often want to pass parameters to it. To do that, you can append the parameters to the end of the URL as shown by the second set of examples in this figure. Here, the question mark after the jsp extension indicates that one or more parameters will follow. Then, you code the parameter name, the equals sign, and the parameter value for each parameter that is passed, and you separate multiple parameters with ampersands (&). If you omit a parameter that's required by the JSP, the getParameter method will return a null value for that parameter.

The third example shows how you can use an A tag to call a JSP. When you use an A tag, it always uses the HTTP Get method, and you can append parameters to the end of the URL. In this example, the A tag appends two parameters to the URL that requests the JSP.

Finally, you can request a JSP by entering its URL into a browser as shown by the last set of examples in this figure. Here, the first example shows the URL for the JSP when it's mapped to the ch05email directory on a local web server using port 8080. Then, the second example shows the URL for the JSP if it was deployed in the email directory of the web server for www.murach.com.

A JSP that's requested with the HTTP Get method

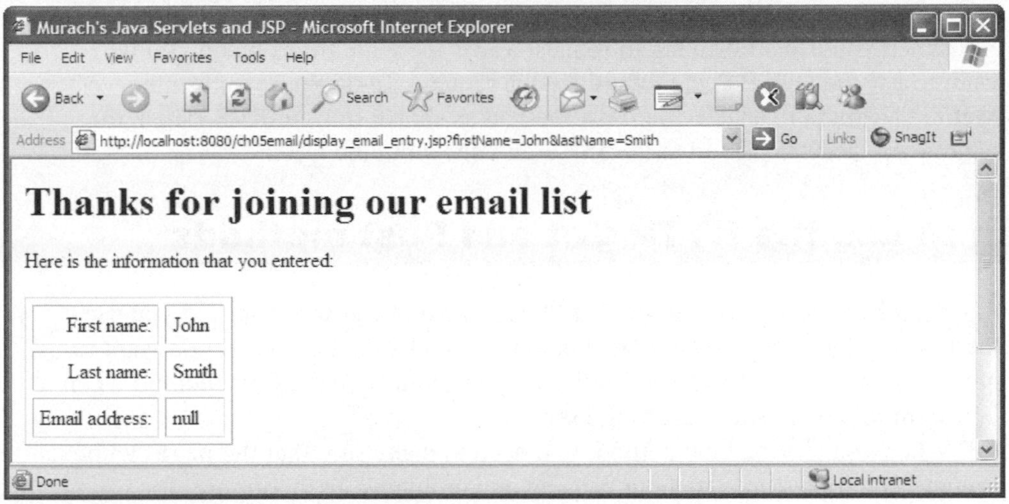

Two Form tags that use the Get method

```
<form action="display_email_entry.jsp">
<form action="display_email_entry.jsp" method="get">
```

How to append parameters to a request

```
display_email_entry.jsp?firstName=John
display_email_entry.jsp?firstName=John&lastName=Smith
```

An Anchor tag that requests a JSP with the Get method

```
<a href="display_email_entry.jsp?firstName=John&lastName=Smith">
    Display Email Entry Test
</a>
```

Two URLs that request a JSP with the Get method

```
http://localhost:8080/ch05email/display_email_entry.jsp?firstName=John
http://www.murach.com/email/display_email_entry.jsp?firstName=John
```

Description

- When you use the HTTP Get method to request a JSP from an HTML form, the parameters are automatically appended to the URL.

- When you code or enter a URL that requests a JSP, you can add a parameter list to it starting with a question mark and with no intervening spaces. Then, each parameter consists of its name, an equals sign, and its value. To code multiple parameters, use ampersands (&) to separate the parameters.

- The A tag always uses the HTTP Get method.

Figure 5-7   How to request a JSP with the HTTP Get method

How to request a JSP with the HTTP Post method

When you use a Form tag to request a JSP, there are times when you will want to use the HTTP Post method for the request. To do that, you use the Method attribute to specify the Post method as shown in figure 5-8. Then, the parameters that are passed to the JSP aren't shown in the URL.

When to use the HTTP Get and Post methods

So, when should you use the HTTP Get method and when should you use the Post method? In general, you should use the Get method when you want to *get* (read) data from the server. Similarly, you should use the Post method when you want to *post* (write) data to the server.

When you use the Get method, you need to make sure that the page can be executed multiple times without causing any problems. In this figure, for example, the JSP just displays the data to the user, so there's no harm in executing this page multiple times. If, for example, the user clicks the Refresh button, the browser requests the page again, and this doesn't cause any problems.

However, if the JSP in this figure wrote the data to a database, you wouldn't want the user to write the same data to the database twice. As a result, it would make more sense to use the Post method. Then, if the user clicks the Refresh button, the browser will display a dialog like the one shown in this figure that warns the user that the data will be submitted again. At that point, the user can click on the Cancel button to cancel the request.

There are also a few other reasons to use the Post method. First, since the Post method doesn't append parameters to the end of the URL, it is more appropriate for working with sensitive data. Second, since the Post method prevents the web browser from including parameters in a bookmark for a page, you'll want to use it if you don't want the parameters to be included in the bookmark. Third, if your parameters contain more than 4 KB of data, the Get method won't work so you'll need to use the Post method.

For all other uses, the Get method is preferred. It runs slightly faster than the Post method, and it lets the user bookmark the page along with the parameters that were sent to the page.

A JSP that's requested with the HTTP Post method

A Form tag that uses the Post method

```
<form action="display_email_entry.jsp" method="post">
```

When to use the Get method

- When the request reads data from the server.
- When the request can be executed multiple times without causing any problems.

When to use the Post method

- When the request writes data to the server.
- When executing the request multiple times may cause problems.
- When you don't want to include the parameters in the URL for security reasons.
- When you don't want users to be able to include parameters when they bookmark a page.
- When you need to transfer more than 4 KB of data.

A typical browser dialog that's displayed if the user tries to refresh a post

Figure 5-8   How to request a JSP with the HTTP Post method

How to use regular Java classes with JSPs

In this topic, you'll learn how to use regular Java classes to do the processing that a JSP requires. In particular, you'll learn how to use two classes named User and UserIO to do the data processing for the JSP of the Email List application.

The code for the User and UserIO classes

Figures 5-9 presents the code for a business class named User and figure 5-10 presents the code for an I/O class named UserIO. The package statement at the start of each class indicates where each class is stored. Here, the User class is stored in the business directory because it defines a business object while the UserIO class is stored in the data directory because it provides the data access for the application.

The User class defines a user of the application. This class contains three instance variables: firstName, lastName, and emailAddress. It includes a constructor that accepts three values for these instance variables. And it includes get and set methods for each instance variable.

The code for the User class

```
package business;

public class User
{
    private String firstName;
    private String lastName;
    private String emailAddress;

    public User()
    {
        firstName = "";
        lastName = "";
        emailAddress = "";
    }

    public User(String firstName, String lastName, String emailAddress)
    {
        this.firstName = firstName;
        this.lastName = lastName;
        this.emailAddress = emailAddress;
    }

    public void setFirstName(String firstName)
    {
        this.firstName = firstName;
    }

    public String getFirstName()
    {
        return firstName;
    }

    public void setLastName(String lastName)
    {
        this.lastName = lastName;
    }

    public String getLastName()
    {
        return lastName;
    }

    public void setEmailAddress(String emailAddress)
    {
        this.emailAddress = emailAddress;
    }

    public String getEmailAddress()
    {
        return emailAddress;
    }
}
```

Figure 5-9   The code for the User class

In contrast, the UserIO class contains one static method named add that writes the values stored in a User object to a text file. This method accepts two parameters: a User object and a string that provides the path for the file. If this file exists, the method will add the user data to the end of it. If the file doesn't exist, the method will create it and add the data at the beginning of the file.

If you've read chapter 6 of *Murach's Java SE 6*, you should understand the code for the User class. And if you've read chapter 19, you should understand the code in the UserIO class.

The code for the UserIO class

```
package data;

import java.io.*;
import business.User;

public class UserIO
{
    public static void add(User user, String filepath) throws IOException
    {
        File file = new File(filepath);
        PrintWriter out = new PrintWriter(
                new FileWriter(file, true));
        out.println(user.getEmailAddress()+ "|"
                + user.getFirstName() + "|"
                + user.getLastName());
        out.close();
    }
}
```

Figure 5-10   The code for the UserIO class

A JSP that uses the User and UserIO classes

Figure 5-11 shows the code for the JSP in the Email List application after it has been enhanced so it uses the User and UserIO classes to process the parameters that have been passed to it. In the first statement of the body, a special type of JSP tag is used to import the business and data packages that contain the User and UserIO classes. You'll learn the details of coding this type of tag in the next figure.

In the scriptlet of the JSP, the getParameter method is used to get the values of the three parameters that are passed to it, and these values are stored in String objects. Then, the next two statements use the getRealPath method of the ServletContext object to get the real path for the EmailList.txt file that's stored in the application's WEB-INF directory. Since the WEB-INF directory isn't web-accessible, the users of this application won't be able to access this file.

The last two statements in this scriptlet create the User object from the three parameters and call the add method of the UserIO class to write this object to the EmailList.txt file. Note, here, that the real path of the EmailList.txt file is passed to the add method of the UserIO class, because that's what this method requires.

After the scriptlet, the code in the JSP defines the layout of the page. Within the HTML table definitions, the JSP expressions use the get methods of the User object to display the first name, last name, and email address values. Although these JSP expressions could use the String objects instead, the code in this figure is intended to show how the get methods can be used. In addition, this makes sure that the data that's displayed by the JSP is the same as the data that was written to the EmailList.txt file.

The code for a JSP that uses the User and UserIO classes

```
<!DOCTYPE HTML PUBLIC "-//W3C//DTD HTML 4.01 Transitional//EN"
    "http://www.w3.org/TR/html4/loose.dtd">

<html>
<head>
    <title>Murach's Java Servlets and JSP</title>
</head>
<body>
    <!-- import packages and classes needed by the scripts -->
    <%@ page import="business.*, data.*" %>

    <%
        // get parameters from the request
        String firstName = request.getParameter("firstName");
        String lastName = request.getParameter("lastName");
        String emailAddress = request.getParameter("emailAddress");

        // get the real path for the EmailList.txt file
        ServletContext sc = this.getServletContext();
        String path = sc.getRealPath("/WEB-INF/EmailList.txt");

        // use regular Java objects
        User user = new User(firstName, lastName, emailAddress);
        UserIO.add(user, path);
    %>

    <h1>Thanks for joining our email list</h1>

    <p>Here is the information that you entered:</p>

    <table cellspacing="5" cellpadding="5" border="1">
        <tr>
            <td align="right">First name:</td>
            <td><%= user.getFirstName() %></td>
        </tr>
        <tr>
            <td align="right">Last name:</td>
            <td><%= user.getLastName() %></td>
        </tr>
        <tr>
            <td align="right">Email address:</td>
            <td><%= user.getEmailAddress() %></td>
        </tr>
    </table>

    <p>To enter another email address, click on the Back <br>
    button in your browser or the Return button shown <br>
    below.</p>

    <form action="join_email_list.html" method="post">
        <input type="submit" value="Return">
    </form>

</body>
</html>
```

Figure 5-11   A JSP that uses the User and UserIO classes

How to use three more types of JSP tags

So far, you've learned how to use the two most common types of JSP tags: the tags for scriptlets and expressions. Now, you'll learn how to use three more types of JSP tags. All five types of JSP tags are summarized at the top of figure 5-12.

How to import classes

After the summary of JSP tags, figure 5-12 shows how to use a *JSP directive* to import classes in a JSP. The type of directive that you use for doing that is called a *page directive*, and the shaded statement at the start of the JSP shows how to code one.

To code a page directive for importing classes, you code the starting tag and the word *page* followed by the Import attribute. Within the quotation marks after the equals sign for this attribute, you code the names of the Java classes that you want to import just as you do in a Java import statement. In the example in this figure, all the classes of the business and data packages are imported, plus the Date class in the java.util package.

Once the page directive imports the packages, the JSP can access the User and UserIO classes and the Date class without needing to fully qualify the name. The scriptlet that follows creates a User object from the User class and uses the add method of the UserIO class to write the data for the User object to a text file. The last line in this example uses the default constructor of the Date class as an expression in an HTML line. This works because the JSP will automatically call the toString method of the Date class to convert the Date object that's created into a string.

The five types of JSP tags

Tag	Name	Purpose
`<% %>`	JSP scriptlet	To insert a block of Java statements.
`<%= %>`	JSP expression	To display the string value of an expression.
`<%@ %>`	JSP directive	To set conditions that apply to the entire JSP.
`<%-- --%>`	JSP comment	To tell the JSP engine to ignore code.
`<%! %>`	JSP declaration	To declare instance variables and methods for a JSP.

JSP code that imports Java classes

```
<%@ page import="business.*, data.*, java.util.Date" %>
<%
    // get parameters from the request
    String firstName = request.getParameter("firstName");
    String lastName = request.getParameter("lastName");
    String emailAddress = request.getParameter("emailAddress");

    // get a relative file name
    ServletContext sc = this.getServletContext();
    String path = sc.getRealPath("/WEB-INF/EmailList.txt");

    // use regular Java objects
    User user = new User(firstName, lastName, emailAddress);
    UserIO.add(user, path);
%>

<p>This email address was added to our list on <%= new Date() %></p>
```

Description

- To define the conditions that the JSP engine should follow when converting a JSP into a servlet, you can use a *JSP directive*.
- To import classes in a JSP, you use the import attribute of the *page directive*. This makes the imported classes available to the entire page.
- You can also use the page directive to define other conditions like error handling and content type conditions. You'll learn more about this directive throughout this book.

Figure 5-12   How to import classes

How to code comments in a JSP

Figure 5-13 shows how to code comments in a JSP. To start, the first example shows how you can use HTML comments within a JSP page. In this example, an HTML comment has been used to comment out a line that includes a JSP expression that displays a date.

Then, the second example shows how to use a *JSP comment* in a JSP page. In this example, a JSP comment has been used to comment out a line that includes a JSP expression that displays a date.

When you code HTML and JSP comments, you need to understand how they work to be able to use them properly. In particular, any Java code within an HTML comment is compiled and executed, but the browser doesn't display it. For instance, the first example creates a new Date object even though it doesn't display the date in the browser. In fact, the value for the date object is returned to the browser as an HTML comment. To check this, you can view the HTML for the page that's returned to the browser by selecting the Source or Page Source command from your browser's View menu.

In contrast, any Java code within a JSP comment isn't compiled or executed or returned to the browser in any way. For instance, the second example doesn't create a Date object and it doesn't return it to the browser as a comment. As a result, if you want to comment out code that contains HTML and JSP tags, you typically use a JSP comment. This is critical if the code you're commenting out performs tasks that you no longer want to perform. If, for example, the code updates a variable that you no longer want to update, you need to make sure to use a JSP comment.

Finally, the third example shows how you can code Java comments within a scriptlet. Here, a single-line comment is coded before the three statements that get the request parameters. Then, a multi-line comment is used to comment out the two statements that create the User object and write it to a text file. Since these types of comments work the same as they do with normal Java code, you shouldn't have any trouble using them.

An HTML comment in a JSP

```
<!--
<p>This email address was added to our list on <%= new Date() %></p>
-->
```

A JSP comment

```
<%--
<p>This email address was added to our list on <%= new Date() %></p>
--%>
```

Java comments in a JSP scriptlet

```
<%
    // get parameters from the request
    String firstName = request.getParameter("firstName");
    String lastName = request.getParameter("lastName");
    String emailAddress = request.getParameter("emailAddress");

    /*
    User user = new User(firstName, lastName, emailAddress);
    UserIO.add(user, path);
    */
%>
```

Description

- When you code HTML comments, the comments are compiled and executed, but the browser doesn't display them.

- When you code *JSP comments*, the comments aren't compiled or executed.

- When you code Java comments within a scriptlet, the comments aren't compiled or executed.

Figure 5-13   How to code comments in a JSP

How to declare instance variables and methods

When a JSP is requested for the first time, one *instance* of the JSP is created and loaded into memory, and a *thread* is started that executes the Java code in the JSP. For each subsequent request for the JSP, another thread is started that can access the one instance of the JSP. When you code variables in scriptlets, they are known as local variables, and each thread gets its own copy of each local variable, which is usually what you want.

However, you can also declare instance variables that can be shared between all of the threads that are accessing a JSP. To do that, you can code *JSP declarations* as shown in figure 5-14. Then, any instance variables are initialized when the JSP is first requested. After that, each thread can access these instance variables. This is illustrated by the globalCount variable that's declared in this figure. This variable is incremented by one each time the JSP is requested. Later, when the variable is displayed, it represents the total number of times that the page has been accessed.

Unfortunately, using an instance variable in a JSP can lead to inaccurate results and is generally considered a bad practice. The problem occurs because Java uses a series of operations to increment the globalCount variable. In particular, it reads the value of the variable, modifies the value, and writes a new value back to the variable. Since multiple threads all have access to this variable, two threads may try to read the variable at the same time, which can result in a lost update. In other words, an instance variable in a JSP is not *thread-safe*.

In some cases, it's okay to include instance variables that are not thread-safe. In this figure, for example, it might be acceptable to lose an update to the globalCount variable every now and then. However, in other cases, you need to make sure that your JSP is thread-safe. If, for example, you were using an instance variable to generate a unique identifier for an object, you would need to make sure that all access to the instance variable was thread-safe.

Although there are several techniques for making instance variables thread-safe, none of these techniques are easy to implement. As a result, when you need to make sure all of your operations are thread-safe, you should use local variables instead of instance variables whenever that's possible. If that isn't possible, you can use one of the thread-safe techniques for working with global variables that are described in chapter 8.

Besides declaring instance variables in a JSP, you can declare methods. In this figure, for example, the code for the JSP declares and calls an add method that writes a User object to a file. Here again, though, this is generally considered a bad practice.

So, instead of declaring methods in a JSP, you should consider restructuring your application. In some cases, you may want to use regular Java classes like the UserIO class. In other cases, you may want to use a servlet as described in the next chapter. But most of the time, the best alternative is to use a combination of servlets, JSPs, and regular Java classes as described in chapter 7.

JSP code that declares an instance variable and a method

```
<%-- import any packages needed by the page --%>
<%@ page import="business.*, data.*, java.util.Date, java.io.*" %>

<%!
    // declare an instance variable for the page
    int globalCount = 0;  // this is not thread-safe
%>
<%!
    // declare a method for the page
    public void add(User user, String filename)
           throws IOException
    {
        PrintWriter out = new PrintWriter(
                new FileWriter(filename, true));
        out.println(user.getEmailAddress()+ "|"
                + user.getFirstName() + "|"
                + user.getLastName());
        out.close();
    }
%>
<%
    String firstName = request.getParameter("firstName");
    String lastName = request.getParameter("lastName");
    String emailAddress = request.getParameter("emailAddress");

    ServletContext sc = getServletContext();
    String path = sc.getRealPath("/WEB-INF/EmailList.txt");

    User user = new User(firstName, lastName, emailAddress);

    // use the declared method
    this.add(user, path);

    // update the instance variable
    globalCount++;  // this is not thread-safe
%>
.
.
.
<p>
    This email address was added to our list on <%= new Date() %><br>
    This page has been accessed <%= globalCount %> times.
</p>
```

Description

- You can use *JSP declarations* to declare instance variables and methods.

- Since instance variables aren't *thread-safe*, two threads may conflict when they try to read, modify, and update the same instance variable at the same time.

- In general, you should avoid coding instance variables for JSPs and servlets. Instead, you should use other thread-safe techniques for working with global variables (see chapter 8).

- In general, you should avoid coding methods within JSPs. Instead, you should use some combination of JSPs, servlets, and regular Java classes (see chapter 7).

Figure 5-14   How to declare instance variables and methods

How to work with JSP errors

As you develop JSPs, you will encounter errors. That's why the last two figures in this chapter show you how to work with JSP errors.

How to fix common JSP errors

Figure 5-15 presents the two most common errors that you will encounter when working with JSPs. HTTP Status 404 means that Tomcat received the HTTP request but couldn't find the requested resource. You've already seen this in chapter 2. To fix this type of problem, make sure that the web server is running, that you have entered the correct path and filename for the request, and that the requested file is in the correct location.

In contrast, HTTP Status 500 means that the server received the request and found the resource but couldn't fill the request. This usually means that the JSP engine wasn't able to compile the JSP due to a coding error in the JSP. To fix this type of error, you can review the information provided by the error page. In this figure, for example, the message displayed by the error page shows that a semicolon is missing at the end of one of the statements in the JSP scriptlet.

To correct this type of error, you should fix the JSP so it will compile correctly. To do this, you can open the JSP, add the semicolon, save it, and request the page again. Then, the JSP engine will recognize that the JSP has been modified and it will automatically attempt to compile, load, and display the JSP.

An error page for a common JSP error

```
Apache Tomcat/6.0.10 - Error report - Microsoft Internet Explorer

File   Edit   View   Favorites   Tools   Help

Back  ·           x  2         Search    Favorites              ·

Address    http://localhost:8080/ch05email/display_email_entry.jsp        Go    Links    SnagIt

HTTP Status 500 -


type Exception report

message

description The server encountered an internal error () that prevented it from fulfilling this request.

exception

org.apache.jasper.JasperException: Unable to compile class for JSP:

An error occurred at line: 14 in the jsp file: /display_email_entry.jsp
Syntax error, insert ";" to complete LocalVariableDeclarationStatement
11:
12:    <%
13:       // get parameters from the request
14:       String firstName = request.getParameter("firstName")
15:       String lastName = request.getParameter("lastName");
16:       String emailAddress = request.getParameter("emailAddress");
17:


Stacktrace:
        org.apache.jasper.compiler.DefaultErrorHandler.javacError(DefaultErrorHandler.java:85)
        org.apache.jasper.compiler.ErrorDispatcher.javacError(ErrorDispatcher.java:330)
        org.apache.jasper.compiler.JDTCompiler.generateClass(JDTCompiler.java:415)
        org.apache.jasper.compiler.Compiler.compile(Compiler.java:308)

Done                                                        Local intranet
```

Common JSP errors

- HTTP Status 404 – File Not Found Error
- HTTP Status 500 – Internal Server Error

Tips for fixing JSP errors

- Make sure the Tomcat server is running.
- Make sure that the URL is valid and that it points to the right location for the requested page.
- Make sure all of the HTML, JSP, and Java class files are in the correct locations.
- Read the error page carefully to get all available information about the error.

Figure 5-15   How to fix common JSP errors

When and how to view the servlet that's generated for a JSP

From a practical point of view, you can almost always use the skills described in figure 5-15 to solve the errors that you encounter when working with JSPs. However, it's sometimes helpful to understand what's going on behind the scenes when you work with JSPs. In particular, you should understand the lifecycle of a JSP.

To start, when a user requests a JSP for the first time, the JSP engine generates a servlet for the JSP, compiles the JSP, and creates one instance of the servlet class. After that, a thread is created for each user, and each thread gets its own copy of the local variables of the servlet methods.

Although you may never need to view the code for the servlet that's generated for a JSP, you can view this code if you're trying to debug a JSP or if you're curious about how the JSP engine works. To view the generated servlet, you can look through the web server's files until you find the appropriate directory. For example, the top of this figure shows the path to the directory that Tomcat uses to store the servlets that are generated for the ch05email application. As a result, to view the source code for any of the JSP pages of the ch05email application, you can navigate to this directory. Then, you can open the .java file that corresponds with the JSP that you want to view.

To give you an idea of what a generated servlet looks like, figure 5-16 shows some key parts of the servlet that's generated for the JSP in figure 5-11. As you read through this code, you may find it to be overwhelming at first. However, if you take a moment to compare the code for the JSP in figure 5-11 with the partial servlet code shown in this figure, you should get a good idea of what's going on. Also, after you read the next chapter, which shows you how to develop servlets, the code for this servlet should make even more sense. For now, you can just note how the JSP directive, scriptlet, and expression tags are translated into plain old Java code.

The JSP work directory for ch05email application

```
C:\tomcat\work\Catalina\localhost\ch05email\org\apache\jsp
```

Part of the servlet class that's generated from the JSP in figure 5-11

```java
package org.apache.jsp;

import javax.servlet.*;
import javax.servlet.http.*;
import javax.servlet.jsp.*;
import business.*;
import data.*;
import java.util.Date;

public final class display_005femail_005fentry_jsp extends
org.apache.jasper.runtime.HttpJspBase
implements org.apache.jasper.runtime.JspSourceDependent {
    ...
  public void _jspService(HttpServletRequest request,
  HttpServletResponse response)
  throws java.io.IOException, ServletException {
      ...
      response.setContentType("text/html");
      ...
      out.write("<html>\n");
      out.write("<head>\n");
      out.write("    <title>Murach's Java Servlets and JSP</title>\n");
      out.write("</head>\n");
      out.write("<body>\n");
      ...
        // get parameters from the request
        String firstName = request.getParameter("firstName");
        String lastName = request.getParameter("lastName");
        String emailAddress = request.getParameter("emailAddress");

        // get the real path for the emaillist file
        ServletContext sc = this.getServletContext();
        String path = sc.getRealPath("/WEB-INF/EmailList.txt");

        // use regular Java objects
        User user = new User(firstName, lastName, emailAddress);
        UserIO.add(user, path);
      ...
      out.write("    <table cellspacing=\"5\" cellpadding=\"5\"
                border=\"1\">\n");
      out.write("        <tr>\n");
      out.write("            <td align=\"right\">First name:</td>\n");
      out.write("            <td>");
      out.print( user.getFirstName() );
      out.write("</td>\n");
      out.write("        </tr>\n");
      ...
      out.write("</body>\n");
      out.write("</html>");
      ...
  }
}
```

Figure 5-16   When and how to view the servlet that's generated for a JSP

Perspective

The goal of this chapter has been to provide you with the basic skills for coding a JSP. At this point, you should be able to code simple, but practical, JSPs of your own. In addition, you should understand how HTML pages communicate with JSPs, how JSPs communicate with regular Java classes, and how to fix some of the common JSP errors.

In the next chapter, you'll learn how to use the same types of skills with servlets. In fact, the next chapter uses the same application that's presented in this chapter, but it uses a servlet instead of a JSP.

Summary

- A *JavaServer Page* (*JSP*) consists of HTML code plus Java code that's embedded in *scriptlets* and *expressions*. Within the scriptlets and expressions, you can use the methods of the *implicit request object* to get the *parameters* that are passed to the JSP.

- You can use the getRealPath method of the ServletContext object to get a relative path to refer to a file that's used by your web application.

- When you use the HTTP Get method to pass parameters to a JSP, the parameters are displayed in the URL. When you use the HTTP Post method, they aren't. If executing a request multiple times may cause problems, you should use the Post method.

- You can use regular Java classes from within scriptlets and expressions just as you use them from other Java classes.

- You use a *JSP directive* known as a *page directive* to import classes for use in a JSP.

- When you use *JSP comments*, the comments aren't compiled or executed or returned to the browser. In contrast, HTML comments are compiled and executed and returned to the browser, but the browser doesn't display them.

- You use *JSP declarations* to declare instance variables and methods for a JSP. However, instance variables are not *thread-safe* and may result in lost updates.

- When working with JSPs, an HTTP Status 500 error usually indicates that the JSP engine wasn't able to compile the servlet class for the JSP.

- When a JSP is requested for the first time, the JSP engine generates a servlet class for the page, compiles it, and creates one instance of the servlet. For each subsequent request, a new thread is created from this single instance of the servlet class. As a result, each thread gets its own copy of the local variables, but all threads share the same instance variables.

Exercise 5-1   Enhance the Email List application

In this exercise, you'll modify the HTML document for the Email List application, and you'll create a new JSP that responds to the HTML document.

Review and test the code for the email application

1. Open the ch05email project in the ex_starts directory.

2. Review the code for the HTML and JSP file for the application.

3. Review the code for the User and UserIO classes that are in the business and data packages.

4. Run the application, enter the name and email address for one user, and click on the Submit button. Then, note how the parameters are used in the URL for calling the JSP. Also, use the Back button and Refresh button to see how they work.

5. Use the Windows Explorer or your IDE to find the text file that the users have been saved in (EmailList.txt), open the file, and review the data that has been stored in it.

6. Change the method used for the form in the HTML file from get to post. Then, test the application again by entering another user. Note that the parameters aren't shown in the URL, and note how the Refresh button works for the JSP.

7. Create a JSP error by deleting the semicolon at the end of the first Java statement in the JSP. Then, run the application to see how Tomcat handles this error.

8. Fix the error by restoring the semicolon in the JSP.

Enhance the application

9. Modify the HTML document so it has this line of text after the Email Address text box: "I'm interested in these types of music." Then, follow this text with a list box that has options for Rock, Country, Bluegrass, and Folk music. This list box should be followed by the Submit button, and the Submit button should submit the form to a new JSP named display_music_choices.jsp.

10. Create a new JSP named display_music_choices.jsp that responds to the changed HTML document. This JSP should start with an H1 line that reads like this:

```
Thanks for joining our email list, John Smith.
```

And this line should be followed by text that looks like this:

```
We'll use email to notify you whenever we have new releases for
these types of music:
```

```
Country
Bluegrass
```

In other words, you list the types of music that correspond to the items that are selected in the list box. And the entire web page consists of just the heading and text lines that I've just described.

Please note that you don't have to provide code that saves the data that the user enters to the EmailList.txt file because that would mean changes to both the User and UserIO classes.

11. Change the method for the form in the HTML document back to the Get method so you can see the parameters in the URL. Then, test the HTML document and the new JSP by running the application. Note how the parameter list stores your music choices when you select more than one item from the list box. (To select more than one item, you can hold down the Ctrl or Shift key as you click on items.)

12. Test the new JSP by entering a URL that includes a parameter list in the browser's address box. To keep this simple, you only need to include parameters for first name and last name.

13. When you're through experimenting, close the project.

6

How to develop servlets

In chapter 5, you learned how to develop a web application that consisted of an HTML page and a JavaServer Page. In this chapter, you'll learn how to create the same application using a servlet instead of a JSP. Along the way, you'll learn that many of the skills for developing JSPs also apply to servlets. When you complete this chapter, you should be able to use servlets to develop simple web applications of your own.

The Email List application

This topic shows how to create the Email List application that was presented in the last chapter with a servlet instead of a JSP. Once you see how the pieces of this application fit together, you'll be ready to learn some specific skills for developing servlets.

The user interface for the application

Figure 6-1 shows the two pages that make up the user interface for the Email List application. These pages are the same as the pages that are shown in the last chapter except that the second page uses a servlet instead of a JSP.

Like the last chapter, the first page is an HTML page that asks the user to enter a first name, last name, and email address. However, when the user clicks on the Submit button for this application, the HTML page calls a servlet instead of a JSP and passes the three user entries to the servlet. This is shown by the URL that's displayed in the browser for the second page.

The HTML page

The servlet page

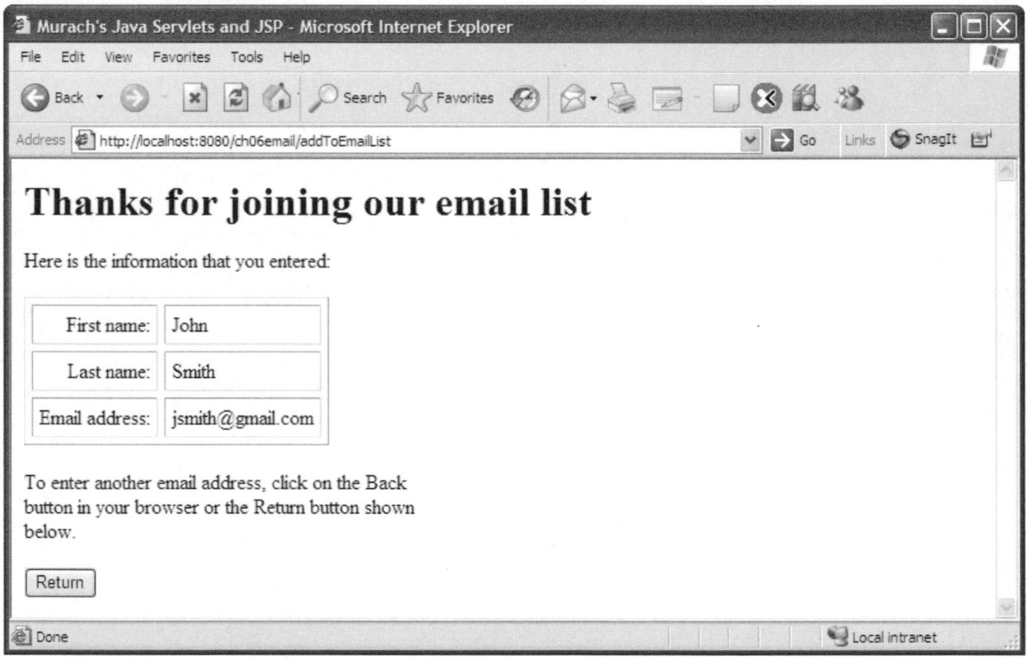

Figure 6-1   The user interface for the application

The code for the HTML page that calls the servlet

Figure 6-2 shows the code for the HTML page that calls the servlet. Except for the Form tag, this code is the same as the code for the HTML page presented in the previous chapter. As a result, you shouldn't have any trouble understanding it.

Within the Form tag, the Action attribute specifies a URL named addToEmailList that's in the same directory as the HTML page. Since this URL is mapped to a servlet, it causes the mapped servlet to be executed. In the next figure, you'll see the code for the servlet and the code that maps the servlet to this URL.

Within the Form tag, the Method attribute specifies the HTTP Post method. As a result, the parameters submitted by this form aren't appended to the end of the URL. To verify this, you can refer to the previous figure. To review the differences between the HTTP Post method and the HTTP Get method, please refer to chapter 5.

The code for the HTML page

```
<!DOCTYPE HTML PUBLIC "-//W3C//DTD HTML 4.01 Transitional//EN">

<html>

<head>
    <title>Murach's Java Servlets and JSP</title>
</head>

<body>
    <h1>Join our email list</h1>
    <p>To join our email list, enter your name and
     email address below. <br>
     Then, click on the Submit button.</p>

    <form action="addToEmailList" method="post">
    <table cellspacing="5" border="0">
        <tr>
            <td align="right">First name:</td>
            <td><input type="text" name="firstName"></td>
        </tr>
        <tr>
            <td align="right">Last name:</td>
            <td><input type="text" name="lastName"></td>
        </tr>
        <tr>
            <td align="right">Email address:</td>
            <td><input type="text" name="emailAddress"></td>
        </tr>
        <tr>
            <td></td>
            <td><br><input type="submit" value="Submit"></td>
        </tr>
    </table>
    </form>
</body>

</html>
```

Description

- This HTML page is the same as the HTML page shown in the previous chapter, except that the Form tag specifies a URL that's mapped to a servlet, and it specifies the HTTP Post method instead of the HTTP Get method.

Figure 6-2   The code for the HTML page that calls the servlet

The code for the servlet

A *servlet* is a Java class that extends the HttpServlet class and runs on the server within a servlet container. In figure 6-3, for example, the declaration for the AddToEmailListServlet class extends the HttpServlet class. Here, the name for the servlet begins with a verb to clearly identify the task that's performed by the servlet.

The first statement for this servlet specifies that the servlet will be stored in a package named email. Then, the next three statements import some packages from the servlet API and from the core Java API that are needed by all servlets. Finally, the last two statements import the User and UserIO classes from the business and data packages. These classes are the same regular Java classes that are described in chapter 5.

After the declaration for this class, the doPost method provides the code that's executed when a browser uses the HTTP Post method to request a servlet. This doPost method accepts two arguments that are passed to it from the web server: an HttpServletRequest object and an HttpServletResponse object. These objects are commonly referred to as the *request object* and the *response object*. In fact, the implicit request object that you learned about in the last chapter is actually an object of the HttpServletRequest class.

Within the doPost method, the first seven statements perform the same processing that was presented in the last chapter. To start, the first three statements use the getParameter method of the request object to return the three parameters entered by the user. Then, the next two statements get the path for the EmailList.txt file that's in the application's WEB-INF directory. Finally, the last two statements create a User object from the three parameters and use the UserIO class to write the data stored in the User object to the specified file.

After the first seven statements, the next two statements create a PrintWriter object that can be used to send a response to the browser. To start, the first statement sets the *content type* that will be returned to the browser. In this case, the content type is set so that the servlet returns an HTML document, but it's possible to return other content types. Then, the second statement gets a PrintWriter object that's used to return data to the browser.

After the PrintWriter object is created, the next statement uses the println method of the PrintWriter object to return HTML to the browser. This is the same HTML that was used in the JSP in the last chapter. However, this HTML is more difficult to code and read now that it's coded as a string argument of the println method. That's why the next chapter shows how to remove this type of tedious coding from your servlets by combining the use of servlets with JSPs.

Within the println string, only the firstName, lastName, and emailAddress variables are displayed outside of quotation marks. Also, the quotation marks within the string, like the quotation marks around HTML attributes, are preceded by a backslash (\). Otherwise, the Java compiler would interpret those quotation marks as the end of the string. Since the quotation marks within the HTML statements aren't actually required, you can remove them to simplify the code, but the code is still clumsy.

The code for the AddToEmailListServlet class   **Page 1**

```java
package email;

import java.io.*;
import javax.servlet.*;
import javax.servlet.http.*;

import business.User;
import data.UserIO;

public class AddToEmailListServlet extends HttpServlet
{
    protected void doPost(
        HttpServletRequest request,
        HttpServletResponse response)
        throws ServletException, IOException
    {
        // get parameters from the request
        String firstName = request.getParameter("firstName");
        String lastName = request.getParameter("lastName");
        String emailAddress = request.getParameter("emailAddress");

        // get a relative file name
        ServletContext sc = getServletContext();
        String path = sc.getRealPath("/WEB-INF/EmailList.txt");

        // use regular Java objects to write the data to a file
        User user = new User(firstName, lastName, emailAddress);
        UserIO.add(user, path);

        // send response to browser
        response.setContentType("text/html;charset=UTF-8");
        PrintWriter out = response.getWriter();
        out.println(
          "<!doctype html public \"-//W3C//DTD HTML 4.0 Transitional//EN\">\n"
        + "<html>\n"
        + "<head>\n"
        + "  <title>Murach's Java Servlets and JSP</title>\n"
        + "</head>\n"
        + "<body>\n"
        + "<h1>Thanks for joining our email list</h1>\n"
        + "<p>Here is the information that you entered:</p>\n"
        + "  <table cellspacing=\"5\" cellpadding=\"5\" border=\"1\">\n"
        + "  <tr><td align=\"right\">First name:</td>\n"
        + "      <td>" + firstName + "</td>\n"
        + "  </tr>\n"
        + "  <tr><td align=\"right\">Last name:</td>\n"
        + "      <td>" + lastName + "</td>\n"
        + "  </tr>\n"
        + "  <tr><td align=\"right\">Email address:</td>\n"
        + "      <td>" + emailAddress + "</td>\n"
        + "  </tr>\n"
        + "  </table>\n"
```

Figure 6-3   The code for the servlet and the web.xml file (part 1 of 2)

The last statement in the doPost method calls the close method of the PrintWriter object. This statement closes the output stream and frees any resources that are associated with it.

After the doPost method, the doGet method provides the code that's executed when a browser uses the HTTP Get method to request a servlet. Here, the doGet method accepts the same arguments and throws the same exceptions as the doPost method. However, the only statement within this doGet method calls the doPost method and passes the request and response objects as parameters. As a result, this doGet method performs the same processing as the doPost method. This is a common programming practice that allows a servlet to use the same code to handle both the Get and Post methods of an HTTP request.

If you don't want to allow the servlet to handle an HTTP Get request, you can omit the doGet method. Then, if an HTTP Get method is used to request the servlet, Tomcat will display an error message that indicates that the Get method isn't supported by the servlet. For instance, since the servlet in this figure writes data to the server, it might make sense to omit its doGet method, especially after you're done testing the servlet.

The mapping for the servlet

Before you can request a servlet, you must use the web.xml file to map the servlet to a URL. This figure shows a complete web.xml file for the Email List application that maps the AddToEmailListServlet to a URL named addToEmailList that's in the root directory for the application.

The first line of code in this file is an XML declaration that indicates the version of XML and the character set for the document. Then, the web-app element specifies the version of the Java EE specification that's being used. These elements are the same from one web application to another, and they are usually generated by your IDE.

After the web-app element, the servlet element declares the servlet. Here, the servlet-name element specifies an internal name that's used to uniquely identify the servlet within the web.xml file. Then, the servlet-class element specifies the package and name of the class for the servlet.

After the servlet element, the servlet-mapping element maps the servlet to a URL. Here, the servlet-name element identifies the servlet by specifying the name that's used in the servlet element. Then, the url-pattern element maps the servlet to the addToEmailList URL in the root directory.

Finally, this web.xml file sets a couple of other configuration settings for the application. First, the session-config element sets the session timeout to 30 minutes. As a result, any resources that are associated with a user will be released if the user hasn't accessed the session within the last 30 minutes. Second, the welcome-file-list element sets the welcome file to join_email_list.html. As a result, when a user requests the root directory of the application, this HTML page will be displayed.

The code for the AddToEmailListServlet class   Page 2

```
            + "<p>To enter another email address, click on the Back <br>\n"
            + "button in your browser or the Return button shown <br>\n"
            + "below.</p>\n"
            + "<form action=\"join_email_list.html\" "
            + "        method=\"post\">\n"
            + "   <input type=\"submit\" value=\"Return\">\n"
            + "</form>\n"
            + "</body>\n"
            + "</html>\n");

        out.close();
    }

    protected void doGet(
        HttpServletRequest request,
        HttpServletResponse response)
        throws ServletException, IOException
    {
        doPost(request, response);
    }
}
```

The web.xml file with the mapping for the servlet

```
<?xml version="1.0" encoding="UTF-8"?>
<web-app version="2.5" xmlns="http://java.sun.com/xml/ns/javaee"
    xmlns:xsi="http://www.w3.org/2001/XMLSchema-instance"
    xsi:schemaLocation="http://java.sun.com/xml/ns/javaee
    http://java.sun.com/xml/ns/javaee/web-app_2_5.xsd">

    <!-- the definitions for the servlet -->
    <servlet>
        <servlet-name>AddToEmailListServlet</servlet-name>
        <servlet-class>email.AddToEmailListServlet</servlet-class>
    </servlet>

    <!-- the mapping for the servlets -->
    <servlet-mapping>
        <servlet-name>AddToEmailListServlet</servlet-name>
        <url-pattern>/addToEmailList</url-pattern>
    </servlet-mapping>

    <!-- other configuration settings for the application -->
    <session-config>
        <session-timeout>30</session-timeout>
    </session-config>
    <welcome-file-list>
        <welcome-file>join_email_list.html</welcome-file>
    </welcome-file-list>
</web-app>
```

Figure 6-3   The code for the servlet and the web.xml file (part 2 of 2)

How to code, map, and request a servlet

Now that you have an overview of how servlets are coded, you're ready to learn more about coding, mapping, and requesting a servlet.

How to code a servlet

Figure 6-4 shows the basic structure for a servlet that performs some processing and returns an HTML document to the browser. You can use this basic structure for all the servlets you write. For now, that's all you need to get started, but you'll learn another way to structure servlets in the next chapter.

Since most servlets are stored in a package, the first statement in this servlet specifies the package for the servlet. This package must correspond to the directory that contains the servlet as described in chapter 3. Then, the next three statements import the classes that are required by all servlets. The javax.servlet.http package is required because it contains the HttpServletRequest and HttpServletResponse classes. The javax.servlet package is required because it contains the ServletException class. And the java.io package is required because it contains the IOException class.

After the first four statements, the class declaration provides the name for the servlet and indicates that it extends the HttpServlet class. In theory, a servlet can extend the GenericServlet class. In practice, however, all servlets extend the HttpServlet class.

The doGet and doPost methods in this figure accept the same arguments and throw the same exceptions. Within these methods, you can use the methods of the request object to get incoming data, and you can use the methods of the response object to set outgoing data. In this figure, the doGet method calls the doPost method. As a result, an HTTP Get request executes the doPost method of the servlet. This is a common programming practice that allows a servlet to use the same code to handle both the Get and Post methods of an HTTP request.

In the doPost method, the first statement calls the setContentType method of the response object. This sets the content type for the HTTP response that's returned to the browser to "text/html," which specifies that the servlet returns text or HTML. In chapter 18, you'll learn how to return other types of data.

The second statement in the doGet method calls the getWriter method of the response object to get a PrintWriter object named out. Once you get this object, you can use one println statement or a series of print and println statements to return HTML or other text to the browser as shown by the third statement. However, as you learned in the last figure, you must code a backslash before any quotation marks that don't start or end a string. Otherwise, the servlet won't compile properly. Then, the last statement closes and flushes the output stream and releases any resources that are being used by this object.

The structure for a simple servlet that returns HTML

```java
package murach;

import java.io.*;
import javax.servlet.*;
import javax.servlet.http.*;

public class TestServlet extends HttpServlet
{
    public void doPost(HttpServletRequest request,
                       HttpServletResponse response)
                throws IOException, ServletException
    {
        //business processing

        response.setContentType("text/html");
        PrintWriter out = response.getWriter();
        out.println("<h1>HTML from servlet</h1>");
        out.close();
    }

    public void doGet(HttpServletRequest request,
                      HttpServletResponse response)
                throws IOException, ServletException
    {
        doPost(request, response);
    }
}
```

Description

- In practice, all servlets extend the HttpServlet class. To extend this class, the servlet must import the java.io, javax.servlet, and javax.servlet.http packages.

- The doGet method overrides the doGet method of the HttpServlet class and processes all HTTP requests that use the Get method, and the doPost method overrides the doPost method of the HttpServlet class and processes all HTTP requests that use the Post method.

- The doGet and doPost methods use two objects that are passed to it by the web server: (1) the HttpServletRequest object, or the *request object*, and (2) the HttpServletResponse object, or the *response object*.

- The setContentType method of the response object sets the *content type* of the response that's returned to the browser. Then, the getWriter method of the response object returns a PrintWriter object that can be used to send HTML to the browser.

- Before you can create a PrintWriter object, you must set the content type. This allows the getWriter method to return a PrintWriter object that uses the proper content type.

Figure 6-4   How to code a servlet

How to map a servlet to a URL

Before you can request a servlet, you need to use the web.xml file for the application to map the servlet to a URL. To illustrate how this works, figure 6-5 shows the XML tags that map two servlets.

The first servlet element in this figure declares a name that refers to the AddToEmailListServlet class that's shown in the previous figure. Here, the servlet-name element provides a unique name for the class. This name is used internally by the web.xml file. Then, the servlet-class element uses a fully-qualified name to identify the class for the servlet. In this example, the servlet-name entry is the same as the name for the class, but it isn't qualified by the package name. This is a common convention for naming a servlet. However, if the same servlet name is used in two or more packages, you can use servlet elements to specify a unique name for each servlet.

The second servlet element declares an internal name for a servlet named TestServlet that's stored in the email package. This servlet element uses the same naming convention as the first servlet element.

The first servlet-mapping element maps the AddToEmailListServlet to a single URL that's available from the root directory of the application. As a result, the user is able to request this servlet by specifying a URL pattern like this one:

```
http://localhost:8080/ch06email/addToEmailList
```

Note that this URL removes the word *Servlet* from the end of the servlet name. I have used this convention throughout this book because it shortens the URL and hides the fact that application uses servlets from the user.

The second servlet-mapping element uses a wildcard character (*) to map the AddToEmailListServlet to any URL that resides within the email directory. This allows this servlet to be requested by multiple URLs. For example, you could request this servlet with this URL:

```
http://localhost:8080/ch06email/email/add
```

Or, you could request this servlet with this URL:

```
http://localhost:8080/ch06email/email/addToList
```

It's important to note that this servlet mapping works even if the email directory is a virtual directory that doesn't actually exist on the server.

The third servlet-mapping element maps the TestServlet to a single URL. This element uses the same naming convention as the first servlet-mapping element.

If you have any trouble working with the web.xml file, you can review the skills for working with the web.xml file that were presented in chapter 3. Or, if necessary, you can get more information about working with XML from chapter 20 of *Murach's Java SE 6*.

XML tags that add servlet mapping to the web.xml file

```
<!-- the definitions for the servlets -->
<servlet>
    <servlet-name>AddToEmailListServlet</servlet-name>
    <servlet-class>email.AddToEmailListServlet</servlet-class>
</servlet>
<servlet>
    <servlet-name>TestServlet</servlet-name>
    <servlet-class>email.TestServlet</servlet-class>
</servlet>

<!-- the mapping for the servlets -->
<servlet-mapping>
    <servlet-name>AddToEmailListServlet</servlet-name>
    <url-pattern>/addToEmailList</url-pattern>
</servlet-mapping>
<servlet-mapping>
    <servlet-name>AddToEmailListServlet</servlet-name>
    <url-pattern>/email/*</url-pattern>
</servlet-mapping>
<servlet-mapping>
    <servlet-name>TestServlet</servlet-name>
    <url-pattern>/test</url-pattern>
</servlet-mapping>
```

XML elements for working with servlet mapping

Element	Description
`<servlet-class>`	Specifies the class for the servlet. Note that this element includes the package and name for the class but not the .class extension.
`<servlet-name>`	Specifies a unique name for the servlet that's used to identify the servlet within the web.xml file. This element is required for both the servlet element and the servlet-mapping element and maps each servlet-mapping element to a servlet element.
`<url-pattern>`	Specifies the URL or URLs that are mapped to the specified servlet. This pattern must begin with a front slash, but the URL pattern can specify a virtual directory or file that doesn't actually exist.

Some URL pattern examples

URL pattern	Description
`/addToEmailList`	Specifies the addToEmailList URL in the root directory of the application.
`/email/*`	Specifies any URL in the email directory.
`/email/add`	Specifies the add URL in the email directory.
`/email/add.jsp`	Specifies the add.jsp URL in the email directory.

Description

- Before you can request a servlet, you should use the application's web.xml file to map a servlet to a URL pattern.

Figure 6-5   How to map a servlet to a URL

How to request a servlet

After you code and map a servlet, you can request the servlet and view it in a web browser. To do that, you typically code a Form tag or an A tag that requests the servlet as shown by the examples in figure 6-6. However, if the web server and servlet engine are running, you can also enter a URL directly into the browser.

The first example shows how to use a Form tag to request a servlet. To start, you can use the Action attribute to provide a URL that requests the servlet. In this example, the assumption is that the Form tag is coded in the root directory of the ch06email application. As a result, the path specified in the Action attribute specifies the URL that was mapped in the previous figure. However, if necessary, you could use any of the skills described in the previous chapter to navigate up or down the directory structure for the application.

After you code the Action attribute for a Form tag, you can use the Method attribute to specify whether you want to use the HTTP Get method or the Post method. In this example, the Form tag uses the Post method. As a result, this tag doesn't append the parameters for the form to the end of the URL.

The second example shows how you can use a Form tag to use a different URL to request the same servlet that was requested in the first example. This is possible because the servlet mapping presented in the previous figure provides for multiple URL patterns that map to the AddToEmailListServlet class. In this case, the URL that's displayed in the browser corresponds with the URL that's specified in the Action attribute for the Form tag.

The third example shows how you can use an A tag to request a servlet. Here, the HRef attribute is used to specify the URL that requests the AddToEmailListServlet. In addition, two parameters have been appended to the end of the URL. This works the same for servlets as it does for JSPs. As a result, if you need to review how this works, you can refer to chapter 5.

The fourth example shows how to request a servlet by entering a URL directly into the browser. In this example, the URL requests the AddToEmailListServlet and appends the firstName parameter to the end of the URL. Since this URL doesn't provide the lastName or emailAddress parameters, this servlet displays null values for these parameters as shown by the screen in this figure.

When you request a servlet by using an A tag or entering a URL into a browser, you need to remember that these techniques automatically use the HTTP Get method. As a result, a servlet will only be able to process these requests if it has implemented the doGet method. If you attempt to use one of these methods with a servlet that doesn't implement the doGet method, Tomcat will return an error message that indicates that the HTTP Get method is not supported by the specified URL.

How to request the mapped servlet

A Form tag that requests the servlet

```
<form action="addToEmailList" method="post">
```

The URL displayed in the browser

```
http://localhost:8080/ch06email/addToEmailList
```

Another Form tag that requests the servlet

```
<form action="email/addToList" method="post">
```

The URL displayed in the browser

```
http://localhost:8080/ch06email/email/addToList
```

An A tag that requests a servlet

```
<a href="addToEmailList?firstName=John&lastName=Smith">
    Display Email Entry Test
</a>
```

A URL that requests a servlet

```
http://localhost:8080/ch06email/addToEmailList?firstName=John
```

Description

• The HTTP Get and Post methods work the same for servlets as they do for JSPs. For more information, refer back to figures 5-7 and 5-8. However, an HTTP Get or Post request will only be processed if the doGet or doPost method has been implemented by the servlet.

Figure 6-6   How to request a servlet

More skills for working with servlets

Now that you have a basic understanding of how to code a servlet, you're ready to learn some other skills for working with servlets.

The methods of a servlet

Figure 6-7 presents some common methods of the HttpServlet class. When you code these methods, you need to understand that the servlet engine only creates one instance of a servlet. This usually occurs when the servlet engine starts or when the servlet is first requested. Then, each request for the servlet starts (or "spawns") a thread that can access that one instance of the servlet.

When the servlet engine creates the instance of the servlet, it calls the init method. Since this method is only called once, you can override it in your servlet to supply any initialization code that's required. In the next figure, you'll see an example of this.

After the servlet engine has created the one instance of the servlet, each request for that servlet spawns a thread that calls the service method of the servlet. This method checks the method that's specified in the HTTP request and calls the appropriate doGet or doPost method.

When you code servlets, you shouldn't override the service method. Instead, you should override the appropriate doGet or doPost methods. To handle a request that uses the Get method, for example, you can override the doGet method. If, on the other hand, you want to handle a request that uses the Post method, you can override the doPost method. To handle both types of requests, you can override both of them and have one call the other as shown in figure 6-4.

If a servlet has been idle for some time or if the servlet engine is shut down, the servlet engine unloads the instances of the servlets that it has created. Before unloading a servlet, though, it calls the destroy method of the servlet. If you want to provide some cleanup code, such as writing a variable to a file or closing a database connection, you can override this method. However, the destroy method can't be called if the server crashes. As a result, you shouldn't rely on it to execute any code that's critical to your application.

Five common methods of a servlet

```
public void init() throws ServletException{}

public void service(HttpServletRequest request,
                    HttpServletResponse response)
                    throws IOException, ServletException{}

public void doGet(HttpServletRequest request,
                    HttpServletResponse response)
                    throws IOException, ServletException{}

public void doPost(HttpServletRequest request,
                    HttpServletResponse response)
                    throws IOException, ServletException{}

public void destroy(){}
```

How the server handles a request for a servlet

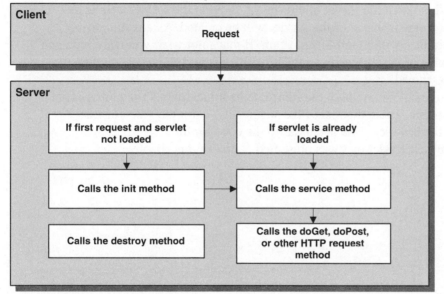

The life cycle of a servlet

- A server loads and initializes the servlet by calling the init method.
- The servlet handles each browser request by calling the service method. This method then calls another method to handle the specific HTTP request type.
- The server removes the servlet by calling the destroy method. This occurs either when the servlet has been idle for some time or when the server is shut down.

Description

- All the methods shown above are located in the abstract HttpServlet class. This means you can override these methods in your own servlets. However, it's generally considered a bad practice to override the service method. Instead, you should override a method like doGet or doPost to handle a specific type of HTTP request.

Figure 6-7   The methods of a servlet

How to code instance variables

Figure 6-8 shows how to code *instance variables* in a servlet. As with JSPs, instance variables are not *thread-safe* and can lead to lost updates. Worse, there's no easy way to make instance variables thread-safe. As a result, it's generally considered a bad practice to code instance variables for servlets or JSPs. As you progress through this book, though, you'll learn several thread-safe techniques for working with global variables so you won't have to use instance variables.

However, if you decide that it's acceptable to occasionally lose updates, you can code instance variables in a servlet as shown in this figure. Here, an instance variable named globalCount is declared immediately after the declaration for the servlet class. Then, the init method is used to initialize this variable. As a result, the variable is initialized when the instance of the servlet is first created.

If you shut down the server and restart it, though, the servlet will be destroyed and a new instance of the servlet will be created. As a result, any instance variables will be initialized again. If that's not what you want, you can write the value of the instance variable to a file so the data isn't lost when the servlet is destroyed.

Within the doPost method, the first statement increments the globalCount instance variable. Then, the rest of the statements return the value of this variable to the browser. This is similar to the code for the AddToEmailListServlet that was presented earlier in this chapter.

Code that adds an instance variable to the EmailServlet class

```
package email;

import java.io.*;
import javax.servlet.*;
import javax.servlet.http.*;

public class AddToEmailListServlet2 extends HttpServlet
{
    // declare an instance variable for the page
    int globalCount; // instance variables are not thread-safe

    public void init() throws ServletException
    {
        globalCount = 0; // initialize the instance variable
    }

    protected void doPost(
        HttpServletRequest request,
        HttpServletResponse response)
        throws ServletException, IOException
    {
        // update global count variable
        globalCount++;    // this is not thread-safe

        // send response to browser
        response.setContentType("text/html;charset=UTF-8");
        PrintWriter out = response.getWriter();
        out.println(
          "<!doctype html public \"-//W3C//DTD HTML 4.0 Transitional//EN\">\n"
        + "<html>\n"
        + "<head>\n"
        + "  <title>Murach's Java Servlets and JSP</title>\n"
        + "</head>\n"
        + "<body>\n"
        + "<h1>Thanks for joining our email list</h1>\n"
        + "<p>This page has been accessed "
        +  globalCount + " times.</p>"
        + "</body>\n"
        + "</html>\n");

        out.close();
    }
}
```

Description

- An *instance variable* of a servlet belongs to the one instance of the servlet and is shared by any threads that request the servlet.

- Instance variables are not *thread-safe*. In other words, two threads may conflict when they try to read, modify, and update the same instance variable at the same time, which can result in lost updates or other problems.

Figure 6-8   How to code instance variables

How to work with servlet errors

When you develop servlets, you will encounter errors. That's why this topic gives you some ideas on how to solve common problems and how to print debugging data to the console or to a log file.

How to solve common servlet problems

Figure 6-9 lists four common problems that can occur when you're working with servlets. Then, it lists some possible solutions for each of these problems. Unfortunately, the solutions to these problems vary depending on the IDE you're using. As a result, the solutions presented here are only described in general terms.

If your servlet won't compile, the error message that's displayed should give you an idea of why the servlet won't compile. If the compiler can't find a class that's in one of the Java APIs, for example, you may need to make the API available to your application. To do that, you can usually use the IDE to add the appropriate library or JAR file to the application. If the compiler can't locate your regular Java classes, the package statement for the class might not correspond with the directory that contains the class. As a result, you may need to modify the package statement or move the servlet file to the correct directory.

If the servlet compiles but won't run, it may be because the servlet engine isn't running. To solve this problem, of course, you can start the servlet engine. However, if the servlet engine is already running, you should double-check the URL to make sure that it's correctly mapped to the servlet. A common mistake, for example, is to change the name of the servlet and forget to update the mapping for the servlet in the web.xml file.

If you make changes to a servlet and the changes don't show up when you run the servlet, it may be because the servlet engine hasn't reloaded the modified class. In this case, you can enable servlet reloading as explained in chapter 2. That way, the servlet engine will automatically detect changes to servlets and reload them. If this doesn't work, you can redeploy the application, and many IDEs do this automatically when you run the web application. Finally, if all else fails, you can shut down Tomcat and restart it so Tomcat has to reload all of the applications that are running on it.

If the HTML page that's returned by a servlet doesn't look right when it's rendered by the browser, the servlet is probably sending bad HTML to the browser. To troubleshoot this problem, you can pull down the browser's View menu and use the Source command (for Internet Explorer) or the Page Source command (for Firefox) to view the HTML that has been returned to the browser. Then, you can identify the problem and modify the servlet to fix it.

Common servlet problems

Problem	Possible solutions
The servlet won't compile	Make sure the compiler has access to the JAR files for all necessary APIs.
	Make sure the Java classes that you code are stored in the correct directories with the correct package statements.
The servlet won't run	Make sure the web server is running.
	Make sure you're using the correct URL.
Changes to the servlet aren't showing up	Make sure servlet reloading is on.
	Redeploy the application.
	Restart the server so it reloads all applications.
The page doesn't display correctly	Select the Source or Page Source command from your browser's View menu to view the HTML code. Then, you can read through the HTML code to identify the problem, and you can fix the problem in the servlet.

Note

- Chapter 3 shows how to make JAR files available to the NetBeans IDE. You can use a similar technique to make a JAR file available to most other modern IDEs.

Figure 6-9   How to solve common servlet problems

How to print debugging data to the console

You can print debugging messages to the console for the servlet engine as shown in figure 6-10. To do that, you can use the println method of the System.out and System.err objects. You can use these messages to help track the methods that are executed or to view the value of a variable.

When you use println statements to check the value of a variable, you'll often want to include the name of the class and the name of the variable. That way, your messages will be easier to understand. This also makes it easier to find and remove the println statements once the error is debugged.

When you use println statements to print debugging data to the console, this data may be printed to different locations depending on your development environment. If, for example, you're using the NetBeans IDE, the data will be printed to the Tomcat tab of the Output window. However, if you're using Tomcat in a stand-alone environment, the data will be printed to a Tomcat console.

Code that prints debugging data to the console

```
public void doPost(HttpServletRequest request,
                   HttpServletResponse response)
                   throws IOException, ServletException
{
    //
    // code
    //
    String emailAddress = request.getParameter("emailAddress");
    System.out.println("AddToEmailListServlet emailAddress: "
        + emailAddress);
    //
    // code
    //
}
```

The output that's printed to the Tomcat console

```
AddToEmailListServlet emailAddress: jsmith@gmail.com
```

Description

- When you're testing an application on your local system, you can use the println method of the System.out or System.err objects to display debugging messages on the console for the servlet engine.

- When you use debugging messages to display variable values, it's a good practice to include the servlet name and the variable name so the messages are easy to interpret.

- When you use an IDE like NetBeans, debugging data that is written to a server console is also available in an output window.

Figure 6-10   How to print debugging data to the console

How to print debugging data to a log file

If you want to keep a permanent history of some key debugging data, you can print debugging data to a *log file* as shown in figure 6-11. Although each servlet engine uses log files a little differently, you should be able to use these log methods with any servlet engine. However, you may need to check the documentation for your servlet engine to see how these methods work.

To write data to a log file, you can use the two log methods of the HttpServlet class. If you just want to write a message to a log file, you can use the first log method. But if you want to write a message to the log file along with the stack trace for an exception, you can use the second log method. A *stack trace* is a series of messages that presents the chain of method calls that precede the current method.

The first example in this figure uses the first log method to write the value for the emailAddress variable to the log file. Here, Tomcat automatically writes some additional information before the message. First, it writes a timestamp that shows the date and time that this data was written to the log file. Then, it writes the word INFO followed by the name of the servlet class. Note, however, that this information will vary from one servlet engine to another.

The second example in this figure uses the second log method to write a message and a stack trace for an IOException. In this case, Tomcat ignores the message and doesn't write it to the log file. Instead, Tomcat writes some other information to the log file. First, it writes a timestamp that shows the date and time that this stack trace was written to the log file. Then, it writes the word WARNING followed by the name of the method that threw the exception and the name of the servlet class. Finally, it writes the stack trace. Note that the stack trace indicates that the exception was thrown by the 11th line of the UserIO class. As a result, this helps you locate the code that's causing the bug.

Tomcat stores its log files in its logs directory. Within this directory, Tomcat stores several types of log files with one file of each type for each date. To view a log file, you can navigate to this directory and open the log file with a text editor. For example, to view the data that's written by the examples in this figure, I opened the log file that's specified at the bottom of this figure. This log file contains the data for any log methods that were executed on the localhost server for June 29th, 2007.

When you use the NetBeans IDE with Tomcat, the server's log file is shown in the Tomcat Log tab of the Output window. As a result, you can view the information that has recently been written to the current log file by displaying that tab.

Two methods of the HttpServlet class used to log errors

Method	Description
`log(String message)`	Writes the specified message to the server's log file.
`log(String message, Throwable t)`	Writes the specified message to the server's log file, followed by the stack trace for the exception.

Servlet code that prints the value of a variable to a log file

```
log("emailAddress=" + emailAddress);
```

The data that's written to the log file

```
Jun 29, 2007 6:26:04 PM org.apache.catalina.core.ApplicationContext log
INFO: AddToEmailListServlet: emailAddress=jsmith@gmail.com
```

Servlet code that prints a stack trace to a log file

```
try
{
    UserIO.add(user, path);
}
catch(IOException e)
{
    log("An IOException occurred.", e);
}
```

The data that's written to the log file

```
Jun 29, 2007 6:30:38 PM org.apache.catalina.core.StandardWrapperValve invoke
WARNING: Servlet.service() for servlet AddToEmailListServlet threw exception
java.io.FileNotFoundException:
C:\murach\servlet_jsp\netbeans\ch06email\build\web\WEB-INF\EmailList.txt
(Access is denied)
        at java.io.FileOutputStream.openAppend(Native Method)
        at java.io.FileOutputStream.<init>(FileOutputStream.java:177)
        at java.io.FileWriter.<init>(FileWriter.java:90)
        at data.UserIO.add(UserIO.java:11)
        at email.AddToEmailListServlet.doPost(AddToEmailListServlet.java:38)
...
...
```

The location of a typical Tomcat log file

```
C:\tomcat\logs\localhost.2007-06-29.log
```

Description

- You can use the log methods of the HttpServlet class to write debugging data to a web server's *log file*.
- A *stack trace* is the chain of method calls for any statement that calls a method.
- The data that's written by the log methods will vary from one server to another. In fact, Tomcat doesn't include the specified message when you use the second method above. The name and location of the log files will also vary from one server to another.
- When you use an IDE like NetBeans, the server log file is also available in an output window.

Figure 6-11   How to print debugging data to a log file

Perspective

The goal of this chapter has been to teach you the basics of coding servlets. Now, you should be able to develop simple, but practical, servlets of your own that return HTML to the browser. However, you usually don't use servlets to send the HTML code back to the browser as shown in this chapter. Instead, you structure your web applications so servlets do the business processing that's required and JSPs send the HTML code back to the browser. In that way, you combine the best features of servlets with the best features of JSPs, and that's what you'll learn how to do in the next chapter.

Before you go on to the next chapter, though, you should know that some of the skills described in this chapter also apply to JSPs. For example, you can use the log method within a JSP scriptlet to write data to a log file. However, if you structure your application as described in the next chapter, you typically won't need to add any log statements to your JSPs since the business processing will be done by servlets, not JSPs.

Summary

- A *servlet* is a Java class that extends the HttpServlet class and runs within a servlet container such as Tomcat.

- When you write servlets, you override the doGet and doPost methods to provide the processing that's required. These methods receive the *request object* and the *response object* that are passed to them by the server.

- After you use the setContentType method of the response object to set the *content type* of the response that's returned to the browser, you use the getWriter method to create a PrintWriter object. Then, you can use the println and print methods of that object to send HTML back to the browser.

- To request a servlet, you request a URL that has been mapped to the servlet. This mapping is specified in the web.xml file by the servlet and servlet-mapping elements.

- You can override the init method of a servlet to initialize its instance variables. These variables are then available to all of the threads that are spawned for the one instance of the servlet.

- Instance variables are not *thread-safe* and can result in lost updates. As a result, it's generally considered a bad practice to use instance variables in a servlet.

- To print debugging data to the server console, you can use the println method of the System.out or System.err object. Or, you can use the log methods of the HttpServlet class to write debugging data to a *log file*.

Exercise 6-1   Modify the servlet for the Email List application

In this exercise, you'll modify the servlet that's used by the email application in this chapter by adding an instance variable and debugging messages to it.

1. Open the ch06email project in the ex_starts directory, and review its files. This is a copy of the book application.

2. Run the application. Then, enter some values in the HTML page and click on the Submit button to run the AddToEmailListServlet class. Note how this requests the /addToEmailList URL.

3. Enter the /addToEmailList URL in your browser and append two parameters to it to send those parameters to the AddToEmailListServlet class.

4. Add the globalCount instance variable to the AddToEmailServlet class as described in figure 6-8. Then, run the servlet and enter another user. This will test whether your IDE automatically reloads servlets after they have been changed. (You may have to refresh your browser for the changes to take effect.) If these changes aren't displayed automatically, you will need to manually reload the servlet. One way to do that is to stop and restart Tomcat.

5. Without closing the browser, enter another user. The globalCount variable should be increased by one.

6. Print a debugging message to the Tomcat console that shows the value of the globalCount variable. If you're using an IDE, the console should be displayed within one of the IDE's output windows. Then, run the servlet two more times to see how this message appears in the console.

7. Repeat step 6, but use a log file this time. If you're using an IDE, the log file should be displayed within one of the IDE's output windows.

Exercise 6-2   Create a new servlet

In this exercise, you'll modify the HTML document for the Email List application, and you'll create a new servlet that responds to the HTML document. This is comparable to what you did for exercise 5-1, but the details are repeated here.

1. With the ch06email project still open, modify the HTML document so it has this line of text after the Email Address text box: "I'm interested in these types of music." Then, follow this line with a list box that has options for Rock, Country, Bluegrass, and Folk music. This list box should be followed by the Submit button, and the Submit button should call a URL that's mapped to a new servlet named DisplayMusicChoicesServlet.

2. Create a new servlet named DisplayMusicChoicesServlet in the email package, and map this servlet to the /displayMusicChoices URL. This servlet should respond to the changed HTML document with an H1 line that looks like this:

   `Thanks for joining our email list, John Smith.`

   And this line should be followed by text that looks like this:

   `We'll use email to notify you whenever we have new releases for`
   `these types of music:`

   `Country`
   `Bluegrass`

   In other words, you list the types of music that correspond to the items that are selected in the list box. And the entire web page consists of just the heading and text lines that I've just described.

3. Please note that you don't have to provide code that saves the data that the user enters to the EmailList.txt file because that would mean changes to both the User and the UserIO classes.

4. Make sure that the servlet only implements the doPost method, not the doGet method. Also, make sure that the HTML page uses the HTTP Post method to request the servlet. Last, be sure to delete any generated code that may interfere with your methods.

5. Test the HTML document and the new servlet by running the application. Note that there is no parameter list since the HTML page uses the HTTP Post method to request the servlet.

6. Test the new servlet by entering a URL that includes a parameter list. Note that this isn't allowed since the new servlet doesn't implement the HTTP Get method.

7. Add a doGet method to the servlet that calls the doPost method.

8. Compile and deploy the changes to the servlet by running the application. Then, test the servlet by entering a URL that includes a parameter list. This should work correctly now that the servlet implements the doGet method.

9. When you're through experimenting, close the project.

7

How to structure a web application with the MVC pattern

In chapter 5, you learned how to use a JSP to create a simple web application. Then, in chapter 6, you learned how to use a servlet to create the same application. In this chapter, you'll learn how to structure an application so it takes advantage of the best features of servlets and JSPs. You'll also learn some other skills for structuring the code in an application so it's easier to code and maintain.

The Email List application

In this topic, you'll learn to modify the Email List application that was presented in the last chapter so it uses a servlet and a JSP. In this application, the servlet will handle all of the processing for the application, and the JSP will handle the presentation. Once you see how this works for this simple application, you'll be ready to learn how to use this technique for more complex applications.

The code for the servlet

Figure 7-1 presents the code for the servlet class that does the processing for the Email List application. Unlike the servlet in chapter 6, this one doesn't use println statements to send HTML back to the browser. Instead, it stores the User object in the request object. Then, it forwards the request and response objects to the JSP shown in the next figure so the JSP can display the data that's stored in the User object.

Later in this chapter, you'll learn the coding details for storing objects in the request object and for forwarding the request and response objects. For now, all you need to know is that the highlighted code stores the User object in the request object and forwards the request and response objects to the JSP named display_email_entry.jsp that's stored in the application's root directory.

The code for the servlet

```java
package email;

import java.io.*;
import javax.servlet.*;
import javax.servlet.http.*;

import business.User;
import data.UserIO;

public class AddToEmailListServlet extends HttpServlet
{
    protected void doPost(HttpServletRequest request,
                          HttpServletResponse response)
                          throws ServletException, IOException
    {
        // get parameters from the request
        String firstName = request.getParameter("firstName");
        String lastName = request.getParameter("lastName");
        String emailAddress = request.getParameter("emailAddress");

        // get a relative file name
        ServletContext context = getServletContext();
        String path = context.getRealPath("/WEB-INF/EmailList.txt");

        // use regular Java classes
        User user = new User(firstName, lastName, emailAddress);
        UserIO.addRecord(user, path);

        // store the User object in the request object
        request.setAttribute("user", user);

        // forward request and response objects to JSP page
        String url = "/display_email_entry.jsp";
        RequestDispatcher dispatcher =
            getServletContext().getRequestDispatcher(url);
        dispatcher.forward(request, response);
    }
}
```

Description

- Instead of sending HTML code to a browser, this servlet stores the User object in the request object and forwards the request and response objects to the JSP shown in the next figure.

Figure 7-1   The code for the servlet

The code for the JSP

Figure 7-2 presents the JSP code for the display_email_entry.jsp file. Since this JSP works like the JSP in chapter 5, you shouldn't have any trouble understanding it. You should realize, though, that this JSP is accessing the request object that has been passed to it from the servlet, not a request object that has been passed to it by the HTTP request. In addition, since the servlet has already used the UserIO class to write the user's data to a file, this JSP doesn't need to use that class. Instead, it only needs to get and display the data in the User object.

For a simple application like this one, the benefits of using servlets for processing and JSPs for presentation may not be obvious. However, as your applications become more complex, you'll realize how this type of structuring results in servlets and JSPs that are easier to code and maintain. In addition, as you read through chapters 9 through 11, you'll learn how to make the code in your JSP pages more readable and elegant by using special JSP tags instead of the JSP directives, scriptlets, and expressions shown here.

The code for the JSP

```
<!DOCTYPE HTML PUBLIC "-//W3C//DTD HTML 4.01 Transitional//EN"
    "http://www.w3.org/TR/html4/loose.dtd">

<html>
<head>
    <title>Murach's Java Servlets and JSP</title>
</head>

<body>
    <h1>Thanks for joining our email list</h1>

    <p>Here is the information that you entered:</p>

    <%@ page import="business.User" %>
    <% User user = (User) request.getAttribute("user"); %>
    <table cellspacing="5" cellpadding="5" border="1">
        <tr>
            <td align="right">First name:</td>
            <td><%= user.getFirstName() %></td>
        </tr>
        <tr>
            <td align="right">Last name:</td>
            <td><%= user.getLastName() %></td>
        </tr>
        <tr>
            <td align="right">Email address:</td>
            <td><%= user.getEmailAddress() %></td>
        </tr>
    </table>

    <p>To enter another email address, click on the Back <br>
    button in your browser or the Return button shown <br>
    below.</p>

    <form action="join_email_list.html" method="post">
        <input type="submit" value="Return">
    </form>

</body>
</html>
```

Description

- The servlet in the last figure forwards the request and response objects to this JSP.

- Since the servlet has already done all of the processing for the requested page, this JSP only needs to handle the presentation for the page.

Figure 7-2   The code for the JSP

Two architectures for web applications

Now that you have a general idea of how to structure a simple application, you're ready to learn about the two architectures that are commonly used for web applications.

The Model 1 architecture

In chapter 5, you learned how to create a simple application that consisted of an HTML page and a JSP. This approach used the *Model 1 architecture* that's shown in figure 7-3. With this architecture, a JSP is responsible for handling both the request and response of the application.

To do that, the JSP interacts with Java classes and objects that represent the data of the business objects in the application and provide the methods that do the business processing. In chapter 5, for example, the application stored the data for a user in a User object.

To save the data of the business classes, the application maps the data to a database or files that can be called the *data store* for the application. This is also known as *persistent data storage* because it exists after the application ends. Usually, data classes like the UserIO class in chapter 5 are used to store the data of the business objects in the data stores. So far in this book, the UserIO class has stored the data for each User object in a file, but you'll learn how to use a database as a data store later in this book.

Although the Model 1 architecture works OK for applications that have limited processing requirements, this architecture is not recommended for most applications. If you notice that your JSPs are becoming cluttered with scriptlets and that your code is becoming difficult to maintain, you should consider using the approach you saw in figures 7-1 and 7-2. That approach is known as the MVC pattern, and you'll learn more about it in the next figure.

The Model 1 architecture

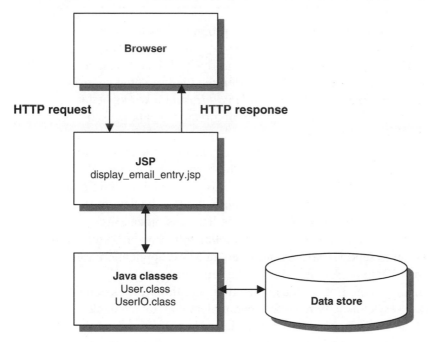

Description

- The *Model 1 architecture* is sometimes adequate for web applications with limited processing requirements. With this architecture, JSPs handle all of the processing and presentation for the application.

- In the Model 1 architecture, the JSPs can use regular Java classes to store the data of the application and to do the business processing of the application.

- The *data store* can be a database or one or more disk files. This is often referred to as *persistent data storage* because it exists after the application ends.

- The application that you studied in chapter 5 uses the Model 1 architecture.

Figure 7-3   The Model 1 architecture

The Model-View-Controller (MVC) pattern

A *pattern* is a standard approach that is used by programmers to solve common programming problems. One of these patterns is the *Model-View-Controller pattern* (*MVC pattern*) that's introduced in figure 7-4. As its name implies, the MVC pattern has three layers: the model, the view, and the controller. This pattern is also known as the *Model 2 architecture*, and it works better than the Model 1 architecture whenever the processing requirements are substantial.

In the MVC pattern, the *model* defines the business layer of the application. This layer is usually implemented by *JavaBeans*, which you'll learn more about in chapter 9. For now, you can think of the User class as the model for the Email List application, and it is a JavaBean. This type of class defines the data for the business objects and provides the methods that do the business processing.

The *view* defines the presentation layer of the application. Since it's cumbersome to use a servlet to send HTML to a browser, an MVC application uses HTML documents or JSPs to present the view to the browser.

The *controller* manages the flow of the application, and this work is done by servlets. To start, a servlet usually reads any parameters that are available from the request, which typically comes from the view. Then, if necessary, the servlet updates the model and saves it to the data store. Finally, based on the logic that's coded in the servlet, the servlet forwards the model to one of several possible JSPs for presentation.

Here again, most applications need to map the data in the model to a data store. But the JavaBeans usually don't provide the methods for storing their own data. Instead, data classes like the UserIO class provide those methods. That separates the business logic from the I/O operations.

When you use the MVC pattern, you should try to keep the model, view, and controller as independent of each other as possible. That makes it easier to modify an application later on. If, for example, you decide to modify an application so it presents the view in a different way, you should be able to modify the view layer without making any changes to the controller or model layers. In practice, it's difficult to separate these layers completely, but in theory complete independence is the goal.

Note, however, that you don't have to use the MVC pattern to implement every page in a web application. For those pages that have substantial processing requirements, this pattern will make it easier to code, test, and maintain the pages. But for web pages with simple processing requirements, it's usually easier to use the Model 1 architecture. In particular, if your model consists entirely of JavaBeans, you can use special JSP tags to work directly with the data in the JavaBeans as described in chapter 9.

The Model-View-Controller pattern

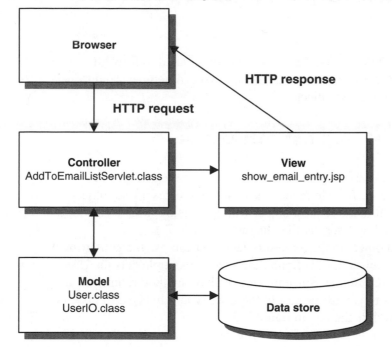

Description

- The *Model-View-Controller (MVC) pattern* is commonly used to structure web applications that have significant processing requirements. That makes them easier to code and maintain. This pattern is also known as the *Model 2 architecture*.

- In the MVC pattern, the *model* consists of business objects like the User object, the *view* consists of HTML pages and JSPs, and the *controller* consists of servlets.

- Usually, the methods of data classes like the UserIO class are used to read and write business objects like the User object to and from the data store.

- When you use the MVC pattern, you try to construct each layer so it's as independent as possible. Then, if you need to make changes to one layer, any changes to the other layers are minimized.

Figure 7-4   The Model-View-Controller (MVC) pattern

How to forward requests and redirect responses

When you use the MVC pattern, your servlets often need to forward a request object to a JSP or another servlet. But first, you sometimes need to store a business object in the request object.

How to get and set request attributes

To store any object in the request object, you can use the setAttribute method as shown in figure 7-5. Here, the first example creates a User object named user and stores it in the request object with a name of "user". This kind of code is typically used by a servlet like the one in figure 7-1.

Once you store an object in the request object, you can use the getAttribute method to retrieve the object. In this figure, the second example gets the User object stored in the first example. Since the getAttribute method returns a value of the Object type, this type must be cast to the User type. This type of code is typically used by a JSP like the one in figure 7-2.

When you work with request attributes, you should realize that the attributes are reset between requests. As a result, if you store a User object as a request attribute and forward that request to a JSP, that User object will only be available to that JSP and won't be available later in the session. In the next chapter, though, you'll learn how to store an object so it's available to any JSP in the current session.

Two methods available from the request object

Method	Description
setAttribute(String name, Object o)	Stores any object in the request as an attribute and specifies a name for the attribute. Attributes are reset between requests.
getAttribute(String name)	Returns the value of the specified attribute as an Object type. If no attribute exists for the specified name, this method returns a null value.

How to set a request attribute

```
User user = new User(firstName, lastName, emailAddress);
request.setAttribute("user", user);
```

How to get a request attribute

```
User user = (User) request.getAttribute("user");
```

How to set a request attribute for a primitive type

```
int id = 1;
request.setAttribute("id", new Integer(id));
```

How to get a request attribute for a primitive type

```
int id = (Integer) request.getAttribute("id");
```

Description

- These methods are most often used in conjunction with a RequestDispatcher object that's used to forward a request as described in the next figure.

Figure 7-5   How to get and set request attributes

How to forward requests

Figure 7-6 shows how to *forward* a request from a servlet to an HTML page, a JSP, or another servlet. Once you understand how to write this type of code, you should be able to implement the MVC pattern in your applications.

To forward the request and response objects from a servlet, you begin by calling the getServletContext method from the HttpServlet class to return a ServletContext object. Then, you call the getRequestDispatcher method of the ServletContext object to return a RequestDispatcher object. Within this method, you must code a URL that starts with a slash so it is relative to the root directory of the current web application. Then, you use the forward method to forward the request and response objects to the HTML page, JSP, or servlet specified by the URL.

In the examples in this figure, the string for the URL is declared and initialized before the statement that creates the RequestDispatcher object. This makes it easier to read the URL than if the URL was coded as an argument of the getRequestDispatcher method.

How to redirect responses

This figure also shows how to *redirect* a response. To do that, you use the sendRedirect method of the response object. This is typically used when you want to transfer control to a URL outside of your application. To use this method, you often supply an absolute URL. However, you can also supply a relative URL because the servlet engine will convert it to an absolute URL. If you begin the pathname with a slash, the servlet engine interprets the path as relative to the root directory for the servlet engine.

When you call the sendRedirect method, the server sends an absolute URL to the browser. Then, the browser sends a request for that URL. Since this processing occurs on the client side rather than the server side, this isn't as efficient as forwarding a request object. In addition, the sendRedirect method doesn't transfer the request and response objects. As a result, you should only use the sendRedirect method when you want to redirect to a URL that's available from another web application.

A method of the ServletContext object for working with paths

Method	Description
`getRequestDispatcher(String path)`	Returns a RequestDispatcher object for the specified path.

A method of the RequestDispatcher object

Method	Description
`forward(ServletRequest request, ServletResponse response)`	Forwards the request and response objects to another resource on the server (usually a JSP or servlet).

How to forward the request to an HTML page

```
String url = "/display_email_entry.html";
RequestDispatcher dispatcher =
    getServletContext().getRequestDispatcher(url);
dispatcher.forward(request, response);
```

How to forward the request to a JSP

```
String url = "/display_email_entry.jsp";
RequestDispatcher dispatcher =
    getServletContext().getRequestDispatcher(url);
dispatcher.forward(request, response);
```

How to forward the request to a servlet

```
String url = "/cart/displayInvoice";
RequestDispatcher dispatcher =
    getServletContext().getRequestDispatcher(url);
dispatcher.forward(request, response);
```

A method of the HttpServletResponse class

Method	Description
`sendRedirect(String path)`	Sends a temporary redirect response to the client using the specified redirect location URL.

How to redirect a response relative to the current directory

```
response.sendRedirect("join_email_list.html");
```

How to redirect a response relative to the servlet engine

```
response.sendRedirect("/musicStore/email/join_email_list.jsp");
```

How to redirect a response to a different web server

```
response.sendRedirect("http://www.murach.com/email/");
```

Figure 7-6   How to forward requests and redirect responses

How to validate data

When a user enters data into an application, the application often needs to check the data to make sure that the data is valid. This is referred to as *data validation*. Then, if the user enters data that isn't valid, the application can display an error message and give the user another chance to enter the data.

How to use JavaScript to validate data on the client

When coding a web application, you can use *JavaScript* to validate data on the client. Although there are other ways to validate data on the client, using JavaScript is one of the most popular ways.

Figure 7-7 shows how to use JavaScript to do some simple data validation. Since all modern web browsers can execute JavaScript, this data validation runs entirely on the client. As a result, it's more efficient than sending a request to the server that includes invalid data only to receive a response that indicates that the data isn't valid.

Although the syntax of JavaScript is similar to the syntax of Java, JavaScript is a different language. As a result, to learn JavaScript, you need to get a book that's devoted to that subject. For now, you can focus on how JavaScript and client-side data validation can be used in a Java web application because that affects the structure of an application.

The JavaScript in this figure checks to make sure the user has entered values into all three text boxes of a form. Here, the opening and closing Script tags identify the JavaScript code to the browser. Usually, JavaScript is coded near the top of an HTML page or a JSP, often between the Head and Body tags. However, you can code JavaScript anywhere within an HTML page or JSP.

Within the Script tags, this example uses a *function* that accepts the HTML form as an argument. This JavaScript function is similar to a Java method. Within this function, an if/else statement checks to make sure that a value has been entered into each text box. If a value hasn't been entered in a text box, the alert method causes the browser to display a dialog box like the one in part 2 of this figure. Then, the focus method moves the focus to that text box. Otherwise, the submit method submits the form.

The HTML in this figure uses a JavaScript button rather than a standard Submit button. Here, the type attribute specifies "button" instead of "submit" to specify the JavaScript button. Then, the onClick attribute of the JavaScript button calls the validate function that's coded within the Script tags. To specify the current form as the argument for the function, this code uses the this keyword and the form keyword.

The JavaScript that validates a form

```
<script language="JavaScript">
function validate(form)
{
    if (form.firstName.value=="")
    {
        alert("Please fill in your first name");
        form.firstName.focus();
    }
    else if (form.lastName.value=="")
    {
        alert("Please fill in your last name");
        form.lastName.focus();
    }
    else if (form.emailAddress.value=="")
    {
        alert("Please fill in your email address");
        form.emailAddress.focus();
    }
    else
    {
        form.submit();
    }
}
</script>
```

The HTML for the form

```
<form action="addToEmailList" method="post">
<table cellspacing="5" border="0">
<tr>
  <td align="right">First name:</td>
  <td><input type="text" name="firstName"
        value="<%= user.getFirstName() %>"></td>
</tr>
<tr>
  <td align="right">Last name:</td>
  <td><input type="text" name="lastName"
        value="<%= user.getLastName() %>"></td>
</tr>
<tr>
  <td align="right">Email address:</td>
  <td><input type="text" name="emailAddress"
        value="<%= user.getEmailAddress() %>"></td>
</tr>
<tr>
  <td></td>
  <td><br><input type="button" value="Submit"
        onClick="validate(this.form)"></td>
</tr>
</table>
</form>
```

Figure 7-7   How to use JavaScript to validate data on the client (part 1 of 2)

Part 2 of figure 7-7 shows the type of dialog box that's displayed when you use JavaScript. In this case, this dialog box is displayed when the user doesn't enter any text in the text box for the email address. When the user clicks the OK button in the dialog box, the focus will move to that text box. Then, the user can enter an email address and submit the form again.

When you validate data, you may not want to display validation messages in a dialog box like this one. In that case, you can validate data on the server as shown in the next two figures. Although this allows you to customize your data validation messages, which can make your application more user-friendly, it isn't as efficient as validating data on the client side.

The dialog box that's displayed when an entry isn't made

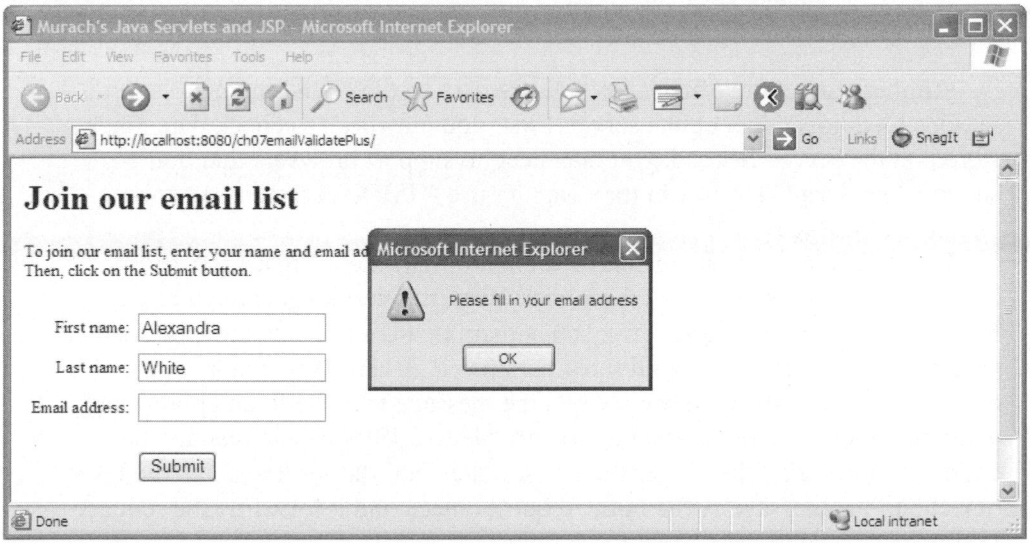

Description

- When you use JavaScript to display validation messages, they appear in standard dialog boxes.
- If you want to display error messages in an HTML page or JSP, you can use servlets to validate data on the server side.

Figure 7-7   How to use JavaScript to validate data on the client (part 2 of 2)

How to use a servlet to validate data on the server

Although it's more efficient to validate data on the client, there are several reasons to validate data on the server. First, you may need to check data that's stored on the server. Second, you may need to support browsers that don't support JavaScript. Third, you may want to use a JSP to customize your data validation messages.

Figure 7-8 presents an enhanced version of the AddToEmailListServlet class that validates the data on the server. Here, this servlet gets the three request parameters from the form, stores them in a User object, and checks that values have been entered for all three parameters. If any of the parameters is equal to an empty string, this code sets the message variable to an appropriate validation message, and it sets the url variable to a JSP that can display the validation message. Then, after the if/else statement, the servlet stores the User object and the message string in the request object, and it forwards the request to the JSP shown in the part 2 of this figure.

On the other hand, if all of the parameters contain strings that aren't empty, this servlet sets the message variable to an empty string so no validation message is displayed, uses the UserIO class to write the data in the User object to a file, and sets the url variable to a string that specifies a JSP that displays the data to the user.

If you study this servlet, it should give you a better idea of how a servlet can function as a controller in the MVC pattern. In particular, this shows how a servlet can get data from the request, update the model based on that data, and forward the request back to appropriate part of the view.

Since this servlet works with strings, you don't need to write any code to convert data. But what if you want to make sure that the user enters an integer? To do that, you can attempt to convert the string to an int value within a try/catch statement. Then, if the parsing fails and an exception is thrown, the servlet can supply code in the catch statement that displays an appropriate validation message and forwards the request to an appropriate JSP.

A servlet that validates data

```java
package email;

import java.io.*;
import javax.servlet.*;
import javax.servlet.http.*;

import business.User;
import data.UserIO;

public class AddToEmailListServlet extends HttpServlet
{
    protected void doPost(HttpServletRequest request,
            HttpServletResponse response)
            throws ServletException, IOException
    {
        // get parameters from the form
        String firstName = request.getParameter("firstName");
        String lastName = request.getParameter("lastName");
        String emailAddress = request.getParameter("emailAddress");

        // create the User object from the parameters
        User user = new User(firstName, lastName, emailAddress);

        // validate the parameters
        String message = "";
        String url = "";
        if (firstName.length() == 0 ||
            lastName.length() == 0  ||
            emailAddress.length() == 0)
        {
            message = "Please fill out all three text boxes.";
            url = "/join_email_list.jsp";
        }
        else
        {
            message = "";

            ServletContext context = getServletContext();
            String path = context.getRealPath("/WEB-INF/EmailList.txt");
            UserIO.addRecord(user, path);

            url = "/display_email_entry.jsp";
        }
        request.setAttribute("user", user);
        request.setAttribute("message", message);

        // forward request and response to the view
        RequestDispatcher dispatcher =
            getServletContext().getRequestDispatcher(url);
        dispatcher.forward(request, response);
    }
}
```

Figure 7-8   How to use a servlet to validate data on the server (part 1 of 3)

Part 2 of figure 7-8 shows the code for the JSP that's displayed when the application starts. To limit the amount of code duplication, this JSP is also used to display the data validation message.

To start, this JSP uses a page directive to import the User class. Then, a scriptlet uses the getAttribute method to get the User object and the message string that have been stored in the request object. Next, this scriptlet uses an if statement to check if these variables contain null objects. If so, the scriptlet sets the message variable equal to an empty string, and it sets the user variable equal to a new User object that's created with the default constructor. This causes the firstName, lastName, and emailAddress variables of the User class to be set to empty strings.

As a result, when a user requests this JSP for the first time, no validation message is displayed, and empty strings are displayed in the three text boxes of the form. However, if the user doesn't enter a valid string for each of the three text boxes, this JSP displays a validation message in italics before the form, and it displays any values that the user has already entered within the text boxes.

A JSP that displays a validation message

```
<!DOCTYPE HTML PUBLIC "-//W3C//DTD HTML 4.01 Transitional//EN"
    "http://www.w3.org/TR/html4/loose.dtd">

<html>
<head>
    <title>Murach's Java Servlets and JSP</title>
</head>
<body>

<%@ page import="business.User" %>
<%
    // get attributes from the request
    User user = (User) request.getAttribute("user");
    String message = (String) request.getAttribute("message");

    // handle null values
    if (user == null) user = new User();
    if (message == null) message = "";
%>

<h1>Join our email list</h1>
<p>To join our email list, enter your name and
 email address below. <br>
 Then, click on the Submit button.</p>

<p><i><%= message %></i></p>

<form action="addToEmailList" method="post">
<table cellspacing="5" border="0">
<tr>
  <td align="right">First name:</td>
  <td><input type="text" name="firstName"
      value="<%= user.getFirstName() %>"></td>
</tr>
<tr>
  <td align="right">Last name:</td>
  <td><input type="text" name="lastName"
      value="<%= user.getLastName() %>"></td>
</tr>
<tr>
  <td align="right">Email address:</td>
  <td><input type="text" name="emailAddress"
      value="<%= user.getEmailAddress() %>"></td>
</tr>
<tr>
  <td></td>
  <td><br><input type="submit" value="Submit"></td>
</tr>
</table>
</form>

</body>
</html>
```

Figure 7-8   How to use a servlet to validate data on the server (part 2 of 3)

The first screen in part 3 of figure 7-8 shows the JSP that's displayed when a user accesses the JSP for the first time. This JSP doesn't display a validation message, and it doesn't display any data in the three text boxes on the form.

The second screen shows the same JSP if the user doesn't enter a value for each of the three text boxes. This JSP displays a validation message that asks the user to fill out all three text boxes, and it displays any values that the user has already entered within the text boxes. That way, the user doesn't have to re-enter any values that have already been entered.

When the user clicks the Submit button, this page sends the values in the text boxes back to the AddToEmailListServlet class. Then, if a value is still missing, this servlet forwards the request to this JSP again. In other words, this request and response cycle continues until the user enters valid data or ends the application. This, of course, is quite inefficient when compared with client-side data validation.

The JSP that's displayed when the application is first started

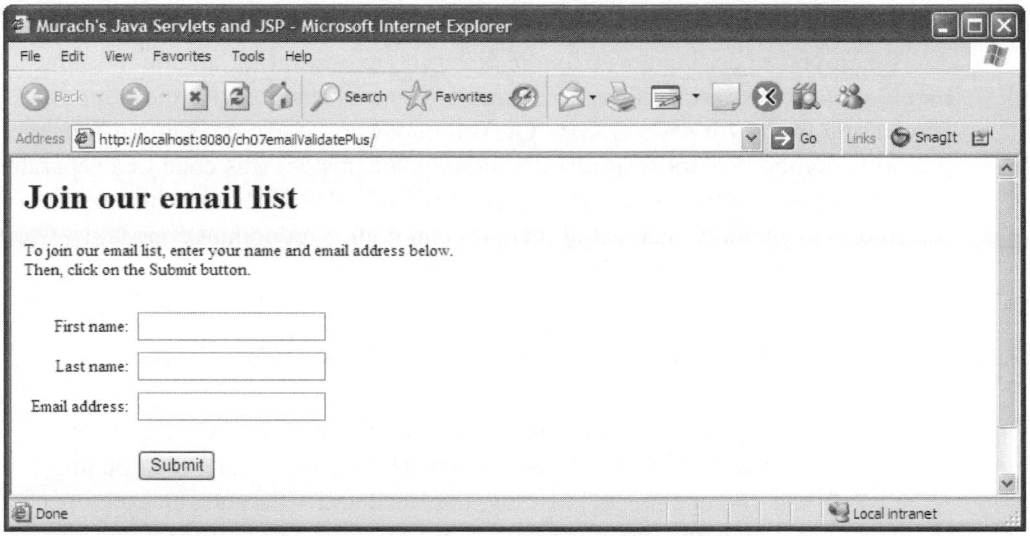

The JSP that's displayed when an entry isn't made

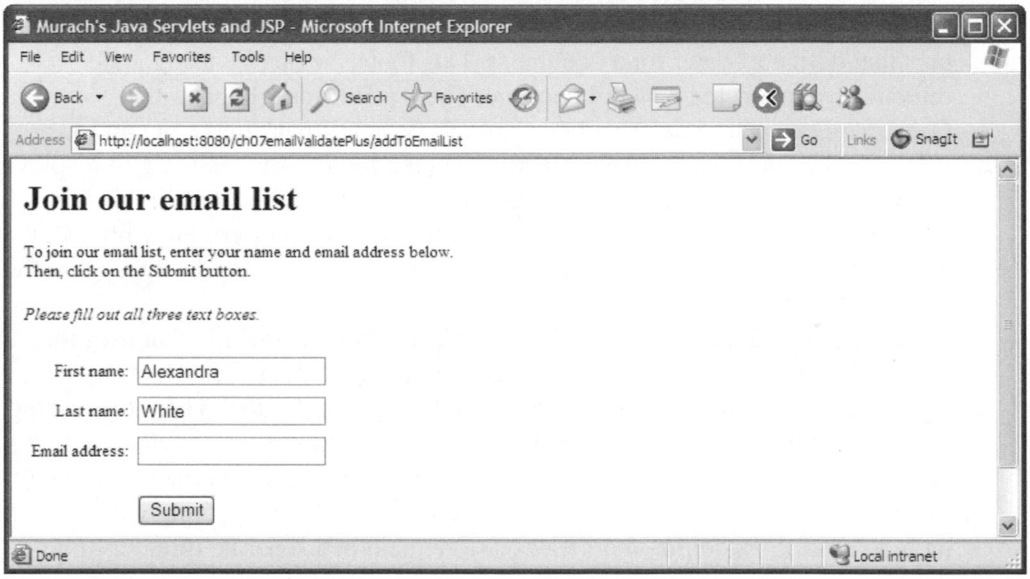

Figure 7-8   How to use a servlet to validate data on the server (part 3 of 3)

How to include a file in a JSP

When you're coding a web application, you may want to include the same block of code in several JSPs. For example, you may want to use the same header and footer for several JSPs. Or, you may want to use the same menus or the same combo box for several JSPs. If so, you can store this code in a separate file. Then, you can include the code in that file in a JSP. Files like this are often referred to as *includes*, and using includes can reduce redundant code and simplify the coding and maintenance of an application.

A JSP that includes a header and footer file

Figure 7-9 begins by showing an HTML file that contains the tags that define the beginning of an HTML document. These tags include the opening DOCTYPE tag, the opening HTML tag, the Head and Title tags, and the opening Body tag. Since this file only contains HTML tags, not any JSP tags, it is stored in an HTML file named header.html. Here, the Title tags set the text that's displayed in the browser's title bar to *Murach's Java Servlets and JSP*.

This figure also shows the footer.jsp file that contains the HTML and JSP tags that define a footer for a document. This footer begins by using a JSP directive to import the java.util package. Then, a JSP scriptlet uses the GregorianDate class that's available from the java.util package to get an int value for the current year. After the scriptlet, the footer uses the P tag to display a copyright notice that uses the int value for the current year. Within this tag, © and & are HTML codes that represents the copyright symbol (©) and the ampersand (&). Finally, the footer provides the closing Body tag and the closing HTML tag.

After the header and footer files, this figure shows a JSP file that uses the shaded statements to include the header.html and footer.jsp files. Here, the first tag in the JSP file includes all the code needed to start the JSP. Then, the last tag in the file includes the code that displays the copyright notice and all code that's needed to finish the JSP. Notice that these statements show that the header and footer files are stored in a directory named includes. When working with include files, it's a common practice to store them in a separate directory like this.

In this figure, the included files are so small that they don't illustrate the power of this technique. Imagine, though, that the included files contain larger blocks of code and that this code is appropriate for dozens or hundreds of JSPs. Then, this coding technique can reduce the total amount of code in the application and make the application easier to maintain. If, for example, you want to change the header for all the JSPs that include the header file, you just have to change one file.

A header file named header.html

```
<!DOCTYPE HTML PUBLIC "-//W3C//DTD HTML 4.01 Transitional//EN"
    "http://www.w3.org/TR/html4/loose.dtd">

<html>
<head>
    <title>Murach's Java Servlets and JSP</title>
</head>
<body>
```

A footer file named footer.jsp

```
<%@ page import="java.util.*" %>
<%
    // initialize the current year that's used in the copyright notice
    GregorianCalendar currentDate = new GregorianCalendar();
    int currentYear = currentDate.get(Calendar.YEAR);
%>

<p><small>
&copy; Copyright <%= currentYear %> Mike Murach &amp; Associates, Inc.
All rights reserved
</small></p>
</body>
</html>
```

A JSP file that uses both include files

```
<%@ include file="/includes/header.html" %>

<h1>Thanks for joining our email list</h1>

<p>Here is the information that you entered:</p>

<%@ page import="business.User" %>
<% User user = (User) request.getAttribute("user"); %>
<table cellspacing="5" cellpadding="5" border="1">
    <tr><td align="right">First name:</td>
        <td><%= user.getFirstName() %></td>
    </tr>
    <tr><td align="right">Last name:</td>
        <td><%= user.getLastName() %></td>
    </tr>
    <tr><td align="right">Email address:</td>
        <td><%= user.getEmailAddress() %></td>
    </tr>
</table>

<p>To enter another email address, click on the Back <br>
button in your browser or the Return button shown <br>
below.</p>

<form action="join_email_list.jsp" method="post">
    <input type="submit" value="Return">
</form>

<%@ include file="/includes/footer.jsp" %>
```

Figure 7-9   A JSP that includes a header and a footer file (part 1 of 2)

Part 2 of figure 7-9 starts by showing the page that's displayed by the JSP in part 1. As you can see, this page includes the header.html and footer.jsp files. Here, the title in the browser is from the header file, and the copyright notice at the bottom of the page is from the footer file.

Part 2 also shows another page that includes the header and footer files. As a result, it displays the same title in the browser, and the same copyright notice at the bottom of the page.

The JSP page

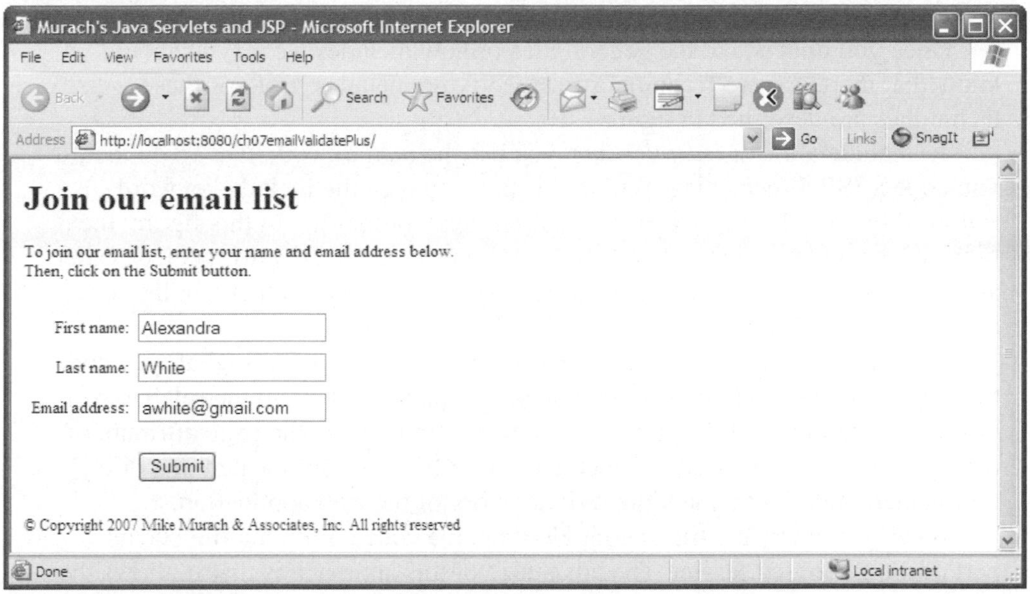

Another JSP page that uses the same header and footer

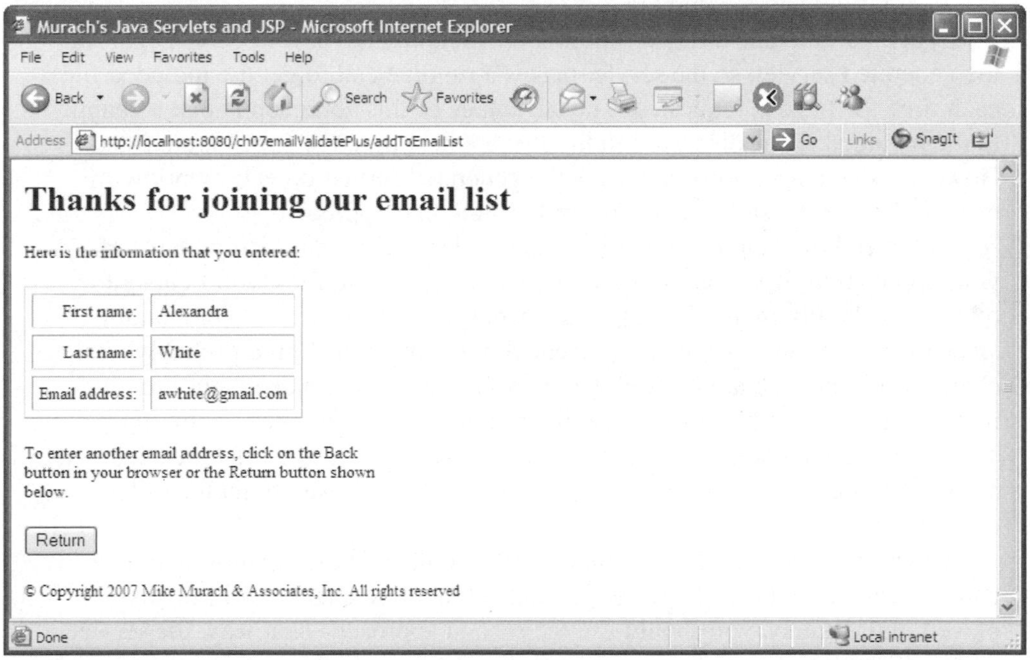

Description

- You can use the include directive to include HTML or JSP files within a JSP.

Figure 7-9   A JSP that includes a header and a footer file (part 2 of 2)

Two techniques for including files in a JSP

Once you understand the general idea of how includes work, you should know that there are two techniques for specifying includes. Both of these techniques are described in figure 7-10.

To include a file at *compile-time*, you use the *include directive*. To do that, you code a JSP directive tag. Within this tag, you type the include keyword followed by the file attribute and the relative path of the file. In this figure, the first two examples use the file attribute of the include directive to specify header and footer files that are located in a directory named includes that's in the root directory of the web application.

To include a file at *runtime*, you use the *include action*. To do that, you code the jsp:include tag. Within this tag, you set the page attribute to the relative path of the include file. In this figure, the last two examples use the page attribute of the jsp:include tag to specify header and footer files that are located in a directory named includes that's in the root directory of the web application.

When you include a file at compile-time, the code within the file becomes part of the generated servlet. The advantage of this approach is that it allows the servlet engine to return a response to the browser more quickly. However, if you make a change to the included file, the change might not be displayed until the JSP is modified and recompiled.

When you include a file at runtime, the included file never becomes part of the generated servlet, so the servlet makes a runtime call to get the included file each time the page is requested. The advantage of this approach is that a change to the included file is displayed in the JSP the next time the page is requested. However, since this approach makes the generated servlet do extra work with each request, it doesn't run as efficiently as the first approach.

In the end, the approach that you choose depends on the requirements of your application. If you are fairly certain that the include files won't change often, you should use the first approach since it's more efficient. For example, since the header and footer files presented in the previous figure probably won't change once the web application is put into production, it makes sense to include them at compile-time. In addition, many servlet engines, including Tomcat 5 and later, are able to automatically detect changes to included files. As a result, if you're using a newer servlet engine, you can usually include files at compile-time.

However, if you want to use include files to display information that may change regularly, and you need to guarantee that these changes will be displayed immediately, you should use the second approach. That way, the servlet for the JSP doesn't need to be regenerated and recompiled to display the updated include file. For example, if you store the code for a weather report in a file that is changed hourly, you'll want to include the file at runtime.

How to include a file in a JSP at compile-time with an include directive

Syntax

```
<%@ include file="fileLocationAndName" %>
```

Examples

```
<%@ include file="/includes/header.html" %>
<%@ include file="/includes/footer.jsp" %>
```

How to include a file in a JSP at runtime with an include action

Syntax

```
<jsp:include page="fileLocationAndName" />
```

Examples

```
<jsp:include page="/includes/header.html" />
<jsp:include page="/includes/footer.jsp" />
```

Description

- To include a file in a JSP at *compile-time*, you use the *include directive*.

- When you use the include directive, the code in the included file becomes part of the generated servlet. As a result, any changes to the included file won't appear in the JSP until the JSP is regenerated and recompiled. However, some of the newer web servers automatically detect changes to included files and automatically regenerate and recompile the servlets for the JSPs that need to be updated.

- To include a file in a JSP at *runtime*, you use the *include action*.

- When you use the include action, the generated servlet uses a runtime call to get the included file, and any changes to the included file appear in the JSP the next time it is requested.

Figure 7-10   Two techniques for including files in a JSP

How to use the web.xml file

In chapter 2, you learned that every application has one web.xml file that contains information about how the application is configured. Then, in chapter 6, you learned how the web.xml file is used for mapping servlets to URLs. Now, you'll learn how to modify some of the tags in the web.xml file that affect how an application is structured.

This topic assumes that you're using Tomcat 6. So if you're using a different servlet engine, you may need to modify the code presented in this topic so it works with your servlet engine. In general, though, the concepts presented here should still apply.

Basic techniques for working with a web.xml file

Figure 7-11 shows the web.xml file that works with the application presented in this chapter. This web.xml file begins with two tags that define the type of XML document that's being used. For now, you don't need to understand this code. However, these tags must be included at the start of each web.xml file. Fortunately, most IDEs create them automatically. Otherwise, you can copy these tags from another web.xml file.

After this code, the web.xml file contains *XML tags* that define *elements*. For example, the opening and closing web-app tags define the web-app element. Since all other elements are coded within this element, the web-app element is known as the *root element*. Any element coded within this element or a lower-level element is known as a *child element*.

To modify a web.xml file, you should be able to use your IDE. As you're making the modifications, if you want to leave code in the XML file but you don't want the servlet engine to use it, you can use XML *comments* to comment out those portions of code. These comments work the same way HTML comments do.

When you're done modifying the file, you must redeploy the application to Tomcat so the changes take effect. With most IDEs, this happens automatically when you run the application. If not, you can always restart Tomcat to make sure that it reads the changes to the web.xml file.

When you modify a web.xml file, you should make sure to code the XML elements in the correct order as shown in this figure. Otherwise, when you start Tomcat or attempt to deploy your application, Tomcat won't be able to read the web.xml file. As a result, it will display an error message. To solve this problem, you can edit the web.xml file and redeploy the application. Or, you can restart Tomcat to read the file again.

The web.xml file for the application in this chapter

```xml
<?xml version="1.0" encoding="UTF-8"?>
<web-app version="2.5" xmlns="http://java.sun.com/xml/ns/javaee"
    xmlns:xsi="http://www.w3.org/2001/XMLSchema-instance"
    xsi:schemaLocation="http://java.sun.com/xml/ns/javaee
    http://java.sun.com/xml/ns/javaee/web-app_2_5.xsd">

    <context-param>
        <param-name>custServEmail</param-name>
        <param-value>custserv@murach.com</param-value>
    </context-param>

    <servlet>
        <servlet-name>AddToEmailListServlet</servlet-name>
        <servlet-class>email.AddToEmailListServlet</servlet-class>
        <init-param>
            <param-name>relativePathToFile</param-name>
            <param-value>/WEB-INF/EmailList.txt</param-value>
        </init-param>
    </servlet>

    <servlet-mapping>
        <servlet-name>AddToEmailListServlet</servlet-name>
        <url-pattern>/addToEmailList</url-pattern>
    </servlet-mapping>

    <!-- you can comment out these tags when the app is in development -->
    <error-page>
        <error-code>404</error-code>
        <location>/error_404.jsp</location>
    </error-page>
    <error-page>
        <exception-type>java.lang.Throwable</exception-type>
        <location>/error_java.jsp</location>
    </error-page>

    <session-config>
        <session-timeout>30</session-timeout>
    </session-config>

    <welcome-file-list>
        <welcome-file>join_email_list.jsp</welcome-file>
    </welcome-file-list>
</web-app>
```

Description

- The web.xml file is stored in the WEB-INF directory for an application. When Tomcat starts, it reads the web.xml file.
- If the elements in the web.xml aren't in the correct order, Tomcat will display an error message when it reads the web.xml file.
- After you modify the web.xml file, you must redeploy the application so the changes take effect. Or, you can restart Tomcat.

Figure 7-11   The web.xml file for the application in this chapter

How to work with initialization parameters

If you want to store some *initialization parameters* for an application in a central location, you can add them to the web.xml file as shown in part 1 of figure 7-12. Then, your servlets can read these parameters as shown in part 2 of this figure.

To define a *context initialization parameter* that will be available to all servlets in the web application, you code a context-param element. Then, you code two child elements: the param-name element and the param-value element. To define multiple context parameters, you can code additional context-param elements after the first one. In this figure, the context-param element defines a parameter named custServEmail that has a value that provides an email address.

To define a *servlet initialization parameter* that will be available to a specific servlet, you can code an init-param element within a servlet element. This element follows the servlet-name and servlet-class elements that you learned about in chapter 6.

Within the init-param element, you must code the param-name and param-value elements to define the name and value of the parameter. To define multiple initialization parameters for a servlet, you can code additional init-param elements after the first one. In this figure, the init-param element defines a parameter named relativePathToFile that has a relative path as its value.

XML tags that set initialization parameters in a web.xml file

```
<context-param>
    <param-name>custServEmail</param-name>
    <param-value>custserv@murach.com</param-value>
</context-param>

<servlet>
    <servlet-name>AddToEmailListServlet</servlet-name>
    <servlet-class>email.AddToEmailListServlet</servlet-class>
    <init-param>
        <param-name>relativePathToFile</param-name>
        <param-value>/WEB-INF/EmailList.txt</param-value>
    </init-param>
</servlet>
```

XML elements for working with initialization parameters

Element	Description
`<context-param>`	Defines a parameter that's available to all servlets within an application.
`<servlet>`	Identifies a specific servlet within the application.
`<servlet-name>`	Defines the name for the servlet that's used in the rest of the web.xml file.
`<servlet-class>`	Identifies the servlet by specifying the servlet's package and class name.
`<init-param>`	Defines a name/value pair for an initialization parameter for a servlet.
`<param-name>`	Defines the name of a parameter.
`<param-value>`	Defines the value of a parameter.

Description

- To create an *initialization parameter* that will be available to all servlets (called a *context initialization parameter*), you code the param-name and param-value elements within the context-param element.

- To create an initialization parameter that will be available to a specific servlet (called a *servlet initialization parameter*), you code the param-name and param-value elements within the init-param element. But first, you must identify the servlet by coding the servlet, servlet-name, and servlet-class elements.

Figure 7-12   How to work with initialization parameters (part 1 of 2)

Part 2 of this figure shows you how to read initialization parameters like those in part 1. To retrieve an initialization parameter that's available to all servlets, you begin by calling the getServletContext method from anywhere in the servlet to get a ServletContext object. Then, you call the getInitParameter method from the ServletContext object.

To retrieve an initialization parameter that's available only to the current servlet, you begin by calling the getServletConfig method from anywhere in the servlet to get a ServletConfig object. Then, you call the getInitParameter method from the ServletConfig object.

Note that the getInitParameter method works the same of whether you call it from the ServletContext object or the ServletConfig object. The only difference is that the ServletContext object returns parameters that are available to all servlets while the ServletConfig object returns parameters that are only available to the current servlet.

When you call the getInitParameter method, you must specify the name of the parameter. If the parameter exists, the getInitParameter method returns the value of the parameter as a string. Otherwise, this method returns a null value.

Two methods of the GenericServlet class

Method	Description
`getServletContext()`	Returns a ServletContext object that contains information about the entire web application's context.
`getServletConfig()`	Returns a ServletConfig object that contains information about a single servlet's configuration.

A method of the ServletContext and ServletConfig interfaces

Method	Description
`getInitParameter(String name)`	Returns a String object that contains the value of the specified initialization parameter. If the parameter doesn't exist, this method returns a null value.

Code that gets an initialization parameter that's available to all servlets

```
ServletContext context = this.getServletContext();
String custServEmail = context.getInitParameter("custServEmail");
```

Code that gets an initialization parameter that's available to the current servlet only

```
ServletConfig config = this.getServletConfig();
String relativePath = config.getInitParameter("relativePathToFile");
```

Description

- To get an initialization parameter that's available to all servlets, you use the getInitParameter method of the ServletContext object.

- To get an initialization parameter for a specific servlet, you use the getInitParameter method of the ServletConfig object.

Figure 7-12   How to work with initialization parameters (part 2 of 2)

How to implement custom error handling

Figure 7-13 shows you how to use the web.xml file to specify custom error pages that apply to the entire application. When you're developing an application, you probably won't want to implement custom error pages. That way, when an error occurs, Tomcat will display an error page that you can use to debug the error. Before you deploy an application, though, you may want to implement custom error pages that present errors in a way that's consistent with the rest of your application.

To specify a custom error page for a specific *HTTP status code*, you begin by coding an error-page element. Within this element, you code two child elements: the error-code element and the location element. The error-code element specifies the HTTP status code for the error. The location element specifies the location of the custom error page.

The first example in this figure shows how to code the error-page element for the HTTP 404 status code. Here, the error-code element specifies the number for the HTTP status code. Then, the location element specifies a URL that points to an error page named error_404.jsp that's stored in the application's root directory. Note that this element must begin with a slash.

The second example shows the code for a custom error page for the 404 status code. This custom error page is a JSP that uses two includes, and this JSP displays a user-friendly message that describes the HTTP 404 status code.

The 404 status code indicates that the server wasn't able to find a file at the requested URL. As you gain more experience with web programming, you'll become familiar with other HTTP status codes. Also, some of the more common ones are summarized in chapter 18.

To specify a custom error page that's displayed when an uncaught exception is thrown, you begin by coding an error-page element. Within this element, you code two child elements: the exception-type element and the location element. The exception-type element specifies the type of exception by identifying the package name and the class name for the exception. The location element specifies the location of the custom error page.

The third example shows how to code an error-page element that handles all Java exceptions. Here, the exception-type element specifies the Throwable class in the java.lang package. Since all exceptions inherit this class, this causes a custom error page to be displayed for all uncaught exceptions. However, if you want to display different error pages for different types of exceptions, you can code multiple error-page elements. For example, you can display one error page for exceptions of the NullPointerException type and another error page for exceptions of the ServletException type.

The fourth example shows the code for a custom error page that handles all Java exceptions. Like the first example, this error page includes a header and footer file. In addition, a page directive is used to identify this page as an error page. As a result, this page is given access to the implicit exception object. From this object, you can call the getClass and getMessage methods to get more information about the type of exception that was thrown.

XML elements for working with error handling

Element	Description
`<error-page>`	Specifies an HTML page or JSP that's displayed when the application encounters an uncaught exception or a certain type of HTTP status code.
`<error-code>`	Specifies the number of a valid HTTP status code.
`<exception-type>`	Uses the fully qualified class name to specify a Java exception.
`<location>`	Specifies the location of the HTML page or JSP that's displayed.

The XML tags that provide error-handling for a HTTP 404 status code

```
<error-page>
    <error-code>404</error-code>
    <location>/error_404.jsp</location>
</error-page>
```

The code for a file named error_404.jsp

```
<%@ include file="/includes/header.html" %>

<%@ page isErrorPage="true" %>

<h1>404 Error</h1>
<p>The server was not able to find the file you requested.</p>
<p>To continue, click the Back button.</p>
<br>

<%@ include file="/includes/footer.jsp" %>
```

The XML tags that provide error-handling for all Java exceptions

```
<error-page>
    <exception-type>java.lang.Throwable</exception-type>
    <location>/error_java.jsp</location>
</error-page>
```

The code for a file named error_java.jsp

```
<%@ include file="/includes/header.html" %>

<%@ page isErrorPage="true" %>

<h1>Java Error</h1>
<p>Sorry, Java has thrown an exception.</p>
<p>To continue, click the Back button.</p>
<br>

<h2>Details</h2>
<p>
    Type: <%= exception.getClass() %><br>
    Message: <%= exception.getMessage() %><br>
</p>

<%@ include file="/includes/footer.jsp" %>
```

Figure 7-13   How to implement custom error handling (part 1 of 2)

When you code a custom error page, you can use an HTML document or a JSP. If you use a JSP, you can use the exception object to customize the error page. In addition, you can use any other techniques that are available to a JSP such as working with the request object or using include files.

Part 2 of figure 7-13 shows how the error pages appear when displayed in a browser. Here, the first screen shows the error page that's displayed for an HTTP 404 status code. By default, however, the Internet Explorer uses its own error pages for HTTP status codes. So if you want to use this browser to view a custom page, you must select the Tools→Internet Options command and use the Advanced tab of the dialog box to deselect the "Show friendly HTTP error messages" option. That's why I used Firefox to display this error page.

The second screen shows the error page that's displayed when Java throws an exception. Here, the details at the bottom of the page show that one of the paths used by the application caused an IllegalArgumentException to be thrown. In addition, the message indicates that exception was thrown because a front slash wasn't coded at the start of the path for the display_email_entry.jsp file.

In this case, this is all the information you need to debug the error. However, this error page doesn't give as much information as the error pages that are provided by Tomcat. As a result, it's easier to debug errors when you're using Tomcat's error pages. That's why you should only use an error page like this when you're ready to put your web application into a production environment. Until then, you can comment out the error-page element in the web.xml file.

The JSP page for the 404 error

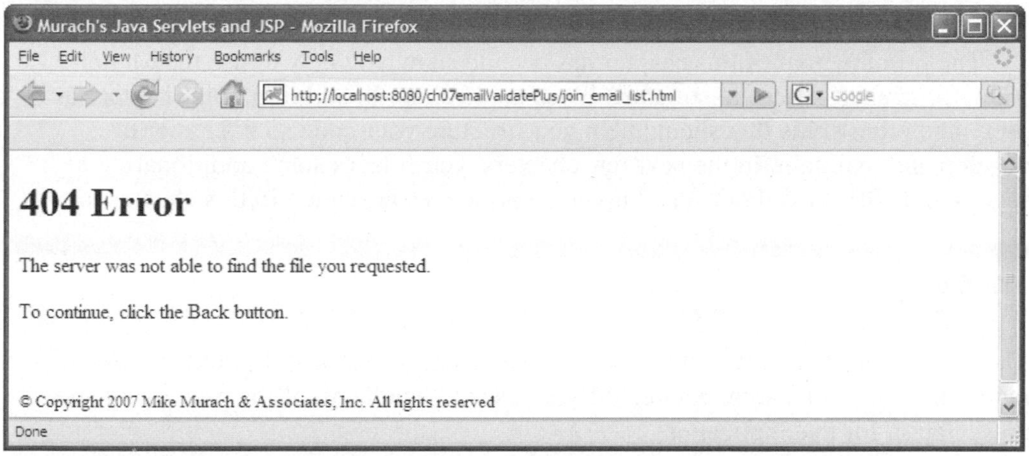

The JSP page that's displayed when a Java exception is thrown

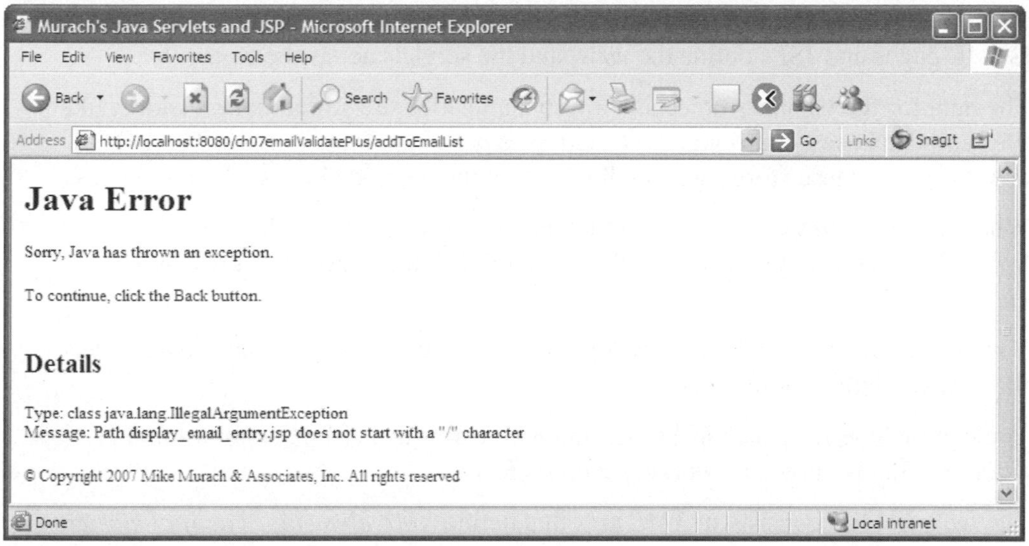

Description

- In the web.xml file, you can use the error-page element to specify the error pages that should be displayed when the application encounters (1) specific HTTP status codes or (2) uncaught exceptions.

- By default, the Internet Explorer uses its own error pages for HTTP status codes. As a result, if you want to use this browser to view a custom page, you must select the Tools→Internet Options command and use the Advanced tab of the dialog box to deselect the "Show friendly HTTP error messages" option.

Figure 7-13   How to implement custom error handling (part 2 of 2)

Perspective

The primary goal of this chapter has been to show you how to use the Model-View-Controller pattern to structure a web application. In addition, this chapter has presented other skills that should help you structure your code so it's easier to develop and maintain. In the next few chapters, you'll learn some additional servlet and JSP skills that expand upon the principles presented in this chapter.

Summary

- The *Model 1 architecture* can be used for web applications with limited processing requirements. In this architecture, JSPs are used to handle all of the processing and presentation for the application.

- The *Model 2 architecture* is commonly used for web applications with significant processing requirements. This architecture is also known as the *Model-View-Controller (MVC) pattern*. In this pattern, business objects define the *model*, the HTML pages and JSPs define the *view*, and the servlets act as the *controller*.

- The data for the business objects in a web application are stored in *data stores* like files and databases. This can be referred to as *persistent data storage*. The I/O operations for these stores are usually done by the methods in data access classes.

- When using the MVC pattern, a servlet uses the RequestDispatcher object to forward the request and response objects to the JSP that's going to present the view.

- You can use JavaScript for *data validation* on the client. Or, you can use a servlet for data validation on the server.

- You can include files such as header and footer files in a JSP at *compile-time* or *runtime*. This is known as working with *includes*.

- The web.xml file consists of *XML tags* that define *XML elements*. The *root element* for this file is the web-app element. When one element is coded within another element, it can be called a *child element*.

- You can use the web.xml file to provide *initialization parameters* that apply to the entire web application or to specific servlets.

- You can use the web.xml file to provide custom error pages for specific Java exceptions or for HTTP errors represented by specific *HTTP status codes*.

Exercise 7-1   Enhance the Email List application

In this exercise, you'll enhance the Email List application so it validates data and uses many of the other features presented in this chapter.

Review and test the code for the email application

1. Open the ch07email project that's in the ex_starts directory.

2. Open the AddToEmailListServer class and view its code. Note how this servlet forwards the request and response to a JSP when it's done with the processing for the request.

3. Run the application and test it with valid and invalid data. Note that this application does not validate data before writing that data to the data store.

Validate data with a servlet

4. Convert the join_email_list.html file to a JSP file. One way to do that is to create a new JSP, cut and paste all code from the HTML file into the JSP, and delete the HTML file.

5. Modify the web.xml file for this application so it starts with the new JSP file when you run the application. Then, test these changes.

6. Modify the servlet for this application as shown in figure 7-8 so it validates the user entries by making sure the user entered each one of them.

7. Modify the join_email_list.jsp file that you created in step 4 so it displays the validation data as shown in figure 7-8.

8. Run the application and test it with invalid data. Note how this application is able to display a message that asks the user to enter values for all three text boxes.

Use includes

9. Modify the join_email_list.jsp and display_email_entry.jsp files so they include the header.html and footer.jsp files at compile-time as described in figure 7-9. These include files are in the includes directory.

10. Run the application and test it to make sure the include files work correctly.

11. Modify the join_email_list.jsp and display_email_entry.jsp files so they include the header.html and footer.jsp files at runtime as described in figure 7-10.

12. Run the application and test it to make sure the include files still work correctly.

Use an initialization parameter

13. Use a servlet initialization parameter to supply a relative path and name for the text file that's passed to the UserIO class as shown in figure 7-12. To do that, you'll need to modify the web.xml file and the servlet for the application.

14. Run the application and test it to make sure the data is still being written to the file correctly.

Use a custom error page

15. Add the error_404.jsp file to the application as described in figure 7-13. Then, edit the web.xml file so the application displays this JSP when it encounters an HTTP 404 error code.

16. Test the application to make sure the error page is displayed when an HTTP 404 error is encountered. To do that, you can enter an invalid page address for the ch07email application in the browser. If you're using the Internet Explorer browser, though, you need to turn off the "Show friendly HTTP error messages" option as described in part 2 of figure 7-13.

17. When you're through experimenting, close the project.

8

How to work with sessions and cookies

In all but the simplest of web applications, you need to keep track of the user as the user moves through the web application. Fortunately, the servlet API makes it relatively easy to do this. In this chapter, you'll learn how to use the servlet API to keep track of sessions, and you'll learn how to use the servlet API to work with cookies.

An introduction to session tracking

Keeping track of users as they move around a web site is known as *session tracking*. So to start, you'll learn how the servlet API tracks sessions, and you'll be introduced to a web application that needs session tracking.

Why session tracking is difficult with HTTP

Figure 8-1 shows why session tracking is more difficult for web applications that use HTTP than it is for other types of applications. To start, a browser on a client requests a page from a web server. After the web server returns the page, it drops the connection. Then, if the browser makes additional requests the web server has no way to associate the browser with its previous requests. Since HTTP doesn't maintain *state*, it is known as a *stateless protocol*. (In contrast, FTP maintains state between requests so it is known as a *stateful protocol*.)

How session tracking works in Java

Figure 8-1 also shows how the servlet API keeps track of sessions. To start, a browser on a client requests a JSP or servlet from the web server, which passes the request to the servlet engine. Then, the servlet engine checks if the request includes an ID for the Java session. If it doesn't, the servlet engine creates a unique ID for the session plus a *session object* that can be used to store the data for the session. From that point on, the web server uses the session ID to relate each browser request to the session object, even though the server still drops the HTTP connection after returning each page.

By default, the servlet API uses a *cookie* to store the session ID within the client's browser. This is an extension of the HTTP protocol. Then, when the next request is made, this cookie is added to the request. However, if cookies have been disabled within a browser, this type of session tracking won't work.

To get around this problem, the servlet API provides a way to rewrite the URL so it includes the session ID. This is known as *URL encoding*, and it works even if cookies have been disabled within a browser. However, you have to provide for this encoding in your servlets and JSPs as shown in figure 8-6. In contrast, cookies are automatically used for session tracking so you don't have to provide any code for them.

Why session tracking is difficult with HTTP

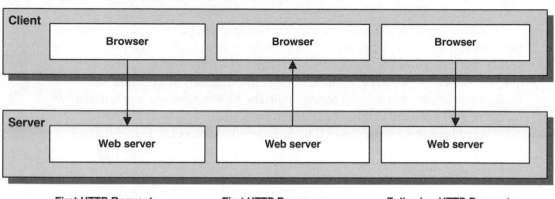

First HTTP Request:
The browser requests a page.

First HTTP Response:
The server returns the requested page and drops the connection.

Following HTTP Requests:
The browser requests a page. The web server has no way to associate the browser with its previous request.

How Java keeps track of sessions

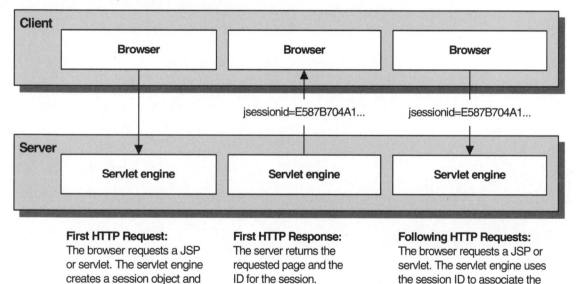

First HTTP Request:
The browser requests a JSP or servlet. The servlet engine creates a session object and assigns an ID for the session.

First HTTP Response:
The server returns the requested page and the ID for the session.

Following HTTP Requests:
The browser requests a JSP or servlet. The servlet engine uses the session ID to associate the browser with its session object.

Description

- HTTP is a *stateless protocol*. Once a browser makes a request, it drops the connection to the server. So to maintain *state*, a web application must use *session tracking*.

- By default, the servlet API uses a *cookie* to store a session ID in each browser. Then, the browser passes the cookie to the server with each request.

- To provide session tracking when cookies are disabled in the browser, you can use *URL encoding* to store the session ID in the URL for each page of an application.

- To store the data for each session, the server creates a *session object*.

Figure 8-1 An introduction to session tracking

An application that needs session tracking

Figure 8-2 shows the user interface for the first two pages of a Cart application. Here, the first page allows the user to add an item to the Cart, and the second page displays the items in the cart and allows the user to update the quantity or remove an item. Without session tracking, this application wouldn't be able to associate the second request with the first request. As a result, the cart would never be able to display more than one item.

Throughout this chapter, you'll be introduced to snippets of code that are used in this Cart application. If necessary, you can refer back to this figure to view the user interface.

The Index page

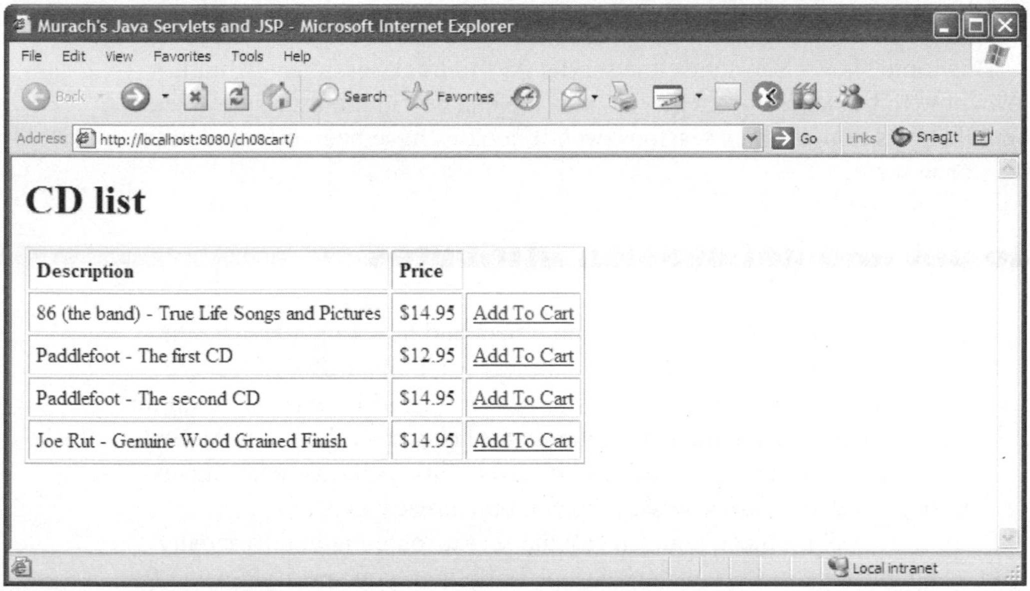

The Cart page

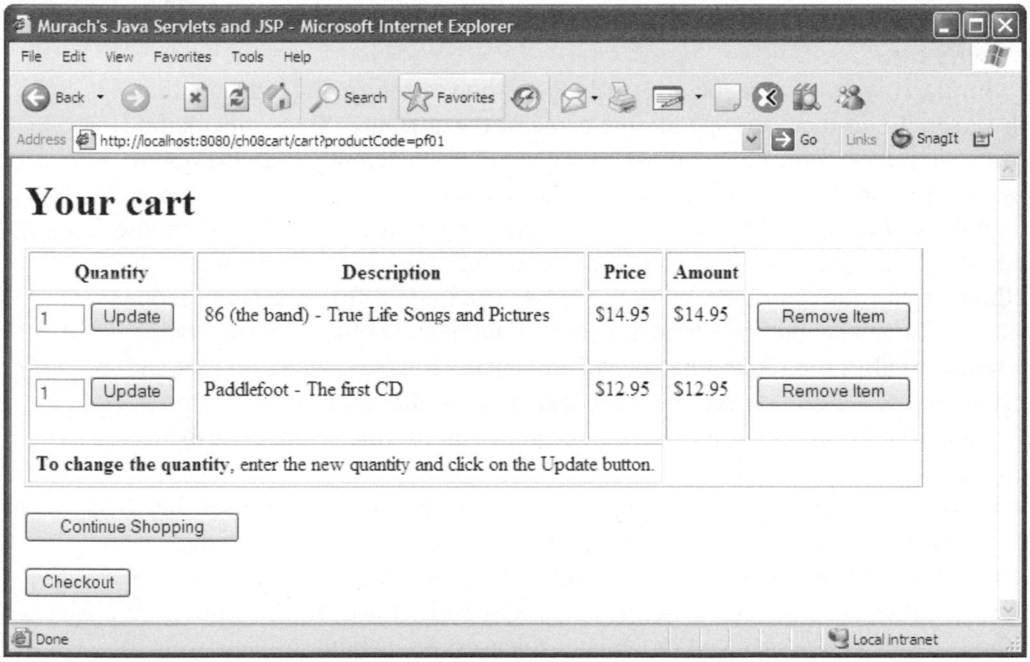

Figure 8-2   An application that needs session tracking

How to work with sessions

This topic shows how to use the servlet API to track sessions. To start, it shows how to track sessions when cookies are enabled in the user's browser. Then, it shows how to track sessions even if cookies have been disabled in the user's browser.

How to set and get session attributes

Figure 8-3 shows how to get a session object and how to get and set the attributes of that object. Since the session object is a built-in JSP object, you only need to get a session object when you're working with servlets. To do that, you can call the getSession method of the request object as shown in the first example. Then, if the session object doesn't exist, this method creates a new one. Usually, though, it just accesses the one that already exists.

From the session object, you can call the setAttribute method to set any object as an attribute of the current session. To do that, you specify a name for the attribute and the name of the object that you want to store. For instance, the second and third examples show how to store a String object and a Cart object. Here, the Cart object is a business object that is used to store all of the items for the user's cart.

Similarly, you can use the getAttribute method to return any attribute that you've set. To do that, you specify the name of the attribute. Since this method returns an object of the Object class, you need to cast each object to the appropriate type as shown by the fourth and fifth examples.

In the last chapter, you learned how to use the getAttribute and setAttribute methods of the request object. Note that the getAttribute and setAttribute methods of the session object work the same. The main difference is the scope of the attributes. When you set an attribute in the request object, the attributes are removed after the request has been completed. However, when you set an attribute in the session object, the attributes are available until the user closes the browser, until the session times out, or until you use the removeAttribute method to remove an attribute from the session object.

If you work with an older web application, you may find that it uses the putValue, getValue, and removeValue methods instead of the setAttribute, getAttribute, and removeAttribute methods. That's because the Attribute methods were introduced in version 2.2 of the servlet API. However, the Value methods have been deprecated in the later releases. As a result, all new web applications should use the Attribute methods.

A method of the request object

Method	Description
getSession()	Returns the HttpSession object associated with this request. If the request is not associated with a session, this method creates a new HttpSession object and returns it.

Three methods of the session object

Method	Description
setAttribute(String name, Object o)	Stores any object in the session as an attribute and specifies a name for the attribute.
getAttribute(String name)	Returns the value of the specified attribute as an Object type. If no attribute exists for the specified name, this method returns a null value.
removeAttribute(String name)	Removes the specified attribute from this session.

Examples

Code that gets a session object

```
HttpSession session = request.getSession();
```

Code that sets a String object as an attribute

```
session.setAttribute("productCode", productCode);
```

Code that sets a user-defined object as an attribute

```
Cart cart = new Cart(productCode);
session.setAttribute("cart", cart);
```

Code that gets a String object

```
String productCode = (String) session.getAttribute("productCode");
```

Code that gets a user-defined object

```
Cart cart = (Cart) session.getAttribute("cart");
if (cart == null)
    cart = new Cart();
```

Code that removes an object

```
session.removeAttribute("productCode");
```

Description

- A session object is created when a browser makes the first request to a site. It is destroyed when the session ends.

- A session ends when a specified amount of time elapses without another request or when the user exits the browser.

- The session object is a built-in JSP object. As a result, you don't need to create the session object when working with JSPs.

Figure 8-3   How to set and get session attributes

More methods of the session object

Most of the time, you'll use the methods presented in the last figure to work with the session object. However, figure 8-4 presents some other methods of the session object that you may want to use.

You can use the getAttributeNames method of the session object to return the names of all attributes stored in the session object. To do that, you use the getAttributeNames method to return an Enumeration object. Then, you can use the hasMoreElements and nextElement methods of the Enumeration object to loop through the names as shown in the first code example. This can be useful for debugging.

You can use the getId method to return the ID that the servlet engine is using for the current session. This ID is a long string that uniquely identifies each Java session. Here again, this can be useful for debugging.

You can use the isNew method to check if the client is new or if the client chooses to not join the session. This method returns a true value if the client is accessing the site for the first time in a new session or if cookies have been disabled on the browser.

You can use the last two methods to control when a session is invalidated. When this happens, all objects that have been stored in the session object are released from the session object. By default, the session will be invalidated if a user is inactive for half an hour, but you can use the setMaxInactiveInterval method to change this default. If, for example, you supply an argument of −1, the session object won't be invalidated until the user exits the browser. If necessary, though, you can call the invalidate method whenever you want to invalidate the session. If you call a method from the session object after it has been invalidated, that method will throw an IllegalStateException.

More methods of the session object

Method	Description
getAttributeNames()	Returns a java.util.Enumeration object that contains the names of all attributes in the HttpSession object.
getId()	Returns a string for the unique Java session identifier that the servlet engine generates for each session.
isNew()	Returns a true value if the client does not yet know about the session or if the client chooses not to join the session. This can happen if the session relies upon cookies and the browser doesn't accept cookies.
setMaxInactiveInterval(int seconds)	By default, the maximum inactive interval for the session is set to 1800 seconds (30 minutes). As a result, if the user is inactive for 30 minutes, the session will be invalidated. To increase or decrease this interval, supply a positive integer value. To create a session that won't end until the user closes the browser, supply a negative integer such as −1.
invalidate()	Invalidates the session and unbinds any objects that are bound to it.

Examples

A method that gets all the names of the attributes for a session

```
Enumeration names = session.getAttributeNames();
while (names.hasMoreElements())
{
    System.out.println((String) names.nextElement());
}
```

A method that gets the ID for a session

```
String jSessionId = session.getId();
```

A method that sets the inactive interval for a session

```
session.setMaxInactiveInterval(60*60*24);  // one day
session.setMaxInactiveInterval(-1);        // until the browser is closed
```

A method that invalidates the session and unbinds any objects

```
session.invalidate();
```

Description

- If the session object has been explicitly or implicitly invalidated, all methods of the session object will throw an IllegalStateException.

- For more information about these and other methods of the session object, you can look up the HttpSession interface in the javax.servlet.http package in the documentation for the Servlet and JavaServer Pages API.

Figure 8-4   More methods of the session object

How to enable or disable cookies

There are two types of cookies. A *per-session cookie* is stored on the browser until the user closes the browser, and a *persistent cookie* can be stored on the user's hard disk for up to 3 years. Since the session tracking code in the previous two figures relies on per-session cookies, it won't work unless per-session cookies are enabled in the user's browser.

That's why figure 8-5 shows how to enable or disable cookies in a browser. To test sessions that rely on cookies, you'll need to enable cookies in your browser. Conversely, to test code that's intended to work even if cookies have been disabled, you'll need to disable cookies in your browser.

If you're using Internet Explorer 6.0, the default privacy setting is Medium. This default setting enables per-session and persistent cookies. To disable both per-session cookies and persistent cookies, you can select a privacy setting that blocks all cookies as shown in this figure. In addition, if you want to disable cookies in a local testing environment, you must use the Security tab to deselect the "Include all local (intranet) sites" option.

For earlier versions of Internet Explorer, you control cookies through the Security tab. Here, the default security level is the Medium security level. The default settings for this level enable per-session and persistent cookies. In contrast, the defaults for the High security level disable both per-session cookies and persistent cookies. However, you can use the Custom tab to modify the defaults for the High security level so this level allows per-session cookies.

If you're using Mozilla Firefox 2.0, the default privacy setting also enables per-session and persistent cookies. To disable both per-session cookies and persistent cookies, you can deselect the "Allow cookies from sites" check box as described in this figure. Or, to allow per-session cookies only, you can allow cookies but use the Keep Until combo box to specify that you only want to keep them until you close the browser.

An Internet Explorer dialog box with disabled cookies

How to disable cookies for Internet Explorer 6.0

1. Pull down the Tools menu and select the Internet Options command.
2. Select the Privacy tab.
3. Use the slider control to set the security level to block cookies.

How to disable local cookies for Internet Explorer 6.0

1. Pull down the Tools menu and select the Internet Options command.
2. Select the Security tab, the Local Intranet icon, and click on the Sites button.
3. Deselect the "Include all local (intranet) sites" check box.

How to disable cookies for Mozilla Firefox 2.0

1. Pull down the Tools menu and select the Options command.
2. Click on the Privacy tab.
3. Deselect the "Accept cookies from sites" check box.

Description

*   To learn how to enable or disable cookies for different versions of Internet Explorer or Firefox, or to learn how to enable or disable cookies for other browsers, please use the browser's Help menu or the Internet to get more information.

Figure 8-5   How to enable or disable cookies

How to use URL encoding to track sessions without cookies

Although cookies are enabled by default on most web browsers, some people choose to disable cookies in their browsers. When you're programming a web application, you have to take this into account. If the web application isn't a critical part of the web site, it may be acceptable to display a message that explains that this part of the site won't work properly if cookies have been disabled. Otherwise, you can make the application work even when cookies have been disabled by using *URL encoding* to track sessions as shown in figure 8-6.

To use URL encoding, you must convert all of the HTML pages in the application to JSPs. Then, you can use the encodeURL method of the response object to encode all the URLs for the JSPs that are used in the application. Once you do that, the session ID is added to a URL whenever the URL is requested from a browser with disabled cookies. In the Address box of the browser in this figure, for example, you can see that a session ID has been added to the end of the URL, but before the parameters.

When you use URL encoding, you must be sure to encode all URLs in the application. If you forget one, the application will lose track of the session as soon as the web server returns a response object that contains a URL that isn't encoded. However, if a servlet forwards a request to a JSP in an MVC pattern, you don't need to encode the URL in the servlet because the JSP returns the response to the browser.

To test an application that uses URL encoding, you need to disable cookies in your browser as shown in the previous figure. Then, the URL for each page in the application should include the ID for the Java session. However, if you enable cookies in your browser, the URLs of the application usually won't display the ID for the Java session. This shows that the encodeURL method only rewrites the URLs of the application when necessary.

A method of the response object

Method	Description
`encodeURL(String url)`	Returns a string for the specified URL. If necessary, this method encodes the session ID in the URL. If not, it returns the URL unchanged.

How to encode a URL in a Form tag

```
<form action="<%=response.encodeURL("cart")%>" method="post">
```

How to encode a URL in an A tag

```
<a href="<%=response.encodeURL("cart?productCode=8601")%>">
Add To Cart
</a>
```

A URL after it has been encoded

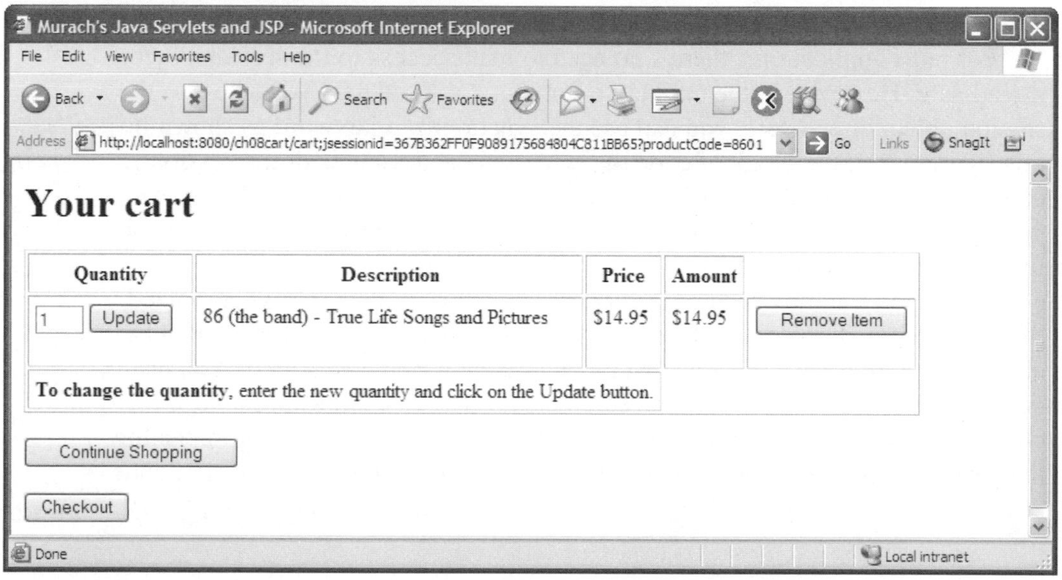

Description

- If the user has disabled per-session cookies, you can use *URL encoding* to keep track of the ID for the session. To do that, you must convert any relevant HTML pages to JSPs, and you must encode all relevant URLs.
- When you encode a URL, the session ID is passed to the browser in the URL.

Figure 8-6   How to use URL encoding to track sessions without cookies

How to provide thread-safe access to the session object

In chapter 6, you learned that the servlet container only creates and loads one instance of a servlet. Then, it uses one thread for each request that's made by a client. Most of the time, that means that there's only one thread for each client that can access the session object. As a result, it's almost always thread-safe to access the session object with the getAttribute and setAttribute methods.

However, it's possible that the user may open multiple windows within a browser as shown in figure 8-7. With the Firefox browser, for example, you can open a new window within the browser by holding down the Ctrl key while you click on a link. In that case, all windows within the browser have access to the same session object. As a result, it's possible (though highly unlikely) that two threads might try to get or set an attribute in the session object at the same time, which might result in a lost update or another type of problem.

For most applications, there's no need to make access to the session object thread-safe. However, in the unlikely event that you need to make access to the session object thread-safe, you can use the synchronized keyword as shown in this figure. Here, the block of code that accesses the attributes of the session object is synchronized on the session object. As a result, when one thread is getting or setting an attribute in the session object, no other threads will be able to access that session object.

When you use the synchronized keyword, you can make the synchronized block of code as large or small as you want. However, no other threads will be able to access the session while this block of code is being executed. As a result, you'll want to make the synchronized block of code as small as possible. Of course, if it improves the readability of your code without negatively impacting the performance of your application, you can synchronize larger blocks of code.

An example that synchronizes access to the session object

```
Cart cart;
synchronized(session)
{
    cart = (Cart) session.getAttribute("cart");
}
```

Another example that synchronizes access to the session object

```
synchronized(session)
{
    session.setAttribute("cart", cart);
}
```

A web browser with three windows accessing the same session object

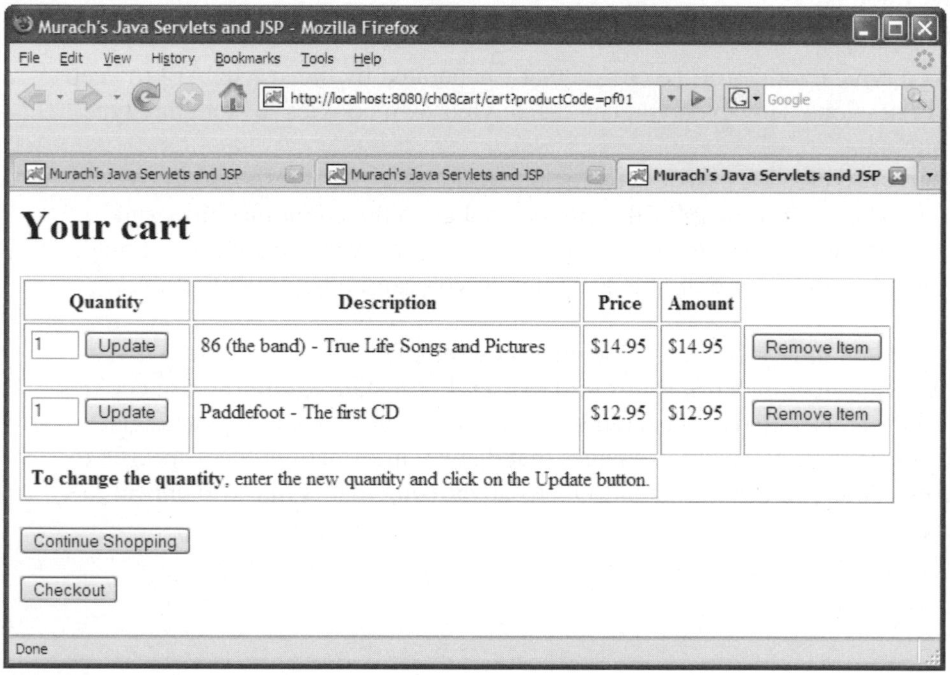

Description

- Each servlet creates one session object that exists for multiple requests that come from a single client.
- If the client has one browser window open, access to the session object is thread-safe.
- If the client has multiple browser windows open, it's possible (though highly unlikely) that two threads from the same client will access the session object at the same time. As a result, the session object isn't completely thread-safe.

Figure 8-7   How to provide thread-safe access to the session object

How to work with cookies

In the last topic, you learned that the servlet API uses per-session cookies. Now, you'll learn more about working with cookies including how to create a persistent cookie that can be stored on the user's computer for up to three years.

An introduction to cookies

Figure 8-8 introduces you to some basic facts about cookies. To start, it shows some examples of cookies. These examples show that a cookie is essentially a name/value pair. For example, the name of the first cookie is jsessionid, and its value is

```
D1F15245171203E8670487F020544490
```

This is a typical value for the cookie that's generated by the servlet API to keep track of sessions. However, you can create your own cookies to store any type of string data.

Once you create a cookie, you include it in the server's response to the browser. Then, the browser will store the cookie on the client machine, and it will send it back to the server with all subsequent requests. Remember, though, that some browsers have disabled cookies so you can't always count on using them.

Once you have stored a cookie on a browser's PC, you can use it to make your web application work better for the user. For instance, you can use cookies to verify that users have registered before so they don't have to register again. You can use them to customize pages that display information that's specific to the users. And you can use them to focus advertising that is likely to appeal to the users.

Examples of cookies

```
jsessionid=D1F15245171203E8670487F020544490
user_id=87
email=jsmith@hotmail.com
userName=jsmith
passwordCookie=opensesame
```

How cookies work

- A cookie is a name/value pair that is stored in a browser.
- On the server, a web application creates a cookie and sends it to the browser. On the client, the browser saves the cookie and sends it back to the server every time it accesses a page from that server.
- Cookies can be set to persist within the user's browser for up to 3 years.
- Some users disable cookies in their browsers. As a result, you can't always count on all users having their cookies enabled.
- Browsers generally accept only 20 cookies from each site and 300 cookies total. In addition, they can limit each cookie to 4 kilobytes.
- A cookie can be associated with one or more subdomain names.

Typical uses for cookies

- **To allow users to skip login and registration forms** that gather data like user name, password, address, or credit card data.
- **To customize pages** that display information like weather reports, sports scores, and stock quotations.
- **To focus advertising** like banner ads that target the user's interests.

Description

- A per-session cookie that holds the session ID is automatically created for each session. That cookie is used to relate the browser to the session object.
- You can also create and send other cookies to a user's browser. You can use these cookies to access user-specific data that's stored in a file or database.

Figure 8-8   An introduction to cookies

How to create and use cookies

To create and use cookies, you use the constructors and methods shown in figure 8-9. After you use the constructor of the Cookie class to create a cookie, you can use the methods of this class to set parameters for the cookie and to get its name and value. Then, you can use the addCookie method of the response object to add a cookie to a browser's PC. And you can use the getCookies method of the request object to get an array of all the cookies on the browser's PC. These methods are illustrated by the two examples.

The first example uses four statements to create a cookie and add it to the response object. The first statement creates the Cookie object. The second statement calls the setMaxAge method to set the life of the cookie on the browser's PC to two years (60 seconds times 60 minutes times 24 hours times 365 days times 2 years). The third statement sets the path for the cookie so it's available to the entire web application. And the fourth statement adds the cookie to the response object so it will be returned to the browser and added to the browser's PC.

The second example retrieves a cookie from the request object that's been sent from a browser. Here, the first statement returns an array of Cookie objects from the request object. Then, the following statements loop through the array to return the cookie that's named userIdCookie. To do that, these statements use the getName and getValue methods of the Cookie object.

Constructor of the Cookie class

Constructor	Description
`Cookie(String name, String value)`	Creates a cookie with the specified name and value.

The methods of the Cookie class

Method	Description
`setMaxAge(int maxAgeInSeconds)`	To create a persistent cookie, set the cookie's maximum age to a positive number.
	To create a per-session cookie, set the cookie's maximum age to –1. Then, the cookie will be deleted when the user exits the browser.
`setPath(String path)`	To allow the entire application to access the cookie, set the cookie's path to "/".
`getName()`	Returns a string for the name of the cookie.
`getValue()`	Returns a string that contains the value of the cookie.

A method of the response object

Method	Description
`addCookie(Cookie c)`	Adds the specified cookie to the response.

A method of the request object

Method	Description
`getCookies()`	Returns an array of Cookie objects that the client sent with this request. If no cookies were sent, this method returns a null value.

Code that creates and sets a cookie

```
Cookie userIdCookie = new Cookie("userIdCookie", userId);
userIdCookie.setMaxAge(60*60*24*365*2); //set the age to 2 years
userIdCookie.setPath("/"); // allow access by the entire application
response.addCookie(userIdCookie);
```

Code that gets the cookie

```
Cookie[] cookies = request.getCookies();
String cookieName = "userIdCookie";
String cookieValue = "";
for (int i=0; i<cookies.length; i++)
{
    Cookie cookie = cookies[i];
    if (cookieName.equals(cookie.getName()))
        cookieValue = cookie.getValue();
}
```

Figure 8-9   How to create and use cookies

How to view and delete cookies

When you're testing or debugging an application, you may want to view all of the cookies for a browser to make sure the right ones are being stored. Similarly, you may want to delete all the cookies from the browser so you can add new cookies to it. In figure 8-10, you can learn how to do both of these tasks.

To display all the cookies for a browser, you can write a JSP that uses the getCookies method of the request object to get an array of cookies. Then, you can code a loop that gets each name in the array and displays it. This is illustrated by the first example.

To delete all the cookies for a browser, you can get the array of cookies again. Then, you can code a loop that uses the setMaxAge method to set the age of each cookie to zero. This is illustrated by the second example.

Four methods of the Cookie class

Method	Description
`setPath(String path)`	By default, when you send a cookie to a browser, the browser will return the cookie to all servlets and JSPs within the directory that sent the cookie and all subdirectories of that directory. To make a cookie available to the entire application, you can set the path to a slash (/).
	To make a cookie available to a directory and its subdirectories, you can specify a path like /cart. Then, the browser will return the cookie to the cart directory and all subdirectories. However, the directory that originally sent the cookie must be within this directory or one of its subdirectories.
`setDomain(String domainPattern)`	By default, the browser only returns a cookie to the host that sent the cookie. To return a cookie to other hosts within the same domain, you can set a domain pattern like .ads.com. Then, the browser will return the cookie to any subdomain of www.ads.com like www.travel.ads.com or www.camera.ads.com.
`setSecure(boolean flag)`	By default, the browser sends a cookie over a regular connection or an encrypted connection. To protect cookies that store sensitive data such as passwords, you can supply a true value for this method. Then, the cookie will only be sent over a secure connection.
`setVersion(int version)`	By default, Java creates cookies that use version 0 of the cookie protocol that was developed by Netscape. Since this is the cookie protocol that has been around the longest, it is the most widely supported. However, you can specify an int value of 1 for this method to use the new version of the cookie protocol, which is version 1.

Description

- All of these set methods have corresponding get methods.
- For more information about these methods and other methods for working with cookies, use your web browser to look up the Cookie class in the javax.servlet.http package that's in the documentation for the Servlet and JavaServer Pages API.

Figure 8-11   Four methods for working with cookies

A utility class for working with cookies

As you've already seen, you must loop through an array of cookies whenever you want to get the value for one cookie. Since this can be tedious, it's common to place the code that loops through the array of cookies in a utility class like the one shown in figure 8-12. Then, you can easily retrieve the value of a cookie by calling the utility class.

The CookieUtil class in this figure contains one static method named getCookieValue. This method accepts an array of cookies and the name of the cookie that you want to get. Then, it loops through the array of cookies and returns the value that matches the name of the cookie. If it doesn't find the name of the cookie in the array, this method returns an empty string.

Since you might want to access this class from more than one servlet or JSP, you should store this class in a central location. For instance, this class is stored in the util package. As a result, you need to import this class before you can use it. Once you do that, you can use Java statements like the two at the bottom of this figure to get the value of any cookie.

A utility class that gets the value of a cookie

```
package util;

import javax.servlet.http.*;

public class CookieUtil
{
    public static String getCookieValue(
        Cookie[] cookies, String cookieName)
    {
        String cookieValue = "";
        Cookie cookie;
        if (cookies != null)
        {
            for (int i=0; i<cookies.length; i++)
            {
                cookie = cookies[i];
                if (cookieName.equals(cookie.getName()))
                {
                    cookieValue = cookie.getValue();
                }
            }
        }
        return cookieValue;
    }
}
```

Code that uses the CookieUtil class to get the value of a cookie

```
Cookie[] cookies = request.getCookies();
String emailAddress = CookieUtil.getCookieValue(cookies, "emailCookie");
```

Description

- To make it easier to get the value of a cookie, you can create a utility class that contains a method that accepts an array of Cookie objects and the name of the cookie and then returns the value of the cookie.

Figure 8-12   A utility class for working with cookies

How to work with URL rewriting and hidden fields

In the early days of web programming, programmers used URL rewriting and hidden fields to track sessions. Today, you can use the servlet API to track sessions. However, you can still use URL rewriting and hidden fields to pass parameters between the browser and the server.

In particular, URL rewriting and hidden fields are handy if you need to pass data for a single request. Rather than storing that type of data in the session object, which takes up memory, you can use URL rewriting and hidden fields to pass data from page to page.

How to use URL rewriting to pass parameters

Figure 8-13 shows how to use *URL rewriting* to pass parameters from the browser to the server. This should already be familiar to you because that's how parameters are passed from HTML documents to a JSP or servlet when the Get method is used.

For instance, the first example shows how to code an A tag that specifies a URL that adds a product to a cart. Here, the URL calls the servlet that's mapped to the /cart URL and passes a parameter named productCode with a value of 8601. Since the A tag always uses the Get method of the HTTP protocol, this will cause the productCode parameter to be displayed in the browser as shown in this figure.

The second example shows that you can also use URL rewriting within a Form tag. Here, the Method attribute of the Form tag specifies the HTTP Post method. As a result, the productCode parameter won't be appended to the end of the URL that's displayed in the browser.

Finally, the third example shows that you can use a JSP expression to pass a value to a URL. Here, the product code is an expression that's evaluated at runtime.

Although URL rewriting works even if cookies have been disabled, it has the two limitations that are summarized in this figure. One way to get around these limitations is to use hidden fields as shown in the next figure. But, as you will see, hidden fields have some limitations too.

The syntax for URL rewriting

```
url?paramName1=paramValue1&paramName2=paramValue2&...
```

An A tag that adds a product code to a URL

```
<a href="cart?productCode=8601">Add to cart</a>
```

The link displayed in a browser

86 (the band) - True Life Songs and Pictures	$14.95	Add To Cart

The URL that's displayed when you click on the link

More examples

A Form tag that calls a JSP

```
<form action="cart.jsp?productCode=jr01" method="post">
```

An A tag that uses a JSP expression for the product code

```
<a href="cart?productCode=<%= productCode %>" >Add to cart</a>
```

Two limitations of URL rewriting

- Most browsers limit the number of characters that can be passed by a URL to 2,000 characters.
- It's difficult to include spaces and special characters such as the ? and & characters in parameter values.

Description

- You can use *URL rewriting* to pass parameters to a servlet or JSP. To do that, you add the parameters to the end of the URL.

Figure 8-13   How to use URL rewriting to pass parameters

How to use hidden fields to pass parameters

In chapter 4, you learned how to code *hidden fields* within an HTML form. Now, figure 8-14 shows how to use hidden fields to pass a parameter from a browser to the server. In particular, it shows how to pass a parameter named productCode to the servlet that's mapped to the /cart URL.

Although the first example in this figure accomplishes the same task as the URL rewriting example in the previous figure, there are a couple advantages to hidden fields. First, a hidden field can contain spaces and other special characters that are difficult to work with when using URL rewriting. Second, there is no limit on the number of characters that can be stored in a hidden field. Of course, in this example, the productCode parameter is short and doesn't contain special characters. As a result, it doesn't illustrate the advantages of using hidden fields.

The second example in this figure shows that you can use a JSP expression to assign a value to a hidden field. Here, the form contains a hidden field that contains the product code, a text box for the quantity, and an Update button. However, the value for the hidden field isn't hard-coded. Instead, a JSP expression retrieves the value for the hidden field. That way, when the user clicks on the Update button, the servlet can tell which product the user wants to update.

A Form tag that uses a hidden text field

```
<form action="cart" method="post">
  <input type="submit" value="Add To Cart">
  <input type="hidden" name="productCode" value="8601">
</form>
```

The form displayed in a browser

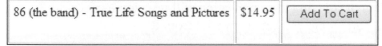

86 (the band) - True Life Songs and Pictures	$14.95	Add To Cart

The URL that's displayed when you click on the button

Murach's Java Servlets and JSP - Microsoft Internet Explorer

File   Edit   View   Favorites   Tools   Help

Back   Search   Favorites

Address http://localhost:8080/ch08cart/cart   Go   Links   SnagIt

Your cart

A Form tag that uses JSP expressions to set hidden field values

```
<form action="cart" method="post">
    <input type="hidden" name="productCode"
        value="<%=product.getCode()%>">
    <input type=text size=2 name="quantity"
        value="<%=lineItem.getQuantity()%>">
    <input type="submit" name="updateButton" value="Update">
</form>
```

One limitation of hidden fields

* Because hidden fields are displayed in the source code for the page that's returned to the browser, anyone can view the parameters by selecting the Source command from the View menu of the browser. As a result, hidden fields aren't appropriate for secure data like passwords.

Description

* You can use *hidden fields* to pass parameters to a servlet or JSP. To do that, you code hidden fields within a Form tag.

Figure 8-14   How to use hidden fields to pass parameters

The Download application

At this point, you should have the basic skills for working with sessions, cookies, URL rewriting, and hidden fields. But it's hard to understand how to use these skills without seeing them in a complete application. That's why figure 8-15 presents an application that lets registered users download sound files from a web site. Although studying this application will take some page flipping because it's seven parts long, you can learn a lot from it.

The user interface

The user interface for the Download application consists of three pages. The Index page lets a user select a CD. Then, if the user hasn't already registered with the site, the Register page registers the user by gathering the user's first name, last name, and email address. Once the user is registered, the Downloads page lets the user select a song to download. If, for example, the user clicks on the MP3 link to the right of a song, that song is downloaded and played.

The Index page

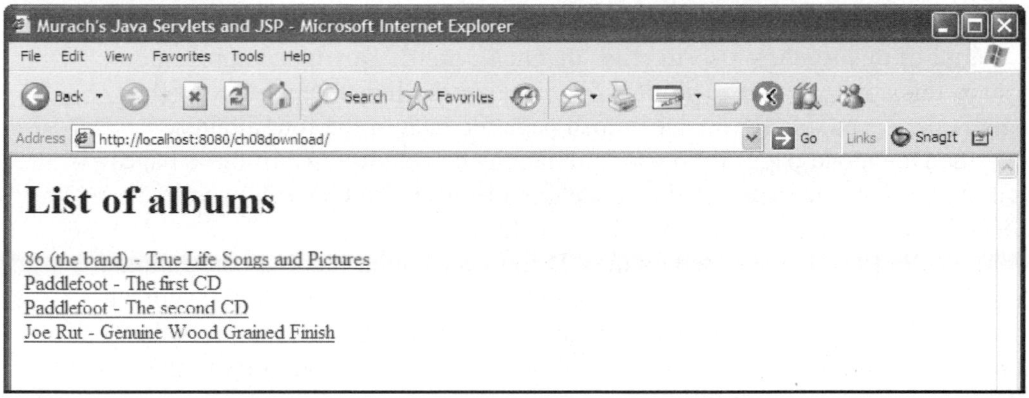

The Register page

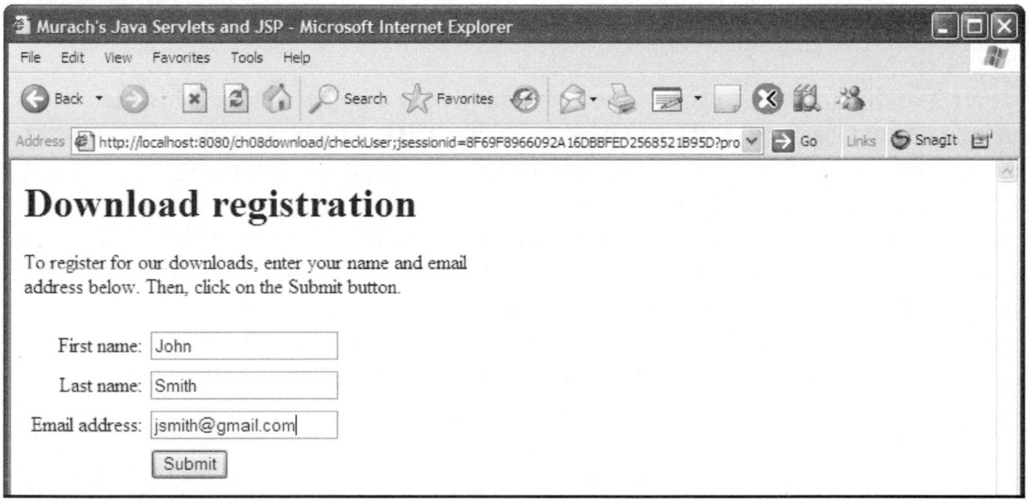

The Downloads page

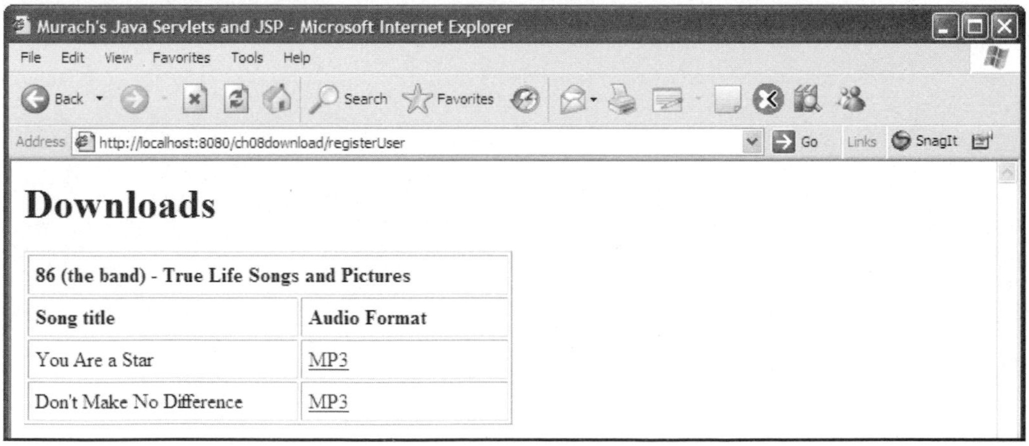

Figure 8-15   The Download application (part 1 of 7)

The file structure

Part 2 of this figure shows the files that make up the Download application. To start, this application uses six JSP files: one for the Index page, one for the Register page, and one for the Download page for each of the four albums. Here, the Download pages follow a rigid naming convention. All of these pages begin with a four-character product code that identifies the CD, followed by an underscore character, followed by "download.jsp".

The MP3 files that are used by the CD follow a similar naming convention. These files are all stored in a subdirectory of the sound directory that's available from another application named musicStore. Here, each subdirectory uses the four-character product code for the CD. When a modern browser goes to the URL for one of these MP3 files, it downloads and plays it.

The web.xml file

Part 2 of this figure also shows the web.xml file for the application. This file maps the CheckUserServlet class to the /checkUser URL, and it maps the RegisterUserServlet class to the /registerUser URL. In addition, it sets the default session timeout to 30 minutes. As a result, unless you change this value in the web.xml file or use the setMaxInactiveInterval method to change the maximum inactive interval for the session, the session will be invalidated if a client doesn't access the session object within 30 minutes. Finally, the web.xml file sets the welcome file list for the application to index.jsp. As a result, if a user requests the root directory of the application, the index.jsp file is displayed.

The names of the jsp files

```
index.jsp
register.jsp
8601_download.jsp
pf01_download.jsp
pf02_download.jsp
jr01_download.jsp
```

The names of the servlet classes

```
download.CheckUserServlet
download.RegisterUserServlet
```

The file structure for the mp3 files

```
musicStore/sound/8601/*.mp3
musicStore/sound/pf01/*.mp3
musicStore/sound/pf02/*.mp3
musicStore/sound/jr01/*.mp3
```

The web.xml file

```xml
<?xml version="1.0" encoding="UTF-8"?>
<web-app version="2.5"
    xmlns="http://java.sun.com/xml/ns/javaee"
    xmlns:xsi="http://www.w3.org/2001/XMLSchema-instance"
    xsi:schemaLocation="http://java.sun.com/xml/ns/javaee
        http://java.sun.com/xml/ns/javaee/web-app_2_5.xsd">

    <servlet>
        <servlet-name>CheckUserServlet</servlet-name>
        <servlet-class>download.CheckUserServlet</servlet-class>
    </servlet>
    <servlet>
        <servlet-name>RegisterUserServlet</servlet-name>
        <servlet-class>download.RegisterUserServlet</servlet-class>
    </servlet>

    <servlet-mapping>
        <servlet-name>CheckUserServlet</servlet-name>
        <url-pattern>/checkUser</url-pattern>
    </servlet-mapping>
    <servlet-mapping>
        <servlet-name>RegisterUserServlet</servlet-name>
        <url-pattern>/registerUser</url-pattern>
    </servlet-mapping>

    <session-config>
        <session-timeout>30</session-timeout>
    </session-config>
    <welcome-file-list>
        <welcome-file>index.jsp</welcome-file>
    </welcome-file-list>
</web-app>
```

Figure 8-15   The Download application (part 2 of 7)

The code for the JSPs and servlets

Part 3 shows the code for the Index page. Here, the A tags for each CD pass the product code for the CD to the CheckUserServlet. Since this JSP uses the encodeURL method of the response object to encode all four URLs, these URLs will track the session even if cookies are disabled in the browser. Remember, though, that all of the URLs for the other JSPs have to be encoded too or session tracking will fail.

The code for the index.jsp file

```
<!doctype html public "-//W3C//DTD HTML 4.0 Transitional//EN">

<html>
<head>
    <title>Murach's Java Servlets and JSP</title>
</head>
<body>

<h1>List of albums</h1>

<p>
<a href="<%=response.encodeURL("checkUser?productCode=8601")%>">
    86 (the band) - True Life Songs and Pictures
</a><br>

<a href="<%=response.encodeURL("checkUser?productCode=pf01")%>">
    Paddlefoot - The first CD
</a><br>

<a href="<%= response.encodeURL("checkUser?productCode=pf02")%>">
    Paddlefoot - The second CD
</a><br>

<a href="<%= response.encodeURL("checkUser?productCode=jr01")%>">
    Joe Rut - Genuine Wood Grained Finish
</a>
</p>

</body>
</html>
```

Figure 8-15   The Download application (part 3 of 7)

Part 4 shows the code for the CheckUserServlet class. This code starts by getting the product code from the request object that was passed from the Index page. Then, it creates a session object by calling the getSession method of the request object, and it sets the product code as an attribute of the session object. From this point on, this product code can be retrieved from the session object.

After that, the code creates a new User object and tries to get the data for this object from the User attribute of the session object. As a result, if the session object contains a User object, which means that the user has called this servlet at least once before in this session, the new User object will get the data from the session object. Otherwise, the getAttribute method will return a null value and the User object will be set to null, which means that the user is calling this servlet for the first time.

The nested if statements that follow provide for three possibilities. First, if the User object is null and a cookie named emailCookie isn't available from previous sessions, the code sets the variable named url to a URL that points to the Register page. Second, if the User object is null but the cookie exists, which means the user has registered before, the code (1) uses the getUser method of the UserIO class to get the data for the User object from a file; (2) sets the User object as an attribute of the session object; and (3) sets the url variable to the appropriate Download JSP. Third, if the User object exists, which means that either the emailCookie was available or the user has already registered in this session, the code sets the url variable to the appropriate Download JSP. Finally, after the nested if statements, the last two statements in the servlet forward the request and response objects to the URL that's stored in the url variable.

If you study this code, you should be able to follow it. It may help to understand, though, that the RegisterUserServlet creates a User object from the user entries and adds this object to the session object. It also creates an emailCookie and adds it to the response object. Then, if your browser has cookies enabled, you won't have to register the next time you use this application. Otherwise, you will have to register each time you use this application. In part 6 of this figure, you can see the code for the RegisterUserServlet.

The code for the CheckUserServlet class

```
package download;

import java.io.*;
import javax.servlet.*;
import javax.servlet.http.*;

import business.User;
import data.UserIO;
import util.CookieUtil;

public class CheckUserServlet extends HttpServlet
{
    public void doGet(HttpServletRequest request,
            HttpServletResponse response)
            throws IOException, ServletException
    {
        String productCode = request.getParameter("productCode");
        HttpSession session = request.getSession();
        session.setAttribute("productCode", productCode);
        User user = (User) session.getAttribute("user");
        String url = "";

        // if the User object doesn't exist, check for the email cookie
        if (user == null)
        {
            Cookie[] cookies = request.getCookies();
            String emailAddress =
                    CookieUtil.getCookieValue(cookies, "emailCookie");

            // if the email cookie doesn't exist, go to the registration page
            if (emailAddress == null || emailAddress.equals(""))
            {
                url = "/register.jsp";
            }
            else
            {
                ServletContext sc = getServletContext();
                String path = sc.getRealPath("WEB-INF/EmailList.txt");
                user = UserIO.getUser(emailAddress, path);
                session.setAttribute("user", user);
                url = "/" + productCode + "_download.jsp";
            }
        }
        // if the User object exists, skip the registration page
        else
        {
            url = "/" + productCode + "_download.jsp";
        }

        // forward to the view
        RequestDispatcher dispatcher =
            getServletContext().getRequestDispatcher(url);
        dispatcher.forward(request, response);
    }
}
```

Figure 8-15   The Download application (part 4 of 7)

Part 5 shows the code for the Register page. Since this code works similarly to the Email List application of the previous chapters, it should be easy to follow. The only difference is that the Register page uses the encodeURL method of the response object to encode the URL in the Form tag, which is essential for browsers with disabled cookies.

What's more interesting is the code for the RegisterUserServlet in part 6 of this figure. It starts by retrieving the parameters that the user entered on the Register page. Then, this servlet creates a User object from these parameters and uses the UserIO class to write the User object to a file that's stored in the WEB-INF directory. After writing the file, this servlet stores the User object in the session object, gets the productCode attribute that has already been stored in the session object, and creates a persistent cookie that stores the user's email address for two years. Last, this servlet uses the productCode variable to forward the request and response objects to the appropriate Download page.

The code for the Download page in part 7 of this figure begins by retrieving the product code from the session object. Then, it uses the product code to locate the MP3 sound files for the CD. On most systems, clicking on one of these links will cause the MP3 file to download and automatically begin playing.

To understand how this application works without cookies, notice that the encodeURL method of the response object has been used to encode every URL that's returned to the client. That makes sure that session tracking will take place so the User object that's stored in the session object will be available until the session ends. Since all of the servlets forward the response object to a JSP, though, you don't have to encode the URLs in the servlets.

The code for the register.jsp file

```
<!doctype html public "-//W3C//DTD HTML 4.0 Transitional//EN">
<html>

<head>
    <title>Murach's Java Servlets and JSP</title>
</head>

<body>

<h1>Download registration</h1>

<p>To register for our downloads, enter your name and email <br>
    address below. Then, click on the Submit button.</p>

<form action="<%= response.encodeURL("registerUser")%>"
      method="post">

  <table cellspacing="5" border="0">
    <tr>
      <td align="right">First name:</td>
      <td><input type="text" name="firstName"></td>
    </tr>
    <tr>
      <td align="right">Last name:</td>
      <td><input type="text" name="lastName"></td>
    </tr>
    <tr>
      <td align="right">Email address:</td>
      <td><input type="text" name="emailAddress"></td>
    </tr>
    <tr>
      <td></td>
      <td><input type="submit" value="Submit"></td>
    </tr>
  </table>

</form>
</body>

</html>
```

Figure 8-15   The Download application (part 5 of 7)

The code for the RegisterUserServlet class

```
package download;

import java.io.*;
import javax.servlet.*;
import javax.servlet.http.*;

import business.User;
import data.UserIO;

public class RegisterUserServlet extends HttpServlet
{
    public void doPost(HttpServletRequest request,
            HttpServletResponse response)
            throws IOException, ServletException
    {
        String firstName = request.getParameter("firstName");
        String lastName = request.getParameter("lastName");
        String emailAddress = request.getParameter("emailAddress");

        User user = new User();
        user.setFirstName(firstName);
        user.setLastName(lastName);
        user.setEmailAddress(emailAddress);

        ServletContext sc = getServletContext();
        String path = sc.getRealPath("WEB-INF/EmailList.txt");

        UserIO.add(user, path);

        HttpSession session = request.getSession();
        session.setAttribute("user", user);
        String productCode = (String) session.getAttribute("productCode");

        Cookie emailCookie = new Cookie("emailCookie", emailAddress);
        emailCookie.setMaxAge(60*60*24*365*2); //set its age to 2 years
        emailCookie.setPath("/"); //allow the entire application to access it
        response.addCookie(emailCookie);

        String url = "/" + productCode + "_download.jsp";
        RequestDispatcher dispatcher =
            getServletContext().getRequestDispatcher(url);
        dispatcher.forward(request, response);
    }
}
```

Figure 8-15   The Download application (part 6 of 7)

The code for the 8601_download.jsp file

```
<html>
<head>
    <title>Murach's Java Servlets and JSP</title>
</head>
<body>

<%
    String productCode = (String) session.getAttribute("productCode");
%>

<h1>Downloads</h1>

<table cellpadding="5" border="1">
<tr><td colspan="2"><b>86 (the band) - True Life Songs and Pictures</b></td>
</tr>
<tr><td width="200"><b>Song title</b></td>
    <td width="150"><b>Audio Format</b></td>
</tr>
<tr><td>You Are a Star</td>
    <td><a href="/musicStore/sound/<%=productCode%>/star.mp3">MP3</a></td>
</tr>
<tr><td>Don't Make No Difference</td>
    <td><a href="/musicStore/sound/<%=productCode%>/no_difference.mp3">MP3</a>
    </td>
</tr>
</table>

<p><a href="<%= response.encodeURL("index.jsp")%>">
    View list of albums</a>.</p>

<p><a href="<%= response.encodeURL("view_cookies.jsp")%>">
    View all cookies</a>.</p>

</body>
</html>
```

Description

- This is one of the four JSPs for downloading songs from CDs. The others are similar.

- When a browser receives the URL for a sound file, it downloads and plays it. That's one of the capabilities of a modern browser.

- This JSP gets the product code from the session object and uses it in the URLs for the sound files. This isn't necessary, though, because the URLs could be hard-coded.

- Another way to handle the downloads is to write one JSP that works for all of the CDs. To implement that, you can store the data for the downloadable songs in one file for each CD. Then, the download JSP can get the product code from the session object, read the related file, and load its data into the table.

Figure 8-15   The Download application (part 7 of 7)

Perspective

The goal of this chapter has been to show you how to use the servlet API to track sessions and work with cookies. If you understand the code in the Download application that's presented at the end of this chapter, this chapter has achieved its goal. As a result, you should now be able to develop web applications that require session tracking.

In the next chapter, you'll learn how to work with a special type of Java class known as a JavaBean. You can use JavaBeans to implement the business classes in a web application. In a typical application, it's common to store a JavaBean in the session object so the next chapter will build on what you've learned here.

Summary

- Because HTTP is a *stateless protocol*, web applications must provide for *session tracking*. That way, an application is able to relate each browser request to a specific browser and to the data for that browser session.

- To provide for session tracking, Java creates one *session object* for each browser session. Then, you can add attributes like variables and objects to this session object, and you can retrieve the values of these attributes in any of the servlets and JSPs that are run during the session.

- One way to implement session tracking is to use *cookies*. Then, the session ID is stored in a cookie on the user's browser and that ID can be related to the session object. This type of session tracking is done automatically by the servlet API, but it doesn't work unless the browser enables cookies.

- The other way to implement session tracking is to use *URL encoding*. With this technique, you have to encode each URL in the JSPs with an ID that identifies the browser for the session, but this works even when the browser doesn't enable cookies.

- *Persistent cookies* are stored on the user's PC, while *per-session cookies* are deleted when the session ends.

- To create cookies, you use the methods of the Cookie class. Then, to add a cookie to the response object so it gets stored on the browser's PC, you use the addCookie method of the response object. And to get the cookies from a browser's PC, you use the getCookies method of the request object.

- To pass parameters to a servlet or a JSP, you can use *URL rewriting* or *hidden fields*. When you use hidden fields, you can easily include spaces and special characters in your parameter values.

Exercise 8-1   Test URL encoding

1. Open the ch08cart project in the ex_starts directory. Then, view the code for index.jsp and cart.jsp files. Note that these JSPs encode the URLs so this application works even if cookies are disabled.

2. Run the application and add two or more items to your cart. Assuming that cookies are enabled in your browser, note how the application encodes the session ID in the URL for the first request, but not for subsequent requests. That's because the application doesn't know whether the browser supports cookies on the first request.

3. Disable cookies in your browser. If you're using Internet Explorer 6, disable cookies on your local system as described in figure 8-5. To do that, you use the Privacy tab to disable cookies, plus the Security tab to disable local cookies.

4. Run the application and add two or more items to your cart. Note how the application encodes the session ID in the URL for every request.

5. Modify the index.jsp and cart.jsp files so they don't encode the URLs. Then, run the application. Note that the URL is only encoded for the first request and that the application doesn't work when you add multiple items to the cart.

6. Enable cookies in your browser. Then, run the application. Note how the application works even though the URLs don't encode the session ID.

7. Close this project.

Exercise 8-2   Use a cookie

1. Open the ch08download project in the ex_starts directory. This application is like the one in figure 8-15, but it also has some other features.

2. Run the Download application and click on an album. Then, when the Register page is displayed, enter your name and email address. That should take you to the Downloads page.

3. If you click on an MP3 link on the Downloads page, the corresponding sound file will be played, *but only if the Music Store application is deployed.* That's because the sound files are stored in that application. You can check the location of these files by looking at the code for one of the download pages for this application. If the Music Store application isn't deployed, an error page is displayed when you click on one of the MP3 links on the Downloads page.

4. Still on the Downloads page, click on the View All Cookies link to see all of the cookies that this application has sent to your browser. Then, click on the Delete All Persistent Cookies link to delete all persistent cookies.

5. Close the browser and run the application again to see that the Register page is displayed again. Now, re-register.

6. Open the RegisterUserServlet class and modify it so it creates a cookie that stores the first name of the user. Then, add code that adds this cookie to the user's browser.

7. Open the index.jsp file and add a line of text to the top of the page that says "Welcome back, *first name*" if the user has the first name cookie. To do this, you can use a JSP scriptlet that uses the getCookieValue method of the CookieUtil class to retrieve the cookie.

8. Test the application to make sure it works correctly.

Exercise 8-3   Use a session attribute

1. With the ch08download project still open, open the CheckUserServlet file. Then, add code that creates a Product object that holds the data for the current product. To get this Product object, you can use the getProduct method of the ProductIO class that's in the data package, like this:

```
ServletContext sc = this.getServletContext();
String productPath = sc.getRealPath("WEB-INF/products.txt");
Product product = ProductIO.getProduct(productCode, productPath);
```

2. Store this Product object as a session attribute.

3. For each product's Download page, retrieve the Product object from the session object and use it to get the product code for the album as well as the description for the album.

4. Run the application and test it to make sure it works correctly. Then, delete all cookies and restart the application to make sure the RegisterUserServlet still works correctly.

5. Close the project.

Exercise 8-4   Use URL rewriting instead of hidden fields

1. Open the ch08cart project in the ex_starts directory.

2. Open the cart.jsp file. Then, convert the Remove button into a Remove link that uses URL rewriting.

3. Run the application and test the Remove link. Note the differences between the Remove link and the Update button.

4. Close the project.

9

How to use standard JSP tags with JavaBeans

In chapters 5 through 7, you learned how to use the User class to create User objects that contain the data for a user of a web application. In this chapter, you'll learn that this class follows all the rules for a JavaBean, which means that you can use standard JSP tags to work with this class. This reduces the amount of Java code that's in your JSPs and makes it easier for non-programmers to create the JSPs that work with business classes.

Before you read this chapter, you should know that the standard JSP tags for working with JavaBeans are an older technology that was widely used before the JSP 2.0 specification. As a result, if you're maintaining the code for an older Java web application, you'll probably need to know how to use these tags.

However, if you're developing new Java web applications, you will probably want to use the Expression Language (EL) tags that were introduced with the JSP 2.0 specification. In that case, you can read the introduction to JavaBeans at the start of this chapter and then skip to the next chapter to learn how to use the EL tags with JavaBeans. For most purposes, you'll find that these tags work better than the JSP tags.

An introduction to JavaBeans

When you code a class that defines a *JavaBean*, or *bean*, you can use special JSP tags to work with it. In this topic, you'll learn how to define a JavaBean, and you'll be introduced to three types of JSP tags that you can use to create a bean and work with its properties.

How to code a JavaBean

Figure 9-1 shows the code for the User class. This class is a JavaBean because it follows the three rules that all JavaBeans must follow.

First, a JavaBean must contain a constructor that doesn't accept any arguments. In this figure, for example, the zero-argument constructor uses three statements to set all three instance variables equal to empty strings. As a result, a newly created User object stores empty strings for its instance variables instead of null values, which is usually what you want.

Second, a JavaBean can't declare any public instance variables. In this figure, for example, all of the instance variables are declared as private. However, it's also possible to declare instance variables as protected.

Third, a JavaBean must contain get and set methods for all of the *properties* that need to be accessed by JSPs. In this figure, for example, the methods provide access to all of the instance variables of the User class, so this class qualifies as a bean. Of course, you can also code get and set methods that provide access to other properties in a bean.

To provide access to a Boolean value, you code is and set methods instead of get and set methods. For example, you could code methods named isEmailUpdated and setEmailUpdated to provide access to a Boolean property named emailUpdated.

When you code the get, set, and is methods, you must follow the capitalization conventions used in this figure. In other words, each method name must start with a lowercase letter and each property name must start with an uppercase letter. In this figure, for example, the setFirstName method uses a lowercase s to start the method name and an uppercase f to start the property name.

In addition to following these three rules, it's common, though not required, for a JavaBean to implement the Serializable interface. The Serializable interface is a tagging interface in the java.io package that indicates that a class contains get, set, and is methods that another class can use to read and write an object's instance variables to and from a persistent data source. In this figure, for example, the User class implements the Serializable interface and contains all the necessary get and set methods. As a result, some servlet engines can save and restore this object if that's necessary. For example, the Tomcat container can save the User object's state before it shuts down, and it can restore the User object's state when it starts up the next time.

The code for the User bean class

```
package business;

import java.io.Serializable;

public class User implements Serializable
{
    private String firstName;
    private String lastName;
    private String emailAddress;

    public User()
    {
        firstName = "";
        lastName = "";
        emailAddress = "";
    }

    public User(String first, String last, String email)
    {
        firstName = first;
        lastName = last;
        emailAddress = email;
    }

    public void setFirstName(String f)
    {
        firstName = f;
    }

    public String getFirstName()
    {
        return firstName;
    }

    public void setLastName(String l)
    {
        lastName = l;
    }

    public String getLastName()
    {
        return lastName;
    }

    public void setEmailAddress(String e)
    {
        emailAddress = e;
    }

    public String getEmailAddress()
    {
        return emailAddress;
    }
}
```

Figure 9-1   How to code a JavaBean

When coding a web application, it's common to use JavaBeans to define the business objects of an application. These beans can be called *invisible JavaBeans* because they don't define visible components. The focus of this book is on this type of JavaBean.

You should realize, though, that JavaBeans are capable of doing much more than defining business objects. For instance, JavaBeans can be used to define buttons and other user interface controls.

You should also realize that there's another type of JavaBean called an *Enterprise JavaBean* (*EJB*). Although EJBs are similar in some ways to JavaBeans, EJBs are more complex and difficult to code than JavaBeans. To learn more about them, you can get a book that's dedicated solely to EJBs.

A JSP that uses a JavaBean

The main benefit that you get from coding your business classes so they qualify as JavaBeans is that you can then use special JSP tags for working with the beans. This is illustrated by the JSP in figure 9-2. Here, the useBean tag accesses the User bean. Then, if a User object with the same name already exists within the session object, this tag accesses that User object. Otherwise, this tag creates the object by calling the zero-argument constructor of the User class. Because the object is created from a bean class, it can be called a *bean*.

After the bean has been created, the three getProperty tags display the values of the properties that have been set in the bean. Later in this chapter, you'll learn more about how this works. For now, you just need to understand that you can use the getProperty tag to get the properties of a bean.

You can also use setProperty tag to set the properties of a bean. However, when you use the MVC pattern, the properties of a bean are usually set by servlet code. As a result, you don't need to code setProperty tags as often as getProperty tags.

This figure also shows a JSP that does the same task by using scriptlets and expressions. Since this code is an unwieldy mix of Java code and HTML, it's easy to see how using JavaBeans and JSP tags can make your JSPs easier to code and maintain. In fact, the JSP that uses the JSP tags doesn't require any Java code at all. This makes it easier for non-programmers to code JSPs.

A JSP that uses JSP tags to access the User bean

```
<jsp:useBean id="user" scope="session" class="business.User"/>
<table cellspacing="5" cellpadding="5" border="1">
    <tr>
        <td align="right">First name:</td>
        <td><jsp:getProperty name="user" property="firstName"/></td>
    </tr>
    <tr>
        <td align="right">Last name:</td>
        <td><jsp:getProperty name="user" property="lastName"/></td>
    </tr>
    <tr>
        <td align="right">Email address:</td>
        <td><jsp:getProperty name="user" property="emailAddress"/></td>
    </tr>
</table>
```

The same JSP without using JSP tags to access the User bean

```
<%@ page import="business.User" %>
<%
    User user = (User) session.getAttribute("user");
    if (user == null)
    {
        user = new User();
    }
%>

<table cellspacing="5" cellpadding="5" border="1">
    <tr>
        <td align="right">First name:</td>
        <td><%= user.getFirstName() %></td>
    </tr>
    <tr>
        <td align="right">Last name:</td>
        <td><%= user.getLastName() %></td>
    </tr>
    <tr>
        <td align="right">Email address:</td>
        <td><%= user.getEmailAddress() %></td>
    </tr>
</table>
```

Description

- JSP tags for using JavaBeans make it easier for non-programmers to use beans because they look more like HTML tags and don't require the use of Java code.

Figure 9-2   A JSP that uses standard JSP tags to access a JavaBean

How to code JSP tags for JavaBeans

How to code the useBean tag

Figure 9-3 shows how to code the useBean tag to access a bean. Although this tag looks and works much like an HTML tag, all of the JSP tags for working with JavaBeans use XML syntax. As a result, when you code these tags, you must use lowercase and uppercase characters as shown in this figure; you must code a front slash to mark the end of the opening tag or the start of a closing tag; and you must code single or double quotation marks around all attributes of a tag.

To code a simple useBean tag, you code the name of the tag followed by the attributes of the tag. In this example, the id attribute specifies the name that's used to access the bean, the class attribute specifies the package and class of the bean, and the scope attribute specifies the *scope* of the bean.

When you code the scope attribute, you can specify one of four values: page, request, session, and application. The value of the scope attribute specifies the object that stores the bean and that determines how long the bean will be available to the rest of the application. For instance, the first example sets the scope attribute to session, which means that the bean is bound to the session object. As a result, any JSP or servlet that has access to the session object will have access to this bean. If you don't specify the scope attribute, the scope will be set to "page" by default, which means that the bean will only be available to the current JSP.

If a bean that matches the attributes specified in the useBean tag exists, this tag creates a reference to that object. Otherwise, the useBean tag creates a new object by calling the zero-argument constructor of the specified class. If you study the first example and its equivalent scriptlet, you should get a better idea of how the useBean tag works.

If you want to initialize a bean the first time it's created, you can use an opening and closing useBean tag. To do that, you code the front slash at the beginning of the closing tag instead of coding it at the end of the opening tag. Then, you can code initialization statements within the opening and closing tags. In this figure, the initialization statements set all of the properties of the User bean to string values. However, these statements will only be executed if a bean that matches the specified attributes isn't found.

The useBean tag

Syntax

```
<jsp:useBean id="beanName" class="package.Class" scope="scopeValue" />
```

Example

```
<jsp:useBean id="user" class="business.User" scope="session" />
```

Equivalent scriptlet

```
<%@ page import="business.User" %>
<%
    User user = (User) session.getAttribute("user");
    if (user == null)
    {
        user = new User();
        session.setAttribute("user", user);
    }
%>
```

How to include initialization statements for a bean

```
<jsp:useBean id="user" class="business.User" scope="session" >
    <!-- Note: these statements run only if a new bean is created -->
    <jsp:setProperty name="user" property="firstName" value="John" />
    <jsp:setProperty name="user" property="lastName" value="Smith" />
    <jsp:setProperty name="user" property="emailAddress"
                     value="jsmith@hotmail.com" />
</jsp:useBean>
```

Scope values

Value	Description
page	The bean is stored in the implicit pageContext object for the JSP and is only available to the current page. This is the default setting.
request	The bean is stored in the HttpServletRequest object and is available to all JSPs and servlets that have access to the current request object.
session	The bean is stored in the HttpSession object and is available to all JSPs and servlets that have access to this object. For more information about session objects, see chapter 8.
application	The bean is stored in the ServletContext object and is available to all JSPs and servlets that have access to this object.

Description

- The useBean tag is used to access a bean and, if necessary, create a bean from the JavaBean class.

- The *scope* of a bean refers to the object that stores the bean. This controls how long the bean is available to the rest of the application.

- The JSP tags for working with beans use XML syntax. As a result, these tags are case-sensitive, a front slash indicates the end of the opening tag or the start of a closing tag, and all attributes must be enclosed by single or double quotes.

Figure 9-3   How to code the useBean tag

How to code the getProperty and setProperty tags

Once you code a useBean tag to access or create a bean, you can use the getProperty tag to get the values stored in the bean, and you can use the setProperty tag to set the values stored in the bean. Figure 9-4 shows how.

To get the value of a property that's stored in a bean, you code a getProperty tag. Here, the name attribute specifies the name of the bean, so it should match the id attribute of the useBean tag. If, for example, you set the name attribute to "user," this attribute accesses the User bean specified by the useBean tag in the last figure. Then, the property attribute specifies the name of the property that you want to access. For example, a value of "firstName" accesses the firstName property of the User bean.

To set a property of a bean, you code a setProperty tag. In this tag, you code the name attribute and the property attribute to specify the name of the bean and the property that you want to set. Then, you code the value attribute to specify the value that you want the property set to as shown in this figure or the param attribute as shown in the next figure.

If you need to code one of the special characters shown in this figure as part of a value attribute, you can use the escape sequences shown here. If, for example, you're using single quotes to identify your attributes, you can use an escape sequence like the one in the first escape sequence example to set the lastName property of the User bean to O'Neil. However, you can often avoid using escape sequences by switching the type of quotation mark that you use to identify an attribute. This is illustrated by the second escape sequence example.

When you work with the getProperty tag, you should be aware that it won't get the value of a property if the value is null or an empty string. Similarly, you can't use the setProperty tag to set the value of a property to null or an empty string. If you need to do that, though, you can do it in the constructor of the bean or in a servlet that accesses the bean.

The getProperty tag

Syntax

```
<jsp:getProperty name="beanName" property="propertyName" />
```

Example

```
<jsp:getProperty name="user" property="firstName" />
```

Equivalent JSP expression

```
<%= user.getFirstName() %>
```

The setProperty tag with a value attribute

Syntax

```
<jsp:setProperty name="beanName" property="propertyName" value="value" />
```

Example

```
<jsp:setProperty name="user" property="firstName" value="John" />
```

Equivalent scriptlet

```
<% user.setFirstName("John"); %>
```

Escape sequences within attributes

Character	Escape sequence
'	\'
"	\"
\	\\
<%	<\%
%>	%\>

How to use an escape sequence

```
<jsp:setProperty name='user' property='lastName' value='O\'Neil' />
```

How to avoid an escape sequence

```
<jsp:setProperty name="user" property="lastName" value="O'Neil" />
```

Description

- The name attribute for the getProperty and setProperty tags must match the id attribute in the useBean tag.

- To code special characters within an attribute, you can use escape sequences. However, if you enclose an attribute in double quotes, you don't need to use escape sequences for single quotes. Conversely, if you enclose an attribute in single quotes, you don't need to use the escape sequence for double quotes.

- The getProperty tag can't be used to get a null value or an empty string, and the setProperty tag can't be used to set a property to a null value or an empty string. However, you can use the constructor of a bean or the code in a servlet to set a property to a null value or an empty string.

Figure 9-4   How to code the getProperty and setProperty tags

How to set the properties of a bean from request parameters

Figure 9-5 shows you how to use the setProperty tag to set the properties of a bean from the parameters of a request object. To do that, you use the param attribute instead of the value attribute. Or, if the name of the property matches the name of the parameter, you can omit the param attribute.

If the names of the property and the parameter are different, you need to code the param attribute to specify the name of the parameter that you want to get from the request object. This is illustrated by the first example. Here, the name of the property is "firstName" and the name of the parameter is "userFirstName," so the value of that parameter will be stored in the property.

If the names of the property and the parameter are the same, you don't need to code the param attribute as shown in the second example. Here, the name of both the property and the parameter is "firstName," so the corresponding parameter value will be stored in the firstName property.

If the names of several properties and parameters are the same, you can take this one step further as shown by the third example. Here, an asterisk is coded for the property attribute. Then, all of the properties in the bean with matching parameter names in the request object will be set to the values of those parameters. Since the parameter names should match the corresponding property names if you use consistent naming conventions, this is a common JSP coding technique.

The syntax of the setProperty tag with a param attribute

```
<jsp:setProperty name="name" property="propertyName" param="paramName" />
```

Example 1: Setting a property that has a different name than the parameter

```
<jsp:setProperty name="user" property="firstName" param="userFirstName" />
```

Equivalent scriptlet

```
<% user.setFirstName(request.getParameter("userFirstName")); %>
```

Example 2: Setting a property that has the same name as the parameter

```
<jsp:setProperty name="user" property="firstName" />
```

Equivalent scriptlet

```
<% user.setFirstName(request.getParameter("firstName")); %>
```

Example 3: Setting all properties to the parameters with the same names

```
<jsp:setProperty name="user" property="*" />
```

Equivalent scriptlet

```
<%
    user.setFirstName(request.getParameter("firstName"));
    user.setLastName(request.getParameter("lastName"));
    user.setEmailAddress(request.getParameter("emailAddress"));
%>
```

Description

- You can use the param attribute of the setProperty tag to set the property of a bean to the value of a parameter of the request object.
- If the parameter name is the same as the property name, you can omit the param attribute.
- If the names of the bean properties are the same as the names of the parameters in the request object, you can set the bean properties by specifying an asterisk in the property attribute.

Figure 9-5   How to set the properties of a bean from request parameters

How to set non-string data types in a bean

So far, all of the examples in this chapter use the setProperty tag to set properties to strings. But what happens if you use the setProperty tag to set properties with primitive data types or their wrapper classes? The good news is that the setProperty method automatically does these conversions for you as shown in figure 9-6. As a result, you set properties with these data types the same way that you set properties with string values.

To convert the data types, the JSP engine uses the valueOf method of the wrapper class and, if necessary, converts the object to the corresponding primitive data type. For instance, the first example assumes that the price property of the Product bean uses a double value. Here, the setProperty tag sets the value of the price property to a value of "15.50". Since the setPrice method in the Product bean class accepts a double data type, the JSP engine uses the static valueOf method of the Double class to return a Double object. Then, it calls the doubleValue method from that object to return a double data type. This sets the price property of the Product bean to the double value of 15.50.

The second example shows that these automatic conversions work even when working with the parameters of the request object, which are always returned as strings. When the JSP engine reads the setProperty tag in this example, it performs the same conversion as in the first example.

The servlet code in this figure shows that the JSP engine has automatically converted the string to the appropriate data type. Here, the getPrice method of the Product object returns a double type. This code also shows how to access a bean that has application scope. To do that, you begin by calling the getServletContext method to return a ServletContext object. Then, you can call the getAttribute method of the ServletContext object to return the Product bean.

How the JSP engine automatically converts data types

Type	Conversion calls
double	**Double.valueOf**(valueOrParamString)**.doubleValue**()
Double	**Double.valueOf**(valueOrParamString)
int	**Integer.valueOf**(valueOrParamString)**.intValue**()
Integer	**Integer.valueOf**(valueOrParamString)
float	**Float.valueOf**(valueOrParamString)**.floatValue**()
Float	**Float.valueOf**(valueOrParamString)
long	**Long.valueOf**(valueOrParamString)**.longValue**()
Long	**Long.valueOf**(valueOrParamString)
short	**Short.valueOf**(valueOrParamString)**.shortValue**()
Short	**Short.valueOf**(valueOrParamString)
byte	**Byte.valueOf**(valueOrParamString)**.byteValue**()
Byte	**Byte.valueOf**(valueOrParamString)
boolean	**Boolean.valueOf**(valueOrParamString)**.booleanValue**()
Boolean	**Boolean.valueOf**(valueOrParamString)
char	**Character.valueOf**(valueOrParamString)**.charValue**()
Character	**Character.valueOf**(valueOrParamString)

How to use the setProperty method to set a non-string value

Example 1

```
<jsp:useBean id="product" class="business.Product" scope="application" />
<jsp:setProperty name="product" property="price" value="15.50"/>
```

Example 2

```
<jsp:useBean id="product" class="business.Product" scope="application" />
<jsp:setProperty name="product" property="price" param="productPrice" />
```

Servlet code that accesses a Product bean that has application scope

```
ServletContext context = getServletContext();
Product product = (Product) context.getAttribute("product");
double price = product.getPrice();
```

Description

- The setProperty method automatically converts all of the primitive data types and their wrapper classes to the data types of the properties.

Figure 9-6   How to set non-string data types in a bean

How to use interface and abstract class types with beans

Most of the time, you won't need to use an interface or abstract class type to refer to a bean. As a result, you may want to skip this complex topic until you face that requirement. If you do need to do that, though, you can code a type attribute in the useBean tag as shown in figure 9-7.

In the examples in this figure, the JavaBean classes named Order and CatalogRequest implement the Addressable interface, and this interface contains set and get methods for instance variables named city and state. As a result, every class that implements this interface must implement the setCity, getCity, setState, and getState methods.

To start, this figure shows how to code a useBean tag to create an Order bean that can be referred to by the Addressable interface. Usually, though, you do that in a servlet. That's why this figure also shows servlet code that creates either an Order or a CatalogRequest bean that can be referred to by the Addressable interface.

Since the Order and CatalogRequest beans implement the Addressable interface, you can use the JSP tags to work with the properties that are defined in the interface. If you use JSP tags to access an existing bean, you don't need to include the class attribute. But if the bean doesn't exist and the class attribute isn't coded, the bean will be set to a null value. For that reason, you should code the class attribute when you aren't sure that the bean exists.

How to create a bean of an interface or abstract class type

Syntax for creating a specific type of bean

```
<jsp:useBean id="beanName" class="package.Class"
             type="package.InterfaceOrAbstractClass" scope="scopeValue" />
```

Example

```
<jsp:useBean id="addr" class="business.Order" type="business.Addressable"
    scope="session" />
```

Equivalent scriptlet

```
<%@ page import="business.*" %>
<%
    Addressable addr = new Order();
    session.setAttribute("addr", addr);
%>
```

Servlet code that creates two Addressable beans in the session

```
Addressable addr = null;
if (source.equals("OrderForm"))
    addr = new Order();
else if (source.equals("Request"))
    addr = new CatalogRequest();
session.setAttribute("addr", addr);
```

How to access beans by interface or abstract class type

Syntax for accessing an interface type

```
<jsp:useBean id="beanName" type="package.InterfaceOrAbstractClass"
             scope="scopeValue" />
```

Example

```
<jsp:useBean id="addr" type="business.Addressable" scope="session" />
<jsp:getProperty name="addr" property="city" />
<jsp:getProperty name="addr" property="state" />
```

Equivalent scriptlet

```
<%@ page import="business.*" %>
<%
    Addressable addr = (Addressable) session.getAttribute("addr");
%>
<%= addr.getCity() %>
<%= addr.getState() %>
```

Description

- If you want to refer to a bean by an interface or abstract class type, you can code a type attribute that specifies the interface or abstract class. For this to work, the bean class must implement the interface or extend the abstract class.

Figure 9-7   How to use interface and abstract class types with beans

The Email List application with JSP tags for JavaBeans

When you develop a web application with JavaBeans and JSP tags, you can use either the MVC pattern or the Model 1 architecture to structure the application. To illustrate, this chapter finishes by showing you the Email List application first when the MVC pattern is used and then when the Model 1 architecture is used.

The application when the MVC pattern is used

Figure 9-8 presents a simple version of the Email List application that uses the MVC pattern. It consists of a first JSP that starts the application, a servlet, and a second JSP that presents the results of the servlet.

The JSP in part 1 of this figure starts the application. It uses the useBean tag to access the User bean and bind it to the current session. Then, it uses three getProperty tags to display the values of the properties that are stored in the User bean. The first time this JSP is requested in a session, though, the bean will contain empty strings for its properties so no values will be displayed in the table for this page.

Why then use a JSP instead of an HTML page to start this application? Because the bean will have properties once the user enters data and clicks the Submit button. Then, if the user returns to this JSP, it will display those values. If, for example, the user clicks the Return button on the second page to return to this page, those values will be displayed. For some applications, this is useful.

When the user clicks the Submit button on the first JSP, the Form tag requests the AddToEmailListServlet class shown in part 2 of this figure. This servlet retrieves the parameters stored in the request object, creates a new User bean, sets the values for the User bean, and writes the User bean to a file. Then, this servlet retrieves the session object and binds the User bean to it, which replaces the bean created by the first JSP with the new bean. Finally, this servlet forwards the request and response objects to the second JSP.

Part 3 of this figure shows that the second JSP begins by using the useBean tag to load the User bean that was stored in the session object by the servlet. Then, this page uses three getProperty tags to display the values that are stored in the bean. This shows that the JSPs for the view don't require any Java code at all.

The code for join_email_list.jsp

```
<!DOCTYPE HTML PUBLIC "-//W3C//DTD HTML 4.01 Transitional//EN">

<html>

<head>
    <title>Murach's Java Servlets and JSP</title>
</head>

<body>

<h1>Join our email list</h1>
<p>To join our email list, enter your name and
    email address below. <br>
    Then, click on the Submit button.</p>

<form action="addToEmailList" method="post">
<jsp:useBean id="user" scope="session" class="business.User"/>
<table cellspacing="5" border="0">
    <tr>
        <td align="right">First name:</td>
        <td><input type="text" name="firstName"
            value="<jsp:getProperty name="user" property="firstName"/>">
        </td>
    </tr>
    <tr>
        <td align="right">Last name:</td>
        <td><input type="text" name="lastName"
            value="<jsp:getProperty name="user" property="lastName"/>">
        </td>
    </tr>
    <tr>
        <td align="right">Email address:</td>
        <td><input type="text" name="emailAddress"
            value="<jsp:getProperty name="user" property="emailAddress"/>">
        </td>
    </tr>
    <tr>
        <td></td>
        <td><br><input type="submit" value="Submit"></td>
    </tr>
</table>
</form>

</body>

</html>
```

Figure 9-8   The Email List application when the MVC pattern is used (part 1 of 3)

The code for the AddToEmailListServlet class

```
package email;

import java.io.*;
import javax.servlet.*;
import javax.servlet.http.*;

import business.User;
import data.UserIO;

public class AddToEmailListServlet extends HttpServlet
{
    protected void doPost(HttpServletRequest request,
                          HttpServletResponse response)
                          throws ServletException, IOException
    {
        // get parameters from the request
        String firstName = request.getParameter("firstName");
        String lastName = request.getParameter("lastName");
        String emailAddress = request.getParameter("emailAddress");

        // create the User object
        User user = new User();
        user.setFirstName(firstName);
        user.setLastName(lastName);
        user.setEmailAddress(emailAddress);

        // write the User object to a file
        ServletContext sc = getServletContext();
        String path = sc.getRealPath("/WEB-INF/EmailList.txt");
        UserIO.addRecord(user, path);

        // store the User object in the session
        HttpSession session = request.getSession();
        session.setAttribute("user", user);

        // forward request and response to JSP page
        String url = "/display_email_entry.jsp";
        RequestDispatcher dispatcher =
            getServletContext().getRequestDispatcher(url);
        dispatcher.forward(request, response);
    }

    protected void doGet(HttpServletRequest request,
                         HttpServletResponse response)
                         throws ServletException, IOException
    {
        this.doPost(request, response);
    }
}
```

Figure 9-8   The Email List application when the MVC pattern is used (part 2 of 3)

The code for display_email_entry.jsp

```
<!DOCTYPE HTML PUBLIC "-//W3C//DTD HTML 4.01 Transitional//EN">

<html>

<head>
    <title>Murach's Java Servlets and JSP</title>
</head>

<body>

<h1>Thanks for joining our email list</h1>

<p>Here is the information that you entered:</p>

<jsp:useBean id="user" scope="session" class="business.User"/>
<table cellspacing="5" cellpadding="5" border="1">
    <tr>
        <td align="right">First name:</td>
        <td><jsp:getProperty name="user" property="firstName"/></td>
    </tr>
    <tr>
        <td align="right">Last name:</td>
        <td><jsp:getProperty name="user" property="lastName"/></td>
    </tr>
    <tr>
        <td align="right">Email address:</td>
        <td><jsp:getProperty name="user" property="emailAddress"/></td>
    </tr>
</table>

<p>To enter another email address, click on the Back <br>
button in your browser or the Return button shown <br>
below.</p>

<form action="join_email_list.jsp" method="post">
    <input type="submit" value="Return">
</form>

</body>
</html>
```

Figure 9-8   The Email List application when the MVC pattern is used (part 3 of 3)

The application when the Model 1 architecture is used

When the processing for an application is simple, the Model 1 architecture sometimes works better than the MVC pattern (or Model 2 architecture). In fact, the JSP setProperty tag is designed to help make the Model 1 architecture easier to implement.

When you use this architecture, as you should remember from chapter 7, you don't use a servlet as the controller. Instead, a JSP handles both the processing and the presentation for the application. For the Email List application, then, the first JSP will call the second JSP instead of the servlet. That's the only change that needs to be made to the first JSP in figure 9-8.

In figure 9-9, you can see the second JSP for the Email List application when the Model 1 architecture is used. Here, the first two JSP tags access the User bean that was created by the first JSP and set the properties of the bean to the parameter values of the request object. This shows that one JSP can access a bean created by another JSP without using a servlet as a controller.

Then, the JSP uses a scriptlet to write the data of the bean to a file. This shows that you often have to use some Java code in a JSP when you use the Model 1 architecture. Unfortunately, that makes it difficult for non-programmers to code JSPs, which usually means that the designers and programmers have to work together to create JSPs, even simple ones like this. That's why it's usually better to use the MVC pattern.

The code for display_email_entry.jsp when Model 1 architecture is used

```
<!DOCTYPE HTML PUBLIC "-//W3C//DTD HTML 4.01 Transitional//EN">

<html>

<head>
    <title>Murach's Java Servlets and JSP</title>
</head>

<body>

<h1>Thanks for joining our email list</h1>

<p>Here is the information that you entered:</p>

<%@ page import="data.*" %>
<jsp:useBean id="user" scope="session" class="business.User"/>
<jsp:setProperty name="user" property="*" />
<%
        ServletContext sc = getServletContext();
        String path = sc.getRealPath("/WEB-INF/EmailList.txt");
        UserIO.addRecord(user, path);
%>
<table cellspacing="5" cellpadding="5" border="1">
    <tr>
        <td align="right">First name:</td>
        <td><jsp:getProperty name="user" property="firstName"/></td>
    </tr>
    <tr>
        <td align="right">Last name:</td>
        <td><jsp:getProperty name="user" property="lastName"/></td>
    </tr>
    <tr>
        <td align="right">Email address:</td>
        <td><jsp:getProperty name="user" property="emailAddress"/></td>
    </tr>
</table>

<p>To enter another email address, click on the Back <br>
button in your browser or the Return button shown <br>
below.</p>

<form action="join_email_list.jsp" method="post">
    <input type="submit" value="Return">
</form>

</body>
</html>
```

Figure 9-9   The second JSP in the application when the Model 1 architecture is used

Perspective

The goal of this chapter has been to show you how to code JavaBeans and how to code the JSP tags that work with JavaBeans. Now, if you understand the Email List applications in figures 9-8 and 9-9, this chapter has achieved its goal. At this point, you should be able to maintain existing applications that use JavaBeans and the standard JSP tags.

In the next chapter, though, you'll learn how to use the Expression Language (EL) tags that were introduced with the JSP 2.0 specification. As you'll see, these tags provide a more elegant way to access JavaBeans. They also provide functionality that isn't available with the standard JSP tags.

Summary

- A *JavaBean*, or *bean*, is a Java class that (1) has a zero-argument constructor, (2) doesn't include any public instance variables, and (3) provides get, set, and is methods for all of its *properties*, which are represented by the instance variables.

- When you use JavaBeans in your web applications, you can use JSP tags to create a bean object and get and set its properties. These tags help reduce the amount of Java code in a JSP and thus make it easier for non-programmers to code JSPs.

- The useBean tag lets you access or create a bean object. Then, the getProperty and setProperty tags let you get and set the properties of the object.

- The setProperty tag automatically converts the primitive data types and their wrapper classes to the data types of the properties.

- You can use JavaBeans and JSP tags with both the MVC pattern and the Model 1 architecture. The choice depends on the processing requirements of the application.

Exercise 9-1   Test the Email List application

In this exercise, you'll view and test the Email List application that's presented in this chapter.

1. Open the ch09email project in the ex_starts directory.

2. Open the User class in the business package. Note how it follows all the rules of a JavaBean and how it implements the Serializable interface.

3. Open the two JSPs. Note how they both use standard JSP tags to work with the User bean.

4. Open the AddToEmailListServlet class in the email package. Note how it stores the User object as an attribute of the session.

5. Run the application and enter valid data for a user. Then, click on the Return button to return to the first page of the application. Note that the text boxes on this page contain the information that you entered.

Exercise 9-2   Use JSP tags to work with beans

In this exercise, you'll enhance the Download application of chapter 8 and exercises 8-2 and 8-3 so its JSPs use the standard JSP tags to access the information that's stored in the Product bean.

1. Open the ch09download project in the ex_starts directory. Then, run this application to refresh your memory about how it works.

2. Open the User and Product classes that are stored in the business package. Make sure that these classes follow the rules for a JavaBean and that they implement the Serializable interface.

3. Open the CheckUserServlet and the RegisterUserServlet classes stored in the download package and note how they store the User and Product objects as attributes of the session object.

4. Open the download.jsp page for each product and use the standard JSP tags to access the product code and description from the Product bean that's stored in the session.

5. Run the ch09download application to make sure it works correctly.

How to use the JSP Expression Language (EL)

In chapter 9, you learned how to code a JavaBean and how to use some of the standard JSP tags to get properties from a JavaBean. Now, in this chapter, you'll learn how to use the Expression Language (EL) that was introduced with JSP 2.0 to get properties from a JavaBean. Along the way, you'll see that EL is a significant improvement over the standard JSP tags.

If you skipped chapter 9, you should still be able to understand this chapter, as long as you know how to code a JavaBean. If you don't, you should go back to chapter 9 and read the introduction to JavaBeans at the start of that chapter. Then, you'll be ready for this chapter.

An introduction to JSP Expression Language

The JSP *Expression Language* (*EL*) provides a compact syntax that lets you get data from JavaBeans, maps, arrays, and lists that have been stored as attributes of a web application. To illustrate, figure 10-1 presents two examples that get data from a User object named user that has been stored as an attribute of the session object.

Both of these examples assume that the User class follows all the rules for creating a JavaBean that are shown in figure 9-1 of chapter 9. Then, the first example uses EL to get the properties of the User bean, and the second example uses standard JSP tags to get those properties. This should give you a quick idea of how EL can improve your JSPs.

Advantages of EL

EL has several advantages over standard JSP tags. First, if you compare the EL example to the standard JSP tag example, I think you'll agree that the EL example is more elegant and compact, which makes it easier to code and to read.

Second, although it isn't shown in this figure, EL makes it easy to access nested properties. For example, you can access a property named code from a JavaBean named product that's in a JavaBean named item like this:

```
${item.product.code}
```

Third, although standard JSP tags only let you access JavaBeans, EL lets you access collections such as arrays, maps, and lists. A *map* is a collection that implements the Map interface, such as a HashMap collection. A *list* is a collection that implements the List interface, such as the ArrayList<> collection. For more information about arrays and collections, you can refer to *Murach's Java SE 6*.

Fourth, EL usually handles null values better than standard JSP tags. For example, instead of returning a null value for a string variable, EL returns an empty string, which is usually what you want.

Fifth, EL provides functionality that isn't available from the standard JSP tags. For example, it lets you work with HTTP headers, cookies, and context initialization parameters. It also lets you perform calculations and comparisons.

Disadvantages of EL

Unlike the standard JSP tags, EL doesn't create a JavaBean if the JavaBean hasn't already been stored as an attribute. In addition, EL doesn't provide a way to set the properties of a JavaBean. However, when you use the MVC architecture, you typically use a servlet to create a JavaBean, set its properties, and store it as an attribute. As a result, these disadvantages aren't an issue.

A JSP that uses EL to access a User object named user that has been stored in the session object

```
<table cellspacing="5" cellpadding="5" border="1">
    <tr>
        <td align="right">First name:</td>
        <td>${user.firstName}</td>
    </tr>
    <tr>
        <td align="right">Last name:</td>
        <td>${user.lastName}</td>
    </tr>
    <tr>
        <td align="right">Email address:</td>
        <td>${user.emailAddress}</td>
    </tr>
</table>
```

The same JSP using standard JSP tags

```
<jsp:useBean id="user" scope="session" class="business.User"/>
<table cellspacing="5" cellpadding="5" border="1">
    <tr>
        <td align="right">First name:</td>
        <td><jsp:getProperty name="user" property="firstName"/></td>
    </tr>
    <tr>
        <td align="right">Last name:</td>
        <td><jsp:getProperty name="user" property="lastName"/></td>
    </tr>
    <tr>
        <td align="right">Email address:</td>
        <td><jsp:getProperty name="user" property="emailAddress"/></td>
    </tr>
</table>
```

Advantages of EL

- EL has a more elegant and compact syntax than standard JSP tags.
- EL lets you access nested properties.
- EL lets you access collections such as maps, arrays, and lists.
- EL does a better job of handling null values.
- EL provides more functionality.

Disadvantages of EL

- EL doesn't create a JavaBean if it doesn't already exist.
- EL doesn't provide a way to set properties.

Description

- The JSP *Expression Language* (*EL*) provides a compact syntax that lets you get data from JavaBeans, maps, arrays, and lists that have been stored as attributes of a web application.

Figure 10-1   An introduction to EL

Essential skills for working with EL

Now that you have a general idea of how EL can simplify and improve your JSP code, you're ready to learn the details of working with it.

How to use the dot operator to work with JavaBeans and maps

As you learned in chapters 7 and 8, you can use the setAttribute method of the HttpServletRequest and HttpSession objects to store an object with request or session scope. If you need a larger scope, you can use the setAttribute method of the ServletContext object to store an object with application scope. Or, if you need a smaller scope, you can use the setAttribute method of the implicit PageContext object to store an object with page scope. Then, you can use the getAttribute method of the appropriate object to retrieve the attribute.

Figure 10-2 shows how to use EL to access an attribute of a web application. Whenever you use EL, you begin by coding a dollar sign ($) followed by an opening brace ({) and a closing brace (}). Then, you code the expression within the braces.

The first example in this figure shows how to retrieve an attribute for a simple object like a String or Date object. Here, the servlet code creates a Date object named currentDate that stores the current date. Then, the servlet code stores this object as an attribute of the request object. Last, the JSP code uses EL to access this attribute, convert it to a string, and display it.

Note here that you don't have to specify the scope when you use EL. Instead, EL automatically searches through all scopes starting with the smallest scope (page scope) and moving towards the largest scope (application scope).

The second example shows how to display a property of an attribute for a more complex object like a JavaBean or a map. Here, the servlet code creates a JavaBean for the user and stores this bean as an attribute of the session. Then, the JSP code uses EL to access this attribute, and it uses the dot operator to specify the property of the JavaBean that it's going to display.

You can use the same technique to work with a map. In that case, though, you code the name of the key after the dot operator to get the associated object that's stored in the map. You'll see this used in the next figure.

An example that accesses an attribute named currentDate

Syntax
```
${attribute}
```

Servlet code
```
Date currentDate = new Date();
request.setAttribute("currentDate", currentDate);
```

JSP code
```
<p>The current date is ${currentDate}</p>
```

An example that accesses the firstName property of an attribute named user

Syntax
```
${attribute.property}
```

Servlet code
```
User user = new User(firstName, lastName, emailAddress);
session.setAttribute("user", user);
```

JSP code
```
<p>Hello ${user.firstName}</p>
```

The sequence of scopes that Java searches to find the attribute

Scope	Description
page	The bean is stored in the implicit PageContext object.
request	The bean is stored in the HttpServletRequest object.
session	The bean is stored in the HttpSession object.
application	The bean is stored in the ServletContext object.

Description

- A JavaBean is a special type of object that provides a standard way to access its *properties*.

- A *map* is a special type of collection that's used to store key/value pairs. For example, a HashMap collection is a map.

- When you use the dot operator, the code to the left of the operator must specify a JavaBean or a map, and the code to the right of the operator must specify a JavaBean property or a map key.

- When you use this syntax, EL looks up the attribute starting with the smallest scope (page scope) and moving towards the largest scope (application scope).

Figure 10-2   How to use the dot operator to work with JavaBeans and maps

How to use EL to specify scope

Since Java automatically searches through the scope objects when you use EL, you typically don't need to use the implicit EL objects shown in figure 10-3 for specifying scope. However, if you have a naming conflict, you may need to use them. When you work with these objects, you should be aware that they are all maps. As a result, you can use the dot operator to specify a key when you want to return the object for that key.

To illustrate the use of these EL objects, this figure presents the same examples as in figure 10-2. However, they will work even if there is an attribute with the same name stored in a larger scope. Here, the first example uses request scope to identify the user object. The second example uses session scope.

The implicit EL objects for specifying scope

Scope	Implicit EL object
page	pageScope
request	requestScope
session	sessionScope
application	applicationScope

An example that specifies request scope

Syntax

```
${scope.attribute}
```

Servlet code

```
Date currentDate = new Date();
request.setAttribute("currentDate", currentDate);
```

JSP code

```
<p>The current date is ${requestScope.currentDate}</p>
```

An example that specifies session scope

Syntax

```
${scope.attribute.property}
```

Servlet code

```
User user = new User(firstName, lastName, emailAddress);
session.setAttribute("user", user);
```

JSP code

```
<p>Hello ${sessionScope.user.firstName}</p>
```

Description

- If you have a naming conflict, you can use the *implicit EL objects* to specify scope.
- All of the implicit EL objects for specifying scope are maps. As a result, you can use the dot operator to specify a key when you want to return the object for that key.

Figure 10-3   How to use EL to specify scope

How to use the [ ] operator to work with arrays and lists

Figure 10-4 shows how to use the [ ] operator. Although this operator can be used to work with JavaBeans and maps, it is commonly used to work with arrays and lists.

The first example in this figure shows how to use the [ ] operator to access the firstName property of an attribute named user. This has the same effect as the second example in figure 10-2. However, the second example in that figure is easier to code and read. That's why you'll typically use the dot operator to access the properties of JavaBeans and the values of maps.

The primary exception to this is if you use a dot in a name. If, for example, you use a map key named "murach.address", you can't use the dot operator to access a value. However, you can use the [ ] operator. If necessary, you can use an implicit EL object to specify the scope so you can use the [ ] operator to access an attribute that uses a dot in its name.

The second example shows how to use the [ ] operator to access an array of strings. Here, the servlet code creates an array of strings that stores three colors. Then, it gets a ServletContext object so it can store the array in this object, which makes it available to the entire application. Finally, the JSP code uses EL to retrieve the first two strings that are stored in the array.

Note that this code is similar to the Java syntax for accessing strings that are stored in an array, and that the index values can be enclosed in quotation marks. Although quotation marks are required for using the [ ] operator to access a property of a JavaBean or a key of a map, they are optional for specifying the index of an array or a list.

The third example shows how to use the [ ] operator to access an array of User objects. Here, the servlet code uses the getUsers method of the UserIO class to retrieve a list of User objects. Then, the servlet code stores the list in the session object. Finally, the JSP code uses the [ ] operator to access the first two User objects, and it uses the dot operator to display the emailAddress property of these objects. This shows that you can mix the [ ] and dot operators if that's required.

The syntax for the [ ] operator

```
${attribute["propertyKeyOrIndex"]}
```

An example that works with a JavaBean property

Servlet code

```
User user = new User("John", "Smith", "jsmith@gmail.com");
session.setAttribute("user", user);
```

JSP code

```
<p>Hello ${user["firstName"]}</p>
```

An example that works with an array

Servlet code

```
String[] colors = {"Red", "Green", "Blue"};
ServletContext application = this.getServletContext();
application.setAttribute("colors", colors);
```

JSP code

```
<p>The first color is ${colors[0]}<br>
   The second color is ${colors[1]}
</p>
```

Another way to write the JSP code

```
<p>The first color is ${colors["0"]}<br>
   The second color is ${colors["1"]}
</p>
```

An example that works with a list

Servlet code

```
ArrayList<User> users = UserIO.getUsers(path);
session.setAttribute("users", users);
```

JSP code

```
<p>The first address on our list is ${users[0].emailAddress}<br>
   The second address on our list is ${users[1].emailAddress}
</p>
```

Another way to write the JSP code

```
<p>The first address on our list is ${users["0"].emailAddress}<br>
   The second address on our list is ${users["1"].emailAddress}
</p>
```

Description

- A *list* is a special type of collection such as an ArrayList<> that uses an index to retrieve an object that's stored in the collection.
- Although the [ ] operator can be used to work with JavaBeans and maps, it is commonly used to work with arrays and lists.
- With EL, the quotation marks are required for specifying a property in a JavaBean or a key in a map, but the quotation marks are optional when specifying an index of an array or a list.

Figure 10-4   How to use the [ ] operator to access arrays and lists

How to use the dot operator to access nested properties

The first example in figure 10-5 illustrates the most commonly used syntax for accessing nested properties. Here, the servlet code creates a Product object that has a property named code. Then, the servlet code stores this Product object in a LineItem object, and stores the LineItem object as a session attribute named item.

Since both the LineItem and Product classes follow the rules for JavaBeans, the JSP code can then use EL to retrieve the code property for the Product object that's stored in the item attribute. Although this figure only shows how to work with one nested property, there is no limit to the number of nested properties that you can access with the dot operator.

The second example shows that you can use the dot operator after the [ ] operator. Here, the only catch is that the object that's returned by the [ ] operator must be a JavaBean or a map. In this example, this works because the [ ] operator returns the same Product bean as the first example.

An example that accesses a nested property

Syntax

```
${attribute.property1.property2}
```

Servlet code

```
Product p = new Product();
p.setCode("pf01");
LineItem lineItem = new LineItem(p, 10);
session.setAttribute("item", lineItem);
```

JSP code

```
<p>Product code: ${item.product.code}</p>
```

Another way to access the same property

Syntax

```
${attribute["property1"].property2}
```

Servlet code

```
Product p = new Product();
p.setCode("pf01");
LineItem lineItem = new LineItem(p, 10);
session.setAttribute("item", lineItem);
```

JSP code

```
<p>Product code: ${item["product"].code}</p>
```

Description

- If a JavaBean has a property that returns another JavaBean, you can use the dot operator to access nested properties.

- There is no limit to the number of nested properties that you can access with the dot operator.

Figure 10-5   How to use the dot operator to access nested properties

Other skills for working with EL

Most of the time, the EL skills that you've learned so far are the ones that you will use when you develop your JSPs. However, there are times when you may need some of the skills presented in the rest of this chapter.

How to use the [ ] operator to access attributes

The first example in figure 10-6 shows how you can use the [ ] operator to access an attribute. To start, the servlet code creates a map named usersMap that contains User objects, and it sets this map as an attribute. Although it isn't shown by this code, this map uses the email address as a key that can be used to get the associated User object. Then, the servlet code gets an email address from the request object, and it sets this string as an attribute named emailAddress.

Next, the JSP code retrieves the User object associated with the emailAddress attribute by coding the attribute within the [ ] operator. Since no quotation marks are coded around the attribute, EL attempts to evaluate the attribute. Here, it uses the value stored in the emailAddress attribute in the expression. In other words, if the emailAddress variable is "jsmith@gmail.com", the expression evaluates to:

```
${usersMap["jsmith@gmail.com"].firstName}
```

As a result, the User object that's mapped to "jsmith@gmail.com" will be returned, and the first name for this user will be displayed.

Note, however, that EL doesn't evaluate the variable within the [ ] operator if you code quotation marks around the emailAddress like this:

```
${usersMap["emailAddress"].firstName}
```

As a result, this expression will return an empty string, except in the unlikely event that a user has an email address of "emailAddress".

The second example shows how you can use nested [ ] operators to access attributes. Here, the servlet code stores a map of User objects and an array of email addresses. Then, the JSP code uses nested [ ] operators to get the User object that's mapped to the first email address in the array of email addresses.

This works because the expression within the [ ] operator isn't enclosed in quotes. As a result, EL evaluates the expression as

```
${usersMap["jsmith@gmail.com"].firstName}
```

This means that the User object that's mapped to "jsmith@gmail.com" will be returned, and the first name for this user will be displayed. Here again, this example won't work if you enclose the expression within quotes.

An example that uses an attribute within the [ ] operator

Syntax

```
${attribute[attribute].property}
```

Servlet code

```
HashMap<String, User> usersMap = UserIO.getUsersMap(path);
session.setAttribute("usersMap", usersMap);

String emailAddress = request.getParameter("emailAddress");
session.setAttribute("emailAddress", emailAddress);
```

JSP code

```
<p>First name: ${usersMap[emailAddress].firstName}</p>
```

JSP code that will return an empty string

```
<!-- this doesn't work because the attribute is enclosed in quotes -->
<p>First name: ${usersMap["emailAddress"].firstName}</p>
```

Another example

Syntax

```
${attribute[attribute[index]].property}
```

Servlet code

```
HashMap<String, User> usersMap = UserIO.getUsersMap(path);
session.setAttribute("usersMap", usersMap);

String[] emailAddresses = {"jsmith@gmail.com", "joel@murach.com"};
session.setAttribute("emailAddresses", emailAddresses);
```

JSP code

```
<p>First name: ${usersMap[emailAddresses[0]].firstName}</p>
```

JSP code that will return an empty string

```
<!-- this doesn't work because the attribute is enclosed in quotes -->
<p>First name: ${usersMap["emailAddresses[0]"].firstName}</p>
```

Description

- If the expression within the [ ] operator isn't enclosed within quotes, EL evaluates the expression. To start, EL checks to see if the expression is an attribute. Then, it attempts to evaluate the expression.

- If multiple [ ] operators exist, the expression will be evaluated from the innermost [ ] operator to the outermost [ ] operator. As a result, you can nest as many [ ] operators as necessary.

Figure 10-6   How to use the [ ] operator to access attributes

How to work with the other implicit EL objects

In figure 10-3, you learned how to use the implicit EL objects to specify scope. Now, figure 10-7 presents some other implicit EL objects that you can use to perform other tasks in a JSP. If you use the MVC pattern, though, you typically won't need to use these implicit objects.

The first example in this figure shows how to use the implicit objects for working with request parameters. Here, the HTML form has a parameter named firstName for the first name text box and a parameter named emailAddress for the next two text boxes. In other words, this form lets you enter one first name and two email addresses. Then, the JSP code shows how you can use the param object to get the value of the firstName parameter. In addition, this JSP code shows how you can use the paramValues parameter to get an array of strings that contains the values for the emailAddress parameter.

The second example shows how you can use the header object to get data from the HTTP header. Here, you can use the dot operator to get the value for any request headers that have a single word name. For instance, you can use the dot operator to get the value of the Accept header.

If a request header has more than one word in its name, you can use the [ ] operator to get its value. For instance, you can use this operator to get the value of the Accept-Encoding header. For now, don't worry if you don't understand how HTTP request headers work because you'll learn more about them in chapter 18.

When you learn more about HTTP request headers, you'll find that some HTTP request headers return a list of values. For example, the Accept header returns a list of MIME types that the browser can accept. If you want to return this list as an array, you can use the implicit headerValues object. Then, you can use the array that's returned to process these values.

The third example shows how to use the implicit cookie object to get the value of a cookie. Here, the servlet code creates a Cookie object with a name of emailCookie that stores an email address. Then, the JSP code uses the implicit cookie object to get the Cookie object, and it uses the value property of the cookie to get the email address that's stored within the cookie.

This works because the Cookie class follows all of the rules for a JavaBean, and it includes a method named getValue that can be used to get the value that's stored within the cookie. If necessary, you can use similar code to retrieve other properties of the cookie. For example, you can use the maxAge property to get the maximum age for the cookie.

Other implicit objects that you can use

EL implicit object	Description
param	A map that returns a value for the specified request parameter name.
paramValues	A map that returns an array of values for the specified request parameter name.
header	A map that returns the value for the specified HTTP request header. For a list of HTTP request headers, see chapter 18.
headerValues	A map that returns an array of values for the specified HTTP request header.
cookie	A map that returns the Cookie object for the specified cookie.
initParam	A map that returns the value for the specified parameter name in the context-param element of the web.xml file.
pageContext	A reference to the implicit pageContext object that's available from any JSP.

How to get parameter values from the request

An HTML form that has two parameters with the same name

```
<form action="addToEmailList" method="post">
    <p>First name: <input type="text" name="firstName"></p>
    <p>Email address 1: <input type="text" name="emailAddress"></p>
    <p>Email address 2: <input type="text" name="emailAddress"></p>
</form>
```

JSP code

```
<p>First name: ${param.firstName}<br>
    Email address 1: ${paramValues.emailAddress[0]}<br>
    Email address 2: ${paramValues.emailAddress[1]}
</p>
```

How to get an HTTP header

JSP code

```
<p>Browser MIME types: ${header.accept}<br><br>
    Browser compression types: ${header["accept-encoding"]}
</p>
```

The text that's returned for Internet Explorer 6.0

```
Browser MIME types: image/gif, image/x-xbitmap, image/jpeg, image/pjpeg,
application/x-shockwave-flash, application/vnd.ms-excel, application/msword,
*/*
Browser compression types: gzip, deflate
```

How to work with cookies

Servlet code

```
Cookie c = new Cookie("emailCookie", emailAddress);
c.setMaxAge(60*60); //set its age to 1 hour
c.setPath("/"); //allow the entire application to access it
response.addCookie(c);
```

JSP code

```
<p>The email cookie: ${cookie.emailCookie.value}</p>
```

Figure 10-7   How to work with the implicit EL objects (part 1 of 2)

The fourth example in figure 10-7 shows how to use the initParam object to get a context initialization parameter. Here, the web.xml file uses the context-param element to store a context initialization parameter named custServEmail with a value of "custserv@murach.com". Then, the JSP code uses the initParam object to retrieve the value for this parameter. Note that this parameter is a context initialization parameter that's available to the entire web application, not a servlet initialization parameter that's only available to the current servlet.

The fifth example shows how to use the implicit pageContext object that's available from any JSP. Since the pageContext object follows the rules for a JavaBean, you can easily access any of its properties. In addition, the properties of the pageContext object allow you to access the objects for request, response, session, and application scope.

For example, you can use the request property to return an HttpRequest object that lets you get information about the current request. You can use the response property to return an HttpResponse object that lets you get information about the current response. You can use the session property to return an HttpSession object that lets you get information about the current session. And you can use the servletContext property to return a ServletContext object that lets you get information about the context for the application.

How to get a context initialization parameter

XML in the web.xml file

```
<context-param>
    <param-name>custServEmail</param-name>
    <param-value>custserv@murach.com</param-value>
</context-param>
```

JSP code

```
<p>The context init param: ${initParam.custServEmail}</p>
```

How to use the pageContext object

JSP code

```
<p>HTTP request method: ${pageContext.request.method}<br>
   HTTP response type: ${pageContext.response.contentType}<br>
   HTTP session ID: ${pageContext.session.id}<br>
   HTTP contextPath: ${pageContext.servletContext.contextPath}<br>
</p>
```

An example of the text that might be displayed in the browser

```
HTTP request method: POST
HTTP response type: text/html
HTTP session ID: 4C1CFDB54B0339B53BE3AC8E9BADC0F5
HTTP servletContext path: /ch10email
```

Description

- The four implicit EL objects for specifying scope are presented in figure 10-3.
- All of the implicit objects used by EL are maps, except for the pageContext object, which is a JavaBean.

Figure 10-7   How to work with the implicit EL objects (part 2 of 2)

How to work with other EL operators

Earlier in this chapter, you learned how to use the dot operator and the [ ] operator that are available from EL. Now, figure 10-8 shows how to use some of the other operators that are available from EL. If necessary, you can use these operators to perform calculations and comparisons.

If you know how to code arithmetic, relational, and logical expressions in Java as described in *Murach's Java SE 6*, you shouldn't have any trouble using these operators since they work similarly to the Java operators. Although you usually won't need to use these operators, they may come in handy from time to time.

You can use the arithmetic operators to perform mathematical calculations. The examples in this figure show that you can use scientific notation for extremely large or small numbers and that you can use parentheses to control or clarify the order of precedence.

These examples also show that EL treats any null values as zero. To illustrate, let's assume that you have an attribute named userID that can store an int value. Then, if the attribute stores an int value, EL will use the int value in the calculation. However, if the attribute stores a null value, EL will use zero in the calculation.

You can use the relational operators to compare two operands and return a true or false value. Although these operators work like the standard Java operators, you can use an alternate syntax that uses two letter combinations instead of symbols. For example, you can use eq instead of ==.

When you create relational expressions, you can use the null keyword to specify a null value, the true keyword to specify a true value, and the false keyword to specify a false value. In addition, when you create relational expressions, EL treats a null value as a false value. To illustrate, let's assume that you have an attribute named isDirty that stores a Boolean value. Then, if the attribute stores a true or false value, EL will use that value in the expression. However, if the attribute stores a null value, EL will use a false value for the isDirty attribute.

Arithmetic EL operators

Operator	Alternative	Description
+		Addition
-		Subtraction
*		Multiplication
/	div	Division
%	mod	Modulus (remainder)

Example	Result
${1+1}	2
${17.5+10}	27.5
${2.5E3}	2500.0
${2.5E3+10.4}	2510.4
${2-1}	1
${7*3}	21
${1 / 4}	0.25
${1 div 4}	0.25
${10 % 8}	2
${10 mod 8}	2
${1 + 2 * 4}	9
${(1 + 2) * 4}	12
${userID + 1}	9 if userID equals 8; 1 if userID equals 0

Relational operators

Operator	Alternative	Description
==	eq	Equal to
!=	ne	Not equal to
<	lt	Less than
>	gt	Greater than
<=	le	Less than or equal to
>=	ge	Greater than or equal to

Example	Result
${"s1" == "s1"}	true
${"s1" eq "s1"}	true
${1 == 1}	true
${1 != 1}	false
${1 ne 1}	false
${3 < 4}	true
${3 lt 4}	true
${3 > 4}	false
${3 gt 4}	false
${3 <= 4}	true
${3 >= 4}	false
${user.firstName == null}	true if firstName returns a null value
${user.firstName == ""}	true if firstName returns an empty string
${isDirty == true}	true if isDirty is true, false if isDirty is false, false if isDirty is null

Figure 10-8   How to work with the other EL operators (part 1 of 2)

You can use logical operators to combine multiple relational expressions and return a true or false value. The examples in this figure show how to use all three types of logical operators. You can use the And operator to specify that both relational expressions must be true for the entire expression to evaluate to true. You can use the Or operator to specify that at least one of the relational expressions must be true. And you can use the Not operator to reverse the value of the relational expression.

In addition, you may occasionally want to use the last two operators described in this figure. First, you may want to use the empty operator to check if a variable contains a null value or an empty string. If so, this operator returns a true value.

Second, you may want to use the ? and : operators to create a simple if statement. Here, you can code the condition for the if statement, followed by the ? operator, followed by the value that's returned for a true value, followed by the : operator, followed by the value that's returned for a false value. In the examples for these operators, the true and false keywords are used for the condition because this clearly shows how the ? and : operators work. However, you can substitute any relational or logical expression for the condition.

Logical operators

Operator	Alternative	Description
&&	and	And
||	or	Or
!	not	Not

Example	Result
`${"s1" == "s1" && 4 > 3}`	true
`${"s1" == "s1" and 4 > 3}`	true
`${"s1" == "s1" && 4 < 3}`	false
`${"s1" == "s1" || 4 < 3}`	true
`${"s1" != "s1" || 4 < 3}`	false
`${"s1" != "s1" or 4 < 3}`	false
`${!true}`	false
`${not true}`	false

Other operators

Syntax	Description
empty *x*	Returns true if the value of x is null or equal to an empty string.
x ? *y* : *z*	If x evaluates to true, returns y. Otherwise, returns z.

Example	Result
`${empty firstName}`	true if firstName returns a null value or an empty string
`${true ? "s1" : "s2"}`	s1
`${false ? "s1" : "s2"}`	s2

Keywords you can use in expressions

Keyword	Description
null	A null value
true	A true value
false	A false value

Description

- For arithmetic expressions, you can use parentheses to control or clarify the order of precedence.
- In arithmetic expressions, EL treats a null value as a zero.
- In logical expressions, EL treats a null value as a false value.

Figure 10-8   How to work with the other EL operators (part 2 of 2)

How to disable EL

For JSP 2.0 and later, the servlet container evaluates any code within the ${ and } characters as an EL expression. Most of the time, this is what you want. However, there's an outside chance that you may have one or more old JSPs that use the EL syntax for another purpose. In that case, you can disable EL as shown in figure 10-9.

To disable EL for a single JSP, you add a page directive to the JSP, and you set the isELIgnored attribute to true. Then, the servlet container won't evaluate any expressions that use the EL syntax. Instead, the servlet container will pass this syntax on to the web browser, which typically causes the web browser to display the expression.

To disable EL for multiple pages, you can edit the jsp-config tag in the web.xml file for the application. In this figure, for example, you can see how to disable scripting for all of the JSPs in the application. If necessary, though, you can modify the url-pattern element to disable EL only for selected JSPs within the application.

How to disable scripting

One of the benefits of EL is that it lets you remove JSP scripts from your JSPs, which makes it easier for web designers to work with them. In fact, once you learn how to use EL with JSTL as described in the next chapter, you can usually remove all scripting from your application.

When you're replacing old JSP scripts with EL and JSTL, it is sometimes hard to tell whether you've removed all scripting from your JSPs. Then, to check if you've done that, you can disable scripting for the entire application as described in this figure. After that, when you request a JSP that contains scripting, the servlet container will display an error page. In that case, you can edit the JSP to replace the scripting with EL, JSTL, or a combination of the two.

When you are developing new web applications, you may want to disable scripting from the start. This forces you (and any other programmers working on the application) to always use standard JSP tags, EL, and JSTL instead of scripting. Although this may require you to do more work up front to get the web application structured correctly with the MVC pattern, it should pay off in the long run by making your code easier to read and maintain.

How to disable EL

For a single page (a page directive)

```
<%@ page isELIgnored ="true" %>
```

For the entire application (the web.xml file)

```
<jsp-config>
    <jsp-property-group>
        <url-pattern>*.jsp</url-pattern>
        <el-ignored>true</el-ignored>
    </jsp-property-group>
</jsp-config>
```

How to disable scripting

For the entire application (the web.xml file)

```
<jsp-config>
    <jsp-property-group>
        <url-pattern>*.jsp</url-pattern>
        <scripting-invalid>true</scripting-invalid>
    </jsp-property-group>
</jsp-config>
```

Description

- For JSP 2.0 and later, the servlet container evaluates any text that starts with ${ and ends with } as an EL expression. Most of the time, this is what you want. If it isn't, you can ignore EL for a single JSP or for all JSPs in the entire application.

- If you want to remove all scripting from all JSPs in your application, you can modify the web.xml file so it doesn't allow scripting. Then, if you request a JSP that contains scripting, the servlet container will display an error page.

Figure 10-9   How to disable EL or scripting

Perspective

The goal of this chapter has been to show you how to use EL to get data from JavaBeans, maps, arrays, and lists that have been stored as an attribute in one of the four scopes of a web application. Along the way, you learned how to use some of the implicit EL objects and operators to perform some other useful tasks. Although there's more to learn about EL, this will probably be all you need to know if you use the MVC pattern in your web applications.

When you use EL, you can remove much of the Java scripting and expressions from your JSPs, and that makes your code easier to read and maintain. That also makes it easier for web designers to work with these pages. To take this a step further, though, the next chapter shows you how to use the JSP Standard Tag Library (JSTL) to remove the rest of the scripting from your JSPs. As you'll see, JSTL tags work well with EL, and the two are often mixed in a JSP.

Summary

- The JSP *Expression Language* (*EL*) provides a compact syntax that lets you get data from JavaBeans, maps, arrays, and lists that have been stored as an attribute of a web application.

- A *JavaBean* is a special type of object that provides a standard way to access its *properties*.

- A *map* is a special type of collection that's used to store *key/value pairs*.

- A *list* is a type of collection that uses an *index* to retrieve an object that's stored in the collection.

- You can use the dot operator to work with JavaBeans and maps.

- You can use the [ ] operator to work with arrays and lists.

- If the expression within an [ ] operator isn't enclosed within quotes, EL evaluates the expression.

- If necessary, you can use the implicit EL objects to explicitly specify scope.

- You can use EL to get nested properties.

- You can use the implicit EL objects to work with request parameters, HTTP headers, cookies, context initialization parameters, and the implicit pageContext object that's available to all JSPs.

- You can use other EL operators to perform calculations and make comparisons.

- If necessary, you can disable EL or scripting for one or more pages in a web application.

Exercise 10-1   Modify the Email List application

In this exercise, you'll enhance the Email List application so it uses EL to display attributes.

Convert standard JSP bean tags to EL

1. Open the ch10email project in the ex_starts directory.

2. Open the join_email_list.jsp file. Then, convert the standard JSP tags to EL. Note how this code is shorter and easier to read than the JSP tags.

3. Run the application. Then, enter data for a user, click on the Return button, and note how the user's data is displayed on the first page.

Use EL to work with a collection and an initialization parameter

4. Open the AddToEmailListServlet class. Note that it stores the current date as a request attribute. Note also that it stores an ArrayList of User objects as a session attribute.

5. Open the web.xml file. Note that it doesn't allow scripting for the current application. Note also that the custserv@murach.com email address is stored as a context initialization parameter named custServEmail.

6. Open the display_email_entry.jsp file. Then, complete the code at the end of the page so it displays the current date, the first two users in the ArrayList of User objects, and the customer service email.

7. Run the application. Then, enter data for a user, click on the Return button, and note how the user's data is displayed on the first page.

Use EL to specify scope

8. In the display_email_entry.jsp file, explicitly specify the scope for the user attribute and the currentDate attribute.

9. Test the application to make sure that it still works correctly.

Exercise 10-2   Use EL in the Download application

In this exercise, you'll enhance the Download application that you worked with in the last chapter so it uses EL access attributes.

Convert standard JSP bean tags to EL

1. Open the ch10download project in the ex_starts directory. Then, run the application to make sure it works correctly.

2. Open the CheckUserServlet and the RegisterUserServlet classes in the download package and note that they store the User and Product objects as attributes of the session object.

3. Open the download.jsp page for each product. Then, use EL instead of the standard JSP tags to access the code and description properties of the Product bean that's stored in the session object.

4. Test the application to make sure that it still works correctly.

Use EL to work with a cookie

5. Open the index.jsp file. Then, delete the scriptlet code that's used to retrieve the cookie for the user's first name; use EL to access the cookie for the user's first name; and display a message like this "Welcome back, *firstName*" at the top of the page. Note that this welcome message will only be displayed correctly if the cookie exists.

6. Test the application to make sure that it works correctly.

11

How to use the JSP Standard Tag Library (JSTL)

In chapter 10, you learned how to use the Expression Language (EL) that was introduced with JSP 2.0 to reduce the amount of scripting in your applications. Now, in this chapter, you'll learn how to use the JSP Standard Tag Library (JSTL) to further reduce the amount of scripting in your applications. In fact, for most applications, using JSTL and EL together makes it possible to remove all scripting.

An introduction to JSTL

The *JSP Standard Tag Library* (*JSTL*) provides tags for common tasks that need to be performed in JSPs.

The JSTL libraries

Figure 11-1 shows the five tag libraries that are included with JSTL 1.1. In this chapter, you'll learn the details for working with the common tags in the core library. This library contains tags that you can use to encode URLs, loop through collections, and code if/else statements. If you use the MVC pattern, the tags in the core library are often the only JSTL tags you'll need as you develop your JSPs. If necessary, though, you can use the other four libraries to work with internationalization, databases, XML, or strings.

How to make the JSTL JAR files available to your application

Before you can use JSTL tags within an application, you must make the jstl.jar and standard.jar files available to the application. With the NetBeans IDE, for example, you can add the JSTL 1.1 library to the application as shown in figure 3-17 in chapter 3. Then, the jstl.jar and standard.jar files will be shown beneath the Libraries folder in the Projects window.

How to code the taglib directive

Before you can use JSTL tags within a JSP, you must code a taglib directive to specify the URI and prefix for the JSTL library. In this figure, for example, the taglib directive specifies the URI for the JSTL core library with a prefix of c, which is the prefix that's typically used for this library. In fact, all of the examples in this chapter assume that the page includes a taglib directive like this one before the JSTL tags are used. Although you can use different prefixes than the ones in this figure, we recommend using the standard prefixes.

How to code a JSTL tag

Once you've added the appropriate JAR files to your application and used the taglib directive to identify a library, you can code a JSTL tag. In this figure, for example, the url tag is used to encode a URL that refers to the index.jsp file in the web applications root directory. Note how the prefix for this tag is c. Also note how this tag looks more like an HTML tag, which makes it easier to code and read than the equivalent JSP script, especially for web designers and other nonprogrammers who are used to HTML syntax.

The primary JSTL libraries

Name	Prefix	URI	Description
Core	c	http://java.sun.com/jsp/jstl/core	Contains the core tags for common tasks such as looping and if/else statements.
Formatting	fmt	http://java.sun.com/jsp/jstl/fmt	Provides tags for formatting numbers, times, and dates so they work correctly with internationalization (i18n).
SQL	sql	http://java.sun.com/jsp/jstl/sql	Provides tags for working with SQL queries and data sources.
XML	x	http://java.sun.com/jsp/jstl/xml	Provides tags for manipulating XML documents.
Functions	fn	http://java.sun.com/jsp/jstl/functions	Provides functions that can be used to manipulate strings.

The NetBeans IDE after the JSTL 1.1 library has been added

The taglib directive that specifies the JSTL core library

```
<%@ taglib prefix="c" uri="http://java.sun.com/jsp/jstl/core" %>
```

An example that uses JSTL to encode a URL

JSP code with JSTL

```
<a href="<c:url value='/index.jsp' />">Continue Shopping</a>
```

Equivalent script

```
<a href="<%=response.encodeURL("index.jsp")%>">Continue Shopping</a>
```

Description

- The *JSP Standard Tag Library* (*JSTL*) provides tags for common JSP tasks.
- Before you can use JSTL tags within an application, you must make the jstl.jar and standard.jar files available to the application. To do that for NetBeans, you can add the JSTL 1.1 class library to your project as in figure 3-17 in chapter 3. Otherwise, you can consult the documentation for your IDE.
- Before you can use JSTL tags within a JSP, you must code a taglib directive that identifies the JSTL library and its prefix.

Figure 11-1   An introduction to JSTL

How to view the documentation for a library

As you progress through this chapter, you'll learn how to code the tags in the JSTL core library that you'll use most of the time. If necessary, though, you can view the documentation for any of the tags in this library as shown in figure 11-2.

If, for example, you want to learn more about the url tag in the core library, you can click on the "JSTL core" link in the upper left window. Then, you can click on the "c:url" link in the lower left window to display the documentation for this tag in the window on the right. This documentation provides a general description of the tag, a list of all available attributes for the tag, and detailed information about each of these attributes.

You can also use this documentation to learn more about the JSTL libraries that aren't covered in this chapter. If, for example, you want to learn more about the formatting library for working with internationalization, you can click on the "JSTL fmt" link in the upper left window. Then, you can click on the tags in the lower left window to display information in the window on the right. Incidentally, *i18n* is sometimes used as an abbreviation for *internationalization* because *internationalization* begins with an *i*, followed by *18* letters, followed by an *n*.

The URL for the JSTL 1.1 documentation

`http://java.sun.com/products/jsp/jstl/1.1/docs/tlddocs/index.html`

A browser that displays the JSTL documentation

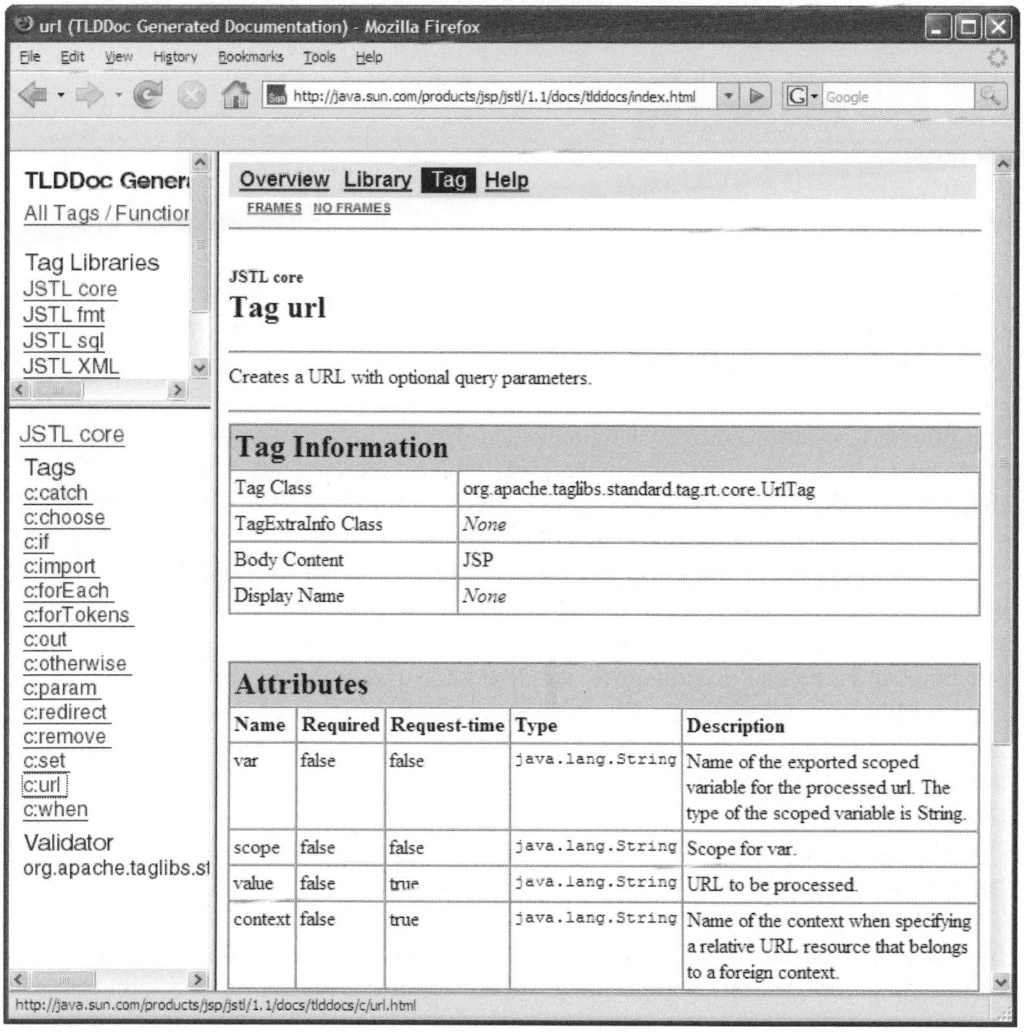

Description

- To view the documentation for the JSTL 1.1 library, use your browser to visit the URL shown above. Then, you can use the upper left window to select the JSTL library, the lower left window to select the tag, and the window on the right to get information about the tag.

Figure 11-2   How to view the documentation for a library

How to work with the JSTL core library

Now that you have a general idea of how JSTL works, you're ready to learn the details for coding the most commonly used JSTL tags. All of these tags are available from the JSTL core library.

How to use the url tag

In chapter 8, you learned how to encode the URLs that are returned to the client so your application can track sessions even if the client doesn't support cookies. Since you usually want your application to do that, you typically encode the URLs in your applications. Without JSTL, though, this requires calling the encodeURL method of the response object from a script within a JSP. With JSTL, you can use the url tag to encode URLs without using scripting.

Figure 11-3 shows how to use the url tag. Here, the first example shows the same url tag that's presented in figure 11-1. This url tag encodes a relative URL that refers to the index.jsp file in the root directory for the web application. Its value attribute is used to specify the URL.

When you specify JSTL tags, you need to be aware that they use XML syntax, not HTML syntax. As a result, you must use the exact capitalization shown in this example for the name of the tag and its attributes. In addition, attributes must be enclosed in either single quotes or double quotes. In this figure, I have used both single and double quotes to differentiate between the href attribute of the A tag (which uses double quotes), and the value attribute of the url tag (which uses single quotes). I think this improves the readability of this code.

The second example shows how to use the url tag to encode a URL that includes a parameter named productCode with a hard-coded value of 8601. Then, the third example shows how to use the url tag to encode a URL that includes a parameter named productCode with a value that's supplied by an EL expression. Here, the EL expression gets the code property of a Product object named product.

The third example also shows how you can code a JSTL param tag within a url tag to specify the name and value for a parameter. The benefit of using this tag is that it automatically encodes any unsafe characters in the URL, such as spaces, with special characters, such as plus signs.

If you compare the url tags in these examples with the equivalent scripting, I think you'll agree that the JSTL tags are easier to code, read, and maintain. In addition, the syntax is closer to HTML than scripting, which makes it easier for web designers and other nonprogrammers to use.

An example that encodes a URL

JSP code with JSTL

```
<a href="<c:url value='/index.jsp' />">Continue Shopping</a>
```

Equivalent scripting

```
<a href="<%=response.encodeURL("index.jsp")%>">Continue Shopping</a>
```

An example that adds a parameter to the URL

JSP code with JSTL

```
<a href="<c:url value='/cart?productCode=8601' />">
    Add To Cart
</a>
```

Equivalent scripting

```
<a href="<%=response.encodeURL("cart?productCode=8601")%>">
    Add To Cart
</a>
```

An example that uses EL to specify the value of a parameter value

JSP code with JSTL

```
<a href="<c:url value='/cart?productCode=${product.code}' />">
    Add To Cart
</a>
```

The same code with the JSTL param tag

```
<a href="
    <c:url value='/cart'>
        <c:param name='productCode' value='${product.code}' />
    </c:url>
">Add To Cart</a>
```

Equivalent scripting

```
<%@ page import="business.Product" %>
<%
    Product product = (Product) session.getAttribute("product");
    String cartUrl = "cart?productCode=" + product.getCode();
%>
<a href="<%=response.encodeURL(cartUrl)%>">Add To Cart</a>
```

Description

- You can use the url tag to encode URLs within your web application. This tag will automatically rewrite the URL to include a unique session ID whenever the client doesn't support cookies.

- You can use the JSTL param tag if you want to automatically encode unsafe characters such as spaces with special characters such as plus signs.

Figure 11-3   How to use the url tag

How to use the forEach tag

You can use the forEach tag to loop through items that are stored in most collections, including arrays. For example, figure 11-4 shows how to use the forEach tag to loop through the LineItem objects that are available from the items property of the cart attribute. Here, the var attribute specifies a variable name of item to access each item within the collection. Then, the items attribute uses EL to specify the collection that stores the data. In this case, the collection is the ArrayList<LineItem> object that's returned by the getItems method of the Cart object for the current session. This Cart object has been stored as an attribute with a name of cart.

Within the forEach loop, the JSP code creates one row with four columns for each item in the cart. Here, each column uses EL to display the data that's available from the LineItem object. In particular, the first column displays the quantity, the second column displays the product description, the third column displays the price per item, and the fourth column displays the total amount (quantity multiplied by price). Note that the LineItem object includes code that applies currency formatting to the price and amount.

If you have trouble understanding the examples in this figure, you may want to study the code for the Cart, LineItem, and Product objects that are presented in figure 11-12. In particular, note how a Cart object can contain multiple LineItem objects and how a LineItem object must contain one Product object. Also, note how the appropriate get methods are provided for all of the properties that are accessed by EL. For example, the Cart class provides a method named getItems that returns an ArrayList of LineItem objects. As a result, with EL, you can use the items property of the cart attribute to get this ArrayList object.

If necessary, you can nest one forEach tag within another. For example, if you wanted to display several Invoice objects on a single web page, you could use an outer forEach tag to loop through the Invoice objects. Then, you could use an inner forEach tag to loop through the LineItem objects within each invoice. However, for most JSPs, you won't need to nest forEach statements.

If you compare the JSTL tags shown in this figure with the equivalent scripting, I think you'll agree that the benefits of the JSTL tags are even more apparent in this figure than in the last one. In particular, the JSP code that uses JSTL is much shorter and easier to read than the equivalent scripting. As a result, it's easier for web designers and other nonprogrammers to work with this code.

An example that uses JSTL to loop through a collection

JSP code with JSTL

```
<c:forEach var="item" items="${cart.items}">
<tr valign="top">
  <td>${item.quantity}</td>
  <td>${item.product.description}</td>
  <td>${item.product.priceCurrencyFormat}</td>
  <td>${item.totalCurrencyFormat}</td>
</tr>
</c:forEach>
```

The result that's displayed in the browser for a cart that has two items

Your cart

Quantity	Description	Price	Amount
1	86 (the band) - True Life Songs and Pictures	$14.95	$14.95
1	Paddlefoot - The first CD	$12.95	$12.95

Equivalent scripting

```
<%@ page import="business.*, java.util.ArrayList" %>
<%
  Cart cart = (Cart) session.getAttribute("cart");
  ArrayList<LineItem> items = cart.getItems();
  for (LineItem item : items)
  {
%>
  <tr valign="top">
    <td><%=item.getQuantity()%></td>
    <td><%=item.getProduct().getDescription()%></td>
    <td><%=item.getProduct().getPriceCurrencyFormat()%></td>
    <td><%=item.getTotalCurrencyFormat()%></td>
  </tr>
<% } %>
```

Description

- You can use the forEach tag to loop through most types of collections, including arrays.
- You can use the var attribute to specify the variable name that will be used to access each item within the collection.
- You can use the items attribute to specify the collection that stores the data.
- If necessary, you can nest one forEach tag within another.

Figure 11-4   How to use the forEach tag

How to use the forTokens tag

You can use the forTokens tag to loop through items that are stored in a string as long as the items in the string are separated by one or more delimiters, which are characters that are used to separate the items. For instance, the string in the first example in figure 11-5 uses a comma as the delimiter. As a result, this string can be referred to as a *comma-delimited string*.

The first example in this figure also shows how to use the forTokens tag to loop through the four product codes that are stored in the string. Here, the var attribute specifies a variable name of productCode to identify each product code in the list. Then, the items attribute uses EL to specify the productCodes attribute as the string that stores the items. Finally, the delims attribute specifies the comma as the delimiter.

To keep this example simple, the servlet code creates the productCodes attribute by storing a hard-coded list of four product codes that are separated by commas. In a more realistic example, of course, the servlet code would dynamically generate this list.

The second example works similarly to the first example, but it uses two delimiters instead of one. In particular, the delims attribute specifies the at symbol (@) as the first delimiter and the period (.) as the second delimiter. As a result, the loop processes three items, one for each part of the email address.

If necessary, you can nest one forTokens tag within another. Or, you can nest a forTokens tag within a forEach tag. However, since you'll rarely need to nest forTokens tags, this technique isn't illustrated in this figure.

An example that uses JSTL to loop through a comma-delimited string

Servlet code

```
session.setAttribute("productCodes", "8601,pf01,pf02,jr01");
```

JSP code

```
<p>Product codes<br>
<c:forTokens var="productCode" items="${productCodes}" delims="," >
    <li>${productCode}</li>
</c:forTokens>
</p>
```

The result that's displayed in the browser

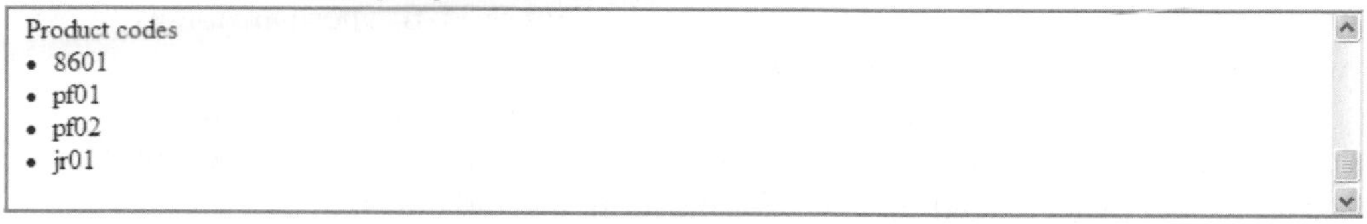

```
Product codes
  • 8601
  • pf01
  • pf02
  • jr01
```

An example that uses JSTL to parse a string

Servlet code

```
session.setAttribute("emailAddress", "jsmith@gmail.com");
```

JSP code

```
<p>Email parts<br>
<c:forTokens var="part" items="${emailAddress}" delims="@.">
    <li>${part}</li>
</c:forTokens>
</p>
```

The result that's displayed in the browser

```
Email parts
  • jsmith
  • gmail
  • com
```

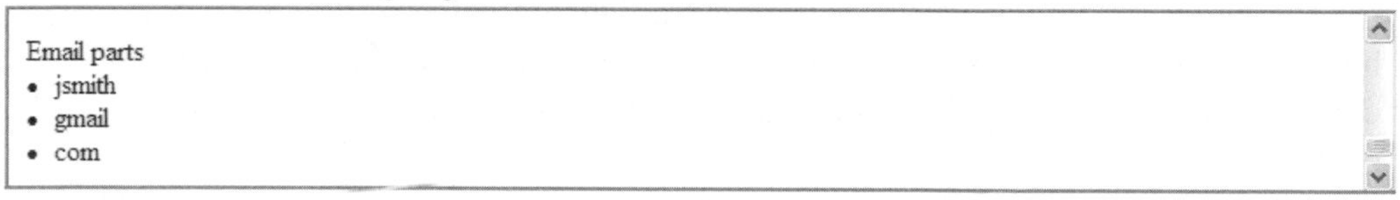

Description

- You can use the forTokens tag to loop through delimited values that are stored in a string.
- You can use the var attribute to specify the variable name that will be used to access each delimited string.
- You can use the items attribute to specify the string that stores the data.
- You can use the delims attribute to specify the character or characters that are used as the delimiters for the string.
- If necessary, you can nest one forTokens tag within another.

Figure 11-5   How to use the forTokens tag

Four more attributes for looping

When working with collections, the servlet code typically creates a collection and passes it to the JSP so the collection can be displayed to the user. Then, the JSP uses the forEach tag to loop through the collection and display it to the user as shown in figure 11-4.

However, there may be times when the JSP will need to do some additional processing. For example, the JSP may need to know whether the item is the first or last item, so it can apply special formatting to that item. Or, the JSP may need to know the item number, so it can apply shading to alternating items. In that case, you can use the attributes described in figure 11-6. These attributes work the same for the forEach and the forTokens tags.

The example in this figure shows how to work with the begin, end, and step attributes that are available for the forEach and forTokens tags. Here, the begin attribute specifies the starting index for the loop; the end attribute specifies the last index for the loop; and the step attribute specifies the amount to increment the index each time through the loop. If you understand how a for loop works in Java, you shouldn't have much trouble understanding these attributes. In this example, these attributes are used to print the first 10 numbers that are stored in an array of 30 int values.

This example also shows how to use the varStatus attribute. This attribute specifies the name of a variable that can be used to get information about the status of the loop. In particular, this variable provides four properties named first, last, index, and count that you can use within the body of a loop. For example, you can use the first and last properties to return a Boolean value that indicates whether the item is the first or last item in the collection. Or, you can use the index and count properties to return an integer value for the item. Note, however, that the index property returns an integer value that's one less than the count value. That's because the index property starts at 0 while the count property starts at 1.

Attributes that you can use for advanced loops

Attribute	Description
begin	Specifies the first index for the loop.
end	Specifies the last index for the loop.
step	Specifies the amount to increment the index each time through the loop.
varStatus	Specifies the name of a variable that can be used to get information about the status of the loop. This variable provides the first, last, index, and count properties.

An example that uses all four attributes

Servlet code

```
int[] numbers = new int[30];
for (int i = 0; i < 30; i++)
{
    numbers[i] = i+1;
}
session.setAttribute("numbers", numbers);
```

JSP code

```
<p>Numbers<br>
<c:forEach items="${numbers}" var="number"
           begin="0" end="9" step="1"
           varStatus="status">
    <li>${number} | First: ${status.first} | Last: ${status.last} |
        Index: ${status.index} | Count: ${status.count} </li>
</c:forEach>
</p>
```

The result that's displayed in the browser

Numbers
- 1 | First: true | Last: false | Index: 0 | Count: 1
- 2 | First: false | Last: false | Index: 1 | Count: 2
- 3 | First: false | Last: false | Index: 2 | Count: 3
- 4 | First: false | Last: false | Index: 3 | Count: 4
- 5 | First: false | Last: false | Index: 4 | Count: 5
- 6 | First: false | Last: false | Index: 5 | Count: 6
- 7 | First: false | Last: false | Index: 6 | Count: 7
- 8 | First: false | Last: false | Index: 7 | Count: 8
- 9 | First: false | Last: false | Index: 8 | Count: 9
- 10 | First: false | Last: true | Index: 9 | Count: 10

Description

- The begin, end, step, and varStatus attributes work for both the forEach and forTokens tags.

Figure 11-6   Four more attributes for looping

How to use the if tag

When coding a JSP, you may need to perform conditional processing to change the appearance of the page depending on the values of the attributes that are available to the page. To do that, you can use the if tag as shown in figure 11-7.

To start, you code an opening if tag that includes the test attribute. In the example in this figure, this test attribute uses EL to get the count property of the cart attribute, which indicates the number of items that are in the cart. Then, the code within the opening and closing if tags displays a message that's appropriate for the number of items in the cart. In particular, the first if tag displays a message if the cart contains 1 item, and the second if tag displays a message if the cart contains more than one item. The main difference between the two messages is that the second message uses the plural (items) while the first uses the singular (item).

If necessary, you can use the var and scope attributes to expose the Boolean condition in the test attribute as a variable with the specified scope. Then, you can reuse the Boolean condition in other if statements. This works similarly to the set tag that's briefly described later in this chapter. However, since you'll rarely need to use these attributes, they aren't illustrated in this figure.

As with the forEach and forTokens tags, you can nest one if tag within another. Or, you can nest an if tag within a forEach or forTokens tag. In short, as you might expect by now, you can usually nest JSTL tags within one another whenever that's necessary.

An example that uses JSTL to code an if statement

JSP code with JSTL

```
<c:if test="${cart.count == 1}">
    <p>You have 1 item in your cart.</p>
</c:if>
<c:if test="${cart.count > 1}">
    <p>You have ${cart.count} items in your cart.</p>
</c:if>
```

The result that's displayed in the browser for a cart that has two items

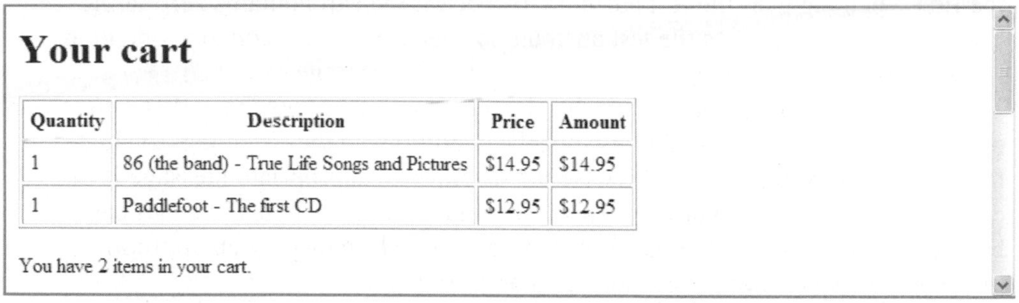

Your cart

Quantity	Description	Price	Amount
1	86 (the band) - True Life Songs and Pictures	$14.95	$14.95
1	Paddlefoot - The first CD	$12.95	$12.95

You have 2 items in your cart.

Equivalent scripting

```
<%@ page import="business.Cart, java.util.ArrayList" %>
<%
  Cart cart = (Cart) session.getAttribute("cart");
  if (cart.getCount() == 1)
    out.println("<p>You have 1 item in your cart.</p>");
  if (cart.getCount() > 1)
    out.println("<p>You have " + cart.getCount() +
                " items in your cart.</p>");
%>
```

Description

- You can use the if tag to perform conditional processing that's similar to an if statement in Java.
- You can use the test attribute to specify the Boolean condition for the if statement.
- If necessary, you can nest one if tag within another.

Figure 11-7   How to use the if tag

How to use the choose tag

In the last figure, you learned how to code multiple if tags. This is the equivalent of coding multiple if statements in Java. However, there are times when you will need to code the equivalent of an if/else statement. Then, you can use the choose tag as described in figure 11-8.

To start, you code the opening and closing choose tags. Within those tags, you can code one or more when tags. For instance, in the example in this figure, the first when tag uses the test attribute to check if the cart contains zero items. Then, the second tag uses the test attribute to check if the cart contains one item. In either case, the when tag displays an appropriate message.

After the when tags but before the closing choose tag, you can code a single otherwise tag that's executed if none of the conditions in the when tags evaluate to true. In this example, the otherwise tag displays an appropriate message if the cart doesn't contain zero or one items. Since the number of items in a cart can't be negative, this means that the otherwise tag uses EL to display an appropriate message whenever the cart contains two or more items.

An example that uses JSTL to code an if/else statement

JSP code with JSTL

```
<c:choose>
    <c:when test="${cart.count == 0}">
        <p>Your cart is empty.</p>
    </c:when>
    <c:when test="${cart.count == 1}">
        <p>You have 1 item in your cart.</p>
    </c:when>
    <c:otherwise>
        <p>You have ${cart.count} items in your cart.</p>
    </c:otherwise>
</c:choose>
```

The result that's displayed in the browser for a cart that has two items

Your cart

Quantity	Description	Price	Amount
1	86 (the band) - True Life Songs and Pictures	$14.95	$14.95
1	Paddlefoot - The first CD	$12.95	$12.95

You have 2 items in your cart.

Equivalent scripting

```
<%@ page import="business.Cart, java.util.ArrayList" %>
<%
  Cart cart = (Cart) session.getAttribute("cart");
  if (cart.getCount() == 0)
    out.println("<p>Your cart is empty.</p>");
  else if (cart.getCount() == 1)
    out.println("<p>You have 1 item in your cart.</p>");
  else
    out.println("<p>You have " + cart.getCount() +
                " items in your cart.</p>");
%>
```

Description

- You can use the choose tag to perform conditional processing similar to an if/else statement in Java. To do that, you can code multiple when tags and a single otherwise tag within the choose tag.

- You can use the test attribute to specify the Boolean condition for a when tag.

- If necessary, you can nest one choose tag within another.

Figure 11-8   How to use the choose tag

How to use the import tag

In chapter 7, you learned two ways to work with includes. The import tag shown in figure 11-9 provides another way to work with includes, and it works like the standard JSP include tag. In other words, it includes the file at *runtime*, not at compile-time.

Neither the standard JSP include tag or the JSTL import tag uses scripting. As a result, it usually doesn't matter which tag you use. However, the JSTL import tag does provide one advantage: it lets you include files from other applications and web servers.

For instance, the second last example in this figure shows how to use the import tag to include the footer.jsp file that's available from the musicStore application that's running on the same local server as the current web application. Then, the last example shows how to use the import tag to include the footer.jsp file that's available from the remote server for the www.murach.com web site.

An example that imports a header file

JSP code with JSTL

```
<c:import url="/includes/header.html" />
```

Equivalent standard JSP tag

```
<jsp:include page="/includes/header.html" />
```

An example that imports a footer file

JSP code with JSTL

```
<c:import url="/includes/footer.jsp" />
```

Equivalent standard JSP tag

```
<jsp:include page="/includes/footer.jsp" />
```

An example that imports a file from another application

```
<c:import url="http://localhost:8080/musicStore/includes/footer.jsp" />
```

An example that imports a file from another web server

```
<c:import url="www.murach.com/includes/footer.jsp" />
```

Description

- The import tag includes the file at *runtime*, not at compile-time, much like the standard JSP include tag described in chapter 7.
- One advantage of the import tag over the standard JSP include tag is that it lets you include files from other applications and web servers.

Figure 11-9   How to use the import tag

Other tags in the JSTL core library

Figure 11-10 shows six more tags in the JSTL core library. However, if you use the MVC pattern, you probably won't need to use these tags. As a result, I've only provided brief examples to give you an idea of how these tags work. If you do need to use them, though, you can look them up in the documentation for the JSTL core library as described in figure 11-2.

If you need to be able to display special characters in your JSPs, you can use the out tag as illustrated by the first example in this figure. Then, this tag automatically handles any special characters before they are displayed on the JSP. If, for example, you try to use EL by itself to display a string that contains the left and right angle brackets (< >), the JSP interprets those brackets as an HTML tag and the string isn't displayed correctly. However, if you use the out tag, these characters display correctly on the JSP.

If you need to set the value of an attribute in a scope, you can use the set tag. For instance, the second example in this figure shows how to set an attribute named message with a value of "Test message" in session scope.

You can also use the set tag if you need to set the value of a property of an attribute within a specified scope. However, instead of using the var attribute to specify the name of the attribute, you use the target attribute to specify the attribute that contains the property. To do that, you use EL within the target attribute to specify a reference to the attribute. This is illustrated by the third example.

The fourth example shows how to use the remove tag to remove an attribute from a scope. When you use this tag, you use the var attribute to specify the name of the attribute that you want to remove, and you use the scope attribute to specify the scope that contains the attribute.

If your JSP includes code that may cause an exception to be thrown, you can use the catch tag to catch the exceptions. This is illustrated by the fifth example. Here, the opening and closing catch tags are coded around a Java scriptlet that causes an ArithmeticException to be thrown due to a divide by zero error. Then, when the exception is thrown, execution jumps over the Java expression that displays the result of the calculation. However, the catch tag also exposes the exception as a variable named e. As a result, the if tag that follows the catch tag is able to display an appropriate error message.

Of course, if you edit the Java scriptlet that's in the catch tag so it performs a legal calculation, no exception will be thrown. In that case, the result of the calculation will be displayed and the error message won't be displayed.

The sixth example shows how to use the redirect tag to redirect a client to a new URL. In this case, the redirect tag is coded within an if tag so the client isn't redirected unless the condition in the if statement is true.

Although this figure doesn't include an example of the param tag, figure 11-3 does illustrate the use of this tag within the url tag. If you read through the documentation for the param tag, you'll find that you can also use it with other tags such as the import tag.

Other tags in the JSTL core library

Tag name	Description
out	Uses EL to display a value, automatically handling most special characters such as the left angle bracket (<) and right angle bracket (>).
set	Sets the value of an attribute in a scope.
remove	Removes an attribute from a scope.
catch	Catches any exception that occurs in its body and optionally creates an EL variable that refers to the Throwable object for the exception.
redirect	Redirects the client browser to a new URL.
param	Adds a parameter to the parent tag.

An out tag that displays a message

Using the Value attribute

```
<c:out value="${message}" default="No message" />
```

Using the tag's body

```
<c:out value="${message}">
    No message
</c:out>
```

A set tag that sets a value in an attribute

```
<c:set var="message" scope="session" value="Test message" />
```

A set tag that sets a value in a JavaBean

JSP code with JSTL

```
<c:set target="${user}" property="firstName" value="John" />
```

Equivalent standard JSP tag

```
<jsp:setProperty name="user" property="firstName" value="John"/>
```

A remove tag that removes an attribute

```
<c:remove var="message" scope="session" />
```

A catch tag that catches an exception

```
<c:catch var="e">
    <%  // this scriptlet statement will throw an exception
        int i = 1/0;
    %>
    <p>Result: <%= i %></p>
</c:catch>
<c:if test="${e != null}">
    <p>An exception occurred. Message: ${e.message}</p>
</c:if>
```

A redirect tag that redirects to another page

```
<c:if test="${e != null}">
    <c:redirect url="/error_java.jsp" />
</c:if>
```

Figure 11-10   Other tags in the JSTL core library

The Cart application

Now that you've learned the details for coding JSTL tags, you're ready to see how they're used within the context of an application. To show that, this chapter finishes by showing a Cart application that maintains a simple shopping cart for a user. Since this application uses the MVC pattern, the JSPs don't require extensive use of JSTL tags. However, the url tag is needed to encode URLs, and the forEach tag is needed to display the items in the user's cart.

The user interface

Figure 11-11 shows the user interface for the Cart application. From the Index page, you can click on the Add To Cart link for any of the four CDs to add the CD to your cart. Then, the Cart page will display all of the items that have been added to your cart.

On the Cart page, you can update the quantity for an item by entering a new quantity in the Quantity column and clicking on the Update button. Or, you can remove an item from the cart by clicking on its Remove Item button. Finally, you can return to the Index page by clicking on the Continue Shopping button, or you can begin the checkout process by clicking on the Checkout button.

The Index page

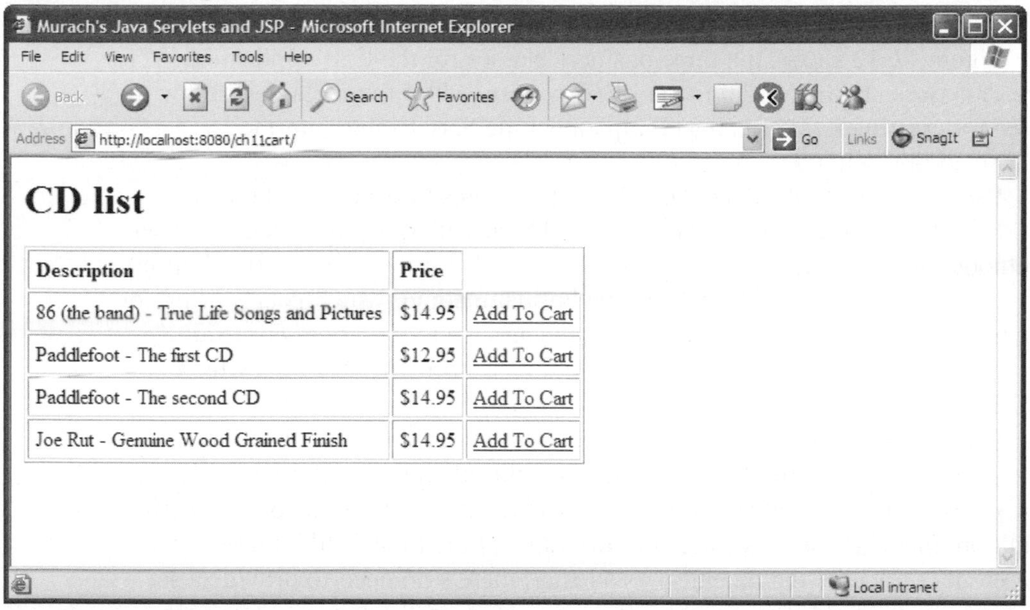

The Cart page

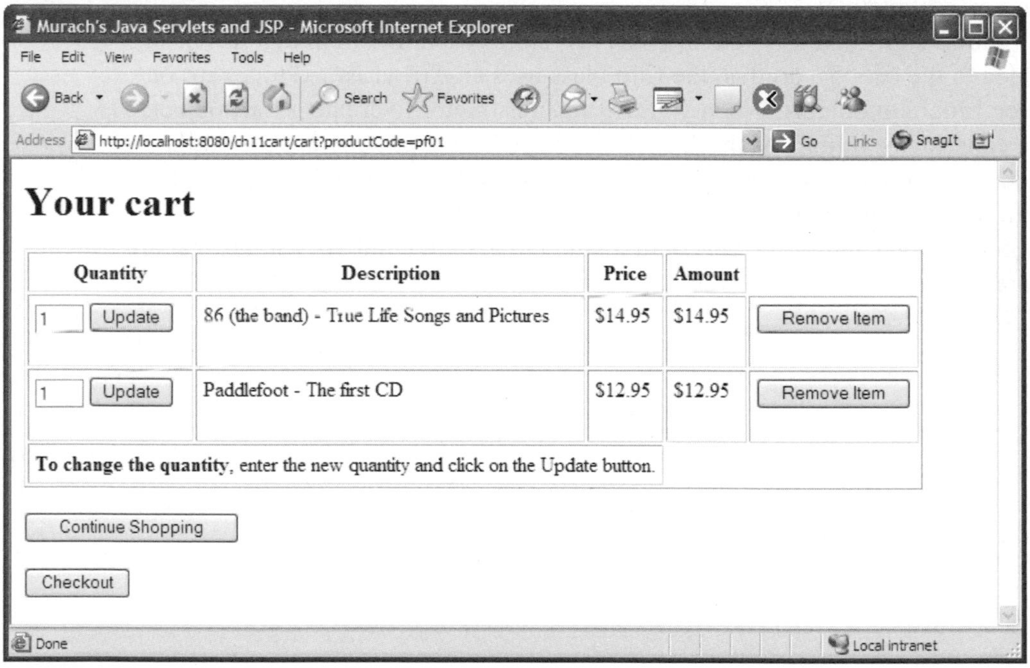

Figure 11-11   The user interface for the Cart application

The code for the business classes

Figure 11-12 shows the three business classes for the Cart application. These classes are the Model in the MVC pattern. All of these classes follow the rules for creating a JavaBean and implement the Serializable interface as described in chapter 9.

Part 1 shows the Product class. This class stores information about each product that's available from the web site. In particular, it provides get and set methods for the code, description, and price fields for the product. In addition, this class provides the getPriceCurrencyFormat method, which gets a string for the price after the currency format has been applied to the price. For example, for a double value of 11.5, this method returns a string of "$11.50", which is usually the format that you want to display on a JSP.

Part 2 shows the LineItem class. This class stores information about each line item that's stored in the cart. To do that, this class uses a Product object as one of its instance variables to store the product information for the line item. In addition, this class always calculates the value of the total field by multiplying the product price by the quantity. As a result, there's no need to provide a set method for this field. Finally, this class provides a getTotalCurrencyFormat method that applies currency formatting to the double value that's returned by the getTotal method.

Part 3 shows the Cart class. This class stores each line item that has been added to the cart. To do that, the Cart class uses an ArrayList to store zero or more LineItem objects. When you use the constructor to create a Cart object, the constructor initializes the ArrayList object. Then, you can use the addItem method to add an item, or you can use the removeItem method to remove an item. In addition, you can use the getItems method to return the ArrayList object, or you can use the getCount method to get the number of items that are stored in the cart.

The code for the Product class

```
package business;

import java.io.Serializable;
import java.text.NumberFormat;

public class Product implements Serializable
{
    private String code;
    private String description;
    private double price;

    public Product()
    {
        code = "";
        description = "";
        price = 0;
    }

    public void setCode(String code)
    {
        this.code = code;
    }

    public String getCode()
    {
        return code;
    }

    public void setDescription(String description)
    {
        this.description = description;
    }

    public String getDescription()
    {
        return description;
    }

    public void setPrice(double price)
    {
        this.price = price;
    }

    public double getPrice()
    {
        return price;
    }

    public String getPriceCurrencyFormat()
    {
        NumberFormat currency = NumberFormat.getCurrencyInstance();
        return currency.format(price);
    }
}
```

Figure 11-12   The code for the business classes (part 1 of 3)

The code for the LineItem class

```
package business;

import java.io.Serializable;
import java.text.NumberFormat;

public class LineItem implements Serializable
{
    private Product product;
    private int quantity;

    public LineItem() {}

    public void setProduct(Product p)
    {
        product = p;
    }

    public Product getProduct()
    {
        return product;
    }

    public void setQuantity(int quantity)
    {
        this.quantity = quantity;
    }

    public int getQuantity()
    {
        return quantity;
    }

    public double getTotal()
    {
        double total = product.getPrice() * quantity;
        return total;
    }

    public String getTotalCurrencyFormat()
    {
        NumberFormat currency = NumberFormat.getCurrencyInstance();
        return currency.format(this.getTotal());
    }
}
```

Figure 11-12   The code for the business classes (part 2 of 3)

The code for the Cart class

```
package business;

import java.io.Serializable;
import java.util.ArrayList;

public class Cart implements Serializable
{
    private ArrayList<LineItem> items;

    public Cart()
    {
        items = new ArrayList<LineItem>();
    }

    public ArrayList<LineItem> getItems()
    {
        return items;
    }

    public int getCount()
    {
        return items.size();
    }

    public void addItem(LineItem item)
    {
        String code = item.getProduct().getCode();
        int quantity = item.getQuantity();
        for (int i = 0; i < items.size(); i++)
        {
            LineItem lineItem = items.get(i);
            if (lineItem.getProduct().getCode().equals(code))
            {
                lineItem.setQuantity(quantity);
                return;
            }
        }
        items.add(item);
    }

    public void removeItem(LineItem item)
    {
        String code = item.getProduct().getCode();
        for (int i = 0; i < items.size(); i++)
        {
            LineItem lineItem = items.get(i);
            if (lineItem.getProduct().getCode().equals(code))
            {
                items.remove(i);
                return;
            }
        }
    }
}
```

Figure 11-12   The code for the business classes (part 3 of 3)

The code for the servlets and JSPs

Figure 11-13 shows the one servlet and two JSPs for the Cart application. Here, the servlet is the Controller and the two JSPs are the View in the MVC pattern.

Part 1 shows the JSP code for the Index page that's displayed when the Cart application first starts. This page includes a taglib directive that imports the JSTL core library. Then, this page displays a table where there is one row for each product. Here, each product row includes an Add To Cart link that uses the JSTL url tag to encode the URL that's used to add each product to the cart. This code works because the CartServlet shown in part 2 of this figure has been mapped to the "/cart" URL.

Although these four rows are hard-coded for this page, the product data could also be read from a database and stored in an ArrayList. Then, you could use a forEach tag to display each product in the ArrayList. The technique for doing this is similar to the technique for displaying each line item in the cart as shown in figure 11-4.

The code for the index.jsp file

```
<!doctype html public "-//W3C//DTD HTML 4.0 Transitional//EN">

<html>
<head>
    <title>Murach's Java Servlets and JSP</title>
</head>
<body>

<%@ taglib prefix="c" uri="http://java.sun.com/jsp/jstl/core" %>

<h1>CD list</h1>

<table cellpadding="5" border=1>

  <tr valign="bottom">
    <td align="left"><b>Description</b></td>
    <td align="left"><b>Price</b></td>
    <td align="left"></td>
  </tr>

  <tr valign="top">
    <td>86 (the band) - True Life Songs and Pictures</td>
    <td>$14.95</td>
    <td><a href="<c:url value='/cart?productCode=8601' />">
        Add To Cart</a></td>
  </tr>

  <tr valign="top">
    <td>Paddlefoot - The first CD</td>
    <td>$12.95</td>
    <td><a href="<c:url value='/cart?productCode=pf01' />">
        Add To Cart</a></td>
  </tr>

  <tr valign="top">
    <td>Paddlefoot - The second CD</td>
    <td>$14.95</td>
    <td><a href="<c:url value='/cart?productCode=pf02' />">
        Add To Cart</a></td>
  </tr>

  <tr valign="top">
    <td>Joe Rut - Genuine Wood Grained Finish</td>
    <td>$14.95</td>
    <td><a href="<c:url value='/cart?productCode=jr01' />">
        Add To Cart</a></td>
  </tr>

</table>

</body>
</html>
```

Figure 11-13   The code for the servlets and JSPs (page 1 of 4)

Part 2 shows the servlet code for the CartServlet. To start, this code gets the value of the productCode parameter from the request object. This parameter uniquely identifies the Product object. Then, this code gets the value of the quantity parameter if there is one. However, unless the user clicked on the Update button from the Cart page, this parameter will be equal to a null value.

After getting the parameter values from the request, this servlet uses the getAttribute method to get the Cart object from a session attribute named cart. If this method returns a null value, this servlet creates a new Cart object.

After the Cart object has been retrieved or created, this servlet sets the value of the quantity variable. To do that, it starts by setting the quantity variable to a default value of 1. Then, if the quantityString variable contains an invalid integer value, such as a null value, the parseInt method of the Integer class will throw an exception. This also causes the quantity to be set to 1. However, if the user enters a valid integer such as 0 or 2, the quantity will be set to that value. Finally, if the quantity is a negative number, the quantity will be set to 1.

After the quantity variable has been set, this servlet uses the getProduct method of the ProductIO class to read the Product object that corresponds with the productCode variable from a text file named products.txt that's stored in the application's WEB-INF directory. To do that, this code specifies the productCode variable as the first argument of the getProduct method. Although this application stores data in a text file to keep things simple, a more realistic application would probably read this data from a database as described in section 3 of this book.

After the Product object has been read from the text file, this servlet creates a LineItem object and sets its Product object and quantity. Then, if the quantity is greater than 0, this code adds the LineItem object to the Cart object. However, if the quantity is 0, this code removes the item from the Cart object.

Finally, this servlet sets the Cart object as a session attribute named cart. Then, it forwards the request and response to the Cart page.

As you review this code, you may notice that the CartServlet only provides an HTTP Get method. As a result, you can't use the HTTP Post method to call this servlet. However, this servlet doesn't write any data to the server, and a user can request this servlet multiple times in a row without causing any problems. As a result, you don't need to implement the HTTP Post method for this servlet.

The code for the CartServlet class

```java
package cart;

import java.io.*;
import javax.servlet.*;
import javax.servlet.http.*;

import business.*;
import data.*;

public class CartServlet extends HttpServlet
{
    protected void doGet(HttpServletRequest request,
                         HttpServletResponse response)
                    throws ServletException, IOException
    {
        String productCode = request.getParameter("productCode");
        String quantityString = request.getParameter("quantity");

        HttpSession session = request.getSession();
        Cart cart = (Cart) session.getAttribute("cart");
        if (cart == null)
            cart = new Cart();

        int quantity = 1;
        try
        {
            quantity = Integer.parseInt(quantityString);
            if (quantity < 0)
                quantity = 1;
        }
        catch(NumberFormatException nfe)
        {
            quantity = 1;
        }

        ServletContext sc = getServletContext();
        String path = sc.getRealPath("WEB-INF/products.txt");
        Product product = ProductIO.getProduct(productCode, path);

        LineItem lineItem = new LineItem();
        lineItem.setProduct(product);
        lineItem.setQuantity(quantity);
        if (quantity > 0)
            cart.addItem(lineItem);
        else if (quantity == 0)
            cart.removeItem(lineItem);

        session.setAttribute("cart", cart);
        String url = "/cart.jsp";
        RequestDispatcher dispatcher =
                getServletContext().getRequestDispatcher(url);
        dispatcher.forward(request, response);
    }
}
```

Figure 11-13   The code for the servlets and JSPs (page 2 of 4)

Part 3 shows the JSP code for the Cart page. Like the Index page, this page uses the taglib directive to import the JSTL core library. Then, it uses a table to display one row for each item in the cart. To do that, it uses a forEach tag to loop through each LineItem object in the ArrayList that's returned by the items property of the cart attribute, and it uses EL to display the data for each line item.

At first glance, the code for this row seems complicated because the first and last columns contain HTML forms that include text boxes, hidden text boxes, and buttons. For example, the first column contains a form that includes a hidden text box that sets the productCode parameter for the form, a text box that allows the user to enter a quantity for the form, and a button that submits the form to the CartServlet. Similarly, the last column contains a hidden text box that sets the productCode parameter for the form, another hidden text box that sets the quantity parameter to 0 (which causes the item to be removed from the cart), and a button that submits the form to the CartServlet. However, if you study this code, you shouldn't have much trouble understanding how it works.

The code for the cart.jsp file   **Page 1**

```
<!doctype html public "-//W3C//DTD HTML 4.0 Transitional//EN">

<html>
<head>
    <title>Murach's Java Servlets and JSP</title>
</head>
<body>

<h1>Your cart</h1>

<table border="1" cellpadding="5">
  <tr>
    <th>Quantity</th>
    <th>Description</th>
    <th>Price</th>
    <th>Amount</th>
  </tr>

<%@ taglib prefix="c" uri="http://java.sun.com/jsp/jstl/core" %>
<c:forEach var="item" items="${cart.items}">

  <tr valign="top">
    <td>
      <form action="<c:url value='/cart' />">
        <input type="hidden" name="productCode"
               value="${item.product.code}">
        <input type=text size=2 name="quantity"
               value="${item.quantity}">
        <input type="submit" value="Update">
      </form>
    </td>
    <td>${item.product.description}</td>
    <td>${item.product.priceCurrencyFormat}</td>
    <td>${item.totalCurrencyFormat}</td>
    <td>
      <form action="<c:url value='/cart' />">
        <input type="hidden" name="productCode"
               value="${item.product.code}">
        <input type="hidden" name="quantity"
               value="0">
        <input type="submit" value="Remove Item">
      </form>
    </td>
  </tr>

</c:forEach>

  <tr>
    <td colspan="3">
      <p><b>To change the quantity</b>, enter the new quantity
            and click on the Update button.</p>
    </td>
  </tr>

</table>
```

Figure 11-13   The code for the servlets and JSPs (page 3 of 4)

Part 4 shows the rest of the JSP code for the Cart page. This code contains two forms where each form contains a single button. The button on the first form displays the Index page, and the button on the second form displays the Checkout page (which isn't shown or described in this chapter).

If you review the use of the JSTL and EL code in the Index and Cart pages, you'll see that the url tag is used to encode all of the URLs. As a result, the Cart application will be able to track sessions even if the user has disabled cookies. You'll also see that the only other JSTL tag that's used is the forEach tag in the Cart page. Finally, you'll see that EL is used to display the nested properties that are available from the Product, LineItem, and Cart objects. This is a typical JSTL and EL usage for applications that use the MVC pattern.

The code for the cart.jsp file   **Page 2**

```
<br>

<form action="<c:url value='/index.jsp' />" method="post">
  <input type="submit" value="Continue Shopping">
</form>

<form action="<c:url value='/checkout.jsp' />" method="post">
  <input type="submit" value="Checkout">
</form>

</body>
</html>
```

Note

- In the web.xml file, the CartServlet class is mapped to the "/cart" URL.

Figure 11-13   The code for the servlets and JSPs (page 4 of 4)

Perspective

The goal of this chapter has been to show you how to use JSTL with EL to eliminate or reduce scripting from your JSPs. However, it isn't always possible to remove all scripting from your applications by using JSTL. In that case, you may occasionally want to use scripting. Another option, though, is to create and use custom tags that are stored in a custom tag library as described in the next chapter.

Summary

- The *JSP Standard Tag Library* (*JSTL*) provides tags for common tasks that need to be performed in JSPs.

- Before you can use JSTL tags, you must make the jstl.jar and standard.jar files available to the application.

- Before you can use JSTL tags in a JSP, you must code a taglib directive for the library that you want to use.

- You can use a web browser to view the documentation for JSTL.

- You can use the url tag to encode URLs so the application can track sessions even if the client browser has cookies disabled.

- You can use the forEach tag to loop through most types of collections, including regular arrays.

- You can use the forTokens tag to loop through items in a delimited string.

- You can use the if tag to code the equivalent of a Java if statement.

- You can use the choose tag to code the equivalent of a Java if/else statement.

- You can use the import tag to include files at runtime. This works like the standard JSP include tag, but it can be used to include files from other web applications even when they're running on remote web servers.

Exercise 11-1   Use JSTL in the Download application

In this exercise, you'll enhance the Download application that you used in exercise 10-2 of the last chapter.

1. Open the ch11download project in the ex_starts directory. Then, run the application to refresh your memory about how it works.

2. Use your IDE to add the JSTL library to this project. With NetBeans, you can do that by right-clicking on the Libraries folder for the project and selecting the Add Libraries command from the resulting menu.

3. Open the JSPs for this project. Then, add the taglib directive for the core JSTL library to the beginning of these pages. Finally, use the url tag to encode all the URLs in this application.

4. Test the application to make sure it works correctly.

5. Open the index.jsp file. Then, modify it so it uses the if tag to only display the welcome message if the cookie for the first name doesn't contain a null value.

6. Test the application to make sure it works correctly.

Exercise 11-2   Use JSTL in the Cart application

In this exercise, you'll use JSTL to loop through an array list of Product objects.

1. Open the ch11cart project in the ex_starts directory.

2. Open the web.xml file. Note that the ProductsServlet class is called when this application starts. This means that the browser will issue an HTTP Get request for the ProductsServlet class so its doGet method will be called.

3. Open the ProductsServlet.java file. Note how this servlet uses the processRequest method to read an ArrayList of Product objects from the projects.txt file and store them as an attribute of the session object. Note too that this method is called from both the doGet and doPost methods.

4. Test the application to make sure it works correctly.

5. Add the JSTL library to this project. Then, open the index.jsp file, and add the taglib directive that imports the core JSTL library.

6. In the index.jsp file, add a forEach tag that loops through the ArrayList of Product objects and displays one row for each product. To do that, you can use EL to display the properties of each Product object. (Be sure to delete any old code that you no longer need.)

7. Test the application to make sure that it works correctly.

12

How to use custom JSP tags

For most applications, you can use the standard JSP tags, EL, and the JSTL tags that you learned about in the last three chapters to eliminate scripting from your JSPs. Sometimes, however, these tags don't provide all the functionality that you need.

In those cases, you can use the skills presented in this chapter to create and use custom JSP tags. Because it's difficult to understand how these tags work without seeing examples, this chapter starts with a simple example and works toward more complex examples.

How to code a custom tag that doesn't have a body

This chapter begins by showing how to code the three components of a custom JSP tag that doesn't have a body. This is the simplest type of tag.

The tag

Part 1 of figure 12-1 shows how to code a *custom tag* that inserts the current date into a JSP. Before you can use a custom tag in a JSP, though, you must code a *taglib directive* in the JSP. Within this directive, the URI attribute must specify the location of the Tag Library Descriptor (or TLD), which you'll learn more about in the next part of this figure. In addition, the prefix attribute must specify a prefix that you can use for the custom tags that are defined by the TLD.

Once you code the taglib directive, you can use any of the custom tags in the TLD. To do that, you code an opening bracket (<), the prefix that's specified in the taglib directive, a colon, the name of the tag, and a slash followed by a closing bracket (/>).

In the example in this figure, you could get the same result by using a JSP scriptlet and expression. However, using a custom tag has a couple of advantages. First, custom tags reduce the amount of Java scripting that's required in your JSP pages. Second, custom tags can help you organize the code of an application so you can reduce code duplication, which can make the code for your application easier to maintain.

As you progress through this chapter, don't forget that all of the custom tag examples assume that a taglib directive like the one in this figure has been coded before the custom tags are used. That's why all of the custom tags in this chapter use a prefix of mma (an abbreviation for Mike Murach & Associates). And that's why all of the custom tags in this chapter use a TLD file named murach.tld that's stored in the application's WEB-INF directory.

A taglib directive that specifies a custom tag library

```
<%@ taglib prefix="mma" uri="/WEB-INF/murach.tld" %>
```

JSP code that uses the custom currentDate tag to display the date

```
<p>The current date is <mma:currentDate />.</p>
```

A JSP that displays the custom tag

Description

- Before you can code a *custom tag* in a JSP, you must code a *taglib directive*. This directive must specify the location of the Tag Library Descriptor (TLD), and it must specify a prefix that can be used for the custom tags that are defined by this TLD.

- All of the custom tag examples in this chapter assume that the taglib directive shown above has been coded before the custom tags are used.

The tag element

Before you can use a custom tag in a JSP, you must create a *Tag Library Descriptor (TLD)* file that describes the tag. To illustrate, part 2 of this figure shows a TLD that contains two custom tags. As you progress through this chapter, you'll learn how to add other types of tags to this TLD. Although you can code as many TLDs as you like for an application, it's typical to code a single TLD that contains all of the custom tags for an application.

Since TLDs are XML documents, you must start a TLD with the standard XML header information. Since you don't need to understand this header information, you can just copy the header from an old TLD to the start of a new one. After the header information, the rest of the tags are XML tags that define the elements of the TLD. Since these tags are similar to HTML tags, you shouldn't have any trouble coding them. However, unlike HTML tags, XML tags are case-sensitive. As a result, when you work with the XML tags in a TLD, you must use the exact capitalization shown in these figures.

After the header information, the taglib element defines the *tag library*. Within this element, you can code the tag library version, a short name for the library, and a URI for the library. Then, if you want to include a brief description of the tag library, you can code the info element. For Tomcat 6.0, the tag library version is the only one of these tags that's required. However, this may vary depending on the JSP engine.

After these elements, you code one tag element for each custom tag in the tag library. When you create a tag element, you're required to code a name element that defines the name of the tag as well as a tagclass element that defines the class that carries out the actions of the tag. This class is sometimes referred to as the *tag class*, or *tag handler class*, and you'll learn more about it in part 3 of this figure.

After the tagclass element, you can code an info element that provides a description of the custom tag. This information should describe the function of the tag so other programmers and web designers can decide whether they want to use it.

When you create a TLD file, you must save the file with a TLD extension. You must also save it in the WEB-INF directory or one of its subdirectories. In the applications that come with this book, for example, the TLD is saved in the murach.tld file of the WEB-INF directory.

A TLD file that contains two tag elements

```xml
<?xml version="1.0" encoding="UTF-8"?>
<taglib version="2.0" xmlns="http://java.sun.com/xml/ns/j2ee"
    xmlns:xsi="http://www.w3.org/2001/XMLSchema-instance"
    xsi:schemaLocation="http://java.sun.com/xml/ns/j2ee
        web-jsptaglibrary_2_0.xsd">

    <tlib-version>1.0</tlib-version>
    <short-name>murach</short-name>
    <uri>/WEB-INF/murach.tld</uri>
    <info>A custom tag library developed by
          Mike Murach and Associates</info>

    <tag>
        <name>currentDate</name>
        <tagclass>tags.CurrentDateTag</tagclass>
        <info>Returns the current date with the SHORT date format</info>
    </tag>

    <tag>
        <name>currentTime</name>
        <tagclass>tags.CurrentTimeTag</tagclass>
    </tag>

</taglib>
```

Description

- The *Tag Library Descriptor (TLD)* is an XML document that describes a *tag library* that contains custom tags that can be used in an application. Although an application typically uses a single TLD to define all of its custom tags, there's no limit to the number of TLDs an application can have.

- The file for a TLD must be saved in the WEB-INF directory or one of its subdirectories, and it must be saved with an extension of TLD.

- If your application doesn't have an existing TLD, you can create one by copying one that's included with the source code for this book. Then, you can add your custom tag elements to this file.

- Within a tag element, you must use the name element to specify the name of the custom tag and the tagclass element to specify the *tag class* for the tag. The tag class is the Java class that does the actions of the tag.

- Within a tag element, you can use the info element to specify descriptive information about the tag, but this element is optional.

- The elements that are required by a TLD may vary depending on the JSP engine. As a result, if a TLD like the one in this figure doesn't work for you, you may need to consult the documentation for your JSP engine.

- Since Tomcat loads the TLD for an application at startup, you must restart your application whenever you modify this file. Otherwise, your changes won't take effect.

Figure 12-1   How to code a custom tag that doesn't have a body (part 2 of 3)

Section 2 *Essential servlet and JSP skills*

The tag class

Part 3 of this figure presents the tag class for the currentDate tag shown in part 1. This class displays the current date with the MM/DD/YY format.

To define a tag class for a custom tag, you must implement the Tag interface. Since you probably don't want to define every method in the Tag interface, though, it's easier to extend the TagSupport class instead. This class is a convenience class that implements the Tag interface. As a result, when you extend this class, you only need to define the methods that you want to use.

To define the actions of a custom tag, you can override the doStartTag method of the TagSupport class. This method is called when the custom tag is read. In this figure, for example, the first three statements in this method use the Date and DateFormat classes to get and format the current date. Then, a try/catch statement uses the built-in pageContext object to return a JspWriter object that's used to return the formatted date to the JSP. Last, the doStartTag method returns the SKIP_BODY constant that's defined in the TagSupport class. Whenever a tag doesn't have a body, you return the SKIP_BODY constant after you use the JspWriter to write the tag's data to the JSP.

When you code tag classes, you can save them in the same location as your other Java classes. However, it's common to store tag classes in a separate package. That's why all the tag classes shown in this chapter are saved in a package named tags.

At this point, you should have a pretty good idea of how custom tags work. When the JSP engine encounters a custom tag, it uses the tag prefix to relate the tag to the taglib directive, which points to the TLD for the tag. Then, the JSP engine uses the TLD to find the tag class that implements the custom tag. Once that's done, the JSP engine can translate the JSP into a servlet that calls the tag class.

A tag class for a tag that doesn't include a body

```
package tags;

import javax.servlet.jsp.*;
import javax.servlet.jsp.tagext.*;
import java.io.*;
import java.util.*;
import java.text.DateFormat;

public class CurrentDateTag extends TagSupport
{
    public int doStartTag() throws JspException
    {
        Date currentDate = new Date();
        DateFormat shortDate =
            DateFormat.getDateInstance(DateFormat.SHORT);
        String currentDateFormatted = shortDate.format(currentDate);

        try
        {
            JspWriter out = pageContext.getOut();
            out.print(currentDateFormatted);
        }
        catch (IOException ioe)
        {
            ioe.printStackTrace();
        }
        return SKIP_BODY;
    }
}
```

Description

- The *tag class,* or *tag handler class,* is the Java class that defines the actions of the tag. A tag class must implement the Tag interface.

- For a tag that doesn't have a body, you can implement the Tag interface by extending the TagSupport class of the javax.servlet.jsp.tagext package. Then, you can override the doStartTag method.

- To display text on the JSP, you use the print method of the JspWriter object that's stored in the javax.servlet.jsp package. Since this print method throws an IOException, you must use a try/catch statement to handle the exception.

- To get a JspWriter object, you use the getOut method of the pageContext object that's defined in the TagSupport class.

- For a tag that doesn't have a body, the doStartTag method must return the SKIP_BODY constant.

- Although you can store tag classes wherever you store your other Java classes, it's common to create a separate package for the tag classes of a tag library.

Figure 12-1   How to code a custom tag that doesn't have a body (part 3 of 3)

How to code a custom tag that has a body

The tag

Part 1 of figure 12-2 shows you how to use a custom tag with a body in a JSP. As with all custom tags, you must code a taglib directive before you can use the custom tag. In this figure, for example, you must code a taglib directive like the one shown in part 1 of figure 12-1 before you code the ifWeekday tag. Then, when you use the ifWeekday tag, you code the opening tag, followed by the body of the tag, followed by the closing tag.

In this figure, the custom tag determines if the body of the tag is displayed. In part 2 of this figure, you will see that the class for this tag displays the body of the tag on Monday through Friday, but doesn't display it on Saturday or Sunday.

JSP code that uses a custom tag with a body

```
<mma:ifWeekday>
    <p>Live support available at 1-800-555-2222</p>
</mma:ifWeekday>
```

A JSP that displays the tag Monday through Friday

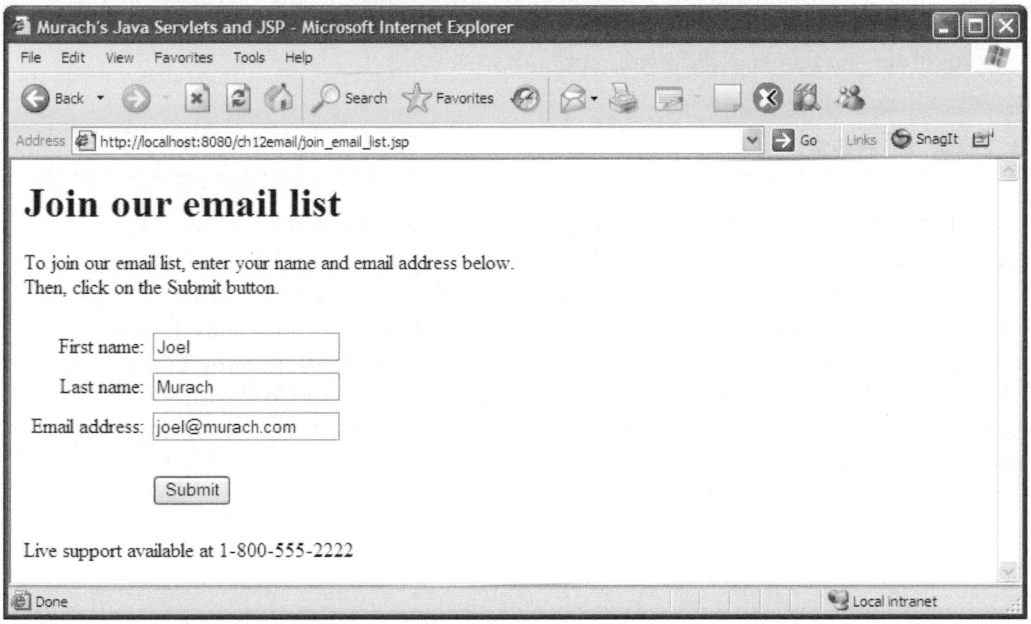

Description

- A tag that has a body must have an opening tag, a body, and a closing tag.
- The body of the tag can contain any HTML or JSP elements.
- The tag class for a custom tag can control whether the body of the tag is displayed in the JSP.

Figure 12-2   How to code a custom tag that has a body (part 1 of 2)

The tag element

Part 2 of this figure shows how to code the tag element for a tag that contains a body. In general, this tag follows the same rules as a tag that doesn't have a body. However, to inform the JSP engine that the tag has a body, you must code a bodycontent element that specifies a value of "JSP". In contrast, when you code a tag that doesn't have a body, you can omit the bodycontent element or you can specify a value of "empty".

The tag class

Part 2 of this figure also shows the tag class for the ifWeekday tag. This class displays the body of the tag if the current day is a weekday.

To start, this class extends the TagSupport class and overrides the doStartTag method. Within the doStartTag method, this class uses an if statement to check if the current day is Saturday or Sunday. If so, this method returns the SKIP_BODY field so the body of the tag is skipped. If not, this method returns the EVAL_BODY_INCLUDE field so the body of the tag is evaluated and displayed.

The tag element in the TLD file

```
<tag>
    <name>ifWeekday</name>
    <tagclass>tags.IfWeekdayTag</tagclass>
    <bodycontent>JSP</bodycontent>
</tag>
```

A tag class that conditionally displays the body of the tag

```
package tags;

import javax.servlet.jsp.*;
import javax.servlet.jsp.tagext.*;
import java.io.*;
import java.util.*;

public class IfWeekdayTag extends TagSupport
{
    public int doStartTag() throws JspException
    {
        Calendar currentDate = new GregorianCalendar();
        int day = currentDate.get(Calendar.DAY_OF_WEEK);
        if (day == Calendar.SATURDAY || day == Calendar.SUNDAY)
        {
            return SKIP_BODY;
        }
        else
        {
            return EVAL_BODY_INCLUDE;
        }
    }
}
```

Description

- When you add a tag that has a body to a TLD, you must specify a value of "JSP" for the bodycontent element. When you add a tag that doesn't have a body to a TLD, you can omit the bodycontent element or specify a value of "empty".

- To create a tag class for a tag that has a body, you can extend the TagSupport class and override the doStartTag method.

- To display the body of the tag in the JSP, the tag class should return the EVAL_BODY_INCLUDE constant. Otherwise, the tag class should return the SKIP_BODY constant.

Figure 12-2   How to code a custom tag that has a body (part 2 of 2)

How to code a custom tag that has attributes

In this topic, you'll learn how to add attributes to a custom tag. Although the example in this topic shows how to add attributes to a tag that doesn't have a body, you can also use attributes with a tag that has a body.

The tag

Part 1 of figure 12-3 shows a JSP that uses a custom tag named ifEmptyMark to display an asterisk after a text box that doesn't contain text. In the JSP, this tag is coded after each of the three text boxes. The two attributes for this tag are color and field, which are used to determine the color of the asterisk and the field that should be checked to see if its empty.

The first code example in this figure shows how to use the ifEmptyMark tag to display a blue asterisk. Here, this color attribute is set to blue and the field attribute is set to an empty string. As a result, the asterisk will be always be displayed.

The second example shows how to use a JSP expression as the value of the field attribute. Here, the field attribute is set to the value that's returned by the getLastName method of the user object. Then, if that method returns a null value or an empty string, this tag will display an asterisk to the right of the text box for that field. If not, the tag handler doesn't do anything. In effect, then, the tag handler provides a type of data validation.

The third example works like the second example except that it uses EL instead of a JSP expression as the value of the field attribute. If you compare the second and third examples, you can see that using EL makes the code easier to read.

So, why would you ever want to use a JSP expression instead of EL? In general, you would only do that if you're working on a legacy application that was developed prior to JSP 2.0. In that case, the web server may not support EL, or you may prefer to use JSP expressions to keep your code consistent with the old code. If you're developing new applications, though, you'll want to use EL in your custom tags.

A JSP that marks required fields with asterisks if the field is empty

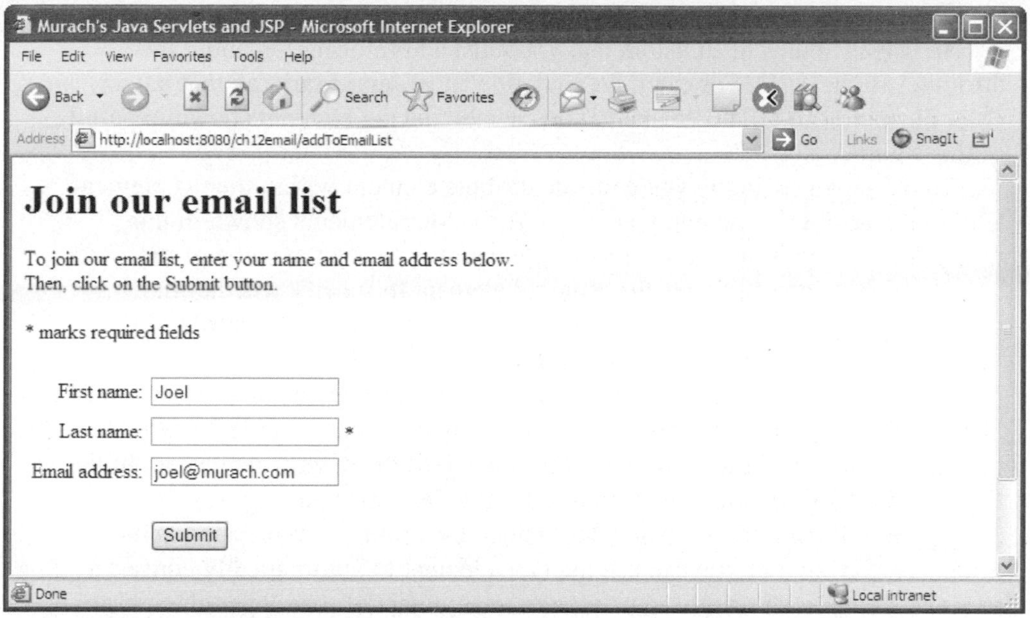

JSP code that uses a custom tag that has attributes

To display the asterisk

```
<p><mma:ifEmptyMark color="blue" field=""/> marks required fields</p>
```

To display the asterisk only if a field is empty (using a JSP expression)

```
<tr>
    <td align="right">Last name:</td>
    <td><input type="text" name="lastName"
        value="<jsp:getProperty name="user" property="lastName"/>">
        <mma:ifEmptyMark color="blue" field="<%= user.getLastName() %>"/>
    </td>
</tr>
```

To display the asterisk only if a field is empty (using EL)

```
<tr>
    <td align="right">Last name:</td>
    <td><input type="text" name="lastName" value="${user.lastName}">
        <mma:ifEmptyMark color="blue" field="${user.lastName}"/>
    </td>
</tr>
```

Description

- The custom tags in this figure use attributes named color and field to send arguments from the JSP to the tag class.

Figure 12-3   How to code a custom tag that has attributes (part 1 of 3)

The tag element

To use attributes in a custom tag, you must add information about the attributes to the TLD. For example, to define an ifEmptyMark tag that has a color attribute and a field attribute, you can add the tag element shown in part 2 of this figure.

To define an attribute, you code an attribute element within the tag element. Within the attribute element, you can code the four elements shown in this figure. To start, you must code a name element to specify the name of the attribute. Then, you can code the required element to specify whether the attribute is required. In the first example in this figure, the color attribute is optional while the field attribute is required.

If an attribute is set to an expression that's determined at runtime, you must also set the rtexprvalue element to true or yes. This informs the JSP engine that the value of the attribute won't be determined until the page is requested. In the first example, this element is set to true for the field attribute.

By default, an attribute that's determined by a runtime expression is returned as a string, but you can use the type element to automatically convert a string attribute to a primitive data type or to an object of a wrapper class of a primitive data type. For instance, the second example in this figure shows the definition for the count attribute of a tag that automatically converts an expression to an int value. Otherwise, you can use the tag class to manually convert the data type.

The syntax for the attribute element in a tag element

```
<attribute>
    <name>attributeName</name>
    <required>true|false|yes|no</required>
    <rtexprvalue>true|false|yes|no</rtexprvalue>
    <type>data_type</type>
</attribute>
```

The tag element with two attributes

```
<tag>
    <name>ifEmptyMark</name>
    <tagclass>tags.IfEmptyMarkTag</tagclass>
    <bodycontent>empty</bodycontent>
    <attribute>
        <name>color</name>
        <required>false</required>
    </attribute>
    <attribute>
        <name>field</name>
        <required>true</required>
        <rtexprvalue>true</rtexprvalue>
    </attribute>
</tag>
```

An attribute element that uses the integer data type

```
<attribute>
    <name>count</name>
    <required>true</required>
    <rtexprvalue>true</rtexprvalue>
    <type>int</type>
</attribute>
```

The attribute child elements

Element	Description
`<name>`	The name of the attribute.
`<required>`	A true/false value that specifies whether this attribute is required. If it isn't required, the tag class should provide a default value.
`<rtexprvalue>`	A true/false value that specifies whether the value of the attribute is determined from a runtime expression. If so, the type element can be any data type. Otherwise, the type element will be a string.
`<type>`	The data type of the attribute value. You only need to code this element when the value of the attribute is determined from a runtime expression and the data type isn't a string.

Description

- The tag element for a tag can include the definitions for one or more attributes.
- For each attribute, you should include at least the name and required elements.

Figure 12-3   How to code a custom tag that has attributes (part 2 of 3)

The tag class

Part 3 of this figure shows how to code a tag class that works with at-tributes. To start, the class must define each attribute as a private instance variable and provide a set method for each attribute.

When you code the set method, you must follow the standard Java naming conventions. For example, if you have an attribute named field, you must code a set method named setField. Similarly, if you have an attribute named height, you must code a set method named setHeight.

When this tag class is executed, it begins by declaring the instance variables named field and color, and it sets the color field to its default value of "red". Then, this class calls the setField method to set the field instance variable. Since this attribute is required, this method will always be called. This sets the value of the field instance variable equal to the value of the Field attribute in the custom JSP tag.

If a color attribute has been coded in the custom JSP tag, this class will also call the setColor method to set the color attribute. Otherwise, the color variable will be equal to its default value of "red".

Once the instance variables have been set, the doStartTag method is called. Within this method, the code checks the value of the field variable. If the field is an empty string, this tag sends an asterisk with the specified color to the JSP. Otherwise, this tag doesn't send any output to the JSP.

A tag class that uses two attributes

```
package tags;

import javax.servlet.jsp.*;
import javax.servlet.jsp.tagext.*;
import java.io.*;

public class IfEmptyMarkTag extends TagSupport
{
    private String field;
    private String color = "red";

    public void setField(String field)
    {
        this.field = field;
    }

    public void setColor(String color)
    {
        this.color = color;
    }

    public int doStartTag() throws JspException
    {
        try
        {
            JspWriter out = pageContext.getOut();
            if (field == null || field.length() == 0)
            {
                out.print("<font color=" + color + "> *</font>");
            }
        }
        catch(IOException ioe)
        {
            ioe.printStackTrace();
        }
        return SKIP_BODY;
    }
}
```

How to code a tag handler that uses attributes

- Declare a private instance variable for each attribute.
- Define a set method for each attribute with the standard naming conventions.

Description

- This tag class will cause the custom JSP tag to display an asterisk if the field attribute is an empty string.
- If the custom tag includes the color attribute, the asterisk that's displayed is that color. Otherwise, the asterisk is red.

Figure 12-3   How to code a custom tag that has attributes (part 3 of 3)

How to code a custom tag that reiterates its body

In this topic, you'll learn how to code a tag class that can repeat the body of a tag multiple times.

The tag

Part 1 of figure 12-4 presents a JSP that uses a custom tag to display all of the items contained in the user's cart. Here, the servlet code starts by getting a Cart object that's stored as an attribute of the session object. Then, this servlet code can add a LineItem object to the cart, or remove a LineItem object from the cart. Finally, this servlet code stores the cart as an attribute of the session. That way, the tag class will be able to access the Cart object.

Once the servlet has set the Cart object as an attribute of the session, the cart tag can display one row of a table for each LineItem object in the Cart object. To do that, the body of the cart tag contains some HTML tags and some JSP expressions or EL. This returns the quantity, product description, product price, and total amount for each line item by calling the getAttribute method of the pageContext object. Although you only need to code this row once, you'll see that the tag handler repeats it once for each line item in the cart.

Here again, if you compare the use of JSP expressions with the use of EL, you can see how much easier it is to code and read EL. As a result, you should only use JSP expressions if you're working with an older version of JSP that doesn't support EL.

A page that displays all line items in the user's cart

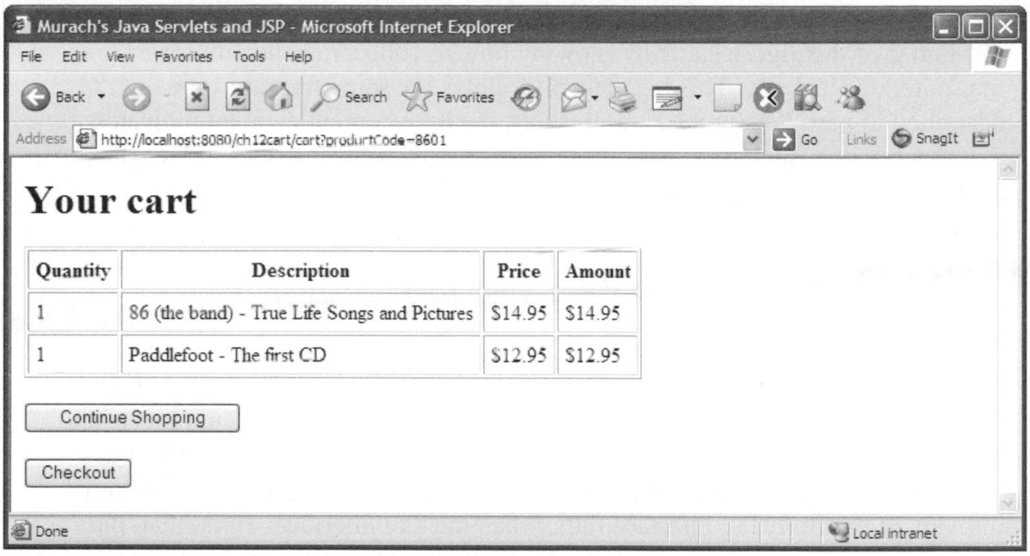

Servlet code that sets the cart attribute

```
Cart cart = (Cart) session.getAttribute("cart");
// code that adds or removes LineItem objects
session.setAttribute("cart", cart);
```

JSP code that displays all items in the cart (using JSP expressions)

```
<mma:cart>
    <tr valign="top">
        <td><%= pageContext.getAttribute("quantity") %></td>
        <td><%= pageContext.getAttribute("productDescription") %></td>
        <td><%= pageContext.getAttribute("productPrice") %></td>
        <td><%= pageContext.getAttribute("total") %></td>
    </tr>
</mma:cart>
```

JSP code that displays all items in the cart (using EL)

```
<mma:cart>
  <tr valign="top">
    <td>${quantity}</td>
    <td>${productDescription}</td>
    <td>${productPrice}</td>
    <td>${total}</td>
  </tr>
</mma:cart>
```

Description

- To pass data to the tag class, you can store that data as a session attribute.
- To use a JSP expression to get an attribute that has been set in the tag class, you can call the getAttribute method of the pageContext object.

Figure 12-4   How to code a custom tag that reiterates its body (part 1 of 3)

The tag element

Part 2 of this figure starts by showing how to code a tag element for a tag that reiterates its body. This tag element follows the same format as the tag described in part 2 of figure 12-2. In short, the bodycontent element indicates that this tag does include a body. Note, however, that this tag doesn't have any attributes.

The tag class

This figure also presents a tag class that gets each line item in the user's cart and displays the data for each LineItem object in the body of the custom JSP tag. In other words, this class loops through a collection of LineItem objects and returns the body of the tag with different attributes for each LineItem object.

To code a tag class that interacts with the body of the tag, the tag class must implement the BodyTag interface rather than the Tag interface. To do that, the tag class usually extends the BodyTagSupport class. Since this convenience class implements all methods of the BodyTag interface, you only need to override the methods that you want to use. Similarly, since the BodyTagSupport class extends the TagSupport class, all methods and fields that you've used so far will be available to any tag class that extends the BodyTagSupport class.

The tag class in this figure contains three instance variables. The first instance variable is an ArrayList object that stores the LineItem objects. The second instance variable is an Iterator object that's used to loop through the LineItem objects stored in the ArrayList object. And the third instance variable is the LineItem object that's used to display data in the tag.

To determine if the tag body should be skipped or evaluated, the doStartTag method retrieves the ArrayList of LineItem objects from the session and checks if it's empty. To do that, this method calls the findAttribute method of the pageContext object. This method will return any attribute stored in the page, request, session, or application scope.

If the array list of line items is empty, the doStartTag method returns the SKIP_BODY constant. As a result, the body of the tag isn't displayed, and the rest of the class is skipped. Otherwise, the doStartTag method returns the EVAL_BODY_BUFFERED constant that's defined in the BodyTagSupport class. As a result, the tag class evaluates the body of the tag by calling the doInitBody and doAfterBody methods.

The doInitBody method initializes the body by preparing the first row of the tag. To do that, this method gets an Iterator object for the collection of LineItem objects. Then, it uses the next method of the Iterator object to get the first LineItem object in the collection and to move the cursor to the second LineItem object in the ArrayList object. After retrieving the first LineItem object, this method calls the setItemAttributes method on the next page, which is a helper method that uses the setAttribute method of the pageContext object to set the five attributes of the LineItem object.

The tag element for the TLD

```
<tag>
    <name>cart</name>
    <tag-class>tags.CartTag</tag-class>
    <body-content>JSP</body-content>
</tag>
```

A tag class that reiterates the body of the tag   Page 1

```
package tags;

import javax.servlet.jsp.*;
import javax.servlet.jsp.tagext.*;
import java.util.*;
import java.io.IOException;

import business.*;

public class CartTag extends BodyTagSupport
{
    private ArrayList<LineItem> lineItems;
    private Iterator iterator;
    private LineItem item;

    public int doStartTag()
    {
        Cart cart = (Cart) pageContext.findAttribute("cart");
        lineItems = cart.getItems();
        if (lineItems.size() <= 0)
            return SKIP_BODY;
        else
            return EVAL_BODY_BUFFERED;
    }

    public void doInitBody() throws JspException
    {
        iterator = lineItems.iterator();
        if (iterator.hasNext())
        {
            item = (LineItem) iterator.next();
            this.setItemAttributes(item);
        }
    }
}
```

Description

- To access a tag that has a body, the tag class must implement the BodyTag interface. The easiest way to do this is to extend the BodyTagSupport class. Since the BodyTagSupport class extends the TagSupport class, this provides access to all of the methods and fields of the TagSupport class.

- If the doStartTag method returns the EVAL_BODY_BUFFERED constant, the body of the tag will be evaluated by calling the doInitBody method and the doAfterBody method.

- The doInitBody method sets the initial values for the first row of the body.

Figure 12-4   How to code a custom tag that reiterates its body (part 2 of 3)

In this example, the custom cart tag doesn't use the productCode attribute. However, the setItemAttributes method of the CartTag class sets the productCode attribute along with the other four attributes. As a result, if you need to access the productCode attribute from within the custom cart tag, you can do that.

After the doInitBody method finishes executing, the body is stored in the bodyContent object that's provided by the BodyTagSupport class. However, the body hasn't yet been displayed. To display the body, you must write the body to the JSP as shown in the doAfterBody method.

The doAfterBody method starts by checking if another element exists in the array list of line items. If so, this method retrieves the LineItem object, and sets the pageContext attributes to the values for that line item. Then, it returns the EVAL_BODY_AGAIN constant. This adds the body to the existing bodyContent object, and it calls the doAfterBody method to evaluate the body again. However, the body still hasn't been displayed.

Eventually, the doAfterBody method finishes looping through all of the line items in the array list. Then, it displays the body. To do that, this method calls the getEnclosingWriter method of the bodyContent object to obtain a JspWriter object. Then, it calls the writeOut method of the bodyContent object and provides the JspWriter object as an argument. This writes the body to the JSP. Last, this method returns the SKIP_BODY constant to indicate that the tag has finished.

Since the writeOut method throws an IOException, you need to catch this exception. That's why all of the code for the doAfterBody method is enclosed in a try/catch statement.

The tag class that reiterates the tag body   **Page 2**

```
    private void setItemAttributes(LineItem item)
    {
        Product p = item.getProduct();
        pageContext.setAttribute(
                "productCode", p.getCode());
        pageContext.setAttribute(
                "productDescription", p.getDescription());
        pageContext.setAttribute(
                "productPrice", p.getPriceCurrencyFormat());
        pageContext.setAttribute(
                "quantity", new Integer(item.getQuantity()));
        pageContext.setAttribute(
                "total", item.getTotalCurrencyFormat());
    }

    public int doAfterBody() throws JspException
    {
        try
        {
            if (iterator.hasNext())
            {
                item = (LineItem) iterator.next();
                this.setItemAttributes(item);
                return EVAL_BODY_AGAIN;
            }
            else
            {
                JspWriter out = bodyContent.getEnclosingWriter();
                bodyContent.writeOut(out);
                return SKIP_BODY;
            }
        }
        catch(IOException ioe)
        {
            System.err.println("error in doAfterBody " + ioe.getMessage());
            return SKIP_BODY;
        }
    }
}
```

Description

- If the doAfterBody method returns the EVAL_BODY_AGAIN constant, the doAfterBody method will be called again.

- You can use the setAttribute method of the PageContext object to set any attributes that you need to access from the JSP tag.

- You can use the getEnclosingWriter and writeOut methods of the bodyContent object to write the body to the JSP.

Figure 12-4   How to code a custom tag that reiterates its body (part 3 of 3)

How to work with scripting variables

If you're using version 2.0 or later of JSP, you can use EL with your custom tags to display attributes that were stored by the tag class. In that case, you don't need to use scripting variables. However, if you're using an older version of JSP, you will need to use JSP expressions to display attributes that were stored by the tag class. In that case, you can create *scripting variables* to make it easier to display these attributes.

An introduction to scripting variables

Figure 12-5 shows how scripting variables can be used to access variables that have been stored as attributes of the pageContext object. Here, the first example shows a custom JSP tag that doesn't use scripting variables. As a result, this tag must use the getAttribute method of the pageContext object to get the three variables that have been stored in the pageContext object by the tag class.

In contrast, the second example uses scripting variables. As a result, you only need to code the name of a scripting variable in an expression when you want to get the related attribute from the pageContext object.

To make this work, you have to do three tasks. First, the tag class must add the scripting variables to the pageContext object as shown in the third example in this figure. Second, you must code a TEI class that defines the scripting variables as shown in the next figure. And third, you must add a tei-class element to the tag element in the TLD as shown in the last example in this figure.

A custom JSP tag without scripting variables

```
<mma:cart>
    <tr valign="top">
        <td><%= pageContext.getAttribute("quantity") %></td>
        <td><%= pageContext.getAttribute("productDescription") %></td>
        <td><%= pageContext.getAttribute("productPrice") %></td>
        <td><%= pageContext.getAttribute("total") %></td>
    </tr>
</mma:cart>
```

A custom JSP tag with scripting variables

```
<mma:cart>
  <tr valign="top">
    <td><%= quantity %></td>
    <td><%= productDescription %></td>
    <td><%= productPrice %></td>
    <td><%= total %></td>
  </tr>
</mma:cart>
```

The code in the tag class that adds the scripting variables to the pageContext object

```
pageContext.setAttribute("productDescription", p.getDescription());
pageContext.setAttribute("productPrice", p.getPriceCurrencyFormat());
pageContext.setAttribute("quantity", new Integer(item.getQuantity()));
pageContext.setAttribute("total", item.getTotalCurrencyFormat());
```

The tag element in the TLD

```
<tag>
    <name>cart</name>
    <tag-class>tags.CartTag</tag-class>
    <tei-class>tags.CartTEI</tei-class>
    <body-content>JSP</body-content>
</tag>
```

How to create a scripting variable

- The tag class must add the scripting variables to the pageContext object.
- The TEI class must define the scripting variables as shown in the next figure.
- The tag element in the TLD must specify both the tag class and the TEI class for the custom tag.

Description

- To make attributes easier to access, you can use *scripting variables*. Then, you can code just the name of a scripting variable in a JSP expression when you want to get the value of an attribute from the pageContext object.

Figure 12-5   An introduction to scripting variables

The TEI class for four scripting variables

Figure 12-6 shows how to code a *TEI class (tag extra information class)* that defines the scripting variables for a tag handler. To code a TEI class, you extend the TagExtraInfo class and override its getVariableInfo method. When you override that method, you must return an array of VariableInfo objects. These objects define the scripting variables.

For each scripting variable, you create a VariableInfo object using the constructor shown in this figure. When you code this constructor, you must provide a string that specifies the name of the variable and you must specify the data type of the variable. For the data type, you can specify a String object, a primitive data type, or a wrapper class for a primitive data type.

After coding the data type, you must code a boolean value that specifies whether the variable is a new scripting variable. If the variable hasn't been declared anywhere else, which is usually the case, you code a true value. Otherwise, you code a false value.

Last, you must define the scope of the scripting variable. Most of the time, you'll want to use the NESTED field. That way, the scripting variables will be available between the opening and closing tags.

The constructor of the VariableInfo class

```
VariableInfo(String varName, String dataType, boolean declare, int scope)
```

A TEI class that creates four scripting variables

```java
package tags;

import javax.servlet.jsp.tagext.*;

public class CartTEI extends TagExtraInfo
{
    public VariableInfo[] getVariableInfo(TagData data)
    {
        return new VariableInfo[]
        {
            new VariableInfo(
                "productDescription", "String", true, VariableInfo.NESTED),
            new VariableInfo(
                "productPrice", "String", true, VariableInfo.NESTED),
            new VariableInfo(
                "quantity", "Integer", true, VariableInfo.NESTED),
            new VariableInfo(
                "total", "String", true, VariableInfo.NESTED),
        };
    }
}
```

The VariableInfo constants that define the scope of a scripting variable

Constant	Scope
AT_BEGIN	From the start of the tag to the end of the JSP.
AT_END	From the end of the tag to the end of the JSP.
NESTED	From the start of the tag to the end of the tag.

Description

- To define scripting variables for a tag class, you create a *tag extra information (TEI) class*. You can store this class in the same location as the tag classes.

- To code a TEI class, you extend the TagExtraInfo class in the javax.servlet.jsp.tagext package. Then, you override the getVariableInfo method to return an array of VariableInfo objects that define the scripting variables.

- For each scripting variable, you create a VariableInfo object that provides this data: the name and data type of the variable, a true/false value that tells whether the variable needs to be declared, and the scope of the variable.

- For the data type of a scripting variable, you can specify a String object, any primitive data type, or any wrapper class for a primitive type.

- To specify whether the scripting variable needs to be declared, you can usually specify a true value to indicate that the variable is new and should be declared.

Figure 12-6   The TEI class for four scripting variables

Classes, methods, and fields for working with custom tags

This topic summarizes the common classes, methods, and fields for working with custom tags. Since this chapter has already presented examples that use these classes, this topic should help you review the skills that you've already learned. In addition, it should give you some ideas for how to use other capabilities of custom tags.

Methods and fields of the TagSupport class

Figure 12-7 presents the common methods of the TagSupport class and shows the fields that these methods can return. When a tag is processed, the doStartTag method is called first, followed by the doEndTag method, followed by the release method. When you extend this class, you only need to override the methods that you want to code.

For many types of tags, you need to override the doStartTag method. If a tag doesn't have a body, you can return the SKIP_BODY field after the statements that process the tag. Then, the body of the tag won't be evaluated. However, if a tag does have a body, you can return the EVAL_BODY_INCLUDE field. Then, the body of the tag will be evaluated.

After the doStartTag method finishes executing, the doEndTag method is called. By default, this method returns the EVAL_PAGE field, which causes the rest of the JSP to be evaluated. Since that's usually what you want, you usually don't need to override this method. However, if you don't want to continue evaluating the JSP below the custom tag, you can override this method and return the SKIP_PAGE field. Then, any part of the JSP below the custom tag won't be displayed.

After the doEndTag method finishes executing, the release method is called. You can use this method to clean up any system resources that are in use. For example, you can use this method to close streams or database connections that you have used in the tag class.

Common methods and fields of the TagSupport class

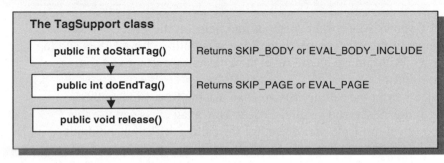

The TagSupport class

public int doStartTag()	Returns SKIP_BODY or EVAL_BODY_INCLUDE
↓	
public int doEndTag()	Returns SKIP_PAGE or EVAL_PAGE
↓	
public void release()	

Description

- The doStartTag method is the first method that's called for a custom tag. Typically, this method contains the statements that perform the processing for the tag.

- If a tag doesn't have a body, the doStartTag method should return the SKIP_BODY field. That way, the body of the tag won't be displayed.

- If a tag has a body, the doStartTag method should return the EVAL_BODY_INCLUDE field. That way, the body of the tag will be displayed.

- If you need to execute any statements at the end of the tag, you can override the doEndTag method.

- To display the rest of the JSP after the custom tag, the doEndTag method should return the EVAL_PAGE field.

- To not display the rest of the JSP after the custom tag, the doEndTag method should return the SKIP_PAGE field.

- If you need to execute any statements that release any system resources that the tag is using, you can code a release method.

Figure 12-7 Methods and fields of the TagSupport class

Methods and fields of the PageContext class

Figure 12-8 shows some of the methods and fields of the PageContext class. Since an instance of this class named pageContext is built-in for all JSPs and tag classes, it allows JSPs and tag classes to communicate by getting and setting objects and attributes.

To get objects from the calling JSP, you can use the first three methods shown in this figure. Since you've already seen how a tag class can use the getOut method to get the JspWriter object for the calling JSP, you shouldn't have much trouble understanding how the getRequest and getResponse methods can return the request and response objects for the calling JSP.

To set and get attributes, you can call any of the set and get methods of the pageContext class. If you don't explicitly specify a scope when setting an attribute, the attribute will only be available within page scope. However, you can use the fields of the PageContext class to specify the scope. Then, you can use these fields to specify the scope when you attempt to get the attribute, or you can use the findAttribute method to search through all four scopes from smallest to largest.

The pageContext object defined in the TagSupport class

```
protected PageContext pageContext
```

Common methods of the PageContext class

Method	Description
getOut()	Returns the JspWriter object from the JSP.
getRequest()	Returns the request object from the JSP.
getResponse()	Returns the response object from the JSP.
setAttribute(String name, Object o)	Sets the named attribute with page scope to the value.
setAttribute(String name, Object o, int scope)	Sets the named attribute with the specified scope to the value. To set the scope, you can use the fields shown below.
getAttribute(String name)	Searches the page scope for an attribute with the specified name. If this method finds the attribute, it returns an object of the Object type. Otherwise, it returns a null value.
getAttribute(String name, int scope)	Searches the specified scope for an attribute with the specified name. If this method finds the attribute, it returns an object of the Object type. Otherwise, it returns a null value. To set the scope, you can use the fields shown below.
findAttribute(String name)	Searches the page, request, session, and application scopes in that sequence for the specified attribute. If this method finds the specified attribute, it returns an object of the Object type. Otherwise, it returns a null value.

The fields of the PageContext class for setting scope

```
PAGE_SCOPE
REQUEST_SCOPE
SESSION_SCOPE
APPLICATION_SCOPE
```

Description

- You can use the pageContext object to set and get JSP objects and attributes.
- For more information about the PageContext class, you can look in the javax.servlet.jsp package of the Java EE API documentation.

Figure 12-8   Methods and fields of the PageContext class

Methods and fields of the BodyTagSupport class

Figure 12-9 shows some of the methods and fields of the BodyTagSupport class. Since this class extends the TagSupport class, you can access the pageContext object and its methods directly from the BodyTagSupport class. In addition, the doEndTag and release methods work much as they do in the TagSupport class.

By default, the doStartTag method of the BodyTagSupport class returns the EVAL_BODY_BUFFERED field. This field indicates that the tag has a body and it causes the doInitBody and doAfterBody methods to be called. As a result, you only need to override this method if you want to add code that writes data to the JSP before the body is evaluated, or if you want to skip the body under certain conditions. To skip the body, the doStartTag method can return the SKIP_BODY field. In that case, the doEndTag and release methods will be called.

If the doStartTag method returns EVAL_BODY_BUFFERED, the doInitBody method is called. Then, you can override this method to initialize any values before the body is evaluated for the first time. After the doInitBody method is executed, the body is evaluated. In other words, the body is read and placed in the built-in bodyContent object, which stores the body. In the next figure, you'll learn more about working with the bodyContent object.

After the doInitBody method finishes executing, the doAfterBody method is called. You can override this method to code statements that need to be executed each time the body is evaluated. If you want to evaluate the body again and add it to the bodyContent object, you return the EVAL_BODY_AGAIN field. Then, when you finish evaluating the body, you return the SKIP_BODY field. But first, you'll probably want to use the bodyContent object to write the body that's stored in the bodyContent object to the JSP.

Once the doAfterBody method returns the SKIP_BODY field, the doEndTag and release methods are called. Since the default values for these methods are usually adequate, you usually don't need to override these methods.

Common methods and fields of the BodyTagSupport class

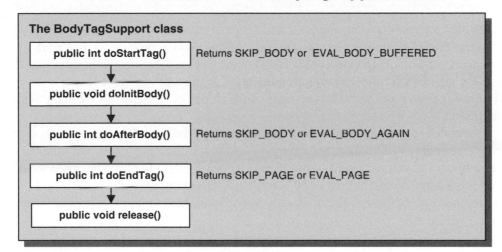

The BodyTagSupport class

public int doStartTag()	Returns SKIP_BODY or EVAL_BODY_BUFFERED
public void doInitBody()	
public int doAfterBody()	Returns SKIP_BODY or EVAL_BODY_AGAIN
public int doEndTag()	Returns SKIP_PAGE or EVAL_PAGE
public void release()	

Description

- The BodyTagSupport class extends the TagSupport class. As a result, the methods and fields that are available in the TagSupport class are also available to the BodyTagSupport class.

- If you want to perform some initial processing for a tag, you can override the doStartTag method of the BodyTagSupport class.

- If the doStartTag method returns the EVAL_BODY_BUFFERED field, the doInitBody and doAfterBody methods will be called to display the body of the tag.

- The doInitBody method should contain all of the initialization statements that are needed for the first evaluation of the body.

- The doAfterBody method should contain all of the statements that are needed for additional evaluations of the body.

- If the doAfterBody method returns the EVAL_BODY_AGAIN field, the body will be added to the bodyContent object and the doAfterBody method will be called again.

- If the doAfterBody method returns the SKIP_BODY field, the processing for the tag will be finished and the body will be skipped.

Figure 12-9   Methods and fields of the BodyTagSupport class

Methods and fields of the BodyContent class

Figure 12-10 shows some methods and fields of the BodyContent class. When you extend the BodyTagSupport class, an instance of this class named bodyContent is automatically available to your tag class and it automatically stores the body of the tag. When the tag class is through evaluating the body of the tag, you can use the getEnclosingWriter and writeOut methods of the BodyContent class to write the body to the JSP.

Sometimes, you may need to use other methods of the BodyContent class. For example, you may need to use the getString method to return the text of the body as a String object. Or, you may need to use the clearBody method to clear the contents of the bodyContent object after the body is evaluated. To learn more about these and other methods of the BodyContent class, you can look them up in the documentation for the Java EE API.

The bodyContent object defined in the BodyTagSupport class

```
protected BodyContent bodyContent
```

Common methods of the BodyContent class

Method	Description
clearBody()	Clears the body.
getEnclosingWriter()	Returns the JspWriter object for the body.
getString()	Returns the body as a String object.
writeOut(Writer out)	Writes the body to the specified out stream.

Description

- The bodyContent object stores the body of the tag before it is written to the JSP.
- To display the body in the JSP, you can use the getEnclosingWriter and writeOut methods of the BodyContent class.
- For more information about the BodyContent class, you can look in the javax.servlet.jsp.tagext package in the Java EE API documentation.

Figure 12-10   Methods and fields of the BodyContent class

Perspective

The goal of this chapter has been to show you how to create and use custom JSP tags. These tags are useful when you need to go beyond the functionality that's available from the standard JSP tags or the JSTL tags. You also need to understand custom tags if you're maintaining legacy code that uses them.

Although it requires a significant amount of effort to create custom tags, there are a couple of advantages to using them. First, custom tags reduce the amount of Java scripting that's required in your JSP pages, which makes it easier for web designers to work with the JSPs. Second, custom tags help organize the code of an application and reduce code duplication, which makes the application easier to maintain.

Summary

- To create a *custom tag* that can be used in a JSP, you must create an XML file called the *Tag Library Descriptor* (*TLD*). This TLD defines the *tag library* that contains the custom tags for an application.

- To implement a custom tag that's defined in the TLD, you code a *tag class*, which can also be referred to as a *tag handler class*. This is a class that implements the Tag interface, usually by extending the TagSupport class.

- Before you can use a custom tag in a JSP, you must code a *taglib directive* that specifies the location of the TLD and a prefix. Then, to use a custom tag, you code the prefix followed by the name of the custom tag.

- You can use custom tags with a body, without a body, with attributes, and with a repeating body.

- Since JSP 2.0, you can use EL with custom tags to get the value of an attribute. Prior to JSP 2.0, you had to use a JSP expression to get the value of an attribute.

- Prior to JSP 2.0, it was a common practice to use *scripting variables* to make it easier to get the value of an attribute. To provide for these variables, you need to code a *tag extra information* (*TEI*) *class* that is related to a tag class by the TLD.

- As you code the tag classes, you can use the methods and fields of the TagSupport, PageContext, BodyTagSupport, and BodyContent classes of the Java EE API.

Exercise 12-1   Create and use a custom tag

In this exercise, you'll enhance the custom tags for the Email List application.

Use the currentDate tag

1. Open the ch12email application that's in the ex_starts folder.

2. Open the murach.tld file that's in the WEB-INF folder. Then, review the information for the custom tag named currentDate.

3. Open the display_email_entry.jsp file. Then, modify it so uses the custom currentDate tag to display the current date below the table that displays information about the user.

4. Run the application to make sure it works correctly.

Modify the ifEmptyMark tag

5. Open the join_email_list.jsp file and modify the ifEmptyMark tags so they use the default color, which is defined as red by the class for the tag.

6. Run the application to make sure it works correctly.

Create and use a currentTime tag

7. Create a custom tag for the current time. To do that, you can create a tag class that works much like the CurrentDateTag class. Then, you can add a tag element for this class to the murach.tld file in the WEB-INF folder.

8. Modify the join_email_list.jsp file so it displays the current date and the current time at the bottom of the page.

9. Modify the display_email_entry.jsp file so it displays the current time after the current date.

10. Run the application to make sure it works correctly.

Modify tag classes

11. Modify the CurrentDateTag and CurrentTimeTag classes so they use the LONG format instead of the SHORT format.

12. Run the application to make sure it works correctly. Note how this changes the tags on both of the JSPs.

13. Modify the IfEmptyMarkTag class so the default color is green.

14. Run the application to make sure it works correctly. This should change the color for all of the tags on the first page.

Exercise 12-2   Create and use a reiterating tag

In this exercise, you'll create a custom tag that reiterates through an array list of
Product objects.

Create a custom tag that displays a table of products

1. Open the ch12cart project that's in the ex_starts folder.

2. Open the ProductsServlet.java file and the web.xml file. Note that the
    ProductsServlet class is called when this application starts. Note also that this
    servlet reads an ArrayList of Product objects from the projects.txt file and
    stores them as an attribute of the session object.

3. Create a tag class named ProductsTag that's like the one in figure 12-4.
    However, the new tag class should display all Product objects that are in the
    ArrayList that has been stored as an attribute of the session object by the
    ProductsServlet class.

4. Open the murach.tld file that's stored in the WEB-INF directory and add a tag
    element for a custom tag named products that uses the ProductsTag class.

5. Open the index.jsp file and modify it so it uses the custom products tag. To do
    that, you'll need to delete all of the hard-coded rows except one. Then, you can
    use the attributes that are available from the tag in place of hard-coded values
    for the row.

6. Run the application to make sure that it works correctly.

Create and use scripting variables

7. Create a TEI class that provides scripting variables for the code, description,
    and price variables of the products tag.

8. Modify the murach.tld file so the products tag uses the TEI class.

9. Modify the index.jsp file so it uses scripting variables to access the code,
    description, and price attributes that are available from the products tag.

10. Run the application to make sure that it works correctly.

Section 3

Essential database skills

For most web applications, the critical data is stored in a database. That's why the two chapters in this section present the essential database skills that you need for developing web applications.

In chapter 13, you'll learn how to use MySQL as the database management system for your databases because MySQL is one of the most popular systems for Java web applications. It is also free. That makes it a great product for learning how to develop web applications that use databases.

Then, in chapter 14, you'll learn how to write servlets that connect to MySQL databases and work with the data that's stored in those databases. Because this works similarly for all database management systems, these chapters present the essential skills that you need for writing Java web applications that work with any database.

13

How to use MySQL as the database management system

Although there are several database management systems that work well with web applications, MySQL is one of the most popular systems for Java web applications. It's also free for the purposes of this book. That's why we used it as the database management system for the applications in this book. In this chapter, you'll learn how to create a MySQL database and how to use SQL statements to work with the data in that database.

Before you start this chapter, you should know that it assumes that you already have some database knowledge or experience. It assumes, for example, that you know that a relational database is made up of tables that consist of columns and rows, that the tables are related by keys, and that you use SQL statements to access and update the data in a database. Although this chapter does review some of these terms, its focus is on the specific skills that you need for using MySQL.

An introduction to MySQL

Figure 13-1 presents an introduction to *MySQL*, which is an open-source database management system (DBMS) that you can download for free from the MySQL web site (www.mysql.com) as described in appendix A. It is also available as part of a hosting package from many Internet Service Providers (ISPs).

What MySQL provides

Figure 13-1 begins by listing some of the reasons that MySQL enjoys such popularity among web developers. To start, it's inexpensive and easy to use when compared with products like Oracle Database or Microsoft SQL Server. It runs fast when compared to those products, especially when you consider the costs. And it runs on most modern operating systems, while Microsoft SQL Server runs only on Windows.

Even though it's free for most uses, MySQL provides most of the features that you would expect from a modern *relational database management system* (*RDBMS*). In particular, it provides support for *Structured Query Language* (*SQL*), which is the industry standard. It provides support for multiple clients. And it provides for connectivity and security.

In terms of web applications, that means you can write Java applications that use SQL statements to access and update the data in a MySQL database. You can connect a Java web application to a MySQL database that's running on an intranet or the Internet. And you can secure your data by restricting access to it.

In the past, MySQL didn't provide some of the features that are typically provided by a relational database. In particular, MySQL didn't provide referential integrity or transaction processing. As a result, referential integrity and transaction processing needed to be implemented on the front end by the application that was using MySQL, which was fine for many types of web applications.

As of release 5.0, however, MySQL provides referential integrity and transaction processing. As a result, referential integrity and transaction processing can be implemented on the backend by MySQL, which reduces the chance that your data will become corrupted. This works similarly to commercial databases such as Oracle Database and Microsoft SQL Server.

MySQL is...

- **Inexpensive.** MySQL is free for most uses and relatively inexpensive for other uses.

- **Fast.** By many accounts, MySQL is one of the fastest relational databases that's currently available.

- **Easy to use.** Compared to other database management systems, MySQL is easy to install and use.

- **Portable.** MySQL runs on most modern operating systems including Windows, Unix, Solaris, and OS/2.

MySQL provides...

- **Support for SQL.** Like any modern database product, MySQL supports SQL, which is the standard language for working with data that's stored in relational databases.

- **Support for multiple clients.** MySQL supports access from multiple clients from a variety of interfaces and programming languages including Java, Perl, PHP, Python, and C.

- **Connectivity.** MySQL can provide access to data via an intranet or the Internet.

- **Security.** MySQL can protect access to your data so only authorized users can view the data.

- **Referential integrity.** If you use the InnoDB tables option, MySQL provides support for referential integrity just like commercial databases such as Oracle Database or Microsoft SQL Server.

- **Transaction processing.** With version 5.0, MySQL provides support for transaction processing just like commercial databases such as Oracle Database or Microsoft SQL Server.

Figure 13-1   An introduction to MySQL

Two ways to interact with MySQL

Figure 13-2 shows two ways that you can interact with MySQL. When you install MySQL as described in appendix A, it includes a command-line tool like the one at the top of this figure. Although this shows the command-line for the Windows operating system, MySQL's command-line tool works similarly on all operating systems. In this example, the user has started the command-line tool, logged into a database named murach, and displayed three rows from the User table in that database. You'll learn more about working with this tool in a moment.

If you install the MySQL GUI tools as described in appendix A, you can use the MySQL Query Browser tool shown in this figure to work with a database. To do that, you can enter a SQL statement in the text area at the top of the tool and click on the Execute button to run the SQL statement. Then, the results for the statement are displayed in a Resultset window. You can also use the Schemata window to view and work with the databases that are running on the current server. In this figure, for example, the Schemata window shows the columns for the User table of the murach database.

When you work with MySQL, you may notice that the terms *database* and *schema* are often used interchangeably. For example, the murach database is sometimes referred to as the murach schema. As a result, when a connect dialog box asks you for a default schema, you can enter murach, music, test, or any other database/schema that's running on the database service.

In general, it's easier to use a GUI tool than a command-line tool to work with databases. For example, the Query Browser tool shown in this figure is relatively self-explanatory. Once you start it, you shouldn't have any trouble using it to execute a SQL statement. That's why this chapter doesn't show you how to use MySQL's GUI tools.

Instead, this chapter focuses on showing you how to use the command-line tool. This tool has one advantage over the Query Browser tool: you can call the command-line tool from a batch file to execute a *SQL script*, which is a file that stores one or more SQL statements. You'll more about that later in this chapter.

A command-line tool

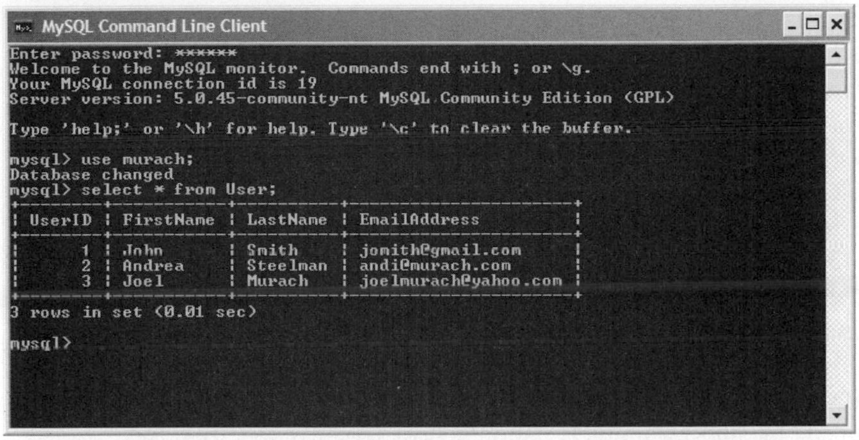

A GUI tool

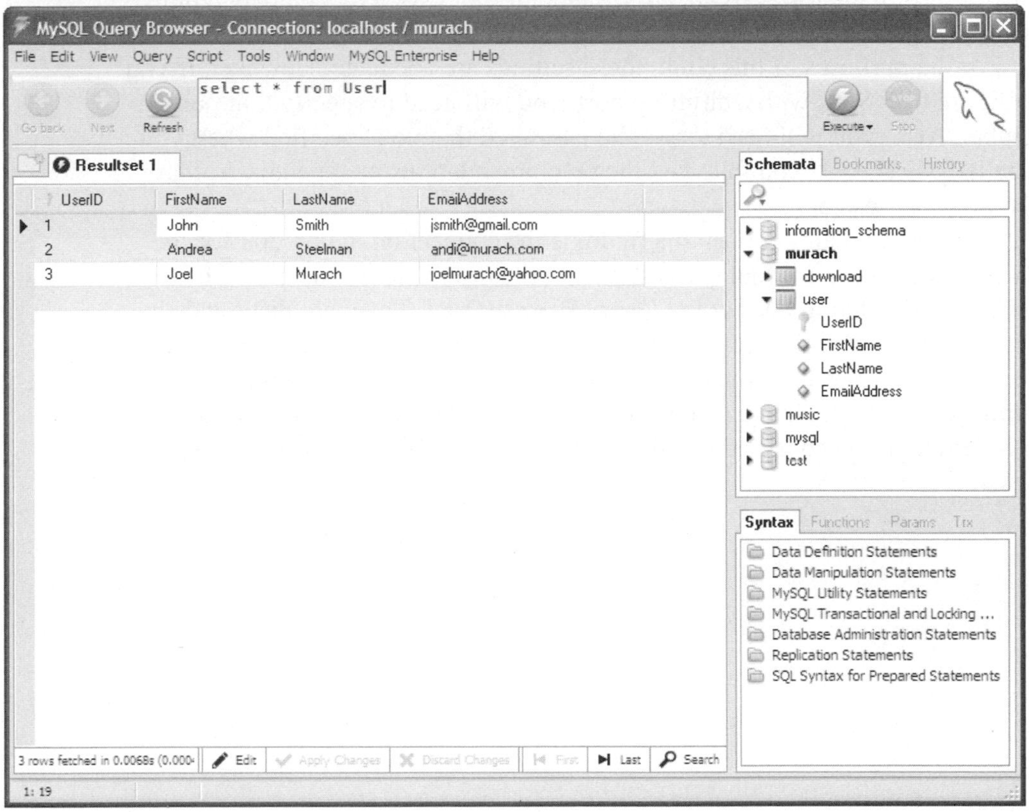

Figure 13-2   Two ways to interact with MySQL

How to connect to the MySQL database service

After you install MySQL, the MySQL *database service* starts automatically whenever you start your computer. This program is often referred to as the *database server* or the *database engine*. This service makes the MySQL databases on your system available to your applications.

If you install the MySQL GUI tools as described in appendix A, you'll be prompted for the information that's needed to connect to the database service as shown in figure 13-3 whenever you start these tools. After you enter the correct information, you can use these GUI tools to work with the databases that are running on that instance of the MySQL service.

The first dialog box in this figure is the connection dialog box for the MySQL Query Browser tool that's shown in the previous figure. Here, the connection is named "localhost – murach", and the host server is specified by the localhost keyword. This dialog box also specifies a port of 3306 (the default port for most database servers), a username of root (MySQL's built-in admin account), a password for the root user, and a default schema of murach.

For the purposes of this book, these settings are adequate. However, if you configured MySQL with a different port, you will need to specify that port number. Also, you will need to use the password that you specified when you installed MySQL. If you followed the recommendations in appendix A, that password is "sesame".

The second dialog box in this figure is the connection dialog box for the MySQL Administrator tool that's shown in the next figure. This dialog box works like the dialog box for the Query Browser tool. The main difference is that you don't need to specify a default schema, and you do need to specify a user, such as the root user, that has adequate permissions to work with the Administrator tool. Here again, if you use root as the user, you need to use the password that you specified when you installed MySQL, which should be "sesame".

The connection dialog box for the Query Browser tool

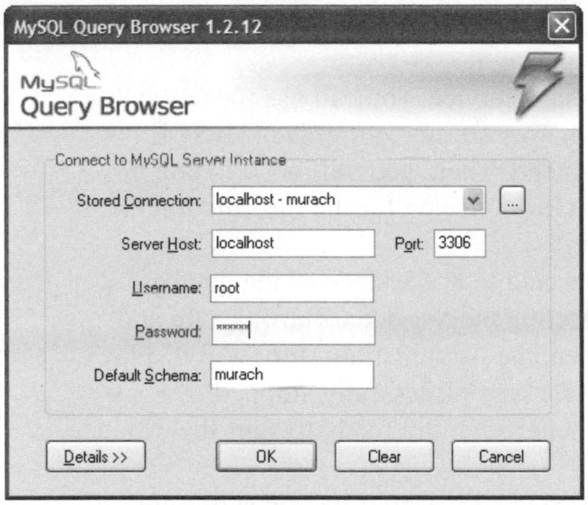

The connection dialog box for the Administrator tool

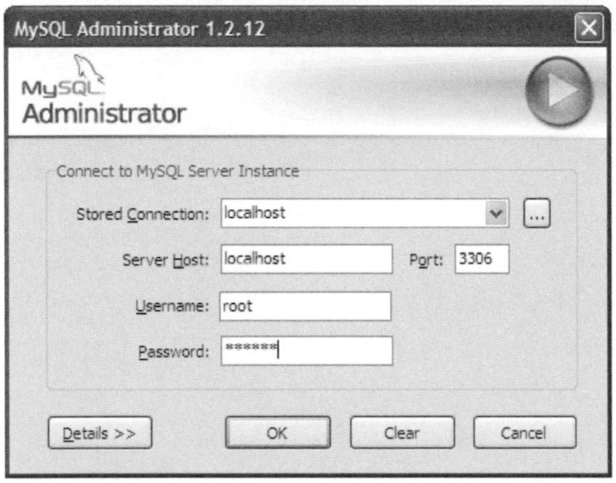

Description

- By default, the MySQL *database service* starts every time you start your computer. This is the piece of software that lets you work with the database, and it is sometimes referred to as the *database server* or the *database engine*.

- To start one of the MySQL GUI tools, you can select the menu item for the tool from the Windows Start menu. Then, you will be prompted by a connection dialog box before you can connect to the database service.

- To store connection information for future sessions, you can click on the dialog box button to the right of the Stored Connection box. Then, in the resulting dialog box, you can click on the New Connection button to display a dialog box that lets you set up and store a connection that you can easily access for future sessions.

Figure 13-3   How to connect to the MySQL database service

How to start and stop the MySQL database service

If you want to start or stop the database service, you can use the MySQL Administrator tool shown in figure 13-4. To start this tool, select MySQL Administrator from the Windows Start menu. Then, you will get a dialog box like the one shown in the last figure that prompts you for the information that's needed to connect to the MySQL server.

Once the Administrator tool is connected to an instance of the database service, you can stop the service by selecting the Service Control group and clicking on the Stop Service button. Then, the Administrator tool will display a message that indicates whether the service was successfully stopped. If so, you can click on the Start Service button whenever you're ready to start the instance of the database service again.

If you don't want the database service to start each time you start your computer, you can use the procedure in this figure to change that. Then, you can use the Administrator tool to manually start the database service whenever you want to work with the database.

The MySQL Administrator tool

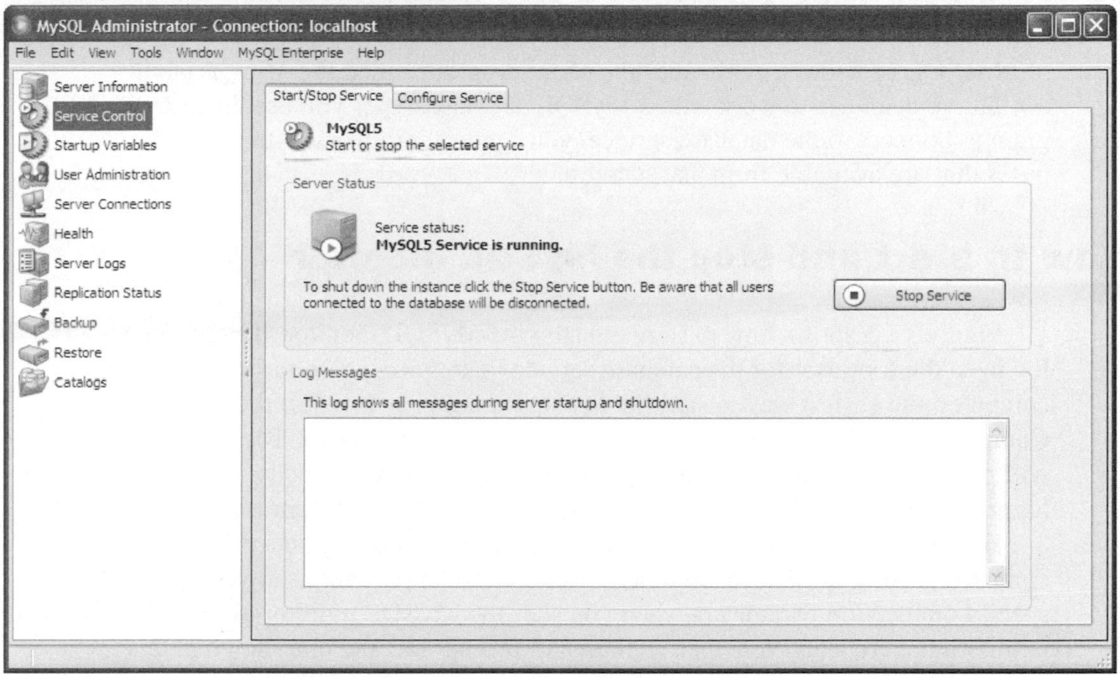

Description

- You can use the MySQL Administrator tool to start and stop the database service.

- To start the MySQL Administrator, select MySQL Administrator from the Windows Start menu. Then, respond to the connection dialog box as in the previous figure.

- To stop the server, start the MySQL Administrator, select the Service Control group, and click on the Stop Service button.

- To start the server, start the MySQL Administrator, select the Service Control group, and click on the Start Service button.

- To change the default settings for the service, start the MySQL Administrator, select the Service Control group, select the Configure Service tab, and select or deselect the "Launch MySQL server on system start" item.

- To install MySQL and the MySQL Administrator, follow the procedures in appendix A.

Figure 13-4   How to start and stop the MySQL database service

How to work with the MySQL monitor

MySQL provides a command-line client program called the *MySQL monitor* that you can use to work with a MySQL database. After you use this program to connect to the database service, you can use it to work with the databases that are available from that server.

How to start and stop the MySQL monitor

Figure 13-5 shows how to start and stop the MySQL monitor. If you want to log in as the root user for the database service that's running on the local computer, the easiest way to start the MySQL monitor is to select the MySQL Command Line Client command from the Windows Start menu. Then, MySQL will prompt you for a password. If you enter the password correctly, you will be logged on to the database service as the root user as shown in figure 13-2.

However, if you want to log into a database that's running on a different computer, or if you want to log in as a user other than the root user, you can specify connection parameters when you start the MySQL monitor as described in this figure. To start, you open a command-prompt like the one shown in this figure and change the directory to the bin directory for the MySQL installation. In the example in this figure, this directory is located here:

    C:\Program Files\MySQL\MySQL Server 5.0\bin

Then, you execute the mysql command and supply the parameters that are needed to connect to the database service.

If the MySQL server is located on a remote computer, you'll need to specify the host name of the computer and a valid username. Then, MySQL will ask you for a valid password. Although it can take some experimentation to get these connection parameters right, you only need to figure this out once.

Once you enter a valid password for the specified username, the program will display a welcome message like the one shown in this figure, and it will display a mysql command prompt that looks like this:

    mysql>

From this prompt, you can enter any MySQL command or SQL statement. To exit from the MySQL monitor, for example, you can enter an Exit or Quit command like this one:

    mysql>quit

Starting the MySQL monitor from a command prompt

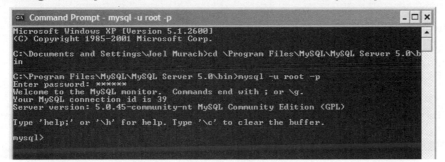

How to start the MySQL monitor from a command prompt

The syntax

```
mysql -h hostname -u username -p
```

Examples

```
c:\mysql\bin>mysql -h localhost -u root -p
c:\mysql\bin>mysql -h murach.com -u jmurach -p
c:\mysql\bin>mysql -u jmurach -p
```

How to start the MySQL monitor from the Windows Start menu

- Select MySQL➔MySQL Server 5.0➔MySQL Command Line Client.

How to exit from the MySQL monitor

The syntax

```
exit | quit
```

Examples

```
mysql>exit
```

Description

- MySQL provides a command-line client program called the *MySQL monitor*. This program lets you enter MySQL commands and SQL statements that work with MySQL databases.

- To start the MySQL monitor and log in as the root user to a MySQL service on the local computer, start the monitor from the Windows Start menu as shown above.

- To specify connection parameters when you start the MySQL monitor, open a command prompt, change to MySQL's bin directory, and enter a mysql command that includes the username and the host name if it isn't the computer that you're logged in on. Then, MySQL will prompt you for a valid password.

- To stop the MySQL monitor, enter "exit" or "quit" at the command prompt.

Figure 13-5   How to start and stop the MySQL monitor

How to create, select, and delete a database

Once the MySQL monitor is connected to a database service, you can use it to run *MySQL commands* and *SQL statements* that work with the databases that are available from that server. As you read the rest of this chapter, you'll see examples of each.

When you enter a command or statement, you must end it with a semicolon. Otherwise, the mysql prompt will display a second line when you press the Enter key like this:

```
mysql> show databases
    ->
```

This shows that the MySQL monitor is waiting for you to finish your command or statement. As you will see, this makes it easy for you to enter commands or statements that require more than one line. To finish a command or statement and have it executed, you just type a semicolon and press the Enter key.

Figure 13-6 shows how use two MySQL commands and two SQL statements. To make it easy to distinguish them, the text in this chapter capitalizes just the first letters in the names of commands and all of the letters in the names of SQL statements. Thus, you use the Show Databases command to list the names of all the databases that are managed by the database service, and you use the CREATE DATABASE statement to create a database. When you enter commands or statements at the prompt for the MySQL monitor, though, you can use all lowercase letters because it's easier to type lowercase letters.

To create a database, you use the CREATE DATABASE statement as illustrated by the first example in this figure. Here, this statement creates a database named "murach_test", and the message after the command indicates that this has been done successfully. Note, however, that this database hasn't been defined yet and it doesn't contain any data. You'll learn how to define it and add data to it in the next two figures.

To list the names of the databases stored on a server, you use the Show Databases command as illustrated by the second example. Here, the "murach" and "music" databases are the databases that are created when you install our downloadable databases as described in appendix A. The "murach_test" database is the one created by the first example. The "information_schema" and "mysql" databases are internal databases that are used by the MySQL server. And the "test" database is a test database that comes with MySQL.

To select the database that you want to work with, you use the Use command as illustrated by the third example. This selects the "murach" database, and the message after this command says "Database changed" to indicate that the statement was successful. After you select a database, the commands and statements that you enter will work with that database.

To delete a database from the server, you use the DROP DATABASE statement as illustrated by the fourth example. Here, the "murach_test" database is deleted. When you successfully delete a database, the MySQL monitor displays a message that says "Query OK" along with the number of rows that were deleted from the tables in the database.

How to create a database

```
mysql> create database murach_test;
Query OK, 1 row affected (0.02 sec)
```

How to list the names of all databases managed by the server

```
mysql> show databases;
+--------------------+
| Database           |
+--------------------+
| information_schema |
| murach             |
| murach_test        |
| music              |
| mysql              |
| test               |
+--------------------+
6 rows in set (0.00 sec)
```

How to select a database for use

```
mysql> use murach_test;
Database changed
```

How to delete a database

```
mysql> drop database murach_test;
Query OK, 0 rows affected (0.08 sec)
```

Description

- You can use the MySQL monitor to work with any of the MySQL databases that are managed by the database service. To do that, you can use MySQL commands and SQL statements.

- You can use the CREATE DATABASE statement to create a database and the DROP DATABASE statement to delete a database. These are *SQL statements*, and the text uses all capital letters to refer to these statements.

- You can use the Use command to select the database that you want to work with and the Show Databases command to list the names of all the databases for a server. These are *MySQL commands*.

- When you use the MySQL monitor, the commands and statements aren't case-sensitive. As a result, most programmers enter them in lowercase letters because they're easier to type.

Figure 13-6   How to create, select, and delete a database

How to create and delete a table

As you probably know, a *relational database* consists of one or more *tables* that consist of *rows* and *columns*. These tables are related by the *keys* in the rows. The *primary key* is a column that provides a unique value that identifies each row in a table. A *foreign key* is a column that is used to relate each row in one table with one or more rows in another table, usually by the primary keys in those rows.

So after you create a database as shown in the last figure, you need to create its tables as shown in figure 13-7. To do that, you use the CREATE TABLE statement. This statement is used to name each table and to define its columns.

In the example in this figure, you can see that a table named User is created that consists of four columns (UserID, FirstName, LastName, and EmailAddress), and the primary key is the UserID field. Here, the UserID column is the INT (integer) data type, it can't contain a null value, and it uses MySQL's auto-increment feature to automatically generate a unique integer for each new row by incrementing the number for the last row. In contrast, the other three columns have the VARCHAR (variable character) data type and can hold a maximum of 50 characters.

Because entering a lengthy statement like this at the prompt is error prone, statements like this are often entered into separate text files known as SQL scripts. In fact, a SQL script can contain more than one statement so a single script can create a database and create all the tables for it. To run a SQL script, you enter the mysql command. This command must include a complete connection string, the name of the database, and the path for the SQL script as shown by the second example in this figure.

Once you've created the tables for a database, you can use the Show Tables command to list them. You can also use the DROP TABLE statement to delete one of them. That's useful when you want to modify the definitions for the columns in a table. An efficient way to do that is to drop the table you want to change, modify the script for the table, and rerun the script to recreate the table.

Please note, however, that the purpose of this figure is *not* to teach you how to create the tables for a database because that's more than can be done in a servlets book. Instead, the purposes of this figure are (1) to introduce you to the commands and statements for creating, listing, and deleting the tables in a database and (2) to show you how to use SQL scripts. That will help you understand the SQL script that's used by the procedure in appendix A to create the databases for this book.

This script is named setup_db.sql and it's stored in a directory named murach/servlet_jsp/db. If you open this script and study it, you should get a better feel for how the tables in a database are defined. In particular, you'll see the definitions for other data types, primary keys, foreign keys, and so on. That in turn will make it easier for you to understand what's happening when you write SQL statements that retrieve and update the data in these databases.

How to use the CREATE TABLE statement

With the MySQL monitor

```
mysql> create table User (
    -> UserID int not null auto_increment,
    -> FirstName varchar(50),
    -> LastName varchar(50),
    -> EmailAddress varchar(50),
    -> primary key (UserID)
    -> );
Query OK, 0 rows affected (0.11 sec)
```

A mysql command that runs a script

```
C:\Program Files\MySQL\MySQL Server 5.0\bin>mysql -u root -p murach_test <
c:\murach\servlet_jsp\db\ch13\UserCreate.sql
Enter password: ******
```

The SQL script that's stored in a file named UserCreate.sql

```
CREATE TABLE User (
    UserID INT NOT NULL AUTO_INCREMENT,
    FirstName VARCHAR(50),
    LastName VARCHAR(50),
    EmailAddress VARCHAR(50),
    PRIMARY KEY(UserID)
)
```

How to list all of the tables in a database

```
mysql> show tables;
+------------------+
| Tables_in_murach |
+------------------+
| download         |
| user             |
+------------------+
2 rows in set (0.00 sec)
```

How to delete a table

```
mysql> drop table User;
Query OK, 0 rows affected (0.08 sec)
```

Description

- A *relational database* consists of one or more *tables* that consist of *rows* (*records*) and *columns* (*fields*). These tables are related by *keys*. The *primary key* in a table is the one that uniquely identifies each of the rows in the table. A *foreign key* is used to relate the rows in one table to the rows in another table.

- When you create a table, you define each of its columns and you identify its primary key. To define a column, you must supply the name and the data type, whether it's automatically generated for new rows, and so on.

- A file that stores one or more SQL statements is a *SQL script*. You can use the mysql command to run a SQL script.

- On Unix systems, the table and column names are case-sensitive.

Figure 13-7   How to create and delete a table

How to insert or load data into a table

After you've created a table, you can fill the table with data. Figure 13-8 shows two ways to do that. First, you can use the INSERT statement to insert one or more rows into a table. Second, you can use the Load command to transfer the data that's stored in a tab-delimited text file into a table. Typically, the INSERT statement is used within the code for a web application to insert one row into a table while the Load command is used to load large amounts of data into a table.

This figure starts by showing two ways to execute an INSERT statement that inserts three rows into the User table that you learned how to create in the last figure. First, you can enter the statement directly into the MySQL monitor. Second, you can store the statement in an SQL script and execute the script.

To begin an INSERT statement, you code the INSERT INTO keywords. Then, you code the table name followed by a set of parentheses. Within the parentheses, you code a list of the column names for the table. Although the SQL keywords aren't case-sensitive, the table and column names are case-sensitive on Unix systems. As a result, it's a good programming practice to code these names using the correct case.

After the list of column names, you code the VALUES keyword followed by a set of parentheses. Within these parentheses, you can code the values that should be inserted into each row. If you want to code more than one row of values, you can separate each row with a comma. In this figure, for example, the INSERT statement inserts three rows. Note that you don't need to include values for columns that use MySQL's auto increment feature or are defined with default values. In this case, since the value for the UserID column is automatically generated, you don't need to include it.

When you use the Load command to load the data from a tab-delimited text file into a table, the file must provide for all of the columns that are defined for the table. This is illustrated by the example in this figure, which has four fields for each record of the User table. Then, the Load command loads the data from this file into the User table on the local computer.

To load data from your system into a table on a remote web server, you may need to use a Load command like the second one in this figure. Because this varies depending on how the remote server is configured, you may need to ask your Internet service provider how Load commands should be coded.

How to use the INSERT statement

With the MySQL monitor

```
mysql> insert into User
    -> (FirstName, LastName, EmailAddress)
    -> values
    -> ('John', 'Smith', 'jsmith@gmail.com'),
    -> ('Andrea', 'Steelman', 'andi@murach.com'),
    -> ('Joel', 'Murach', 'joelmurach@yahoo.com');
Query OK, 3 rows affected (0.06 sec)
```

A mysql command that runs a SQL script

```
C:\Program Files\MySQL\MySQL Server 5.0\bin>mysql -u root -p murach_test <
c:\murach\servlet_jsp\db\ch13\UserInsert.sql
Enter password: ******
```

The SQL script stored in a file named UserInsert.sql

```
INSERT INTO User
   (FirstName, LastName, EmailAddress)
VALUES
   ('John', 'Smith', 'jsmith@gmail.com'),
   ('Andrea', 'Steelman', 'andi@murach.com'),
   ('Joel', 'Murach', 'joelmurach@yahoo.com')
```

How to use the Load command

A tab-delimited text file that's stored in Users.txt

```
1   John    Smith   jsmith@gmail.com
2   Andrea  Steelman        andi@murach.com
3   Joel    Murach  joelmurach@yahoo.com
```

A Load command that loads the data into a local table

```
mysql> load data local infile "c:/murach/servlet_jsp/db/ch13/Users.txt"
into table User;
Query OK, 3 rows affected (0.06 sec)
Records: 3   Deleted: 0   Skipped: 0   Warnings: 0
```

A Load command that loads the data into a table on a remote Unix server

```
load data infile "/usr/local/etc/httpd/sites/murach.com/htdocs/Users.txt"
into table User
```

Description

- The INSERT statement lets you insert one or more rows into one table of a database. When you code it, you need to include data for all columns that aren't defined with default values or aren't automatically generated.

- The Load command lets you load a tab-delimited text file into a table. In this case, the text file must have the same number of columns as the table.

- On a Unix system, table and column names are case-sensitive.

- If you're loading data into a table on a remote web server, you need to find out how the Load command should be coded.

Figure 13-8   How to insert or load data into a table

The SQL statements for data manipulation

With the exception of the INSERT statement, the SQL statements that you've seen thus far have been part of SQL's *Data Definition Language* (*DDL*). These statements let you create databases, create tables, drop tables, and so on, but they don't work with the data in the tables.

In contrast, the statements that you'll learn about next make up SQL's *Data Manipulation Language* (*DML*). These statements work with the data in a database, and they include the SELECT, INSERT, UPDATE, and DELETE statements. As a result, these are the statements that you will use in your Java applications.

How to select data from a single table

The SELECT statement is the most commonly used SQL statement. It can be used to retrieve data from one or more tables in a database. When you run a SELECT statement, it is commonly referred to as a *query* (although the execution of any SQL statement can also be referred to as a query). The result of this query is always a table known as a *result set*, or a *result table*.

In figure 13-9, the first example shows how to use this statement to retrieve all rows and columns from the User table. Here, the SELECT clause uses the asterisk wildcard to indicate that all of the columns in the table should be retrieved. Then, the FROM clause identifies the User table. In the result table, you can see the three rows and four columns that are returned by this query.

The second example shows how to use this statement to retrieve two columns and two rows from the User table. Here, the SELECT clause identifies the two columns, and the FROM clause identifies the table. Then, the WHERE clause limits the number of rows that are retrieved by specifying that the statement should only retrieve rows where the value in the UserID field is less than 3. Last, the ORDER BY clause indicates that the retrieved rows should be sorted in ascending order (from A to Z) by the LastName field.

The result set is a logical table that's created temporarily within the database. Then, the *current row pointer*, or *cursor*, keeps track of the current row. You can use this pointer from your web applications.

As you might guess, queries can have a significant effect on the performance of a database application. In general, the more columns and rows that a query returns, the more traffic the network has to bear. As a result, when you design queries, you should try to keep the number of columns and rows to a minimum.

The syntax for a SELECT statement that gets all columns

```
SELECT *
FROM table-1
[WHERE selection-criteria]
[ORDER BY field-1 [ASC|DESC] [, field-2 [ASC|DESC] ...]]
```

Example

```
SELECT * FROM User
```

Result set

```
+--------+-----------+----------+----------------------+
| UserID | FirstName | LastName | EmailAddress         |
+--------+-----------+----------+----------------------+
|      1 | John      | Smith    | jsmith@gmail.com     |
|      2 | Andrea    | Steelman | andi@murach.com      |
|      3 | Joel      | Murach   | joelmurach@yahoo.com |
+--------+-----------+----------+----------------------+
```

The syntax for a SELECT statement that gets selected columns

```
SELECT field-1 [, field-2] ...
FROM table-1
[WHERE selection-criteria]
[ORDER BY field-1 [ASC|DESC] [, field-2 [ASC|DESC] ...]]
```

Example

```
SELECT FirstName, LastName
FROM User
WHERE UserID < 3
ORDER BY LastName ASC
```

Result set

```
+-----------+----------+
| FirstName | LastName |
+-----------+----------+
| John      | Smith    |
| Andrea    | Steelman |
+-----------+----------+
```

Description

- A SELECT statement is a SQL DML statement that returns a *result set* (or *result table*) that consists of the specified rows and columns.
- To specify the columns, you use the SELECT clause.
- To specify rows, you use the WHERE clause.
- To specify the table that the data should be retrieved from, you use the FROM clause.
- To specify how the result set should be sorted, you use the ORDER BY clause.

Figure 13-9   How to select data from a single table

How to select data from multiple tables

Figure 13-10 shows how to use the SELECT statement to retrieve data from two tables. This is commonly known as a *join*. The result of any join is a single result table.

An *inner join* is the most common type of join. When you use one, the data from the rows in the two tables are included in the result set only if their related columns match. In the example in this figure, the SELECT statement joins the data from the rows in the User and Download tables only if the value of the UserID field in the User table is equal to the UserID field in the Download table. In other words, if there isn't any data in the Download table for a user, that user won't be added to the result set.

Another type of join is an *outer join*. With this type of join, all of the records in one of the tables are included in the result set whether or not there are matching records in the other table. In a *left outer join*, all of the records in the first table (the one on the left) are included in the result set. In a *right outer join*, all of the records in the second table are included. To illustrate, assume that the SELECT statement in this figure had used a left outer join. In that case, all of the records in the User table would have been included in the result set...even if no matching record was found in the Download table.

To code a join, you use the JOIN clause to specify the second table and the ON clause to specify the fields to be used for the join. If a field in one table has the same name as a field in the other table, you code the table name, a dot, and the field name to specify the field that you want to use. You can see this in the ON clause of the example in this figure.

Although this figure only shows how to join data from two tables, you can extend this syntax to join data from additional tables. If, for example, you want to create a result set that includes data from three tables named User, Download, and Product, you can code the FROM clause of the SELECT statement like this:

```
FROM User
    INNER JOIN Download
        ON User.UserID = Download.UserID
    INNER JOIN Product
        ON Download.ProductCode = Product.ProductCode
```

Then, you can include any of the fields from the three tables in the field list of the SELECT statement.

The syntax for a SELECT statement that joins two tables

```
SELECT field-1 [, field-2] ...
FROM table-1
    {INNER | LEFT OUTER | RIGHT OUTER} JOIN table-2
    ON table-1.field-1 {=|<|>|<=|>=|<>} table-2.field-2
[WHERE selection-criteria]
[ORDER BY field-1 [ASC|DESC] [, field-2 [ASC|DESC] ...]]
```

A statement that gets data from related User and Download tables

```
SELECT EmailAddress, DownloadFilename, DownloadDate
FROM User
    INNER JOIN Download
    ON User.UserID = Download.UserID
WHERE DownloadDate > '2007-04-01'
ORDER BY EmailAddress ASC
```

Result set

```
+------------------------+-------------------+---------------------+
| EmailAddress           | DownloadFilename  | DownloadDate        |
+------------------------+-------------------+---------------------+
| andi@murach.com        | jr01_filter.mp3   | 2007-09-18 10:31:38 |
| joelmurach@yahoo.com   | jr01_so_long.mp3  | 2007-09-18 10:31:38 |
| jsmith@gmail.com       | jr01_so_long.mp3  | 2007-05-01 00:00:00 |
| jsmith@gmail.com       | jr01_filter.mp3   | 2007-09-18 10:31:38 |
+------------------------+-------------------+---------------------+
4 rows in set (0.13 sec)
```

Description

- To return a result set that contains data from two tables, you *join* the tables. To do that, you can use a JOIN clause. Most of the time, you'll want to code an *inner join* so that rows are only included when the key of a row in the first table matches the key of a row in the second table.

- In a *left outer join*, the data for all of the rows in the first table (the one on the left) are included in the table, but only the data for matching rows in the second table are included. In a *right outer join*, the reverse is true.

Figure 13-10   How to select data from multiple tables

How to insert, update, and delete data

Figure 13-11 shows how to use the INSERT, UPDATE, and DELETE statements to add, update, or delete one or more records in a database. Because these statements modify the data in a database, they are sometimes referred to as *action queries*.

The syntax and examples for the INSERT statement show how to use this statement to add one record to a database. To do that, the statement supplies the names of the fields that are going to receive values in the new record, followed by the values for those fields. Here, the first example inserts one row into the Download table. The second example also inserts one row into the Download table, but it uses the NOW function provided by MySQL to automatically insert the current date and time into the DownloadDate field.

Similarly, the syntax and examples for the UPDATE statement show how to update records. In the first example, the UPDATE statement updates the FirstName field in the record where the EmailAddress is equal to jsmith@gmail.com. In the second example, the ProductPrice field is updated to 36.95 in all of the records where the ProductPrice is equal to 36.50.

Last, the syntax and examples for the DELETE statement show how to delete records. Here, the first example deletes the record from the User table where the EmailAddress equals jsmith@gmail.com. Since each record contains a unique value in the EmailAddress field, this only deletes a single record. However, in the second example, multiple records in the Download table may have a DownloadDate field that's less than June 1, 2007. As a result, this statement will delete all records that satisfy this condition.

When you issue an INSERT, UPDATE, or DELETE statement from a Java application, you usually work with one record at a time. You'll see this illustrated by the Email List application in the next chapter. Action queries that affect more than one record are often issued by database administrators.

The syntax for the INSERT statement

```
INSERT INTO table-name [(field-list)]
   VALUES (value-list)
```

A statement that adds one row to the Download table

```
INSERT INTO Download (UserID, DownloadDate, DownloadFilename, ProductCode)
   VALUES (1, '2007-05-01', 'jr01_so_long.mp3', 'jr01')
```

A statement that uses the MySQL Now function to get the current date

```
INSERT INTO Download (UserID, DownloadDate, DownloadFilename, ProductCode)
   VALUES (1, NOW(), 'jr01_filter.mp3', 'jr01'),
```

The syntax for the UPDATE statement

```
UPDATE table-name
   SET expression-1 [, expression-2] ...
   WHERE selection-criteria
```

A statement that updates the FirstName column in one row

```
UPDATE User
   SET FirstName = 'Jack',
   WHERE EmailAddress = 'jsmith@gmail.com'
```

A statement that updates the ProductPrice column in selected rows

```
UPDATE Product
   SET ProductPrice = 36.95
   WHERE ProductPrice = 36.50
```

The syntax for the DELETE statement

```
DELETE FROM table-name
   WHERE selection-criteria
```

A statement that deletes one row from the User table

```
DELETE FROM User WHERE EmailAddress = 'jsmith@gmail.com'
```

A statement that deletes selected rows from the Downloads table

```
DELETE FROM Download WHERE DownloadDate < '2007-06-01'
```

Description

- Since the INSERT, UPDATE, and DELETE statements modify the data that's stored in a database, they're sometimes referred to as *action queries*. These statements don't return a result set. Instead, they return the number of rows that were affected by the query.

Figure 13-11   How to insert, update, and delete data

Perspective

The primary goal of this chapter is to present the basic skills that you need for using MySQL. A secondary goal is to introduce you to the SELECT, INSERT, UPDATE, and DELETE statements that you'll use as you develop database applications with Java. If this chapter has succeeded, you should now be able to use the MySQL monitor to run commands, SQL statements, and SQL scripts.

In the next chapter, you'll learn how to use a servlet to connect to a MySQL database. You'll also learn how to use the SELECT, INSERT, UPDATE, and DELETE statements in your web applications.

Keep in mind, though, that this chapter has presented just a small subset of SQL skills. In particular, it has presented the least you need to know about SQL statements for understanding the Java code that is presented in the next chapter. For a complete mastery of SQL, you'll probably want to get a book about SQL for the database that you're using. If, for example, you're using Microsoft SQL Server for your applications, *Murach's SQL Server 2005 for Developers* presents all of the SQL statements that you'll need for your applications.

Summary

- *MySQL* is a *relational database management system* (*RDBMS*) that can manage one or more *databases*. To retrieve and modify the data in one of its databases, MySQL provides support for *Structured Query Language* (*SQL)*, which is the standard language for working with databases.

- Whenever you use MySQL, its *database service* must be running. Usually, this server starts automatically whenever you start your system.

- To work with a MySQL database, you can use a client tool called the *MySQL monitor*. It provides a command-line interface that lets you enter and run *MySQL commands* and *SQL statements*.

- A *SQL script* is a file that stores SQL statements. To run a script from the MySQL monitor, you use the Mysql command.

- The SQL statements that you use for creating and deleting databases and tables are part of the *Data Definition Language* (*DDL*).

- The SQL statements that you use for retrieving and modifying the data in a database make up the *Data Manipulation Language* (*DML*). These are the SELECT, INSERT, UPDATE, and DELETE statements.

- The SELECT statement is used to get data from one or more tables and put it in a *result set*, or *result table*. This is commonly referred to as a *query*.

- The INSERT, UPDATE, and DELETE statements are used to add one or more rows to a table, update the data in one or more rows, and delete one or more rows. These statements don't return a result set, and they're sometimes referred to as *action queries*.

Before you do the exercises for this chapter

If you haven't already done so, you should install MySQL, the source files for this book, and the databases for this book as described in appendix A.

Exercise 13-1   Use the MySQL monitor

1. Start the MySQL monitor by selecting MySQL→MySQL Server 5.0→MySQL Command Line Client from the Start menu.

2. Run the Show Databases command to see which databases are installed on your system. If the murach and music databases aren't installed, you need to install them before you continue. To do that, skip to exercise 13-2, and then return to the next step.

3. Select the murach database. Then, run the first SELECT statement in figure 13-9 to view the data stored in the User table.

4. Run the first UPDATE statement in figure 13-11 to see how that works. Then, run the SELECT statement for the User table again to see how it has been changed.

5. Exit from the MySQL monitor.

Exercise 13-2   Review the scripts for creating the murach and music databases

1. Use a text editor to open the batch file named create_db.bat that's in the c:\murach\servlet_jsp\db directory. One way to do that is to find the file in the Windows Explorer, right-click on it, and select Edit.

2. Note that the create_db.bat file starts the MySQL monitor as shown in figure 13-5 and runs the script in the create_db.sql file. Then, close the file.

3. Open the create_db.sql file that's in the c:\murach\servlet_jsp\db directory.

4. Note that this script contains the statements that create and build the murach and music databases. Note also that this script uses the DROP command to delete the murach and music databases before it builds them so you can run this script at any time to rebuild the initial versions of the databases. Then, close the file.

5. If you haven't already created the databases for our book or if you want to re-create them, you can do so now by running the batch file that you reviewed in step 1. The easiest way to run it is to find it in the Windows Explorer and double-click on it. When the MySQL monitor starts, it will ask you for the password for the root user, which should be "sesame" if you used our recommendation when you installed MySQL.

Exercise 13-3 Use the MySQL GUI tools

This exercise gives you a chance to use two of the MySQL GUI tools.

Use the MySQL Administrator

1. Start the MySQL Administrator tool and use it to stop and restart the MySQL database service as shown in figure 13-4.

2. Pull down the Tools menu, and note that you can start other MySQL tools from that menu including the Query Browser and the Command Line Client (or MySQL monitor). Then, exit from this tool.

Use the Query Browser

3. Start the MySQL Query Browser from the Windows Start menu as shown in figure 13-3, and note the default schema that's used in the connection dialog box. When the Browser starts, note that the default schema (database) is highlighted (boldfaced) in the Schemata window.

4. In the Schemata window, click on the icon before the music database to show its tables, and click on the icon before one of its tables to show its fields. Then, right-click on one of the tables and select the Edit command, which shows the details for how the fields in the table are defined. These techniques make it easy for you to review the design of a database.

5. If it isn't already highlighted, right-click on the murach database in the Schemata window and select Make Default Schema so the murach database is the one that will be used by any queries that you run.

6. Enter the query shown in figure 13-2 in the text box at the top of the Query Browser window, and click on the Execute button to run the query.

7. Enter the second query example in figure 13-9 and run it.

8. Enter the query shown in figure 13-10 and run it. Then, modify the date in the query so fewer records will be selected, and run the query again.

9. Continue to experiment until you have a good feel for how the murach database is designed and how to run queries against it. Then, exit the Query Browser.

14

How to use JDBC to work with a database

The basic skills for using Java to work with a database are the same for web applications as they are for other types of applications. So if you've used Java to work with a database before, you're probably already familiar with some of the skills presented in this chapter. In addition, though, you're going to see database programming in the context of web applications. And you're going to learn how to use a connection pool for a web application, which can improve the performance of the application.

How to work with JDBC

To write Java code that works with a database, you can use *JDBC*, which is sometimes referred to as *Java Database Connectivity*. The core JDBC API is stored in the java.sql package, which comes as part of the Standard Edition of Java. In this topic, you'll learn how to use JDBC to connect to a database, and you'll learn how to retrieve and modify the data that's stored in a database.

An introduction to database drivers

Before you can connect to a database, you must make a *database driver* available to your application. Figure 14-1 lists the four types of JDBC database drivers that you can use. Then, it shows how to download a database driver and make it available to your web applications.

Since type-1 and type-2 database drivers require installation on the client side, they aren't ideal for allowing an application that's running on the client to directly access a database that's running on the server. As a result, you'll typically want to use a type-3 or type-4 driver for this type of application.

With a web application, of course, all of the data access code runs on the server side. As a result, you can use any type of driver to connect to the database. However, you'll typically want to use a type-4 driver whenever one is available for the database that you're using.

If you want to connect to a MySQL database, you can use the type-4 driver named Connector/J that's available for free from the MySQL web site. You can usually download drivers for other types of databases from the web site for that database. The documentation for these drivers typically shows how to install and configure the driver.

To install the database driver, you must add the JAR file that contains the database driver to the classpath. The easiest way to do that is to copy the JAR file for the driver into the JDK's jre\lib\ext directory as described in appendix A. If that doesn't work, you can try using your IDE to add the JAR file to the libraries that are available to your application.

The four types of JDBC database drivers

Type 1   A *JDBC-ODBC bridge driver* converts JDBC calls into ODBC calls that access the DBMS protocol. For this data access method, the ODBC driver must be installed on the client machine.

Type 2   A *native protocol partly Java driver* converts JDBC calls into calls in the native DBMS protocol. Since this conversion takes place on the client, some binary code must be installed on the client machine.

Type 3   A *net protocol all Java driver* converts JDBC calls into a net protocol that's independent of any native DBMS protocol. Then, middleware software running on a server converts the net protocol to the native DBMS protocol. Since this conversion takes place on the server side, no installation is required on the client machine.

Type 4   A *native protocol all Java driver* converts JDBC calls into a native DBMS protocol. Since this conversion takes place on the server side, no installation is required on the client machine.

How to download a database driver

- For MySQL databases, you can download a JDBC driver named Connector/J from the MySQL web site as described in appendix A. This driver is an open-source, type-4 driver that's available for free.

- For other databases, you can usually download a type-4 JDBC driver from the database's web site.

How to make a database driver available to an application

- Before you can use a database driver, you must make it available to your application. One easy way to do that is to copy the JAR file for the driver into the JDK's jre\lib\ext directory.

Figure 14-1   An introduction to database drivers

How to connect to a database

Before you can access or modify the data in a database, you must connect to the database as shown in figure 14-2. At the start of this figure, you can see the syntax that you need to use for identifying the database within the code that gets the connection. Then, the first example in this figure shows how to use a type-4 MySQL driver to connect to the murach database.

To get a connection to a database, you use the getConnection method of the DriverManager class to return a Connection object. This method requires three arguments: the URL for the database, a username, and a password. In the first example, that URL consists of jdbc, the subprotocol for MySQL drivers (mysql), the host machine (localhost), the port for the database service (3306), and the name of the database. This code also uses root as the user and sesame as the password.

In the second example, you can see similar code for connecting to an Oracle database. Here again, you provide the URL for the database, a user name, and a password. This is true no matter what type of database you're using with JDBC.

In practice, though, connecting to the database is often frustrating because it's hard to figure out what the URL, username, and password need to be. So if your colleagues have already made a connection to the database that you need to use, by all means try to get this information from them.

Since the getConnection method of the DriverManager class throws an SQLException, you need to handle this exception whenever you connect to a database. With JDBC 4.0 (the version of JDBC that comes with Java SE 6), you can use an enhanced for statement to loop through any exceptions that are nested within the SQLException object. In this figure, the catch block in the first example loops through all the exceptions that are nested in the SQLException object.

To do that, this loop retrieves a Throwable object named t for each nested exception. Then, it prints the stack trace for this exception. This works because the Throwable class is the superclass for all exceptions, and a Throwable object is returned by the iterator for the SQLException class.

The first two examples in this figure illustrate a new feature of JDBC 4.0 called *automatic driver loading*. This feature loads the database driver automatically based on the URL for the database.

If you're working with an older version of Java, though, you need to use the forName method of the Class class to explicitly load the driver before you call the getConnection method. This is illustrated by the third example in this figure. Since this method throws a ClassNotFoundException, you also have to handle this exception.

With JDBC 4.0, you can still use the forName method of the Class class to explicitly load a driver. However, it usually makes sense to remove this method call from your code. That way, you can connect to the database with less code, and you don't have to hard code the name of the database driver. As a result, you can typically upgrade a database driver by swapping in a new jar file for the database driver.

Database URL syntax

```
jdbc:subprotocolName:databaseURL
```

How to connect to a MySQL database with automatic driver loading

```java
try
{
    String dbURL = "jdbc:mysql://localhost:3306/murach";
    String username = "root";
    String password = "sesame";
    Connection connection = DriverManager.getConnection(
        dbURL, username, password);
}
catch(SQLException e)
{
    for (Throwable t : e)
        t.printStackTrace();
}
```

How to connect to an Oracle database with automatic driver loading

```java
Connection connection = DriverManager.getConnection(
    "jdbc:oracle:thin@localhost/murach", "scott", "tiger");
```

How to load a MySQL database driver prior to JDBC 4.0

```java
try
{
    Class.forName("com.mysql.jdbc.Driver");
}
catch(ClassNotFoundException e)
{
    e.printStackTrace();
}
```

Description

- Before you can get or modify the data in a database, you need to connect to it. To do that, you use the getConnection method of the DriverManager class to return a Connection object.

- When you use the getConnection method of the DriverManager class, you must supply a URL for the database, a username, and a password. This method throws a SQLException.

- With JDBC 4.0, the SQLException class implements the Iterable interface. As a result, you can use an enhanced for statement to loop through any nested exceptions.

- With JDBC 4.0, the database driver is loaded automatically. This new feature is known as *automatic driver loading*. Prior to JDBC 4.0, you needed to use the forName method of the Class class to load the driver. This method throws a ClassNotFoundException.

- Although the connection string for each driver is different, the documentation for the driver should explain how to write a connection string for that driver.

- Typically, you only need to connect to one database for an application. However, it's possible to load multiple database drivers and establish connections to multiple types of databases.

Figure 14-2   How to connect to a database

How to return a result set and move the cursor through it

Once you connect to a database, you're ready to retrieve data from it as shown in figure 14-3. Here, the first two examples show how to use Statement objects to create a *result set*, or *result table*. Then, the next two examples show how to move the *row pointer*, or *cursor*, through the result set.

Both of the result sets in this figure are read-only, forward-only result sets. This means that you can only move the cursor forward through the result set, and that you can read but not write records in the result set. Although JDBC 4.0 supports other types of scrollable, updateable result sets, these features require some additional overhead, and they aren't necessary for most web applications.

In the first example, the createStatement method is called from a Connection object to return a Statement object. Then, the executeQuery method is called from the Statement object to execute an SQL SELECT statement that's coded as a string. This returns a ResultSet object that contains the result set for the SELECT statement. In this case, the SELECT statement only retrieves a single column from a single row (the user ID for a specific email address) so that's what the ResultSet object contains. This object can be checked to see whether a record exists.

The second example works like the first example. However, it returns all of the rows and columns for the Product table and puts this result set in a ResultSet object named products. This object can be used to display all products.

The third example shows how to use the next method of the ResultSet object to move the cursor to the first row of the result set that's created by the first example. When you create a result set, the cursor is positioned before the first row in the result set so the first use of the next method attempts to move the cursor to the first row in the result set. If the row exists, the cursor will be moved to that row and the next method will return a true value. Otherwise, the next method will return a false value. In the next figure, you'll learn how to retrieve values from the row that the cursor is on.

The fourth example shows how to use the next method to loop through all of the records in the result set that's created in the second example. Here, the while loop calls the next method. Then, if the next row is a valid row, the next method will move the cursor to the row and return a true value. As a result, the code within the while loop will be executed. Otherwise, the next method will return a false value and the code within the while loop won't be executed.

Since all of the methods described in this figure throw an SQLException, you either need to throw or catch this exception when you're working with these methods. The applications presented later in this chapter show how this works.

Although there are other ResultSet methods, the one you'll use the most with a forward-only, read-only result set is the next method. In this figure, though, three other methods are summarized that you may occasionally want to use for this type of result set.

How to create a result set that contains 1 row and 1 column

```
Statement statement = connection.createStatement();
ResultSet userIDResult = statement.executeQuery(
    "SELECT UserID FROM User " +
    "WHERE EmailAddress = 'jsmith@gmail.com'");
```

How to create a result set that contains multiple columns and rows

```
Statement statement = connection.createStatement();
ResultSet products = statement.executeQuery(
    "SELECT * FROM Product ");
```

How to move the cursor to the first record in the result set

```
boolean userIDExists = userIDResult.next();
```

How to loop through a result set

```
while (products.next()) {
    // statements that process each record
}
```

ResultSet methods for forward-only, read-only result sets

Method	Description
next()	Moves the cursor to the next row in the result set.
last()	Moves the cursor to the last row in the result set.
close()	Releases the result set's resources.
getRow()	Returns an int value that identifies the current row of the result set.

Description

- To return a *result set*, you use the createStatement method of a Connection object to create a Statement object. Then, you use the executeQuery method of the Statement object to execute a SELECT statement that returns a ResultSet object.

- By default, the createStatement method creates a forward-only, read-only result set. This means that you can only move the *cursor* through it from the first record to the last and that you can't update it. Although you can pass arguments to the createStatement method that create other types of result sets, the default is appropriate for most web applications.

- When a result set is created, the cursor is positioned before the first row. Then, you can use the methods of the ResultSet object to move the cursor. To move the cursor to the next row, for example, you call the next method. If the row is valid, this method moves the cursor to the next row and returns a true value. Otherwise, it returns a false value.

- The createStatement, executeQuery, and next methods throw an SQLException. As a result, any code that uses these methods needs to catch or throw this exception.

Figure 14-3   How to return a result set and move the cursor through it

How to retrieve data from a result set

When the cursor is positioned on the row that you want to get data from, you can use the methods in figure 14-4 to get that data. Although the examples show how to use the getString and getDouble methods of the ResultSet object to return String values and double values, you can use similar get methods to return other types of data.

The methods in this figure show the two types of arguments accepted by the get methods. The first method accepts an int value that specifies the index number of the column in the result set, where 1 is the first column, 2 is the second column, and so on. The second method accepts a string value that specifies the name of the column in the result set. Although the get methods with column indexes run slightly faster and require less typing, the get methods with column names lead to code that's easier to read and understand.

The first example shows how to use column indexes to return data from a result set named products. Here, the first two statements use the getString method to return the code and description for the current product while the third statement uses the getDouble method to return the price of the product. Since these methods use the column index, the first column in the result set must contain the product code, the second column must contain the product description, and so on.

The second example shows how to use column names to return data from the products result set. Since this code uses the column names, the order of the columns in the result set doesn't matter. However, the column names must exist in the result set or an SQLException will be thrown that indicates that a column wasn't found.

The third example shows how you can use the get methods to create a Product object. Here, the constructor for the Product object uses three values that are returned by the get methods to create a new product. Since objects are often created from data that's stored in a database, code like this is commonly used.

If you look up the ResultSet interface in the java.sql package of the documentation for the Java API, you'll see that get methods are available for all of the primitive types and for other types of data too. For example, get methods are available for the Date, Time, and Timestamp classes that are a part of the java.sql package. For many purposes, though, like displaying numbers and dates, you can use the getString method to return a string representation of the data type.

Methods of a ResultSet object that return data from a result set

Method	Description
getXXX(int columnIndex)	Returns data from the specified column number.
getXXX(String columnName)	Returns data from the specified column name.

Code that uses column indexes to return fields from the products result set

```
String code = products.getString(1);
String description = products.getString(2);
double price = products.getDouble(3);
```

Code that uses column names to return the same fields

```
String code = products.getString("ProductCode");
String description = products.getString("ProductDescription");
double price = products.getDouble("ProductPrice");
```

Code that creates a Product object from the products result set

```
Product product = new Product(products.getString(1),
                              products.getString(2),
                              products.getDouble(3));
```

Description

- The getXXX methods can be used to return all eight primitive types. For example, the getInt method returns the int type and the getLong method returns the long type.

- The getXXX methods can also be used to return strings, dates, and times. For example, the getString method returns any object of the String class, and the getDate, getTime, and getTimestamp methods return objects of the Date, Time, and Timestamp classes of the java.sql package.

Figure 14-4   How to retrieve data from a result set

How to insert, update, and delete data

Figure 14-5 shows how to use JDBC to modify the data in a database. To do that, you use the executeUpdate method of a Statement object to execute SQL statements that add, update, and delete data. Since this method has been a part of Java since version 1.0 of JDBC, it should work for all JDBC drivers.

When you work with the executeUpdate method, you just pass an SQL statement to the database. In these examples, the code adds, updates, and deletes a product in the Product table. To do that, the code combines data from a Product object with the appropriate SQL statement. For the UPDATE and DELETE statements, the SQL statement uses the product's code in the WHERE clause to select a single product.

How to use the executeUpdate method to modify data

How to add a record

```
String query =
    "INSERT INTO Product (ProductCode, ProductDescription, ProductPrice) " +
    "VALUES ('" + product.getCode() + "', " +
            "'" + product.getDescription() + "', " +
            "'" + product.getPrice() + "')";
Statement statement = connection.createStatement();
int rowCount = statement.executeUpdate(query);
```

How to update a record

```
String query = "UPDATE Product SET " +
    "ProductCode = '" + product.getCode() + "', " +
    "ProductDescription = '" + product.getDescription() + "', " +
    "ProductPrice = '" + product.getPrice() + "' " +
    "WHERE ProductCode = '" + product.getCode() + "'";
Statement statement = connection.createStatement();
int rowCount = statement.executeUpdate(query);
```

How to delete a record

```
String query = "DELETE FROM Product " +
            "WHERE ProductCode = '" + productCode + "'";
Statement statement = connection.createStatement();
int rowCount = statement.executeUpdate(query);
```

Description

- The executeUpdate method is an older method that works with most JDBC drivers. Although there are some newer methods that require less SQL code, they may not work properly with all JDBC drivers.

- The executeUpdate method returns an int value that identifies the number of records that were affected by the SQL statement.

Figure 14-5   How to insert, update, and delete data

How to work with prepared statements

Each time a Java application sends a new SQL statement to the database server, the server checks the statement for syntax errors, prepares a plan for executing the statement, and executes the statement. If the same statement is sent again, though, the database server checks to see whether it has already received one exactly like it. If so, the server doesn't have to check its syntax and prepare an execution plan for it so the server just executes it. This improves the performance of the database operations.

To take advantage of this database feature, Java provides for the use of *prepared statements* as shown in figure 14-6. This feature lets you send statements to the database server that get executed repeatedly by accepting the parameter values that are sent to it. That improves the database performance because the database server only has to check the syntax and prepare the execution plan once for each statement.

To illustrate, the first example in this figure shows how to use a prepared statement to create a result set that contains a single product. Here, the first statement uses a question mark (?) to identify the parameter for the SELECT statement, which is the product code for the book, and the second statement uses the prepareStatement method of the Connection object to return a PreparedStatement object. Then, the third statement uses a set method (the setString method) of the PreparedStatement object to set a value for the first parameter in the SELECT statement, and the fourth statement uses the executeQuery method of the PreparedStatement object to return a ResultSet object.

The result is that the prepared statement is the same each time the query is executed, which improves database performance, even though the product code changes each time based on the parameter value that's sent to the SQL statement. In contrast, if you don't use a prepared statement, the database server treats each statement as a new statement, which degrades database performance. For this reason, you should consider the use of prepared statements whenever performance is an issue and the SQL statements that you're using are complex.

The second example shows how to use a prepared statement to execute an UPDATE query that requires four parameters. Here, the first statement uses four question marks to identify the four parameters of the UPDATE statement, and the second statement creates the PreparedStatement object. Then, the next four statements use set methods to set the four parameters in the order that they appear in the UPDATE statement. The last statement uses the executeUpdate method of the PreparedStatement object to execute the UPDATE statement.

The third and fourth examples show how to insert and delete records with prepared statements. Here, you can see that the type of SQL statement that you're using determines whether you use the executeQuery method or the executeUpdate method. If you're using a SELECT statement to return a result set, you use the executeQuery method. But if you're using an INSERT, UPDATE, or DELETE statement, you use the executeUpdate method. This holds true whether you're using a Statement object or a PreparedStatement object.

How to use a prepared statement

To return a result set

```
String preparedSQL = "SELECT ProductCode, ProductDescription, ProductPrice "
                   + "FROM Product WHERE ProductCode = ?";
PreparedStatement ps = connection.prepareStatement(preparedSQL);
ps.setString(1, productCode);
ResultSet product = ps.executeQuery();
```

To modify data

```
String preparedSQL = "UPDATE Product SET "
                   + "    ProductCode = ?, "
                   + "    ProductDescription = ?, "
                   + "    ProductPrice = ?"
                   + "WHERE ProductCode = ?";
PreparedStatement ps = connection.prepareStatement(preparedSQL);
ps.setString(1, product.getCode());
ps.setString(2, product.getDescription());
ps.setDouble(3, product.getPrice());
ps.setString(4, product.getCode());
ps.executeUpdate();
```

To insert a record

```
String preparedQuery =
    "INSERT INTO Product (ProductCode, ProductDescription, ProductPrice) "
  + "VALUES (?, ?, ?)";
PreparedStatement ps = connection.prepareStatement(preparedQuery);
ps.setString(1, product.getCode());
ps.setString(2, product.getDescription());
ps.setDouble(3, product.getPrice());
ps.executeUpdate();
```

To delete a record

```
String preparedQuery = "DELETE FROM Product "
                     + "WHERE ProductCode = ?";
PreparedStatement ps = connection.prepareStatement(preparedQuery);
ps.setString(1, productCode);
ps.executeUpdate();
```

Description

- When you use *prepared statements* in your Java programs, the database server only has to check the syntax and prepare an execution plan once for each SQL statement. This improves the efficiency of the database operations.

- To specify a parameter for a prepared statement, type a question mark (?) in the SQL statement.

- To supply values for the parameters in a prepared statement, use the set methods of the PreparedStatement interface. For a complete list of set methods, look up the PreparedStatement interface of the java.sql package in the documentation for the Java API.

- To execute a SELECT statement, use the executeQuery method. To execute an INSERT , UPDATE, or DELETE statement, use the executeUpdate method.

Figure 14-6   How to work with prepared statements

The SQL Gateway application

This topic presents the SQL Gateway application that allows you to use a web-based interface to execute any type of SQL statement. An application like this makes it easy to view and modify the data in a database. For example, you can cut and paste SQL scripts into this application and execute them. In addition, if you enter an SQL statement with incorrect syntax, this application will display an error message when you try to execute it. Then, you can edit the SQL statement and attempt to execute it again.

When working with a database, you'll usually want to use an application like this one instead of a command-line interface. If you're working with a database that's hosted by an ISP, the ISP will usually include a web-based way to work with the database that's similar to this tool. If not, you can upload this application to work with the database.

The user interface

Figure 14-7 shows the user interface for the SQL Gateway application. To use this application, you enter an SQL statement in the SQL Statement text area. Then, you click on the Execute button to run the SQL statement. When you do that, the result will be displayed at the bottom of the page.

If the SQL statement is a SELECT statement that runs successfully, the result set will be displayed within an HTML table as in the second page in this figure. For other types of statements, the result will be a message that indicates the number of rows that were affected by the statement as in the first page in this figure. Of course, if the SQL statement doesn't execute successfully, the result will be a message that displays information about the SQLException that was thrown.

The SQL Gateway application after executing an INSERT statement

The SQL Gateway application after executing a SELECT statement

Figure 14-7   The user interface for the SQL Gateway application

The code for the JSP

Figure 14-8 shows the code for the single JSP for the SQL Gateway application. Here, the JSTL if tag at the start of the page checks if the sqlStatement attribute contains a null value. If so, this code uses a JSTL set tag to set the value of this attribute to "select * from User". That way, this SQL statement will be displayed when a user requests this page for the first time in a session.

The form for this JSP contains a text area and a submit button. Here, the text area allows the user to enter the SQL statement. This code creates a text area that's approximately 60 characters wide and 8 lines tall. Within this area, the sqlStatement attribute is displayed. Then, when the user clicks the submit button, this JSP calls the sqlGateway URL, which is mapped to the SQLGatewayServlet that's shown in the next figure.

The end of this JSP displays the string that contains the result of the SQL statement. If the SQL statement returns a result set, this string will contain all the HTML tags needed to display the result set within an HTML table. Otherwise, this string will contain some text that indicates the success or failure of the SQL statement.

The code for the JSP (sqlGateway.jsp)

```
<!doctype html public "-//W3C//DTD HTML 4.0 Transitional//EN">
<html>

<head>
    <title>Murach's Java Servlets and JSP</title>
</head>

<body>

<%@ taglib prefix="c" uri="http://java.sun.com/jsp/jstl/core" %>
<c:if test="${sqlStatement == null}">
    <c:set var="sqlStatement" value="select * from User" />
</c:if>

<h1>The SQL Gateway</h1>
<p>Enter an SQL statement and click the Execute button. Then, information
about the <br>
statement will appear at the bottom of this page.</p>

<p>
<b>SQL statement:</b><br>
<form action="sqlGateway" method="post">
    <textarea name="sqlStatement" cols="60" rows="8">${sqlStatement}
    </textarea><br><br>
    <input type="submit" value="Execute">
</form>
</p>

<p>
<b>SQL result:</b><br>
    ${sqlResult}
</p>

</body>
</html>
```

Figure 14-8   The code for the JSP

The code for the servlet

Figure 14-9 shows the code for the SQLGatewayServlet. To start, this servlet imports the java.sql package so it can use the JDBC classes.

Within the doPost method of this servlet, the first statement gets the SQL statement that the user entered in the JSP, and the second statement declares the sqlResult variable. Then, within the try block, the first four statements create a Connection object for the murach database that's running on the local MySQL service, and the fifth statement uses this object to create a Statement object.

Once the Statement object has been created, a series of if statements are used to parse the SQL string. To start, the first statement uses the trim method to remove any leading or trailing spaces from the SQL string. Then, an if statement checks to makes sure that the SQL string contains 6 or more characters, which is the minimum amount of characters needed to prevent a NullPointerException from being thrown by the following substring method. If the SQL string contains more than 6 characters, the substring method returns the first six letters of the SQL statement.

If the first six letters of the SQL statement are "select", the executeQuery method of the Statement object returns a ResultSet object. Then, this object is passed to the getHtmlTable method of the SQLUtil class that's shown in the next figure, and it returns the result set formatted with all the HTML tags needed to display all rows and columns of the result set in an HTML table.

However, if the first six letters of the SQL statement aren't "select", the executeUpdate method of the Statement object is called, which returns the number of rows that were affected. If the number of rows is 0, the SQL statement was a DDL statement like a DROP TABLE or CREATE TABLE statement. Otherwise, the SQL statement was an INSERT, UPDATE, or DELETE statement. Either way, the code sets the sqlResult variable to an appropriate message.

The SQLGatewayServlet class   **Page 1**

```java
package sql;

import java.io.*;
import javax.servlet.*;
import javax.servlet.http.*;

import java.sql.*;

public class SqlGatewayServlet extends HttpServlet
{
    protected void doPost(HttpServletRequest request,
                          HttpServletResponse response)
                    throws ServletException, IOException
    {
        String sqlStatement = request.getParameter("sqlStatement");
        String sqlResult = "";

        try
        {
            // get a connection
            String dbURL = "jdbc:mysql://localhost:3306/murach";
            String username = "root";
            String password = "sesame";
            Connection connection = DriverManager.getConnection(
                dbURL, username, password);

            // create a statement
            Statement statement = connection.createStatement();

            // parse the SQL string
            sqlStatement = sqlStatement.trim();
            if (sqlStatement.length() >= 6)
            {
                String sqlType = sqlStatement.substring(0, 6);
                if (sqlType.equalsIgnoreCase("select"))
                {
                    // create the HTML for the result set
                    ResultSet resultSet =
                            statement.executeQuery(sqlStatement);
                    sqlResult = SQLUtil.getHtmlTable(resultSet);
                    resultSet.close();
                }
                else
                {
                    int i = statement.executeUpdate(sqlStatement);
                    if (i == 0) // a DDL statement
                        sqlResult = "The statement executed successfully.";
                    else        // an INSERT, UPDATE, or DELETE statement
                        sqlResult = "The statement executed successfully.<br>"
                                + i + " row(s) affected.";
                }
            }
            statement.close();
            connection.close();
        }
```

Figure 14-9   The SQLGatewayServlet class (part 1 of 2)

If any of the statements within the try block throw an SQLException, the catch block sets the sqlResult variable to display information about the SQLException. If, for example, you enter an SQL statement that contains incorrect syntax, this message will help you troubleshoot your syntax problem.

After the catch block, the next three statements get the session object and set the sqlStatement and sqlResult variables as attributes of that object. Then, the last three statements return a RequestDispatcher object that forwards the request and response objects to the JSP shown in the previous figure.

The SQLGatewayServlet class   **Page 2**

```
        catch(SQLException e)
        {
            sqlResult = "Error executing the SQL statement: <br>"
                    + e.getMessage();
        }

        HttpSession session = request.getSession();
        session.setAttribute("sqlResult", sqlResult);
        session.setAttribute("sqlStatement", sqlStatement);

        String url = "/sql_gateway.jsp";
        RequestDispatcher dispatcher =
            getServletContext().getRequestDispatcher(url);
        dispatcher.forward(request, response);
    }
}
```

Note

*   The web.xml file for this application maps the SQLGatewayServlet class to the /sqlGateway URL.

Figure 14-9   The SQLGatewayServlet class (part 2 of 2)

The code for the utility class

Figure 14-10 shows the code for the utility class named SQLUtil. This class contains a static method named getHtmlTable that is called by the servlet in the last figure. Since this utility class is used to work with SQL statements, it is stored in the sql package.

The getHtmlTable method accepts a ResultSet object and returns a String object that contains the HTML tags that are needed to display the columns and rows in the result set within an HTML table. To build the information for that String object, the getHtmlTable method declares a StringBuffer object named htmlRows and appends data to it as the method is executed. At the end of the method, the toString method is used to convert the StringBuffer object to the String object that is returned to the servlet.

To get the column headings that are returned, the getHtmlTable method uses the getMetaData method of the ResultSet object to create a ResultSetMetaData object. This type of object contains information about the result set including the number of columns and the names of the columns. To get that information, the getHtmlTable method uses the getColumnCount and getColumnName methods of the ResultSetMetaData object.

To get the data from the result set, the getHtmlTable method uses a for loop within a while loop to get the data for each column in each row. Within these loops, the code uses the getString method of the result set to get the data for each field. That converts the data to a string no matter what data type the field is.

The SQLUtil class

```
package sql;

import java.util.*;
import java.sql.*;

public class SQLUtil
{
    public static String getHtmlTable(ResultSet results)
            throws SQLException
    {
        StringBuffer htmlRows = new StringBuffer();
        ResultSetMetaData metaData = results.getMetaData();
        int columnCount = metaData.getColumnCount();

        htmlRows.append("<table cellpadding=\"5\" border=\"1\">");
        htmlRows.append("<tr>");
        for (int i = 1; i <= columnCount; i++)
            htmlRows.append("<td><b>" + metaData.getColumnName(i) +
                "</b></td>");
        htmlRows.append("</tr>");

        while (results.next())
        {
            htmlRows.append("<tr>");
            for (int i = 1; i <= columnCount; i++)
                htmlRows.append("<td>" + results.getString(i) + "</td>");
            htmlRows.append("</tr>");
        }
        htmlRows.append("</table>");
        return htmlRows.toString();
    }
}
```

Description

- The getHtmlTable method in this class accepts a ResultSet object and returns a String object that contains the HTML code for the result set so it can be displayed by a browser.

- The getMetaData method of a ResultSet object returns a ResultSetMetaData object.

- The getColumnCount method of a ResultSetMetaData object returns the number of columns in the result set.

- The getColumnName method of a ResultSetMetaData object returns the name of a column in the result set.

Figure 14-10   The SQLUtil class

How to work with connection pooling

Opening a connection to a database is a time-consuming process that can degrade an application's performance. As a result, it's a common programming practice to create a collection of Connection objects and store them in another object that's commonly known as a *database connection pool* (*DBCP*). Then, the Connection objects in the pool are shared by all the users of a web application. This limits the number of times that connections are opened as well as the total number of Connection objects.

How connection pooling works

Figure 14-11 shows how connection pooling works. To start, when the connection pool is created for the first time, a ConnectionPool object that contains multiple Connection objects is created. Then, when a user accesses a servlet, the servlet spawns a thread. This thread gets a Connection object from the ConnectionPool object, uses that Connection object to access the database, and returns the Connection object to the connection pool.

Typically, you create a single connection pool for a web application. Then, all of the servlets in the application use the same connection pool to access the database. In the next two figures, you'll learn how to install, customize, and share a connection pool among all of the servlets in an application.

How to make a connection pool available

Although you can write the Java code for your own connection pool, this code is already available from third-party sources. As a result, you'll almost always want to use a connection pool that has already been developed and tested by someone else. Then, you can install and customize that connection pool so it works with your database.

For instance, Tomcat 6 includes the database connection pool that's available from the Jakarta-Commons project. The files for this database connection pool are stored in the JAR file named tomcat-dbcp.jar that's in Tomcat's lib directory. To make this connection pool available to your system, you can copy it from Tomcat's lib directory to the JDK's jre\lib\ext directory. If you did the procedure in figure 2-1 of chapter 2, you have already done this.

How connection pooling works

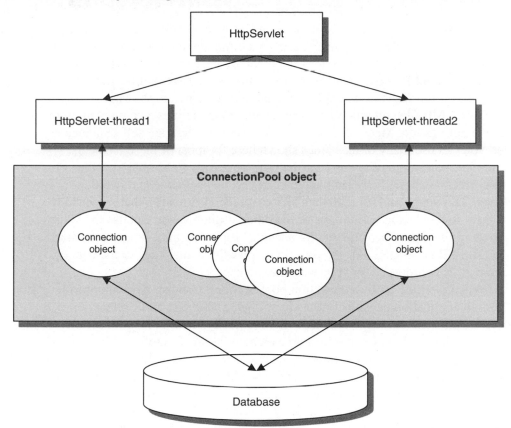

Description

- When *database connection pooling* (*DBCP*) is used, a limited number of connections are opened for a database and these connections are shared by the users who connect to the database. This improves the performance of the database operations.

- When one of the threads of a servlet needs to perform a database operation, the thread gets a Connection object from the ConnectionPool object and uses that Connection object to do the operation. When it is finished, it returns the Connection object to the pool.

- Tomcat 6 includes the database connection pool that's available from the Jakarta-Commons project. The files for this database connection pool are stored in the JAR file named tomcat-dbcp.jar. To make this connection pool available to your system, you can copy it from Tomcat's lib directory to the JDK's jre\lib\ext directory.

Figure 14-11   How connection pooling works

How to implement a connection pool

To customize the Jakarta-Commons database connection pool so it's appropriate for your application, you can start by editing the context.xml file for your application so it specifies the parameters that are needed to configure the connection pool for your application. In figure 14-12, for example, the context.xml file for the web application named ch14email is shown.

This XML file contains a Resource element that defines a connection pool for the application. Many of the attributes for this element are self-explanatory, and you can use many of the values shown here for most of these elements. However, you can modify these attributes as necessary to be able to connect to the correct database. For example, you can use the username, password, driverClassName, and url attributes to specify the information that's needed to connect to the database. For most of the other attributes, you can use the values shown in this figure because they're adequate for most small- to medium-sized web sites. If necessary, though, you can modify these attributes so the connection pool is appropriate for your web site.

When working with a connection pool, a connection can be abandoned if the web application doesn't close its ResultSet, Statement, and Connection objects. This can cause a "leak" that will eventually result in no connections being available. However, the Resource element in this figure is configured to return any abandoned connections to the pool. In particular, this element sets the removeAbandoned attribute to true, and it sets the removeAbandonedTimeout attribute to 60. That way, abandoned connections are returned to the pool after they have been idle for 60 seconds. In addition, this element sets the logAbandoned attribute to true so the code that caused the connection to be abandoned will be written to the log file for the connection pool.

Once you've configured the context.xml file correctly, you can create a class to make it easy to get a connection to the database. In this figure, for example, the ConnectionPool class makes it easy for any class in the application to get a connection from the connection pool for the murach database that's running on the MySQL database server.

To start, the ConnectionPool class imports the interfaces and classes that it needs to be able to get a connection from the connection pool. This includes the DataSource interface that the Jakarta-Commons connection pool uses to store the connections, and it includes the InitialContext class that's used to get a DataSource object.

After the class declaration, this class declares a private static instance variable that holds the ConnectionPool pool object, and it declares a private static instance variable that holds the DataSource object.

After these declarations, the ConnectionPool class uses a private constructor to create an instance of the connection pool. To do that, it uses the InitialContext object to return a DataSource object. Note that this code works because the end of the string that's passed to the lookup method (jdbc/murach) matches the name attribute that's specified in the context.xml file.

A context.xml file that configures a connection pool

```xml
<?xml version="1.0" encoding="UTF-8"?>
<Context path="/ch14email">

    <Resource name="jdbc/murach" auth="Container"
        maxActive-"100" maxIdle="30" maxWait-"10000"
        username="root" password="sesame"
        driverClassName="com.mysql.jdbc.Driver"
        url="jdbc:mysql://localhost:3306/murach?autoReconnect=true"
        logAbandoned="true" removeAbandoned="true"
        removeAbandonedTimeout="60" type="javax.sql.DataSource" />

</Context>
```

A class that defines a connection pool   Page 1

```java
package data;

import java.sql.*;
import javax.sql.DataSource;
import javax.naming.InitialContext;

public class ConnectionPool
{
    private static ConnectionPool pool = null;
    private static DataSource dataSource = null;

    private ConnectionPool()
    {
        try
        {
            InitialContext ic = new InitialContext();
            dataSource = (DataSource)
                ic.lookup("java:/comp/env/jdbc/murach");
        }
        catch(Exception e)
        {
            e.printStackTrace();
        }
    }

    public static ConnectionPool getInstance()
    {
        if (pool == null)
        {
            pool = new ConnectionPool();
        }
        return pool;
    }
```

Figure 14-12   How to implement and use a connection pool (part 1 of 2)

After the constructor, the static getInstance method returns a reference to the ConnectionPool object. To start, this method checks to see if the ConnectionPool object exists. Most of the time, the object will exist so this method will just return a reference to the ConnectionPool object. However, if the ConnectionPool object hasn't been created, this method will create the ConnectionPool object and return a reference to this object.

Please note that the private constructor and getInstance method of the ConnectionPool class allow only a single instance of the ConnectionPool class to be created. This is known as the *singleton pattern*, and it's commonly used by programmers when they want to make sure that only a single instance of an object is created.

Once the connection pool has been created, the application can use the getConnection method in this figure to return a Connection object that can be used to access the database. To get a connection object, this method calls the getConnection method of the DataSource object. If this method throws an SQLException, this code prints a stack trace and returns a null value.

Finally, the freeConnection method can be used to close the specified Connection object. This returns the connection to the connection pool. If the close method of the Connection object throws an SQLException, this method prints a stack trace.

How to use a connection pool

Figure 14-12 also shows the code that you can use to get a Connection object from a ConnectionPool object. This should give you a clearer idea of how you can use this ConnectionPool object in your own code.

To start, you can call the static getInstance method of the ConnectionPool class to return a ConnectionPool object. Then, you can call the getConnection method of the ConnectionPool object to return a Connection object that can be used to access the database. Finally, after all the code that uses the Connection object has been executed, you can call the freeConnection method of the connection pool to return the Connection object to the pool. Since a typical database operation takes only a fraction of a second, a relatively low number of Connection objects can handle a high volume of user requests.

A class that defines a connection pool   **Page 2**

```java
public Connection getConnection()
{
    try
    {
        return dataSource.getConnection();
    }
    catch (SQLException sqle)
    {
        sqle.printStackTrace();
        return null;
    }
}

public void freeConnection(Connection c)
{
    try
    {
        c.close();
    }
    catch (SQLException sqle)
    {
        sqle.printStackTrace();
    }
}
}
```

Code that uses the connection pool

```java
ConnectionPool pool = ConnectionPool.getInstance();
Connection connection = pool.getConnection();

// code that uses the connection to work with the database

pool.freeConnection(connection);
```

Description

- With Tomcat 6, you can use the context.xml file to configure connection pooling for an application.

- The ConnectionPool class provides the getConnection and freeConnection methods that make it easy for programmers to get connections and to return connections to the connection pool.

Figure 14-12   How to implement and use a connection pool (part 2 of 2)

The Email List application

In section 2 of this book, you learned how to code an Email List application that uses a class named UserIO to write the User data to a text file. Now, you'll learn how to code an Email List application that uses a class named UserDB to write the user data to a database. This application also uses the connection pool described in the last topic so it quickly connects its threads to the database. This illustrates how easy it is to modify an application when you use the MVC pattern and keep the presentation, business, and data layers independent of each other.

The user interface

Figure 14-13 shows the user interface for the new Email List application. This is similar to the interface that you've seen in earlier versions of this application, but it displays an error message if a user enters an email address that already exists in the database.

The code for the JSP

Since you already know how to code JSPs like the one for this interface, this figure only shows the beginning of the JSP code. In particular, the shaded line of code displays an error message if the servlet sets this message as a session attribute.

The Email List application as it displays an error message

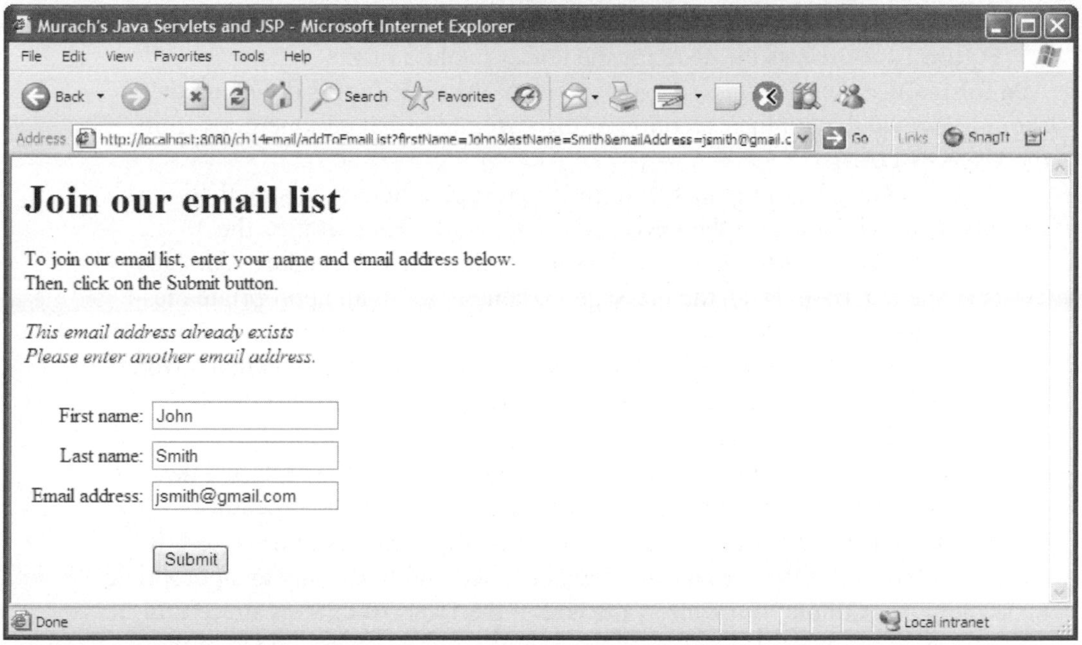

The code for this JSP

```
<!DOCTYPE HTML PUBLIC "-//W3C//DTD HTML 4.01 Transitional//EN">
<html>

<head>
    <title>Murach's Java Servlets and JSP</title>
</head>

<body>
  <h1>Join our email list</h1>
  <p>To join our email list, enter your name and
     email address below. <br>
     Then, click on the Submit button.</p>

  <p><i>${message}</i></p>

  <form action="addToEmailList" method="get">
  <table cellspacing="5" border="0">
    <tr>
      <td align="right">First name:</td>
      <td><input type="text" name="firstName"
          value="${user.firstName}">
      </td>
    </tr>

    <!-- the rest of the code for the JSP -- >
```

Figure 14-13   The user interface and JSP for the Email List application

The code for the servlet

Figure 14-14 shows the code for the doGet method of the AddToEmailListServlet class. By now, most of the code in this doGet method should be review, with the exception of the statements that call methods from the UserDB class.

After creating a User object from the request parameters, this method defines string variables for the URL and the message. Then, it uses the emailExists method of the UserDB class to check if the email address already exists in the database. If so, the message variable is set to an appropriate message, and the url variable is set to the JSP that's shown in the previous figure. If not, the insert method of the UserDB class is used to write the data that's stored in the User object to the database, and the url variable is set to a JSP that displays the data that has been entered.

Since the methods of the UserDB class don't throw any exceptions, the servlet class doesn't need to handle any of these exceptions. If necessary, though, it can use the values that are returned by the methods of the UserDB class to determine if the action succeeded or failed and to display an appropriate message. For example, if the insert method of the UserDB class is successful, it will return an int value that indicates the number of rows that it added to the database. If this method returns a value of 0, no rows were added to the database. Although the code in this figure doesn't check this value, you could easily add code that does.

If you review this code, I think you'll agree that the methods of the UserDB class are easy to use. That's because these methods handle all of the details for working with the database. For example, these methods handle all the details for getting a connection to the database from the connection pool, and they handle all the details for executing the appropriate SQL statements. To see how this works, you can view the code shown in the next figure. For now, though, note how separating the database layer from the rest of the application lets the servlet focus on its job as the controller in the MVC pattern.

The code for the servlet

```
package email;

import java.io.*;
import javax.servlet.*;
import javax.servlet.http.*;

import business.User;
import data.UserDB;

public class AddToEmailListServlet extends HttpServlet
{
    protected void doGet(HttpServletRequest request,
                         HttpServletResponse response)
                         throws ServletException, IOException
    {
        // get parameters from the request
        String firstName = request.getParameter("firstName");
        String lastName = request.getParameter("lastName");
        String emailAddress = request.getParameter("emailAddress");

        // create the User object
        User user = new User();
        user.setEmailAddress(emailAddress);
        user.setFirstName(firstName);
        user.setLastName(lastName);

        String url = "";
        String message = "";

        if (UserDB.emailExists(user.getEmailAddress()))
        {
            message = "This email address already exists<br>" +
                      "Please enter another email address.";
            url = "/join_email_list.jsp";
        }
        else
        {
            UserDB.insert(user);
            url = "/display_email_entry.jsp";
        }

        // store the user and message in the session
        HttpSession session = request.getSession();
        session.setAttribute("user", user);
        request.setAttribute("message", message);

        // forward the request and response to the view
        RequestDispatcher dispatcher =
            getServletContext().getRequestDispatcher(url);
        dispatcher.forward(request, response);
    }
}
```

Figure 14-14   The servlet for the Email List application

The code for the database class

Figure 14-15 shows the code for the UserDB class. This class contains the emailExists and insert methods that are used by the servlet in the previous figure. In addition, this class contains three more methods (update, delete, and selectUser) that can be used to modify and retrieve user data.

The methods in this class map the User object to the User table in the murach database. In particular, the insert method stores a User object in a new row in the User table. Conversely, the getUser method creates a User object from the data that's stored in a row in the User table. This is known as *object-to-relational mapping,* or *OR mapping.*

Although writing all of the OR mapping for an application gives you complete control over how it works, this can also be tedious and time-consuming. As a result, for larger projects, you may want to try using a framework, such as Hibernate, that automatically generates the OR mapping code from your database tables. That, however, is a subject that's worthy of its own book.

In the UserDB class, the methods begin by getting a Connection object from the ConnectionPool object that allows them to connect to the database. Then, these methods declare the PreparedStatement object, the ResultSet object (if necessary), and a string that contains the SQL statement. Within the try block for these methods, the statements create the PreparedStatement object, set its parameters, execute the PreparedStatement statement, and return an appropriate value. If an exception occurs, the catch block prints a stack trace and returns an appropriate value. Either way, the finally block closes any PreparedStatement, ResultSet, or Connection objects that have been opened. To do that, it uses the DBUtil class that's described in figure 14-16.

The insert method adds a new row to the User table. To do that, it executes an INSERT statement that includes the data from the User object that was passed to the method. If this method executes successfully, it returns an integer value of 1 to the calling method. Otherwise, it prints a stack trace and returns an integer value of 0 to indicate that the row was not inserted.

The update method works like the insert method, but it uses an UPDATE statement instead of an INSERT statement. Within the UPDATE statement, the WHERE clause uses the email address to find the record to be updated.

The UserDB class   **Page 1**

```java
package data;

import java.sql.*;
import business.User;

public class UserDB
{
    public static int insert(User user)
    {
        ConnectionPool pool = ConnectionPool.getInstance();
        Connection connection = pool.getConnection();
        PreparedStatement ps = null;

        String query =
                "INSERT INTO User (FirstName, LastName, EmailAddress) " +
                "VALUES (?, ?, ?)";
        try
        {
            ps = connection.prepareStatement(query);
            ps.setString(1, user.getFirstName());
            ps.setString(2, user.getLastName());
            ps.setString(3, user.getEmailAddress());
            return ps.executeUpdate();
        }
        catch(SQLException e)
        {
            e.printStackTrace();
            return 0;
        }
        finally
        {
            DBUtil.closePreparedStatement(ps);
            pool.freeConnection(connection);
        }
    }

    public static int update(User user)
    {
        ConnectionPool pool = ConnectionPool.getInstance();
        Connection connection = pool.getConnection();
        PreparedStatement ps = null;

        String query = "UPDATE User SET " +
                "FirstName = ?, " +
                "LastName = ?, " +
                "WHERE EmailAddress = ?";
        try
        {
            ps = connection.prepareStatement(query);
            ps.setString(1, user.getFirstName());
            ps.setString(2, user.getLastName());
            ps.setString(3, user.getEmailAddress());

            return ps.executeUpdate();
        }
```

Figure 14-15   The database class for the Email List application (part 1 of 3)

The delete method works like the update method, but it uses the DELETE statement instead of the UPDATE statement.

The emailExists method checks if the specified email address already exists in the User table. To do that, this method executes a SELECT statement that searches for the specified email address. If this method finds the address, it returns a true value. Otherwise, it returns a false value.

The UserDB class **Page 2**

```
        catch(SQLException e)
        {
            e.printStackTrace();
            return 0;
        }
        finally
        {
            DBUtil.closePreparedStatement(ps);
            pool.freeConnection(connection);
        }
    }

    public static int delete(User user)
    {
        ConnectionPool pool = ConnectionPool.getInstance();
        Connection connection = pool.getConnection();
        PreparedStatement ps = null;

        String query = "DELETE FROM User " +
                "WHERE EmailAddress = ?";
        try
        {
            ps = connection.prepareStatement(query);
            ps.setString(1, user.getEmailAddress());

            return ps.executeUpdate();
        }
        catch(SQLException e)
        {
            e.printStackTrace();
            return 0;
        }
        finally
        {
            DBUtil.closePreparedStatement(ps);
            pool.freeConnection(connection);
        }
    }

    public static boolean emailExists(String emailAddress)
    {
        ConnectionPool pool = ConnectionPool.getInstance();
        Connection connection = pool.getConnection();
        PreparedStatement ps = null;
        ResultSet rs = null;

        String query = "SELECT EmailAddress FROM User " +
                "WHERE EmailAddress = ?";
        try
        {
            ps = connection.prepareStatement(query);
            ps.setString(1, emailAddress);
            rs = ps.executeQuery();
            return rs.next();
        }
```

Figure 14-15   The database class for the Email List application (part 2 of 3)

The selectUser method creates a User object that gets the data from the row in the User table that corresponds with the email address that's passed to the method. If the email address is found in the User table, this method uses the set methods of the User class to fill the User object with values from the database. Then, this method returns the User object to the calling method. Otherwise, this method prints a stack trace and returns a null value.

So far in this book, the User and UserDB classes have only worked with three fields: first name, last name, and email address. In the real world, though, a single business class or database table may contain dozens of fields. To give you some idea of this complexity, section 5 presents a more realistic application. When you code an application like that, the good news is that all the skills you've just learned still apply. The bad news is that you have to write many more lines of code as you develop typical business and database classes.

If you configure your connection pool as described in figure 14-12, the connection pool will automatically return abandoned connections to the pool. However, it's still a good programming practice to close all database resources when you're done with them as illustrated by the methods in this figure. This will help your database code run more efficiently, and it will reduce the likelihood of running into resource usage problems.

The UserDB class   **Page 3**

```java
        catch(SQLException e)
        {
            e.printStackTrace();
            return false;
        }
        finally
        {
            DBUtil.closeResultSet(rs);
            DBUtil.closePreparedStatement(ps);
            pool.freeConnection(connection);
        }
    }

    public static User selectUser(String emailAddress)
    {
        ConnectionPool pool = ConnectionPool.getInstance();
        Connection connection = pool.getConnection();
        PreparedStatement ps = null;
        ResultSet rs = null;

        String query = "SELECT * FROM User " +
                       "WHERE EmailAddress = ?";
        try
        {
            ps = connection.prepareStatement(query);
            ps.setString(1, emailAddress);
            rs = ps.executeQuery();
            User user = null;
            if (rs.next())
            {
                user = new User();
                user.setFirstName(rs.getString("FirstName"));
                user.setLastName(rs.getString("LastName"));
                user.setEmailAddress(rs.getString("EmailAddress"));
            }
            return user;
        }
        catch (SQLException e){
            e.printStackTrace();
            return null;
        }
        finally
        {
            DBUtil.closeResultSet(rs);
            DBUtil.closePreparedStatement(ps);
            pool.freeConnection(connection);
        }
    }
}
```

Figure 14-15   The database class for the Email List application (part 3 of 3)

The code for the utility class

Before you close a Statement, PreparedStatement, or ResultSet object, it's a good practice to check if the object is null. Then, if the object is null, you can avoid a NullPointerException by not calling the close method. On the other hand, if the object isn't null, you can safely call the close method to close it. However, you still need to catch the SQLException that's thrown by the close method.

Since this requires a significant amount of code, and since you often need to close these objects, it often makes sense to create a utility class like the DBUtil class shown in figure 14-16. A class like this can make it easier to close database objects. Note, for example, how this class makes it easier to code the UserDB class shown in the previous figure.

The DBUtil class

```
package data;

import java.sql.*;

public class DBUtil
{
    public static void closeStatement(Statement s)
    {
        try
        {
            if (s != null)
                s.close();
        }
        catch(SQLException e)
        {
            e.printStackTrace();
        }
    }

    public static void closePreparedStatement(Statement ps)
    {
        try
        {
            if (ps != null)
                ps.close();
        }
        catch(SQLException e)
        {
            e.printStackTrace();
        }
    }

    public static void closeResultSet(ResultSet rs)
    {
        try
        {
            if (rs != null)
                rs.close();
        }
        catch(SQLException e)
        {
            e.printStackTrace();
        }
    }
}
```

Description

- To make it easier to close statements and result sets, you can use a utility class like the one shown in this figure.

Figure 14-16   The utility class for the Email List application

Perspective

The goal of this chapter has been to show you how to use JDBC and connection pooling within the context of a web application. Although there's a lot more to database programming than that, this should get you off to a good start. In fact, the skills in this chapter are adequate for most small- to medium-sized web sites.

For large web sites, though, the skills presented in this chapter may not be adequate. In that case, you may want to use other third-party tools to design and create a database, to map objects to a database, and to manage a connection pool. For example, you may want to use Hibernate to map your objects to a relational database. Or, you may need to use Enterprise JavaBeans (EJBs). To learn more about these subjects, you can read about them on the Internet, or you can get books that are dedicated to these subjects.

Summary

- To write Java code that works with a database, you use *Java Database Connectivity* (*JDBC*). To do that, you use the classes in the JDBC API.

- Before you can access a database, you must install a database driver on the database server. Then, before you can work with the database, you must load the driver and create a Connection object that connects to the database.

- With JDBC 4.0, the database driver is loaded automatically. This new feature is known as *automatic driver loading*.

- You use the createStatement method of the Connection object to create a Statement object that contains the SQL statement that you want to run. Then, you use the executeQuery or executeUpdate method to run the SQL statement.

- When you run a SELECT statement, it returns a result set to your program. Then, you can use the methods of the ResultSet object to move the cursor through the rows of the result set and to get the data from the rows.

- Prepared statements can improve the performance of database operations because the database server only checks their syntax and prepares execution plans for them the first time they are executed. To use them, you create PreparedStatement objects that contain SQL statements, and you use the methods of these objects to pass parameters to them and run them.

- A ResultSetMetaData object contains information about a result set like the number of columns in the table and the names of the columns.

- *Database connection pooling* (*DBCP*) can improve the performance of a web application by sharing the connections to a database between all of the users of the application.

Before you do the exercises for this chapter

The exercises for this chapter assume that you've already installed MySQL and the JDBC driver for MySQL as described in appendix A. They also assume that you've made the connection pool jar file available to your application as described in figure 14-11 (and figure 2-1). Last, if you're using NetBeans and you haven't yet registered the murach database, you may need to use the procedure in figure 3-4 to do that when you open the projects for these exercises.

Exercise 14-1   Implement connection pooling

In this exercise, you'll enhance the SQL Gateway application shown in this chapter so that it uses connection pooling.

1. Open the ch14sqlGateway project in the ex_starts directory.

2. Run the application and execute some SELECT statements to see how this application works.

3. Open the context.xml file in the META-INF folder. Then, modify it so it includes a Resource element that configures a connection pool. The easiest way to do this is to copy the Resource element from the ch14email application's context.xml file.

4. Create a ConnectionPool class in a package named data that you can use to get or free a connection. The easiest way to do this is to copy the ConnectionPool class from the ch14email application.

5. Open the SQLGatewayServlet.java file that's stored in the sql package. Then, modify this servlet so it uses the ConnectionPool class to get a connection.

6. Run the application and make sure it works as before.

Exercise 14-2   Create an Administration application

In this exercise, you'll create an application that allows you to view all users, update existing users, and delete users in the User table in the murach database.

1. Open the project named ch14userAdmin in the ex_starts directory.

2. Review the existing code for this application. Note that the context.xml file configures connection pooling and that the web.xml file maps servlets to URLs. Note also the Java code that's available from the business, data, and user packages.

3. Open the UserDB class that's located in the data package. Then, add code to the selectUsers method to return an ArrayList of User objects that corresponds with the rows in the User table.

4. Add code to the DisplayUsersServlet in the user package that gets an ArrayList of User objects from the User table, sets the ArrayList as a session attribute, and forwards the request to the users.jsp to display the list of users.

5. Open the users.jsp file. Then, note that the Update link requests the DisplayUserServlet class and the Delete link requests the DeleteUserServlet.

6. Add code to the DisplayUserServlet class that gets the User object that corresponds with the specified email address from the User table, stores this object in the session, and forwards the request to the user.jsp.

7. Open the user.jsp file. Then, note that it displays user data and submits it to the UpdateUserServlet class.

8. Add code to the UpdateUserServlet class that gets all request parameters from the user.jsp and updates the user in the User table. This servlet should forward the request to the DisplayUsersServlet so the list of users is displayed after a user is updated.

9. Add code to the DeleteUserServlet class that retrieves the request parameter for the email address and deletes the specified user. This servlet should forward the request to the DisplayUsersServlet so the list of users is displayed after a user is deleted.

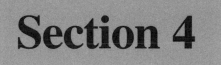

Section 4

Advanced servlet and JSP skills

This section contains six chapters that present other servlet and JSP skills that you may need for some of your web applications. Because each of these chapters is written as an independent module, you can read these chapters in whatever sequence you prefer. If, for example, you want to learn how to use listeners to respond to events that occur during a web application's lifecycle, you can skip to chapter 19. Or, if want to learn how to work with a secure connection, you can skip to chapter 16. Eventually, though, you should read all of the chapters in this section because they all provide useful capabilities.

15

How to use JavaMail to send email

When you create a web application, you sometimes need to send email to the users of the application. For example, when a user makes a purchase from an e-commerce site, the web application usually sends a confirmation email that contains information about the order. In this chapter, you'll learn how to use the JavaMail API to send an email from a servlet.

An introduction to the JavaMail API

The *JavaMail API* is a programming interface that makes it easy for Java developers to write code that automatically sends an email. This API depends on another API known as the JavaBeans Activation Framework (JAF) API. Figure 15-1 introduces you to these APIs and several of the protocols that these APIs use.

How email works

You're probably familiar with *mail client* software such as Microsoft Outlook or Eudora that allows you to send and retrieve messages. This type of software communicates with the *mail server* software that actually sends and retrieves your email. Most likely, your mail server software is provided by your Internet Service Provider (ISP) or through your company.

The diagram in figure 15-1 shows how this works. The protocol that's most commonly used to send email messages is *SMTP*. When you send an email message, the message is first sent from the mail client software on your computer to your mail server using the SMTP protocol. Then, your mail server uses SMTP to send the mail to the recipient's mail server. Finally, the recipient's mail client uses the *POP* protocol or the *IMAP* protocol to retrieve the mail from the recipient's mail server.

A fourth protocol you should know about is *MIME*. Unlike the other protocols described in this figure, MIME isn't used to transfer email messages. Instead, it defines how the content of an email message and its attachments are formatted. In this chapter, you'll learn how to send messages that consist of simple text messages as well as messages that use HTML format.

How email works

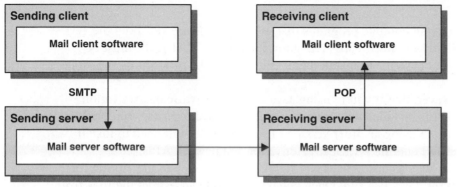

Three protocols for sending and retrieving email messages

Protocol	Description
SMTP	*Simple Mail Transfer Protocol* is used to send a message from one mail server to another.
POP	*Post Office Protocol* is used to retrieve messages from a mail server. This protocol transfers all messages from the mail server to the mail client. Currently, POP is in version 3 and is known as POP3.
IMAP	*Internet Message Access Protocol* is used by web-based mail services such as Hotmail, Yahoo, and Gmail. This protocol allows a web browser to read messages that are stored on the mail server. Currently, IMAP is in version 4 and is known as IMAP4.

Another protocol that's used with email

Protocol	Description
MIME	The *Multipurpose Internet Message Extension* type, or *MIME* type, specifies the type of content that can be sent as a message or attachment.

The JAR files for the JavaMail API

File	Description
mail.jar	Contains the Java classes for the JavaMail API.
activation.jar	Contains the Java classes for the JavaBean Activation Framework. These classes are necessary for the JavaMail API to run.

Description

- The *JavaMail API* is a high level API that allows you to use a mail protocol to communicate with a mail server. It depends upon another API known as the JavaBeans Activation Framework (JAF) API.

Figure 15-1   An introduction to the JavaMail API

How to install the JavaMail API

Before you can compile programs that use the JavaMail API, both the JavaMail API and the JavaBeans Activation Framework (JAF) API must be installed on your system. To install them, you can use the procedures shown in figure 15-2.

Note, however, that if you're using Java SE 6, the JavaBeans Activation Framework API is installed with it so you will only have to install the JavaMail API. But if you're using an older version of Java SE, you will need to install both the JavaMail and the JavaBeans Activation Framework APIs.

The easiest way to install the JavaMail API is to download the zip file for this API from the Java web site. Once you do that, you can extract the files from the zip file onto your computer. Then, you can copy the mail.jar file to the JDK's jre\lib\ext directory. That way, the classes needed by the JavaMail API will be available to your system. To install the JavaBeans Activation Framework API, you use a similar procedure.

When you unzip the zip file for an API, the documentation for that API is installed on your system. To view this documentation, you can navigate to the directory that contains the index.html file for the API and view that page in your web browser. For example, if you unzipped the JavaMail API into the c:\murach\servlet_jsp directory, the index file for the documentation will be in this directory:

```
c:\murach\servlet_jsp\javamail-1.4\docs\javadocs
```

Then, if you open the index file in a web browser, you'll be able to get more information about the interfaces and classes that make up the JavaMail API.

How to install the JavaMail API

1. Locate the download page for the JavaMail API on the Java web site (www.java.sun.com).
2. Click on the Download button and follow the instructions.
3. Save the zip file for the JavaMail API to your hard disk. This file is typically named something like javamail-1_4.zip.
4. Extract the files from the zip file.
5. Copy the mail.jar file to the JDK's jre\lib\ext directory.

How to install the JavaBeans Activation Framework API

1. Locate the download page for the JavaBeans Activation Framework API on the Java web site (www.java.sun.com).
2. Click on the Download button and follow the instructions.
3. Save the zip file for the JavaMail API to your hard disk. This file is typically named something like jaf-1_1.zip.
4. Extract the files from the zip file.
5. Copy the activation.jar file to the JDK's jre\lib\ext directory.

Description

*   Both the JavaMail and JavaBeans Activation Framework (JAF) APIs need to be installed to send email from a servlet.
*   The JavaBeans Activation Framework API is included with Java SE 6. As a result, if you're using Java SE 6 or later, you don't need to install this API.
*   If you want to use different versions of these APIs, you can use the procedure shown above to download and install the version that you want to use.
*   After you unzip the zip file for an API into a directory on your computer, you can view the documentation for the API by navigating to the docs\javadocs subdirectory and opening the index.html page.

Figure 15-2   How to install the JavaMail API

Code that uses the JavaMail API to send an email message

Figure 15-3 shows the packages that you need to import to be able to send an email, and it shows some Java code that creates and sends an email message that contains plain text. Although you may not understand every line in this example, you can see how the Java API makes it easy to create and send an email. In the next four figures, you'll learn the details for writing code like this.

Three packages for sending email

Package	Description
java.util	Contains the Properties class that's used to set the properties for the email session.
javax.mail	Contains the Session, Message, Address, Transport, and MessagingException classes needed to send a message.
javax.mail.internet	Contains the MimeMessage and InternetAddress classes needed to send an email message across the Internet.

Code that uses the JavaMail API to send an email

```
try
{
    // 1 - get a mail session
    Properties props = new Properties();
    props.put("mail.smtp.host", "localhost");
    Session session = Session.getDefaultInstance(props);

    // 2 - create a message
    Message message = new MimeMessage(session);
    message.setSubject(subject);
    message.setText(body);

    // 3 - address the message
    Address fromAddress = new InternetAddress(from);
    Address toAddress = new InternetAddress(to);
    message.setFrom(fromAddress);
    message.setRecipient(Message.RecipientType.TO, toAddress);

    // 4 - send the message
    Transport.send(message);
}
catch (MessagingException e)
{
    log(e.toString());
}
```

Description

- This code uses the classes that are available from the JavaMail API to send a simple email message that displays plain text.

Figure 15-3   Code that uses the JavaMail API to send an email message

How to create and send an email message

Now that you have a general idea of how to use the JavaMail API to create and send an email message, you'll learn the coding details.

How to create a mail session

Figure 15-4 shows how to create a *mail session* so you can create and send an email message. Before you create a mail session, you need to create a Properties object that contains any properties that the session needs to send or receive mail. A Properties object stores a list of properties where each property has a name, which is often referred to as a key, and a value. To specify properties for a mail session, you can use the put method of the Properties class to define any of the standard properties available from the JavaMail API.

To create a mail session, you can call the static getDefaultInstance method of the Session class to get a Session object that has all of the default settings for a mail session. Before you do that, though, you at the least need to use the Properties class to specify the property for the SMTP host as shown in the first example. Here, the localhost keyword is used to specify that the SMTP server is running on the same computer as the web application. This is often the case when you deploy a web application to a production server.

Like the first example, the second example uses the localhost keyword to specify that the SMTP server is running on the same server as the web application. However, this example explicitly sets two other properties. First, it sets the protocol to SMTP. Then, it sets the port to 25. Since these are the default values, this isn't necessary, but it does show how to set the protocol and port for a server.

After it creates the session object, the second example uses the setDebug method of the Session object to turn on debugging for the session. As a result, the Session object will print debugging information to the Tomcat console. This can be helpful when you're troubleshooting a connection to a new SMTP server.

The third example shows how to use an SMTP server that's running on a remote server. In particular, it shows how to use an SMTP server that's running on a GMail server. Like many remote SMTP servers, this one uses the SMTPS protocol. Unlike SMTP, SMTPS always uses a secure connection and allows for authentication. For more information about secure connections and authentication, see chapters 16 and 17.

This third example starts by setting the protocol to SMTPS. Then, it sets the host, port, auth, and quitwait properties for the SMTPS protocol. Here, the auth property indicates that the user must be authenticated before the session can connect to the SMTP server, and the quitwait property prevents an SSLException that sometimes occurs when you use a GMail SMTP server.

If you're running Tomcat on your computer, it can be difficult to find the right settings for testing the JavaMail API. One option is to install an SMTP

Common properties that can be set for a Session object

Property	Description
mail.transport.protocol	Specifies the protocol that's used for the session. For sending email, the protocol is usually smtp or smtps.
mail.smtp.host	Specifies the host computer for the SMTP server.
mail.smtp.port	Specifies the port that the SMTP server is using.
mail.smtp.auth	Specifies whether authentication is required to log in to the SMTP server.
mail.smtp.quitwait	This property can be set to false to prevent an SSLException from occurring when you attempt to connect to a GMail SMTP server.

How to get a mail session for a local SMTP server

```
Properties props = new Properties();
props.put("mail.smtp.host", "localhost");
Session session = Session.getDefaultInstance(props);
```

Another way to get a mail session for a local SMTP server

```
Properties props = new Properties();
props.put("mail.transport.protocol", "smtp");
props.put("mail.smtp.host", "localhost");
props.put("mail.smtp.port", 25);
Session session = Session.getDefaultInstance(props);
session.setDebug(true);
```

How to get a mail session for a remote SMTP server

```
Properties props = new Properties();
props.put("mail.transport.protocol", "smtps");
props.put("mail.smtps.host", "smtp.gmail.com");
props.put("mail.smtps.port", 465);
props.put("mail.smtps.auth", "true");
props.put("mail.smtps.quitwait", "false");
Session session = Session.getDefaultInstance(props);
session.setDebug(true);
```

Description

- A Session object contains information about the *mail session* such as the procotol, the host, the port, and so on. (This isn't the same as the HttpSession object.)

- To set the properties of a Properties object, you can use the put method to specify a property name and value for each property.

- The static getDefaultInstance method of the Session class returns the default Session object for the application.

- The setDebug method of the Session object can be used to print debugging information about the session to a log file.

- If you change the properties for a Session object, you must restart Tomcat before the changes take effect.

- If the Java application is running on the same computer as the SMTP server, you can usually use the localhost keyword to specify the SMTP host.

Figure 15-4   How to create a mail session

server on your computer. Then, you can use the localhost keyword to connect to that server. Another option is to work with your network administrator or your ISP to get the details that you need for connecting to a remote SMTP server.

When you work with a mail session, keep in mind that there are many other mail session properties that aren't shown in this figure. If necessary, you can set these properties using the techniques that you've just learned.

Note, however, that when you change the properties that are stored in the Session object, you need to restart Tomcat to put them in force. That's because the static getDefaultInstance method of the Session object returns the existing Session object if one already exists. So if you want to create a new Session object that uses the new properties, you must get rid of the old Session object. The easiest way to do that is to restart Tomcat.

How to create a message

Once you've created the Session object, you can create an object that defines an email message as shown in figure 15-5. To do that, you pass a Session object to the constructor of the MimeMessage class to create a MimeMessage object. Then, you can set the subject, body, and addresses for the message. To set the subject, you use the setSubject method. To set the message body as plain text, you use the setText method. Then, you use the methods shown in the next figure to set the addresses for the message.

When you use the setText method to set the body of the message, the MIME type for the message is automatically set to text/plain. For many text messages, this is adequate. However, since most modern mail clients can display text that's formatted with HTML tags, it's also common to use the setContent method to change the MIME type for a message to text/html. Then, the body of the message can include HTML tags that format the text, display images, and provide links to web resources.

How to create a message

```
Message message = new MimeMessage(session);
```

How to set the subject line of a message

```
message.setSubject("Order Confirmation");
```

How to set the body of a plain text message

```
message.setText("Thanks for your order!");
```

How to set the body of an HTML message

```
message.setContent("<H1>Thanks for your order!</H1>", "text/html");
```

Description

- You can use the MimeMessage class that's stored in the javax.mail.internet package to create a message. This message extends the Message class that's stored in the java.mail package.

- To create a MimeMessage object, you supply a valid Session object to the MimeMessage constructor.

- Once you've created a MimeMessage object, you can use the setSubject and setText methods to set the subject line and body of the email message. This automatically sets the MIME type to text/plain.

- You can use the setContent method to include an HTML document as the body of the message. To do that, the first argument specifies a string for the HTML document, and the second argument specifies text/html as the MIME type.

- All of the methods in this figure throw a javax.mail.MessagingException. As a result, you must handle this exception when you use these methods.

Figure 15-5   How to create a message

How to address a message

Figure 15-6 shows how to address a MimeMessage object like the one in the last figure. This allows you to specify the From address as well as the To, CC (*carbon copy*), and BCC (*blind carbon copy*) addresses. When you send a carbon copy, the CC addresses will appear in the message, but when you send a blind carbon copy, the BCC addresses won't appear in the message.

Before you can set an address within a MimeMessage object, though, you must create an Address object that defines at least an email address. To do that, you create an object from the InternetAddress subclass of the Address class. When you create this object, the first argument specifies the email address.

If you want to associate a name with the email address, you can include a second argument. Then, the name will be displayed next to the email address like this: andi@yahoo.com (Andrea Steelman). However, this constructor throws an exception of the java.io.UnsupportedEncodingException type. As a result, you must handle this exception if you associate a name with the email address.

To set the From address, you can use the setFrom method of the MimeMessage object. When you use this method, you must supply an Address object that defines the email address you wish to be displayed in the From attribute of the email message.

To set the To, CC, and BCC addresses, you can use the setRecipient method of the MimeMessage object. With this method, the first argument specifies the type of recipient for the address. Then, the second argument specifies an Address object. To specify the recipient type, you use one of the fields defined in the Message.RecipientType class.

If you want to send your message to multiple recipients, you can use the setRecipients method of the MimeMessage class. This method allows you to send a message to an array of Address objects. When you use this method, it replaces any recipients that were already set in the message. However, if you want to add recipients to an existing message, you can use the addRecipient or addRecipients methods. These methods work like the setRecipient and setRecipients methods, but they add recipients to an existing list.

Since the methods of the MimeMessage class throw a MessagingException, you must handle this exception in any code that uses these methods. In addition, the InternetAddress constructor throws an AddressException when an illegally formatted address is found. However, since the AddressException class extends the MessagingException class, you can catch both exceptions by catching the MessagingException.

How to set the From address

```
Address fromAddress = new InternetAddress("cds@murach.com");
message.setFrom(fromAddress);
```

How to set the To address

```
Address toAddress = new InternetAddress("andi@yahoo.com");
message.setRecipient(Message.RecipientType.TO, toAddress);
```

How to set the CC address

```
Address ccAddress = new InternetAddress("ted@yahoo.com");
message.setRecipient(Message.RecipientType.CC, ccAddress);
```

How to set the BCC address

```
Address bccAddress = new InternetAddress("jsmith@gmail.com");
message.setRecipient(Message.RecipientType.BCC, bccAddress);
```

How to include an email address and a name

```
Address toAddress =
    new InternetAddress("andi@yahoo.com", "Andrea Steelman");
```

How to send a message to multiple recipients

```
Address[] mailList = { new InternetAddress("andi@hotmail.com"),
                       new InternetAddress("joelmurach@yahoo.com"),
                       new InternetAddress("jsmith@gmail.com") };
message.setRecipients(Message.RecipientType.TO, mailList);
```

How to add recipients to a message

```
Address toAddress = new InternetAddress("joelmurach@yahoo.com");
message.addRecipient(Message.RecipientType.TO, toAddress);
```

Description

- To define an email address, use the InternetAddress class that's stored in the javax.mail.internet package. This class is a subclass of the Address class that's stored in the javax.mail package.

- To set the From address, use the setFrom method of the MimeMessage object.

- To set the To, CC (*carbon copy*), and BCC (*blind carbon copy*) addresses, use the setRecipient and setRecipients methods of the MimeMessage object.

- To include a name that's associated with an email address, you can add a second argument to the InternetAddress constructor. However, this constructor throws an exception of the java.io.UnsupportedEncodingException type.

- To send an email message to multiple recipients, you can pass an array of Address objects to the setRecipients method. This replaces any existing addresses.

- To add email addresses to any existing addresses for a message, use the addRecipient and addRecipients methods.

- All of the methods in this figure throw a javax.mail.MessagingException. As a result, you must handle this exception when using these methods.

Figure 15-6   How to address a message

How to send a message

Once you've created and addressed a MimeMessage object as shown in the last two figures, you can send the message as shown in figure 15-7. For an SMTP server that doesn't require authentication, you can call the static send method of the Transport class with the MimeMessage object as the argument.

However, if the SMTP server requires authentication, you use the getTransport method of the session object to return a Transport object. Then, you can use the connect method to specify a username and password that can be used to connect to the server. In this figure, for example, the connect method specifies a username of "johnsmith@gmail.com" and a password of "sesame".

Once you've connected to the SMTP server, you can use the sendMessage method to send the message. When you use this method, you can specify the MimeMessage object as the first argument, and you can specify the second argument by calling the getAllRecipients method of the MimeMessage object. Finally, you can use the close method to close the connection.

If the message can't be sent, the send or sendMessage method will throw an exception of the SendFailedException type. This exception contains a list of (1) invalid addresses to which the message could not be sent, (2) valid addresses to which the message wasn't sent, and (3) valid addresses to which the message was sent. If necessary, you can use this exception to perform some processing such as writing these addresses to a log file.

How to send a message when no authentication is required

```
Transport.send(message);
```

How to send a message when authentication is required

```
Transport transport = session.getTransport();
transport.connect("johnsmith@gmail.com", "sesame");
transport.sendMessage(message, message.getAllRecipients());
transport.close();
```

Description

- If the SMTP server doesn't require authentication, you can use the static send method of the Transport class to send a message to the specified SMTP server.

- If the SMTP server requires authentication, you can use the getTransport method of the session object to return a Transport object. Then, you can use the connect method to specify a username and password that can be used to connect to the server; the sendMessage method to send the message; and the close method to close the connection.

- If the SMTP host is incorrect in the session object, the send method will throw a SendFailedException object.

- The send method also throws a SendFailedException object when a message can't be sent. You can use this object to return the invalid addresses, the valid addresses that have been sent, and the valid addresses that haven't been sent.

- Since the SendFailedException class inherits the MessagingException class, you can catch both types of exceptions by catching the MessagingException.

Figure 15-7   How to send a message

Example classes that send an email message

Now that you know the coding details for creating and sending an email message, here are three classes that put that code into use. The first is a helper class that can be used to send a message to a local SMTP server. The second is a servlet that uses the helper class to send a message. The third is a helper class that can be used to send a message to a remote SMTP server.

A helper class for sending an email with a local SMTP server

Figure 15-8 shows a helper class named MailUtilLocal that you can use to send an email. This class contains a static method named sendMail that creates and sends a message from a single email address to a single email address. Since this method throws an exception of the MessagingException type, any class that calls this method must catch this exception.

The fifth parameter of the sendMail method is a Boolean value that specifies whether the body of the message contains HTML formatting. As a result, if this parameter is set to true, this method uses the setContent method to set the body of the message and to indicate that the body contains HTML formatting. Otherwise, this method uses the setText method to set the body of the message as plain text.

Although this MailUtil class is simple, it is useful. To enhance it, you can add sendMail methods that provide for CC and BCC addresses. Or, you can add sendMail methods that provide for multiple TO, CC, and BCC addresses.

A helper class for sending an email with a local SMTP server

```java
package util;

import java.util.Properties;
import javax.mail.*;
import javax.mail.internet.*;

public class MailUtilLocal
{
    public static void sendMail(String to, String from,
        String subject, String body, boolean bodyIsHTML)
        throws MessagingException
    {
        // 1 - get a mail session
        Properties props = new Properties();
        props.put("mail.transport.protocol", "smtp");
        props.put("mail.smtp.host", "localhost");
        props.put("mail.smtp.port", 25);
        Session session = Session.getDefaultInstance(props);
        session.setDebug(true);

        // 2 - create a message
        Message message = new MimeMessage(session);
        message.setSubject(subject);
        if (bodyIsHTML)
            message.setContent(body, "text/html");
        else
            message.setText(body);

        // 3 - address the message
        Address fromAddress = new InternetAddress(from);
        Address toAddress = new InternetAddress(to);
        message.setFrom(fromAddress);
        message.setRecipient(Message.RecipientType.TO, toAddress);

        // 4 - send the message
        Transport.send(message);
    }
}
```

Description

- You can use the static sendMail method of this MailUtil class to send an email message with a From address and a To address.

- Since the sendMail method throws the MessagingException, any class that uses this method must handle this exception.

Figure 15-8   A helper class for sending an email with a local SMTP server

A servlet that uses a helper class to send an email message

Figure 15-9 presents the code for the AddToEmailListServlet class. Since you've seen variations of this class throughout this book, you shouldn't have any trouble understanding how it works. This time, though, the servlet uses the MailUtilLocal class presented in the last figure to send an email message to the email address that the user entered.

After the servlet writes the User object to a file, the servlet creates four strings that contain the information for the email message. First, it sets the To address to the email address that was passed with the request. Then, it sets the From address, the subject line, and the text for the body of the message.

In addition, this servlet creates a Boolean variable that specifies whether the body of the email contains HTML formatting. In this case, this variable is set to false. As a result, the email will use plain text formatting.

A servlet that sends an email   **Page 1**

```java
package email;

import java.io.*;
import javax.servlet.*;
import javax.servlet.http.*;

import javax.mail.MessagingException;

import business.User;
import data.UserIO;
import util.*;

public class AddToEmailListServlet extends HttpServlet
{
    protected void doPost(HttpServletRequest request,
                          HttpServletResponse response)
                          throws ServletException, IOException
    {
        // get parameters from the request
        String firstName = request.getParameter("firstName");
        String lastName = request.getParameter("lastName");
        String emailAddress = request.getParameter("emailAddress");

        // create the User object and write it to a file
        User user = new User(firstName, lastName, emailAddress);
        ServletContext sc = getServletContext();
        String path = sc.getRealPath("/WEB-INF/EmailList.txt");
        UserIO.addRecord(user, path);

        // store the User object in the session
        HttpSession session = request.getSession();
        session.setAttribute("user", user);

        // send email to user
        String to = emailAddress;
        String from = "email_list@murach.com";
        String subject = "Welcome to our email list";
        String body = "Dear " + firstName + ",\n\n" +
            "Thanks for joining our email list. We'll make sure to send " +
            "you announcements about new products and promotions.\n" +
            "Have a great day and thanks again!\n\n" +
            "Kelly Slivkoff\n" +
            "Mike Murach & Associates";
        boolean isBodyHTML = false;
```

Figure 15-9   A servlet that uses a helper class to send an email message (part 1 of 2)

To create and send the message, the servlet calls the sendMail method of the MailUtilLocal class. Since this method throws a MessagingException, the servlet catches that exception. Then, it stores a custom error message in a String variable named errorMessage, and it sets that message as an attribute of the request object. That way, the next JSP can display the error message.

Finally, this code uses the log method of the servlet to write the email that you were trying to send to a log file. That way, you can view the email even if the sendMail method isn't able to successfully send the email.

If you can't send an email message with a servlet, there are several possible causes. First, you might not be able to connect to your SMTP server. To solve this problem, you may need to make sure that you are connected to the Internet. Second, you might not have the correct name for the SMTP server or you might not have the proper security clearance for accessing the server. To solve this problem, you might need to contact your network administrator or ISP.

A servlet that sends an email   **Page 2**

```
        try
        {
            MailUtilLocal.sendMail(to, from, subject, body, isBodyHTML);
        }
        catch (MessagingException e)
        {
            String errorMessage =
                "ERROR: Unable to send email. " +
                    "Check Tomcat logs for details.<br>" +
                "NOTE: You may need to configure your system " +
                    "as described in chapter 15.<br>" +
                "ERROR MESSAGE: " + e.getMessage();
            request.setAttribute("errorMessage", errorMessage);
            this.log(
                "Unable to send email. \n" +
                "Here is the email you tried to send: \n" +
                "=====================================\n" +
                "TO: " + emailAddress + "\n" +
                "FROM: " + from + "\n" +
                "SUBJECT: " + subject + "\n" +
                "\n" +
                body + "\n\n");
        }

        // forward request and response to JSP page
        String url = "/display_email_entry.jsp";
        RequestDispatcher dispatcher =
            getServletContext().getRequestDispatcher(url);
        dispatcher.forward(request, response);
    }
}
```

Figure 15-9   A servlet that uses a helper class to send an email message (part 2 of 2)

A helper class for sending an email with a remote SMTP server

Figure 15-10 shows a helper class named MailUtilYahoo that you can use to send an email with a remote SMTP server. In particular, you can use this class to send an email with an SMTP server that's available from Yahoo!. Of course, this only works if you have a Yahoo! Mail account with a valid username and password.

If you compare this class with the MailUtilLocal class shown in figure 15-8, you'll see that it works similarly. The primary differences are that the properties for the Session object specify that the session should use the SMTPS protocol, an SMTP server from Yahoo!, and port 465. In addition, the auth property requires authentication for the SMTP server. As a result, the connect method of the Transport object must specify a valid username and password for a Yahoo! Mail account.

A helper class for sending an email with a remote SMTP server

```java
package util;

import java.util.Properties;
import javax.mail.*;
import javax.mail.internet.*;

public class MailUtilYahoo
{
    public static void sendMail(String to, String from,
        String subject, String body, boolean bodyIsHTML)
        throws MessagingException
    {
        // 1 - get a mail session
        Properties props = new Properties();
        props.put("mail.transport.protocol", "smtps");
        props.put("mail.smtps.host", "smtp.mail.yahoo.com");
        props.put("mail.smtps.port", 465);
        props.put("mail.smtps.auth", "true");
        Session session = Session.getDefaultInstance(props);
        session.setDebug(true);

        // 2 - create a message
        Message message = new MimeMessage(session);
        message.setSubject(subject);
        if (bodyIsHTML)
            message.setContent(body, "text/html");
        else
            message.setText(body);

        // 3 - address the message
        Address fromAddress = new InternetAddress(from);
        Address toAddress = new InternetAddress(to);
        message.setFrom(fromAddress);
        message.setRecipient(Message.RecipientType.TO, toAddress);

        // 4 - send the message
        Transport transport = session.getTransport();
        transport.connect("johnsmith", "sesame");
        transport.sendMessage(message, message.getAllRecipients());
        transport.close();
    }
}
```

Figure 15-10   A helper class for sending an email with a remote SMTP server

Perspective

In this chapter, you learned how to use the JavaMail API to send email from your servlets. Keep in mind, though, that you can use the JavaMail API to do more than that. For instance, you can use that API to send messages that have attachments and to retrieve messages. If you need to do tasks like that, you should be able to use the documentation for the JavaMail API to build on the skills you've learned in this chapter.

Summary

- When an email message is sent it goes from the *mail client* software to that client's *mail server* software to the receiving client's mail server and then to the receiving mail client.

- To send email messages from server to server, the *Simple Mail Transfer Protocol* (*SMTP*) is commonly used. Then, to retrieve messages from a server, *Post Office Protocol* (*POP*) and *Internet Message Access Protocol* (*IMAP*) are commonly used.

- To send email messages from your Java programs, you use the classes of the *JavaMail API*. In particular, you create a Session object that contains information about the *mail session* including an address for the SMTP server.

Exercise 15-1   Send an email from a servlet

1. Open the ch15email project in the ex_starts directory. If NetBeans displays error markers next to the classes in the email and util directories, install the JavaMail and Java Activation Framework APIs on your system as described in figure 15-2.

2. Review the helper classes in the util package, including the one for Yahoo email users and the one for Gmail users. Then, choose the class that's closest to what you're going to need for sending email on your system, and modify it so it will work on your system.

    If possible, get help from someone who knows what the properties for the mail session need to be. But if that isn't possible and you don't know what the properties should be, continue with this exercise anyway.

3. Review the servlet named AddToEmailListServlet that's in the email package. Note that it sends a message to the person who joins the email list. Then, modify this servlet so it uses the sendMail method of the helper class that you modified in step 2.

4. Test the application by entering your name and email address and clicking on the Submit button. If the application works, you should receive an email message. Otherwise, you should see error messages at the bottom of the JSP that's displayed. Then, you can look at the Tomcat log file to see what the email message would have looked like if it had worked.

16

How to use SSL to work with a secure connection

If your application requires users to enter sensitive data such as credit card numbers and passwords, you should use a secure connection when you send data between the client and the server. Otherwise, a hacker might be able to intercept and view this data. In this chapter, you'll learn how to transfer data over a secure connection.

An introduction to SSL

To prevent others from reading data that is transmitted over the Internet, you can use the *Secure Sockets Layer* (*SSL*). This is the protocol that lets you transfer data between the server and the client over a secure connection.

How SSL works

Figure 16-1 shows a web page that uses SSL to transfer data between the server and the client over a *secure connection*. To determine if you're transmitting data over a secure connection, you can read the URL. If it starts with https rather than http, then you're transmitting data over a secure connection. In addition, a small lock icon appears in the lower right of the browser when you're using a secure connection.

With a regular HTTP connection, all data is sent as unencrypted plain text. As a result, if a hacker intercepts this data, it is easy to read. With a secure connection, though, all data is encrypted before it's transferred between the client and server. Although a hacker can still intercept this data, he won't be able to read it unless he can break the encryption code.

How TLS works

Transport Layer Security (*TLS*) is another protocol that's used for working with secure connections. This protocol is more advanced than SSL, but it works similarly. As a user, it's hard to tell whether you're using an SSL connection or a TLS connection. Although TLS is only supported by newer browsers, any server that implements TLS also implements SSL. That way, the newer browsers can use TLS, and the older browsers can still use SSL.

When you're working with secure connections, you'll find that SSL is often used to describe the connection instead of TLS. That's because SSL is the older, more established protocol for working with secure connections. In this chapter, the term SSL is used even though the connection could also be a TLS connection.

When to use a secure connection

Due to the time it takes to encrypt and decrypt the data that's sent across a secure connection, secure connections are noticeably slower than regular HTTP connections. As a result, you usually use secure connections only when your application passes sensitive data between the client and the server.

A request made with a secure connection

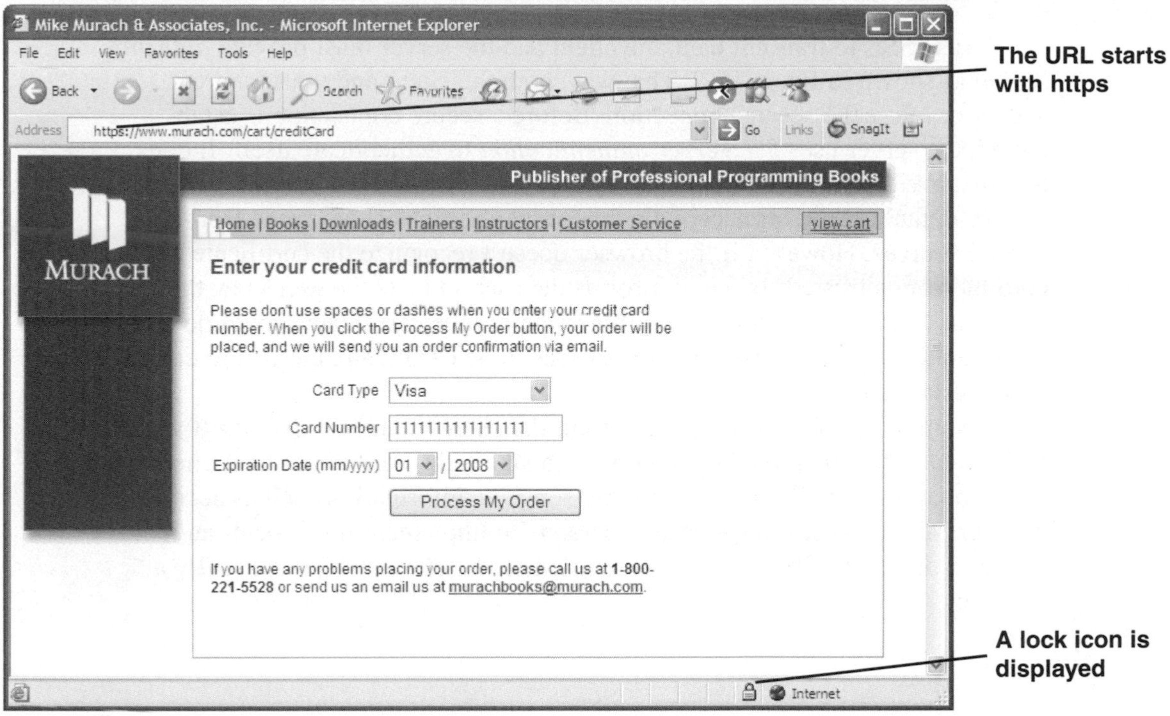

The URL starts with https

A lock icon is displayed

Description

- *Transport Layer Security* (*TLS*) and *Secure Sockets Layer* (*SSL*) are the two protocols used by the Internet that allow clients and servers to communicate over a *secure connection*.

- TLS is the successor to SSL. Although there are slight differences between SSL and TLS, the protocol remains substantially the same. As a result, they are sometimes referred to as the TLS/SSL protocol or these terms are used interchangeably.

- With SSL, the browser encrypts all data that's sent to the server and decrypts all data that's received from the server. Conversely, the server encrypts all data that's sent to the browser and decrypts all data that's received from the browser.

- SSL is able to determine if data has been tampered with during transit.

- SSL is also able to verify that a server or a client is who it claims to be.

- The URL for a secure connection starts with HTTPS instead of HTTP.

- A web browser that is using a secure connection displays a lock in the lower right corner.

Figure 16-1   An introduction to SSL

How SSL authentication works

To use SSL to transmit data, the client and the server must provide *authentication* as shown in figure 16-2. That way, both the client and the server can accept or reject the secure connection. Before a secure connection is established, the server uses *SSL server authentication* to authenticate itself. It does this by providing a *digital secure certificate* to the browser.

By default, browsers accept digital secure certificates that come from trusted sources. However, if the browser doesn't recognize the certificate as coming from a trusted source, it informs the user and lets the user view the certificate. Then, the user can determine whether the certificate should be considered valid. If the user chooses to accept the certificate, the secure connection is established.

In some rare cases, a server may want the client to authenticate itself with *SSL client authentication*. For example, a bank might want to use SSL client authentication to make sure it's sending sensitive information such as account numbers and balances to the correct person. To implement this type of authentication, a digital certificate must be installed on the client, which is usually a browser.

A digital secure certificate

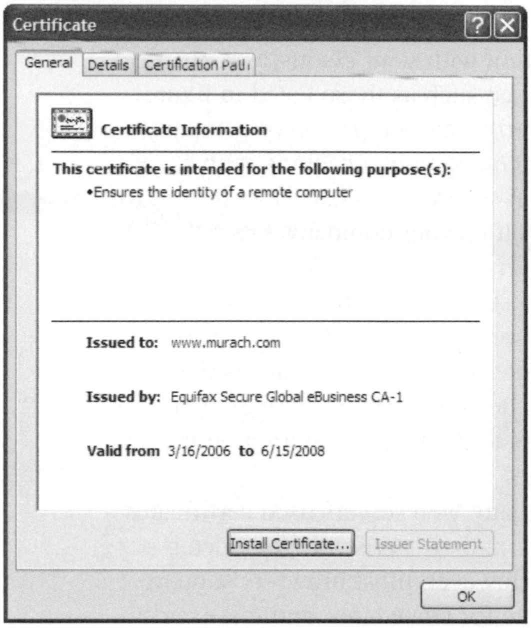

Types of digital secure certificates

Certificate	Description
Server certificate	Issued to trusted servers so client computers can connect to them using secure connections.
Client certificate	Issued to trusted clients so server computers can confirm their identity.

How authentication works

- *Authentication* is the process of determining whether a server or client is who and what it claims to be.
- When a browser makes an initial attempt to communicate with a server over a secure connection, the server authenticates itself by providing a *digital secure certificate*.
- If the digital secure certificate is registered with the browser, the browser won't display the certificate by default. However, the user still has the option to view the certificate.
- In some rare cases, the server may request that a browser authenticate itself by presenting its own digital secure certificate.

Figure 16-2   How SSL authentication works

How to get a digital secure certificate

If you want to establish a secure connection with your clients, you must get a *digital secure certificate* from a trusted source such as those listed in figure 16-3. These *certification authorities (CAs)* verify that the person or company requesting the certificate is a valid person or company by checking with a *registration authority (RA)*. To obtain a digital secure certificate, you'll need to provide an RA with information about yourself or your company. Once the RA approves the request, the CA can issue the digital secure certificate.

A digital secure certificate from a trusted source is not free, and the cost of the certificate will depend on a variety of factors such as the level of security. As a result, when you purchase a digital certificate, you want one that fits the needs of your web site. In particular, you'll need to decide what *SSL strength* you want the connection to support. SSL strength refers to the level of encryption that the secure connection uses when it transmits data.

In the early days of web programming, many web servers used certificates with 40-bit or 56-bit SSL strength. At this strength, it's possible for a determined hacker to break the encryption code. However, most browsers support these strengths, these strengths are appropriate for some sites, and these certificates are reasonably priced.

Today, most web servers use 128-bit or higher SSL strength. Although these certificates are more expensive than 40-bit certificates, it's extremely hard for a hacker to break the encryption code. Since most modern web browsers support 128-bit encryption, they are able to use this SSL strength. Meanwhile, older browsers that don't support this strength can use whatever lesser strength they support.

Once you purchase a secure certificate, you typically send it to your web host who installs it for your site. Once the certificate is installed, you can use SSL to transmit data over a secure connection.

Common certificate authorities that issue digital secure certificates

```
www.verisign.com
www.thawte.com
www.geotrust.com
www.instantssl.com
www.entrust.com
```

SSL strengths

Strength	Pros and Cons
40-bit	Most browsers support it, but it's relatively easy to break the encryption code.
56-bit	It's thousands of times stronger than 40-bit strength and most browsers support it, but it's still possible to break the encryption code.
128-bit	It's over a trillion times a trillion times stronger than 40-bit strength, which makes it extremely difficult to break the encryption code, but it's more expensive and not all browsers support it.

Description

- To use SSL in your web applications, you must first purchase a digital secure certificate from a trusted *certificate authority* (*CA*). Once you obtain the certificate, you send it to the people who host your web site so they can install it on the server.

- A CA is a company that issues and manages security credentials. To verify information provided by the requestor of the secure certificate, a CA must check with a *registration authority* (*RA*). Once the RA verifies the requestor's information, the CA can issue a digital secure certificate.

- Since SSL is built into all major browsers and web servers, installing a digital secure certificate enables SSL.

- *SSL strength* refers to the length of the generated key that is created during the encryption process. The longer the key, the more difficult to break the encryption code.

- The SSL strength that's used depends on the strength provided by the certificate, the strength supported by the web server, and the strength supported by the browser. If a web server or browser isn't able to support the strength provided by the certificate, a lesser strength is used.

Figure 16-3   How to get a digital secure certificate

How to configure a testing environment for SSL

If you're using a commercial web server, you probably won't need to configure the server for SSL. To implement SSL, you just purchase a secure certificate and provide it to the web hosting company. Then, your web hosting company should configure SSL for you.

However, if you want to be able to test secure connections before you deploy them to your web server, you'll need to configure your testing environment. To do that, you can create and install a self-signed digital secure certificate for free.

Since a self-signed certificate doesn't come from a trusted source, it will cause a warning dialog box to be displayed when you use it. However, it will allow you to configure a secure connection for your local testing environment as described in this topic. Although this topic shows how to work with Tomcat 6.0, similar skills apply to other web servers.

The *Java Secure Socket Extension (JSSE)* API is a collection of Java classes that let you use secure connections within your Java programs. Without it, your application won't be able to connect to the server that transmits data over a secure connection. Fortunately, the JSSE API has been included as part of the Java SE library since version 1.4 of the JDK. As a result, if you're using Java SE 6, the JSSE API should already be installed on your system.

How to create a certificate for testing

Figure 16-4 shows how to create a self-signed digital secure certificate for your system. To start, you must create a *keystore file*. To do that, you can open a Command Prompt window and use the cd command to change the current directory to the bin directory of your JDK. Next, you enter the keytool command with the parameters shown in this figure. Then, the keytool program will prompt you to enter some passwords and other information.

When you're asked for the keystore password, you must enter "changeit". If you don't, the certificate won't work properly. Later, when the keytool program asks for the key password for Tomcat, you should press Enter to use the same password as the keystore password.

For the rest of the prompts, you can enter any information about yourself and your company that you want. This information will be displayed on the secure certificate that's used for testing purposes.

When you finish responding to the prompts, the keytool program creates a keystore file named

`.keystore`

and it stores this file in your home directory. For Windows XP, this directory is C:\Documents and Settings*user.name*, but this will vary depending on your operating system.

The entries for creating a secure certificate for testing purposes

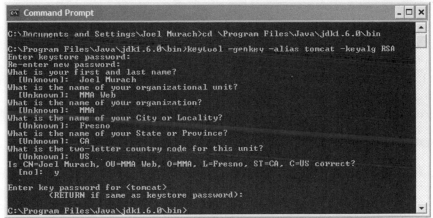

The keytool command for creating a keystore file

```
keytool -genkey -alias tomcat -keyalg RSA
```

The Connector element for an SSL connection in Tomcat's server.xml file

```
<!-- Define a SSL HTTP/1.1 Connector on port 8443 -->
<Connector port="8443" protocol="HTTP/1.1" SSLEnabled="true"
           maxThreads="150" scheme="https" secure="true"
           clientAuth="false" sslProtocol="TLS" />
```

The procedure for configuring SSL on a local system

1. Use a command prompt to create a keystore file. To do that, open the command prompt, and use the cd command to navigate to the bin directory of your JDK. Then, run the keytool command shown above and respond to the prompts. Be sure to use "changeit" as the keystore password, and to press Enter to use the same password for the key password.

2. Edit the server.xml file in Tomcat's conf directory, and remove the comments from the Connector element shown above. Then, restart Tomcat.

Description

- The *Java Secure Socket Extension* (JSSE) API is a collection of Java classes that enable secure connections within Java programs by implementing a version of the SSL and TLS protocols. The JSSE API is included with versions 1.4 and later of the JDK.

- To test SSL connections in a local environment, you can create a self-signed certificate. However, you'll need to purchase a valid certificate before you deploy the application to a commercial web server.

- To create a self-signed certificate, you create a *keystore file* as shown above. The keystore file is named .keystore and it's stored in your operating system's home directory. For Windows XP, the home directory is C:\Documents and Settings*user.name*.

- By default, Tomcat's server.xml file defines the protocol as TLS, not SSL. As a result, newer browsers will use TLS, and older browsers will use SSL.

Figure 16-4   How to configure SSL on a local system

How to enable SSL in Tomcat

After you create the keystore file, you need to enable SSL in Tomcat by editing the server.xml file located in Tomcat's conf directory. To do that, you open this file in a text editor like NotePad and remove the comments from the SSL Connector element that's shown in the previous figure. This Connector element defines a secure connection on port 8443, and it specifies the TLS protocol. As a result, newer browsers will use the TLS protocol, and older browsers will use the SSL protocol.

How to test a local SSL connection

Once you've configured your testing environment as described in the last figure, you can test your local SSL connection by starting or restarting Tomcat and entering this URL:

```
https://localhost:8443
```

Note that this URL begins with https and includes the port number for the SSL connection. Although it's possible to change the SSL port to another value when you're using a testing environment, you must specify the number of a valid SSL port.

If the SSL connection works, your browser will display one or two warning dialog boxes. To start, you usually get a dialog box that indicates that you're about to view pages over a secure connection. This is normal, and you can click the OK button to continue. Then, if you're using a temporary testing certificate, you usually get a dialog box that indicates that the certificate does not come from a trusted source. At this point, you can read the warning and click the OK button or the Yes button to continue.

After you respond to the warning dialog boxes, you should be able to view the page shown in figure 16-5 if your SSL connection is configured correctly. Otherwise, you'll need to troubleshoot your connection. To do that, you can check the problems described in this figure, and you can review the previous figure. If there's a problem with the keystore file, you may need to find the keystore file, delete it, and create a new one.

The URL you can use to test the local SSL connection

```
https://localhost:8443
```

The page that's displayed if SSL is set up correctly on the local system

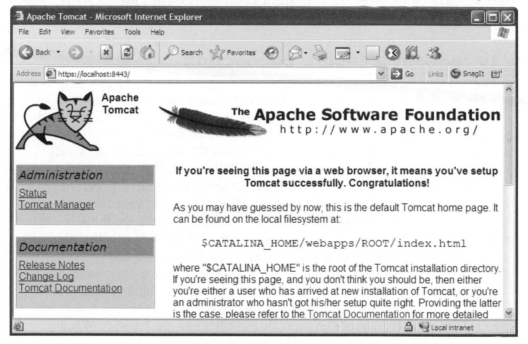

Common problems when configuring the local SSL connection

Problem 1

Problem: Tomcat can't find the keystore file. When you start Tomcat, it will throw a java.io.FileNotFoundException.

Solution: Make sure the .keystore file is located in your home directory, which will vary from system to system. For Windows XP, the home directory is C:\Documents and Settings*user.name*.

Problem 2

Problem: The keystore password and key passwords that you used to create the keystore file don't match. When you start Tomcat, it will display a java.io.FileNotFoundException that says, "keystore was tampered with" or "password was incorrect."

Solution: Delete the old keystore file and create a new keystore file.

Note

- After you enter the URL, your web browser will prompt you with dialog boxes like those in the next figure.

Figure 16-5   How to test a local SSL connection

How to work with a secure connection

Once a remote or local server has been configured to work with SSL, it's easy to request a secure connection, and it's easy to return to a regular HTTP connection.

How to request a secure connection

Figure 16-6 shows how to code a URL that requests a secure connection. To do that, you code an absolute URL that begins with https. If you're using a local server, you need to include the port number that's used for SSL connections. Although the two examples show how to request a JSP, you can use the same technique to request secure connections for HTML pages, JSPs, and servlets.

When a secure connection is requested, the server authenticates itself by sending its secure certificate to the browser. Then, if the certificate doesn't come from a certification authority that's registered with the browser, the browser should display a dialog box like the first one in this figure. Since a self-signed certificate doesn't come from a trusted source, you should see a dialog box like this when you request a secure connection in your local testing environment.

Even if the certificate does come from a certification authority that's registered with the browser, you may get a dialog box like the second one in this figure. However, this depends on the security settings for the browser. When you begin working with secure connections, this dialog box is helpful since it tells you when you're about to use a secure connection and when you're about to return to a regular HTTP connection.

A URL that requests a secure connection over the Internet

```
https://www.murach.com/email/join_email_list.jsp
```

A URL that requests a secure connection from a local system

```
https://localhost:8443/ch16email/join_email_list.jsp
```

A dialog box that may be displayed for secure connections

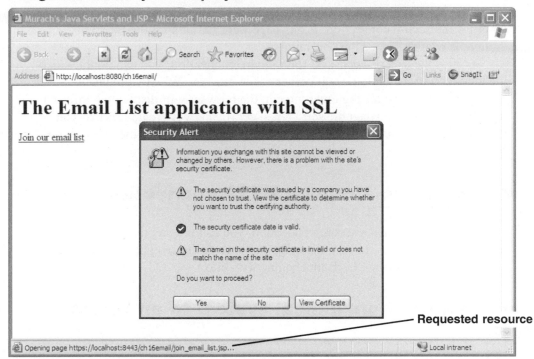

Requested resource

Another dialog box that may be displayed for secure connections

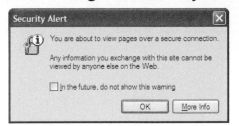

Description

- To request a secure connection, you use an absolute URL that starts with https. If you're requesting a resource from a local system, you also need to specify the port that's used for secure connections. For Tomcat, that port is usually 8443.

- Once you establish a secure connection, you can use relative URLs to continue using the secure connection.

Figure 16-6   How to request a secure connection

A JSP that uses a secure connection

Once the authentication process is complete, the server sends the response to the browser. For example, figure 16-7 shows the join_email_list.jsp page when it's displayed over a secure connection. This means that when the user submits data in this page, the data is encrypted before it's sent to the server.

You can tell that this page uses a secure connection since the URL starts with https. In addition, since this page is running on the local server, it uses port 8443 for the secure connection. If this page were running on the Internet, though, it wouldn't need the port number.

To view the secure certificate for a secure connection, you can double-click the lock icon in the bottom right corner of the browser. When you view a certificate for a local testing environment, the browser will display the information that was entered when the self-signed certificate was created. When you view a certificate on the web, you'll see a certificate similar to the one in figure 16-2.

How to return to a regular HTTP connection

Once you establish a secure connection, you can use relative paths to request web resources. In fact, the only way to return to a regular HTTP connection is to use an absolute URL that begins with http.

How to switch from a local system to an Internet server

When you transfer a web site from a local testing environment to a web server on the Internet, you need to modify the absolute URLs used in the application so they refer to the web site. If, for example, your web site is named www.trout.com, then you need to change all URLs that begin with

```
https://localhost:8443
```

to

```
https://www.trout.com
```

You also need to change all URLs that begin with

```
http://localhost:8080
```

to

```
http://www.trout.com
```

To make this switch easier, you can store variables that refer to the secure connection and the regular HTTP connection in a central location. Then, you only need to make two changes before you deploy your web application to a web server that's running on the Internet.

A JSP that uses a secure connection

```
Murach's Java Servlets and JSP - Microsoft Internet Explorer

File   Edit   View   Favorites   Tools   Help

Back ▾         ✕  🔄  🏠   🔎 Search  ⭐ Favorites  🔄   🖉 ▾ 🖨 🖃 ▾ 🗌 ⊗ 🔍 🖧

Address  🖉  https://localhost:8443/ch16email/join_email_list.jsp       ▾ → Go   Links  🌀 Snagit 🖳
```

Join our email list

To join our email list, enter your name and email address below.
Then, click on the Submit button.

First name: [   ]

Last name: [   ]

Email address: [   ]

[Submit]

**Double-click the
lock icon to view
the certificate**

🖉 Done   🔒 🖧 Local intranet

A URL that returns to a regular connection over the Internet

```
http://www.murach.com/email/index.jsp
```

A URL that returns to a regular connection from a local system

```
http://localhost:8080/ch16email/index.jsp
```

Description

- Once you establish a secure connection, the application will continue using that connection as long as you use relative URLs.
- To return to a regular HTTP connection after using a secure connection, you code an absolute URL that starts with http.

Figure 16-7   How to return to a connection that isn't secure

Perspective

Now that you're done with this chapter, you should be able to modify your applications so they use a secure connection whenever that's needed. In the next chapter, you'll learn how to restrict access to certain portions of your web site by requiring the user to supply a username and a password. This is another form of security known as authentication that is often used in conjunction with a secure connection.

Summary

- *Secure Sockets Layer (SSL)* is an older protocol that's used by the Internet to allow clients and servers to communicate over a *secure connection*. When a secure connection is used, the data that's passed between client and server is encrypted.

- *Transport Layer Security (TLS)* is the successor to SSL, and it works similarly. Since SSL is the older and more established protocol, it is often used to refer to a secure connection even when the connection is most likely using the TLS protocol.

- When a browser attempts to communicate with a server using a secure connection, the server *authenticates* itself by providing a *digital secure certificate*. This is referred to as *SSL server authentication*.

- To get a *digital secure certificate*, you contact a *certificate authority* that uses a *registration authority* to authorize your certificate. This certificate specifies the *SSL strength* of the encryption that's used. When you get the certificate, you install it on your web site.

- The *Java Secure Socket Extension (JSSE)* API makes it possible for a Java application to use a secure connection. This API is included with most modern versions of the Java SE, including Java SE 6.

- To use a secure connection, you need to install a digital secure certificate on your web server, and you need to configure your web server so it defines a secure connection.

- To request a secure connection from a web application, you use an absolute URL that starts with https. Then, you use relative URLs to continue using the secure connection. To return to a regular connection, you use an absolute URL that starts with http.

Exercise 16-1   Test a secure connection

1. Configure a secure connection for your local testing environment as shown in figure 16-4. To do that, you need to create a self-signed certificate. You also need to remove the comments in Tomcat's server.xml file from the Connector element that's shown in this figure.

2. Test the connection by entering the URL shown in figure 16-5 into your browser. This should display the Security Alert dialog box and give you a chance to view the secure certificate that you installed. If this connection doesn't work, you need to fix the configuration as described in figure 16-5, and test it again.

3. Open the ch16email application in the ex_starts directory, and restart Tomcat. Then, run this application and click on the "Join our email list" link. This will test your secure connection and display the Security Alert dialog box. When the "Join our email list" page is displayed, double-click on the lock icon at the bottom of the browser to display the secure certificate again.

4. Click on the Back button until you return to the index.jsp page. Note how this page returns to a regular HTTP connection.

5. Open the display_email_entry.jsp file and view the code for the Return button. Note how this button uses an absolute URL to specify a regular HTTP connection. Also, make sure that the port is set right for your system. If it isn't, change it. Then, test the application and the Return button to make sure that this works.

17

How to restrict access to a web resource

In this chapter, you'll learn how to restrict access to parts of a web site. Then, you'll learn how to allow authorized users to access the restricted parts of the web site. For example, many web sites have an administrative section that can only be accessed by a user who logs in to the site with an authorized username and password.

An introduction to authentication

Although you can restrict access to certain parts of a web application by writing custom servlets and JSPs to work directly with HTTP requests and responses, doing that can be time-consuming and error-prone. That's why most modern servlet containers such as Tomcat provide a built-in way to restrict access to certain parts of a web application. This is known as *container-managed security*, or *container-managed authentication*.

How container-managed authentication works

Figure 17-1 shows what happens when a user requests a resource that has been restricted. Here, the user has run the application for chapter 17 and clicked a link to access a web page within the admin subdirectory of this application. Since this resource has been restricted, a dialog box appears that requests a username and password. Then, if the user enters an authorized username and password, the user will be able to access the resource. Otherwise, the user won't be able to access that resource.

To restrict access to a resource, a *security constraint* must be coded in the web.xml file for the application. In this figure, for example, the security constraint restricts access to all files in the admin subdirectory of the application. As a result, when a browser requests any URL in this directory, the server notifies the browser that the user must identify himself or herself. This is known as *authentication*.

When the user sends the username and password to the server, the server attempts to authenticate the user. If the user provides a valid username and password, the server checks to see if that username is associated with a *role* that has the right to access the resource. In this figure, for example, users with the programmer and service roles can access the resource. This is known as *authorization*.

To authorize the username and password, the server uses a *security realm*. A security realm is an interface that provides a flexible way to store the usernames and passwords for the roles that are authorized. This makes it possible for the web developer to store the usernames and passwords for the authorized roles in an XML file, a database, or another type of data store.

In the example in this figure, the browser has requested a page in the admin subdirectory. Since this subdirectory is restricted, Tomcat has displayed a dialog box that requests a username and password. Then, if the user is authorized to view the requested page, that authorization will remain in effect for subsequent requests for any of the pages in the admin directory.

An authentication dialog box for a restricted web resource

The security-constraint and login-config elements in the web.xml file

```
<!-- Restrict access to all files in the /admin folder -->
<security-constraint>
    <web-resource-collection>
        <web-resource-name>Protected Area</web-resource-name>
        <url-pattern>/admin/*</url-pattern>
    </web-resource-collection>
    <!-- Authorize the programmer and service roles -->
    <auth-constraint>
        <role-name>programmer</role-name>
        <role-name>service</role-name>
    </auth-constraint>
</security-constraint>

<!-- Use basic authentication -->
<login-config>
    <auth-method>BASIC</auth-method>
    <realm-name>Admin Login</realm-name>
</login-config>
```

How to implement container-managed authentication with Tomcat

- To restrict access to a web resource, you code a security-constraint element in the application's web.xml file that specifies the URL patterns that you want to restrict and the *roles* that are authorized to access these URLs.

- To allow access to the restricted resources, you code a login-config element in the application's web.xml file that specifies the *authentication* method.

- You also need to implement a *security realm* that provides the usernames, passwords, and roles for the authorized users as in figures 17-4 through 17-6.

Figure 17-1   An introduction to container-managed authentication

Three types of authentication

Figure 17-2 presents three common types of authentication. *Basic authentication* causes the browser to display a dialog box like the one in the last figure that requests a username and password. Then, when the user enters a username and password, it sends this data as plain text to the server so the server can attempt to authorize the user. Since you don't have to code a form for this type of authentication, it is easy to implement. However, you can't control the appearance of this dialog box.

Digest authentication also causes the browser to display a dialog box that requests a username and password. However, when the user enters a username and password, digest authentication encrypts the username and password before it sends them to the server. Although this seems to be more secure, it isn't as secure as using a secure connection as described in chapter 16, and you don't have as much control over the encryption that's used. As a result, digest authentication isn't used as often as the other types of authentication.

Form-based authentication uses a web form instead of a login dialog box to request the username and password. This type of authentication allows a developer to control the look and feel of the web page. As a result, it's the most common type of authentication for production web sites.

Since basic authentication and form-based authentication send the username and password as plain text, a hacker can possibly intercept an unencrypted username and password and gain access to a restricted web resource. As a result, it's common to use a secure connection as described in chapter 16 with these types of authentication. That way, the username and password are encrypted before they are sent to the server.

Basic authentication

- Causes the browser to display a dialog box like the one shown in the previous figure.
- Doesn't encrypt the username and password before sending them to the server.

Digest authentication

- Causes the browser to display a dialog box like the one shown in the previous figure.
- Encrypts the username and password before sending them to the server.

Form-based authentication

- Allows the developer to code a login form that gets the username and password.
- Doesn't encrypt the username and password before sending them to the server.

Description

- Since *basic authentication* and *form-based authentication* don't automatically encrypt the username and password before sending them to the server, these types of authentication are typically used over a secure connection as described in chapter 16.
- Since *digest authentication* isn't as secure as using a secure connection, it isn't used as often as basic authentication or form-based authentication over a secure connection.

Figure 17-2   Three types of authentication

How to restrict access to web resources

Now that you understand the general concept of how container-managed authentication works, you're ready to learn how to use Tomcat to create a constraint that restricts access to web resources. Although this topic uses Tomcat 6 to create a constraint, these concepts apply to other versions of Tomcat and to other servlet containers.

How to add a security role

Before you restrict access to a web resource, you often want to add one or more security-role elements to the web.xml file for the application as shown in figure 17-3. These elements are used to define the security roles that are allowed to access restricted web resources. In this figure, for example, two security roles have been added: one named service and one named programmer. Although your application may function correctly without these security roles, if you don't add them, Tomcat may display a warning message when it starts that indicates that these security-role elements are missing.

How to add a security constraint

To restrict access to a web resource, you add a security-constraint element to the web.xml file for the application as shown in figure 17-3. This XML element specifies the web resources that are restricted and it specifies the roles that can access these resources.

When you code the url-pattern element, you can code a URL that specifies a single file. Or, you can use the asterisk character to restrict access to multiple files. In this figure, for example, the asterisk restricts access to all URLs in the admin directory. This includes all HTML and JSP files as well as any servlets or other resources that are mapped to this directory.

If you want to restrict access to a resource, but only for specified HTTP methods, you can use the http-method element to do that. In this figure, for example, access is restricted only for the HTTP Get and Post methods. If you want to restrict access for all HTTP methods (and you usually do), you just omit the http-method element.

When you code the auth-constraint element, you define the user roles that are authorized to access the restricted resource. In this figure, for example, any user associated with the programmer role or the service role is authorized to access the resources available from the admin directory.

To restrict access to multiple files or directories, you can define several url-pattern elements within a single security-constraint element. Or, if you want to specify different roles for different URL patterns, you can create multiple security-constraint elements.

How to set a security constraint in a web.xml file

```
<security-role>
    <description>customer service employees</description>
    <role-name>service</role-name>
</security-role>

<security-role>
    <description>programmers</description>
    <role-name>programmer</role-name>
</security-role>

<security-constraint>
  <web-resource-collection>
      <web-resource-name>Protected Area</web-resource-name>
      <url-pattern>/admin/*</url-pattern>
      <http-method>GET</http-method>
      <http-method>POST</http-method>
  </web-resource-collection>
  <auth-constraint>
      <role-name>programmer</role-name>
      <role-name>service</role-name>
  </auth-constraint>
</security-constraint>
```

The elements used to create a security roles and constraints

Element	Description
`<security-role>`	Creates a security role for one or more web resources.
`<description>`	Specifies the description for a security role.
`<role-name>`	Specifies the name for a security role.
`<security-constraint>`	Creates a security constraint for one or more web resources.
`<web-resource-collection>`	Specifies a collection of restricted web resources.
`<web-resource-name>`	Specifies a name for the collection of web resources.
`<url-pattern>`	Specifies the URL pattern for the web resources that you wish to restrict. You can use the asterisk character (*) to specify several files at once.
`<http-method>`	Specifies the HTTP methods that require authentication. By default, a constraint will restrict access to all HTTP methods.
`<auth-constraint>`	Specifies the security roles that are permitted to access a restricted web resource.

Figure 17-3   How to add security roles and constraints to the web.xml file

How to implement a security realm

When you use Tomcat to manage security, you need to determine what type of *security realm* (or just *realm*) you want to implement. A realm is the mechanism that identifies authorized users. In this topic, you'll learn how to use three of the most common types of security realms that are available with Tomcat.

How to implement the UserDatabaseRealm

By default, Tomcat stores usernames, passwords, and roles in the tomcat-users.xml file that's in its conf directory. To do that, the server.xml file that's stored in Tomcat's conf directory uses the Realm element shown in figure 17-4 to specify a UserDatabaseRealm named UserDatabase. Then, the server.xml file uses a Resource element to specify the tomcat-users.xml file as the user database. Since these elements are configured by default when you install Tomcat, you don't need to change them or understand how they work.

To add a user to the tomcat-users.xml file, you can open this file in a text editor. Then, you can add role elements that specify new roles. Or, you can add user elements that specify the username, password, and roles for each new user. When you do this, you can specify multiple roles for a user by separating them with commas.

In this figure, for example, the tomcat-users.xml file specifies three roles (manager, programmer, and service) and three users (admin, joel, and andrea). Of these users, andrea belongs to two roles (programmer and server). Then, to put these users into effect, you need to restart Tomcat.

When you edit the tomcat-users.xml file, the changes apply to all applications running on the current server, including the Tomcat Web Application Manager described in chapter 2. As a result, you won't want to remove any roles or users unless you're sure they're not being used by other applications. In this figure, for example, the admin username and the manager role is used to access the Tomcat Web Application Manager.

The default Realm element in Tomcat's server.xml file

```
<Realm className="org.apache.catalina.realm.UserDatabaseRealm"
       resourceName="UserDatabase"/>
```

The default Resource element in Tomcat's server.xml file

```
<Resource name="UserDatabase" auth="Container"
          type="org.apache.catalina.UserDatabase"
          description="User database that can be updated and saved"
          factory="org.apache.catalina.users.MemoryUserDatabaseFactory"
          pathname="conf/tomcat-users.xml" />
```

A tomcat-users.xml file that specifies three roles and three users

```
<?xml version='1.0' encoding='utf-8'?>
<tomcat-users>
    <role rolename="manager"/>
    <role rolename="programmer"/>
    <role rolename="service"/>
    <user username="admin" password="sesame" roles="manager"/>
    <user username="joel" password="sesame" roles="programmer"/>
    <user username="andrea" password="sesame" roles="programmer,service"/>
</tomcat-users>
```

Description

- A *realm* is an interface that's used to authenticate users so they can access web resources that have been restricted.

- By default, the server.xml file in Tomcat's conf directory uses the UserDatabaseRealm to use the usernames, passwords, and roles that are defined in the tomcat-users.xml file that's stored in Tomcat's conf directory. However, you can change this default to one of the other realms.

- If you use the UscrDatabaseRealm for authentication, you can edit the tomcat-users.xml file so it contains the role and user elements that you need.

Figure 17-4   How to implement the UserDatabaseRealm

How to implement the JDBCRealm

For simple applications, the UserDatabaseRealm provides a quick and easy way to implement a realm. However, for more serious web applications, you'll often want to use the JDBCRealm to store usernames, passwords, and roles in a relational database. In addition, you'll often want to implement a security realm for a specific application rather than for all applications on the current server.

To implement security for a specific application, you can add a Realm element to the application's context.xml file. In figure 17-5, for example, you can see the context.xml file for the ch17admin application, which implements the JDBCRealm. Here, the JDBC realm uses the Connector/J MySQL driver to connect to a MySQL database named murach with a username of root and a password of sesame.

The rest of the attributes in the JDBC Realm element define the names of the tables and columns that are used to store the usernames, passwords, and roles for the application. These tables can be created and filled by using a SQL script like the one in part 2 of this figure.

A context.xml file that implements the JDBCRealm

```
<?xml version="1.0" encoding="UTF-8"?>
<Context path="/ch17admin">

    <Realm className="org.apache.catalina.realm.JDBCRealm" debug="99"
        driverName="com.mysql.jdbc.Driver"
        connectionURL="jdbc:mysql://localhost:3306/murach"
        connectionName="root" connectionPassword="sesame"
        userTable="UserPass" userNameCol="Username" userCredCol="Password"
        userRoleTable="UserRole" roleNameCol="Rolename" />

</Context>
```

The attributes of the Realm element for a JDBCRealm

Attribute	Description
className	The fully qualified name for the JDBCRealm class.
driverName	The fully qualified class name for the JDBC driver.
connectionURL	The database URL for the connection.
connectionName	The username for the connection.
connectionPassword	The password for the connection.
userTable	The name of the table that contains the usernames and passwords. This table must include at least the columns named by the userNameCol and userCredCol attributes.
userNameCol	The name of the column that contains usernames.
userCredCol	The name of the column that contains passwords.
userRoleTable	The name of the table that contains the usernames and their associated roles. This table must include the columns named by the userNameCol and roleNameCol attributes.
roleNameCol	The name of the column that contains the roles.

Description

- To specify a realm for a single application, you can code a Realm element within the context.xml file in the application's META-INF folder. This overrides the default Realm element that's specified in the server.xml file in Tomcat's conf folder.

- Tomcat's JDBCRealm uses a database to check a username and password against a table of valid usernames and passwords. In addition, the JDBCRealm uses a second table to associate a username with a role.

- For the JDBCRealm to work, the JAR file for the database driver that's specified must be stored in Tomcat's lib directory. To learn more about database drivers, databases, and connecting to databases, please see chapter 14.

Figure 17-5   How to implement the JDBCRealm (part 1 of 2)

If the tables for the JDBC realm don't already exist, you can create a table of users that contains a username and password for each user, and you can create a table of roles that can be associated with each user. To do that, you can use a SQL script like the one in part 2 of figure 17-5. Note how the table and column names in this script match the table and column names specified in the Realm element shown in part 1 of this figure.

After it creates the UserPass table, this script creates the UserRole table. Here, you can see that the user named "joel" is associated with the programmer role, and the user named "andrea" is associated with both the service and programmer roles. Note, however, that the user named "anne" isn't associated with any role, so she won't be authorized to access restricted portions of the application.

A SQL script that creates the tables used by the JDBCRealm

```sql
CREATE TABLE UserPass (
    Username varchar(15) NOT NULL PRIMARY KEY,
    Password varchar(15) NOT NULL
);

INSERT INTO UserPass VALUES ('andrea', 'sesame'),
                            ('joel', 'sesame'),
                            ('anne', 'sesame');

CREATE TABLE UserRole (
    Username VARCHAR(15) NOT NULL,
    Rolename VARCHAR(15) NOT NULL,

    PRIMARY KEY (Username, Rolename)
);

INSERT INTO UserRole VALUES ('andrea', 'service'),
                            ('andrea', 'programmer'),
                            ('joel', 'programmer');
```

Description

- The table and column names must match the table and column names specified by the Realm element for the JDBCRealm.
- A user can be associated with zero roles, one role, or multiple roles.
- The table that stores the username and password can contain other columns.

Figure 17-5   How to implement the JDBCRealm (part 2 of 2)

How to implement the DataSourceRealm

If your application is using connection pooling as described in chapter 14, you will probably want to implement the DataSourceRealm as shown in figure 17-6. This realm is similar to the JDBCRealm.

Compared to the JDBCRealm, though, there are two advantages to using the DataSourceRealm. First, this realm can take advantage of connection pooling, which can allow your application to authenticate and authorize users more quickly.

Second, if you've already specified the database connection information for your application in a Resource element, you don't need to duplicate this information in the Realm element. Instead, you can code a Realm element that uses the dataSourceName and localDataSource attributes to use the same connection information as the Resource element. In this figure, for example, the Resource element specifies all the connection information that's needed to connect to the music database that's used by the Music Store application presented in section 5.

After you code the Realm attributes to connect to a data source, you code the rest of the attributes just as you would for a JDBCRealm. In this figure, for example, the Realm element uses the same tables and columns as the JDBCRealm shown in the previous figure.

A context.xml file that implements the DataSourceRealm

```
<?xml version="1.0" encoding="UTF-8"?>
<Context path="/musicStore">

    <Resource name="jdbc/musicDB" auth="Container"
        maxActive="100" maxIdle="30" maxWait="10000"
        username="root" password="sesame"
        driverClassName="com.mysql.jdbc.Driver"
        url="jdbc:mysql://localhost:3306/music?autoReconnect=true"
        logAbandoned="true" removeAbandoned="true"
        removeAbandonedTimeout="60" type="javax.sql.DataSource" />

    <Realm className="org.apache.catalina.realm.DataSourceRealm" debug="99"
        dataSourceName="jdbc/musicDB" localDataSource="true"
        userTable="UserPass" userNameCol="Username" userCredCol="Password"
        userRoleTable="UserRole" roleNameCol="Rolename" />

</Context>
```

The attributes of the Realm element for a DataSourceRealm

Attribute	Description
className	The fully qualified name for the DataSourceRealm class.
dataSourceName	The name that specifies the data source. If the Realm element is coded in the same context.xml file as the Resource element that's used to connect to the database, you can specify the same name that's specified by the Resource element.
localDataSource	By default, this attribute is set to false, which allows you to use the dataSourceName attribute to specify a global data source. However, if the Realm element is coded in the same context.xml file as the Resource element, you can set this attribute to true to specify a local data source.

Description

- Tomcat's DataSourceRealm works similarly to the JDBCRealm but it uses a data source that's specified by a Resource element. It can also take advantage of connection pooling.
- The userTable, userNameCol, userCredCol, userRoleTable, and roleNameCol attributes work the same for a DataSourceRealm as they do for a JDBCRealm.

Figure 17-6   How to implement the DataSourceRealm

How to allow access to authorized users

Once you've restricted access to web resources and implemented a security realm, you're ready to allow access to authorized users.

How to use basic authentication

Figure 17-7 shows how to use basic authentication to provide access to a restricted resource. In particular, it shows how to use basic authentication to provide access to the application for chapter 17.

If you request a restricted web resource that uses basic authentication, your browser will display an authentication dialog box like the one in this figure. This box requests a username and password. Then, when the user selects the OK button, the username and password are sent to the server.

When the server gets the username and password, it checks the security realm to see whether the username and password are valid, and it checks whether the user is associated with a role that is authorized to access the resource. If so, the user will be allowed to access the resource.

Since basic authentication is the simplest type of authentication, the web.xml file only requires a few XML elements. To start, you code the login-config element. Within this element, you specify that you want to use basic authentication. Then, you specify a name for the realm. This name will be displayed in the dialog box. When you add the XML tags for the login-config element to the web.xml file, they must immediately follow the security-constraint element that they relate to as shown in figure 17-1.

How to use digest authentication

If you have basic authentication working, you can easily switch to digest authentication by specifying DIGEST instead of BASIC in the auth-method element. Then, the username and password will be encrypted even if the request isn't being sent over a secure connection. However, as mentioned earlier, it's more common to use basic authentication or form-based authentication over a secure connection.

Basic authentication

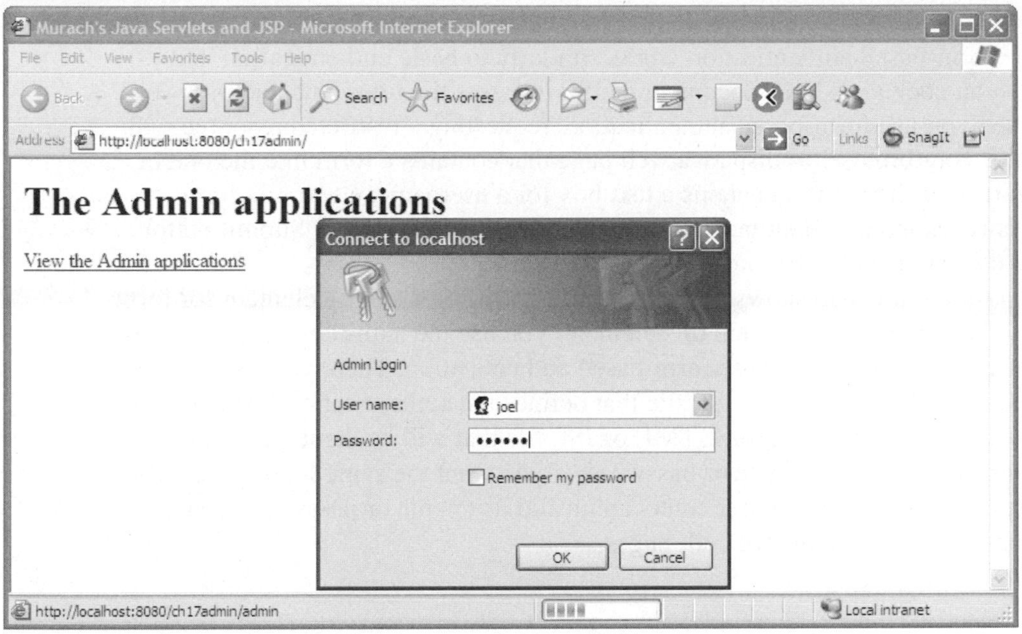

The web.xml elements that specify basic authentication

```
<login-config>
    <auth-method>BASIC</auth-method>
    <realm-name>Admin Login</realm-name>
</login-config>
```

The elements for basic authentication

Element	Description
`<login-config>`	Creates the authentication type to use.
`<auth-method>`	Specifies the authentication method. Valid entries include BASIC, DIGEST, FORM, and CLIENT-CERT. BASIC and DIGEST authentication display a dialog box like the one shown in this figure. FORM authentication displays a form as described in the next figure. And CLIENT-CERT uses SSL client authentication as described in chapter 16.
`<realm-name>`	Specifies the name that's displayed in the dialog box, but this is optional.

Figure 17-7   How to use basic authentication

How to use form-based authentication

Form-based authentication works similarly to basic authentication, but it lets you code an HTML document or JSP that gets the username and password. When you use form-based authentication, requesting a restricted resource will cause your browser to display a web page that contains a form like the one in figure 17-8. This form contains a text box for a username, a text box for a password, and a Submit button. Then, when the user clicks the Submit button, the username and password are sent to the server.

This figure also shows how to code the form-login-config element for form-based authentication. Within this element, you use the auth-method element to specify that you want to use form-based authentication. Then, you can specify the name of the HTML or JSP file that defines the authentication form, and you can specify the name of the HTML or JSP file that will be displayed if the user enters an invalid username or password. If you want the same login page to be displayed again when a user enters an invalid username or password, you can specify the same name for both pages.

Form-based authentication

The web.xml elements that specify form-based authentication

```
<login-config>
    <auth-method>FORM</auth-method>
    <form-login-config>
        <form-login-page>/admin/login.html</form-login-page>
        <form-error-page>/admin/login_error.html</form-error-page>
    </form-login-config>
</login-config>
```

The additional web.xml elements for form-based authentication

Element	Description
`<form-login-config>`	Specifies the login and error pages that should be used for form-based authentication. If form-based authentication isn't used, these elements are ignored.
`<form-login-page>`	Specifies the location of the login page that should be displayed when a restricted resource that's set in the security constraint is accessed. This page can be an HTML page, JSP, or servlet.
`<form-error-page>`	Specifies the location of the page that should be displayed when an invalid username or password is entered in the login form.

Description

- When you use form-based authentication, you can use HTML to code the login form that's displayed when someone attempts to access a restricted resource. This form can be coded within an HTML document or a JSP.

Figure 17-8   How to use form-based authentication (part 1 of 2)

Part 2 of figure 17-8 shows the code for the login page that's shown in part 1. Although you can place any HTML or JSP tags in a login page, this page must at least provide an HTML form that contains a submit button and two text boxes, and this form must use the three highlighted attributes shown in this figure. Here, the action attribute for the form must be j_security_check. The name of the text box that gets the username must be j_username. And the name of the text box that gets the password must be j_password.

In this example, the text box that requests the password uses the password type. As a result, the password won't be displayed on the screen when the user types it. Instead, this text box will display a special character such as a bullet or an asterisk for each character. You can see how this works by looking at part 1 of this figure.

The code for a login web page

```
<!DOCTYPE HTML PUBLIC "-//W3C//DTD HTML 4.0 Transitional//EN">
<html>
<head>
    <title>Murach's Java Servlets and JSP</title>
</head>

<body>
<h1>Admin Login Form</h1>
<p>Please enter your username and password to continue.</p>
<table cellspacing="5" border="0">
  <form action="j_security_check" method="get">
    <tr>
      <td align="right">Username</td>
      <td><input type="text" name="j_username"></td>
    </tr>
    <tr>
      <td align="right">Password</td>
      <td><input type="password" name="j_password"></td>
    </tr>
    <tr>
      <td><input type="submit" value="Login"></td>
    </tr>
  </form>
</table>
</body>
</html>
```

Description

- The login form for form-based authentication must contain the three attributes highlighted above.
- The login form can be stored in any directory where HTML and JSP files can be stored.

Figure 17-8   How to use form-based authentication (part 2 of 2)

Perspective

Now that you've finished this chapter, you should be able to use Tomcat 6 to implement container-managed security in your applications. However, you should keep in mind that this chapter doesn't cover all aspects of using Tomcat for authentication.

In particular, Tomcat provides several other security realms that aren't presented in this chapter. For example, the JNDIRealm allows you to look up users in an LDAP directory server that's accessed by a JNDI provider. So, if the security realms presented in this chapter aren't adequate for your applications, you can consult the documentation that's available from the Tomcat website.

Summary

- To restrict access to web resources such as HTML documents, JSPs, and servlets, you can use *container-managed security*, which is also known as *container-managed authentication*.

- You can use the web.xml file to specify the type of *authentication* for an application.

- *Basic authentication* displays a pre-defined dialog box to get the username and password. *Digest authentication* works similarly to basic authentication, but it encrypts the username and password. And *form-based authentication* lets the application use a custom web form to get the username and password.

- You can use the web.xml file to specify a *security constraint* that identifies the URL patterns that should have restricted access, and also to specify the *roles* that have the proper *authorization* to access the restricted pages.

- You can use Tomcat's server.xml file or an application's context.xml file to specify a *security realm* that uses an interface to provide the usernames, passwords, and roles for the authorized users.

- Three of the realms that are commonly used with Tomcat are the UserDatabaseRealm, the JDBCRealm, and the DataSourceRealm. You can use any of these realms with any of the authentication methods.

- When you use form-based authentication, the HTML code for the login page must include a form and two text boxes that use the required names for specific attributes.

Exercise 17-1　Work with authentication types

Review the application

1. Open the ch17admin project in the ex_starts folder.

2. Open the web.xml file for the application. Note that it restricts access to all URLs in the admin folder, that it authorizes the programmer and service roles, and that it uses form-based authentication.

3. Open the context.xml file for the application. Note that the Realm element specifies the JDBCRealm. Note also that this element specifies the murach database and columns from the UserPass and UserRole tables.

4. If you're interested, use the MySQL Query Browser tool to review the data in the UserPass and UserRole tables of the murach database.

5. Open the admin/login.html file that's specified by the web.xml file for form-based authentication. Then, review the attributes that this form uses.

Use form-based authentication

6. Run the application and click on the link to access the admin subdirectory. That should display the login form. Then, test the application by entering an invalid username and password, and note that the login_error.html page is displayed.

7. Test the application by entering a valid username and password for the programmer role such as "joel" and "sesame". This should give you access to the restricted pages.

8. Modify the web.xml file so the programmer role is no longer authorized. Then, test the application with a valid username and password for the programmer role such as "joel" and "sesame". Now, you should no longer be able to view the restricted page. However, if you enter a valid username and password for the service role such as "andrea" and "sesame", you should be able to view the restricted page.

Use basic authentication

9. Modify the web.xml file so the application uses basic authentication instead of form-based authentication.

10. Restart Tomcat, and test the application with a valid username and password from the murach database for the service role such as "andrea" and "sesame". The application should still work because the Realm element in the context.xml file for the application specifies the use of the murach database.

11. Comment out the Realm element in the context.xml file. This means that the default UserDatabaseRealm will be in use, which means that the valid usernames and passwords are in the tomcat-users.xml file in Tomcat's conf directory. To view the data in this file, you can find it in the Windows Explorer and double-click on it. Then, modify the web.xml file for the application so it will authorize a user who has the "admin" role.

12. Test the application by using "admin" and "sesame" for the user that is authorized for the "admin" role.

18

How to work with HTTP requests and responses

When you write servlets and JSPs, the classes and methods of the servlet API shelter you from having to work directly with HTTP. Sometimes, though, you need to know more about HTTP requests and responses, and you need to use the methods of the servlet API to work with them. So that's what you'll learn in this chapter. Along the way, you'll get a better idea of how HTTP works.

An introduction to HTTP

This topic introduces you to some of the most common headers and status codes that make up the *Hypertext Transfer Protocol* (*HTTP*). This protocol can be used to request a resource from a server, and it can be used to return a response from a server.

An HTTP request and response

Figure 18-1 shows the components of a typical HTTP request and a typical HTTP response. As you learn more about these components, you'll get a better idea of how HTTP requests and responses work.

The first line of an HTTP request is known as the *request line*. This line contains the request method, the request URL, and the request protocol. Typically, the request method is Get or Post, but other methods are also supported by HTTP. Similarly, the request protocol is usually HTTP 1.1, but could possibly be HTTP 1.0 or HTTP 1.2.

After the request line, an HTTP request contains the *request headers*. These headers contain information about the client that's making the request. In the example in this figure, the HTTP request contains eight request headers with one header per line, but a request can include more headers than that. Each request header begins with the name of the request header, followed by a colon and a space, followed by the value of the request header.

After the request headers, an HTTP request that uses the Post method may include a blank line followed by the parameters for the request. Unlike a Get request, a Post request doesn't include its parameters in the URL.

The first line of an HTTP response is known as the *status line*. This line specifies the version of HTTP that's being used, a *status code*, and a message that's associated with the status code.

After the status line, an HTTP response contains the *response headers*. These headers contain information about the server and about the response that's being returned to the client. Like request headers, each response header takes one line. In addition, each line begins with the name of the header, followed by a colon and a space, followed by the value of the header.

After the response headers, an HTTP response contains a blank line, followed by the *response entity*, or *response body*. In this figure, the response entity is an HTML document, but it could also be an XML document, plain text, tab-delimited text, an image, a PDF file, a sound file, a video file, and so on.

To learn more about HTTP 1.1, you can search the web for "HTTP 1.1 specification" and view the documentation that's available from www.w3.org. This documentation provides a highly technical description of HTTP 1.1 including a complete list of headers and status codes.

An HTTP request

```
GET http://www.murach.com/email/join_email_list.html HTTP/1.1
referer: http://www.murach.com/murach/index.html
connection: Keep-Alive
user-agent: Mozilla/4.0 (compatible; MSIE 6.0; Windows NT 5.1; SV1)
host: www.murach.com
accept: image/gif, image/jpeg, application/vnd.ms-excel, */*
accept-encoding: gzip, deflate
accept-language: en-us
cookie: emailCookie=joel@murach.com; firstNameCookie=Joel
```

An HTTP response

```
HTTP/1.1 200 OK
date: Sat, 17 Mar 2008 10:32:54 GMT
server: Apache/2.2.3 (Unix) PHP/5.2.4
content-type: text/html
content-length: 201
last-modified: Fri, 16 Aug 2007 12:52:09 GMT

<!DOCTYPE HTML PUBLIC "-//W3C//DTD HTML 4.01 Transitional//EN">
<html>
<head>
  <title>Murach's Java Servlets and JSP</title>
</head>
<body>
  <h1>Join our email list</h1>
</body>
</html>
```

Description

- *Hypertext Transfer Protocol* (*HTTP*) is the primary protocol that's used to transfer data between a browser and a server. Three versions of HTTP exist: 1.0, 1.1., and 1.2. Of these, HTTP 1.1 is the most commonly used. Since HTTP 1.1 is a superset of HTTP 1.0, all HTTP 1.0 request headers arc also available in HTTP 1.1.

- The first line of an HTTP request is known as the *request line*. This line specifies the request method, the URL of the request, and the version of HTTP.

- After the first line of a request, the browser sends *request headers* that give information about the browser and its request.

- The first line of an HTTP response is known as the *status line*. This line specifies the HTTP version, a *status code*, and a brief description associated with the status code.

- After the first line of a response, the server sends *response headers* that give information about the response. Then, it sends the *response entity*, or *response body*. The body of a response is typically HTML, but it can also be other types of data.

- To learn more about HTTP 1.1, you can search the web for "HTTP 1.1 specification" and view the documentation that's available from www.w3.org.

Figure 18-1   An HTTP request and response

Common MIME types

Figure 18-2 shows some of the most common *Multipurpose Internet Mail Extension (MIME)* types that are used by HTTP. You can use them in the accept header of a request or the content-type header of a response.

To specify an officially registered MIME type, you can use this format:

```
type/subtype
```

To specify a MIME type that isn't officially registered, you can use this format:

```
type/x-subtype
```

Although the "text/plain" MIME type is the default MIME type for a servlet, the most commonly used MIME type is the "text/html" type. Later in this chapter, you'll see examples of how MIME types can be used in HTTP requests and responses.

If you want to learn more about MIME types, you can search the web for "MIME types" and view the documentation that's available from www.iana.org. This documentation provides a highly technical description of MIME types. Or, you can view other web sites that provide less technical descriptions of MIME types.

Common MIME types

Type/Subtype	Description
text/plain	Plain text document
text/html	HTML document
text/css	HTML cascading style sheet
text/xml	XML document
image/gif	GIF image
image/jpeg	JPEG image
image/png	PNG image
image/tiff	TIFF image
image/x-xbitmap	Windows bitmap image
application/msword	Microsoft Word document
application/vnd.ms-excel	Microsoft Excel spreadsheet
application/pdf	PDF file
application/postscript	PostScript file
application/zip	ZIP file
application/x-java-archive	JAR file
application/x-gzip	GZIP file
application/octet-stream	Binary data
audio/x-midi	MIDI sound file
audio/mpeg	MP3 sound file
audio/wav	WAV sound file
audio/x-wav	WAV sound file
video/mpeg	MPEG video file
video/quicktime	QuickTime video file

Description

- The *Multipurpose Internet Mail Extension* (*MIME*) types provide standards for the various types of data that can be transferred across the Internet.
- MIME types can be included in the accept header of a request or the content-type header of a response.
- For more information about MIME types, you can search the web for "MIME types" and view the documentation that's available from www.iana.org.

Figure 18-2   MIME types

Common HTTP request headers

Figure 18-3 lists some of the most common HTTP request headers. Today, most web browsers support HTTP 1.1 so you can usually use HTTP 1.1 headers. However, some older browsers only support HTTP 1.0. As a result, if your web application needs to support these older browsers, you should only use headers that were specified in the HTTP 1.0 version.

Most of the time, a web browser automatically sets these request headers when it makes a request. Then, when the server receives the request, it can check these headers to learn about the browser. In addition, though, you can write servlets that set some of these request headers. For example, chapter 8 shows how to use the servlet API to set the cookie header. And chapter 17 shows how to use the servlet container to automatically set the authorization header.

Common HTTP request headers

Name	Description
accept	Specifies the preferred order of MIME types that the browser can accept. The "*/*" type indicates that the browser can handle any MIME type.
accept-encoding	Specifies the types of compression encoding that the browser can accept.
accept-charset	Specifies the character sets that the browser can accept. Although the Internet Explorer doesn't usually return this header, Firefox usually does.
accept-language	Specifies the standard language codes for the languages that the browser prefers. The standard language code for English is "en" or "en-us".
authorization	Identifies the authorization level for the browser. When you use container-managed security as described in chapter 17, the servlet container automatically sets this header.
connection	Indicates the type of connection that's being used by the browser. In HTTP 1.0, a value of "keep-alive" means that the browser can use a persistent connection that allows it to accept multiple files with a single connection. In HTTP 1.1, this type of connection is the default.
cookie	Specifies any cookies that were previously sent by the current server. In chapter 8, you learned how to use the servlet API to work with this header.
host	Specifies the host and port of the machine that originally sent the request. This header is optional in HTTP 1.0 and required in HTTP 1.1.
pragma	A value of "no-cache" indicates that any servlet that's forwarding requests shouldn't cache this page.
referer	Indicates the URL of the referring web page. The spelling error was made by one of the original authors of HTTP and is now part of the protocol.
user-agent	Indicates the type of browser. Although both Internet Explorer and Firefox identify themselves as "Mozilla", the Internet Explorer always includes "MSIE" somewhere in the string.

Figure 18-3   HTTP request headers

Common HTTP status codes

Figure 18-4 summarizes the five categories of status codes. Then, this figure lists some of the most common status codes.

For successful requests, the server typically returns a 200 (OK) status code. However, if the server can't find the requested file, it typically returns the infamous 404 (Not Found) status code. Or, if the server encounters an error while trying to retrieve the file, it may return the equally infamous 500 (Internal Server Error) status code.

Status code summary

Number	Type	Description
100-199	Informational	The request was received and is being processed.
200-299	Success	The request was successful.
300-399	Redirection	Further action must be taken to fulfill the request.
400-499	Client errors	The client has made a request that contains an error.
500-599	Server errors	The server has encountered an error.

Status codes

Number	Name	Description
200	OK	The default status indicating that the response is normal.
301	Moved Permanently	The requested resource has been permanently moved to a new URL.
302	Found	The requested resource resides temporarily under a new URL.
400	Bad Request	The request could not be understood by the server due to bad syntax.
401	Unauthorized	The request requires authentication. The response must include a www-authenticate header. If you use container-managed security as described in chapter 17, the web server automatically returns this status code when appropriate.
404	Not Found	The server could not find the requested URL.
405	Method Not Allowed	The method specified in the request line is not allowed for the requested URL.
500	Internal Server Error	The server encountered an unexpected condition that prevented it from fulfilling the request.

Figure 18-4   HTTP status codes

Common HTTP response headers

Figure 18-5 lists some of the most common HTTP response headers. Most of the time, the web server automatically sets these response headers when it returns the response. However, there are times when you may want to use Java code to set response headers that control the response sent by your web server.

For example, you can use the cache-control header to control how your web server caches a response. To do that, you can use the cache-control values specified in this figure to turn off caching, to use a private cache, to use a public cache, to specify when a response must be revalidated, or to increase the duration of the cache. You'll see an example of this later on in this chapter.

Common HTTP response headers

Name	Description
cache-control	Controls when and how a browser caches a page. For more information, see figure 18-9 and the list of possible values shown below.
content-disposition	Can be used to specify that the response includes an attached binary file. For an example, see figure 18-11.
content-length	Specifies the length of the body of the response in bytes. This allows the browser to know when it's done reading the entire response and is necessary for the browser to use a persistent, keep-alive connection.
content-type	Specifies the MIME type of the response document. You can use the "maintype/subtype" format shown earlier in this chapter to specify the MIME type.
content-encoding	Specifies the type of encoding that the response uses. Encoding a document with compression such as GZIP can enhance performance. For an example, see figure 18-10.
expires	Specifies the time that the page should no longer be cached.
last-modified	Specifies the time when the document was last modified.
location	Works with status codes in the 300s to specify the new location of the document.
pragma	Turns off caching for older browsers when it is set to a value of "no-cache".
refresh	Specifies the number of seconds before the browser should ask for an updated page.
www-authenticate	Works with the 401 (Unauthorized) status code to specify the authentication type and realm. If you use container-managed security as described in chapter 17, the servlet container automatically sets this header when necessary.

Values for the cache-control header

Name	Description
public	The document can be cached in a public, shared cache.
private	The document can only be cached in a private, single-user cache.
no-cache	The document should never be cached.
no-store	The document should never be cached or stored in a temporary location on the disk.
must-revalidate	The document must be revalidated with the original server (not a proxy server) each time it is requested.
proxy-revalidate	The document must be revalidated on the proxy server but not on the original server.
max-age=x	The document must be revalidated after x seconds for private caches.
s-max-age=x	The document must be revalidated after x seconds for shared caches.

Figure 18-5   HTTP response headers

How to work with the request

This topic shows how to use the methods of the request object to get the data that's contained in an HTTP request.

How to get a request header

You can use the first group of methods in figure 18-6 to get any of the headers in an HTTP request. The getHeader method lets you return the value of any header. The getIntHeader and getDateHeader methods make it easier to work with headers that contain integer and date values. And the getHeaderNames method returns an Enumeration object that contains the names of all of the headers for the request.

You can use the second group of methods to get the request headers more easily. For example, this statement:

```
int contentLength = request.getIntHeader("Content-Length");
```

returns the same value as this statement:

```
int contentLength = request.getContentLength();
```

The first example in this figure uses the getHeader method to return a string that includes all of the MIME types supported by the browser that made the request. Then, it uses the indexOf method within an if statement to check if a particular MIME type exists in the string. If it does, the code calls a method that returns a PNG image if the browser supports that type. Otherwise, the code calls a method that returns a GIF image.

The second example uses the getHeader method to return a string that identifies the type of browser that made the request. Since the Internet Explorer always includes the letters "MSIE" in its string, this example uses an indexOf method within an if statement to check if the string contains the letters "MSIE". If so, it calls a method that executes some code that's specific to the Internet Explorer. Otherwise, it calls a method that executes some code that's specific to the Firefox browser.

Although you may never need to write code that checks the MIME types or the browser type, these examples illustrate general concepts that you can use to check any request header. First, you use the getHeader, getIntHeader, or getDateHeader methods to return a header. Then, you can use an if statement to check the header. For a String object, you can use the indexOf method to check if a substring exists within the string. For int values and Date objects, you can use other comparison operators.

General methods for working with request headers

Method	Description
getHeader(String headerName)	Returns a String value for the specified header.
getIntHeader(String headerName)	Returns an int value for the specified header.
getDateHeader(String headerName)	Returns a Date value for the specified header.
getHeaderNames()	Returns an Enumeration object that contains the names of all headers.

Convenience methods for working with request headers

Method	Description
getContentType()	Returns the MIME type of the body of the request. If the type is not known, this method returns a null value.
getContentLength()	Returns an int value for the number of bytes in the request body that are made available by the input stream. If the length is not known, this method returns -1.
getCookies()	Returns an array of Cookie objects. For information about this method, see chapter 8.
getAuthType()	Returns the authentication type that's being used by the server.
getRemoteUser()	Returns the username of the user making this request, if the user has been authenticated. If the user has not been authenticated, this method returns a null value.

An example that checks the MIME types accepted by the browser

```
String mimeTypes = request.getHeader("Accept");
if (mimeTypes.indexOf("image/png") > -1)
    returnPNG();
else
    returnGIF();
```

An example that checks the browser type

```
String browser = request.getHeader("User-Agent");
if (browser.indexOf("MSIE") > -1)
    doIECode();
else
    doFirefoxCode();
```

Description

- All of these methods can be called from the request object to return information about the HTTP request.

- For more information about these and other methods and fields of the HttpServletRequest interface, you can refer to the documentation for the Java EE API.

Figure 18-6   How to get a request header

How to display all request headers

Part 1 of figure 18-7 shows a JSP that displays all of the request headers for a request. If you're developing a web application that needs to check other request headers, you can use this JSP to quickly view the request headers for all of the different browsers that your web application supports. Then, you can write the code that checks the request headers and works with them.

This JSP begins by defining the table that will contain the request headers. In the first row of the table, the first column is the Name column, and the second column is the Value column.

After the first row of the table, this page imports the Enumeration class in the java.util package. Then, it uses the getHeaderNames method of the request object to return an Enumeration object that contains the names of all of the request headers. After that, a while loop cycles through all of the header names. To do that, this loop uses the hasMoreElements method to check if more elements exist, and it uses the nextElement method to return the current header name and move to the next header name. Once the loop has returned the name of the header, the getHeader method of the request object uses this name to return the value of the header. Last, the loop displays the name and value for the current header in a row.

JSP code that displays all request headers

```
<html>
<head>
    <title>Murach's Java Servlets and JSP</title>
</head>
<body>

<h1>Request Headers</h1>

<table cellpadding="5" border="1">

  <tr align="left">
    <th>Name</th>
    <th>Value</th>
  </tr>
<%@ page import="java.util.Enumeration" %>
<%
  Enumeration headerNames = request.getHeaderNames();
  while (headerNames.hasMoreElements())
  {
    String name = (String) headerNames.nextElement();
    String value = request.getHeader(name);
%>
  <tr>
    <td width="120"><%= name %></td>
    <td><%= value %></td>
  </tr>
<% } %>

</table>

</body>
</html>
```

Figure 18-7   How to display all request headers (part 1 of 2)

Since the request headers and their values vary depending on the client that makes the request, part 2 of figure 18-7 shows how the JSP in the last figure looks when displayed by different clients. First, it shows how the JSP will look when requested by version 6.0 of the Internet Explorer. Then, it shows how the JSP will look when requested by version 2.0 of Firefox. If you compare the values sent by each of these browsers, you'll see some of the differences between them.

For example, the accept header for Internet Explorer 6.0 indicates that it prefers documents in Microsoft Word or Microsoft Excel formats. Of course, this is what you would expect from a Microsoft product. Since Firefox supports the */* type, it also support these formats. However, by not specifying these formats in its accept header, Firefox indicates that it doesn't prefer the Microsoft formats.

If you compare the user-agent headers, you'll see that Firefox identifies itself as a "Mozilla" browser while Internet Explorer identifies itself as being compatible with "Mozilla". However, Internet Explorer includes the "MSIE" string that indicates that it's the Microsoft Internet Explorer. Also, if you check the accept-charset headers for these browsers, you'll see that Firefox sends this header while Internet Explorer does not.

Although the request headers that are sent by version 7.0 of Internet Explorer 7.0 aren't shown in this figure, they are nearly identical to the request headers for Internet Explorer 6.0. The only significant difference is that the user-agent header identifies the browser as MSIE 7.0 instead of MSIE 6.0.

All request headers sent by Internet Explorer 6.0

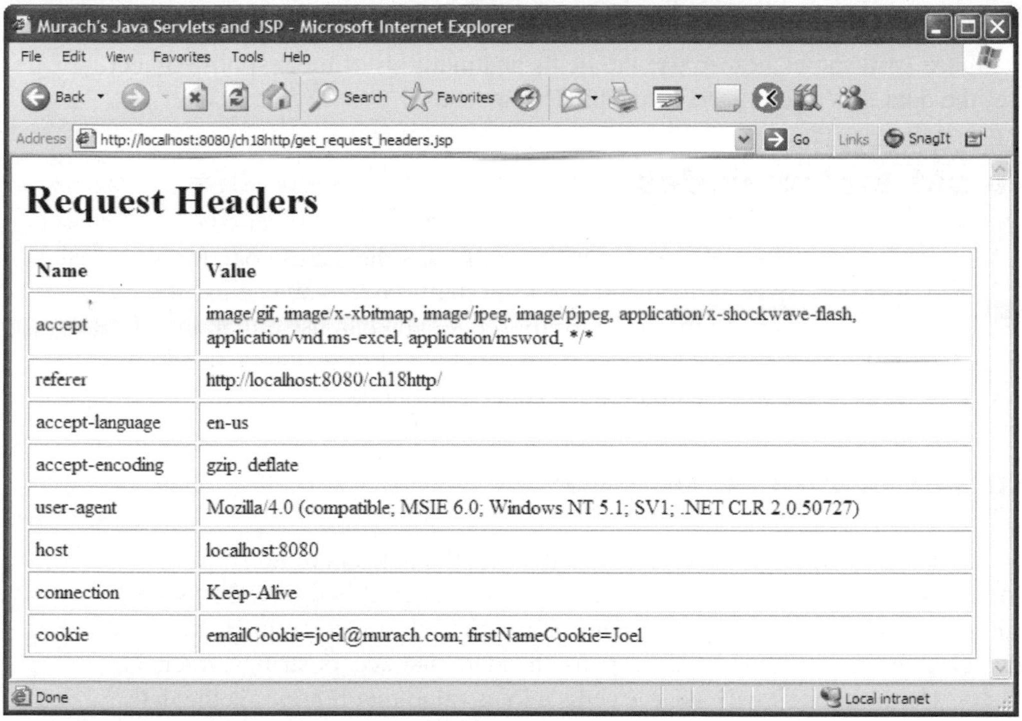

Request Headers

Name	Value
accept	image/gif, image/x-xbitmap, image/jpeg, image/pjpeg, application/x-shockwave-flash, application/vnd.ms-excel, application/msword, */*
referer	http://localhost:8080/ch18http/
accept-language	en-us
accept-encoding	gzip, deflate
user-agent	Mozilla/4.0 (compatible; MSIE 6.0; Windows NT 5.1; SV1; .NET CLR 2.0.50727)
host	localhost:8080
connection	Keep-Alive
cookie	emailCookie=joel@murach.com; firstNameCookie=Joel

All request headers sent by Firefox 2.0

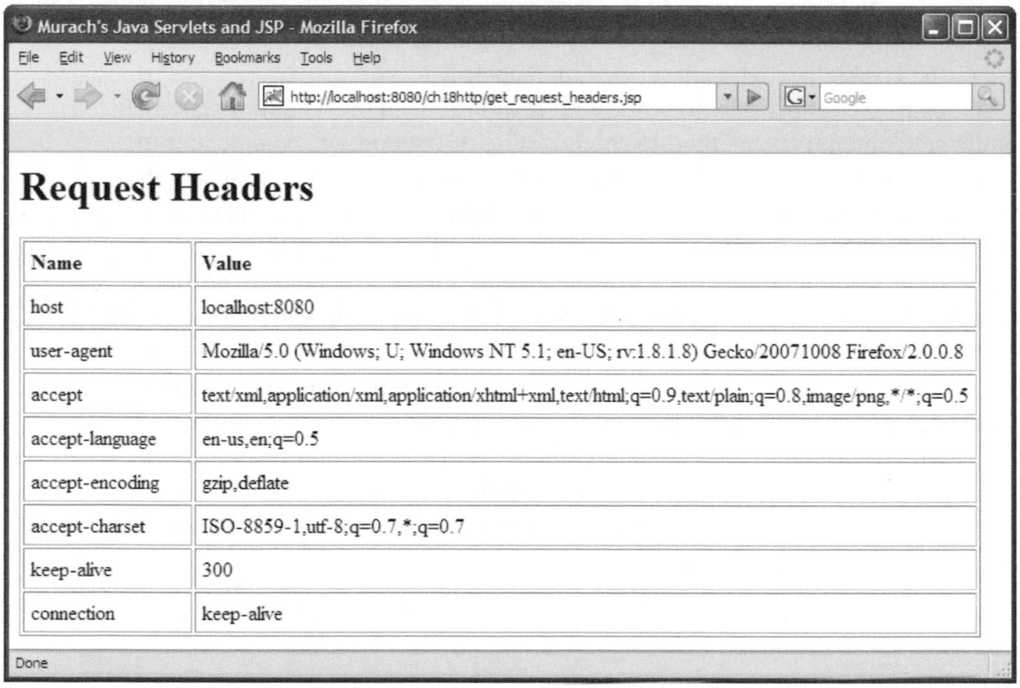

Request Headers

Name	Value
host	localhost:8080
user-agent	Mozilla/5.0 (Windows; U; Windows NT 5.1; en-US; rv:1.8.1.8) Gecko/20071008 Firefox/2.0.0.8
accept	text/xml,application/xml,application/xhtml+xml,text/html;q=0.9,text/plain;q=0.8,image/png,*/*;q=0.5
accept-language	en-us,en;q=0.5
accept-encoding	gzip,deflate
accept-charset	ISO-8859-1,utf-8;q=0.7,*;q=0.7
keep-alive	300
connection	keep-alive

Figure 18-7 How to display all request headers (part 2 of 2)

How to work with the response

Figure 18-8 shows how to use the fields and methods of the response object to set the data that's contained in an HTTP response.

How to set status codes

Most of the time, the web server automatically sets the status code for an HTTP response. However, if you need to set the status code, you can use the setStatus method. To specify the value for this code, you can use either an integer value or one of the fields of the response object. For example, this figure shows two ways to specify the 404 (Not Found) status code.

How to set response headers

Like status codes, the web server usually sets the headers of an HTTP response. However, if you need to set a response header, this figure shows six methods that you can use. To start, you can use the setHeader, setIntHeader, and setDateHeader methods to set all response headers that accept strings, integers, or dates. Here, the setDateHeader accepts a long value that represents the date in milliseconds since January 1, 1970 00:00:00 GMT.

On the other hand, if you're working with commonly used headers, such as the content-type or content-length headers, you can use the setContentType and setContentLength methods. And you can use the addCookie method to add a value to the cookie header as described in chapter 8.

The examples show how to work with response headers. The first statement uses the setContentType method to set the value of the content-type header to the "text/html" MIME type. The second statement uses the setContentLength method to set the content-length header to 403 bytes, although you usually won't need to set this header.

The third statement uses the setHeader method to set the pragma header to "no-cache" to turn off caching for older browsers. The fourth statement uses the setIntHeader method to set the refresh header to 60 seconds. As a result, the browser will request an updated page in 1 minute. Last, the fifth statement uses the setDateHeader to set the expires header so caching for the page will expire after 1 hour. To do that, this statement calls the getTime method from a Date object named currentDate to return the current time in milliseconds. Then, it adds 3,600,000 milliseconds to that date (1000 miliseconds times 60 seconds times 60 minutes equals one hour).

The main method for setting the status codes

Method	Description
`setStatus(int code)`	Sets the status code for this response.

How status codes map to fields of the response object

Code	HttpServletResponse field
200 (OK)	SC_OK
404 (Not Found)	SC_NOT_FOUND
XXX (Xxx Xxx)	SC_XXX_XXX

Examples that set the status code

```
response.setStatus(404);
response.setStatus(response.SC_NOT_FOUND);
```

General methods for setting response headers

Method	Description
`setHeader(String name, String value)`	Sets a response header with the specified name and value.
`setIntHeader(String name, int value)`	Sets a response header with the specified name and int value.
`setDateHeader(String name, long value)`	Sets a response header with the specified name and date value.

Convenience methods for setting response headers

Method	Description
`setContentType(String mimeType)`	Sets the MIME type of the response being sent to the client in the Content-Type header.
`setContentLength(int lengthInBytes)`	Sets the length of the content body in the Content-Length header.
`addCookie(Cookie cookie)`	Adds the specified cookie to the response. For more information about this method, see chapter 8.

Examples that set response headers

```
response.setContentType("text/html");
response.setContentLength(403);
response.setHeader("pragma", "no-cache");
response.setIntHeader("refresh", 60);
response.setDateHeader("expires", currentDate.getTime() + 60 * 60 * 1000);
```

Description

- For more information about these and other methods and fields of the HttpServletResponse interface, you can refer to the documentation for the Java EE API.

Figure 18-8   How to set a response status code or header

Practical skills for working with HTTP

Now that you understand the concepts behind using the servlet API to work with HTTP requests and responses, you're ready to learn some practical skills for working with HTTP. These skills illustrate some situations when you might want to work with the request and response headers.

How to return a tab-delimited file as an Excel spreadsheet

Most modern browsers can use Microsoft Excel to read tab-delimited text. As a result, to display tab-delimited text as a spreadsheet, you can create some tab-delimited text, set the Content-Type response header to the "application/ vnd.ms-excel" MIME type, and return the tab-delimited text to the browser. Then, the browser will open the tab-delimited text in Excel as shown in figure 18-9.

The code in this figure starts by storing the column headings for the spreadsheet in a StringBuilder object named report. Then, it retrieves all of the columns and rows of the User table from a database and stores this data in tab-delimited format in the StringBuilder object.

When the code finishes storing the tab-delimited data in the StringBuilder object, the first statement in the highlighted code uses the setContentType method to set the content-type header of the response object. Here, the value in the header indicates that the response body contains data that's intended to be opened with Microsoft Excel.

Then, the second highlighted statement sets the cache-control header, as explained in a moment. And the last two statements in this method get a PrintWriter object that's used to return the StringBuilder object to the client.

How to control caching

The second statement in the highlighted code uses the setHeader method to set the cache-control response header so the document that's returned won't be cached. Otherwise, the server might automatically cache the response. Although it's usually more efficient to allow a document to be cached, preventing caching makes sure that the browser updates the data with every visit.

An Excel spreadsheet displayed within the Internet Explorer

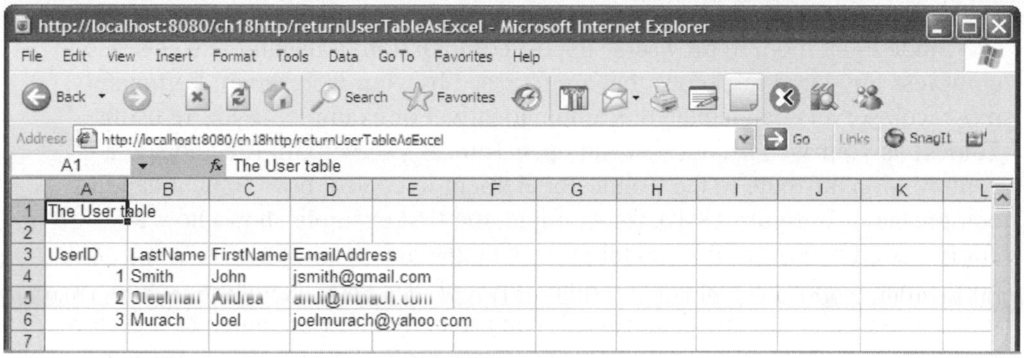

Servlet code that returns a tab-delimited file as an Excel spreadsheet

```
public void doGet(HttpServletRequest request,
        HttpServletResponse response)
        throws IOException, ServletException
{
    String query = "SELECT * FROM User ORDER BY UserID";
    String d = "\t";
    StringBuilder report = new StringBuilder("The User table\n\n"
            + "UserID" + d
            + "LastName" + d
            + "FirstName" + d
            + "EmailAddress" + "\n");
    try
    {
        ConnectionPool pool = ConnectionPool.getInstance();
        Connection connection = pool.getConnection();
        Statement statement = connection.createStatement();
        ResultSet results = statement.executeQuery(query);
        while (results.next())
        {
            report.append(results.getInt("UserID") + d
                    + results.getString("LastName")+ d
                    + results.getString("FirstName") + d
                    + results.getString("EmailAddress") + "\n");
        }
        results.close();
        statement.close();
        connection.close();
    }
    catch(SQLException e)
    {
        this.log(e.toString());
    }

    response.setContentType("application/vnd.ms-excel");
    response.setHeader("cache-control", "no-cache");

    PrintWriter out = response.getWriter();
    out.println(report);
}
```

Figure 18-9   How to return a tab-delimited file as an Excel spreadsheet

How to compress a response with GZIP

Since most modern browsers support compression, it usually makes sense to compress any large responses that are returned by your web server. Fortunately, most web servers can handle this automatically. For example, if you're using Tomcat as your web server, you can open Tomcat's server.xml file and add a compression attribute to the Connector element to control how Tomcat handles compression. In figure 18-10, for example, the first example shows how to compress all responses that contain text data that are returned on Tomcat's 8080 port. Since responses that contain other types of data such as images, sound, or video are usually already compressed, you typically don't get much of a performance gain by compressing these types of responses. As a result, the setting shown in this figure is the setting that's most commonly used.

However, if your web server doesn't automatically handle compression, you can manually encode a response with GZIP compression by checking and modifying the HTTP headers for requests and responses. This can dramatically improve download times for large documents. For example, if the table named User contains a large amount of data, it might make sense to encode the tab-delimited document that's returned in the last figure with GZIP compression. To do that, you can add the code shown in the second example.

Here, the first statement uses the getHeader method to return the accept-encoding request header. This request header is a string that contains the types of encoding that the browser supports. Then, the second statement declares a PrintWriter object.

In the if block, the if statement tests whether the browser supports GZIP encoding. If it does, this code creates a PrintWriter object that uses a GZIPOutputStream object to compress the output stream. This code also uses the setHeader method to set the content-encoding response header to GZIP. That way, the browser knows to use GZIP to decompress the stream before trying to read it.

However, if the browser doesn't support GZIP encoding, the getWriter method of the response object is used to return a normal PrintWriter object. Either way, the PrintWriter object is used to return the report to the browser.

How to modify Tomcat's server.xml to automatically handle compression

```
<Connector port="8080" protocol="HTTP/1.1"
           maxThreads="150" connectionTimeout="20000"
           redirectPort="8443" compression="on" />
```

Valid values for the compression attribute of the Connector element

Value	Description
on	Enables compression for text data.
force	Forces compression for all types of data.
int value	Enables compression for text data but specifies a minimum amount of data before the output is compressed.
off	Disables compression.

How to write code that manually encodes a response with GZIP compression

```
String encodingString = request.getHeader("accept-encoding");
PrintWriter out;
if (encodingString != null && encodingString.indexOf("gzip") > -1)
{
    OutputStream outputStream = response.getOutputStream();
    out = new PrintWriter(
            new GZIPOutputStream(outputStream), false);
    response.setHeader("content-encoding", "gzip");
}
else
{
    out = response.getWriter();
}
```

Description

- The GZIPOutputStream class is included in the java.util.zip package of the JDK. For more information about this class, you can refer to the documentation for the Java SE API.

- The getOutputStream method of the response object returns a binary output stream. The getWriter method of the response object returns a text output stream.

Figure 18-10   How to compress a response with GZIP

How to display the File Download dialog box

Within a web application, you can code an HTML link that points to a downloadable file. For example, you can code a link that points to a *Portable Document Format* (*PDF*) file. Then, when a user clicks on this link, most browsers automatically try to display the PDF file within Adobe Reader.

Although this is adequate for some applications, the Adobe Reader doesn't indicate how long it will take to open the file. As a result, for a large PDF file, the user may be left staring at a blank page for several minutes while the document downloads. In that case, you might want to display a File Download dialog box like the one shown in figure 18-11. That way, the user will have the choice of opening the PDF file or saving the file to disk, and the user will see a dialog box that indicates the progress of the download.

The code in this figure begins by showing how to code an HTML link to a MP3 sound file. On many systems, clicking on a link like this automatically launches an audio player that plays the sound file. If that's not what you want, you can code an HTML link to a servlet that forces the File Download dialog box to be displayed by setting a content-disposition header. This type of servlet is illustrated by the example in this figure.

The first three statements in this servlet get the path and name of the file that was sent as a request parameter. Then, the fourth statement sets the content-type response header to indicate that the response will contain generic binary data, and the fifth statement sets the content-disposition header to indicate that the response contains an attached file. This will force the File Download dialog box to be displayed.

Once the response headers have been set, this code uses a while loop to read each byte from the specified file. Then, it uses the PrintWriter object to write each byte to the response. Finally, this code closes the input and output streams.

The File Download dialog box

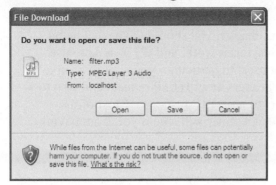

An HTML link to an MP3 sound file

```
<a href="filter.mp3">Joe Rut - Filter</a>
```

An HTML link to the servlet for downloading the file

```
<a href="downloadFile?name=filter.mp3">Joe Rut - Filter</a>
```

The servlet code that causes the File Download dialog box to be displayed

```
public void doGet(HttpServletRequest request,
        HttpServletResponse response)
        throws IOException, ServletException
{
    ServletContext sc = getServletContext();
    String path = sc.getRealPath("/");
    String name = request.getParameter("name");

    response.setContentType("application/octet-stream");
    response.setHeader("content-disposition",
        "attachment; filename=" + name);

    FileInputStream in = new FileInputStream(path + name);
    PrintWriter out = response.getWriter();

    int i = in.read();
    while (i != -1)
    {
        out.write(i);
        i = in.read();
    }
    in.close();
    out.close();
}
```

Description

- To force a File Download dialog box to be displayed, set the content-disposition header as shown above.

Figure 18-11   How to display the File Download dialog box

Perspective

Now that you have finished reading this chapter, you should (1) have a better understanding of how HTTP requests and responses work, and (2) be able to use Java to work with HTTP requests and responses. In particular, you should be able to use Java code to check the values in the headers of an HTTP request and also to set the status code and values of the headers of an HTTP response. Most of the time, though, the servlet API and the servlet container will shield you from having to work directly with HTTP.

Summary

- An HTTP request consists of a *request line* followed by *request headers*, while an HTTP response consists of a *status line* followed by *response headers* and then by a *response body*. The headers specify the attributes of a request or a response.

- The *Multipurpose Internet Mail Extension* (*MIME*) types provide standards for various types of data that can be transferred across the Internet.

- You can use the get methods of the request object to get the values of request headers, and you can use the set methods of the response object to set the values of response headers.

Exercise 18-1 Work with requests and responses

1. Open the ch18http project in the ex_starts folder.

2. Run the application. Then, test the first three links to see how the request headers can be returned in different formats.

3. View the index.html page to see how the first three links are coded. Then, view the JSP and servlet code that returns the request headers for the first three links in the HTML, XML, and Excel formats. Note how the different MIME types are specified.

4. Run the application. Then, test the two links that display the User table in an Excel spreadsheet. For this to work, the murach database must be installed on your system as described in appendix A.

5. View the servlets for these links to see how they work. Note that the only difference between these servlets is the code that adds the GZIP compression.

6. Run the application. Then, test the links that download the MP3 and PDF file. Note how two of the links display the File Download dialog box, and two don't.

7. View the index.html page to see how the href attributes for the MP3 and PDF files are coded. Then, note that these files are included in the root directory for this application.

8. View the servlet code for the links that display dialog boxes. Note that one servlet is used for downloading both MP3 and PDF files. Note also how this servlet sets the content-disposition response header.

19

How to work with listeners

Starting with the servlet 2.3 specification, you can add a listener to a web application. For example, you can create a listener class that contains code that's executed when your web application starts. Or, you can create a listener class that contains code that's executed every time a user starts a new session. In this chapter, you'll learn how to use listeners.

How to use a ServletContextListener

A *listener* is a class that listens for various events that can occur during the lifecycle of a web application and provides methods that are executed when those events occur. For instance, you can use a ServletContextListener to determine when an application is started, and you can use its contextInitialized method to initialize one or more global variables when that event occurs. This lets you initialize the global variables before the first JSP or servlet of an application is requested.

Because this is a common use of a listener, this chapter is going to use a ServletContextListener as its only example. That, however, should give you a good background for using any of the other listeners.

How to code a class for the listener

To code the class for a listener, you must implement one of the listener interfaces that are stored in the javax.servlet and javax.servlet.http packages. In part 1 of figure 19-1, for example, the CartContextListener class implements the ServletContextListener interface that's in the javax.servlet package. In other words, the CartContextListener is a ServletContextListener.

A class that implements a listener interface must override all of the methods of that interface. In this figure, for example, the CartContextListener class overrides the two methods of the ServletContextListener interface: the contextInitialized method and the contextDestroyed method. Both of these methods include a ServletContextEvent object as a parameter.

The contextInitialized method contains the code that's executed right after the application starts. In the method in this figure, the first statement calls the getServletContext method from the event parameter to return the ServletContext object. Note that a listener class doesn't extend the HttpServlet class so it isn't a servlet. As a result, you can't call the getServletContext method of the HttpServlet class directly from the listener class. Instead, you must call this method from the event parameter.

After getting the context object, the rest of the statements in this method initialize global variables and set them as attributes of the ServletContext object. As a result, these attributes are available to all of the JSPs and servlets for the application. Here, the code gets the customer service email address from the application's web.xml file. Then, it gets an int value for the current year. Next, it gets the path for the text file named products.txt that's stored in the WEB-INF directory. Finally, this code uses this path and the ProductsIO class to create an ArrayList of Product objects from the values that are stored in the text file.

In contrast, the contextDestroyed method is used for the code that's executed when the application stops and destroys the ServletContext object. This method typically contains cleanup code that frees any resources such as database connections that are used by the contextInitialized method. In this figure, though, the contextInititalized method doesn't use any resources that need to be cleaned up. As a result, this method doesn't contain any code.

A listener class that implements the ServletContextListener interface

```
package util;

import javax.servlet.*;
import java.util.*;

import business.*;
import data.*;

public class CartContextListener implements ServletContextListener
{
    public void contextInitialized(ServletContextEvent event)
    {
        ServletContext sc = event.getServletContext();

        // initialize the customer service email address
        String custServEmail = sc.getInitParameter("custServEmail");
        sc.setAttribute("custServEmail", custServEmail);

        // initialize the current year that's used in the copyright notice
        GregorianCalendar currentDate = new GregorianCalendar();
        int currentYear = currentDate.get(Calendar.YEAR);
        sc.setAttribute("currentYear", currentYear);

        // initialize the path for the products text file
        String productsPath = sc.getRealPath("WEB-INF/products.txt");
        sc.setAttribute("productsPath", productsPath);

        // initialize the list of products
        ArrayList<Product> products = new ArrayList<Product>();
        products = ProductIO.getProducts(productsPath);
        sc.setAttribute("products", products);
    }

    public void contextDestroyed(ServletContextEvent event)
    {
        // no cleanup necessary
    }
}
```

Description

- A *listener* is a class that listens for various events that can occur in an application and provides methods that respond to those events when they occur.

- To code the class for a listener, you must implement one of the listener interfaces that are stored in the javax.servlet and javax.servlet.http packages.

- A class that implements a listener interface must override the methods of that interface. For more information about the listener interfaces, see figures 19-2 and 19-3.

Figure 19-1   How to use a ServletContextListener (part 1 of 3)

How to register the listener

After you code the class for a listener, you must register the listener with the web application. To do that, you must add a listener element to the application's web.xml file as shown in part 2 of figure 19-1. Here, the shaded code contains the listener element. Within the listener element, the listener-class element specifies the fully qualified name of the class. In this case, it specifies the CartContextListener class in the util package, which is the class that's shown in part 1 of this figure.

Below the listener element in this figure, you can see the context-param element that defines the context initialization parameter for the customer service email address. This, of course, has nothing to do with the use of listeners, except that this parameter is read by the listener class that's presented in part 1. As you can see, this parameter has a name of custServEmail and a value of "custserv@murach.com".

A web.xml file that includes a listener element

```xml
<?xml version="1.0" encoding="UTF-8"?>
<web-app version="2.5" xmlns="http://java.sun.com/xml/ns/javaee"
         xmlns:xsi="http://www.w3.org/2001/XMLSchema-instance"
         xsi:schemaLocation="http://java.sun.com/xml/ns/javaee
         http://java.sun.com/xml/ns/javaee/web-app_2_5.xsd">

    <servlet>
        <servlet-name>CartServlet</servlet-name>
        <servlet-class>cart.CartServlet</servlet-class>
    </servlet>
    <servlet-mapping>
        <servlet-name>CartServlet</servlet-name>
        <url-pattern>/cart</url-pattern>
    </servlet-mapping>

    <listener>
        <listener-class>util.CartContextListener</listener-class>
    </listener>

    <context-param>
        <param-name>custServEmail</param-name>
        <param-value>custserv@murach.com</param-value>
    </context-param>

    <session-config>
        <session-timeout>30</session-timeout>
    </session-config>
    <welcome-file-list>
        <welcome-file>index.jsp</welcome-file>
    </welcome-file-list>
</web-app>
```

The listener elements

Element	Description
listener	Adds a listener to the application.
listener-class	Specifies the fully qualified name of a class that implements a listener.

Description

- After you code the class for a listener, you must register the listener with the application by adding a listener element to the application's web.xml file.

Figure 19-1   How to use a ServletContextListener (part 2 of 3)

How to code a JSP that uses the attributes set by the listener

Part 3 of figure 19-1 shows how a JSP within a web application can use the attributes set by the listener. Here, the three shaded portions use EL to get the attributes of the ServletContext object that were set by the listener presented in parts 1 and 2. This code works because EL automatically searches through all scopes, including application scope.

However, if you are worried about possible naming conflicts, you can explicitly specify application scope like this:

```
${applicationScope.products}
```

That way, you can be sure that this JSP will only use the products attribute that has been set in the ServletContext object. In this case, that attribute contains an ArrayList object that stores all of the Product objects for the application.

A JSP file that uses attributes that have been set by a listener

```html
<!DOCTYPE HTML PUBLIC "-//W3C//DTD HTML 4.01 Transitional//EN"
    "http://www.w3.org/TR/html4/loose.dtd">
<html>
<head>
    <title>Murach's Java Servlets and JSP</title>
</head>
<body>

<%@ taglib prefix="c" uri="http://java.sun.com/jsp/jstl/core" %>

<h1>CD list</h1>

<table cellpadding="5" border=1>

  <tr valign="bottom">
    <td align="left"><b>Description</b></td>
    <td align="left"><b>Price</b></td>
    <td align="left"></td>
  </tr>


<c:forEach var="product" items="${products}">
  <tr valign="top">
    <td>${product.description}</td>
    <td>${product.priceCurrencyFormat}</td>
    <td><a href="<c:url value='/cart?productCode=${product.code}' />">
        Add To Cart</a></td>
</tr>
</c:forEach>

</table>

<p>
For customer service, please send an email to ${custServEmail}.
</p>

<p>
&copy; Copyright ${currentYear} Mike Murach &amp; Associates, Inc.
All rights reserved.
</p>

</body>
</html>
```

Description

- Any of the attributes that are set by the class that implements the ServletContextListener interface are available to the rest of the servlets and JSPs in the application.

Figure 19-1   How to use a ServletContextListener (part 3 of 3)

How to work with other types of listeners

Now that you know how to use a ServletContextListener, you're ready to learn how to work with other types of listeners.

A summary of the listener interfaces

Figure 19-2 summarizes the eight listener interfaces. Of these interfaces, the ServletContext and ServletRequest interfaces are stored in the javax.servlet package, and the HttpSession interfaces are stored in the javax.servlet.http package. If you review the descriptions of these interfaces, you'll see that they let you listen for a variety of events that occur on the ServletContext, HttpSession, and ServletRequest objects. In other words, they let you listen for events that occur at application, session, or request scope.

For example, the HttpSessionListener works like the ServletContextListener. However, it lets you write code that's executed when a new session is created or destroyed. Typically, a session is destroyed when the user hasn't requested a URL from the web application within 30 minutes, but that time is determined by the web.xml file for the application.

As this figure shows, other listeners let you respond to events that occur when an attribute is added to, removed from, or replaced in the ServletContext, session, or request objects. You can also respond to events that occur when an object is bound or unbound from a session or when a session is activated or deactivated. For most web applications, though, the only listener that you're likely to use is the ServletContextListener.

The ServletContext interfaces

Interface	Description
ServletContextListener	Provides methods that are executed when the ServletContext object is initialized and destroyed. This happens when the application is started and stopped.
SerlvetContextAttributeListener	Provides methods that are executed when attributes are added to, removed from, or replaced in the ServletContext object.

The HttpSession interfaces

Interface	Description
HttpSessionListener	Provides methods that are executed when the session object is created and destroyed for a user. This happens every time a new user accesses an application and when the session for a user is destroyed.
HttpSessionAttributeListener	Provides methods that are executed when attributes are added to, removed from, or replaced in the session object.
HttpSessionBindingListener	Provides methods that are executed when an object is bound to or unbound from the session.
HttpSessionActivationListener	Provides methods that are executed when the session is activated or deactivated. This happens when the session is migrating to another JVM.

The ServletRequest interfaces

Interface	Description
ServletRequestListener	Provides methods that are executed when a request object is initialized and destroyed. This happens every time the server receives and processes a request.
ServletRequestAttributeListener	Provides methods that are executed when attributes are added to, removed from, or replaced in the request object.

Description

- The ServletContext and ServletRequest interfaces are stored in the javax.servlet package, and the HttpSession interfaces are stored in the javax.servlet.http package.

Figure 19-2   A summary of the listener interfaces

The methods of the listener interfaces

To round out your understanding of listeners, figure 19-3 presents the methods of the listener interfaces that are summarized in the previous figure. If you study these methods, you'll see that they all include an event object as the sole parameter. Then, you can use the methods that are provided by the event object in your listener methods as described in the next figure.

The ServletContext interfaces

The ServletContextListener interface

`contextInitialized`(ServletContextEvent e)
`contextDestroyed`(ServletContextEvent e)

The ServletContextAttributeListener interface

`attributeAdded`(ServletContextAttributeEvent e)
`attributeRemoved`(ServletContextAttributeEvent e)
`attributeReplaced`(ServletContextAttributeEvent e)

The HttpSession interfaces

The HttpSessionListener interface

`sessionCreated`(HttpSessionEvent e)
`sessionDestroyed`(HttpSessionEvent e)

The HttpSessionAttributeListener interface

`attributeAdded`(HttpSessionBindingEvent e)
`attributeRemoved`(HttpSessionBindingEvent e)
`attributeReplaced`(HttpSessionBindingEvent e)

The HttpSessionBindingListener interface

`valueBound`(HttpSessionBindingEvent e)
`valueUnbound`(HttpSessionBindingEvent e)

The HttpSessionActivationListener interface

`sessionDidActivate`(HttpSessionEvent e)
`sessionWillPassivate`(HttpSessionEvent e)

The ServletRequest interfaces

The ServletRequestListener interface

`requestInitialized`(ServletRequestEvent e)
`requestDestroyed`(ServletRequestEvent e)

The ServletRequestAttributeListener interface

`attributeAdded`(ServletRequestAttributeEvent e)
`attributeRemoved`(ServletRequestAttributeEvent e)
`attributeReplaced`(ServletRequestAttributeEvent e)

Description

- All of these methods include a parameter for the event that has occurred.
- Since none of these methods return a value, you can use the void keyword for the return type.

Figure 19-3   The methods of the listener interfaces

The methods of the event objects

Figure 19-4 presents the methods of the event objects that are available from the methods of the listener interfaces. For example, if you implement the HttpSessionListener interface, the sessionCreated and sessionDestroyed methods of this interface must include an HttpSessionEvent object as the parameter. Then, you can use the getSession method of the HttpSessionEvent object to return the HttpSession object that raised the event.

Similarly, the ServletContextAttributeEvent object provides getName and getValue methods that return the name and value of the attribute that raised the event. In addition, since the ServletContextAttributeEvent class inherits the ServletContextEvent class, you can also call the getServletContext method from this event object.

The ServletContextEvent class

Method	Description
`getServletContext()`	Returns the ServletContext object that was initialized or destroyed.

The ServletContextAttributeEvent class

Method	Description
`getName()`	Returns a string for the name of the attribute that was added to, removed from, or replaced in the ServletContext object.
`getValue()`	Returns an object for the value of the attribute that was added to, removed from, or replaced in the ServletContext object.

The HttpSessionEvent class

Method	Description
`getSession()`	Returns the HttpSession object that was changed.

The HttpSessionBindingEvent class

Method	Description
`getName()`	Returns a string for the name of the attribute that was added to, removed from, or replaced in the HttpSession object.
`getValue()`	Returns an object for the value of the attribute that was added to, removed from, or replaced in the HttpSession object.

The ServletRequestEvent class

Method	Description
`getServletRequest()`	Returns the ServletRequest object that was initialized or destroyed.

The ServletRequestAttributeEvent class

Method	Description
`getName()`	Returns a string for the name of the attribute that was added to, removed from, or replaced in the ServletRequest object.
`getValue()`	Returns an object for the value of the attribute that was added to, removed from, or replaced in the ServletRequest object.

Description

- The ServletContextAttributeEvent class inherits the ServletContextEvent class. As a result, the getServletContext method is available to this class.
- The HttpSessionBindingEvent class inherits the HttpSessionEvent class. As a result, the getSession method is available to this class.
- The ServletRequestAttributeEvent class inherits the ServletRequestEvent class. As a result, the getServletRequest method is available to this class.

Figure 19-4   The methods of the event objects

Perspective

Now that you've finished this chapter, you should be able to code a ServletContextListener that initializes the global variables for a web application when the application starts. You should also know what events the other listeners can respond to, and with a little experimentation you should be able to figure out how to code one of those listeners if your application requires that.

Summary

- A *listener* is a class that listens for various events that can occur during the lifecycle of a web application and provides methods that are executed when specific events occur.

- To create a listener, you must code a class that implements one of the listener interfaces, and you must register the listener by adding a listener element to the application's web.xml file.

- All of the methods of a listener interface have an event object as its sole parameter. You can call the methods of this event object in your listener methods.

Exercise 19-1   Work with listeners

Review the application

1. Open the ch19cart project in the ex_starts folder.

2. Open the CartContextListener.java file. Note how this class sets four attributes in the ServletContext object.

3. Open the web.xml file. Note how the listener element registers the listener class. Note also how the context-param element stores the context initialization parameter that's read by the listener class.

4. Open the index.jsp and cart.jsp files. Note how these JSPs use attributes of the ServletContext object that were set by the CartContextListener class.

5. Run the application. Note how the two JSPs display the data that was initialized by the CartContextListener class.

Add a listener class

6. Add a class to the util package named CartSessionListener. This class should implement the HttpSessionListener interface. Then, code the declarations for the two methods that are required by the HttpSessionListener interface.

7. In the body of the sessionCreated method, use the getSession method of the event object to get the session object. Use the getServletContext method of the session object to get the ServletContext object. And use the log method of the ServletContext object to print a message to Tomcat's log file that says, "Session created."

8. Modify the web.xml file for the application so it includes a listener element that registers the CartSessionListener class with the web application.

9. Restart Tomcat so it reads the modified web.xml file.

10. Run the application. Then, check the Tomcat log file and note the information that's written to the log file.

11. The "Session created" message should be written each time a new browser window requests a valid URL within the application. To test this, open one or more browser windows and request a URL for any of the JSPs within the application from each window.

20

How to work with filters

Starting with the servlet 2.3 specification, you can add a filter to your web application. For example, you can code a filter class that examines an HTTP request and does some processing based on the values of the HTTP request headers. Sometimes, this processing may include modifying the HTTP response that's returned to the client. Since filters often work closely with HTTP requests and responses, you may want to read chapter 18 before you read this chapter.

An introduction to filters

A *filter* can intercept an HTTP request and execute code before or after the requested servlet or JSP is executed. As a result, filters are ideal for handling *cross-cutting concerns*, which are aspects of an application that cut across different parts of an application

How filters work

The diagram in figure 20-1 shows how filters work. Here, the application uses two filters (Filter1 and Filter2) and two servlets (Servlet1 and Servlet2). In this diagram, Filter1 has been mapped to Servlet1, while Filter1 and Filter2 have been mapped to Servlet2.

When a client requests Servlet1, Filter1 can execute some code before the code for Servlet1 is executed. Then, after the code for Servlet1 is executed, Filter1 can execute more code before the response is returned to the client.

When a client requests Servlet2, both Filter1 and Filter2 can execute some code before the code for Servlet2 is executed. Then, after the code for Servlet2 is executed, Filter2 and Filter1 can execute more code before the response is returned to the client.

Two benefits of filters

One benefit of filters is that they allow you to create modular code that can be applied to different parts of an application. In other words, the requested servlet doesn't need to have any knowledge of the filter. As a result, you should be able to turn a filter on or off without affecting the behavior of the servlet.

Another benefit of filters is that they allow you to create flexible code. This works because you use an application's web.xml file to control when filters are executed. As a result, you can easily apply filters to different parts of an application, and you can easily turn a filter on or off.

When to use filters

As mentioned earlier, filters are ideal for handling cross cutting concerns. For example, a filter can be used to write data to a log file, handle authentication, or compress a response. In addition, a filter can be used to handle image type conversions, localization, XSL transformations, caching, and so on.

Of course, if your servlet container already provides the type of functionality that you need, it's usually easier and less error-prone to use the built-in functionality. As a result, before you code a custom filter to handle a complex task such as compressing responses, you should check the documentation for your servlet container to see if it already provides this type of functionality.

How filters work

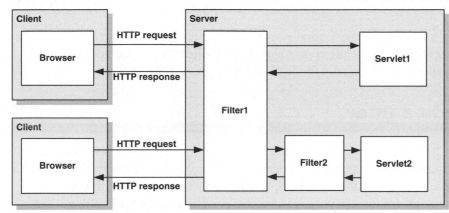

Two benefits of using filters

- **Modular code.** Filters allow you to store code in a single location that can be applied to multiple parts of an application.
- **Flexible code.** You can use the web.xml file to control when filters are executed. This allows you to apply filters to different parts of an application, and it allows you to turn a filter on or off.

Types of tasks that can be performed by filters

- **Logging.** You can use a filter to log the requests and responses of a web application.
- **Authentication.** You can use a filter to only allow authorized users to access certain parts of a web site.
- **Compression.** You can use a filter to compress responses to improve the performance of your web application.

Description

- You can use a filter to intercept an HTTP request and do some processing before the requested servlet or JSP is executed. Conversely, you can use a filter to intercept an HTTP response and to do some processing after the requested servlet or JSP is executed but before the HTTP response is returned to the browser.
- Filters are ideal for addressing *cross-cutting concerns*, which are aspects of an application that cut across different parts of an application.
- You can chain two or more filters together.
- Filters were introduced with the servlet 2.3 specification.

Figure 20-1   How filters work

How to add a filter

Adding a filter to an application works similarly to adding a servlet to an application. To start, you must code a class for the filter. Then, you add some code to the web.xml file to map the filter to one or more URL patterns.

How to code a filter

Figure 20-2 shows how to code the class for a simple filter that writes some basic information about the request and response to a log file. To start, the package statement stores the class in a package named filters. Then, the three import statements import the packages that are needed to work with a filter. Note that these packages are the same ones that are used to work with a servlet.

After the import statements, the code declares a class named TestFilter1 that implements the Filter interface. This class implements all three methods of the Filter interface: init, doFilter, and destroy. These methods are called when the filter is initialized, executed, and destroyed.

After the declaration for the class, a private instance variable is declared for a FilterConfig object named filterConfig. This object is initialized in the init method. To do that, the init method assigns the filterConfig instance variable to the FilterConfig object that's passed to the init method as an argument.

After the init method, the doFilter method contains the code that's executed by the filter. To start, the first two statements cast the ServletRequest and ServletResponse parameters to HttpServletRequest and HttpServletResponse objects. That way, the doFilter method can call all of the same methods of the request and response objects that are available to servlets. Then, the third statement gets the application's ServletContext object by calling the getServletContext method of the filterConfig instance variable.

After the request, response, and ServletContext objects have been set up, the fourth statement gets the name of the filter from the FilterConfig object, and the fifth statement gets the servlet path from the request object. Then, the sixth statement uses the log method of the ServletContext object to write this data to a log file. And the seventh statement uses the doFilter method of the FilterChain parameter to pass the request and response to the next filter or servlet in the chain. At this point, execution is passed along the chain.

After the servlet is executed, the last statement in the doFilter method is executed. This statement writes the same data to the log file as the sixth statement. However, it appends "after request" to the end of the data to show that this code was executed after the requested servlet was executed but before the response was returned to the client.

The last method in this class is the destroy method, which assigns a null value to the filterConfig instance variable. Although assigning this value isn't necessary, this is generally considered a good programming practice.

As simple as this class is, it illustrates all of the principles that you need for coding a filter, including how to initialize the FilterConfig object and how to get the request, response, and ServletContext objects. In this case, the class just logs

A class that implements the Filter interface

```
package filters;

import java.io.*;
import javax.servlet.*;
import javax.servlet.http.*;

public class TestFilter1 implements Filter
{
    private FilterConfig filterConfig = null;

    public void init(FilterConfig filterConfig)
    {
        this.filterConfig = filterConfig;
    }

    public void doFilter(
            ServletRequest request,
            ServletResponse response,
            FilterChain chain) throws IOException, ServletException
    {
        HttpServletRequest httpRequest = (HttpServletRequest) request;
        HttpServletResponse httpResponse = (HttpServletResponse) response;
        ServletContext sc = filterConfig.getServletContext();

        String filterName = filterConfig.getFilterName();
        String servletPath = "Servlet path: " + httpRequest.getServletPath();

        sc.log(filterName  + " | " + servletPath + " | before request");

        chain.doFilter(httpRequest, httpResponse);

        sc.log(filterName  + " | " + servletPath + " | after request");
    }

    public void destroy()
    {
        filterConfig = null;
    }
}
```

Description

- A filter class must implement the Filter interface that includes the init, doFilter, and destroy methods that are called when the filter is initialized, executed, and destroyed.

- The init method accepts a FilterConfig object as a parameter. You can use this object's getFilterName method to get the name of the filter, and you can its getServletContext method to get the ServletContext object for the application.

- The doFilter method accepts ServletRequest and ServletResponse objects as parameters. You can cast these objects to the HttpServletRequest and HttpServletResponse objects.

- The doFilter method also accepts a FilterChain object. You can use the doFilter method of this object to forward the request and response to the next filter or servlet in the chain.

Figure 20-2   How to code a filter

some data from the FilterConfig object and the request objects, but it could easily vary the processing based on the data that's in the request. If, for example, you want to block requests for unauthorized users, you can check the authorization header of the request to see if the user is authorized. If so, you can call the doFilter method of the FilterChain object to forward the request. If not, you can use a RequestDispatcher object to forward the request to a login page.

How to configure a filter

Part 1 of figure 20-3 shows a web.xml file for an application that configures three filters. Except for the name of the class, all three filters contain the same code as the filter presented in figure 20-2. To start, the three filter elements register the classes named TestFilter1, TestFilter2, and TestFitler3 that are stored in the package named filters. Then, the three filter-mapping elements map the three filters to a URL pattern.

The first filter-mapping element maps TestFilter1 to all URL requests within the current application. To do that, the url-pattern element uses a front slash followed by an asterisk (/*). As a result, this filter is executed for all URLs within the root directory.

The second filter-mapping element also maps TestFilter2 to all URL requests within the current application. However, this element includes two dispatcher elements that indicate that this filter should be executed for (1) requests coming from clients and (2) requests that are forwarded from within the application. By contrast, TestFilter1 is only executed for requests coming from clients.

The third filter-mapping element uses the servlet-name element to map TestFilter3 to all requests for the CheckUserServlet. In this web.xml file, this servlet is only mapped to one URL (/checkUser). However, if this servlet was mapped to multiple URLs, TestFilter3 would be mapped to those URLs as well.

This web.xml file shows how easy it is to configure filters. For example, you can easily turn off TestFilter1 by commenting out its servlet-mapping element. Or, you can change the URLs that cause TestFilter2 to be executed by modifying its url-pattern element. Once you do that, you don't have to recompile or modify your filter or servlet classes. As a result, it's easy to experiment with filters. More importantly, it's easy to add or remove features that apply to multiple parts of an application.

A web.xml file that contains three filters

```xml
<?xml version="1.0" encoding="UTF-8"?>
<web-app version="2.5"
    xmlns="http://java.sun.com/xml/ns/javaee"
    xmlns:xsi="http://www.w3.org/2001/XMLSchema-instance"
    xsi:schemaLocation="http://java.sun.com/xml/ns/javaee
    http://java.sun.com/xml/ns/javaee/web-app_2_5.xsd">

    <filter>
        <filter-name>TestFilter1</filter-name>
        <filter-class>filters.TestFilter1</filter-class>
    </filter>
    <filter>
        <filter-name>TestFilter2</filter-name>
        <filter-class>filters.TestFilter2</filter-class>
    </filter>
    <filter>
        <filter-name>TestFilter3</filter-name>
        <filter-class>filters.TestFilter3</filter-class>
    </filter>

    <filter-mapping>
        <filter-name>TestFilter1</filter-name>
        <url-pattern>/*</url-pattern>
    </filter-mapping>
    <filter-mapping>
        <filter-name>TestFilter2</filter-name>
        <url-pattern>/*</url-pattern>
        <dispatcher>REQUEST</dispatcher>
        <dispatcher>FORWARD</dispatcher>
    </filter-mapping>
    <filter-mapping>
        <filter-name>TestFilter3</filter-name>
        <servlet-name>CheckUserServlet</servlet-name>
    </filter-mapping>

    <servlet>
        <servlet-name>CheckUserServlet</servlet-name>
        <servlet-class>download.CheckUserServlet</servlet-class>
    </servlet>

    <!-- The rest of the servlet elements go here -->

    <servlet-mapping>
        <servlet-name>CheckUserServlet</servlet-name>
        <url-pattern>/checkUser</url-pattern>
    </servlet-mapping>

    <!-- The rest of the web.xml file goes here -->

</web-app>
```

Figure 20-3   How to configure a filter (part 1 of 2)

Part 2 of figure 20-3 begins by summarizing the elements that are used within the web.xml file to map a filter to a URL pattern. If you understand the web.xml file presented in part 1, you shouldn't have much trouble understanding how these elements work. Note, however, that the dispatcher element wasn't introduced until the servlet 2.4 specification. As a result, you can't use this element if you're working with a servlet container that implements the 2.3 specification.

The log data for the first request shows the filters that are executed when the index.jsp file for the application is requested. To start, TestFilter1 is executed, followed by TestFilter2, followed by the servlet for the index.jsp file. Here, it's important to note that the filters are executed in the order that they are specified in the web.xml file. Then, after the servlet for the index.jsp file is executed, TestFilter2 is executed, followed by TestFilter1. Here, it's important to note that the filters are executed in the reverse order.

The log data for the second request shows the filters that are executed when the CheckUserServlet that's mapped to the /checkUser URL is requested. To start, all three test filters are executed, just as you would expect. Then, the CheckUserServlet forwards the request to the 8601_download.jsp file. At this point, since TestFilter2 is the only filter that handles requests that are forwarded from other parts of the application, it is the only filter that's executed. Finally, the servlet for the 8601_download.jsp file is executed. After this servlet is executed, TestFilter2 is executed again since it was the last filter to be executed. Then, TestFilter3 is executed, followed by TestFilter2, followed by TestFilter1.

The filter and filter-mapping elements

Element	Description
filter	Adds a filter to the application.
filter-name	Specifies a name for the filter.
filter-class	Specifies the fully qualified name of a class that implements a filter.
filter-mapping	Adds filter-mapping to the application.
url-pattern	Specifies the URLs that cause the filter to be executed.
servlet-name	Specifies a servlet that causes the filter to be executed. The value for this element should match the value of the servlet-name element for the servlet element.
dispatcher	Specifies the types of requests that cause the filter to be executed. Valid values include REQUEST, FORWARD, ERROR, and INCLUDE. REQUEST (the default) executes the filter on requests from the client. FORWARD executes the filter on forwards from within the application. INCLUDE executes the filter when the application uses an include. And ERROR executes the filter when the application uses an error handler. This element was introduced with the servlet 2.4 specification.

The log data when the index.jsp file is requested

```
Nov 5, 2007 11:28:20 AM org.apache.catalina.core.ApplicationContext log
INFO: TestFilter1 | Servlet path: /index.jsp | before request
Nov 5, 2007 11:28:20 AM org.apache.catalina.core.ApplicationContext log
INFO: TestFilter2 | Servlet path: /index.jsp | before request
Nov 5, 2007 11:28:20 AM org.apache.catalina.core.ApplicationContext log
INFO: TestFilter2 | Servlet path: /index.jsp | after request
Nov 5, 2007 11:28:20 AM org.apache.catalina.core.ApplicationContext log
INFO: TestFilter1 | Servlet path: /index.jsp | after request
```

The log data when the servlet that's mapped to /checkUser is requested

```
Nov 5, 2007 11:28:21 AM org.apache.catalina.core.ApplicationContext log
INFO: TestFilter1 | Servlet path: /checkUser | before request
Nov 5, 2007 11:28:21 AM org.apache.catalina.core.ApplicationContext log
INFO: TestFilter2 | Servlet path: /checkUser | before request
Nov 5, 2007 11:28:21 AM org.apache.catalina.core.ApplicationContext log
INFO: TestFilter3 | Servlet path: /checkUser | before request
Nov 5, 2007 11:28:21 AM org.apache.catalina.core.ApplicationContext log
INFO: TestFilter2 | Servlet path: /8601_download.jsp | before request
Nov 5, 2007 11:28:21 AM org.apache.catalina.core.ApplicationContext log
INFO: TestFilter2 | Servlet path: /8601_download.jsp | after request
Nov 5, 2007 11:28:21 AM org.apache.catalina.core.ApplicationContext log
INFO: TestFilter3 | Servlet path: /checkUser | after request
Nov 5, 2007 11:28:21 AM org.apache.catalina.core.ApplicationContext log
INFO: TestFilter2 | Servlet path: /checkUser | after request
Nov 5, 2007 11:28:21 AM org.apache.catalina.core.ApplicationContext log
INFO: TestFilter1 | Servlet path: /checkUser | after request
```

Description

- The request filters are executed in the order that they are declared in the web.xml file.
- The response filters are executed in the reverse order that they are executed for the request.

Figure 20-3   How to configure a filter (part 2 of 2)

Two filter classes

Now that you've learned how to code and configure a simple filter, you're ready to learn how to code filters that do processing on only one side of the request. With request-side processing, the processing is done before the request reaches the target servlet. With response-side processing, the processing is done after the requested servlet has been executed but before the response is returned to the client.

When you code filters that that only perform processing on one side of the request, the resulting code can be more modular and give you more flexibility when you configure the filter. However, as you'll see later in this chapter, there are times when a filter must perform both request-side and response-side processing.

How to code a filter that performs request-side processing

Figure 20-4 shows how to code a filter named LogRequestFilter that executes code before the requested servlet is executed. If you study the code for this filter, you'll see that it works similarly to the TestFilter1 presented in figure 20-2. However, there are a few differences.

First, the LogRequestFilter class includes the value of a cookie in the data that it writes to the log file. To do that, this code calls the getCookies method of the HttpServletRequest object to get an array of Cookie objects. Then, it uses the getCookieValue method of the custom CookieUtil class to get the value of the cookie named emailCookie.

Second, this class doesn't do any processing after the requested servlet is executed. In other words, this servlet doesn't do any response-side processing. To do that, all of the code for the doFilter method is coded before the statement that calls the doFilter method of the FilterChain object.

Third, since this class doesn't call any methods from the request object, it doesn't bother to cast the ServletResponse object that it receives as a parameter to the HttpServletResponse object. Instead, it passes the ServletResponse object to the doFilter method of the FilterChain object.

The code for a filter that performs request-side processing

```
package filters;

import java.io.*;
import javax.servlet.*;
import javax.servlet.http.*;

public class LogRequestFilter implements Filter
{
    private FilterConfig filterConfig = null;

    public void init(FilterConfig filterConfig)
    {
        this.filterConfig = filterConfig;
    }

    public void doFilter(
            ServletRequest request,
            ServletResponse response,
            FilterChain chain) throws IOException, ServletException
    {
        HttpServletRequest httpRequest = (HttpServletRequest) request;
        ServletContext sc = filterConfig.getServletContext();

        String logString = filterConfig.getFilterName() + " | ";
        logString += "Servlet path: " + httpRequest.getServletPath() + " | ";

        Cookie[] cookies = httpRequest.getCookies();
        String emailAddress = util.CookieUtil.getCookieValue(
                cookies, "emailCookie");
        logString += "Email cookie: ";
        if (emailAddress.length() != 0)
            logString += emailAddress;
        else
            logString += "Not found";

        sc.log(logString);

        chain.doFilter(httpRequest, response);
    }

    public void destroy()
    {
        filterConfig = null;
    }
}
```

Description

- To code a filter that executes code before the requested servlet is executed, you code all of the code for the filter before you call the doFilter method of the FilterChain parameter.

Figure 20-4   How to code a filter that performs request-side processing

How to code a filter that performs response-side processing

Figure 20-5 shows how to code a filter named LogResponseFilter that executes code after the requested servlet is executed but before the response is returned to the client. If you study the code for this filter, you'll see that it works similarly to the TestFilter1 presented in figure 20-2. However, there are a couple differences.

First, the LogResponseFilter class does all of its processing after the requested servlet is executed. In other words, this servlet doesn't do any request-side processing. To do that, all of the code in the doFilter method is after the statement that calls the doFilter method of the FilterChain object.

Second, this class includes the content type of the response in the log file. To do that, this code calls the getContentType method of the HttpServletResponse object to get the MIME type of the response.

The code for a filter that performs response-side processing

```
package filters;

import java.io.*;
import javax.servlet.*;
import javax.servlet.http.*;

public class LogResponseFilter implements Filter
{
    private FilterConfig filterConfig = null;

    public void init(FilterConfig filterConfig)
    {
        this.filterConfig = filterConfig;
    }

    public void doFilter(ServletRequest request,
                         ServletResponse response,
                         FilterChain chain)
                         throws IOException, ServletException
    {
        chain.doFilter(request, response);

        HttpServletRequest httpRequest = (HttpServletRequest) request;
        HttpServletResponse httpResponse = (HttpServletResponse) response;
        ServletContext sc = filterConfig.getServletContext();

        String logString = filterConfig.getFilterName() + " | ";
        logString += "Servlet path: " + httpRequest.getServletPath() + " | ";
        logString += "Content type: " + httpResponse.getContentType();

        sc.log(logString);
    }

    public void destroy()
    {
        filterConfig = null;
    }
}
```

Description

- To code a filter that executes code after the requested servlet is executed but before the response is returned to the client, you code all of the code for the filter after you call the doFilter method of the FilterChain parameter.

Figure 20-5   How to code a filter that performs response-side processing

Other skills for working with filters

Now that you know how to code a filter that performs request-side or response-side processing, you're ready to learn two more skills that are sometimes useful when working with filters. First, you'll learn how to add functionality to a request or response object by creating a custom request or response object. Second, you'll learn how to add initialization parameters to a filter.

How to wrap a request or response

Figure 20-6 begins by summarizing two wrapper classes that you can use to create custom request or response objects. These classes implement a design pattern known as the *wrapper pattern* or the *decorator pattern*.

The HttpServletRequestWrapper class implements the HttpServletRequest interface by providing methods that call the methods of the underlying HttpServletRequest interface. As a result, if you code a class that extends the HttpServletRequestWrapper class, all of the existing methods already work. Then, to add new functionality, you can add a method that doesn't exist in the HttpServletRequest interface. Or, to modify the existing functionality, you can override one of the methods of the HttpServletRequest class.

As you would expect, the HttpServletResponseWrapper class wraps the HttpServletResponse interface just as the HttpServletRequestWrapper class wraps the HttpServletRequest interface. As a result, once you understand how to use one of these classes, you should understand how to use the other. Since the HttpServletRequestWrapper class is more commonly used, this figure shows how to use that class.

If you review the two pages of code in this figure, you'll see that the first page presents the LogResponseCookiesFilter class and the second page presents the ResponseCookiesWrapper class. Since this wrapper class is only used by the LogResponseCookiesFilter class, the wrapper class is nested within the same file as the filter class. Also, since this wrapper class is nested, it can't be declared as public. Instead, it is declared with the default scope.

If you study the LogResponseCookiesFilter class, you can see that it works much like the filters presented earlier in this chapter. However, it uses the ResponseCookiesWrapper class to create a custom response object. This custom response class includes a new method named getCookies that returns all of the Cookie objects that have been stored in the response object. This custom response class also overrides the addCookie method in the underlying response object so it can keep track of the cookies that are added to the response.

Once this filter creates the custom response object, it passes it to the doFilter method of the FilterChain object. That way, any filters or servlets that are called later in the chain will use the custom response object instead of the standard response object. As a result, the response-side processing for this filter can call the getCookies method that's available from the custom response

Two classes for creating custom request and response objects

Class	Description
HttpServletRequestWrapper	This class implements the HttpServletRequest interface by providing methods that call the methods of the HttpServletRequest interface.
HttpServletResponseWrapper	This class implements the HttpServletResponse interface by providing methods that call the methods of the HttpServletResponse interface.

The code for a filter that uses a custom response object   Page 1

```
package filters;

import java.io.*;
import java.util.*;
import javax.servlet.*;
import javax.servlet.http.*;

public class LogResponseCookiesFilter implements Filter
{
    private FilterConfig filterConfig = null;

    public void init(FilterConfig filterConfig)
    {
        this.filterConfig = filterConfig;
    }

    public void doFilter(
            ServletRequest request,
            ServletResponse response,
            FilterChain chain) throws IOException, ServletException
    {
        HttpServletResponse httpResponse = (HttpServletResponse) response;
        ResponseCookiesWrapper wrappedResponse =
            new ResponseCookiesWrapper(httpResponse);

        chain.doFilter(request, wrappedResponse);

        HttpServletRequest httpRequest = (HttpServletRequest) request;
        ServletContext sc = filterConfig.getServletContext();
        String filterName = filterConfig.getFilterName();
        String servletPath = "Servlet path: " + httpRequest.getServletPath();
        ArrayList<Cookie> cookies = wrappedResponse.getCookies();
        String cookiesString = "";
        for (Cookie c : cookies)
            cookiesString += c.getName() + "=" + c.getValue() + " ";

        sc.log(filterName + " | " + servletPath + " | cookies: " +
                cookiesString);
    }

    public void destroy()
    {
        filterConfig = null;
    }
```

Figure 20-6   How to wrap a request or response (part 1 of 2)

object, but isn't available from the standard HttpServletResponse object. Then, this filter can write the cookies that are stored in the response object to the log file.

The ResponseCookiesWrapper class begins by declaring an ArrayList of Cookie objects as an instance variable. Then, the constructor for this subclass uses the super method to pass the standard response object to the super class, which is the wrapper class for the underlying response object. In addition, the constructor initializes the ArrayList of Cookie objects that's used by the custom response object.

After the constructor, this class adds a new method to the custom response object named getCookies. This method contains a single statement that returns the ArrayList of Cookie objects.

After the getCookies method, this class overrides the addCookie method of the HttpServletRequest class. To start, it adds the Cookie object parameter to the instance variable for the ArrayList of Cookie objects. Then, this method calls the getResponse method of the HttpServletResponseWrapper class to get the underlying HttpServletResponse object. Finally, this method calls the addCookie method of the underlying HttpServletResponse object so the Cookie object parameter is added to the underlying response object.

Since the overridden addCookie method passes the Cookie object parameter to the addCookie method of the underlying response object, the addCookie method of the response object will work as expected for any components down the chain. In other words, as long as the custom response object implements all the methods of a standard response object, the components that come later in the chain don't know the difference between the standard object and the custom object.

Although this example is simple, you can apply the same principles to create custom request and response objects that perform more complex tasks. If, for example, you want to compress the response that's returned to the client, you can create a custom response object to do that. However, this requires overriding the getOutputStream() and getWriter() methods of the ServletResponse object, which requires a good understanding of working with output streams.

If you want to see an example of this type of filter, Tomcat 6 provides an example within this Tomcat folder:

```
webapps\examples\WEB-INF\classes\compressionFilters
```

The classes in this folder include a wrapper class for a custom response object and a filter class that uses the custom response object. Of course, before you code a custom filter to compress your application's HTTP responses, you should check to see if your web server or servlet container provides built-in compression.

The code for a filter that uses a custom response object   Page 2

```
class ResponseCookiesWrapper extends HttpServletResponseWrapper
{
    private ArrayList<Cookie> cookies = null;

    public ResponseCookiesWrapper(HttpServletResponse response)
    {
        super(response);
        cookies = new ArrayList<Cookie>();
    }

    // provide a new method for the ResponseWrapper class
    public ArrayList<Cookie> getCookies()
    {
        return cookies;
    }

    // override the addCookie method of the HttpServletResponse object
    public void addCookie(Cookie cookie)
    {
        // store the cookie in the response wrapper object
        cookies.add(cookie);

        // store the cookie in the original response object
        HttpServletResponse httpResponse =
                (HttpServletResponse) this.getResponse();
        httpResponse.addCookie(cookie);
    }
}
}
```

Description

- The HttpServletRequestWrapper and HttpServletResponseWrapper classes implement a design pattern known as the *wrapper pattern* or the *decorator pattern*.

- The HttpServletRequestWrapper and HttpServletResponseWrapper classes contain methods that call all of the methods of the underlying interface or class. As a result, when you extend these classes, you only need to add new methods or override existing methods.

- When you extend the HttpServletResponseWrapper class, you can use the getResponse method to return the underlying HttpServletResponse object.

Figure 20-6   How to wrap a request or response (part 2 of 2)

How to use an initialization parameter

Figure 20-7 shows how you can supply an initialization parameter for a filter. Since this works much like initialization parameters for servlets, you shouldn't have much trouble understanding how this works.

To start, you add one or more initialization parameters to the web.xml file. In this figure, for example, one initialization parameter with a name of logFilename and a value of "test_init_params.log" has been added to the filter named TestInitParamsFilter. Then, you can use the getInitParameter method of the FilterConfig object to return the value of the parameter.

A filter element that includes an initialization parameter

```
<filter>
    <filter-name>TestInitParamsFilter</filter-name>
    <filter-class>filters.TestInitParamsFilter</filter-class>
    <init-param>
        <param-name>logFilename</param-name>
        <param-value>test_init_params.log</param-value>
    </init-param>
</filter>
```

The initialization parameter elements

Element	Description
`<init-param>`	Defines a name/value pair for an initialization parameter for a servlet.
`<param-name>`	Defines the name of a parameter.
`<param-value>`	Defines the value of a parameter.

Filter code that reads the initialization parameter

```
String logFilename = filterConfig.getInitParameter("logFilename");
```

Description

- To create an initialization parameter that will be available to a specific filter, you code the param-name and param-value elements within the init-param element. But first, you must identify the filter by coding the filter, filter-name, and filter-class elements.

- You can code multiple init-param elements for a single filter.

- Initialization parameters work similarly for filters and servlets. For more information about initialization parameters, refer to chapter 7.

Figure 20-7   How to use an initialization parameter

Perspective

Now that you have finished this chapter, you should (1) be able to code and deploy filters, and (2) understand when a filter might be useful. However, before you use a filter to write custom code, you should check to see if this type of functionality is already available to you from your web server or servlet container.

For example, since most web servers (including Apache 2.x) and servlet containers (including Tomcat 4.x and later) provide for compressing responses before they are returned to the client, you don't need to use filters to do that. Instead, you just need to configure your web server or servlet container so it takes advantage of the feature that you want to use. This is easier and less error-prone than coding a filter. For instance, chapter 18 shows how to turn on compression for Tomcat 6.

Summary

- You can use a *filter* to intercept an HTTP request and do some processing before or after the requested servlet or JSP is executed.

- Filters are ideal for addressing *cross-cutting concerns*, which are aspects of an application that cut across different parts of an application.

- You can *chain* two or more filters together.

- To code a filter, you must code a class that implements the Filter interface. In addition, you must map the Filter to a URL pattern by adding a filter element and a filter-mapping element to the application's web.xml file.

- The HttpServletRequestWrapper and HttpServletResponseWrapper classes implement a design pattern known as the *wrapper pattern* or the *decorator pattern*. You can use them to create custom request and response objects.

Exercise 20-1   Run the sample applications

1. Open the ch20download project in the ex_starts folder.

2. Open the code for the classes named TestFilter1, TestFilter2, and TestFilter3. Then, review this code. Note that the code for these classes is the same.

3. Open the web.xml file and review it. Note how the TestFilter1, TestFilter2, and TestFilter3 classes are mapped to different URL patterns.

4. Run the application and click on some of its links. After each click, view the data in the log file. Note when the code for the TestFilter1, TestFilter2, and TestFilter3 classes is executed.

5. Open and review the code for the LogResponseCookiesFilter class. Note how this class prints information about the cookies that are stored in the response to the log file.

6. Open the code for the LogRequestFilter class. Then, review this code. Note how this class prints information about the email cookie that's stored in the request to the log file.

7. Modify the LogRequestFilter class so it prints information about all of the cookies that are stored in the request to the log. To do that, you can use the code in the LogResponseCookiesFilter as a model. In addition, you'll need to use an if statement to make sure that the array of Cookie objects isn't null. Otherwise, a NullPointerException may be thrown when you run the application.

8. Modify the web.xml file to turn off the three TestFilter classes and to turn on the LogRequestFilter and LogResponseCookiesFilter classes. Then, restart Tomcat.

9. Run the application and click on some of its links. After each click, view the data in the log file. Make sure to click on the "View all cookies" link and the "Delete all cookies" link. Then, note the cookies that are stored in the response object.

10. Close your browser and run the application again. Then, after you register for the download, check the log file and note that the email cookie is added to the response object.

Section 5

The Music Store web site

One of the best ways to improve your web programming skills is to study web sites and applications that have been developed by others. That's why you can download a complete Music Store web site from www.murach.com. And that's why this section presents some of the key components of that web site.

In chapter 21, you'll be introduced to this web site and to the components that are common to all three of its applications. In chapters 22 and 23, you'll learn more about the Download and Cart applications that let users download songs and order albums. Finally, in chapter 24, you'll learn about the Admin application that lets the employees of the company process the orders and prepare reports.

Although the Music Store web site isn't a real web site, it illustrates the skills that you need for developing a real site. As you study it, you'll see that it requires only the skills that are presented in this book. In other words, this book presents everything you need to know for developing a complete e-commerce web site.

21

An introduction to the Music Store web site

The Music Store web site is a web site for a fictional record company that allows a user to navigate between several web applications. This chapter shows how the Music Store web site works, and it describes the common resources that are used by its web applications.

The user interface

The Music Store application uses JSPs to present the user interface of the application. Although these pages are more complex than the web pages you've seen so far in this book, they don't use any HTML tags that aren't described in chapter 4.

The Home and Catalog pages

Figure 21-1 shows two JSPs of the Music Store application: the Home page and the Catalog page. Both of these pages use the same header and footer, and both use left and right columns. The left column contains five links that let the user navigate through the site, and the right column displays a new release. If, for example, the user clicks on the "Browse through our catalog" link in the left column, the Catalog page is displayed in the middle column, but the right column remains the same.

The code for the Home page

Figure 21-2 shows the JSP code for the Home page. This code divides the page into a table that contains five main parts: the header, the left column, the middle column, the right column, and the footer. To do that, this JSP code uses include files for the header, the left column, the right column, and the footer. Here, the header.html file contains all the code for the beginning of each JSP, including the definition for the table and the first row of the table. Then, the three JSP files provide the code for the left column, the right column, and the footer. As a result, the code for the Home page only needs to include the code for the middle column of the table.

When you review this code, note that all of the include files are stored in the includes subdirectory of the root directory. Note also that the header.html file includes a "Delete Cookies" link that allows you to delete all cookies that the current browser is sending to this application. This makes it easy for you to test how cookies work with this application. However, this link is included for testing purposes and wouldn't be included in most production environments.

Although this code is more complex than the code for most of the JSPs presented in earlier chapters, it's actually simpler than the code for most real-world applications. Nevertheless, it's common for a real-world application to use nested tables to control the layout of its pages. And that's how the JSPs in the Music Store web site are coded.

Another common technique for creating a three-column layout like the one used by the Music Store application is to use the HTML Div tag with a CSS file. Although this technique has several advantages over using tables to create columns, we have used tables for this application because tables are commonly used in the real world and they are conceptually easier to understand than using the Div tag with a CSS file.

The Home page

The Catalog page

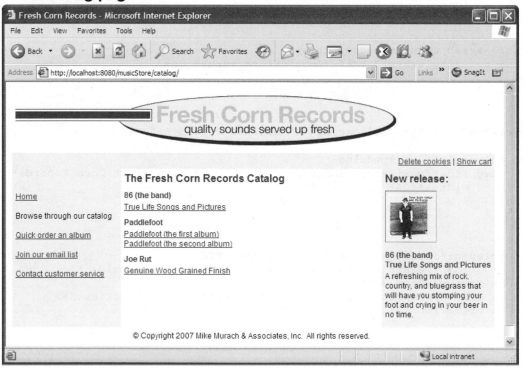

Figure 21-1   The Home and Catalog pages

The code for the Home page

```
<jsp:include page="/includes/header.html" />
<jsp:include page="/includes/column_left_home.jsp" />

<!-- start the middle column -->

    <td width="404" valign="top">
      <h1>Welcome to Fresh Corn Records!</h1>
      <p>
      Thanks for visiting. Make yourself at home. Feel free to browse through
      our musical catalog. When you do, you can listen to samples from the
      albums on our site, or you can download selected sound files and listen
      to them later. We think our catalog contains some great music, and we
      hope you like it as much as we do.
      </p>
      <p>
      If you find an album that you like, we hope that you'll use this site
      to order it. Most of the albums we carry aren't available anywhere else!
      </p>
    </td>

<!-- end the middle column -->

<jsp:include page="/includes/column_right_news.jsp" flush="true" />
<jsp:include page="/includes/footer.jsp" />
```

The code for the header.html file

```
<!DOCTYPE HTML PUBLIC "-//W3C//DTD HTML 4.01 Transitional//EN"
    "http://www.w3.org/TR/html4/loose.dtd">

<html>
<head>
    <title>Fresh Corn Records</title>
    <link rel="stylesheet" href="/musicStore/murach.css">
</head>

<body>

<table cellpadding="5" cellspacing="0" border="0" width="756">
<tr>
    <td colspan="3" cellpadding="0">
        <img src="/musicStore/images/storelogo.gif" alt="Fresh Corn Records"
            width="606" height="79">
    </td>
</tr>

<tr>
    <td colspan="3" align="right" bgcolor="#FFFFCC">
        <!-- The "Delete cookies" link is for testing and should
        be removed from a production environment -->
        <a href="/musicStore/catalog/deleteCookies">Delete cookies</a> |
        <a href="/musicStore/cart/displayCart">Show cart</a>
    </td>
</tr>

<tr>
```

Figure 21-2   The HTML for the Home page (part 1 of 2)

The code for the column_left_home.jsp file

```
<td width="160"  valign="top" bgcolor="#FFFFCC" cellpadding="0">
  <p>
    <br><br>
    Home<br><br>
    <a href="/musicStore/catalog">
        Browse through our catalog
    </a><br><br>
    <a href="/musicStore/cart">
        Quick order an album
    </a><br><br>
    <a href="/musicStore/email/join_email_list.jsp">
        Join our email list
    </a><br><br>
    <a href="/musicStore/customer_service.jsp">
        Contact customer service
    </a>
  </p>
</td>
```

The code for the column_right_news.jsp file

```
<td width="166" valign="top" bgcolor="#FFFFCC">
    <h1>New release:</h1>
    <img src="/musicStore/images/8601_cover_t.jpg" width="80" height="80"><br>
    <h4>86 (the band)<br>
    True Life Songs and Pictures</h4>
    <p>A refreshing mix of rock, country, and bluegrass that will have you
    stomping your foot and crying in your beer in no time.</p>
</td>
```

The code for the footer.jsp file

```
</tr>
<tr>
    <td colspan="3">
        <p class="copyright" align="center">&copy; Copyright ${currentYear}
        Mike Murach &amp; Associates, Inc. All rights reserved.</p>
    </td>
</tr>
</table>

</body>
</html>
```

Figure 21-2   The HTML for the Home page (part 2 of 2)

The structure

This topic shows the overall structure of the Music Store web site including the web.xml and context.xml files that are used by the web site.

The structure of the web site

Figure 21-3 shows how the pages of the Music Store web application lead to three smaller applications. In particular, it shows how you can start the Download application that's described in chapter 22, the Cart application that's described in chapter 23, and an Email application that's similar to the Email application described in chapter 14. In addition, in chapter 24, you'll learn how to start another application that's included with the Music Store web site: the Admin application.

The directory structure

Figure 21-4 shows the directory structure for the files of the Music Store web site after it is deployed to a servlet container like Tomcat. If you read chapter 2, you should understand how this directory structure works. Since the Music Store web site contains four products, the JSP files for each product are stored in a subdirectory of the catalog directory that corresponds with the product's code. Similarly, the MP3 sound files for each album are stored in a subdirectory of the sound directory that corresponds with the product's code.

The web.xml file

Figure 21-5 shows the web.xml file for the application. If you've read chapters 1-19, you shouldn't have any trouble understanding this web.xml file. However, this shows a realistic web.xml file that provides for a context initialization parameter, servlet mapping, a listener, welcome files, custom error pages, and authentication. To save space, this web.xml file doesn't show all of the servlet and servlet-mapping elements, but the same pattern that's used for the first two servlet and servlet-mapping elements is applied to all servlets within the application.

The context.xml file

Figure 21-6 shows the context.xml file for the application. If you've read chapters 14 and 17, you shouldn't have any trouble understanding this file. In short, it configures the DataSource class that's used by the connection pool, and it configures the DataSourceRealm that's used to authorize users.

The structure

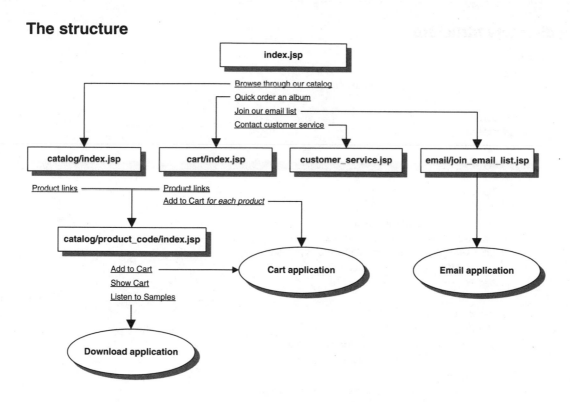

Description

- You can start the Download application by clicking on the Listen to Samples button from any Product page.
- You can start the Cart application by clicking on the Add to Cart button from any Product page or by clicking the Add to Cart link from the Index page for the Cart application.
- You can start the Email List application by clicking on the "Join our email list" link from the Home page.

Figure 21-3   The structure of the web site

The directory structure

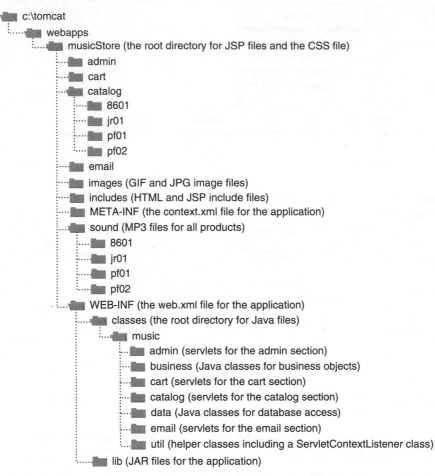

Description

- The JSP files are stored in the root directory for the application or in one of its subdirectories.

- The context.xml file is stored in the META-INF directory.

- The web.xml file is stored in the WEB-INF directory.

- The Java classes, including servlets, are stored in a subdirectory of the WEB-INF directory that corresponds with the name of the package for the class.

- The JAR files for the class libraries that are used by the application are stored in the WEB-INF\lib directory.

Figure 21-4   The directory structure of the web site

The web.xml file   **Page 1**

```xml
<?xml version="1.0" encoding="UTF-8"?>
<web-app version="2.5" xmlns="http://java.sun.com/xml/ns/javaee"
    xmlns:xsi="http://www.w3.org/2001/XMLSchema-instance"
    xsi:schemaLocation="http://java.sun.com/xml/ns/javaee
    http://java.sun.com/xml/ns/javaee/web-app_2_5.xsd">

    <!-- define a context initialization parameter -->
    <context-param>
        <param-name>custServEmail</param-name>
        <param-value>custserv@freshcornrecords.com</param-value>
    </context-param>

    <!-- servlet definitions (alphabetical by complete class name) -->
    <servlet>
        <servlet-name>DisplayInvoicesServlet</servlet-name>
        <servlet-class>music.admin.DisplayInvoicesServlet</servlet-class>
    </servlet>
    <servlet>
        <servlet-name>ProcessInvoiceServlet</servlet-name>
        <servlet-class>music.admin.ProcessInvoiceServlet</servlet-class>
    </servlet>
    <!-- the rest of the servlet elements go here -->

    <!-- servlet mappings -->
    <servlet-mapping>
        <servlet-name>DisplayInvoicesServlet</servlet-name>
        <url-pattern>/admin/displayInvoices</url-pattern>
    </servlet-mapping>
    <servlet-mapping>
        <servlet-name>ProcessInvoiceServlet</servlet-name>
        <url-pattern>/admin/processInvoice</url-pattern>
    </servlet-mapping>
    <!-- the rest of the servlet-mapping elements go here -->

    <!-- define a servlet context listener -->
    <listener>
        <listener-class>
            music.util.MusicStoreContextListener
        </listener-class>
    </listener>

    <!-- define the welcome files -->
    <welcome-file-list>
        <welcome-file>index.jsp</welcome-file>
        <welcome-file>index.html</welcome-file>
    </welcome-file-list>
```

Figure 21-5   The web.xml file (part 1 of 2)

The web.xml file

```xml
<!-- enable the custom error pages -->
<error-page>
    <error-code>404</error-code>
    <location>/error_404.jsp</location>
</error-page>
<error-page>
    <exception-type>java.lang.Throwable</exception-type>
    <location>/error_java.jsp</location>
</error-page>

<!-- define two security roles -->
<security-role>
    <description>customer service employees</description>
    <role-name>service</role-name>
</security-role>
<security-role>
    <description>programmers</description>
    <role-name>programmer</role-name>
</security-role>

<!-- restrict access to the URLs in the admin directory -->
<security-constraint>
    <web-resource-collection>
        <web-resource-name>Admin</web-resource-name>
        <url-pattern>/admin/*</url-pattern>
    </web-resource-collection>
    <!-- authorize the service and programmer roles -->
    <auth-constraint>
        <role-name>service</role-name>
        <role-name>programmer</role-name>
    </auth-constraint>
</security-constraint>

<!-- use form-based authentication to provide access -->
<login-config>
  <auth-method>FORM</auth-method>
  <form-login-config>
    <form-login-page>/login.jsp</form-login-page>
    <form-error-page>/login_error.jsp</form-error-page>
  </form-login-config>
</login-config>

</web-app>
```

Figure 21-5   The web.xml file (part 2 of 2)

The context.xml file

```xml
<?xml version="1.0" encoding="UTF-8"?>
<Context path="/musicStore">

    <Resource name="jdbc/musicDB" auth="Container"
        maxActive="100" maxIdle="30" maxWait="10000"
        username="root" password="sesame"
        driverClassName="com.mysql.jdbc.Driver"
        url="jdbc:mysql://localhost:3306/music?autoReconnect=true"
        logAbandoned="true" removeAbandoned="true"
        removeAbandonedTimeout="60" type="javax.sql.DataSource" />

    <Realm className="org.apache.catalina.realm.DataSourceRealm" debug="99"
        dataSourceName="jdbc/musicDB" localDataSource="true"
        userTable="UserPass" userNameCol="Username" userCredCol="Password"
        userRoleTable="UserRole" roleNameCol="Rolename" />

</Context>
```

Figure 21-6   The context.xml file

The business layer

The business objects of the Music Store web site are stored in the music.business package. All of these business objects follow the rules for coding a JavaBean.

The class diagrams

Figure 21-7 shows the class diagrams for the six business objects for the Music Store web application. These diagrams show that the User class that's used by the Music Store web site is more complex than the User class that was used earlier in this book. However, the same concepts still apply to this object.

In addition, these class diagrams show that a business object can contain another business object as an instance variable. For example, the Download and Invoice objects can set and get a User object. Similarly, the LineItem object can get and set a Product object. And the Invoice and Cart items can get and set an ArrayList object that can contain zero or more LineItem objects.

The Product class

Figure 21-8 shows the code for the Product class that implements the Product diagram in the last figure. Although this class is one of the simpler classes used by the Music Store web site, all of the other classes have the same structure. That is, they all provide private instance variables, get and set methods for each instance variable, and one zero-argument constructor. In other words, they all follow the rules for creating a JavaBean.

In addition, a business class may provide other convenience methods that do some additional work beyond getting and setting instance variables. With the Product class, for example, the getArtistName and getAlbumName methods parse the description instance variable to return useful information. Similarly, the getImageURL and getProductType methods provide more information about the product. Finally, the getPriceCurrencyFormat method applies the currency format to the price instance variable.

If you want to view the code for the other business classes, you can open them in an IDE or a text editor. In fact, due to the highlighting and color-coding that's provided by any text editor that's designed for working with Java, you may find it easier to read these classes when they're opened in a text editor. If not, you can print the code for the classes that you want to review.

The class diagrams for the business objects

User

-firstName : String
-lastName : String
-emailAddress : String
-companyName : String
-address1 : String
-address2 : String
-city : String
-state : String
-zip : String
-country : String
-creditCardType : String
-creditCardNumber : String
-creditCardExpirationDate : String

+User()
+setFirstName(f : String)
+getFirstName() : String
+setLastName(l : String)
+getLastName() : String
+setEmailAddress(e : String)
+getEmailAddress() : String
+setCompanyName(c : String)
+getCompanyName() : String
+setAddress1(a : String)
+getAddress1() : String
+setAddress2(a : String)
+getAddress2() : String
+getAddressHTMLFormat() : String
+setCity(c : String)
+getCity() : String
+setState(s : String)
+getState() : String
+setZip(z : String)
+getZip() : String
+setCountry(c : String)
+getCountry() : String
+setCreditCardType(c : String)
+getCreditCardType() : String
+setCreditCardNumber(n : String)
+getCreditCardNumber() : String
+setCreditCardExpirationDate(d : String)
+getCreditCardExpirationDate() : String

Download

-user : User
-downloadDate: Date
-productCode : String

+Download()
+setUser(user : User)
+getUser() : User
+setDownloadDate(date : Date)
+getDownloadDate() : Date
+setProductCode(code : String)
+getProductCode() : String

Invoice

-user : User
-lineItems : ArrayList<LineItem>
-invoiceDate : Date
-invoiceNumber : int

+Invoice()
+setUser(user : User)
+getUser() : User
+setLineItems(
   items : ArrayList<LineItem>)
+getLineItems() : ArrayList<LineItem>
+setInvoiceDate(date : Date)
+getInvoiceDate() : Date
+getInvoiceDateDefaultFormat() : Date
+setInvoiceNumber(num : int)
+getInvoiceNumber() : int
+getInvoiceTotal() : double
+getInvoiceTotalCurrencyFormat() : String

Product

-code : String
-description: String
-price : double

+Product()
+seCode(c: String)
+getCode() : String
+setDescription(d : String)
+getDescription() : String
+getArtistName() : String
+getAlbumName() : String
+setPrice(p : double)
+getPrice() : double
+getPriceCurrencyFormat() : String
+getImageURL() : String
+getProductType() : String

Cart

-items : ArrayList<LineItem>

+Cart()
+setItems(
   lineItems: ArrayList<LineItem>)
+getItems() : ArrayList<LineItem>
+addItem(item : LineItem)
+removeItem(item : LineItem)

LineItem

-item : Product
-quantity: int

+LineItem()
+setProduct(product: Product)
+getProduct() : Product
+setQuantity(qty : int)
+getQuantity() : int
+getTotal() : double
+getTotalCurrencyFormat() : String

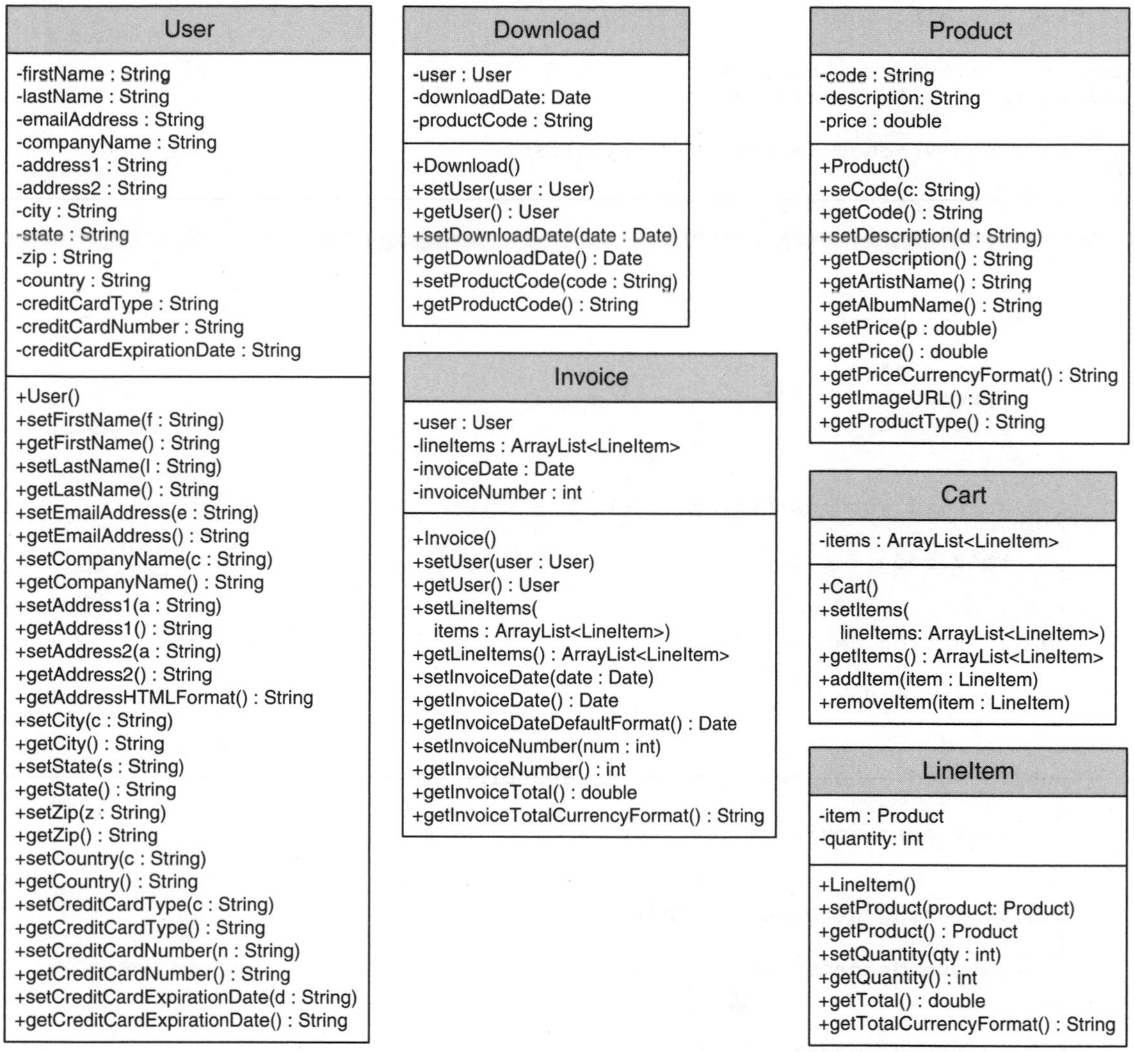

Description

- These business classes are stored in the music.business package. These classes are all coded as JavaBeans (see chapter 9).
- Some of these business objects can get and set other business objects.

Figure 21-7   The class diagrams for the business objects

The Product class

```java
package music.business;

import java.text.NumberFormat;
import java.io.Serializable;

public class Product implements Serializable
{
    private String code;
    private String description;
    private double price;

    public Product()
    {
        code = "";
        description = "";
        price = 0;
    }

    public void setCode(String code)
    {
        this.code = code;
    }

    public String getCode()
    {
        return code;
    }

    public void setDescription(String description)
    {
        this.description = description;
    }

    public String getDescription()
    {
        return description;
    }

    public String getArtistName()
    {
        String artistName =
            description.substring(0, description.indexOf(" - "));
        return artistName;
    }

    public String getAlbumName()
    {
        String albumName =
            description.substring(description.indexOf(" - ") + 3);
        return albumName;
    }
```

Figure 21-8   The Product class (part 1 of 2)

The Product class   **Page 2**

```java
    public void setPrice(double price)
    {
        this.price = price;
    }

    public double getPrice()
    {
        return price;
    }

    public String getPriceCurrencyFormat()
    {
        NumberFormat currency = NumberFormat.getCurrencyInstance();
        return currency.format(price);
    }

    public String getImageURL()
    {
        String imageURL = "/musicStore/images/" + code + "_cover.jpg";
        return imageURL;
    }

    public String getProductType()
    {
        return "Audio CD";
    }
}
```

Description

- Like all the business classes for this application, the Product class is defined by a class diagram in figure 21-7 and it is coded as a JavaBean.

Figure 21-8   The Product class (part 2 of 2)

The database

The Music Store web site uses a MySQL database named music to store the data for the web site in its tables. For more information about working with MySQL, you can refer to chapter 13.

The database diagram

Figure 21-9 shows the database diagram for the Music Store database. This diagram shows that this database stores the bulk of its data in five tables that correspond to five of the business objects. The asterisk used in this diagram shows that one row in the User table can correspond with zero or more rows in the Download or Invoice table. Similarly, one row in the Invoice table can correspond with one or more rows in the LineItem table. However, a row in the Download table and a row in the LineItem table can have one and only one row in the Product table.

In addition to these five tables, the Music Store database provides two more tables that are used to store the usernames, passwords, and roles. These tables are used by the Admin application that's described in chapter 24.

The SQL script for the database

Figure 21-10 shows the SQL script that you can use to create the Music Store database. This script creates a database named music, and it creates the seven tables in the database diagram. To do that, it uses seven CREATE TABLE statements that identify the column names, data types, primary keys, and so on. In addition, this script uses three INSERT INTO statements to insert data into the Product, UserPass, and UserRole tables. If you want to use your own usernames and passwords for the Admin application, you can modify the INSERT INTO statements for the UserPass and UserRole tables before you run this script.

The database diagram

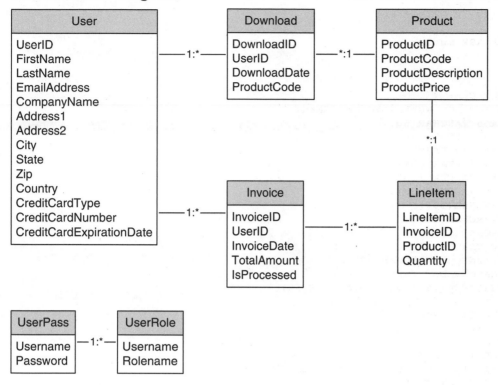

Description

- This database diagram shows the tables that are used to store the data for the Music Store web site.

- The User, Invoice, LineItem, Download, and Product tables correspond to the business classes that are defined in figure 21-7.

- The UserPass and UserRole tables are used to store the usernames and passwords that can be used to access the Admin application that's shown in chapter 24.

Figure 21-9   The database diagram

The SQL script for the database

```sql
DROP DATABASE IF EXISTS music;

CREATE DATABASE music;

USE music;

CREATE TABLE User (
    UserID INT NOT NULL AUTO_INCREMENT,
    FirstName VARCHAR(50),
    LastName VARCHAR(50),
    EmailAddress VARCHAR(50),
    CompanyName VARCHAR(50),
    Address1 VARCHAR(50),
    Address2 VARCHAR(50),
    City VARCHAR(50),
    State VARCHAR(50),
    Zip VARCHAR(50),
    Country VARCHAR(50),
    CreditCardType VARCHAR(50),
    CreditCardNumber VARCHAR(50),
    CreditCardExpirationDate VARCHAR(50),

    PRIMARY KEY (UserID)
);

CREATE TABLE Invoice(
    InvoiceID INT NOT NULL AUTO_INCREMENT,
    UserID INT NOT NULL,
    InvoiceDate DATETIME NOT NULL DEFAULT '0000-00-00 00:00:00',
    TotalAmount FLOAT NOT NULL DEFAULT '0',
    IsProcessed enum('y','n') DEFAULT NULL,

    PRIMARY KEY (InvoiceID),
    FOREIGN KEY (UserID) REFERENCES User (UserID)
);

CREATE TABLE LineItem(
    LineItemID INT NOT NULL AUTO_INCREMENT,
    InvoiceID INT NOT NULL DEFAULT '0',
    ProductID INT NOT NULL DEFAULT '0',
    Quantity INT NOT NULL DEFAULT '0',

    PRIMARY KEY (LineItemID),
    FOREIGN KEY (InvoiceID) REFERENCES Invoice (InvoiceID)
);

CREATE TABLE Product(
    ProductID INT NOT NULL AUTO_INCREMENT,
    ProductCode VARCHAR(10) NOT NULL DEFAULT '',
    ProductDescription VARCHAR(100) NOT NULL DEFAULT '',
    ProductPrice DECIMAL(7,2) NOT NULL DEFAULT '0.00',

    PRIMARY KEY (ProductID)
);
```

Figure 21-10   The SQL script for the database (part 1 of 2)

The SQL script for the database   **Page 2**

```
INSERT INTO Product VALUES
    ('1', '8601', '86 (the band) - True Life Songs and Pictures', '14.95'),
    ('2', 'pf01', 'Paddlefoot - The first CD', '12.95'),
    ('3', 'pf02', 'Paddlefoot - The second CD', '14.95'),
    ('4', 'jr01', 'Joe Rut - Genuine Wood Grained Finish', '14.95');

CREATE TABLE Download (
    DownloadID INT NOT NULL AUTO_INCREMENT,
    UserID INT NOT NULL,
    DownloadDate DATETIME NOT NULL,
    ProductCode VARCHAR(10)  NOT NULL,

    PRIMARY KEY (DownloadID),
    FOREIGN KEY (UserID) REFERENCES User (UserID)
);

CREATE TABLE UserPass (
  Username varchar(15) NOT NULL PRIMARY KEY,
  Password varchar(15) NOT NULL
);

INSERT INTO UserPass VALUES ('andrea', 'sesame'),
                            ('joel', 'sesame'),
                            ('anne', 'sesame');

CREATE TABLE UserRole (
  Username VARCHAR(15) NOT NULL,
  Rolename VARCHAR(15) NOT NULL,

  PRIMARY KEY (Username, Rolename)
);

INSERT INTO UserRole VALUES ('andrea', 'service'),
                            ('andrea', 'programmer'),
                            ('joel', 'programmer');
```

Description

- This SQL script creates the tables needed by the Music Store application. You can download this SQL script from www.murach.com, and appendix A shows how to execute it to create the tables needed by the Music Store application.

Figure 21-10   The SQL script for the database (part 2 of 2)

The data layer

The data access classes that let the Music Store web site access the database are stored in the music.data package. In addition, this package includes a ConnectionPool class and a DBUtil class that are used by the data access classes. For more information about coding these classes, you can refer to chapter 14.

The class diagrams

Figure 21-11 shows the class diagrams for five data access classes. These classes use static methods to read and write business objects to a database. As a result, they don't contain instance variables or constructors.

Most of the methods that read a business object from a database accept a single argument that uniquely identifies the business object. For example, the selectProduct method of the ProductDB class can read a Product object from a database using either a string for the product code or an int value for the product ID.

Most of the methods that write a business object to a database accept the business object as an argument. For example, the insert method of the UserDB class accepts a User object as a parameter. Then, most of these methods return an int value that indicates whether the write operation was successful. Here, a value of 1 or more typically indicates that 1 or more rows were successfully written, and a value of 0 or less indicates that the write operation wasn't successful.

Class diagrams for the data access classes

ProductDB
+selectProduct(productCode : String) : Product
+selectProduct(productID: int) : Product
+selectProductID(product: Product) : int
+selectProducts() : ArrayList<Product>

UserDB
+insert(user : User) : int
+update(user : User) : int
+emailExists(emailAddress : String) : boolean
+selectUserID(user : User) : int
+selectUser(emailAddress : String) : User

InvoiceDB
+insert(invoice : Invoice) : int
+selectUnprocessedInvoices() : ArrayList<Invoice>
+updateInvoiceIsProcessed(invoiceNumber : int) : int

LineItemDB
+insert(invoiceID: int, lineItem : LineItem) : int
+selectLineItems(invoiceID : int) : ArrayList<LineItem>

DownloadDB
+insert(download : Download) : int

Description

- These data access classes are stored in the music.data package. You can use them to read business objects from the database and write them to the database.

- The Admin application uses another data access class that isn't shown here: the ReportDB class. You can learn about this class in chapter 24.

Figure 21-11   The class diagrams for the data access classes

The ProductDB class

Figure 21-12 shows the code for the ProductDB class. This code implements the ProductDB class diagram in the previous figure. If you read chapter 14, you shouldn't have much trouble understanding this code.

And if you understand this code, you shouldn't have much trouble understanding how the other classes in the data access layer work since they all follow the same pattern. To view the code for the other data access classes, you can open them in an IDE or a text editor. They're all stored in the music.data package.

The ProductDB class   **Page 1**

```java
package music.data;

import java.sql.*;
import java.util.*;

import music.business.*;

public class ProductDB
{
    public static Product selectProduct(String productCode)
    {
        ConnectionPool pool = ConnectionPool.getInstance();
        Connection connection = pool.getConnection();
        PreparedStatement ps = null;
        ResultSet rs = null;

        String query = "SELECT * FROM Product " +
                "WHERE ProductCode = ?";
        try
        {
            ps = connection.prepareStatement(query);
            ps.setString(1, productCode);
            rs = ps.executeQuery();
            if (rs.next())
            {
                Product p = new Product();
                p.setCode(rs.getString("ProductCode"));
                p.setDescription(rs.getString("ProductDescription"));
                p.setPrice(rs.getDouble("ProductPrice"));
                return p;
            }
            else
            {
                return null;
            }
        }
        catch(SQLException e)
        {
            e.printStackTrace();
            return null;
        }
        finally
        {
            DBUtil.closeResultSet(rs);
            DBUtil.closePreparedStatement(ps);
            pool.freeConnection(connection);
        }
    }
}
```

Figure 21-12   The ProductDB class (part 1 of 3)

The ProductDB class

```java
//This method will return 0 if productID isn't found.
public static int selectProductID(Product product)
{
    ConnectionPool pool = ConnectionPool.getInstance();
    Connection connection = pool.getConnection();
    PreparedStatement ps = null;
    ResultSet rs = null;

    String query = "SELECT ProductID FROM Product " +
            "WHERE ProductCode = ?";
    try
    {
        ps = connection.prepareStatement(query);
        ps.setString(1, product.getCode());
        rs = ps.executeQuery();
        rs.next();
        int productID = rs.getInt("ProductID");
        return productID;
    }
    catch(SQLException e)
    {
        e.printStackTrace();
        return 0;
    }
    finally
    {
        DBUtil.closeResultSet(rs);
        DBUtil.closePreparedStatement(ps);
        pool.freeConnection(connection);
    }
}

//This method returns null if a product isn't found.
public static Product selectProduct(int productID)
{
    ConnectionPool pool = ConnectionPool.getInstance();
    Connection connection = pool.getConnection();
    PreparedStatement ps = null;
    ResultSet rs = null;

    String query = "SELECT * FROM Product " +
            "WHERE ProductID = ?";
    try
    {
        ps = connection.prepareStatement(query);
        ps.setInt(1, productID);
        rs = ps.executeQuery();
        if (rs.next())
        {
            Product p = new Product();
            p.setCode(rs.getString("ProductCode"));
            p.setDescription(rs.getString("ProductDescription"));
            p.setPrice(rs.getDouble("ProductPrice"));
            return p;
        }
```

Figure 21-12   The ProductDB class (part 2 of 3)

The ProductDB class

```java
                else
                {
                    return null;
                }
            }
            catch(SQLException e)
            {
                e.printStackTrace();
                return null;
            }
            finally
            {
                DBUtil.closeResultSet(rs);
                DBUtil.closePreparedStatement(ps);
                pool.freeConnection(connection);
            }
        }

        //This method returns null if a product isn't found.
        public static ArrayList<Product> selectProducts()
        {
            ConnectionPool pool = ConnectionPool.getInstance();
            Connection connection = pool.getConnection();
            PreparedStatement ps = null;
            ResultSet rs = null;

            String query = "SELECT * FROM Product";
            try
            {
                ps = connection.prepareStatement(query);
                rs = ps.executeQuery();
                ArrayList<Product> products = new ArrayList<Product>();
                while (rs.next())
                {
                    Product p = new Product();
                    p.setCode(rs.getString("ProductCode"));
                    p.setDescription(rs.getString("ProductDescription"));
                    p.setPrice(rs.getDouble("ProductPrice"));
                    products.add(p);
                }
                return products;
            }
            catch(SQLException e)
            {
                e.printStackTrace();
                return null;
            }
            finally
            {
                DBUtil.closeResultSet(rs);
                DBUtil.closePreparedStatement(ps);
                pool.freeConnection(connection);
            }
        }
    }
```

Figure 21-12   The ProductDB class (part 3 of 3)

Perspective

Once you understand the components of the Music Store web site that are described in this chapter, you're ready to learn more about the Download, Cart, and Admin applications that are presented in the next three chapters. If you had trouble understanding the components in this chapter, though, you may want to review some of the earlier chapters in this book.

To get the most from the Music Store web site, you should install it on your computer as described in appendix A. Then, you can review the figures in any of the chapters in this section as you run the related pages on your computer. If at any time you want to review the code for a component, you can find the component in its directory, open it, and review it.

22

The Download application

Users browsing through the Music Store web site can download and listen to the sound files that are available. But first, they must use the Download application to register with the web site by providing a name and email address. This chapter describes how this Download application works.

The Download application

The Download application presented in this topic is an expanded version of the Download application presented in chapter 8. This version uses a more sophisticated user interface, and it writes a record for each download to the database for the Music Store web site.

The user interface

Figure 22-1 shows the web pages that make up the user interface of the Download application. The Product page contains a "Listen to Samples" link that the user can click on to start the Download application. If the user has already registered with this web site, the Download application displays a Sound page that lets the user download MP3 files by clicking on links. Otherwise, the Download application displays the Register page. Then, the user must register by entering a name and email address.

The structure

Figure 22-2 shows how the JSPs and servlets that are used by the Download application are structured and organized. This diagram shows that the servlet files for the Download application are stored in the music.catalog package. In addition, it shows that most servlets forward the request and response to a corresponding JSP. However, if a user has already registered for downloads, the CheckUserServlet class skips the RegisterUserServlet and the Register page by calling the WriteDownloadServlet class.

A Product page

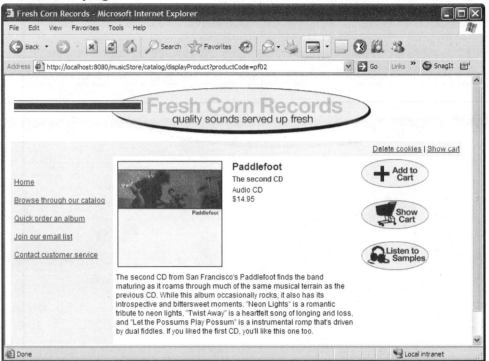

The Register page

Figure 22-1   The user interface (part 1 of 2)

A Sound page

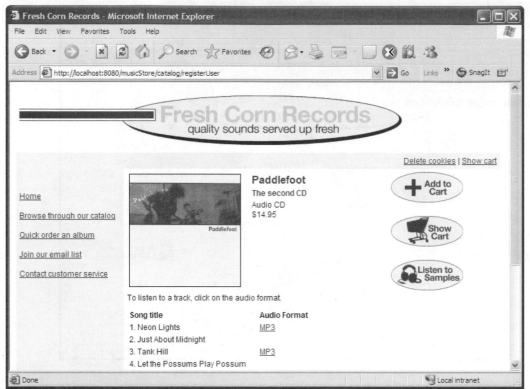

Description

- The Register page will only be displayed if the user hasn't already registered with the web site. A user can register with the web site by using this Register page or by using the Cart application described in the next chapter to make a purchase. Then, the user's browser will send a cookie to the web site that indicates that the user has registered.

- To test the Register page, you can click on the "Delete cookies" link that's displayed at the top of the page to remove cookies from the user's browser. After you do that, you can display the Register page by closing your web browser and running this application again.

Figure 22-1   The user interface (part 2 of 2)

The structure of the Download application

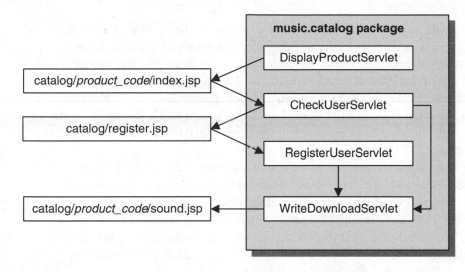

Description

- The JSPs for this application are stored in the musicStore\catalog directory or one of its subdirectories.

- The servlet classes for this application are stored in the music.catalog package.

- The DisplayProductServlet reads a Product object from the database, stores the Product object as a session attribute, and forwards the request to the appropriate Product page.

- The CheckUserServlet checks to see if the user has registered. If so, it proceeds to the WriteDownloadServlet. Otherwise, it displays the Register page.

- The RegisterUserServlet gets the data entered in the Register page, creates a User object from that data, writes the User object to the database, stores the User object as a session attribute, and returns a cookie to the user's browser so the user won't have to register again.

- The WriteDownloadServlet creates a Download object, writes the Download object to the database, and returns the appropriate Sound page to the user.

Figure 22-2   The structure of the Download application

The code

In this application, the Product and Sound pages are JSPs. Since the code for these pages is easy to understand, figures 22-3 through 22-6 don't show them. However, figure 22-3 shows the table that's used to display the product data at the top of the Product and Sound pages. This data is stored as a session attribute by the DisplayProductServlet. In addition, figure 22-3 shows the link on the Product page that calls the CheckUserServlet class that's shown in figure 22-4. This link contains an image tag that specifies a GIF file for the "Listen to Samples" image.

If you study figures 22-5 and 22-6, you can see the code for the Register page and the RegisterUserServlet class. Then, in figure 22-7, you can see that the WriteDownloadServlet creates a Download object and uses the DownloadDB class to write the Download object to the database. This writes a row to the Download table that includes a reference to a row in the User table, the current date, and a reference to a row in the Product table. As a result, the database keeps track of every download that a user makes.

Since the code for the business objects and data access classes was described in chapter 21, this chapter doesn't show any of those classes. In addition, this chapter doesn't show any of the utility classes stored in the music.util package. However, these classes are included in the download that's available for this book. So once you've installed the Music Store web site, you can view these files by opening them.

The DisplayProductServlet class

```
package music.catalog;

import java.io.*;
import javax.servlet.*;
import javax.servlet.http.*;

import music.business.*;
import music.data.*;

public class DisplayProductServlet extends HttpServlet
{
    public void doGet(HttpServletRequest request,
                      HttpServletResponse response)
                      throws ServletException, IOException
    {
        // get request parameters
        String productCode = request.getParameter("productCode");

        // update the Model
        Product product = ProductDB.selectProduct(productCode);
        HttpSession session = request.getSession();
        session.setAttribute("product", product);

        // forward to the View
        String url = "/catalog/" + productCode + "/index.jsp";
        RequestDispatcher dispatcher =
            getServletContext().getRequestDispatcher(url);
        dispatcher.forward(request, response);
    }
}
```

The Product page table that displays product information

```
<table border="0">
<tr>
  <td width="179">
    <img src="${product.imageURL}" width="175" height="175">
  </td>
  <td width="5">
  </td>
  <td width="187" valign="top">
    <h2>${product.artistName}</h2>
    <h3>${product.albumName}</h3>
    <p>${product.productType}<br>
    ${product.priceCurrencyFormat}</p>
  </td>
</tr>
</table>
```

The Product page link that calls the CheckUserServlet

```
<a href="<c:url value='/catalog/checkUser'/>">
    <img src="/musicStore/images/listen.gif" width="113" height="47">
</a>
```

Figure 22-3   The code for the DisplayProductServlet class

The CheckUserServlet class

```
package music.catalog;

import java.io.*;
import javax.servlet.*;
import javax.servlet.http.*;

import music.business.*;
import music.data.*;
import music.util.*;

public class CheckUserServlet extends HttpServlet
{
    public void doGet(HttpServletRequest request,
            HttpServletResponse response)
            throws IOException, ServletException
    {
        HttpSession session = request.getSession();
        User user = (User) session.getAttribute("user");
        String url = "";

        // if the User object doesn't exist, check for the email cookie
        if (user == null)
        {
            Cookie[] cookies = request.getCookies();
            String emailAddress =
                    CookieUtil.getCookieValue(cookies, "emailCookie");

            // if the email cookie doesn't exist, go to the registration page
            if (emailAddress == null || emailAddress.equals(""))
            {
                url = "/catalog/register.jsp";
            }

            // if the email cookie does exist, create the User object
            // from the email cookie and skip the registration page
            else
            {
                user = UserDB.selectUser(emailAddress);
                session.setAttribute("user", user);
                url = "/catalog/writeDownload";
            }
        }

        // if the User object exists, skip the registration page
        else
        {
            url = "/catalog/writeDownload";
        }

        RequestDispatcher dispatcher =
            getServletContext().getRequestDispatcher(url);
        dispatcher.forward(request, response);
    }
}
```

Figure 22-4   The code for the CheckUserServlet class

The Register page

```
<jsp:include page="/includes/header.html" />
<jsp:include page="/includes/column_left_all.jsp" />

<!-- start the middle column -->

<td>

  <h1>Download registration</h1>

  <p>Before you can download and listen to these sound files,
  you must register with us by entering your name and email
  address below.</p>

  <!-- Import the core JSTL library -->
  <%@ taglib prefix="c" uri="http://java.sun.com/jsp/jstl/core" %>

  <!-- Use the JSTL url tag to encode the URL -->
  <form action="<c:url value='/catalog/registerUser'/>"
        method="post">
    <table cellpadding="5" border="0">
      <tr>
        <td align="right"><p>First name:</td>
        <td><input type="text" name="firstName"></td>
      </tr>
      <tr>
        <td align="right"><p>Last name:</td>
        <td><input type="text" name="lastName"></td>
      </tr>
      <tr>
        <td align="right"><p>Email address:</td>
        <td><input type="text" name="emailAddress"></td>
      </tr>
      <tr>
        <td></td>
        <td><input type="button" value="Submit"
                   onClick="validate(this.form)"></td>
      </tr>
    </table>
  </form>

</td>

<!-- end the middle column -->

<jsp:include page="/includes/column_right_buttons.jsp" />
<jsp:include page="/footer.jsp" />
```

Note

- This JSP uses JavaScript code that isn't shown in this figure to validate the entries made by the user.

Figure 22-5   The register.jsp file

The RegisterUserServlet class

```
package music.catalog;

import java.io.*;
import javax.servlet.*;
import javax.servlet.http.*;

import music.business.*;
import music.data.*;

public class RegisterUserServlet extends HttpServlet
{
    public void doPost(HttpServletRequest request,
            HttpServletResponse response)
            throws IOException, ServletException
    {
        HttpSession session = request.getSession();

        String firstName = request.getParameter("firstName");
        String lastName = request.getParameter("lastName");
        String emailAddress = request.getParameter("emailAddress");

        User user = new User();
        user.setFirstName(firstName);
        user.setLastName(lastName);
        user.setEmailAddress(emailAddress);

        if (UserDB.emailExists(emailAddress))
            UserDB.update(user);
        else
            UserDB.insert(user);

        session.setAttribute("user", user);

        Cookie emailCookie = new Cookie("emailCookie", emailAddress);
        emailCookie.setMaxAge(60*60*24*365*2);
        emailCookie.setPath("/");
        response.addCookie(emailCookie);

        String url = "/catalog/writeDownload";
        RequestDispatcher dispatcher =
            getServletContext().getRequestDispatcher(url);
        dispatcher.forward(request, response);
    }
}
```

Figure 22-6   The code for the RegisterUserServlet class

The WriteDownloadServlet class

```
package music.catalog;

import java.io.*;
import javax.servlet.*;
import javax.servlet.http.*;

import music.business.*;
import music.data.*;

public class WriteDownloadServlet extends HttpServlet
{
    public void doPost(HttpServletRequest request,
                       HttpServletResponse response)
                  throws IOException, ServletException
    {
        HttpSession session = request.getSession();

        User user = (User) session.getAttribute("user");
        Product product = (Product) session.getAttribute("product");
        Download download = new Download();
        download.setUser(user);
        download.setProductCode(product.getCode());

        DownloadDB.insert(download);

        String url = "/catalog/" + product.getCode() + "/sound.jsp";
        RequestDispatcher dispatcher =
            getServletContext().getRequestDispatcher(url);
        dispatcher.forward(request, response);
    }

    public void doGet(HttpServletRequest request,
            HttpServletResponse response)
            throws IOException, ServletException
    {
        doPost(request, response);
    }
}
```

Note

- The constructor for the Download class sets the download date to the current date. As a result, it isn't necessary to use the setDownloadDate method to set the download date in this servlet.

Figure 22-7   The code for the WriteDownloadServlet class

Perspective

If you study the code for this application, you may notice a couple of minor flaws. For example, since the Sound pages are JSPs, it's possible for a user to access these pages without registering by entering a URL that points directly to the page. However, to do this, the user would have to know the URL for the sound page. As a result, it's unlikely that a first time user would be able to guess the URL. Besides, since the worst case scenario is that a user will be able to download a sound file without registering, this isn't a critical security issue. To solve this problem, though, you can use a security constraint as shown in chapter 17.

In addition, you may notice that the record that's written to the database for each download isn't as complete as it could be. Specifically, the Download object contains only a User object, a date, and a product code. In a more complete application, this object could also contain the name and type of the sound file for each download.

Despite these flaws, this Download application is adequate for instructional purposes. In particular, you can see how the Download application writes a record to the database. Then, in chapter 24, you'll see how you can create an administrative application that lets selected users view reports that summarize this data.

23

The Cart application

A user browsing through the Music Store web site can add any album on the site to a virtual shopping cart. Then, the user can use the Cart application to buy the items in the shopping cart. This chapter describes how this e-commerce application works.

The Cart application

Although some aspects of the Cart application have been simplified for instructional purposes, this application introduces all of the elements of a real e-commerce application. As a result, if you need to build an e-commerce site, you can use the code that's presented in this book as a starting point.

The user interface

Figure 23-1 presents some of the key pages of the Cart application. The first two pages provide links that start the Cart application. For example, the Product page provides a link that surrounds the "Add to Cart" graphic. This link adds the current product to the cart and displays the cart. In addition, the Product page contains a link that surrounds the "Show Cart" graphic. This link displays the items that are already in the cart. In contrast, the Quick Order page for the Cart application shows a list of the four albums available from the site. Each of these albums contains an "Add To Cart" link. Like the "Add to Cart" graphic, this link adds the related product to the cart and displays the cart.

The Cart page displays the items that have been added to the cart. To change the quantity for an item, the user can enter a new quantity and click on the Update button. To remove an item, the user can click on the Remove button. To add more items to the cart, the user can select the Continue Shopping button, which returns the user to the Quick Order page. To proceed to checkout, the user can click on the Checkout button. When the user clicks on this button, the application uses a secure connection for the rest of the pages in the Cart application.

If the user has a valid cookie and a record for the user exists in the database, the Cart application skips the User page and proceeds directly to the Invoice page. Otherwise, the Cart application displays the User page.

No matter how the user gets to the Invoice page, the user can verify that the shipping and order data is correct. To modify the shipping data, the user can select the Edit Address button to display the User page again. Then, the application displays the User page with the current data in its text boxes so the user can modify the current data.

When the user clicks on the Continue button from the Invoice page, the application displays the Credit Card page. On this page, the user selects a payment type, enters a credit card number, and chooses an expiration date. To submit the order, the user can click on the Submit Order button. This should display another page that informs the user that the order was successful.

A Product page

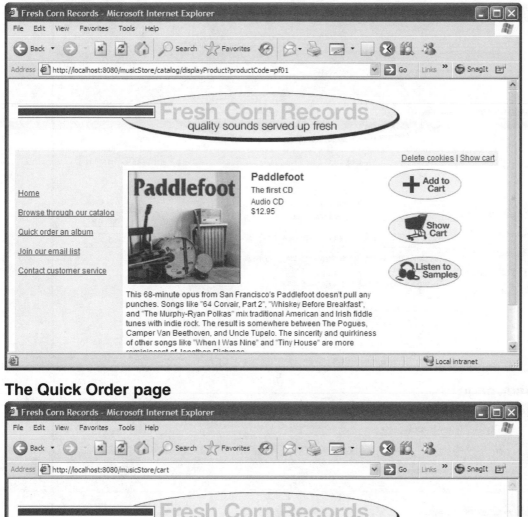

The Quick Order page

Figure 23-1   The user interface (part 1 of 3)

The Cart page

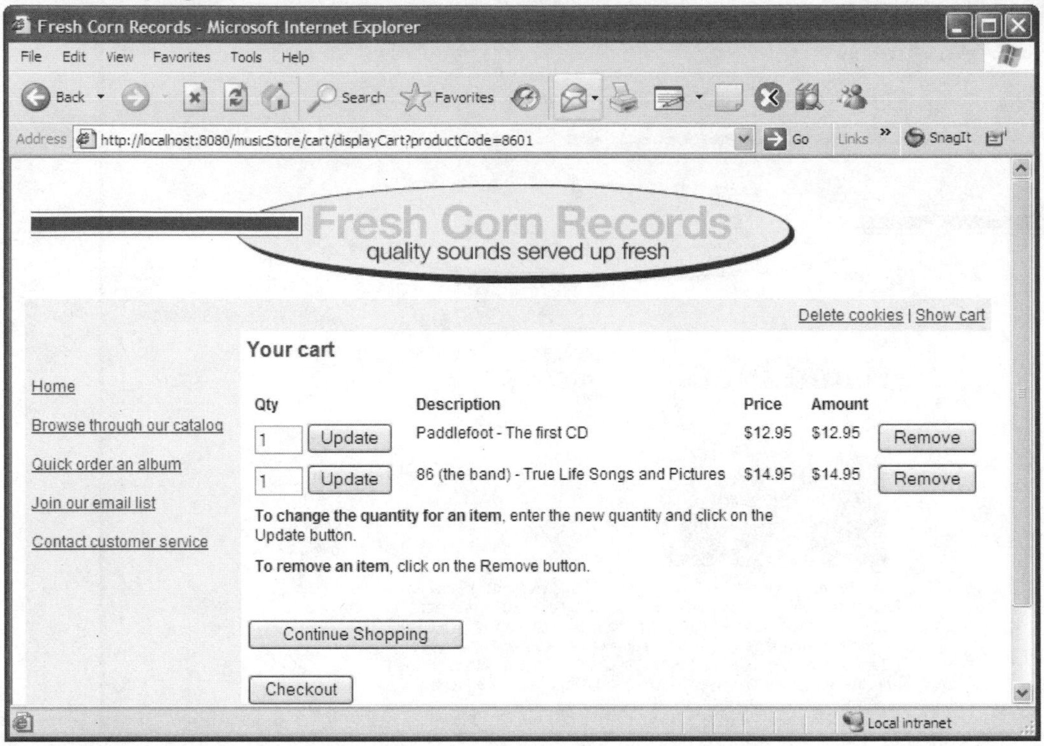

The User page

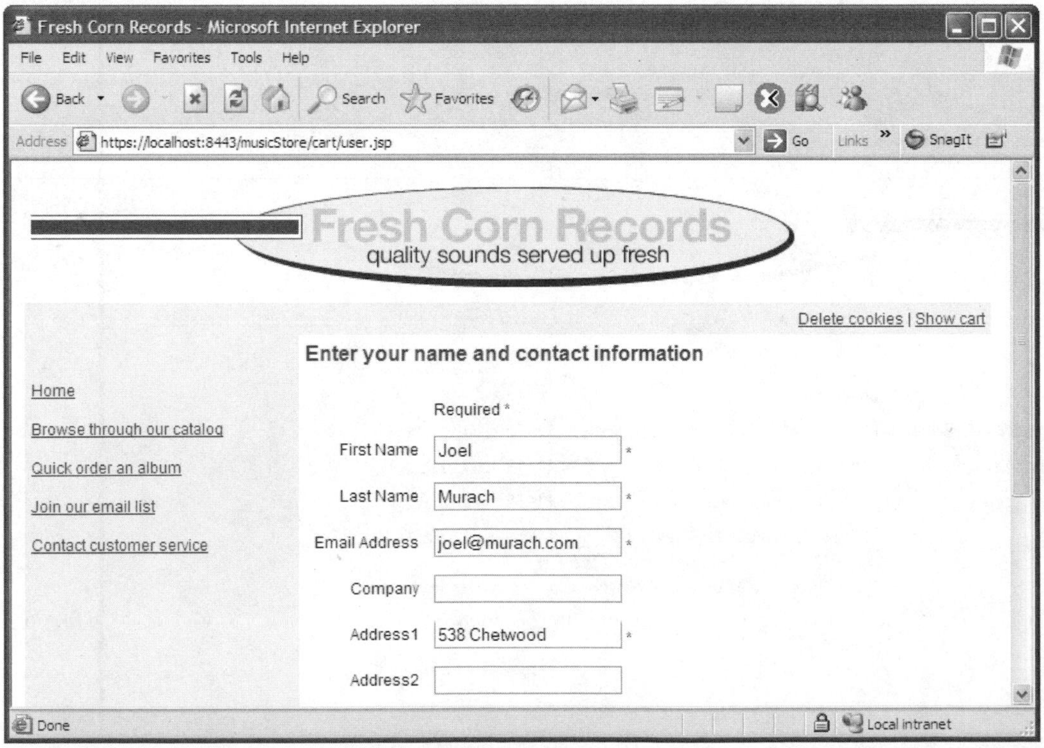

Figure 23-1 The user interface (part 2 of 3)

The Invoice page

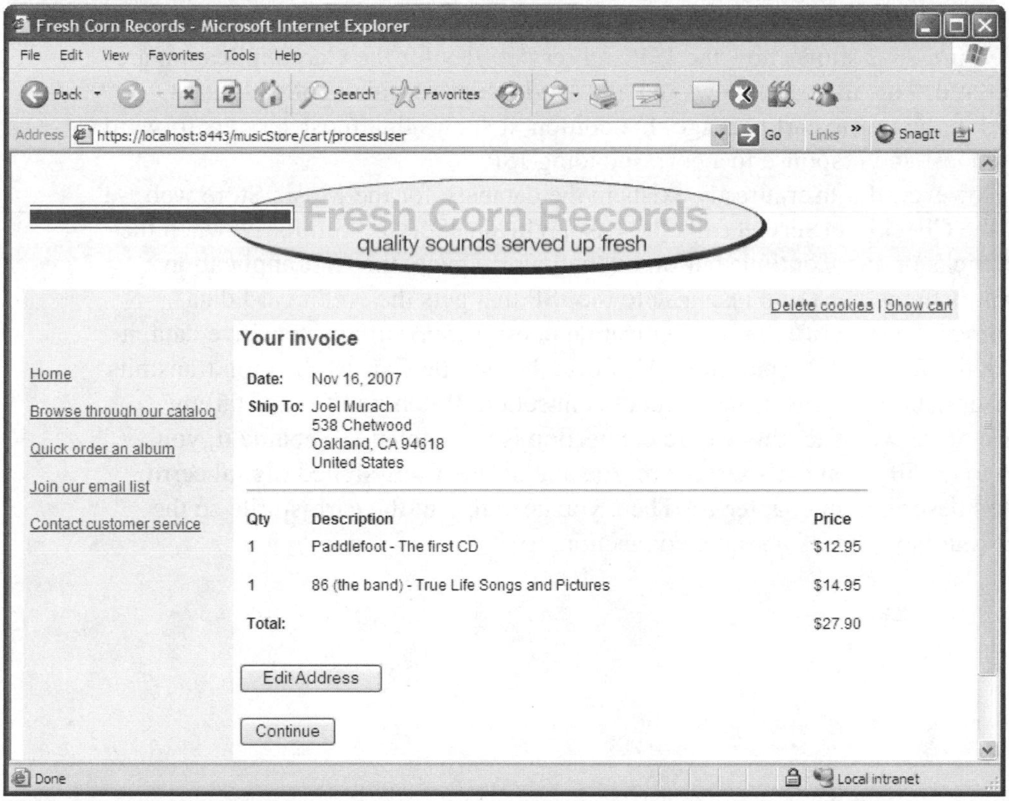

The Credit Card page

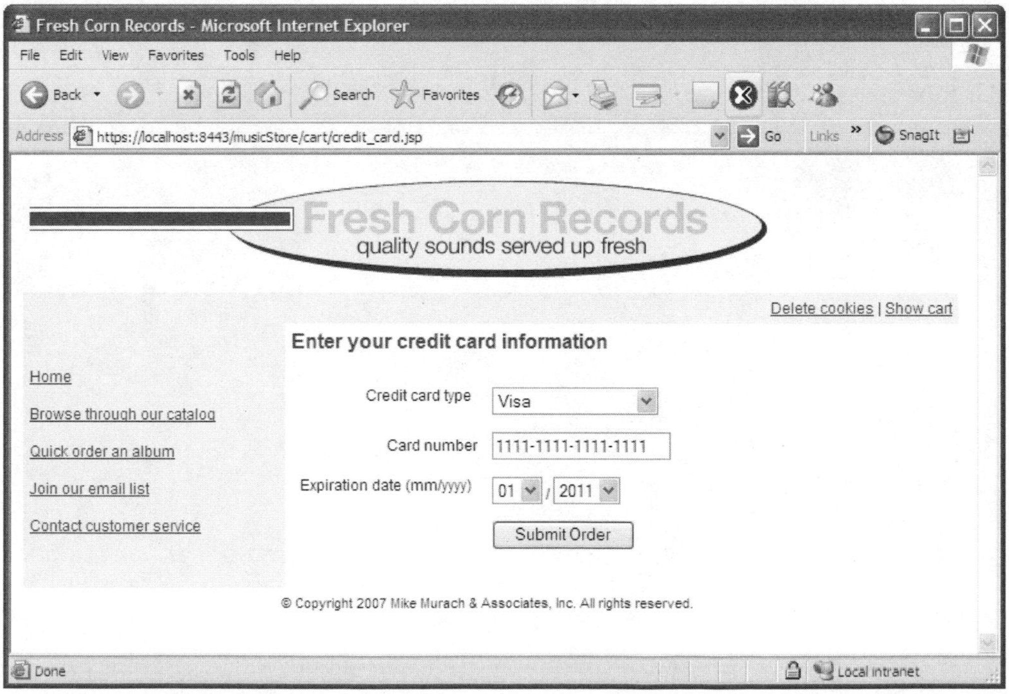

Figure 23-1   The user interface (part 3 of 3)

The structure

Figure 23-2 shows how the JSP and servlet files for the Cart application are structured. This diagram shows that the servlet files for this application are stored in the music.cart package. In addition, it shows that most servlets forward the request and response to a corresponding JSP.

However, if a user already exists in the database for the Music Store web site, the CheckUserServlet calls the DisplayInvoiceServlet. Similarly, when the user clicks on the Continue button on the Invoice page, the Cart application forwards the request and response to the JSP that gets the credit card data.

Since the start of the Cart application doesn't transmit any sensitive data, it uses a regular HTTP connection. However, before the Cart application transmits the user data, it begins using a secure connection. When you first install the Music Store web site, this secure connection isn't enabled. To enable it, you need to modify Tomcat's server.xml file and create a self-signed digital certificate as described in chapter 16. Then, you need to edit the cart.jsp file so the Checkout button uses a secure connection.

The structure of the Cart application

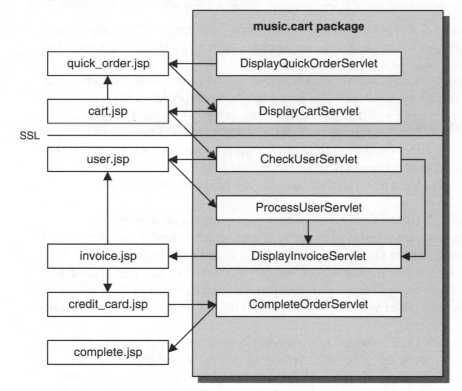

Description

- The JSPs for this application are stored in the musicStore\cart directory.
- The servlets for this application are stored in the music.cart package.
- The JSPs and servlets that transmit sensitive data use a secure connection.
- The DisplayQuickOrderServlet reads the products from the database and displays the Quick Order page. This servlet is mapped to the /cart URL. As a result, if you call the /cart URL, the Quick Order page is displayed.
- The DisplayCartServlet finds the user's cart and displays it. If the user's cart doesn't contain any items, this servlet displays the Quick Order page for the Cart application.
- The CheckUserServlet checks if a user has already entered his personal information. If so, this servlet creates a User object from the database and skips the User page and the ProcessUserServlet.
- The ProcessUserServlet creates a User object from information entered on the User page. Then, it saves the User object as an attribute of the session.
- The DisplayInvoiceServlet creates the Invoice object and displays the Invoice page. From the Invoice page, the user can call the User page to edit any personal information that isn't correct.
- The CompleteOrderServlet writes the data for the user and the invoice to the database, sends a confirmation email, and displays the Complete page.

Figure 23-2   The structure of the Cart application

The code

Figures 23-3 through 23-13 show some of the code for the JSPs and servlets used by this application. By now, you shouldn't have much trouble understanding this code, but here are a few notable points.

In figure 23-3, the DisplayQuickOrderServlet reads the product data from the database once for each session. The advantage of this approach is that the product data will be current for each user even when the product information is updated in the database. The disadvantage is that the product data will be read from the database many times and stored in multiple memory locations. As a result, if the product data doesn't change often, you may want to store the product data in the ServletContext object so the product data is only read once and stored in one location.

In figure 23-10, the constructor of the Invoice object could set the invoiceDate instance variable to the current date, which is usually what you want. Then, the code for the DisplayInvoiceServlet wouldn't need to create a Date object and set it in the Invoice object. Instead, this would be handled automatically by the constructor of the Invoice object. In general, it makes an application easier to develop when you design the business objects so they do as much work as possible.

In figure 23-12, EL and JSTL are used to loop through an ArrayList of String objects that store the possible valid credit card years. This ArrayList was created by the MusicStoreContextListener that's in the music.util package. If you open the source code for this class, you'll see that it runs when the application starts, and it creates the ArrayList and stores it as a ServletContext attribute.

In figure 23-13, the CompleteOrderServlet uses the MailUtil class that's stored in the music.util class to send an email. Since both of these classes use the JavaMail API that's stored in the mail.jar file, this JAR file has been included in the WEB-INF\lib folder for this application and added to the NetBeans project. For information about working with the JavaMail API, see chapter 15.

Since the code for the business objects and data access classes are described in chapter 21, these figures don't show any of those classes. In addition, these figures don't list the code for the utility classes that are used by the Cart application. If you're interested in them, though, you can use your IDE or a text editor to open and review them.

The DisplayQuickOrderServlet class

```
package music.cart;

import java.io.*;
import javax.servlet.*;
import javax.servlet.http.*;

import java.util.ArrayList;

import music.business.*;
import music.data.*;

public class DisplayQuickOrderServlet extends HttpServlet
{
    public void doGet(HttpServletRequest request,
                      HttpServletResponse response)
                      throws ServletException, IOException
    {
        HttpSession session = request.getSession();

        // if list of products doesn't exist, initialize it,
        // and store it for the remainder of the session
        if (session.getAttribute("products") == null)
        {
            ArrayList<Product> products = ProductDB.selectProducts();
            session.setAttribute("products", products);
        }

        // forward to the Quick Order page
        String url = "/cart/quick_order.jsp";
        RequestDispatcher dispatcher =
            getServletContext().getRequestDispatcher(url);
        dispatcher.forward(request, response);
    }

    public void doPost(HttpServletRequest request,
                       HttpServletResponse response)
                       throws ServletException, IOException
    {
        doGet(request, response);
    }
}
```

Figure 23-3   The DisplayQuickOrderServlet class

The code for the Quick Order page

```
<jsp:include page="/includes/header.html" />
<jsp:include page="/includes/column_left_order.jsp" />

<!-- begin middle column -->

<td width="570" valign="top" colspan="2">
<%@ taglib prefix="c" uri="http://java.sun.com/jsp/jstl/core" %>

<h1>Quick order an album</h1>

<table cellpadding="5" border="0">
  <tr valign="bottom">
    <th align="left">Description</th>
    <th align="left">Price</th>
    <th align="left"> </th>
  </tr>
  <c:forEach var="product" items="${products}">
  <tr valign="top">
    <td>
      <a href="
      <c:url value='/catalog/displayProduct?productCode=${product.code}'/>">
      ${product.description}
     </a>
    </td>
    <td>${product.priceCurrencyFormat}</td>
    <td>
      <a href="
      <c:url value='/cart/displayCart?productCode=${product.code}'/>">
      Add To Cart
    </a></td>
  </tr>
  </c:forEach>
</table>

</td>

<!-- end middle column -->

<jsp:include page="/includes/footer.jsp" />
```

The links from a Product page that call the DisplayCartServlet class

```
<%@ taglib prefix="c" uri="http://java.sun.com/jsp/jstl/core" %>
<a href="<c:url value='/cart/displayCart?productCode=${product.code}'/>">
    <img src="/musicStore/images/addtocart.gif" width="113" height="47">
</a><br><br>
<a href="<c:url value='/cart/displayCart'/>">
    <img src="/musicStore/images/showcart.gif" width="113" height="47">
</a><br><br>
```

Note

- Each Product page contains two links that call the DisplayCartServlet class. These links surround a tag that specifies a GIF file. As a result, when the user clicks on the graphic, the DisplayCartServlet is called.

Figure 23-4   The quick_order.jsp file

The DisplayCartServlet class   **Page 1**

```
package music.cart;

import java.io.*;
import javax.servlet.*;
import javax.servlet.http.*;

import music.business.*;
import music.data.*;

public class DisplayCartServlet extends HttpServlet
{
    public void doPost(HttpServletRequest request,
            HttpServletResponse response)
            throws IOException, ServletException
    {
        String quantityString = request.getParameter("quantity");
        String productCode = request.getParameter("productCode");
        String removeButtonValue = request.getParameter("removeButton");

        HttpSession session = request.getSession();

        Cart cart = (Cart) session.getAttribute("cart");
        if (cart == null)
        {
            cart = new Cart();
            session.setAttribute("cart", cart);
        }

        // If the user enters a negative or invalid number in the
        // Update text box, the quantity is automatically reset to 1.
        int quantity = 1;
        try
        {
            quantity = Integer.parseInt(quantityString);
            if (quantity < 0)
                quantity = 1;
        }
        catch(NumberFormatException nfe)
        {
            quantity = 1;
        }

        // If the user clicks the Remove button
        if (removeButtonValue != null)
        {
            quantity = 0;
        }

        // Get product from product code
        Product product = ProductDB.selectProduct(productCode);
        session.setAttribute("product", product);
```

Figure 23-5   The DisplayCartServlet class (part 1 of 2)

The DisplayCartServlet class

```
    // If product exists, add or remove from cart
    if (product != null)
    {
        LineItem lineItem = new LineItem();
        lineItem.setProduct(product);
        lineItem.setQuantity(quantity);
        if (quantity > 0)
            cart.addItem(lineItem);
        else
            cart.removeItem(lineItem);
    }
    session.setAttribute("cart", cart);

    // If no items exist in cart, forward to the Quick Order page.
    // Otherwise, forward to the Cart page.
    String url = "";
    if (cart.getItems().size() <= 0)
    {
        url = "/cart/displayQuickOrder";
    }
    else
    {
        url = "/cart/cart.jsp";
    }

    RequestDispatcher dispatcher =
            getServletContext().getRequestDispatcher(url);
    dispatcher.forward(request, response);
}

public void doGet(HttpServletRequest request,
        HttpServletResponse response)
        throws IOException, ServletException
{
    doPost(request, response);
}
}
```

Note

*   The Remove button on the Cart page includes a name and a value. As a result, you can use the getParameter method of the request object to get the value of this button, and you can check if this button was clicked by checking if its value is not null.

Figure 23-5   The DisplayCartServlet class (part 2 of 2)

The cart.jsp file

```
<jsp:include page="/includes/header.html" />
<jsp:include page="/includes/column_left_all.jsp" />

<!-- begin middle column -->
<td>
<%@ taglib prefix="c" uri="http://java.sun.com/jsp/jstl/core" %>

<h1>Your cart</h1>
<table cellspacing="5" border="0">
  <tr>
    <th align="left">Qty</th>
    <th align="left">Description</th>
    <th align="left">Price</th>
    <th align="left">Amount</th>
  </tr>

<c:forEach var="item" items="${cart.items}">
<form action="<c:url value='/cart/displayCart' />" method="post">
  <tr valign="top">
    <td>
      <form action="<c:url value='/cart/displayCart' />" method="post">
        <input type="hidden" name="productCode" value="${item.product.code}">
        <input type="text" size="2" name="quantity" value="${item.quantity}">
        <input type="submit" value="Update">
      </form>
    </td>
    <td>${item.product.description}</td>
    <td>${item.product.priceCurrencyFormat}</td>
    <td>${item.totalCurrencyFormat}</td>
    <td><input type="submit" name="removeButton" value="Remove"></td>
  </tr>
</form>
</c:forEach>

  <tr>
    <td colspan="3">
      <p><b>To change the quantity for an item</b>, enter the new quantity
          and click on the Update button.</p>
      <p><b>To remove an item</b>, click on the Remove button.</p>
    </td>
  </tr>
</table>

<form action="<c:url value='/cart/displayQuickOrder' />" method="post">
  <input type="submit" value="Continue Shopping">
</form>

<form action="<c:url
          value='https://localhost:8443/musicStore/cart/checkUser' />"
      method="post">
  <input type="submit" value="Checkout">
</form>
<!-- end middle column -->

<jsp:include page="/includes/footer.jsp" />
```

Figure 23-6   The cart.jsp file

The CheckUserServlet class

```
package music.cart;

import java.io.*;
import javax.servlet.*;
import javax.servlet.http.*;

import music.business.*;
import music.data.*;
import music.util.*;

public class CheckUserServlet extends HttpServlet
{
    public void doGet(HttpServletRequest request,
            HttpServletResponse response)
            throws IOException, ServletException
    {
        HttpSession session = request.getSession();
        User user = (User) session.getAttribute("user");
        String url = "/cart/user.jsp";

        // if the User object exists with address1, skip User page
        if (user != null && !user.getAddress1().equals("") )
        {
            url = "/cart/displayInvoice";
        }
        // otherwise, check the email cookie
        else
        {
            Cookie[] cookies = request.getCookies();
            String emailAddress =
                    CookieUtil.getCookieValue(cookies, "emailCookie");
            if (emailAddress.equals(""))
            {
                user = new User();
            }
            else
            {
                user = UserDB.selectUser(emailAddress);
                if (user != null && !user.getAddress1().equals("")  )
                    url = "/cart/displayInvoice";
            }
        }
        session.setAttribute("user", user);
        RequestDispatcher dispatcher =
            getServletContext().getRequestDispatcher(url);
        dispatcher.forward(request, response);
    }

    public void doPost(HttpServletRequest request,
                    HttpServletResponse response)
                    throws ServletException, IOException
    {
        doGet(request, response);
    }
}
```

Figure 23-7   The CheckUserServlet class

The user.jsp file

```
<jsp:include page="/includes/header.html" />
<jsp:include page="/includes/column_left_all_absolute.jsp" />

<!-- begin middle column -->

<td>
<%@ taglib prefix="c" uri="http://java.sun.com/jsp/jstl/core" %>

<h1>Enter your name and contact information</h1>

<form action="<c:url value='/cart/processUser' />" method=post>
<table border="0" cellpadding="5">
  <tr>
    <td></td>
    <td align=left>Required <font color=red>*</font></td>
  </tr>
  <tr>
    <td align=right>First Name</td>
    <td><input type="text" name="firstName"  size="20" maxlength=20
            value="${user.firstName}">
            <font color=red>*</font></td>
  </tr>
  <tr>
    <td align=right>Last Name</td>
    <td><input type=text name="lastName" size=20
            value="${user.lastName}">
            <font color=red>*</font></td>
  </tr>
  .
  .
  .
  <tr>
    <td align=right>Country</td>
    <td><input type=text name="country" size=20
            value="${user.country}">
            <font color=red>*</font></td>
  </tr>
  <tr>
    <td align=right> </td>
    <td><input type="button" value="Continue"
        onClick="validate(this.form)"></td>
  </tr>
</table>

</form>

</td>

<!-- end middle column -->

<jsp:include page="/includes/footer.jsp" />
```

Note

- Although it isn't shown in this figure, this page uses JavaScript to validate the entries. For more information about using JavaScript, see chapter 7.

Figure 23-8   The user.jsp file

The ProcessUserServlet class

```
package music.cart;

import java.io.*;
import javax.servlet.*;
import javax.servlet.http.*;

import music.business.*;

public class ProcessUserServlet extends HttpServlet
{
    public void doGet(HttpServletRequest request,
            HttpServletResponse response)
            throws IOException, ServletException
    {
        String firstName = request.getParameter("firstName");
        String lastName = request.getParameter("lastName");
        String companyName = request.getParameter("companyName");
        String emailAddress = request.getParameter("emailAddress");
        String address1 = request.getParameter("address1");
        String address2 = request.getParameter("address2");
        String city = request.getParameter("city");
        String state = request.getParameter("state");
        String zip = request.getParameter("zip");
        String country = request.getParameter("country");

        HttpSession session = request.getSession();
        User user = (User) session.getAttribute("user");

        user.setFirstName(firstName);
        user.setLastName(lastName);
        user.setEmailAddress(emailAddress);
        user.setCompanyName(companyName);
        user.setAddress1(address1);
        user.setAddress2(address2);
        user.setCity(city);
        user.setState(state);
        user.setZip(zip);
        user.setCountry(country);

        session.setAttribute("user", user);

        String url = "/cart/displayInvoice";
        RequestDispatcher dispatcher =
                getServletContext().getRequestDispatcher(url);
        dispatcher.forward(request, response);
    }

    public void doPost(HttpServletRequest request,
            HttpServletResponse response)
            throws IOException, ServletException
    {
        doGet(request, response);
    }
}
```

Figure 23-9   The ProcessUserServlet class

The DisplayInvoiceServlet class

```
package music.cart;

import java.io.*;
import javax.servlet.*;
import javax.servlet.http.*;

import music.business.*;

public class DisplayInvoiceServlet extends HttpServlet
{
    public void doGet(HttpServletRequest request,
            HttpServletResponse response)
            throws IOException, ServletException
    {
        HttpSession session = request.getSession();

        User user = (User) session.getAttribute("user");
        Cart cart = (Cart) session.getAttribute("cart");

        java.util.Date today = new java.util.Date();

        Invoice invoice = new Invoice();
        invoice.setUser(user);
        invoice.setInvoiceDate(today);
        invoice.setLineItems(cart.getItems());

        session.setAttribute("invoice", invoice);

        String url = "/cart/invoice.jsp";
        RequestDispatcher dispatcher =
                getServletContext().getRequestDispatcher(url);
        dispatcher.forward(request, response);
    }

    public void doPost(HttpServletRequest request,
            HttpServletResponse response)
            throws IOException, ServletException
    {
        doGet(request, response);
    }
}
```

Figure 23-10   The DisplayInvoiceServlet class

The invoice.jsp file

```jsp
<jsp:include page="/includes/header.html" />
<jsp:include page="/includes/column_left_all_absolute.jsp" />

<!-- begin middle column -->

<td>
<%@ taglib prefix="c" uri="http://java.sun.com/jsp/jstl/core" %>

<h1>Your invoice</h1>

<table border="0" cellspacing="5">
  <tr><td><b>Date:</b></td>
      <td width="400">${invoice.invoiceDateDefaultFormat}</td>
      <td></td>
  </tr>
  <tr valign="top">
    <td><b>Ship To:</b></td>
    <td>${user.addressHTMLFormat}</td>
    <td></td>
  </tr>
  <tr><td colspan="3"><hr></td></tr>
  <tr><td><b>Qty</b></td>
      <td><b>Description</b></td>
      <td><b>Price</b></td>
  </tr>

  <c:forEach var="item" items="${invoice.lineItems}">
  <tr>
    <td><p>${item.quantity}</td>
    <td><p>${item.product.description}</td>
    <td><p>${item.totalCurrencyFormat}</td>
  </tr>
  </c:forEach>

  <tr>
    <td><b>Total:</b></td>
    <td></td>
    <td>${invoice.invoiceTotalCurrencyFormat}</td>
  </tr>
</table>

<form action="<c:url value='/cart/user.jsp' />" method="post">
    <input type="submit" value="Edit Address">
</form>

<form action="<c:url value='/cart/credit_card.jsp' />" method="post">
    <input type="submit" value="Continue">
</form>

</td>

<!-- end middle column -->

<jsp:include page="/includes/footer.jsp" />
```

Figure 23-11   The invoice.jsp file

The creditcard.jsp file

```
<td>
<%@ taglib prefix="c" uri="http://java.sun.com/jsp/jstl/core" %>

<h1>Enter your credit card information</h1>

<form action="<c:url value='/cart/completeOrder' />" method="post">
    <table border="0" cellpadding="5">
    <tr>
        <td align="right"><p>Credit card type</td>
        <td><select name="creditCardType" size="1">
            <option value="Visa">Visa</option>
            <option value="Mastercard">Mastercard</option>
            <option value="AmEx">American Express</option>
          </select>
        </td>
    </tr>
    <tr>
        <td align="right">Card number</td>
        <td><input type="text" size="20" name="creditCardNumber"
                maxlength="25"></td>
    </tr>
    <tr>
        <td align="right"><p>Expiration date (mm/yyyy)</td>
        <td><select name="creditCardExpirationMonth">
                <option value="01">01
                <option value="02">02
                <option value="03">03
                <option value="04">04
                <option value="05">05
                <option value="06">06
                <option value="07">07
                <option value="08">08
                <option value="09">09
                <option value="10">10
                <option value="11">11
                <option value="12">12
          </select>
          /
          <select name="creditCardExpirationYear">
                <c:forEach var="year" items="${creditCardYears}">
                  <option value="${year}">${year}
                </c:forEach>
          </select>
        </td>
    </tr>
    <tr>
        <td></td>
        <td align="left"><input type="submit" value="Submit Order"></td>
    </tr>
    </table>
</form>

</td>
```

Figure 23-12   The creditcard.jsp file

The CompleteOrderServlet class   **Page 1**

```java
package music.cart;

import java.io.*;
import javax.servlet.*;
import javax.servlet.http.*;

import java.util.*;
import javax.mail.*;

import music.business.*;
import music.data.*;
import music.util.*;

public class CompleteOrderServlet extends HttpServlet
{
    public void doPost(HttpServletRequest request,
            HttpServletResponse response)
            throws IOException, ServletException
    {
        HttpSession session = request.getSession();
        User user = (User)session.getAttribute("user");
        Invoice invoice = (Invoice)session.getAttribute("invoice");

        String creditCardType =
                request.getParameter("creditCardType");
        String creditCardNumber =
                request.getParameter("creditCardNumber");
        String creditCardExpMonth =
                request.getParameter("creditCardExpirationMonth");
        String creditCardExpYear =
                request.getParameter("creditCardExpirationYear");

        user.setCreditCardType(creditCardType);
        user.setCreditCardNumber(creditCardNumber);
        user.setCreditCardExpirationDate(creditCardExpMonth
                + "/" + creditCardExpYear);

        // If a record for the User object exists, update it
        if (UserDB.emailExists(user.getEmailAddress()))
        {
            UserDB.update(user);
        }
        // Otherwise, write a new record for the User object
        else
        {
            UserDB.insert(user);
        }

        // Write a new invoice record
        InvoiceDB.insert(invoice);
```

Figure 23-13   The CompleteOrderServlet class (part 1 of 2)

The CompleteOrderServlet class   **Page 2**

```java
            // Set the emailCookie in the user's browser.
            Cookie emailCookie = new Cookie("emailCookie",
                    user.getEmailAddress());
            emailCookie.setMaxAge(60*24*365*2*60);
            emailCookie.setPath("/");
            response.addCookie(emailCookie);

            // Remove all items from the user's cart
            Cart cart = (Cart) session.getAttribute("cart");
            cart.setItems(new ArrayList<LineItem>());

            // Send an email to the user to confirm the order.
            String to = user.getEmailAddress();
            String from = "confirmation@freshcornrecords.com";
            String subject = "Order Confirmation";
            String body = "Dear " + user.getFirstName() + ",\n\n" +
                "Thanks for ordering from us. " +
                "You should receive your order in 3-5 business days. " +
                "Please contact us if you have any questions.\n" +
                "Have a great day and thanks again!\n\n" +
                "Joe King\n" +
                "Fresh Corn Records";
            boolean isBodyHTML = false;
            try
            {
                MailUtil.sendMail(to, from, subject, body, isBodyHTML);
            }
            catch(MessagingException e)
            {
                this.log(
                    "Unable to send email. \n" +
                    "You may need to configure your system as " +
                    "described in chapter 15. \n" +
                    "Here is the email you tried to send: \n" +
                    "=====================================\n" +
                    "TO: " + to + "\n" +
                    "FROM: " + from + "\n" +
                    "SUBJECT: " + subject + "\n" +
                    "\n" +
                    body + "\n\n");
            }

            String url = "/cart/complete.jsp";
            RequestDispatcher dispatcher =
                    getServletContext().getRequestDispatcher(url);
            dispatcher.forward(request, response);
    }
}
```

Note

* This class uses the MailUtil class that's stored in the music.util package to send a confirmation email. For more information about working with this class, see chapter 15.

Figure 23-13   The CompleteOrderServlet class (part 2 of 2)

Perspective

Now that you're done with this chapter, you should understand how the skills taught in this book can be integrated into an e-commerce application. However, you should also understand that this application has been simplified for instructional purposes. As a result, some real-world issues aren't completely resolved. Nevertheless, this application is a good starting point for developing e-commerce applications.

When you do develop your own applications, for example, you will need to validate all user entries including credit card information. If you have many products, you will probably want to generate the Product pages from data that's stored in the database. In addition, you will probably want to add functionality to the application shown in the next chapter so it allows employees to easily add new products to the database. If you've mastered chapters 1 through 19, though, you have all the skills you need for making enhancements like that.

In the next chapter, you'll see how an administrative application lets employees with proper security clearance process the orders that the Cart application writes to the database. You'll also see how this application lets the users view reports that summarize the orders that have been written to the database. Once you read this chapter, you'll have a complete view of how you can use JSPs and servlets to create an e-commerce site.

24

The Admin application

In the last two chapters, you were introduced to the applications of the Music Store web site that allow anyone in the world with an Internet connection and a web browser to download sound files and order albums. Now, you'll learn about the Admin application. This application provides the administrative functions for the web site, but it's only available to a user who has a valid username and password.

An introduction to the Admin application

The Admin application provides two main functions. The first one lets the user display and process invoices, and the second one lets the user view reports.

The Index page

Figure 24-1 shows the Index page for the Admin application. Each button on this page leads to a different part of this application. The Process Invoices button lets the user display and process the orders that have been placed by users of the Cart application. The Display Reports button lets the user view reports that summarize data about users, invoices, and downloads.

The structure

Figure 24-2 shows the JSPs and servlets that are used by the Admin application. To display and process invoices, this application calls the DisplayInvoicesServlet. This class reads all invoices that have not been processed yet and stores them as a session attribute. Then, the Invoices page displays these invoices. When the user of the application selects an invoice, the DisplayInvoiceServlet displays the Invoice page for the specified invoice. This page shows the data for a single invoice. Then, the user can choose to process the invoice or return to the Invoices page.

To access reports, this application calls the Reports page. Depending on the report requested by the user, the application either calls the DisplayReportServlet or the Parameters page. Either way, the DisplayReportServlet is eventually called and the report is then displayed.

The security

Since the Admin application should only be available to employees of the Music Store web site, it uses a security constraint to restrict access to all URLs in the admin directory. To see this security constraint, you can view the web.xml file that's presented in chapter 21. As a result, before you can access the Admin application, you must use the login form shown in figure 24-3 to specify a valid username and password.

Since this application transmits sensitive data, you should use a secure HTTPS connection for all URLs of this application. To do that, you can start the application by requesting a secure connection like the one shown in figure 24-1. However, before this connection will work, you need to configure a secure connection on your system by modifying the server.xml file and installing a self-signed certificate as described in chapter 16. Until you do that, you can use a regular HTTP connection to test the Admin application.

The URL for accessing the Admin application without SSL

```
http://localhost:8080/musicStore/admin
```

The URL for accessing the Admin application with SSL

```
https://localhost:8443/musicStore/admin
```

The Index page for the Admin application

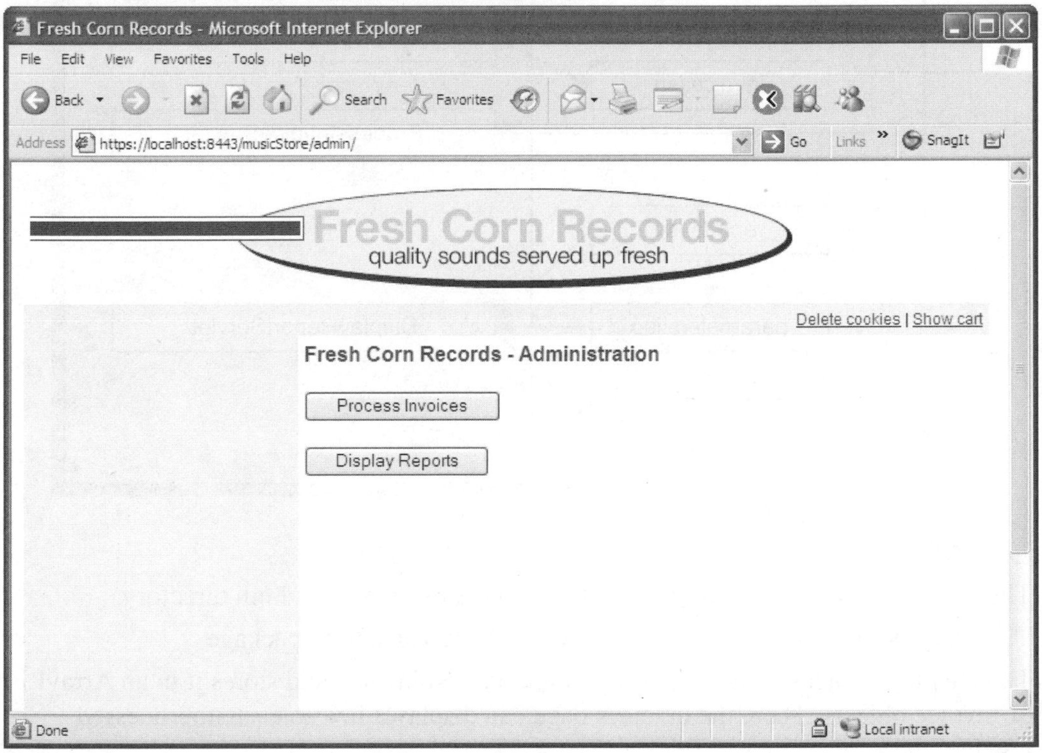

Description

- The Index page for the Admin application lets the user choose between the two main administrative functions: (1) processing invoices, and (2) viewing reports.

- You can start the Admin application by entering the URL for the index page in your browser. If you have configured a secure connection, you can access this application with the secure HTTPS connection shown above. Otherwise, you can use the regular HTTP connection shown above to access the application.

- To learn how to configure a secure connection, see chapter 16.

Figure 24-1   The Index page for the Admin application

The structure of the Admin application

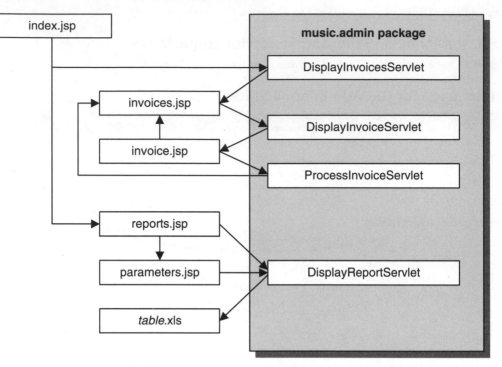

Description

- The JSP files for this application are stored in the musicStore\admin directory.
- The servlets for this application are stored in the music.admin package.
- The DisplayInvoicesServlet reads each unprocessed invoice and stores it in an ArrayList of Invoice objects. Then, the Invoices page can display a link to each unprocessed invoice.
- The DisplayInvoiceServlet gets the selected invoice from the ArrayList of Invoice objects. Then, the Invoice page can display the invoice so the user can decide whether to process it.
- The ProcessInvoiceServlet processes the selected invoice.
- The DisplayReportServlet accepts the name of the report and its parameters and creates a tab-delimited string that contains the data of the report. Then, it returns that string as an Excel spreadsheet.

Figure 24-2   The structure of the Admin application

The Login page

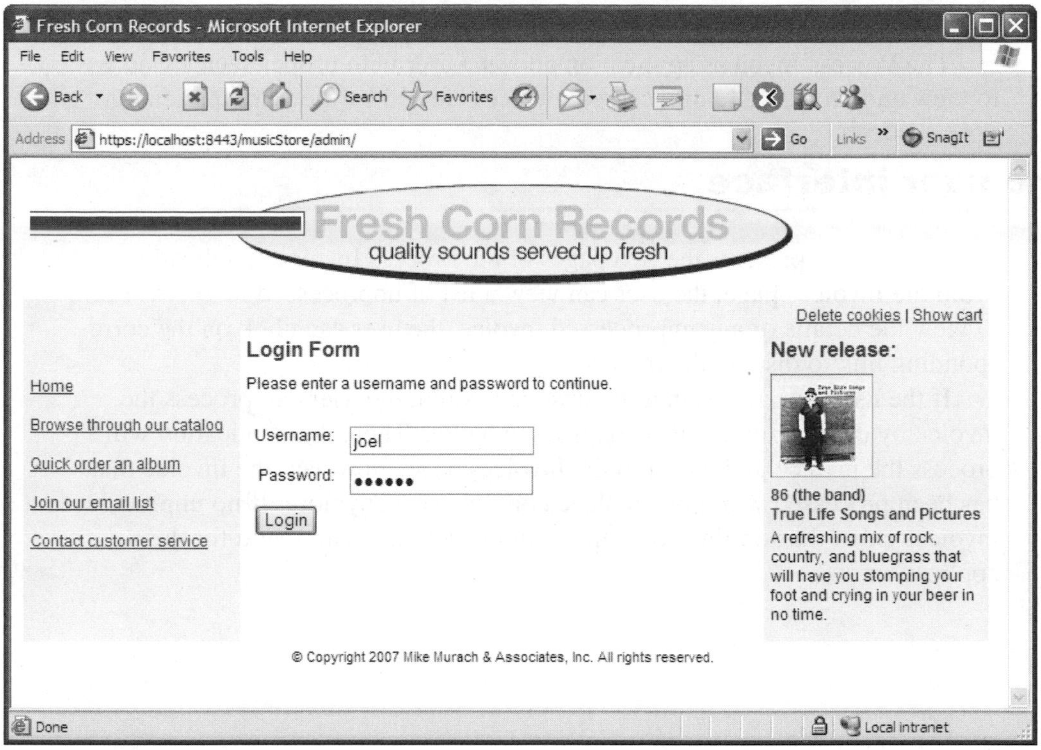

Description

- The web.xml file for this application uses a security constraint to restrict access to all URLs in the admin directory. To view this web.xml file, see chapter 21.

- The security constraint causes a Login page like the one above to be displayed the first time the user requests any page from the admin directory. To learn how to enable a security constraint, see chapter 17.

- The entire Admin application should use a secure connection so all data that's passed between the browser and server is encrypted. To learn how to configure and use a secure connection, see chapter 16.

Figure 24-3   The security for the Admin application

The Process Invoices application

The Process Invoices application allows a user with proper security access to view and process all unprocessed invoices created by the Cart application.

The user interface

Figure 24-4 presents the two pages of the Process Invoices application. From the Invoices page, the user can view a list of unprocessed invoices. Then, to view the details of any unprocessed invoice, the user can click on the corresponding link to display the Invoice page.

If the user determines that the invoice is valid, the user can process the invoice by clicking on the Process Invoice button. Then, the application will process the invoice and return to the Invoices page. However, the invoice that has been processed won't be displayed on this page anymore. If no unprocessed invoices exist, the Admin application will display the main menu for the application.

The Invoices page

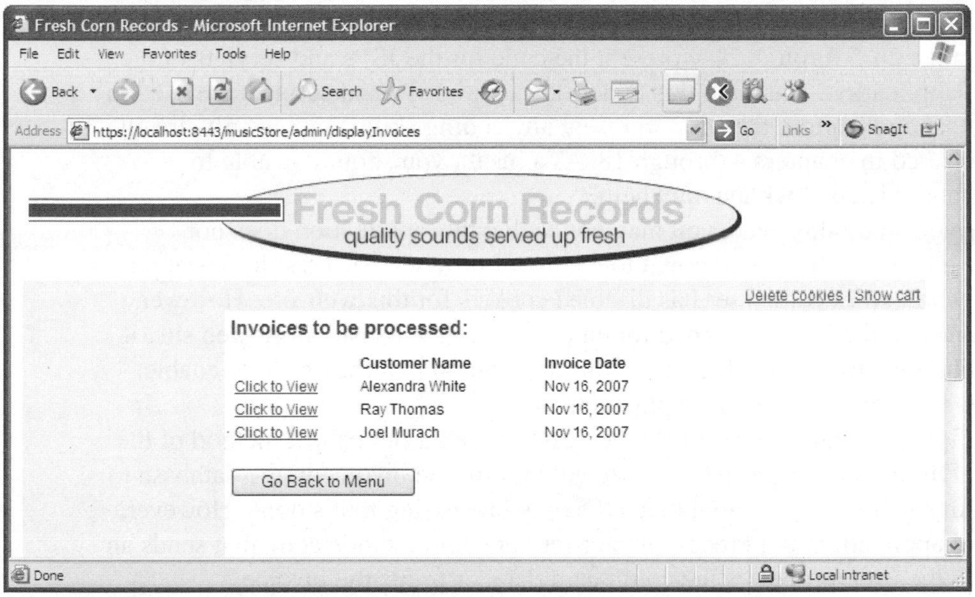

The Invoice page

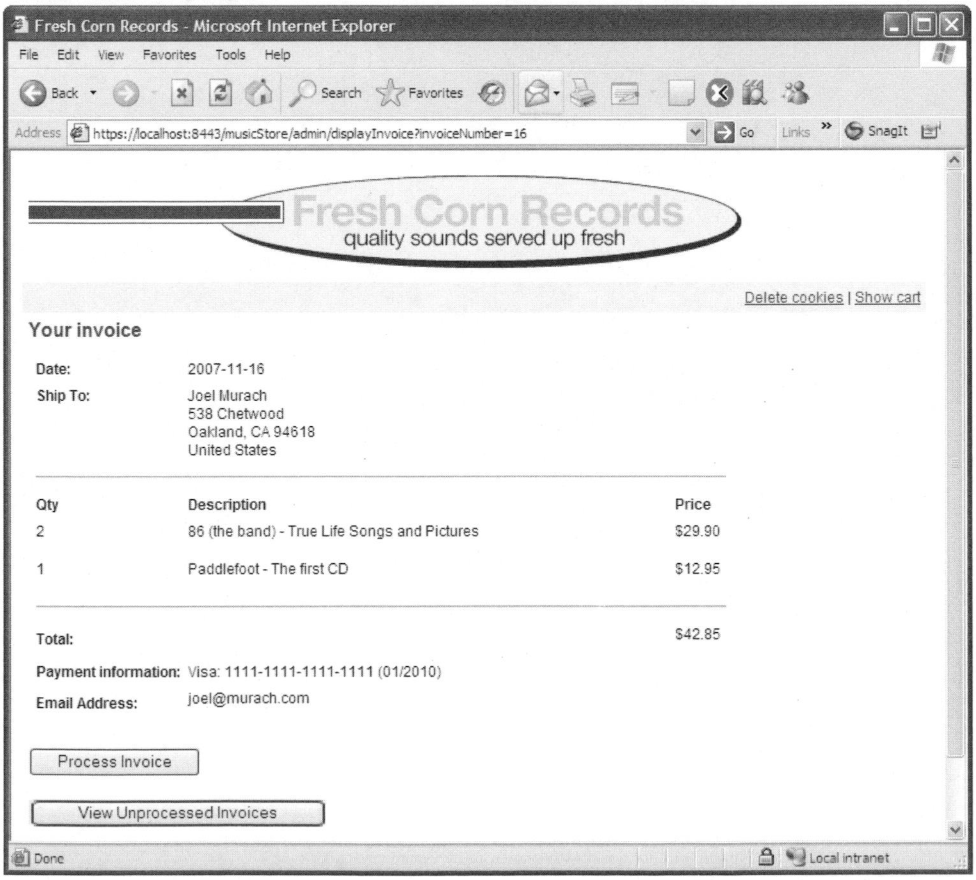

Figure 24-4   The user interface for the Process Invoices application

The code

Figures 24-5 through 24-9 present the code for the JSPs and servlets of the Admin application. Although this code shows how JSPs and servlets are used in a practical application, they don't present any coding skills that haven't already been covered in chapters 4 through 18. As a result, you should be able to understand this code without any help.

As you study this code, you may notice that this application does not encode the URLs that are returned to the user's browser. As a result, this application won't work if the user has disabled cookies for this web site. However, since this application is designed for employees of the Music Store web site, it should be easy to inform all users of this application that they need to enable cookies to be able to use this application.

In figure 24-9, the code for the ProcessInvoiceServlet calls a method of the InvoiceDB class to set the IsProcessed column for the invoice in the database to 'y'. In this simple application, that's the only processing that's done. However, in a real application, the ProcessInvoiceServlet could include code that sends an email to the user, processes the credit card data, or prints the invoice.

The DisplayInvoicesServlet class

```java
package music.admin;

import java.io.*;
import javax.servlet.*;
import javax.servlet.http.*;

import java.util.ArrayList;

import music.data.*;
import music.business.*;

public class DisplayInvoicesServlet extends HttpServlet
{
    public void doGet(HttpServletRequest request,
            HttpServletResponse response)
            throws IOException, ServletException
    {
        HttpSession session = request.getSession();

        ArrayList<Invoice> unprocessedInvoices =
            InvoiceDB.selectUnprocessedInvoices();

        if (unprocessedInvoices == null ||
            unprocessedInvoices.size() <= 0)
        {
            response.sendRedirect("/musicStore/admin");
        }
        else
        {
            session.setAttribute("unprocessedInvoices", unprocessedInvoices);

            String url = "/admin/invoices.jsp";
            RequestDispatcher dispatcher =
                getServletContext().getRequestDispatcher(url);
            dispatcher.forward(request, response);
        }
    }

    public void doPost(HttpServletRequest request,
            HttpServletResponse response)
            throws IOException, ServletException
    {
        doGet(request, response);
    }
}
```

Figure 24-5   The DisplayInvoicesServlet class

The invoices.jsp file

```jsp
<jsp:include page="/includes/header.html" />
<jsp:include page="/includes/column_left_no_links.jsp" />

<!-- begin middle column -->

<td valign="top">
<%@ taglib prefix="c" uri="http://java.sun.com/jsp/jstl/core" %>

<h1>Invoices to be processed:</h1>

<table>

<tr>
  <td width="100"></td>
  <td width="150"><b>Customer Name</b></td>
  <td><b>Invoice Date</b></td>
</tr>

<c:forEach var="invoice" items="${unprocessedInvoices}">
<tr>
  <td>
    <a href="displayInvoice?invoiceNumber=${invoice.invoiceNumber}">
      Click to View
    </a>
  </td>
  <td>${invoice.user.firstName} ${invoice.user.lastName}</td>
  <td>${invoice.invoiceDateDefaultFormat}</td>
</tr>
</c:forEach>

</table>

<br>

<form action="index.jsp" method="post">
    <input type=submit value="Go Back to Menu">
</form>

</td>

<!-- end middle column -->

<jsp:include page="/includes/footer.jsp" />
```

Figure 24-6   The invoices.jsp file

The DisplayInvoiceServlet class

```
package music.admin;

import java.io.*;
import javax.servlet.*;
import javax.servlet.http.*;

import java.util.ArrayList;

import music.business.*;

public class DisplayInvoiceServlet extends HttpServlet
{
    public void doGet(HttpServletRequest request,
            HttpServletResponse response)
            throws IOException, ServletException
    {
        HttpSession session = request.getSession();

        String invoiceNumberString = request.getParameter("invoiceNumber");
        int invoiceNumber = Integer.parseInt(invoiceNumberString);
        ArrayList<Invoice> unprocessedInvoices =
            (ArrayList<Invoice>) session.getAttribute("unprocessedInvoices");

        Invoice invoice = null;
        for (int i = 0; i < unprocessedInvoices.size(); i++)
        {
            invoice = unprocessedInvoices.get(i);
            if (invoice.getInvoiceNumber() == invoiceNumber)
            {
                break;
            }
        }

        User user = invoice.getUser();
        ArrayList<LineItem> lineItems = invoice.getLineItems();

        session.setAttribute("user", user);
        session.setAttribute("invoice", invoice);
        Cart cart = new Cart();
        cart.setItems(lineItems);
        session.setAttribute("cart", cart);

        String url = "/admin/invoice.jsp";
        RequestDispatcher dispatcher =
            getServletContext().getRequestDispatcher(url);
        dispatcher.forward(request, response);
    }

    public void doPost(HttpServletRequest request,
            HttpServletResponse response)
            throws IOException, ServletException
    {
        doGet(request, response);
    }
}
```

Figure 24-7   The DisplayInvoiceServlet class

The invoice.jsp file

```
<td valign="top">
<%@ taglib prefix="c" uri="http://java.sun.com/jsp/jstl/core" %>

<h1>Your invoice</h1>

<table border="0" cellspacing="5">
  <tr>
    <td><b>Date:</b></td>
    <td width="400">${invoice.invoiceDate}</td>
    <td></td>
  </tr>
  <tr valign="top">
    <td><b>Ship To:</b></td>
    <td>${user.addressHTMLFormat}</td>
    <td></td>
  </tr>
  <tr><td colspan="3"><hr></td></tr>
  <tr>
    <td><b>Qty</b></td>
    <td><b>Description</b></td>
    <td><b>Price</b></td>
  </tr>

  <c:forEach var="item" items="${invoice.lineItems}">
  <tr>
    <td>${item.quantity}</td>
    <td>${item.product.description}</td>
    <td>${item.totalCurrencyFormat}</td>
  </tr>
  </c:forEach>

  <tr><td colspan="3"><hr></td></tr>
  <tr>
    <td><b>Total:</b></td>
    <td></td>
    <td><p>${invoice.invoiceTotalCurrencyFormat}</td>
  </tr>
  <tr>
    <td><b>Payment information:</b></td>
    <td>${user.creditCardType}: ${user.creditCardNumber}
        (${user.creditCardExpirationDate})</td>
  </tr>
  <tr>
    <td><b>Email Address:</b></td>
    <td><p>${user.emailAddress}</td>
  </tr>
</table>
<form action="processInvoice" method="post">
  <input type="submit" value="Process Invoice">
</form>
<form action="invoices.jsp" method="post">
  <input type="submit" value="View Unprocessed Invoices">
</form>

</td>
```

Figure 24-8   The invoice.jsp file

The ProcessInvoiceServlet class

```java
package music.admin;

import java.io.*;
import javax.servlet.*;
import javax.servlet.http.*;

import music.data.*;
import music.business.*;

public class ProcessInvoiceServlet extends HttpServlet
{
    public void doPost(HttpServletRequest request,
            HttpServletResponse response)
            throws IOException, ServletException
    {
        HttpSession session = request.getSession();

        Invoice invoice = (Invoice) session.getAttribute("invoice");
        int invoiceID = invoice.getInvoiceNumber();

        InvoiceDB.updateInvoiceIsProcessed(invoiceID);

        String url = "/admin/displayInvoices";
        RequestDispatcher dispatcher =
            getServletContext().getRequestDispatcher(url);
        dispatcher.forward(request, response);
    }
}
```

Figure 24-9   The ProcessInvoiceServlet class

The Reports application

The Reports application lets the user view the data that's stored in the database for the Music Store web site. In particular, this application provides access to four reports that summarize data about users, invoices, and downloads.

The user interface

Figure 24-10 shows the pages of the Reports application. To start, the Reports page displays a list of available reports. If the user selects the first report, the report is displayed. But if the user selects one of the next three reports, the Parameters page is displayed. This page lets the user enter a start and end date for the report.

This figure also shows three of the reports that can be generated from the Admin application. This shows that the reports are returned as Excel spreadsheets. As a result, the user can view the data, or the user can save the data as an Excel spreadsheet. However, these reports could also be returned as HTML tables or XML documents.

The code

Figures 24-11 and 24-12 show the code for the Reports application. Although this code shows how JSPs and servlets are used in a practical application, they don't present any coding skills that haven't already been covered in chapters 4 through 18. As a result, you should be able to understand this code without any help.

Unlike most of the other applications, the Reports application doesn't use any business objects. Instead, the DisplayReportServlet in figure 24-11 calls a method from the ReportDB class directly. Then, the ReportDB class gets a result set from the database and creates a tab-delimited string that contains the data in the result set. Here, the ReportDB class uses a StringBuilder object instead of a String object to create the string. This can make a large report run noticeably faster.

The Reports page

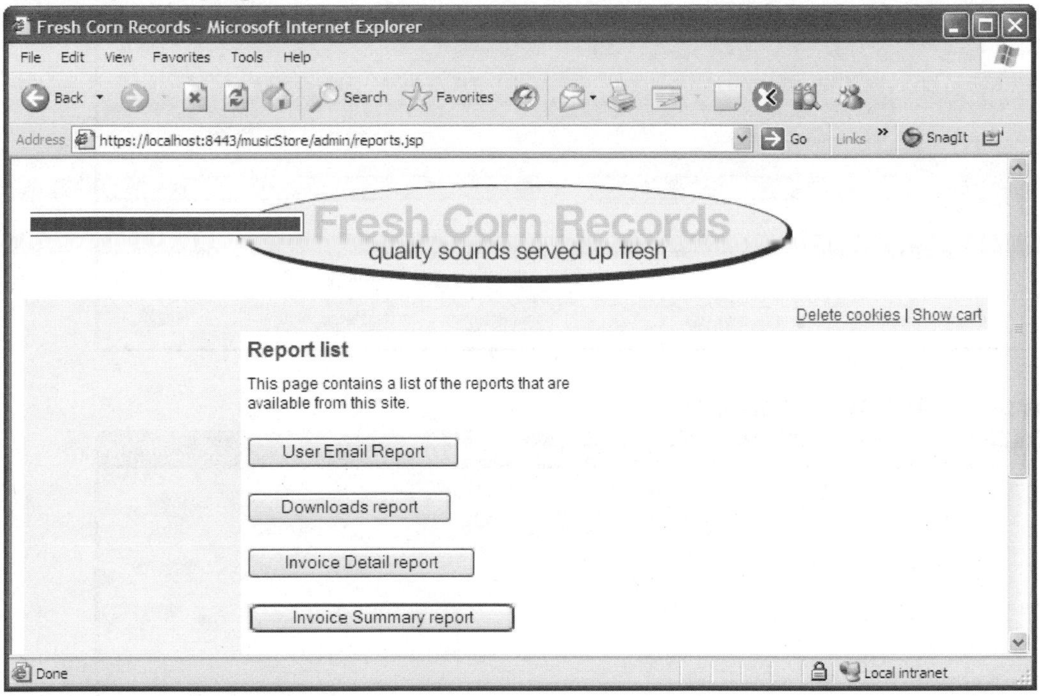

The Parameters page

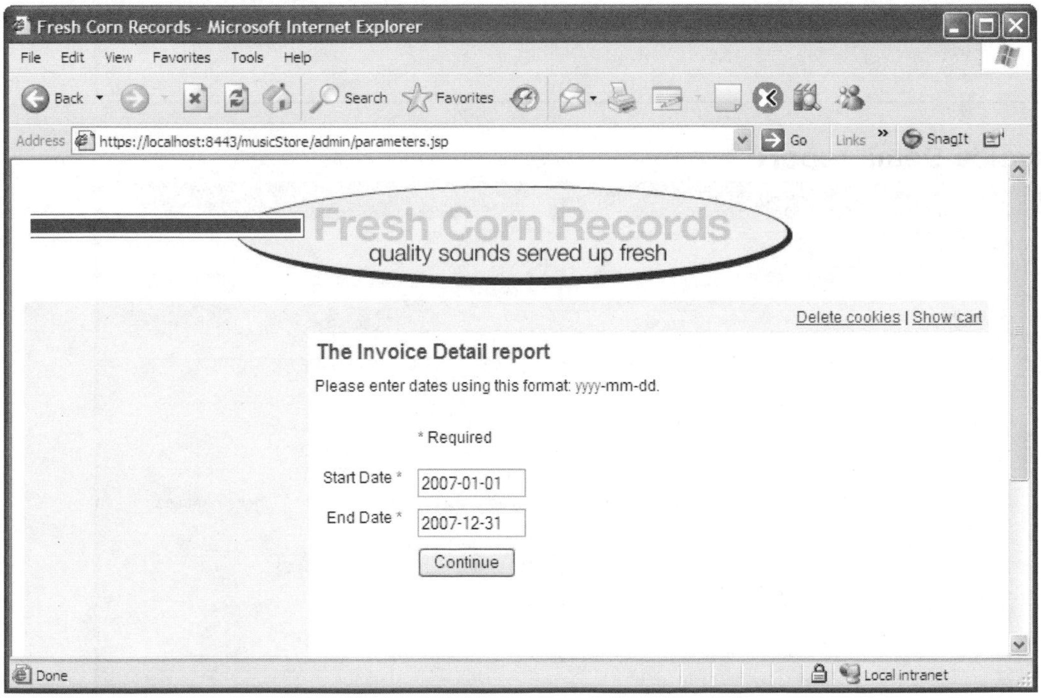

Figure 24-10   The user interface for the Reports application (part 1 of 2)

The User Email report

	A	B	C	D	E	F	G	H	I	
1	The User Email report									
2										
3	LastName	FirstName	EmailAddress	CompanyName	Address1	Address2	City	State	Zip	Co
4	Murach	Joel	joel@murach.com		538 Chetwood		Oakland	CA	94618	Un
5	Thomas	Ray	raythomas@hotmail.com		186 Derby St.		Berkeley	CA	94711	Un
6	White	Alexandra	alexandrawhite@gmail.com		19 Martin St.		Hazleton	PA	18222	Un
7										

Address: https://localhost:8443/musicStore/admin/displayReport — Cell A17

The Invoice Summary report

	A	B	C	D	E	F	G	H	
1	The Invoice Summary report								
2									
3	Start Date: 2007-01-01								
4	End Date: 2007-12-31								
5									
6	ProductCode	ProductDescription	ProductPrice	Quantity	Total				
7	8601	86 (the band) - True Life Songs and Pictures	14.95	3	44.85				
8	jr01	Joe Rut - Genuine Wood Grained Finish	14.95	2	29.9				
9	pf01	Paddlefoot - The first CD	12.95	2	25.9				
10	pf02	Paddlefoot - The second CD	14.95	1	14.95				
11									

Address: https://localhost:8443/musicStore/admin/displayReport — Cell A18

The Invoice Detail report

	A	B	C	D	E	F	G	H	I	J	
1	The Invoice Detail report										
2											
3	Start Date: 2007-01-01										
4	End Date: 2007-12-31										
5											
6	Date	Time	InvoiceID	EmailAddress	UserID	oductCode	ProductPri	Quantity	LineItemAmount		
7											
8	11/16/2007	16:22:09	16	joel@murach.com	1	pf01	12.95	1	12.95		
9	11/16/2007	16:22:09	16	joel@murach.com	1	8601	14.95	2	29.9		
10	11/16/2007	16:09:23	15	raythomas@hotmail.com	3	pf01	12.95	1	12.95		
11	11/16/2007	16:09:23	15	raythomas@hotmail.com	3	jr01	14.95	1	14.95		
12	11/16/2007	16:05:12	14	alexandrawhite@gmail.com	2	jr01	14.95	1	14.95		
13	11/16/2007	16:05:12	14	alexandrawhite@gmail.com	2	pf02	14.95	1	14.95		
14	11/16/2007	16:02:36	13	joel@murach.com	1	8601	14.95	1	14.95		
15											
16	Totals:							8	115.6		
17											

Address: https://localhost:8443/musicStore/admin/displayReport — Cell A19

Figure 24-10   The user interface for the Reports application (part 2 of 2)

The DisplayReportServlet class

```
package music.admin;

import java.io.*;
import javax.servlet.*;
import javax.servlet.http.*;

import music.data.*;

public class DisplayReportServlet extends HttpServlet
{
    public void doGet(HttpServletRequest request,
            HttpServletResponse response)
            throws IOException, ServletException
    {
        response.setContentType("application/vnd.ms-excel");
        PrintWriter out = response.getWriter();

        String reportName = request.getParameter("reportName");
        String reportTitle = request.getParameter("reportTitle");
        String startDate = request.getParameter("startDate");
        String endDate = request.getParameter("endDate");

        String reportString = null;
        if (reportName.equalsIgnoreCase("userEmail"))
        {
            reportString = ReportDB.getUserEmail(reportTitle);
        }
        else if (reportName.equalsIgnoreCase("downloadDetail"))
        {
            reportString = ReportDB.getDownloadDetail(
                    reportTitle, startDate, endDate);
        }
        else if (reportName.equalsIgnoreCase("invoiceSummary"))
        {
            reportString = ReportDB.getOrderSummary(
                    reportTitle, startDate, endDate);
        }
        else if (reportName.equalsIgnoreCase("invoiceDetail"))
        {
            reportString = ReportDB.getOrderDetail(
                    reportTitle, startDate, endDate);
        }
        out.println(reportString);
    }

    public void doPost(HttpServletRequest request,
            HttpServletResponse response)
            throws IOException, ServletException
    {
        doGet(request, response);
    }
}
```

Figure 24-11   The DisplayReportServlet class

The ReportDB class

```
package music.data;

import java.sql.*;

public class ReportDB
{
    // The Order Summary report
    public static String getOrderSummary(String reportTitle,
        String startDate, String endDate)
    {
        ConnectionPool pool = ConnectionPool.getInstance();
        Connection connection = pool.getConnection();
        Statement statement = null;
        ResultSet rs = null;

        String query =
            "SELECT ProductCode, ProductDescription, "
        +  "    ProductPrice, Quantity, "
        +  "    SUM(Quantity) AS ProductQuantity, "
        +  "    SUM(ProductPrice*Quantity) AS ProductTotal "
        +  "FROM Invoice "
        +  "    INNER JOIN LineItem ON Invoice.InvoiceID = LineItem.InvoiceID "
        +  "    INNER JOIN Product ON LineItem.ProductID = Product.ProductID "
        +  "WHERE InvoiceDate >= '" + startDate + "' "
        +  "    AND InvoiceDate <= '" + endDate + "' "
        +  "GROUP BY ProductCode, ProductDescription "
        +  "ORDER BY ProductTotal DESC";

        try
        {
            statement = connection.createStatement();
            rs = statement.executeQuery(query);
            String d = "\t";
            StringBuilder report = new StringBuilder(
                reportTitle + "\n\n"
                + "Start Date: " + startDate + "\n"
                + "End Date: " + endDate + "\n\n"
                + "ProductCode" + d
                + "ProductDescription" + d
                + "ProductPrice" + d
                + "Quantity" + d
                + "Total" + "\n");
            while (rs.next())
            {
                report.append(rs.getString("ProductCode") + d
                        + rs.getString("ProductDescription") + d
                        + rs.getDouble("ProductPrice") + d
                        + rs.getInt("ProductQuantity") + d
                        + rs.getDouble("ProductTotal") + "\n");
            }
            return report.toString();
        }
```

Figure 24-12   The ReportsDB class (part 1 of 2)

The ReportDB class   **Page 2**

```
        catch(SQLException e)
        {
            e.printStackTrace();
            return null;
        }
        finally
        {
            DBUtil.closeResultSet(rs);
            DBUtil.closeStatement(statement);
            pool.freeConnection(connection);
        }
    }

    // the methods for the other reports

}
```

Note

- The code that generates the User Email, Order Detail, and Download Detail reports isn't shown in this figure. However, it is included with the source code for this book.

Figure 24-12   The ReportsDB class (part 2 of 2)

Perspective

Now that you've finished this chapter, you should understand how to provide administrative access to the Music Store web site. In addition, you should be able to use the principles illustrated here to provide administrative access to any web site.

Although the Admin application only provides two functions, it's common for an Admin application to provide many functions. For example, an Admin application can be used to add, update, or delete products from a Products table. This is useful in an application that generates the product pages from the data in the Products table.

Although this chapter shows how to return a report as an Excel spreadsheet, you will only want to use this option for very simple reports. If you need to create professional quality reports, you will probably want to use third-party software. In that case, you may want to use commercial reporting software such as Crystal Reports. Or, you may want to use open-source reporting software such as JasperReports. Either way, good reporting software will save you development time and allow you to create professional quality reports.

Appendix A

How to set up your computer for this book

This appendix shows how to install and configure all of the software and source code that you need for running the web applications that are presented in this book. This includes the software for Java and MySQL that's available for free from the Internet. And it includes the source code for this book that's available for free from www.murach.com.

The master list

Figure A-1 presents three procedures that you can use for installing the software and source code that you need for this book. All of this software and source code is available for free from the web sites that are described in the figures that follow.

The first procedure in this figure has you install Java SE 6, plus the source code for the applications that are presented in this book. You need to do this procedure before you do the exercises for chapter 2, and you can find the procedures for doing these installations in figures A-2 and A-3.

The second procedure in this figure has you (1) install MySQL, (2) create the MySQL databases that are used by the applications in this book, (3) install the MySQL GUI tools, and (4) install the JDBC driver that you need for MySQL. You should also do this procedure before you do the exercises for chapter 2, and you can find the procedures for doing these tasks in figures A-4 through A-7.

The third procedure in this figure has you first read chapter 2 and install Tomcat. That's the web server that you need for running Java servlets and JavaServer Pages. Then, this procedure has you read chapter 3 and install the NetBeans IDE. That's the IDE that we recommend for doing the exercises and developing the applications for this book. When you finish these chapters and installations, you'll be able to run all of the book's applications. In addition, your system will be set up for doing the exercises for any of the chapters that follow.

As you do these procedures, please keep in mind that they are for the current releases of the software as this book goes to press. Most likely, these procedures will still work for any new releases of the software. However, if the new releases cause problems that you need to know about, we will post updated information about installing these products on our web site (www.murach.com).

The basic installation

1. Install the Java Development Kit (JDK) as described in figure A-2.
2. Download and install the source code for this book as described in figure A-3.

The MySQL installation

1. Install the MySQL database management system as described in figure A-4.
2. Create the databases as described in figure A-5.
3. Install the MySQL GUI tools as described in figure A-6.
4. Install a JDBC driver for MySQL as described in figure A-7.

The Tomcat and NetBeans installations

1. Read chapter 2 and install and configure the Tomcat web server and servlet container.
2. Read chapter 3 and install and configure the NetBeans IDE.

Description

- You should do the basic and MySQL installations before you do the exercises for chapter 2.
- By the time you complete chapter 3, you should have all the software that you need for this book installed.

Figure A-1   How to install the software and source code for this book

The basic installation procedure

Figures A-2 and A-3 present the procedures for installing the JDK for Java SE 6 and the source code for this book.

How to install the Java Development Kit (JDK)

If you've been using Java for a while, it is probably installed on your computer already. In that case, you can skip this topic. Otherwise, figure A-2 shows how to install Java SE 6, the version of Java that's designed to work with Tomcat 6.

Since Sun is continually updating the Java web site, the procedure in this figure may not be up-to-date by the time you read this. As a result, you may have to do some searching to find the current version of the JDK. In general, you can start by looking for products for the Standard Edition of Java (Java SE). Then, you can find the most current version of Java SE for your operating system.

The Java web site

`http://java.sun.com`

How to install the JDK from the Java web site

1. Go to the Java web site.
2. Locate the download page for Java SE 6.
3. Click on the Download button for JDK 6 and follow the instructions.
4. Save the exe file for the setup program to your hard disk.
5. Run the exe file and respond to the resulting dialog boxes. When you're prompted for the JDK directory, use the default directory.

For Windows, the default installation directory should be something like

`c:\Program Files\Java\jdk1.6.0`

Description

- If you already have the JDK for Java SE 6 installed on your computer, you can of course skip this step. However, if you have an earlier release of the JDK installed, we recommend that you upgrade to SE 6.
- For more information about installing the JDK, you can refer to the Java web site.

Figure A-2   How to install the Java Development Kit (JDK)

How to install the source code for this book

Figure A-3 shows how to install the source code for this book. This includes the source code for the applications shown in this book, the source code for the exercise starts, and the files that can be used to create the databases for this book.

The Murach web site

www.murach.com

The default installation directory for the source code

c:\murach\servlet_jsp

The NetBeans directory for the book applications

c:\murach\servlet_jsp\netbeans\book_apps

The NetBeans directory for the exercise starting points

c:\murach\servlet_jsp\netbeans\ex_starts

How to download and install the source code

1. Go to www.murach.com.
2. Find the page for *Murach's Java Servlets and JSP (Second Edition)*.
3. Click the link for "FREE download of the book examples."
4. Select the "All book files" link and respond to the resulting pages and dialog boxes. This will download a setup file named jsp2_allfiles.exe onto your hard drive.
5. Use the Windows Explorer to find the setup file on your hard drive.
6. Double-click this file and respond to the dialog boxes that follow. If you accept the defaults, this installs the source code into the directories shown above.

Description

- All of the source code for this book is contained in a self-extracting zip file (an exe file) that can be downloaded from www.murach.com. When the file is executed, the source code is installed into the directories shown above.

Figure A-3   How to install the source code for this book

The MySQL installation procedure

Figures A-4 through A-7 present the procedures for installing MySQL and its related components. If you're comfortable with the use of a database, you can do these procedures right after you do the basic installation procedures. Otherwise, you can wait until you read chapters 13 and 14. Once you've done these procedures, you'll be able to run the database applications for chapter 14 as well as the Music Store web site that's presented in chapters 21 through 24.

How to install the MySQL database

Figure A-4 figure shows how to install version 5.0 of MySQL on a Windows machine. If you're using Windows, the easiest way to do that is to download the msi file for the MySQL Community Server from the MySQL web site. Then, you can navigate to the directory for the msi file and run it. As it runs, you can accept all of the default options until you reach the MySQL Configuration Wizard.

At the end of the installation procedure, the MySQL Configuration Wizard helps you configure MySQL for your computer. Here again, you can accept all of the default options until you are asked for the password for the root user. At this point, because our downloadable applications use "sesame" as the password for the root user, we recommend that you use "sesame" as the password. *At the least, though, be sure to remember the password that you use because you will need it to connect to MySQL.* You will learn more about this in chapters 13 and 14.

If you want to install a different version of MySQL, or if you want to install MySQL on a different operating system, you can follow the instructions that are available from the MySQL web site to do that. When you install MySQL on most systems, the MySQL database server starts every time you start your computer, which is usually what you want. If it isn't, you can use the MySQL Administrator tool to change this behavior as described in chapter 13.

The MySQL web site

`www.mysql.com`

How to download and install MySQL

1. Go to the MySQL web site.
2. Locate the download page for the MySQL Community Server – Generally Available (GA) Release. To do that, you may need to start by clicking on the Community link.
3. Select the Essentials package. This package contains the minimum set of files needed to install MySQL on Windows and is recommended for most users.
4. Save the installation file to your hard disk. This file is typically named something like mysql-essential-5.0.45-win32.msi.
5. Run the msi file by double-clicking on it.
6. Respond to the MySQL installation prompts to install MySQL on your computer. On most systems, you can accept all default options.
7. Respond to the MySQL Configuration Wizard to configure MySQL on your computer. On most systems, you can accept most of the default options. *However, when you are prompted to enter a password for the root user, use "sesame" for the password.*
8. If you use a password other than "sesame", write it down in a safe location so you'll know what it is later on.

The default installation directory for MySQL

`C:\Program Files\MySQL\MySQL Server 5.0`

Recommended username and password

Username: root
Password: sesame

About the username and password for MySQL

*   In step 7 above, we recommend using "sesame" as the password for the root user because those are the entries that are used by the downloadable applications for this book.
*   If you've already installed MySQL with root as the username and another password, you can change the password by running the MySQL Server Instance Config Wizard that's available from the MySQL→MySQL Server 5.0 group that's available from the Start menu.

Description

*   For more information about working with MySQL, see chapter 13.

Figure A-4   How to install the MySQL database management system

How to create the databases for this book

Figure A-5 shows how to create the databases for this book. To do that, you can navigate to the db directory of the source code for this book. Then, you can double-click on the create_db.bat file. This will run a SQL script named create_db.sql that will create the databases used by this book.

Of course, for this procedure to work, you must install the source code as described in figure A-3, you must install MySQL as described in figure A-4, and the MySQL database server must be running. You must also enter the password for the root MySQL user when the batch file runs.

The directory that contains the create_db.bat file

```
c:\murach\servlet_jsp\db
```

The databases that are created

Database	Description
murach	The database that's used for section 3 of this book.
music	The database that's used for the Music Store application that's presented in section 5 of this book

How to create the databases for this book

1. Use the Windows Explorer to find the create_db.bat file that's in the directory shown above.

2. Double-click on this file to run it. This should display a DOS window like the one below.

3. For the password, enter the password that you used for the MySQL root user. This should be "sesame" if you've followed the procedure in figure A-4.

4. When the bat file finishes, press any key to continue.

The DOS window after a successful install

```
C:\WINDOWS\system32\cmd.exe
Enter password: ******
If no error message is shown, the databases named murach and music were created
successfully.
Press any key to continue . . .
```

Description

- For the create_db.bat file to work, the database server must be running. By default, the database server is automatically started when you start your system. If it isn't running, you can start it as described in chapter 13.

- The create_db.bat file specifies the default installation directory for MySQL that's shown in figure A-4. If this directory is different on your PC, you can use a text editor to change this directory in the bat file before you run it.

- If you receive an error that indicates that the database is in use, you may need to close any applications that are using the database.

Figure A-5   How to create the databases for this book

How to install the MySQL GUI tools

Figure A-6 shows how to install the MySQL GUI tools, which include the MySQL Administrator tool and the MySQL Query Browser tool. Since this is similar to the procedure for installing any application, you shouldn't have much trouble using it. In chapter 13, you'll learn how to use the MySQL Administrator tool to start and stop the database server, and you'll learn how to use the MySQL Query Browser tool to run a SQL statement.

How to download and install the MySQL GUI tools

1. Go to the MySQL web site.

2. Locate the download page for the MySQL GUI Tools Downloads – Generally Available (GA) Release. To do that, you may need to start by clicking on the Community link.

3. Save the installation file to your hard disk. This file is typically named something like mysql-gui-tools-5.0-r12-win32.msi.

4. Run the msi file by double-clicking on it.

5. Respond to the installation prompts to install the MySQL GUI tools on your computer. On most systems, you can accept all default options.

The default installation directory for the MySQL GUI tools

```
C:\Program Files\MySQL\MySQL Tools for 5.0
```

Description

- For more information about installing and configuring the MySQL GUI tools, check the MySQL website.

- For more information about working with the MySQL GUI tools, see chapter 13.

Figure A-6   How to install the MySQL GUI tools

How to install a JDBC driver for MySQL

Before you can use Java to access a MySQL database, you need to install a database driver for MySQL. To do that, you can download a JDBC driver named Connector/J from the MySQL web site, as described in figure A-7, and copy it into the proper JDK directory.

How to download and install a JDBC driver for MySQL

1. Go to the MySQL web site.

2. Locate the download page for the Connector/J. To do that, you may need to start by clicking on the Community link, and then on the Connectors link.

3. Save the zip file for the connector to your hard disk. This file is typically named something like mysql-connector-java-5.0.7.zip.

4. Unzip the zip file onto your hard disk. The unzipped files should include a JAR file for the driver. This file is typically named something like mysql-connector-java-5.0.7-bin.jar.

5. Copy the JAR file for the driver into this JDK directory:

   `jre\lib\ext`

Description

- For more information about installing and configuring the Connector/J driver, check the MySQL website or the HTML pages that are available from the docs directory that's included when you unzip the zip file for the driver.

- For more information about working with the Connector/J driver, see chapter 14.

Figure A-7   How to install a JDBC driver for MySQL

Index

H

Post Office Protocol, 488, 489
Prepared statement (JDBC), 452, 453
Presentation layer, 22, 23
Primary key (database), 428, 429
Privileged attribute (context.xml file), 56, 57
Project (NetBeans), 72, 73
Projects window (NetBeans), 74, 75
Properties object, 494, 495
Property (JavaBean), 288, 289
Protocol, 38, 39

Q

Query, 432, 436, 437
Query Browser (MySQL), 418-421

R

RA, 518, 519
Radio button, 126, 127
RDBMS, 416
Read-only result set, 446, 447
Realm, 538-545
Redirect response, 212, 213
redirect tag (JSTL), 356, 357
Referential integrity, 416, 417
Refresh button, 152
Registration authority, 518, 519
Relational database, 428, 429
   management system, 416
Relative link (HTML), 110, 111
Reload an application, 52-55
Reloadable attribute (context.xml file), 54, 55
remove tag (JSTL), 356, 357
removeAttribute method (session object), 248, 249
Request forwarding, 212, 213
Request header (HTTP request), 556, 557, 560, 561, 566-571
Request line (HTTP request), 556, 557
request object, 142, 143, 146, 147, 178, 179, 182, 183, 248, 249, 260, 261
Request scope, 248, 249, 292, 293
RequestDispatcher object, 212, 213
requestScope object (EL), 316, 317
Reset button, 124, 125
Response body (HTTP response), 556, 557
Response entity (HTTP response), 556, 557

Response header (HTTP response), 556, 557, 564, 565, 572, 573
response object, 178, 179, 182, 183, 260, 261
Result set, 432, 433, 446-449
Result table, *see Result set*
ResultSet object, 446-449, 462, 463
ResultSetMetaData object, 462, 463
Right outer join, 434, 435
Role, 532, 533, 536, 537
role element (tomcat-users.xml), 50, 51
Root directory, 46, 47
Root element, 230, 231
Row, 112, 113
Row (database), 428, 429
Row pointer (database), 446, 447
Run application, 44, 45
   with NetBeans, 78, 79

S

Schema, 418
Scope, 248, 249, 292, 293, 314-317, 356, 357
   PageContext class, 404, 405
   scripting variable, 400, 401
Scripting disabling, 332, 333
Scripting variable, 398-401
Scriptlet, 142-145
Secure connection, 514, 515, 524-527
   cookies, 264, 265
Secure Sockets Layer, 513-528
Security (Music Store web site), 684, 685
Security realm, 532, 533, 538-545
Security role, 532, 533, 536, 537
Select database, 426, 427
SELECT statement (SQL), 432-435, 446, 447
send method (Transport class), 500, 501
SendFailedException object, 500, 501
sendMessage method (Transport class), 500, 501
sendRedirect method (response object), 212, 213
Serializable interface, 288, 289
Server computer, 6, 7
Server.xml file, 42, 43
   realms, 538, 539
Service method (servlet), 188, 189
Services window (NetBeans), 94, 95
Servlet, 18, 19, 173-198
   element, 48, 49

What software you need for this book

- Java SE 6 (JDK 1.6): You can download this software for free from java.sun.com. Then, you can install this software as described in appendix A.

- Tomcat 6.0 (servlet 2.5/JSP 2.1): You can download this software for free from tomcat.apache.org. Then, you can install and configure this software as described in chapter 2.

- NetBeans IDE 6.0: You can download this software for free from netbeans.org. Then, you can install and configure this software as described in chapter 3.

- MySQL 5.0: You can download this software for free from mysql.com. Then, you can install and configure this software as described in appendix A.

- When new versions of this software become available, please check murach.com for updates that describe how to use this book with the newer software.

The downloadable source code for this book

- Complete source code for the applications presented in this book so you can view, compile, and run the code for the applications as you read each chapter.

- Starting source code for the exercises presented at the end of each chapter so you can get more practice in less time.

- All source code is compatible with the NetBeans IDE.

How to download the source code for this book

- Go to murach.com, and go to the page for *Murach's Java Servlets and JSP (2nd Edition)*.

- Click the link for "FREE download of the book applications." Then, download "All book files." This will download a file named jsp2_allfiles.exe to your computer.

- Use the Windows Explorer to find the exe file that you downloaded. Then, double-click this file and respond to the dialog boxes that follow. This installs the files in subdirectories of the c:\murach\servlet_jsp directory.

How to use another IDE with this book

- Although we recommend using the NetBeans IDE with this book, you can use another IDE if you prefer. To do that, you will need to figure out how to import the source code for this book into your IDE so you can compile and run the sample applications and complete the exercises. In addition, you will need to learn how to use your IDE to perform the tasks presented in chapter 3.